The Rationale of Publicity in the Law of Corporeal Movables and Claims

Meeting the Requirement of Publicity by Registration?

The Rationale of Publicity in the Law of Corporeal Movables and Claims

Meeting the Requirement of Publicity by Registration?

Jing Zhang

eleven
international publishing

Published, sold and distributed by Eleven International Publishing
P.O. Box 85576
2508 CG The Hague
The Netherlands
Tel.: +31 70 33 070 33
Fax: +31 70 33 070 30
e-mail: sales@elevenpub.nl
www.elevenpub.com

Sold and distributed in USA and Canada
Independent Publishers Group
814 N. Franklin Street
Chicago, IL 60610, USA
Order Placement: +1 800 888 4741
Fax: +1 312 337 5985
orders@ipgbook.com
www.ipgbook.com

Eleven International Publishing is an imprint of Boom uitgevers Den Haag.

ISBN 978-94-6236-210-9

Acknowledgements

China Scholarship Council (CSC) provided financial supports for this research in the period between 1 September 2014 and 31 August 2018. Hereby I express my sincere appreciation to the CSC.
Publication of this dissertation is funded by Istituto Italo-Cinese of Zhongnan University of Economics and Law.

Abbreviations

AcP	Archiv für die civilistische Praxis
Art.	Article
BEA	Bills of Exchange Act
BGB	Bürgerliches Gesetzbuch (German Civil Code)
BGH	Bundesgerichtshof (German Supreme Court)
BW	Burgerlijk Wetboek (Dutch Civil Code)
CC	Code Civil (French Civil Code)
CCC	Chinese Civil Code
CEAL	Center for the Economic Analysis of Law
DCFR	Draft Common Frame of Reference
FA	Factors Act
FATF	Financial Action Task Force
HGB	Handelsgesetzbuch (German Commercial Code)
HPI	Hire Purchase Inspection
HR	Hoge Raad (Dutch Supreme Court)
LPA	Law of Property Act
No.	Number
Nr.	Nummer (Number)
NJ	Nederlandse Jurisprudentie
NJW	Neue Juristische Wochenschrift
NTBR	Nederlands Tijdschrift voor Burgerlijk Recht
NTHR	Nederlands Tijdschrift voor Handelsrecht
P.	Page
PEL	Principles of European Law
PMC	Purchase Money Charge
PMSI	Purchase Money Security Interest
PPSA	Personal Property Security Act
Rn.	Randnummer (Marginal Number)
S.	Section
SGA	Sales of Goods Act
UCC	Uniform Commercial Code
UN	United Nations
UNCITRAL	United Nations Commission on International Trade Law
UNIDROIT	International Institute for the Unification of Private Law
VIN	Vehicle Identification Number
WG	Wechselgesetz (Law of Bills)
WPNR	Weekblad voor Privaatrecht, Notariaat en Registratie
WvK	Wetboek van Koophandel (Dutch Commercial Code)

Brief Table of Contents

Detailed Table of Contents

1 Introduction: Context, Question, Methodology and Outline

1.1 The Research Context and Questions

1.1.1 General Context: Property Rights, Third Parties, Information and Publicity

The law of patrimony (in Dutch *vermogensrecht*, in German *Vermögensrecht*) takes the distinction between property rights (rights *in rem*) and personal rights (rights *in personam*) as its structural basis. The prominent difference between these two types of rights lies in the breadth of enforceability: property rights can bind third parties, while personal rights only have an effect *inter partes*. This broad enforceability of property rights makes publicity become a principle in the law of property. As the starting point, every property right should have a form of publicity so that third parties can easily know of the existence and content of this right. From the perspective of information economics, publicity is a way of addressing the problem of information asymmetry, a problem that can be triggered by the broad effect of property rights.[1] Information asymmetry arises when one party has more or better information than another party, especially under the circumstance of the conveyance of property. In the aspect of knowing of the proprietary relationships over a thing which is going to be transferred, the potential transferee, compared with the transferor, is often in a disadvantageous situation. For the transferee, there is always a burden of investigating, *inter alia*, whether the transferor has authority to transfer and whether there is any proprietary encumbrance over the thing. In general, publicity allows the transferee to obtain relevant information, alleviating this burden to a large extent.[2]

In general, there are different types of third parties against whom property rights are enforceable. One type of third party's demand for information may differ from another type of third party's demand. For example, general creditors may have no interest in knowing the proprietary legal relationships with respect to a certain asset of the debtor, while a potential acquirer often investigates the legal relationships regarding the

---

1 Arruñada 2011, p. 238-239.

2 For example, if A wants to buy a house from B, he needs to investigate whether B has ownership of this house and whether the house has been mortgaged. In general, B owns more information than A, and A is in a disadvantageous situation. However, by searching the land register, A can collect relevant information and avoid this situation to a large extent.

asset. Hence, the discussion of publicity in the law of property has to be conducted on the basis of the categorization of third parties. The different demands for information by different types of third parties may influence the scope of the legal effect of publicity. Failure to perform publicity perhaps means that the property right has no effect over one type of third party, but the right might still be able to be effective against another type of third party. For example, where a bicycle is transferred under the declaratory system, ownership of this bicycle passes to the transferee upon the effect of the agreement.[3] In the absence of delivery, a method of publicity for corporeal movables, the transferee is protected from the illegal act by thieves, one type of third party, but the ownership acquired may be ineffective against a subsequent buyer acting in good faith, another type of third party. Therefore, we need to pay attention to the specialty in the aspect of the demand for information by different types of third parties.

Unlike property rights, personal rights (or claims) are not subject to the principle of publicity. This is because the parties of a personal right already know the details of this right. However, it should be noted that personal rights have the same problem of publicity as property rights once they are included in transactions (such as assignment and pledge) and taken as an object of disposal. This problem is considered by some writers as an example showing that personal rights have a "proprietary status (*goederenrechtelijk statuut*)" or a proprietary aspect.[4] Like tangible things (such as bicycles), personal rights, which are intangible *per se*, also have a problem of "belonging (*toebehoren* or *Zuordnung*)" when they are seen not only as a legal relationship between the debtor and the creditor, but also as a type of asset that can be alienated and pledged. When a claim is assigned to another person, the question arises of whether the assignor has full authority of disposal. This question concerning the authority further affects the possibility of the assignee becoming the new creditor and obtaining the performance. For example, if a creditor assigns a claim to two different persons, which person can require the debtor to perform the debt and preserve the performance? In a nutshell, like the disposal of tangible things, the disposal of personal rights is also linked to the principle of publicity.

Generally speaking, the form of publicity is determined by the nature of the object of property rights. "Public registration" is used to publicize proprietary interests in immovable property as well as some special movable

---

3 Under the declaratory system, publicity is not a condition for the acquisition of property rights and only "declares" property rights to third parties. In general, what matters is the parties' consent. Therefore, this system is also known as consensual system. However, publicity might be necessary for a property right acquired to be effective against some third parties with competing rights. See Sagaert 2008, p. 18. The declaratory system forms a contrast to the translative system, which is shown below (see 1.3.4) and discussed in detail in Chapter 5 (see 5.1.4.1).

4 Lebon 2010, p. 4; Lubbe 2006, p. 316.

things, such as vessels and aircraft. Here, public registration refers to registration that is made available to the public, especially third parties in the law of property. Not all registration is public. For example, the register for the non-possessory pledge and undisclosed pledge in Dutch law is not available to third parties (art. 3:237 and 3:329 BW).[5] In this research, the system of registration not made available to the public is called "private registration", as opposed to public registration. It is commonly accepted that public registration is an eligible method of publicity. At present, the main issue is how to define the legal effect of, and improve the efficiency of, this method of publicity.[6] Publicity of immovable property is beyond the scope of our research. It will be referred to, only when necessary, as an illustration in discussing the publicity of movables, the theme of this research.

Here, the term "movables" (or movable things, movable property) is used in a very broad sense. It not only covers tangible things that are not immovable (such as bicycles), but also intangible things, such as claims, shares (stocks), and intellectual property. This way of use is alien to German and Dutch lawyers. In German law and Dutch law, movable things (*bewegliche Sachen* in German law and *roerende zaken* in Dutch law) are necessarily corporeal.[7] In English law, however, movable things are divided into two categories: corporeal movables and incorporeal movables. Things, which are neither immovable property nor corporeal movables, are covered by the term incorporeal movables.[8] As a result, incorporeal movables include a large number of assets, such as claims, intellectual property, and shares. In this research, the term "movables" is used as in English law: it covers both tangible and intangible things that are not immovable property.

However, as the title of this dissertation shows, we do not include every type of movable within this research. Only corporeal movables and claims are included. In addition to claims, incorporeal movables also include intellectual property, shares, and emerging intangible property, such as carbon emissions units[9] and agricultural products quotas.[10] These incorporeal movables differ significantly in nature as well as the way of transactions. Moreover, the other types of incorporeal movables (such as intellectual property and shares) are regulated by special laws (such as intellectual

5 Heilbron 2011, p. 44.
6 Dekker 2003, p. 116.
7 Wieling 2007, p. 21; Snijders and Rank-Berenschot 2017, p. 20.
8 Bridge, Gullifer, McMeel and Worthington 2013, p. 10.
9 Cole 2016, p. 10. There is a system of registration for the transaction of carbon emissions units. However, the register is not open to the public, and this type of property is not "registerable property (*registergoederen*)" under Dutch law. See Snijders and Rank-Berenschot 2017, p. 44.
10 Quotas are a device used by the government to control production, importation, exportation and so on. For example, this device is used by the European Communities to control the production of milk and livestock. The milk quotas and livestock quotas are tradable and deemed by some scholars as a type of property. See Cardwell 2000, p. 168.

property law, company law and the law of securities), and the problem of publicity has been addressed to a large extent.[11] For the sake of comprehensiveness, "documental rights" concerning corporeal movables (such as warehouse receipts) and payment (such as bills of exchange) are included in this research. This type of right is documental because the right is embodied in a document or security. Securities to corporeal movables are often termed securities to or document to "goods (*Gütern* in German)".[12] In this research, goods are defined to be corporeal and movable. This term is used in the discussion of securities to goods (see 4.2.2). In general, securities still play a role in transactions involving corporeal movables and claims. For example, the transfer of things stored in a warehouse is usually associated with the transfer of the warehouse receipt, and the alienation of the claim embodied within a bill of exchange is, in principle, dependent on the transfer of the bill of exchange *per se*.

1.1.2 Question I: Is the Principle of Publicity Tenable?

At present, a main problem concerning the principle of publicity is whether this principle remains tenable in the law of corporeal movables and claims. Specifically speaking, whether the existing means of publicity can sufficiently support the saying that the principle of publicity is still tenable. Traditionally, possession is treated as a method of publicity for the transaction of corporeal movables,[13] and notification to debtors is treated as a method of publicity for the disposal of claims in some jurisdictions.[14] However, are these two methods qualified as a means of publicity?

Possession is a complicated concept, a concept used with different meanings in different jurisdictions. For example, there is a distinction between "possession (*bezit*)" and "detention (*houderschap*)" in Dutch law: possession is detention for oneself.[15] German law, however, prescribes a broader concept of "possession (*besitz*)" and differentiates "ownership possession (*Eigenbesitz*)", "limited-right possession (*Fremdbesitz*)" and "control

11 Nowadays, registration has been used in transactions concerning uncertificated shares and debentures (bonds). Moreover, these securities are registered in electronic accounts and transferred through a central exchange system which operates electronically. This is known as the phenomenon of "*dematerialisation*" of securities. See Haentjens 2007, p. 33. A system of registration for intellectual property, especially patents and trademarks, has already been constructed and operates well in the practice. See WIPO 2012, p. 22-23.

12 Bridge, Gullifer, McMeel and Worthington 2013, p. 841; Zöllner 1978, p. 4-5.

13 Clarke and Kohler 2005, p. 390; Wolf and Wellenhofer 2011, p. 76; Snijders and Rank-Berenschot 2017, p. 63.

14 DCFR 2009, p. 1076; Guest and Liew 2018, no. 6-06; Von Wilmowsky 1996, p. 392; Snijders and Rank-Berenschot 2017, p. 302.

15 Rank-Berenschot 2012, p. 13-14.

by agents (*Besitzdienerschaft*)".[16] The distinction made by Dutch law cannot be found in English law. Like German law, English law also has a broader concept of possession which, on the other hand, does not include a distinction between ownership possession and limited-right possession.[17] In this research, the concept of possession is used in a wide sense, not only including possession by owners, but also possession by lessees, pledgees and the like. The differences just mentioned are related to the possessory intention (*animus*). This implies a question regarding publicity: whether possession can independently show the intention, which is invisible, to third parties. In other words, for example, can a third party distinguish ownership possession (or *bezit* in Dutch law) from limited-right possession (or *houderschap* in Dutch law) only on the basis of possession *per se*?

In addition to viewing possession from the aspect of possessory intention, we can also analyze the concept according to the element of factual control (*corpus*). Possession can be either visible through factual control by the possessor himself or invisible as a result of factual control by another person than the possessor himself. In the jargon of law, possession can be direct (actual) or indirect (constructive). Indirect possession, often deemed as "mental control (*vergeistigte Sachherrschaft*)", means that the possessor does not factually control the object in a direct way.[18] Because of the absence of direct control, indirect possession is invisible.[19] This casts doubt on the capability of indirect possession to show property rights to outsiders. Direct possession is also open to criticisms, despite the fact that the direct possessor himself often exercises factual control. In the viewpoint of some scholars, even direct possession is too ambiguous to qualify as a means of publicity.[20] This criticism is raised against the background that corporeal movables are transacted in a great variety of ways nowadays, such as reservation of ownership, transfer of ownership for security reasons, and lease. Typically, the qualification of possession as a method of publicity is questioned because it triggers a problem of "*ostensible ownership*" or "*false wealth*" in the secured transaction in corporeal movables: possession is no longer a method of publicity, but a source of misleading information.[21]

16 Baur and Stürner 2009, p. 89. Here, "ownership possession" means factual control by the owner, "limited-right possession" refers to factual control on the basis of a limited right, while "control by agents" is used in the situation where an agent holds factual control on behalf of and subject to the instructions of ownership possessors or limited-right possessors. A detailed discussion of the concept of possession is provided in 3.1.

17 Bridge, Gullifer, McMeel and Worthington 2013, p. 55.

18 Wolf and Wellenhofer 2011, p. 82.

19 Quantz 2005, p. 41-42.

20 Hamwijk 2012, p. 310-311; Füller 2006, p. 280.

21 Baird 1983, p. 54; Drobnig 2011, p. 1027.

Notification to debtors is traditionally deemed as a method of publicity for the disposal of claims, at least by some lawyers in some jurisdictions.[22] It requires that a creditor who will dispose of or has disposed of the claim must notify his debtor of the disposal. Afterwards, third parties can obtain information concerning the disposal from the notified debtor. In some sense, it can be said that notification represents, like possession, a kind of factual control over the claim: when a debtor is notified of the assignment or pledge, he has to pay to the designated assignee or pledgee.[23] However, it might be still problematic to say that the notification is a method of publicity for claims.[24] Can third parties easily know about the disposal after the debtor involved is notified? Can the act of notification be so objective and reliable that the reliance of third parties is protected in the situation where the creditor's authority of disposal is defective? Does the debtor involved have a legal duty to disclose the disposal to third parties who inquire with him? Moreover, the formality of notification might bring a heavy burden for the transaction, in particular when a large number of claims are involved. This casts doubt on the appropriateness of notification as a form of publicity for the transaction of claims.

1.1.3 Question II: Is Registration Desirable?

The questions raised above require us to turn to another question: whether and to what extent the principle of publicity is properly implemented in the law of corporeal movables and claims. To answer this question, we need to conduct comprehensive research into the role played by possession and notification in different types of transactions, examining whether and to what extent the two methods can provide information concerning property rights to third parties who, in turn, can make decisions with safety according to the information. The comprehensive research will be conducted in Chapter 3 and Chapter 4. On the basis of a comparative law study, these two Chapters examine possession and notification to the debtor respectively.

If the research leads to a negative answer, namely that the principle of publicity only exists in a weak sense in the law of corporeal movables and claims, then we need to further explore the desirability and possibility of having a new method of publicity for corporeal movables and claims. This is the central task of Chapter 5. In general, this new method of publicity is (public) registration: whether and how registration should be introduced into the law of corporeal movables and claims to meet the requirement of publicity?

22 DCFR 2009, p. 1076; Proprietary Security in Movable Assets 2014, p. 447; Snijders and Rank-Berenschot 2017, p. 63.
23 Lebon 2010, p. 173.
24 Rongen 2012, p. 498; Von Wilmowsky 1996, p. 392-393.

The formality of registration might have merits as well as disadvantages. Thus, a trade-off seems inevitable in answering this question. In general, scholars' opinions are divided. Some writers approve a system of registration and raise certain criteria for introducing registration for the transaction of corporeal movables and claims.[25] However, other writers take an opposite view and believe that the formality of registration is harmful to the smoothness of transactions; thus, registration should not be allowed to intrude in the law of corporeal movables and claims.[26]

1.1.4 Specific Cases: Secured Transactions, Trusts, and Property Rights of Motor Vehicles

In practice, the fierce debate on the desirability of registration mainly occurs in relation to the secured transaction of movables. In making use of corporeal movables for a security purpose, there is a strong demand that the security provider can continue possessing and using the collateral. This gives rise to a problem of publicity: under the precondition of allowing the debtor to preserve possession, how can a proprietary right of security be shown to third parties over whom it has binding force? In the situation where claims are used as collateral, a problem of publicity also arises. Claims are incorporeal and thereby invisible. How to make proprietary rights of security over claims (such as the right of pledge) transparent is an important matter in the financial practice.

In general, the debate not only concerns whether registration should be employed, but also how and to what extent it should be introduced. Nowadays, neither German law nor Dutch law has any general public system of registration for movables, and the secured transaction of movables remains hidden to third parties.[27] English law has a registration system for the

25 Bridge, Macdonald, Simmonds and Walsh 1999, p. 567-664; Baird and Jackson 1984, p. 299-320.

26 Van den Boezem and Goosmann 2010, p. 751-753; Lwowski 2008, p. 174-179.

27 Brinkmann 2016, p. 340; Heilbron 2011, p. 44. There is a system of registration for aircraft and vessels in German law and Dutch law. In Dutch law, these two special types of corporeal movables fall under the concept of "registerable property (*registergoederen*)" (art. 3:10 BW), and disposal of them requires registration. See Snijders and Rank-Berenschot 2017, p. 44. Slightly different from Dutch law, German law does not require registration for the transfer of "seagoing vessels (*Seeschiffe*)", and even delivery is unnecessary. However, registration is a condition for the mortgage of seagoing vessels. Differently, registered "riverboats (*Binnenschiffe*)" cannot be validly transferred and mortgaged until registration is completed under German law. Pursuant to German law, aircraft can be transferred without registration, and it is general rules concerning the transfer of corporeal movables that are applied to the transfer of aircraft. However, mortgage of aircraft is subject to registration. See Baur and Stürner 2009, p. 406-407; Rakob 2007, p. 89-90; Steppler and Brecke 2015, p. 55.

charge and mortgage of movables.[28] However, the system follows a formal approach, which means that registration is not applied to those transactions that only have a security function in the economic sense, such as reservation of ownership and sale and leaseback.[29] Under the formal approach, only the security interests enumerated by law and having a legal form are registerable. Different from the English law, Article 9 of the Uniform Commercial Code (UCC) takes a functional approach, as opposed to the formal approach, and creates a more comprehensive regime of publicity: all security interests are registerable, irrespective of their legal form.[30] Under Article 9, what matters is the economic function of transactions. As a result, such security devices as reservation of ownership and sale and leaseback are also registerable.

On the EU level, Book IX of the Draft Common Frame of Reference (DCFR), an achievement of academic attempts on the harmonization of security interests in movable assets, takes a middle path. Book IX requires registration for those transactions that only have a function of security in the economic sense (such as reservation of ownership), thereby following a functional approach. However, a formal approach is adopted in some other aspects, such as the enforcement of security interests. For example, the creditor who reserves ownership is entitled to terminate the contract and reclaim the property on the basis of ownership.[31] In the Personal Property Security Act (PPSA) system, accepted by Canada, Australia, and New Zealand, a further step has been taken. Registration is not only required for secured transactions, whether in the economic or legal sense, but also for certain outright transactions that do not serve any function of security.[32] A typical example is that the long lease of movable things with a term of more than one year is subject to the requirement of registration.[33] This is not surprising since the legal relationship of lease serving a security function

---

28 However, this system is different from the systems of registration for vessels and aircraft. In the case of aircraft, registration is not a condition for transfer, but there is a special register for the mortgage of aircraft. Entry into this special register allows the mortgage to be effective against third parties. Remarkably, the mortgage of aircraft can also be recorded in the register for movables, provided that the mortgagor is a company. As a result, there are two registers for the mortgage of aircraft, and the priority between two mortgages recorded in different registers is determined by the date of registration. See Bridge 2007, p. 152; Bisset 2015, p. 44-45. In the case of vessels, transfer of ownership is effected by "*a bill of sale satisfying the prescribed requirements*" and must be registered, and mortgage takes registration as a condition for the legal effectiveness against third parties. See Bridge 2007, p. 153; Beale, Bridge, Gullifer and Lomnicka 2018, no. 14.34-14.37.

29 Goode 2013, p. 4-5; Bridge, Gullifer, McMeel and Worthington 2013, p. 14.

30 Walsh 2016, p. 76-86.

31 DCFR 2009, p. 4458-4459; De Groot 2012, p. 139-140. The Principles of European Law (PEL) Group takes a similar approach. See Proprietary Security in Movable Assets 2014, p. 243-244.

32 Whittaker and Partner 2015, p. 56.

33 Whittaker and Partner 2015, p. 76.

(such as financial lease) has no substantial difference from the legal relationship of lease having no purpose of providing security (true lease or outright lease). Both give rise to ownership being invisible.

The brief introduction above indicates that two central divergences exist with respect to the issue of publicity of secured transactions of movables. One concerns the desirability of registration, and the other the scope of registration. Though being the most important and controversial, the secured transaction of movables is not the only example related to the matter of publicity for corporeal movables and claims. Another one is the trust.

Trust is a common law concept. The reception of trust in civil law is a traditional and controversial topic. A relevant difficulty is that the trust runs counter to the principle of publicity. Weiser deems this principle as the "*public enemy*" of the reception of trust.[34] In a relationship of trust, the trustee does not have, with respect to the entrusted assets, legal ownership in the civil law sense: the trustee's "ownership" is not full, but subject to the beneficiary's interest which has certain proprietary features. The beneficiary's right can bind certain third parties, especially the trustee's personal creditors (the effect of separation) and *mala fide* subsequent acquirers of the entrusted asset (the effect of tracing). Due to these particular legal consequences, a question of publicity arises: whether registration should be employed, as a supportive regime for the reception, to show third parties the relationship of trust and the proprietary limitations caused over the right of ownership.

As to the issue of reception, the French *fiducie* introduced in 2007 provides an example.[35] However, it seems that the 2007 legal reform gave insufficient attention to the problem of publicity. The trust of immovable property is required to be registered and thus is visible to third parties.[36] However, the registration for the trust of movables is mainly for the purpose of administrative regulations and is not publicly available to third parties, thereby failing to be a private registration. This is deemed as "*a weakness of the French legal framework*".[37] The Convention on the Law Applicable to Trusts and on Their Recognition (1984) requires registration under article 12.[38] However, this requirement is thought of as "*surprising*" by some common law experts.[39] In their opinion, the fact that the trust is hidden is a merit rather than a problem: thanks to this feature, transferees do not

34 Weiser 1936, p. 8.

35 Mallet-Bricout 2013, p. 143.

36 Fix 2014, p. 211.

37 Barrière 2013, p. 123.

38 Article 12 Convention on the Law Applicable to Trusts and on Their Recognition (1984): "*Where the trustee desires to register assets, movable or immovable, or documents of title to them, he shall be entitled, in so far as this is not prohibited by or inconsistent with the law of the State where registration is sought, to do so in his capacity as trustee or in such other way that the existence of the trust is disclosed.*"

39 Lupoi 2000, p. 173.

have to worry about whether the property involved is under a trust, which smooths the progress of transactions.[40]

From this brief introduction, it can be seen that there is a deep divide between common law and civil law in the aspect of publicity of the trust. In this research, we pay particular attention to the issue of the publicity of trust, but only to the extent that the entrusted asset is corporeal movables and/or claims.

Registration of secured transactions and trusts are two examples related to the content of transactions; another example, however, concerns the object of transactions: registration of motor vehicles.[41] Though motor vehicles have become a common product in our daily life and an important type of collateral in secured transactions, many jurisdictions lack a system of public registration. As a result, property rights of motor vehicles still use possession as a method of publicity. The question is, however, whether possession is sufficient for showing proprietary interests of motor vehicles to third parties.

In the aspect of value, longevity and the possibility of identification, motor vehicles bear significant similarities to vessels and aircraft. Nevertheless, they are treated differently. For example, motor vehicles under Dutch law are not "registerable property (*registergoederen*)", a kind of property taking public registration as the method of publicity and includes immovable property, certain vessels, and aircraft.[42] The proprietary interest of motor vehicles also lacks registration under English law, German law, and Dutch law, which causes a problem of information to third parties. As a market response, two registers, the Hire Purchase Inspection (HPI) and the AutoCheck, have been implemented by several large finance companies in England.[43] In Australia, secured transactions of motor vehicles have been noted by legislators. In constructing a system of registration for movables,

---

40 Lupoi 2000, p. 173; Lau 2011, p. 154-155.

41 Roughly speaking, motor vehicle is self-propelled with an engine and commonly wheeled. Unlike trains and trams, it does not operate on rails. It is used for the transportation of people or cargo. It includes cars, buses, motorcycles, off-road vehicles, and trucks. The term motor vehicle is not a legal concept in private law, and motor vehicles are regulated under the concept of corporeal movable. However, motor vehicle is a term technically defined by traffic law. In general, traffic law stipulates the requirements concerning the number of wheels, the type of engine (internal combustion engine and/or electronic engine), the speed, the cylinder capacity, the weight and so on. See s. 185 Road Traffic Act (1988) of Great Britain, art. 1 *Wegenverkeerswet* (1994) of the Netherlands, and § 1 *Straßenverkehrsgesetz* (1909) of Germany. In this research, an accurate definition is not provided for motor vehicles, which, nevertheless, does not prevent us from discussing the publicity of motor vehicles. In general, if a motor vehicle has to be registered for the purpose of public regulation according to traffic law, then this motor vehicle falls within the scope of our discussion. This is because, as will be shown later, a system of public registration should be introduced on the basis of the current administrative system of registration (see 5.6).

42 Reehuis and Heisterkamp 2019, p. 7.

43 Beale, Bridge, Gullifer and Lomnicka 2018, no. 9.26-9.33.

the Australian PPSA describes motor vehicles as a typical category of "*serial-numbered property*", and the registration of security interests of motor vehicles requires an indication of the serial number, namely the Vehicle Identification Number (VIN).[44] On account of the existing divergences, this research will explore the question of whether public registration should be introduced for motor vehicles.

In summary, this research focuses on two central questions:
(1) is the principle of publicity still tenable on the basis of existing means of publicity (possession and notification to the debtor) in the law of corporeal movables and claims and to what extent?
(2) should registration be employed to meet the requirement of publicity for property rights created on corporeal movables and claims?

Moreover, we also conduct three case studies in this research because of their relevance to the issue of publicity: the secured transaction in corporeal movables and claims, the trust of corporeal movables and claims, and registration of motor vehicles.

1.2 Research Methodology

The central methodology of this research is a comparative law study mainly involving legislation, cases and scholarly commentaries. As a research method, comparative law studies serve certain purposes, among which the principal one is to facilitate the development of law on a national level and the harmonization of law on a regional or international level.[45] This purpose is supposed to be a reason why this research is conducted.

In general, English law, German law and Dutch law are taken as the main body of the comparative study here. The reason for choosing these three jurisdictions involves several aspects. The first aspect concerns comprehensiveness. The aim of this research is to provide a general discussion of the principle of publicity in the law of corporeal movables and claims. This requires the jurisdictions selected to be diverse and typical. In the field of private law, especially property law, common law and civil law differ significantly. Among the three jurisdictions, English law represents common law, and the other two jurisdictions belong to the family of civil law. For example, the concept of possession in English law is apparently different from the concept of "possession (*Besitz*)" in German law as well as from the concept of "possession (*bezit*)" in Dutch law (see 3.1). Moreover, the legal effect of notification to the debtor in English law is different from that in German law and Dutch law (see 4.1).

---

44 Whittaker and Partner 2015, p. 178-179.
45 Wilson 2007, p. 87-88.

There is a distinction within the family of civil law between the Germanic law group and the French law group, which are represented by the German Civil Code (*Bürgerliches Gesetzbuch*, abbreviated as BGB) and the French Civil Code (*Code Civil*, abbreviated as CC) respectively.[46] This distinction is, more or less, a result of the fact that some jurisdictions are more affected by the BGB, while others by the CC.[47] Historically, Dutch private law was heavily influenced by French law.[48] For this reason, it belongs to the French law group. Yet, the later recodification in the second half of 20th century has made the new Dutch Civil Code (*Burgerlijk Wetboek*, abbreviated as BW) more similar to German law.[49] However, in some aspects closely related to this research, Dutch law still differs from German law. One example is that the concept of *bezit* in Dutch law differs from the concept of *Besitz* in German law: the two are different in the aspect of the possessory intention (see 3.1). This has been mentioned above. Moreover, how the legal effect of notification to debtors over the disposal of claims is prescribed by German law and Dutch law differently (see 4.1). Notification has nothing to do with the assignment of claims under German law, but it is a requirement for the "disclosed assignment (*openbare cessie*)" under Dutch law.[50] In the end, the new BW is quite modern, which implies that recent developments of private law can be reflected by it or, at least, discussed during the process of the recodification. For example, E.M. Meijers, the spiritual father of the new BW, proposed to construct a system of registration for the undisclosed pledge, but his proposal met with fierce resistance and was not accepted in the end.[51]

In this research, the comparative study is not confined to the three jurisdictions in some parts, especially the case study on publicity of secured transactions in corporeal movables and claims. In that part, Article 9 UCC and the PPSA systems in Canada, Australia and New Zealand are also discussed. Article 9 UCC and the PPSA systems are quite different from the current system operating in the three jurisdictions selected. As has been indicated above, both German law and Dutch law do not have any system of public registration for the secured transaction, and English law only has a system under the formal approach, which means that the scope of registration does not include such security devices as reservation of ownership and sale and leaseback. The UCC first introduced a comprehensive system of registration, namely the notice-filing system, under the functional approach.

46 Zweigert and Kötz 1998, p. 132.

47 The two groups differ in, for example, how to define the concept of possession, whether ownership can be transferred upon the conclusion of the contract, and whether a defect of the underlying contract can affect the transfer of ownership. See Ritaine 2012, p. 52, 98-100; McGuire 2012, p. 42, 73-77.

48 Hondius 1982, p. 351.

49 Tallon 1993, p. 197. Drobnig pointed out, from an outsider's perspective, that in terms of the requirements for a valid transfer the new BW is "*on the half of the way between Paris and Berlin* (*auf halbem Wege zwischen Paris und Berlin*)". See Drobnig 1993, p. 181.

50 Kötz 2010, p. 1296; Snijders and Rank-Berenschot 2017, p. 302.

51 Hamwijk 2014, p. 62.

As a result, registration is applicable to every proprietary security interest, regardless of the legal form it takes. Inspired by but somewhat different from the UCC, the PPSA systems also construct a notice-filing system and extend registration to some non-security transactions of movables, such as the long lease of movable things.[52] In another case study, registration of trust, the recent development in French law and Belgian law is included.

The comparative law study also has another dimension: at the end of this research, we examine the new Chinese Civil Code (2020) and provide some proposals for the construction of a system of registration for corporeal movables and claims. Here, the author should mention that despite his expertise in Chinese law, he did not choose Chinese law as a subject matter of the comparative study. This is because most of its legal concepts and rules can find their origin from other jurisdictions, in particular German law and Japanese law.[53] In addition, another reason is that the current rules of Chinese law concerning the research topic are not sufficiently concise, which would create some difficulties for the comparative study if Chinese law had been selected. For example, the concept of possession is not defined by Chinese law, despite the fact that most Chinese lawyers refer to German law (namely the rules of *Besitz*) in understanding this concept.

Before comparing the jurisdictions selected, it is necessary to find and then clarify relevant sources of law. The sources of law mainly include statutes and precedents. In general, case law is more important in English law than in both German law and Dutch law. This, however, does not mean that statutes are irrelevant for understanding English law. It will be found that the Sales of Goods Act (1979), the Law of Property Act (1925), the Bills of Exchange Act (1882) and the Companies Act (2006) are of great importance for transactions involving corporeal movables and claims. In the course of understanding English statutes, it should be borne in mind that case law, especially precedents based on equity, might change the content of statutory rules. As a result, the whole image of English law is co-shaped by statutes and precedents. German law and Dutch law are quite different from English law in this aspect. The former two jurisdictions have codified most rules of private law into codes (such as the BGB and the BW). It is codes that serve as the principal source of law in Germany and the Netherlands. However, merely paying attention to the codes is insufficient. Case law is also relevant, at least, in two aspects: one is that the court might create a new rule or regime, such as the security transfer of ownership in German law;[54] the other is that judicial cases might further develop statutory rules.

In understanding the sources of law mentioned above, a doctrinal approach is adopted. The central function of the doctrinal approach is to

52 Whittaker and Partner 2015, p. 56.

53 For Chinese legislation in the field of private law, Japanese law always has significant importance, perhaps due to geographic reasons. At present, a large number of Chinese scholars are engaging in the comparative study between Chinese law and Japanese law.

54 Brinkmann 2016, p. 341.

"identify, analyse and synthesise the content of the law".[55] Moreover, to clarify how the present regime of publicity for corporeal movables and claims operates in each of the selected jurisdictions, we also focus on academic commentaries and sometimes legislative materials. For example, this research often refers to the DCFR, an achievement of academic attempts for the harmonization of European private law, and related commentaries, in particular the commentaries concerning Book VIII ("Acquisition and Loss of Ownership of Goods") and Book IX ("Proprietary Security Rights in Movable Assets").

From the introduction above on research methodology, it is not difficult to see that this research as a whole has a doctrinal characteristic.[56] Empirical research, a non-doctrinal approach which can be either quantitative or qualitative, plays a limited role in this dissertation. Briefly stated, quantitative research *"deals with numbers, statistics or hard data"*.[57] It is not involved in this dissertation. The qualitative method is different from the quantitative method in that the former is non-numerical and *"mostly in the form of words"*.[58] The qualitative empirical method also should be carefully distinguished from the doctrinal research, because the former is used to explore *"social relations and reality as experience"* rather than to reveal the content of applicable laws.[59] Here, we make use of some non-numerical data or facts related to the theme of this research, such as in the analysis of the information demanded by different types of third parties. However, these data or facts are mainly obtained through analysis of the literature.

1.3 Research Outline

In addition to this Introduction Chapter, the dissertation includes six other Chapters, including the summary Chapter.

1.3.1 Chapter 2: Property Rights, Third Parties, Information, and Publicity

Chapter 2 seeks to lay a theoretical foundation and to construct a framework for the whole research. It addresses two questions: (1) what is the essence of property rights and what are their distinctive features compared to other types of rights, especially the personal right (see 2.1); and (2) what is the

55 Hutchinson 2013, p. 9.
56 To avoid misunderstandings, saying that the whole research is doctrinal does not mean that we only compare legal concepts or rules in doing comparative law studies. In the contemporary study of comparative law, the fundamental method should be the functional approach, an approach that focuses on the effect and legal consequences of law, as has been asserted by Zweigert and Kötz. See Zweigert and Kötz 1998, p. 34.
57 Chui 2007, p. 48.
58 Chui 2007, p. 48.
59 Dobinson and Johns 2007, p. 21.

connection between the third-party effect of property rights with "proprietary information", a term raised by this research, and publicity (see 2.2).

In Chapter 2, we first discuss the traditional debate on whether property rights are a subject-object relationship or a subject-subject relationship. There, property rights are argued as a legal relationship between persons. After that, we explore the most important feature of property rights, namely absoluteness. Property rights can bind third parties. In dealing with this feature, we categorize third parties into three types: strange interferers, subsequent acquirers, and general creditors. Strange interferers, such as the illegal dispossessor, are third parties who bear a duty to not interfere. Violation of this duty will trigger certain legal consequences, such as the return of the thing and pecuniary compensation. Subsequent acquirers are third parties who enjoy a property right but bear a duty to respect the already existing property rights on the same thing.[60] General creditors are third parties who, in the event of the debtor's insolvency, have an unsecured claim and fall into a position inferior to secured creditors.

After that, we explain how the feature of absoluteness gives rise to a problem of information asymmetry to third parties. The existence of this problem makes it desirable to have a proper means of publicity to reliably communicate proprietary information, i.e. information concerning property rights. As is pointed out, the content of proprietary information demanded varies from one type of third party to another. It is obvious that subsequent acquirers demand much more intensive proprietary information than strange interferers. For example, knowing the specific identity of the owner of a bicycle is unnecessary for strange interferers, but essential for a person who wants to purchase this bicycle.

1.3.2 Chapter 3: Corporeal Movables and Possession

Chapter 3 focuses on possession, which is traditionally deemed as a means of publicity for corporeal movables. In that chapter, a conceptual analysis of possession is provided first by comparing the three jurisdictions, namely English law, German law, and Dutch law (see 3.1). In general, possession is a "functional" concept: how to define it is mainly contingent on legislative policies. This explains why significant differences exist in the way of defining the concept between the three jurisdictions. After the conceptual comparison, we then turn to the issue whether and to what extent possession can serve as a means of publicity for corporeal movables (see 3.2). There, we find that possession is a defective means of publicity because it cannot clearly show third parties proprietary interests of corporeal movables. Possession can only indicate that the possessor has a *right* to the possessed

60 For example, where A wants to obtain ownership of a bicycle that has already been pledged to B, then A is a subsequent acquirer, a third party, in relation to B. Here A has to respect B's right of pledge.

object. It does not indicate the content and type of this right. In this sense, possession is an ambiguous method of publicity.

After the general discussion, we examine the importance of possession for different types of third parties, namely strange interferers (see 3.3), subsequent acquirers (see 3.4), and general creditors (see 3.5). It will be further argued that the information conveyed by possession, namely that the possessor enjoys a right to the possessed thing, is sufficient for strange interferers. Possession can function as a system of navigation for human beings to avoid conducting illegal interference. However, the information is insufficient for subsequent acquirers and general creditors. Where only possession is used as a means of publicity for corporeal movables, property rights remain hidden to these two types of third parties. As a result, the problem of information asymmetry is still existent in the transaction of corporeal movables. In this sense, we can say that the principle of publicity based on possession has significantly faded in the law of corporeal movables.

1.3.3 Chapter 4: Claims, Notification to Debtors, and Documental Recordation

In Chapter 4 attention shifts to notification to debtors and documental recordation, the means of publicity for claims and "documental rights" respectively. Documental rights are documental because they are embodied within documents or securities. In essence, documental rights are a kind of claim (personal right). This Chapter includes two parts: one focuses on notification to debtors (see 4.1), and the other deals with securities concerning goods and payments (see 4.2). As pointed out above, claims have a proprietary aspect once they are included in the transaction: the disposal of claims also involves a problem of information. For example, in the situation of assignments of claims, the potential assignee needs to identify whether the assignor has qualified authority to dispose. In this Chapter, we examine whether and to what degree the two methods can communicate proprietary information to the three types of third parties: strange interferers, subsequent acquirers, and general creditors.

The conclusion on the notification to debtors is negative: just notifying the debtor involved cannot make the disposal of a claim visible to third parties. After notifying the debtor, third parties can, at most, be provided with a possibility to know of the disposal through inquiry with the debtor. However, the debtor has no legal duty to provide information, nor will the information provided be assumed to be correct for the benefit of the inquirer. Moreover, where a large number of claims are involved, notifying all the debtors will be very costly. This casts doubt on the appropriateness of the notification as a means of publicity for claims. In the end, the requirement of notification creates an obstacle to the disposal of future claims, claims that have not come into existence yet, because the identity of the debtor of future claims cannot be ascertained.

In contrast, securities qualify for being a means of publicity for rights embodied in the security: they are often treated as an outward appearance of rights.[61] From securities, third parties can know about disposals of the embodied right because law requires the transacting parties to provide a simple record on the face of the securities. For example, where a bill of exchange to order is pledged, a mark of pledge might be made on the face of the bill of exchange; as a result, third parties can know of the pledge after glancing at the bill of exchange.[62] To avoid misunderstandings, it is necessary to mention here that securities to goods (such as warehouse receipts) only embody a personal claim for recovery of the goods, rather than ownership or any proprietary limited right to the goods. On account of this, recordation on the securities to goods is discussed in the same Chapter as the notification to the debtor, even though the transfer of securities to goods is closely linked to the disposal of the goods involved.

1.3.4 Chapter 5: The Rationale of Publicity in the Law of Corporeal Movables and Claims

Chapter 5 offers a conclusive analysis on the basis of the preceding two Chapters. It seeks to reveal the rationale of publicity as a special formality in transactions and to disclose its importance for different types of third parties (see 5.1). After that, we explore the role publicity plays in the course of the derivative acquisition of property rights. In general, the system of derivative acquisitions can be divided according to two criteria: one leads to the distinction between the declaratory system and the translative system, and the other gives to the causation principle and the abstraction principle.[63] Here, the difference between the two systems lies in whether the valid acquisition of property rights requires the formality of publicity as a condition.[64] The two principles differ in whether a defect in the underlying contract can affect the acquisition *per se*. The connection of publicity with the two systems and the two principles are discussed in 5.1.

After concluding, on the basis of Chapter 3 and Chapter 4, that the principle of publicity has faded in the law of corporeal movables and claims (see 5.2), we address another central question of this research: whether and how registration should be employed to meet the requirement of publicity. The question is discussed in two stages. The first stage is to propose the essential aspects that need to be considered for employing registration for corporeal movables and claims (see 5.3). This stage involves a general discussion. In the second stage, we analyze three specific cases, namely the

61 Hueck and Canaris 1986, p. 82; Schnauder 1991, p. 1648; Scheltema 1993, p. 96-99.
62 Zevenbergen 1951, p. 70.
63 Snijders and Rank-Berenschot 2017, p. 276-278.
64 Krimphove 2006, p. 59.

secured transaction (see 5.4), the trust (see 5.5), and the transaction of motor vehicles (see 5.6).

1.3.5 Chapter 6: Implications for Chinese Law

Chapter 6 examines the new Chinese Civil Code (2020) and provides some observations for the construction of a system of registration for corporeal movables and claims. The observations mainly concern how to improve the current Chinese system of registration for corporeal movables and claims in the context of the new civil code. In general, the old system under the Property Law (2007) is not comprehensive or efficient. The system only applies to the mortgage (charge) of corporeal movables and pledge of receivables (monetary claims). Thus, a number of property rights concerning these two types of property remain hidden to third parties. For example, reservation of ownership and sale and leaseback are excluded from the system. Moreover, the ways in which the present system operates are costly, which hampers the smoothness of transactions. For example, the system is regionally fragmented and not fully automated, which creates inconvenience to the legal practice.

The drafters of the new Chinese Civil Code (CCC) have been aware of the problems presented above. Under the new civil code, reservation of ownership, financial lease and factoring are subject to registration for the legal effectiveness against third parties. However, the extension of the scope of registration is insufficient, since sale and leaseback, true lease, and non-factoring assignment remain outside the register. In addition, the CCC leaves space for the State Coucil to construct a unified system of registration in the future by not specifying the registry intentionally. The fragmented systems will be unified as one comprehensive system. In this research, several proposals are raised for the construction of a future register in China.

1.3.6 Chapter 7: Summary

The last Chapter provides a summary of this research. In sum, this research focuses on the rationale of publicity in the law of corporeal movables and claims and includes a comparative study mainly involving English law, German law, and Dutch law. After providing a general introduction to property rights and publicity, we examine the qualification of possession, notification to debtors and securities as a method of publicity. The result of this examination is that the principle of publicity is only implemented in a very weak sense by these methods. Therefore, a system of (public) registration should be introduced into the law of corporeal movables and claims, making proprietary rights over these two types of property transparent. The current Chinese system of registration for corporeal movables and claims are defective in many aspects and needs to be improved.

2 Property Rights and Publicity

The theme of this research is publicity for property rights of corporeal movables and claims. In light of the doctrinal viewpoint, property rights are a kind of private right that has binding force over third parties. Thus, these parties should be provided with a channel through which property rights can be known easily and securely. This is the core of the principle of publicity. To have a further understanding of this principle, it is necessary to first outline what property rights are.

This Chapter consists of two sections. In the first section, we discuss the essence and characteristics of property rights (see 2.1). In this section, we have a general view on the similarities as well as differences between property rights and another type of patrimonial interest, namely personal rights. The borderline between the two types of rights has long been a topic in the theory of private law. It will be argued that property rights and personal rights have the same essence: both are an inter-personal relationship. However, they differ in the breadth of legal effect. Property rights have a feature of absoluteness or exclusivity, which means that they are enforceable against third parties. As will be presented, third parties include three main categories: strange interferers, subsequent acquirers, and general creditors. Personal rights, as a legal relationship *inter partes*, in principle bind the creditor and the debtor only.

In the second section, we show that the feature of exclusivity makes publicity of property rights important for third parties (see 2.2). This feature gives rise to an asymmetry of "proprietary information" between the holder of property rights (i.e. the proprietor) and third parties. This information problem can be addressed to a large extent by different methods, such as the disclosure of transacting counterparties, the inquiry with independent intermediaries, and publicity. Among these methods, publicity seems to be most important: it is supposed to not only make property rights transparent to third parties, but also provide a basis for the protection of the reliance of third parties. In other words, publicity is a *secure* source of proprietary information. This section also outlines the specific proprietary information demanded by different types of third parties.

2.1 Definition of Property Rights

2.1.1 Initial Difficulties

Property law textbooks often begin with an introduction to the concept of property rights. This concept is commonly used, but not easy to define. The common usage of a concept usually implies difficulty in definition, since many nuanced meanings will be given to this concept. In general, the context in which a concept is used significantly affects its meaning. For example, the concept of ownership in ancient Germanic law differs from that in modern German law, as a result of socio-economic changes.[1] Moreover, the concept of ownership may be used with some distinctions in different subjects of law. For example, this concept in the German Fundamental Law is broader than that in the German private law.[2] Therefore, a universal definition of a concept is difficult as well as undesirable due to the fact that the meaning of the concept changes over time and varies in different contexts. This research confines itself to property rights in modern property law. Yet, despite such limitation, defining the concept of property rights is still not easy.

2.1.1.1 The Closed System of Property Rights

In most jurisdictions, property law usually provides a closed system of property rights under the principle of *numerus clausus*. The principle requires that both the type and content of property rights must be defined by property law, and individual parties are not allowed to craft a new property right as they like.[3] The principle, therefore, serves a function of drawing a boundary between property rights and other kinds of rights. On account of this principle, defining the concept of property rights amounts to describing the property rights that are already recognized by law. The work of definition concerns exploring the common core of the property rights recognized and distinguishing them from other rights. In this sense, we can

1 In ancient Germanic law, ownership of land had different layers. In relation to one parcel of land, there could be two or more persons holding an interest in the form of ownership, but with different rankings. Land ownership was fragmented and distributed to different persons, which can be seen as a remarkable feature of the feudal land system. See Hübner 1918, p. 232. On the contrary, the right of ownership in the current civil law system is in principle unitary, and fragmentation of ownership is not allowed. However, the unitary feature is eroded in some sense, such as in the situation of trust and security transfer of ownership.

2 In German law, the term "*Eigentum*" in art. 13 of the Fundamental Law (*Grundgesetz*) is broader than that in § 903 BGB. "*This has resulted in a property concept that is specifically formulated for purposes of the constitutional property guarantee, and that is wider than the private-law concept of corporeal things.*" See Van der Walt 1999, p. 151.

3 Van Erp 2012, p. 67-69.

say that the principle of *numerus clausus* makes the work of definition less complex.

However, the principle also brings some difficulties with it. Firstly, the principle does not eliminate the possibility that different jurisdictions might recognize different types of property rights. A right might be treated differently in different jurisdictions. For example, the right of land lease is proprietary in some jurisdictions (such as English law), but it is shaped as a personal right with some proprietary features in other jurisdictions (such as German law and Dutch law).[4] Ownership might be allowed to be fragmented in one jurisdiction, but it is subject to the unitary principle in another legal system.[5] In addition, the principle of *numerus clausus* is implemented to different degrees by different systems of law. For example, compared with civil law, common law has a longer list of property rights; thus, individual parties under common law enjoy more autonomy in creating a legal relationship of property rights.[6] Some common law scholars even hold that "*the possibility of overreaching beneficial interests renders the concept of the numerus clausus redundant*".[7] In other words, the recognition of trust and equity law allow individuals to circumvent the principle without difficulty, which in essence makes the system open.[8]

Moreover, the principle should not be viewed as it appears: courts are always preparing to add new property rights into the list to cater to the demand in practice. The principle of *numerus clausus* can easily cause a problem of rigidity: property law fails to respond to the social demand for new forms of property rights immediately. The social-economic evolution requires that the list should be updated correspondingly. Before the list is updated by legislators, the judicial authority often recognizes some emerging property rights, which can be seen as an expedient. A famous illustration is what is known as the "right of expectation (*Anwartschaftsrecht*)" in German law: this right is not a "mature" property right, but it has certain proprietary effects and thus obscures the boundary between property rights and personal rights.[9] The possibility of the judicial recognition of new property rights means that only focusing on codes and statutes is not adequate, and the system of property rights in practice is often more diverse.

2.1.1.2 The Dynamic Aspect of Property Rights

Property rights are a concept used not only in a static dimension (namely the preservation against illegal interference) but also in a dynamic dimension (namely the transaction of rights). In reality, people seek to keep

4 See s. 1 LPA (1925), § 535 BGB, and art. 7:201 BW.
5 Matthews 2013, p. 319.
6 Swadling 2013, p. 181-182.
7 Sparkes 2012, p. 769.
8 Dalhuisen 2001, p. 289.
9 Baur and Stürner 2009, p. 30.

property rights as well as to transact them for a certain purpose. In the latter situation, it often concerns the question of how to distribute interests between the transferor and the transferee: what is acquired and retained by the transferee and the transferor respectively, and what do we mean by saying that a property right shifts from the transferor to the transferee. Once we take into consideration the dynamic dimension of property rights, the work of definition becomes more complicated.

For example, under the declaratory system in which publicity does not affect the acquisition of property rights, ownership is transferred upon the effect of the underlying contract, provided that the other conditions are fulfilled. Here, publicity has nothing to do with the acquisition of ownership *per se*. However, the transfer is not complete in the absence of publicity: the ownership acquired might be unenforceable against third parties in good faith with a competing interest.[10] For example, in the case of double sales, the ownership acquired by the first buyer might be subject to the second sale where the subsequent buyer acts in good faith and first completes the publicity. In this very situation, what do we mean when saying that the first transferee has acquired ownership upon the conclusion of the contract? Is a property right unenforceable against *bona fide* third parties still a (typical) property right? This question is closely related to another issue: what legal effects are essential for property rights and can make a right qualify as a property right?

The translative system, in contrast to the declaratory system, requires publicity as a condition for the derivative acquisition of property rights. Under a translative system, corporeal movables cannot be transferred until delivery occurs (the *traditio* rule), and transfer of immovable property only takes effect when entry into the land register is completed.[11] As property rights are only acquired at the moment of the completion of publicity, the rights acquired are effective against third parties, even if they are in bad faith. Under this system, the concept of property rights is used in a simpler and more consistent way. However, this does not mean that the questions mentioned at the end of the last paragraph do not exist for a translative system. For example, this system allows corporeal movables to be transferred in the absence of actual delivery, especially in the case of *traditio per constitutum possessorium*. Where the thing is still in factual control by other persons than the acquirer himself, the acquirer is always subject to the possibility of *bona fide* acquisition by third parties. As a result, the question also arises of whether a property right that cannot bind third parties in good faith can still be treated as proprietary. Notably, under Dutch law, ownership acquired in the way of *traditio per constitutum possessorium* cannot be effective against the property right existing on the object earlier and thus become "relativized (*gerelativeerd*)" (art. 3:90 (2) BW).[12]

10 Sagaert 2008, p. 18-19.
11 Sagaert 2008, p. 29; Krimphove 2006, p. 155.
12 Brahn 1992, p. 67.

In general, the application of the rule of *bona fide* acquisition means that the original property right loses its enforceability against third parties in good faith. The application causes a phenomenon of the "relativization" of property rights, as pointed out by some writers.[13] This phenomenon is a consequence of facilitating the "dynamic security": to promote the certainty of transactions and to protect the acquisition by third parties, the original proprietor's interest of preserving his proprietary right (the "static security") is sacrificed to some extent.[14] Truly, the *bona fide* protection only forms an exceptional restriction. However, it does imply that the exclusivity of property rights is limited under certain circumstances. Therefore, it can be said that all property rights are exclusive, but in varying degrees.

2.1.2 The Essence of Property Rights

In defining the concept of property rights, two questions are relevant. One concerns the essence, and the other concerns the characteristics of property rights. The concept of essence is used to describe what "property rights", as an umbrella term for a number of rights, are. In general, there are three approaches to the issue of essence: the subject-object approach, the subject-subject approach, and the mixed approach. The question of characteristics of property rights concerns how to differentiate property rights from other categories of rights, especially personal rights. The first question is addressed below, and the question of characteristics is discussed in another section (see 2.1.3).

2.1.2.1 The Subject-Object Approach

In the subject-object viewpoint, property rights are rights exercised by persons over things in the external world. Property rights imply a relationship of control between persons and things. The ownership of a house, for example, means that its owner is free to possess, use, enjoy and dispose of the house. According to this notion, the essence of property rights is a kind of legal control or domination over things.[15]

Blackstone, a famous common law scholar, expressed his notion of property rights in the following oft-cited excerpt.

> *"There is nothing which so generally strikes the imagination, and engages the affections of mankind, as the right of property; or that sole and despotic dominion which one man claims and exercises over the external things of the world, in total exclusion of the right of any other individual in the universe."*[16]

---

13 Nieuwenhuis 2015, p. 9; Snijders and Rank-Berenschot 2017, p. 56-57; Wieling 2006, p. 670.
14 O'Connor 2005, p. 47-49.
15 Füller 2006, p. 38.
16 Blackstone 1893, p. 3.

In his perception, property rights amount to absolute dominion over external things, and the starting point (or the essence) of property rights is the relationship between proprietors and things. Though Blackstone points out, at the end of the excerpt, that property rights are exclusive to the world, the effect of exclusivity seems to be a feature or a further explanation of the subject-object relationship only.

Like Blackstone, German scholar Dernburg also held that property rights represented a kind of relationship between the subject and the object.[17]

> *"Dinglich sind die Rechte, welche uns eine körperliche Sache unmittelbar unterwerfen [...]. Die Forderungsrechten oder Obligationen sind Rechte des Gläubigers auf eine vermögenswertige Leistung durch den Schuldner. Auch bei Forderungsrechten handelt es sich meistens um körperliche Sachen. Aber die Forderung gibt nur ein Rechte gegen den Schuldner, sie heißt den Berechtigten nicht in eine unmittelbar Beziehung zu der geschuldeten Sache. Die Leistung durch den Schuldner ist also der Durchgangspunkt, um die Sache zu gewinnen."*[18]

From Dernburg's notion, it is the direct domination by the proprietor over a specific object that distinguishes property rights from personal rights. Different from proprietors, creditors cannot gain by virtue of personal rights direct domination over the object. The power of domination over external things implies that property rights are a relationship of persons with respect to things. Wolf, another German scholar, also explicitly follows this approach.[19] Nowadays, property law scholars still hold the subject-object approach in understanding property rights.[20]

2.1.2.2 *The Subject-Subject Approach*

Under this approach, property rights are not a right to a thing, but to other persons. In other words, property rights give rise to a relationship between proprietors and their obligors, rather than a relationship between proprietors and things. The law is to regulate the interaction of human beings with respect to things. In this line of reasoning, things only serve as a "platform" for interpersonal interactions. The law focuses on the interactions *per se* rather than the "platform" on which they take place. Here a case in point

17 Gordley 2013, p. 225.

18 Dernburg 1894, p. 49-50. English translation: *"The proprietary right is a right based on which we can dominate tangible things [...]. The personal right or obligation is a right of the creditor with respect to a performance by the debtor. Most personal rights also concern tangible things. However, the personal right only gives rise to a right against the debtor, and the creditor has no direct relationship with the burdened thing. For acquiring the thing, performance by the debtor is a point of connection."*

19 Wolf and Wellenhofer 2011, p. 2.

20 MacCormick 1990, p. 1100; Penner 1996, p. 711; Snijders and Rank-Berenschot 2017, p. 3; Ritaine 2012, p. 13; Clarke and Kohler 2005, p. 17; Donahue 1980, p. 30.

is Robinson's isolated island. There is not any other person on the island except for Robinson himself. This implies that the social origin (the possibility of conflicts between persons) of property law is absent. As a result, it is nonsensical to say that Robinson has ownership of the island and of the things on the island in law.

Kant considers property rights as a relationship between the free will of different persons. The Kantian theory on the nature of rights is will-oriented. In the opinion of Kant, only human beings, as rational agents, have free will (freedom). Rights denote the province of free will of different persons. This implies that property rights represent a relationship between persons.

> *"A property right initially looks to be a strictly person-to-thing relation. On closer inspection, however, it does have a relational dimension, one that Kant certainly did not ignore [...]. In Kant's scheme, property is not merely relational; it involves a special kind of relationship. If I own an apple, your duty with respect to my property rights to that apple is negative in nature."*[21]

Von Savigny articulates his notion of property rights in constructing a theory of the private law system. The system is based on the concept of "legal relationship (*Rechtsbeziehung*)". In his opinion, a legal relationship *"appears to us a relation between person and person, determined by a rule of law."*[22] The categorization of legal relationships (the original self, the self-widened into the family, and the outer world) determines the system of private law as well as the system of private rights (family rights, property rights, and obligational rights).[23] Among the three categories of private rights, property rights represent domination over things. His view regarding the distinction between property rights and personal rights can be shown in the following except.

> *"All now is dependent upon whether the thing in itself, independently of an act of others, is the object-matter of our right or whether our right is immediately directed to an act of others as the object-matter subjected to our mastery and without regard to whether this act has for its end to invest us with the right to a thing or to the enjoyment of it [...]. The distinction between the two indeed for the most part, by no means however universally, coincides with the difference between an opponent undetermined and determined."*[24]

This excerpt indicates that property rights and personal rights can be distinguished according to two factors: one is the nature of their object, and the other is whether the obligor is definite. The theory of legal relationship implies that property rights are no more than an instrument to demarcate

21 Alexander and Peñalver 2012, p. 75-76.
22 Von Savigny 1867, p. 271.
23 Von Savigny 1867, p. 280.
24 Von Savigny 1867, p. 302-304.

the province of free will. Thus, property rights are necessarily a relationship between persons. The view is followed by some later German lawyers, such as Windschied.[25]

In the common law world, Hohfeld is a representative theorist who articulates property rights as a relationship between persons.

> *"A right in rem is not a right 'against a thing' [...]. A man may indeed sustain close and beneficial physical relations to a given physical thing: he may physically control and use such thing, and he may physically exclude others from any similar control or enjoyment. But, obviously, such purely physical relations could as well exist quite apart from, or occasionally in spite of, the law of organized society: physical relations are wholly distinct from juridical relations."*[26]

The subject-subject approach is approved by some contemporary scholars.[27]

2.1.2.3 *The Mixed Approach*

The mixed approach is the result of an attempt to combine the preceding two arguments. According to this approach, property rights are not only a relationship between persons and things or a relationship between persons and persons. Instead, property rights are a compound of both. For example, ownership of a house is deemed to embody two relationships: the owner's relationship to the house and the owner's relationship with other persons. The former concerns a positive dimension of ownership: the owner has a right to dominate the house. The latter implies a negative dimension: the domination is protected from outside interferences.[28] The mixed approach is popular among contemporary scholars.[29]

An advantage of the mixed approach is that the approach, after combining the subject-object and subject-subject approach, can respond to criticism of the two approaches. However, the combination leads to an internal paradox. Upon treating property rights as a relationship between proprietors and things, how can we also deem that they are also a relationship with other persons? Essence (*esse* in Latin) denotes "*the basic or primary element in the being of a thing; the thing's nature, or that without which it could not be what it is*".[30] In this research, the essence of property rights refers to the "most basic" element of property rights. Thus, it is single and pure.

Indeed, property rights have the feature of thinghood and must exist on a tangible or intangible thing, as will be shown later (see 2.1.3.1). However, as will also be shown below, the essence of property rights should not be confused with their features. In fact, the issue of essence is a preliminary matter

---

25 Lebon 2010, p. 37.
26 Hohfeld 1917, p. 721.
27 Wolf and Neuner, p. 240-245; Cohen 1954, p. 374.
28 Yin 2002, p. 281.
29 Xie 2011, p. 8.
30 Blackburn 2008, online.

for comparison. Before starting to compare property rights and personal rights, it is necessary to make sure that the two types of rights are homogeneous: they share the same essence. Moreover, the subsequent discussion also criticizes the subject-object approach in different aspects. In general, the mixed approach is open to the same criticism because it includes the subject-object notion as an essential part.

2.1.2.4 *Property Rights as an Interpersonal Relationship*

A *What Does Law Concern?*

Law regulates persons' conduct. In this aspect, law is similar to other social norms, such as ethics and religions: they all regulate behaviors by persons.[31] On the other hand, law is different from other social norms. Law only regulates persons' external conduct, while ethics, for example, goes further and also concentrates on internal conscience.[32] In general, internal ideas of human beings are beyond the regulation of law, except when the idea is an origin of conduct that has occurred or might occur in the future.[33] In the field of private law, contracts and torts are all a result of conduct. When a valid contract is created, private law focus on performance by the debtor, and whether the debtor has internal willingness to perform the debt is irrelevant.[34] However, ethics not only requires keeping the promise, but also doing so voluntarily. Criminal law might impose punishment over those who only have an internal intention to commit crimes, this is because this intention is an origin of the imminent criminal act. If the criminal act will not happen, then just having the internal intention does not violate law. However, merely having the intention might breach an ethical duty.

> *"The conception of law, so as it relates to an obligation corresponding to it (that is, its moral conception), concerns first the external and practical relation only of one person towards another, so far as their actions as facts can influence on one another (either immediately or mediately) [...]. Law, then, is the aggregation of the conditions, on which the arbitrement of one can be united with that of the other according to the universal law of liberty."*[35]

> *"The latter take significance from the law; and, since the purpose of the law is to regulate the conduct of human beings, all juridical relations must, in order to be clear and direct in their meaning, be predicated of such human beings."*[36]

31 Giese 1948, p. 22; Schumann 1959, p. 31.
32 Giese 1948, p. 22; Schumann 1959, p. 31.
33 Radbruch 1929, p. 17.
34 Hedemann 1927, p. 43-44.
35 Kant 1799, p. 28-29.
36 Hohfeld 1917, p. 26.

As a result, property law, as a part of the entire legal system, also regulates interpersonal relationships only.[37]

B Objects or Things Lack Will

The fact that objects or things have no free will implies that the relationship between persons and things merely exists in the physical sense. In Kant's view, for example, freedom is the only original or natural right belonging to every person.[38] The ability of human beings to decide and reason by rationality makes them different from other creatures and things. Only between persons, can there be social interactions susceptible to regulation by law.

> *"Dem Berechtigten einer Sache steht damit die rechtliche Macht zu, mit einer Sache im Verhältnis zu anderen Personen zu verfahren. Die Beziehung zwischen dem Berechtigten und der Sache besteht in der Gebrauchsmöglichkeit."*[39]

The owner of a house may live in the house for a long period. However, the house cannot interact with the owner because the house lacks free will. Therefore, no conflict can occur between the person and the house. Property law is created to solve conflicts between different persons with respect to the enjoyment, use and ownership of property and to maintain the order of property. The right of ownership is just a legal device used to regulate the relationship between the owner and other persons. For example, if a person has ownership of a bicycle, then this person is entitled to request others not to damage this bicycle. Moreover, the person can also transfer ownership of the bicycle, and, in principle, others cannot intervene in the process of transfer. In general, whether and how the owner makes use of the bicycle is not regulated by law, provided that no other persons are adversely influenced. Therefore, the problem of the subject-object theory is that it mistakenly confuses the physical (*de facto*) relationship with the legal (*de jure*) relationship. In practice, different persons may have competing claims with respect to things. The principal purpose of property law is to determine the priority or relative strength between these claims.

C A Systematic Concern

Thirdly, the subject-subject approach is also required to maintain the consistency of the entire private law system. In general, only objects of the same kind can be coherently arrayed within one system. In other words, all individual components in a given system should share the same essence. Otherwise, the system will be prey to becoming contradictory. In the sphere of private law, there is a fundamental dichotomy between patrimonial

---

37 Wolf and Neuner 2012, p. 205.

38 Alexander and Peñalver 2012, p. 71.

39 Füller 2006, p. 43. English translation: "*Therefore, the legal authority owned by the holder of a thing lies in dealing with the thing in relation to others. The relationship between the holder and the thing lies in the possibility of use.*"

rights and personality rights. The reason why both can be incorporated into the system of private law is that they share the same essence or the same denominator: both are a relationship between persons. In this line of reasoning, if one recognizes that personal rights are a relationship between persons (the creditor and the debtor), then he or she has to also treat property rights as an interpersonal relationship. It is impossible to categorize two kinds of rights of different essence into one system without undermining the systematic consistency.

> *"In the first place, it is striking that in the Pandecist approach to property law, emphasis is placed on the relationship between the person and the thing. This is not a very transparent means of presentation: the law is always concerned with regulating the legal relationship between persons after all. It is true that sometimes also a relationship to a thing can be construed, but that needlessly complicates the matter because different standards are then used for the law of obligations and the law of property [...]. Thus the law of obligations and law of property are brought back to the same denominator: the question of both legal areas is to determine to whom one is bound, independent of any relationship to the thing."*[40]

As mentioned above, the fact that property rights and personal rights have the same essence is a precondition for comparing them and revealing the characteristics of property rights.

D Remedies for Property Rights

The legal maxim *"no remedy, no right"* also implies that property rights are not a relationship between persons and things. Remedies and subjective rights are closely intertwined in the sense that rights are valueless in the absence of legal remedies. Rights are a legal basis for remedies, which will ensue when rights are infringed. Remedies must involve two or more persons. The interpersonal nature of remedies implies that property rights are a relationship between persons.[41]

> *"Although the relationship of a person to a thing may have meaning in philosophical discourse, it does not in legal discourse, because a thing cannot defend or bring a lawsuit."*[42]

Therefore, treating property rights as an interpersonal relationship helps us to understand how the law of property functions in the real world. The relational attribute of property rights becomes evident when disputes, which necessarily involve different persons, occur.

---

40 Smits 2002, p. 252.

41 Füller 2006, p. 43.

42 Donahue 1980, p. 30.

2.1.2.5 *Two Irrelevant Issues*

The subject-subject approach is often questioned from two angles. The first criticism is that the approach is useless. According to this criticism, the subject-subject approach fails to indicate how to distinguish property rights from personal rights.[43] If property rights are viewed as an interpersonal relationship, then they are not distinguished from personal rights. This is because personal rights are also a relationship between persons. The criticism is based on a concern about utility: the approach fails to provide anything useful for the differentiation. In contrast, the subject-object approach creates such utility: in light of this approach, one can tell whether a given right is personal or proprietary.

Indeed, the preceding criticism correctly points out the "weakness" of the subject-subject approach. However, it fails to note the distinction between the issue of essence and the issue of differentiation. The subject-subject approach only concerns the essence of property rights. It does not intend to tell us how to distinguish them from personal rights. To identify a property right, one should pay attention to the "external features (*externe kenmerken*)" of property rights, which will be explored later (see 2.1.3).[44] As has been reiterated, essence is a preliminary issue for the differentiation. Only after demonstrating that property rights and personal rights share the same essence or the same denominator, does comparing them become possible.

The second criticism is that the subject-subject approach is rooted in, besides law, public policies and other extra-legal factors, which opens the door for public regulations and restrictions of private property rights. The criticism is raised against the background that the essence of property rights is discussed in relation to the movement of legal realism in the world of common law.[45] According to some scholars, the subject-subject approach takes extra-legal factors into consideration, an approach that disintegrates property rights and leads to the "*death of property*".[46] As a result, the subject-subject approach weakens the value of property rights for protecting individuals' freedom against public regulation.[47]

In general, the criticism from the political perspective is irrelevant to the essence of property rights. The subject-subject perception is merely a result of a conceptual analysis, irrespective of any political concerns and social values. The interpersonal relationship advocated by this approach is malleable. In other words, the notion that property rights are an interpersonal relationship can fit into each theory of property law, whether the social-

43 Smith 2012, p. 1697-1700; Penner 1996, p. 714.
44 Sagaert, Tilleman and Laurent 2013, p. 5-6.
45 William 1998, p. 296-297.
46 Krier 1990, p. 75.
47 Grey 1980, p. 69-70; William 1998, p. 298-299; Smith 2012, p. 1697.

obligation theory,[48] the personhood theory,[49] the social-relation theory,[50] or the individual-liberty theory.[51] The subject-subject approach should not be deemed as an "accomplice" of the anti-liberalism idea. For example, Kant, though as an advocate of individuals' liberty, approves that property rights are a subject-subject relationship, as has been pointed out above. In a nutshell, the subject-subject approach is value-neutral.

2.1.3 The Features of Property Rights

After describing the essence of property rights, we explore the distinctive features that enable property rights to stand out from other rights, especially personal rights. In general, property rights have two important features: thinghood and absoluteness. The term thinghood is borrowed from Penner's article, *The "Bundle of Rights" Picture of Property*.[52] In this research, thinghood means that property rights should be created on a specific thing, whether tangible or intangible. The other feature, absoluteness, amounts to the third-party effect or the effect of exclusivity in this research. It is used to describe the legal consequence that property rights can be enforced against third parties in general.[53] The feature forms a sharp contrast to the principle of privity in contract law as well as the principle of *paritas creditorum* in the law of obligations. These two features are elaborated on in the following parts.

2.1.3.1 Thinghood

Property rights are rights on a specific thing, as required by the principle of specificity in property law. It is impossible to create or transfer a property right where things are not ascertained or where no things are involved.[54]

> *"It follows from the principle of general enforceability that, if my right in a thing is to be a property right, it must be possible to identify the thing in question. Because a property right in a thing is enforceable against everyone who comes into contact with the thing, it must be possible to identify whether or not any particular thing has become burdened in this way."*[55]

---

48 Alexander 2009, p. 745.
49 Radint 1982, p. 957.
50 Singer and Beermann 1993, p. 217.
51 William 1998, p. 277.
52 *"The essential feature distinguishing property is that it consists of a right to a thing which is only contingently connected to any particular person,"* and it *"[...] characterizes the objects of property which serves to mediate between an owner and his legal relation to all others who have that duty."* See Penner 1996, p. 711.
53 Snijders and Rank-Berenschot 2017, p. 48.
54 Schwab and Prütting 2006, p. 9.
55 Clarke and Kohler 2005, p. 156.

The feature of thinghood, including the requirement of specificity, helps distinguish property rights from other types of rights in the following sense.

A What Does Thinghood Mean?

Firstly, thinghood implies an economic attribute of the object of property rights, thereby drawing a line between patrimonial rights and non-patrimonial rights. Property law forms a part of the patrimonial law, and property rights are of economic nature.

> *"The first feature of the composition of a patrimony is that it is limited to economic values. As diverse as these values might be, all patrimonial components share the possibility of being converted into money."*[56]

Property rights emerge against the background that there is a motivation to maximize the utility of limited resources and to prevent low efficiency caused by externalities in managing resources.[57] On the basis of the economic attribute implied by the thinghood, it is possible to separate property rights from the other rights that have no economic value, such as the right to names, the right to "bodily integrity (*lichamelijke interiteit*)",[58] and the political right to vote.

Secondly, the feature of thinghood implies the existence of a thing, whether tangible or intangible. This makes it possible to distinguish property rights from some personal rights that concern no things. For example, in the situation of employment we cannot say that the employer has any property right to the employee's labor. Labor is not a thing in property law. In contemporary law, requiring a debtor to do or not to do something is possible, but any direct force over the debtor's body for the purpose of performance is in principle immoral and illegal.[59]

Thirdly, the requirement of specificity distinguishes those personal rights merely concerning unspecific or generic things from property rights. The requirement of specificity blocks a number of personal rights outside the door of property rights. For example, a claim based on a contract of sale with respect to a certain amount of generic goods (such as 10 bicycles of certain make and type) is doomed to be personal, provided that individualization is not completed yet.[60] This is why only specific corporeal movables can be transferred even under the declaratory system, as opposed to the translative system, despite the irrelevance of delivery to the acquisition of ownership.

---

56 Christian Atias, Droit Civil: Les Biens (11th ed.), cited from Van Erp 2012, p. 38.

57 Demsetz 1967, p. 347-359. In economics, externalities refer to the costs or benefits that affect a party who did not choose to incur those costs or benefits.

58 Meijers 1948, p. 266.

59 Nowadays, imprisonment for debts may be still possible as a measure of indirect execution. However, it is subject to strict restrictions and only permitted in rare situations. See De Jong, Krans and Wissink 2018, p. 78.

60 Martinson 2006, p. 15.

> *"As a result of the principle of specificity, ownership of generic goods can pass only when certain goods are separated and appropriated for delivery to the acquirer. And, where there is a contract for the transfer of future goods, ownership can pass only after the goods have come into existence."*[61]

However, the requirement of specificity has been relaxed to some extent. An example is what is known as bulk ownership in English law (see 3.4.2.1.B). In this situation, a purchaser of generic goods which form a part of a specific bulk, but are not individualized, may still gain a proprietary interest, namely ownership of a share of the bulk involved.[62] Another example is that in the secured transaction of movables, the requirement of *specificity* is eased to the requirement of *ascertainability* in some jurisdictions.[63] As a result, parties do not have to specify each object involved in advance; only a general description with adequate accuracy suffices. Thanks to this transformation, it is possible to dispose of future assets, namely assets that have not come into existence yet.[64]

It is worthwhile mentioning that personal rights, such as the right of lease, might also exist on a specific object. This implies that the feature of thinghood is not exclusively owned by property rights.[65] The difference lies in that property rights *must*, while personal rights *can*, take a specific or an ascertainable thing as the object.

B What Does Thinghood Not Mean?

The preceding discussion has shown that the feature of thinghood requires that property rights are only available with respect to a specific, at least ascertainable, thing. The feature does not mean that the object must be tangible. In current society, property rights can also be created on intangible things. For example, the BGB prescribes that "things (*Sachen*)" have to be tangible (§ 90 BGB); nevertheless, property rights can also be created on incorporeal things, such as the pledge of rights and the usufruct of rights.[66] In the Netherlands, only corporeal things (*zaken*) can be the object of ownership (art. 5:1 and art. 3:2 BW), but incorporeal things, such as claims and intellectual property rights, can be the object of pledge and usufruct.[67]

The continuing emergence of new forms of wealth, such as stocks, bonds, intellectual property and Bitcoins, has made the dogma obsolete that the object of property rights should be tangible.[68] In fact, it is the specificity (at least the ascertainability) rather than the tangibility that matters for the creation, transfer and acquisition of property rights.

---

61 Van Vliet 2012, p. 892.
62 Clarke and Kohler 2005, p. 484-486.
63 Struycken 1999, p. 582; Bülow 2012, Rn. 1293.
64 Dalhuisen 2016, p. 323.
65 Sagaert 2005, p. 991.
66 Wilhelm 2010, p. 3.
67 Akkermans 2008, p. 289-293.
68 Krier 1990, p. 76.

> *"Indeed, it is not the physicality of the asset but rather the reasonable description possibility that is the key in a modern rights-based system of proprietary rights no longer constrained by physical notions."*[69]

The dichotomy between tangibility and intangibility only reflects the physical attribute of objects, but property law should take the social effect as the prominent criterion in defining the scope of the object of property rights. Truly, the nature of the object of property rights sometimes affects the types of rights that can be created. However, it should not be deemed to be decisive for demarcating the scope of application of property law rules.[70] The notion of equally treating tangible and intangible assets lays a foundation for the general part of the patrimonial law (Book 3) in the new BW.[71] Tangible things can be specified and individualized, and property rights can exist on them. By the same token, where intangible things are sufficiently specific, they can also be an object of property rights.

> *"Virtual property shares three legally relevant characteristics with real world property: rivalrousness, persistence, and interconnectivity. Based on these shared characteristics, subsequent sections will show that virtual property should be treated like real world property under the law."*[72]

Here, it should be noted that once personal rights are taken as the object of disposals, such as assignment and pledge, they begin to have a proprietary aspect.[73] As is shown in this research, like the transfer of corporeal movables, the assignment of claims also faces a problem of multiple disposals (see 4.1.1.1). This implies that the disposal of corporeal tangibles and that of claims have the same problem concerning publicity: how to address the problem of information asymmetry to potential acquirers. Nevertheless, the proprietary aspect does not mean that claims *per se* are a property right. At most, we can say that the disposal of claims is proprietary in the sense that relevant rules of property law are applicable, but claims *per se* are in nature not proprietary.

2.1.3.2 Absoluteness

In differentiating property rights from personal rights, another critical criterion is absoluteness. Property rights are an absolute right with *erga omnes* effect, while personal rights are a relative right governed by the principle of *paritas creditorum*. Thus, the effect of exclusivity is a distinctive feature of property rights. If property rights are understood as a bundle of rights,

---

69 Dalhuisen 2016, p. 321.
70 Dalhuisen 2016, p. 330.
71 Meijers 1954, p. 159.
72 Fairfield 2005, p. 1047.
73 Sagaert 2005, p. 1000; Lebon 2010, p. 4.

as often held in common law, then the right to exclude is deemed to be a fundamental element.[74] The effect of exclusivity allows property rights to be a more secure and reliable device for the utilization of things.[75] This is not difficult to understand. For example, different from a proprietary right to use, a contractual right to use is always under threats from competing claims held by others.[76] In the subsequent discussion, we elaborate on this feature of property rights by disclosing their legal consequences or effects.

A The Duty to Refrain

Absoluteness is first shown by the fact that third parties have a general duty to refrain from illegal interference with the property right. Property rights, needless to say, should be respected by others. The duty to refrain from interference also requires that the law should provide sufficient protection to proprietors. The protection may take the form of recovering the object, removing the imminent danger, suspending the existing interference, or providing compensation for the loss caused. Interferers are treated as a type of third party.

Typically, interferers are strangers who lack a legal reason to take any action with respect to the thing in question. Unlike subsequent acquirers, another type of third party, interferers have no intention to participate in a consensual relationship with the proprietor. Moreover, interferers are also different from general creditors: the latter are in a competing relationship with the secured creditors with respect to the debtor's assets. Thus, we can say that interferers often do not have any specific legal interest in the infringed thing. As interferences trigger obligations, how to avoid conducting illegal interventions becomes important. Following Merrill's opinion, this type of third party is called "strange interferers" in this research.

> *"By stranger, I mean any person who has no interest in particular objects of value other than to avoid interfering with those claimed by others."*[77]

In reality, each of us tries to not interfere with others' things and to avoid becoming a strange interferer. Otherwise, the world would fall into chaos.

In respect of the duty to refrain from interference, property rights and personal rights appear to bear some similarity. If we acknowledge that rights mean a legal interest enjoyed by the holder of rights, then personal rights should also be protected from illegal interference by third parties.

---

74 Merrill 1998, p. 730.
75 Kelly 2014, p. 860.
76 Hijma, Van Dam, Valk and Van Schendel 2016, p. 323.
77 Merrill 2015, p. 29.

> *"De passieve verbintenis van eenieder om geen inbreuk te plegen op een zakelijk recht, bestaat immers ook ten aanzien van persoonlijke rechten. Derden hebben de verplichting om zich te onthouden van inbreuken op persoonlijke rechten waarvan ze kennis hebben."*[78]

Indeed, personal rights might be protected from illegal interference in practice. For instance, a third party who intentionally induces the debtor to breach a contract may be required to compensate the damage suffered by the creditor.[79] This tort law protection constitutes an exception to the principle of privity as well as the relative effect of obligations, thereby blurring the line between property rights and personal rights.[80]

Nevertheless, the blurring effect should not be overstated. Personal rights are a legal relationship only between the creditor and the debtor. This determines that they can only in rare cases be interfered with by a third party. In principle, where the creditor does not obtain performance, it is the rules on default by debtors that will be applied.[81] When the creditor requires a third party to compensate for the damage of his personal right, strict conditions have to be fulfilled. For example, the interferer has to be malicious, and the act of interference is illegal or immoral.[82] Therefore, even though personal rights might be said to have a general effect against illegal interference, we have to acknowledge that such interference only arises in rare situations.

B The Right of Preference

Absoluteness is also reflected by the "right of preference" (or the preferential effect). In this research, this term is used to describe two different situations: one is the priority of secured creditors over unsecured creditors, and the other is the priority of older property rights over younger property rights.

B1: Property Rights as an Exception to Paritas Creditorum

Preferential effect first occurs where the holder of property rights has a prior position over unsecured creditors in the event of the debtor's insolvency. The principle of equality between creditors is the starting point for the distribution of the insolvent debtor's assets. It can only be overridden when statutory law prescribes otherwise.[83] The device of proprietary security constitutes an important exception to this principle. In practice, limited property rights of security, such as mortgage and pledge, can typically give

78 Sagaert, Tilleman and Laurent 2013, p. 5-6. English translation: "*The passive obligation borne by every person of causing no infringement on a property right also exists in relation to personal rights. Third parties have a duty to refrain themselves from interfering with personal rights they know.*"

79 Non-Contractual Liability Arising out of Damage Caused to Another, p. 546-555.

80 Hijma, Van Dam, Valk and Van Schendel 2016, p. 325.

81 Reehuis 2015, p. 358; Rank-Berenschot 1992, p. 133; Wolf and Neuner 2012, p. 227.

82 Non-Contractual Liability Arising out of Damage Caused to Another 2009, p. 546.

83 Sagaert 2005, p. 1029.

rise to a preferential effect. However, the purpose of security can also be realized in other ways, such as the reservation of ownership, a device which realizes the purpose of security by allowing the owner to recover the object. In general, the effect of preference is deemed by some scholars as the "*most important difference in practice between proprietary rights and non-proprietary rights*"[84] or "*the most significant practical application of the distinction between in personam and in rem rights*".[85]

This preferential effect is related to another type of third party: unsecured creditors or general creditors.[86] Different from strange interferers, unsecured creditors have a stake in the existence of proprietary security rights. In the event of the debtor's insolvency, whether and to what extent the debtor's assets are encumbered will affect how much property is available for unsecured creditors. In this sense, we can consider unsecured creditors as a type of third party in relation to proprietary security rights.

What should be noted here is that the law may provide, for policy reasons, a statutory privilege for some personal rights, such as the right of employees to salaries. With such privilege, these personal rights can also be enforced in priority to unsecured claims and even some property rights in the event of insolvency. Nevertheless, the statutory privilege is by no means a property right.[87] One reason is that, unlike pledgees and mortgagees, a creditor owning a statutory privilege cannot exercise his right outside the insolvency procedure: he lacks an executory title.[88] Moreover, the statutory privilege might not exist with respect to specific things, forming the "general privilege (*algemene voorrecht*)".[89] Even the "specific privilege (*bijzondere voorrecht*)", a kind of privilege existing with respect to certain specific assets, lacks the effect of tracing (*droit de suite*). The privileged creditor is not allowed to enforce his right against a third party who has acquired the asset from the debtor.[90] In other words, the specific privilege does not have an effect of preference over subsequent acquirers, a type of third party discussed below.

B2: Property Rights Subject to the Rule of Prior Tempore

The right of preference can also exist where the rule of *prior tempore* is applied. According to this rule, older property rights are in principle prior

84 Clarke and Kohler 2005, p. 163.

85 Bridge, Gullifer, McMeel and Worthington 2013, p. 4.

86 Here two points should be noted. The first is that the term "preference" is confined to the situation of two competing property rights by some scholars, while the legal effect of preference of proprietary security rights in relation to unsecured creditors is called the effect of separation. The other is that the effect of separation involves not only the situation of insolvency, but also that of judicial attachment. See Snijders and Rank-Berenschot 2017, p. 49.

87 Reehuis and Heisterkamp 2019, p. 757.

88 Reehuis and Heisterkamp 2019, p. 757.

89 Reehuis and Heisterkamp 2019, p. 765.

90 Reehuis and Heisterkamp 2019, p. 758.

to younger ones. It aims at dealing with the conflict between two or more property rights existing on the same object, rather than the conflict between personal rights and property rights.

> *"In case of a collision between two property rights the issue is decided by the principle of priority; the oldest property right is stronger than the younger one (droit de preference; prior tempore, potior iure)."*[91]

The rule implies *"the absolute nature of the pre-existing property right"*.[92] Different from property law, the law of obligations applies the principle of equality to the conflict between different personal rights.

In light of this rule, we can say that the holder of younger property rights is a third party in relation to the holder of older property rights. This type of third party is termed "subsequent acquirers" in this research. Different from strange interferers, subsequent acquirers have a specific legal interest with respect to a specific object. The term has significant similarity with the concept of potential transactors in Merrill's theory.

> *"The audience of potential transactors [...] consists of persons interested in engaging in exchange of rights to particular things having significant value and duration [...]. I mean anyone who has an interest in purchasing, selling, leasing, or borrowing [...]. Thus potential transactors are not just buyers and sellers, but include secured lenders, insurers, judgement creditors, asset securitization bundlers, and any others [...]."*[93]

A subsequent acquirer is "subsequent" in the sense that he is a latecomer: at the moment of his acquisition of a property right, there might already be one or more property rights existing on the object. The existing property rights precede and thereby have priority to the property right obtained by the subsequent acquirer. For example, where a thing that has been encumbered with a pledge is transferred, the acquirer is a subsequent acquirer in relation to the pledgee. The security right comes into existence prior to the occurrence of the transfer of ownership. Thus, it can bind the new owner.

However, it should be borne in mind that the *prior tempore* rule may also exist in some situations in the law of obligations, giving rise to an exception to the principle of *paritas creditorum*. For example, the BW provides that where there are two competing personal claims for delivery of the same object, the older claim can under certain conditions prevail over the younger claim.[94]

---

91 Salomon 2008, p. 15.

92 *"A property right can only be impaired by a new property right if the holder of the existing property right is a party to the creation of the new property right. If not, the absolute nature of the pre-existing property right protects the holder of such a property right against later property rights."* See Van Erp 2006 (1), p. 16.

93 Merrill 2015, p. 30.

94 Salomon 2008, p. 82.

> Art. 3:298 BW: *"Vervolgen twee of meer schuldeisers ten aanzien van één goed met elkaar botsende rechten op levering, dan gaat in hun onderlinge verhouding het oudste recht op levering voor, tenzij uit de wet, uit de aard van hun rechten, of uit de eisen van redelijkheid en billijkheid anders voortvloeit."*[95]

Indeed, this provision blurs the boundary between property rights and personal rights.[96] However, this should not be overstated. The priority enjoyed by the older creditor does not elevate the claim to be a proprietary right. Art. 3:298 BW is only a specific rule which, under several conditions and subject to exceptions, grants a priority to the older claim. The legal nature of the older claim is not changed, remaining to be a personal right.[97]

C The Right to Follow

In understanding the feature of absoluteness, the *right to follow* (*droit de suite*) needs to be mentioned. This right means that the proprietor is entitled to exercise the property right wherever the thing exists. It mainly arises in the situation where the thing is not factually controlled by the proprietor.

> *"Property rights are characterized by the notion of droit de suite: the titleholder is allowed to follow and claim his property from whoever holds that property without any title to it (e.g. a lease contract or a right of usufruct)."*[98]

> *"Het volgrecht (droit de suite), naar oud recht meestal aangeduid als zaakgevolg, is ook een consequentie van het absolute karakter van goederenrechtelijke rechten: de rechthebbende kan zijn recht uitoefenen ongeacht onder wie het object van zijn recht zich bevindt."*[99]

Some scholars argue that the decisive difference between personal rights and property rights lies in the right to follow.[100] According to this viewpoint, property rights are in essence a "qualitative obligation (*kwalitatieve verbintenis*)" between the owner and the holder of a property right granted by the former. However, unlike personal rights, property rights can exist independently from the circulation of the object: the latter can bind automatically the person who later acquires the object. Here, it should be noted that this "qualitative obligation" approach may confine the concept of property rights to limited property rights, and the concept of ownership is

95 English translation: Art. 3:298 BW: *"Where two or more creditors have conflicting claims for delivery of one thing, the oldest debt-claim has priority in their mutual relation, unless law, the nature of the claims or the requirement of reasonableness and fairness requires otherwise."*

96 Nieuwenhuis 2015, p. 10.

97 Snijders and Rank-Berenschot 2017, p. 274-275.

98 Salomon 2008, p. 15.

99 Snijders and Rank-Berenschot 2017, p. 50. English translation: *"The right to follow (droit de suite), which was called thing-attaching in the old legal system, is also an outcome of the absolute feature of property rights: the entitled can exercise his right irrespective of where the object of the right situates."*

100 Ginossar 1979, p. 286; Sagaert 2005, p. 997.

used in the general sense of belonging.[101] The object of ownership includes both tangible and intangible things, giving rise to a distinction between tangible ownership and intangible ownership. Regardless of whether the approach is convincing, it implies that the right to follow is not embodied within personal rights.[102]

The right to follow can take place in various situations. For example, an owner has a right to recover his property from the person who commits illegal dispossession. The right of recovery involves the duty to refrain from interference as discussed above, and the dispossessor is in fact a strange interferer. In addition, a secured creditor can keep his right of preference with respect to the collateral, despite the fact that the collateral has been purchased and controlled by a third party. The purchaser of the collateral is, in fact, a subsequent acquirer who has to respect the secured creditor. The two examples indicate that where the right to follow exists, the third party involved can be either a strange interferer or a subsequent acquirer. Therefore, the right to follow overlaps with the duty to refrain from interference and the effect of preference. As just mentioned, the right to follow shows the effect of exclusivity of property rights from a special angle: it highlights that the location of the object has nothing to do with the enforcement of property rights.

D Conclusion

In the preceding discussion, we have shown that property rights are absolute in relation to three types of third parties. The feature of absoluteness includes three aspects (the duty to refrain from interference, the right of preference, and the right to follow), and third parties can be categorized into three groups (strange interferers, general creditors, and subsequent acquirers). Some personal rights also have an absolute effect under some circumstances. This, however, only means that these personal rights are "propertized (*verdinglicht* in German or *verzakelijkt* in Dutch)" without becoming a property right.[103]

The three groups of third parties all bear a negative duty or a duty of respect to the proprietor, but they differ in terms of the situations where they appear.[104] In general, strange interferers appear in the case of illegal interference, general creditors in the case of insolvency, and subsequent acquirers in the situation of the acquisition of property rights. Moreover, they have different interests: (1) strange interferers usually have a need to avoid conducting illegal interventions in order to avert associated liabilities;

---

101 Gretton 2007, p. 810-811.

102 Ghestin and Goubeaux 1994, p. 185; Valsan 2013, p. 498-499.

103 Wolf and Neuner 2012, p. 228; Snijders and Rank-Berenschot 2017, p. 57-59.

104 In contemporary property law, positive duties can become part of the relationship of property rights in an increasing number of situations. However, positive duties must be supplementary and have a sufficiently close connection with the property right. See Sagaert 2005, p. 998; McFarlane 2011, p. 311.

(2) general creditors have a stake in whether and to what extent the debtor's assets have been encumbered; and (3) subsequent acquirers want to know whether their counterparty has the power of disposal and whether there are existing property rights on the object concerned. As will be shown later, this difference means that the three types of third parties demand different proprietary information (see 2.2.2.2).

2.1.4 A Possible Definition

The preceding two sections have shown the most important characteristics that differentiate property rights from other types of rights: thinghood and absoluteness. The feature of thinghood requires that the object of property rights, whether tangible or intangible, should be specific and of economic value. The feature of absoluteness or exclusivity means that property rights can be enforced against general third parties. After discussing the essence and the two characteristics of property rights, we can say that property rights are a right that can be effective against third parties with respect to specific things, whether tangible or intangible.

2.2 Property Rights, Proprietary Information and Publicity

As the preceding section shows, property rights must exist on specific or ascertainable things and can be enforced against third parties (see 2.1). The crucial criterion that distinguishes property rights from personal rights is that the former can be enforced against third parties. In this section, our attention shifts from property rights to publicity, the theme of this research. Property rights are enforceable against third parties. Therefore, these parties should be made aware of the existence of property rights. As will be shown later, publicity serves as the principal method of communicating information concerning property rights, though not being the only method. In this sense, property rights and publicity are closely linked.

> *"Der absolute Geltungsanspruch der dinglichen Rechte macht es nicht nur erforderlich, die gesetzlich zugelassenen Sachenrechtstypen zu begrenzen, das Bestehen konkreter dinglicher Rechte muss vielmehr auch erkennbar sein."*[105]

> *"Furthermore, again given the strength of any property right, third parties must be able to obtain information about such a right: publicity is vital in property relations."*[106]

105 Wolf and Wellenhofer 2011, p. 16. English Translation: *"The absolute effect of property rights not only makes it necessary to limit the types of property rights recognized by law, but also to ensure that the existence of a specific property right is transparent."*

106 Van Erp 2012, p. 76.

This section seeks to provide a general discussion of the link between property rights and publicity. Here we introduce an intermediary concept that connects property rights and publicity. Based on this concept, a framework is provided for the subsequent discussion. The intermediary concept is "proprietary information". In this research, proprietary information refers to information concerning property rights. It includes the information regarding the subject (the person who holds the property right), the object (the thing on which the property right exists), and the content of the property right (the entitlements enjoyed by the subject with respect to the object).

After introducing the concept of proprietary information, this section further discusses the question whether and in what sense proprietary information is important for transacting parties and third parties. Here, transacting parties of a property right refer to the parties who establish or transfer this right, and third parties are the parties who are not transacting parties and bear a duty to respect this property right. As has been shown above, there are three types of third parties: strange interferers, subsequent acquirers, and general creditors (see 2.1.3.2). In this section, we describe the proprietary information demanded by every type of third party. At the end of this section, we show that publicity serves as the most important, though not the sole, means of providing proprietary information for third parties. As a regime in property law, publicity has its special aspects.

2.2.1 Information and Proprietary Information

2.2.1.1 Information

Information implies knowing something. In the economics of information, information refers to the *"data available to individuals, firms, or governments at the time economic decisions have to be taken. Information in this sense refers to economic statistics and the collection, use, and interpretation of those statistics."*[107] This definition is an outcome of the understanding of information by economists, thereby being not universally applicable. It indicates two aspects of information: one is that information is essential for making decisions (the value of information), and the other is that information involves some activities that are not without costs (the cost of information). Therefore, information can be seen as a "product" that gives rise to costs as well as yields benefits.[108] As a type of information, proprietary information also involves these two aspects: collecting proprietary information is necessary for the creation and transfer of property rights and requires the collector to afford time, money and energy.

107 Black, Hashimzade and Myles 2013, online.
108 Stiglitz 2000, p. 1443.

The value of information is not difficult to understand. For example, knowing what the weather will be helps us to decide whether to take an umbrella with us before walking out the door. In general, before making a decision, people have to evaluate the possible consequences the decision will bring. The evaluation requires information. More reliable information implies higher certainty of the evaluation. In the absence of sufficient information, the evaluation will become uncertain.[109] If we do not know what the weather will be, then it becomes uncertain what the eventual result will be after we decide to take an umbrella with us. In general, uncertainty is undesirable. It may discourage actions. In the absence of sufficient information, people might be discouraged from taking actions, because they fear that these actions fall to be fruitless or give rise to an undesirable outcome.[110] When the weather is unknown, some people, who will definitely take an umbrella if they know that it will rain, choose to not take an umbrella. Therefore, we can say that the information a person obtains can affect whether he/she will make a decision and which decision he/she will make.

On the other hand, the definition also shows that information involves such activities as collection, use and interpretation of information. These activities, especially the collection of information, are not without costs. For example, to know what the weather will be, we need to watch the weather forecast. The costs of collecting information imply that one will not use all possible means to obtain all possible information in reality. As a result, a trade-off is usually inevitable: one has to balance the value of the information he or she is going to collect and the costs of the collection of the information.[111]

2.2.1.2 Proprietary Information

A Introduction of Proprietary Information

The preceding introduction on information indicates that information is a very broad concept. As this research focuses only on property rights, we will only devote attention to "proprietary information", namely the information about the legal relationship of property rights. For example, where a buyer wants to purchase a bicycle, the information concerning the ownership of this bicycle is a piece of proprietary information.

As proprietary information is information concerning property rights, the composition of the legal relationship of property rights determines the content of proprietary information. In general, a legal relationship of property right contains three elements: the subject, the object, and the content of this right. The subject refers to the person, whether natural or legal, who holds the property right. The object means the thing, whether tangible

109 Mackaay 1982, p. 107.
110 Mackaay 1982, p. 108.
111 Stiglitz 2000, p. 1443.

or intangible, with respect to which the property right exists. The content represents the interests and entitlements the subject enjoys with respect to the object. In a nutshell, property rights can be seen as the interests and entitlements a particular person enjoys with respect to a specific thing.

> *"In einer Rechts- und Gesellschaftsordnung, welche die vorhandenen Sachen nicht allen zum beliebigen Gemeingebrauch überlässt, sondern von der Institution des Privateigentums ausgeht (Art. 14 GG), muss geregelt werden, welche Sachen welcher Person zustehen und welche Befugnisse diese Person an der Sache hat."*[112]

Correspondingly, the proprietary information of a property right consists of the information concerning the subject, the object, and the content. In principle, these three categories of information are important for a third party. They determine the person with whom this third party has to negotiate, the object with respect to which he will negotiate, and the existing legal relationships he needs to respect and consider. Here the information concerning the object reminds us of the principle of specificity: property rights need to exist with respect to specific, or at least ascertainable, things (see 2.1.3.1). If the object of a property right is unascertainable, which implies that the information concerning the object is insufficient, then the certainty of this property right would be hampered.[113]

In understanding the concept of proprietary information, we need to note the following aspects. Firstly, proprietary information does not include physical or functional attributes of the object. Truly, mere proprietary information is not adequate for transactions in reality because purchasers are also concerned about, for example, the quality and function of the thing in question. However, these attributes have nothing to do with the proprietary condition of the thing. Thus, they are not covered by the concept of proprietary information. For example, the right of ownership can not only exist on a flawless bicycle, but also on a defective bicycle. Property law does not prescribe different forms of ownership according to the physical or functional features of bicycles.

Secondly, proprietary information does not involve personal rights or claims. In principle, information concerning personal rights is not proprietary information. For example, as the starting point, contractual relationships cannot affect third parties under the principle of privity: they only have binding force over the particular parties who create the relationship. The existence of a contract has no effect on the legal position of third parties. However, exceptions exist. As has been shown above, some personal rights also affect third parties under certain circumstances (see 2.1.3.2). For

112 Wolf and Wellenhofer 2011, p. 1. English Translation: "*In a legal and social order, which does not leave things for arbitrary use by the public and takes the regime of private ownership as its starting point (art. 14 of the Fundamental Law), it is necessary to determine which things belong to which person, and which entitlements are enjoyed by the person with respect to these things.*"

113 Clarke and Kohler 2005, p. 156; Wolf and Wellenhofer 2011, p. 17.

example, a lease contract has a proprietary feature in the civil law system: the new owner of the leased thing may be subject to the already existing lease due to the rule of "sale does not break lease" (such as art. 7:226 BW and § 566 BGB). Due to this rule, potential purchasers need to pay attention to whether the thing in question has been leased out, so that they will not be surprised. Thus, the information concerning the legal relationship of lease is important for subsequent acquirers.[114] In this sense, we can say that the information is proprietary or at least quasi-proprietary.

B Value of Proprietary Information

After introducing proprietary information above, we now will demonstrate the value of proprietary information here. It will be contended that proprietary information is closely related to individuals' liberty. In the area of property law, the possibility of obtaining reliable proprietary information inexpensively is a precondition of facilitating individuals' liberty with respect to property.

Briefly speaking, liberty means individuals can do as they deem appropriate in the absence of the intervention by the state. Individuals are usually supposed to have a right to manage their own affairs and to assume the associated consequences, whether beneficial or detrimental. An important basis of liberty is personal rationality, the capacity to reason, evaluate and determine in an independent way.[115] Presumably, nobody is in a better position than a person himself in understanding what he desires and how to achieve it. Liberty lays a basis for and manifests itself in private law as "party autonomy (*Privatautonomie*)", a fundamental principle that makes private law distinctive from public law.[116] According to this principle, individuals are entitled to create a private law relationship with others freely and independently.[117] Under the principle of party autonomy, individuals' liberty is respected and guaranteed in private law.

Liberty can find its ethical root from the notion of personality. In light of Kantian ethics, moral personality is nothing "*but the liberty of a rational being under moral Laws*".[118] As liberty is the moral essence of human beings who should treat themselves as an end rather than a means, liberty can be seen as an ultimate end.[119] "*Liberty is not a means to a higher political end. It is itself the highest political end*", as Lord Acton asserted.[120] Moreover, liberty might also be deemed as a means of achieving certain purposes. From the view-

114 For this reason, some scholars argue that the lease of immovable property needs entry into the land register, at least when the lease is supposed to exist for a long period of time. After registration, the lease can be easily seen by subsequent acquirers, such as buyers and mortgagee. However, opposite opinions exist. See Westrik 2001, p. 257-263.

115 Lucy 2007, p. 82.s

116 Meijers 1948, p. 22; Medicus 2010, p. 7; Bork 2016, Rn. 99.

117 Bork 2016, Rn. 99; Wolf and Wellenhofer 2011, p. 98.

118 Kant 1799, p. 16.

119 Kant 1799, p. 31.

120 Acton 1909, p. 23.

point of some economists, such as Hayek, liberty is *"a means to the end of the satisfaction of overall interests"*.[121] Mill, a utilitarian and libertarian, deems liberty as *"pursuing our own good in our own way"*, which seems to imply that liberty is a means to realize the end of the maximization of happiness.[122]

It might be better to say that liberty is a means as well as an end. Liberty is a means because it is necessary for realizing such purposes as the maximization of overall welfare or happiness. On the other hand, liberty is also an end pursued by individuals because it is an ethical attribute of human beings. If one accepts this general conclusion, then one cannot deny that party autonomy has a double value in the law of property: efficient utilization of property and self-realization of individuals.[123] The first value, often a central topic in the economics of property law, is easy to understand. In general, allowing individuals to freely dispose of property guarantees that property can shift to the person who can make better use of it.[124] The second value means that property is an object with respect to which individuals' liberty is exercised and realized. Liberty with respect to property is also an end. This value is often overlooked but has been articulated by Hegel in the following excerpt.

> *"To have something in my power, even though it be externally, is possession. The special fact that I make something my own through natural want, impulse or caprice, is the special interest of possession. But, when I as a free will am in possession of something, I get a tangible existence, and in this way first became an actual will. This is the true and legal nature of property, and constitutes its distinctive character."*[125]

On the basis of the double value of liberty, it can be further argued that the value of proprietary information lies in two aspects: facilitating liberty with respect to property and improving efficient utilization of property.

Proprietary information is useful for the interaction between different parties with respect to property. Every person has the liberty to act, which creates a possibility of conflicts between two persons. If justice means that one's liberty is harmonious with another's liberty, then how to coordinate the two liberties becomes a central issue for the law. To avoid illegal infringement of others' liberty, a person should first know of the boundaries between his and others' liberty. The knowledge of boundaries is

121 Gamble 2013, p. 350.
122 Mill 1859, p. 24; Kateb 2003, p. 48.
123 Here we do not intend to discuss the tension between party autonomy and the principle of *numerus clausus*. This principle requires that the type and content of property rights should be determined by property law, and individuals cannot create a new property right. Indeed, the principle forms a severe restriction over party autonomy. In this part, however, we focus on the party autonomy in the following sense: individuals are entitled to freely decide whether to transfer property rights and to create a property right that has been recognized by property law. This autonomy is by no means restricted by the principle of *numerus clausus*.
124 Shavell 2004, p. 18.
125 Hegel 2005, p. 58.

often essential for managing one's personal affairs in harmony with others' liberty. In this sense, proprietary information is important for the interaction between different people with respect to property. The information about a property right shows the boundaries of this right, i.e. the scope of the proprietor's liberty, thereby indicating the remaining area others can enter without fear of interfering with this right. If the proprietary information is insufficient, the boundaries are ambiguous, then a risk of conflicts will ensue. Due to this risk, individuals might be discouraged from participating in the utilization of the property: they worry about the occurrence of a conflict. This implies that the scope of individuals' liberty is narrowed. In a word, proprietary information has great importance for the realization of liberty, and the impossibility of obtaining proprietary information amounts to a restriction on liberty.

Secondly, proprietary information is necessary for efficient utilization of property. In general, free transactions ensure that property can flow to the hands of the person who can make the most of it. This is a precondition for the end of maximizing the utility of property. However, a heavy burden of information will often hinder free transactions and cause a risk of the occurrence of conflicts. If a person cannot obtain sufficient proprietary information concerning a thing cost-effectively, then he may choose to take no actions. This inhibits the circulation of this thing. Even if the person takes actions, despite the insufficiency of information, the consequence is likely to be a conflict with other rights that already exist on the thing. In fact, we have indicated this in introducing the concept of information: information can alleviate uncertainty, and potential decision-makers might be discouraged from taking actions when they do not have sufficient information.

> *"An advantage of registration systems is that they may ease sale and resale of things by assuring buyers of the validity of sellers' claims of ownership. In the absence of a registration system, uncertainty as to the validity of ownership might cause a wary buyer not to purchase. Alternatively, this uncertainty might cause the buyer to spend greater effort investigating the validity of ownership than would be necessary if there were a registry."*[126]

In a word, proprietary information also has great importance for efficient utilization of property by reducing uncertainty, a potential impediment to free transactions.[127]

C *Costs of Proprietary Information*

Proprietary information gives rise to costs. The collection and interpretation of proprietary information are activities that are not without costs. This is not difficult to understand. Here we use the collection of proprietary information concerning immovable property as an example. If a potential buyer

126 Shavell 2004, p. 47.
127 Miceli 2005, p. 253.

wants to know whether his or her counterparty, the seller, has ownership of the house intended to be sold, this buyer or his or her agent usually needs to search the land register. The search of the register and further analysis of the information contained by the register book give rise to some costs. Thanks to the development of information technology, land registers might have been digitalized and become accessible online. This reduces the cost of collecting the proprietary information concerning immovable property significantly. Nevertheless, costs still exist.[128]

2.2.2 Parties and Proprietary Information

After introducing the concept of proprietary information, we explore the demand for proprietary information by different types of third parties in this part. Before doing this, a discussion concerning proprietary information and transacting parties will be provided.

2.2.2.1 Transacting Parties and Proprietary Information

Transfer and creation of property rights take place between two or more particular parties. These parties can, for example, be the owner and the usufructuary in the case of creating a right of usufruct, the pledgor and the pledgee in the case of granting a right of pledge, and the transferor and the transferee in the case of transfer of ownership. In this research, where a property right is created or transferred by two or more parties, these parties are termed "transacting parties" of this right, as opposed to third parties. In general, proprietary information concerning a property right is not a problem for the transacting parties of this right. This is easy to understand. The transacting parties are creators of the property right. They have negotiated the creation or transfer of the property right. There is no reason to say that they do not know what they have created and transferred. Therefore, every transacting party can be assumed to have obtained the proprietary information about the property right he or she transfers or creates. As will be seen in Chapter 5, this conclusion is important for defining the legal effect of publicity (see 5.1.3-5.1.4).

For example, to acquire a right of usufruct with respect to a parcel of land, the usufructuary usually has to conclude a contract with the owner of that parcel of land. This contract includes specific terms concerning the location of the parcel of land, the identity of the parties, the manner of use

128 For example, proprietary information concerning immovable property can be collected easily and cheaply from the land registry (*Kadaster*) in the Netherlands. The information can be downloaded from the website of the registry by paying a small amount of fee, such as 2.60 Euros for the information of land ownership. There is no doubt that the convenient and cheap system facilitates the smooth transaction of immovable property in the Netherlands.

and enjoyment, and the period of the right. The owner of the parcel of land and the usufructuary are assumed to have an understanding of these terms. In principle, it is unimaginable that these parties would not know the right of usufruct they created. Thus, the property right of usufruct does not cause any concern about lack of information to the transacting parties.

To avoid misunderstandings, we note that a transacting party of a property right may be a third party in relation to another property right. This is because multiple property rights might exist on the same object. In the example above, the usufructuary is assumed to have full knowledge of the right of usufruct. At the same time, he might be a third party in relation to another property right that already exists on the parcel of land, such as a right of mortgage. In relation to this mortgage, the usufructuary is a third party (a subsequent acquirer): he must respect that right, and yet it cannot be assumed that he knows of the existence of that right.

2.2.2.2 *Third Parties and Proprietary Information*

It has been shown that third parties bear a negative duty to respect property rights (see 2.1.3.2). This duty gives rise to a problem of information asymmetry to third parties: they need to know about the existence of property rights.[129] Obviously, third parties are different from transacting parties in this respect. Unlike transacting parties, third parties do not participate in the transfer or creation of property rights. Thus, it cannot be assumed that third parties know about the transfer or creation. In this part, we outline the proprietary information required by the three types of third parties: strange interferers, subsequent acquirers, and general creditors. It will be found that the information required varies from one type of third party to another.

A *Strange Interferers*

As already shown above (see 2.1.3.2.A), the term "strange interferer" refers to persons who have no particular interests in a specific object other than avoiding conducting illegal interference.[130] The principal purpose of strange interferers is to avert interfering in others' property rights. This type of third party has a very "low" demand for proprietary information. In general, for a person who intends to avert interfering with a property right, he only needs to know that he cannot act in a certain manner with respect to this right. The details of the property right are irrelevant. For example, if a person has already known that he has no right to step onto a parcel of land, then the other information about the proprietary interests of the parcel is useless for this person. This means that the person, upon trespassing on the parcel, cannot be exempted from corresponding liabilities by, for example, claiming that he does not know the identity of the landowner.

---

129 McFarlane 2011, p. 318.
130 Merrill 2015, p. 29.

"But most of the time virtually no one knows the identity of the owners of all the thousands of other cars they see on the streets and in parking lots. In order to maintain a semblance of stability in this system, not only must each owner recognize and exercise dominion over his own car, but virtually all members of society—owners and nonowners alike—must recognize and respect the unique claims of owners to their own particular auto. In other words, virtually everyone must recognize and consider themselves bound by general duties not to interfere with autos that they know are owned by some anonymous other."[131]

"Thus, if a person is to avoid trespassing on land, it is sufficient for that person to know that he owns no rights in the land. It is a matter of some irrelevance whether or not rights in the land are all held by a single individual or, alternatively, have been carved up among various persons to include a fee tail, a joint tenancy, an easement, a lease, and/or a mortgage."[132]

To understand the low demand for proprietary information by strange interferers, we need to note the following two aspects. Firstly, interference with others' property only causes detriment and is contrary to morality in most situations; thus, it should be deterred to the largest extent.[133] If a person knows or should know that his behavior exceeds the boundaries drawn by law for him, then there is sufficient reason for him to cease and, if not, compensate for the damage caused. Secondly, property should be protected equally, irrespective of who the owner or proprietor is. This idea of equal protection requires that the specific identity of the proprietor is irrelevant in judging whether an illegal interferer needs to bear a duty of respect. That the interferer knows no details about the legal relationships of the property damaged is never a sufficient ground for impunity.[134]

Human beings live in a world crowded with things belonging to one or another. This means that a person might easily interfere with or damage another person's property when this person fails to be careful with his behavior. If interference or damage happens, then corresponding liabilities will often be triggered. Therefore, every person needs to know the boundaries of his or her free behavior with respect to property. However, a question is how to obtain such information. It will be shown later that people rely on possession to know the boundary of their behaviors (see 3.3). In general, possession can provide sufficient proprietary information for strange interferers, helping them to know whether their behavior constitutes illegal interference.

B Subsequent Acquirers

It has been shown that subsequent acquirers are another type of third party (see 2.1.3.2.B). They can be an acquirer of ownership or limited property rights. For this type of third party, proprietary information has great

131 Smith and Merrill 2007, p. 1853-1854.
132 Hansmann and Kraakman 2002, p. 411.
133 Smith and Merrill 2007, p. 1854.
134 Hansmann and Kraakman 2002, p. 411; Smith and Merrill 2007, p. 1853-1854.

importance. This is because, unlike strange interferers, subsequent acquirers intend to have a proprietary interest with respect to a specific object. In order to realize this purpose without falling into conflict with others, potential acquirers need to investigate in advance the already existing property rights on the object.

For example, where a potential purchaser wants to acquire a parcel of land, he usually has to pay attention to the following aspects: (1) whether the seller is the legal owner and has the authority of disposal; (2) whether there are any proprietary encumbrances on the parcel of land; and (3) whether the parcel has been attached by the seller's creditors.[135] If, for example, the land has already been encumbered with a right of mortgage, then the purchaser has to respect the mortgage. Therefore, the information about the mortgage is important for the purchaser. In the absence of this proprietary information, the purchaser has no chance to properly react to the encumbrance by, for example, lowering the purchase price, canceling the purchase, or reaching an additional agreement with the mortgagee.

In general, the difference in the need for proprietary information between strange interferers and subsequent acquirers implies that these two types of third parties take advantage of different means of publicity. As mentioned above, the former relies on possession to guide their behaviors, whereas the latter often conducts a detailed investigation by, if possible, searching the register for the property in question.[136] In general, possession cannot satisfy the demand for proprietary information by subsequent acquirers and general creditors, which is discussed in Chapter 3 (see 3.4 and 3.5). In the situation where claims are assigned or pledged, notification to the debtor cannot qualify as a method of publicity for subsequent acquirers (see 4.1.1).

C General Creditors

C1: The Concept of General Creditors

General creditors are another type of third party, which has been discussed above (see 2.1.3.2.B). As a starting point, general creditors can only use the debtor's property to realize their claims. In other words, one's property cannot be used to perform another's obligations, provided there is neither a legal prescription or agreement by the parties to the contrary.[137] Moreover, unlike secured creditors, general creditors have no priority interest with respect to specific collateral and fall in a position inferior to secured creditors. In the situation of the debtor's insolvency, general creditors only have a right to distribute the residual assets, i.e. assets remaining after the discharge of secured debts, in proportion to the sum of their claims. This often means that general creditors cannot fully realize their unsecured

135 Shavell 2004, p. 30.
136 Hansmann and Kraakman 2002, p. 416.
137 Van Buchem-Spapens and Pouw 2008, p. 21.

claims. As a result, general creditors are not only concerned about the assets owned by the debtor, but also the proprietary encumbrances on the debtor's assets. Roughly speaking, only unencumbered assets of the debtor (i.e. assets owned by the debtor and not encumbered with proprietary security interests) are available for general creditors.

For the sake of protecting certain types of general creditors, such as employees and tax authorities, a privilege is granted. As has been demonstrated in 2.1.3.2.B, there is a differentiation between general privilege and specific privilege. The former exists with respect to all the assets of the debtor, while the latter exists on specific assets. In general, the preferential position enjoyed by the privileged general creditor is an outcome of the operation of law. Moreover, different jurisdictions differ in the aspect of the number and type of privileged claims.[138] It should be noted that granting a statutory privilege only means that the creditor benefited will obtain payment in priority to other general creditors. If the asset involved has been transferred to others or encumbered with a limited property right before the beginning of bankruptcy, the transfer and limited property right will not be affected by the statutory privilege, provided that there is no contrary stipulation (art. 3:279 BW).[139]

As a result, privileged creditors are unsecured creditors, despite their having a preferential position over the unsecured creditors. In general, the statutory privilege remains to be a legal issue concerning the distribution of the unencumbered assets of the debtor to general creditors. Having a statutory privilege does not mean that the creditor has a property right.[140]

C2: The Demand of Information by General Creditors

Seemingly, the preceding introduction implies that general creditors have an interest in obtaining information about the debtor's unencumbered assets. This information involves two aspects: the belonging of assets to the debtor (information of belonging) and the proprietary encumbrance over the assets (information of proprietary encumbrance).[141] As both aspects are related to property rights or proprietary issues, the information is generally termed as "proprietary information of unencumbered property" in this research. For the following reasons, the information is only of very limited importance for general creditors.

In general, unsecured creditors rely on the overall financial health of the debtor, in particular "*the debtor's general earning power for repayment*", and

138 Keay, Boraine and Burdette 2001, p. 168.

139 Art. 3:279 BW: "*Pand en hypotheek gaan boven voorrecht, tenzij de wet anders bepaalt.*" English translation: Art. 3:279 BW: "*Pledge and mortgage are superior than the right of privilege, unless the law stipulates otherwise.*"

140 Snijders and Rank-Berenschot 2017, p. 596.

141 Here the term "belonging" is used as an equivalent to "*toebehoren*" in Dutch law and "*Inhaberschaft*" or "*Zuordnung*"in German law. "Belonging" amounts to the concept of ownership, provided that this concept is not confined to corporeal things. See Snijders and Rank-Berenschot 2017, p. 26-27.

usually do not have any direct stake with respect to a specific asset owned by the debtor.[142] Financial health is a term used to describe the state of a person's financial situation. Specifically, the debtor's overall financial health mainly refers to the ability of payment for creditors. This is easy to understand: what creditors principally concern about is whether the debtor is able to perform the obligations on the due date.

In this aspect, general creditors' demand for information differs from secured creditors'. Secured creditors usually have a particular concern about the existing proprietary relationships over the specific collateral, despite the fact that they may also pay attention to the debtor's overall financial health. This is because proprietary security rights are affected by, for example, whether the debtor has lawful ownership of the collateral, and whether the collateral has already been mortgaged or pledged to another person. In contrast, detailed information about specific assets is often beyond the concern of general creditors. Merely knowing the legal relationships of specific assets is neither sufficient nor necessary for general creditors. That a debtor has ownership of certain assets does not mean that this debtor will be able to perform unsecured obligations on the due date. Moreover, pledging or mortgaging certain assets to some creditors does not mean that the debtor will lack the ability to perform unsecured obligations in the future. In general, the realization of an unsecured claim is largely dependent on the debtor's overall financial health.

> *"An unsecured creditor relies on his debtor's overall financial health, which may be difficult to diagnose month to month or day to day. A secured creditor relies on specific property. As long as he knows that the debtor owns that property, his loan is safe, even if the debtor engages in a risky enterprise."*[143]

Even if all the debtor's assets have been mortgaged or pledged, some creditors are still willing to provide credits without requiring any security when they have confidence in the debtor's ability to pay.[144] However, measuring the financial health of a debtor is not always easy. If a potential creditor finds it difficult to measure the overall financial health of the debtor, then he might require a property right of security, especially when the credit is granted by the creditor for a long period.[145]

That general creditors mainly concern about the debtor's overall financial health does not mean that a risky enterprise cannot obtain any credit without providing proprietary security. In reality, even if the overall financial state of a debtor is not sufficiently healthy, it is still possible for this debtor to transact with suppliers and acquire loans from banks in the absence of providing any proprietary security. This is because supplies and

142 Schwartz 1989, p. 221.
143 Baird 1983, p. 57.
144 LoPucki 1994, p. 1938; Hamwijk 2011, p. 620.
145 Finch 1999, p. 639.

banks can capture the risk of underpayment by, for example, adjusting the purchase price and the rate of interest respectively.[146] With these measures, the risk of underpayment can also be countered to some extent.

The proprietary information concerning unencumbered assets does not have great importance for general creditors also for another two reasons. The first reason is that the information obtained will soon become outdated. Even though a general creditor, after exerting much effort, learns about how many assets are owned by the debtor and how many proprietary encumbrances have been created over these assets, this information he obtains will become imprecise afterwards. This is easy to understand. The debtor is always disposing of or preparing to dispose of the assets.[147] For example, suppliers as a debtor need to transfer ownership of their products to the purchaser and are often required to mortgage or pledge their property to banks granting a loan. This can decrease the amount of unencumbered property. On the other hand, suppliers also need to acquire ownership of materials, and existing proprietary encumbrances over the suppliers' property might cease to exist due to the performance of the secured debt. This will increase the amount of unencumbered property. Therefore, the amount of unencumbered property is always in fluctuation. The proprietary information obtained today might become incorrect tomorrow. It cannot be expected that general creditors will investigate the amount of unencumbered property every day.

The second reason is that the proprietary information is useless for a special type of general creditors: involuntary creditors. Roughly speaking, involuntary creditors are those who acquire a claim from the debtor on a non-contractual basis. Tort victims are a typical type of involuntary creditor: they are "forced" to become a general creditor without expressing any consent to the debtor, namely the tortfeasor.[148] Involuntary creditors have no chance to decide whether and under what conditions they will have a relationship of obligation with the debtor. The legal relationship is often a result of the operation of law. Therefore, involuntary creditors cannot react to the existence of security rights on property by, for example, adjusting the price or the rate of interest, and thus are a *"non-adjusting creditor"*.[149] Moreover, involuntary creditors often do not know about the amount of assets owned by the debtor at the moment when the obligation arises. In sum, due to the special way this type of unsecured claim comes into existence, there is no reason to say that the proprietary information of unencumbered property is useful for involuntary creditors.

The preceding observations require us to properly assess the value of proprietary information concerning unencumbered property for general creditors. In general, even if this information is relevant, we have to

146 Bouckaert 2006, p. 180.
147 Hamwijk 2011, p. 619.
148 LoPucki 1994, p. 1893.
149 Bebchuk and Fried 1996, p. 882-891.

acknowledge that its importance is very limited. The amount of unencumbered property can be seen as an indicator of the overall financial state of the debtor, but it is neither the only nor the most important indicator.

> *"Dieser hebt hervor, dass die Vermögensverhältnisse über eine Kreditvergabe jedenfalls nicht an erster Stelle entscheiden. Für die Kreditwürdigkeit einer Person sind andere Kriterien, wie die Einschätzung der Entwicklung der Leistungs- und Ertragskraft, von größerer Bedeutung."*[150]

This is easy to understand. After all, more proprietary encumbrance means that unsecured creditors gain less in the event of the debtor's insolvency.

Therefore, the view that unsecured creditors neglect the debtor's unencumbered property is not completely correct.[151] Truly, unsecured creditors only suffer underpayment when the debtor becomes insolvent, and the debtor's overall financial health, in particular the ability of payment, is more important for them. However, as the preceding excerpt points out, the amount of unencumbered property owned by the debtor is an indicator of the debtor's creditability. Moreover, the clause of "negative pledge" used in practice also implies that the proprietary information of unencumbered property might be of some importance. Negative pledge clause is often used in unsecured transactions, especially unsecured loan agreements. Under this clause, the debtor is required by the unsecured creditor to refrain from granting security interests over certain property to other creditors in the future.[152] The creation of this clause indicates that the unsecured creditor has a concern about the proprietary encumbrance created by the debtor.[153] The unsecured creditor wants to avert the situation that no assets are left after the enforcement of security interests by secured creditors. As to the legal effect of negative pledge clauses, especially whether these clauses have binding force on third parties when being breached by the debtor, different opinions exist.[154]

In another aspect, the proprietary information of unencumbered property might be important for general creditors when the debtor becomes insolvent. This aspect concerns the date when ownership of property is validly transferred by the debtor and when proprietary encumbrances are validly granted to other creditors. In general, the debtor loses the authority to dispose upon the declaration of insolvency.[155] However, the transferee and secured creditors might conspire with the insolvent creditor to antedate the transfer and the creation of proprietary encumbrances. As a result, gen-

---

150 Von Wilmowsky 1996, p. 162. English translation: *"This highlights that the proprietary relationship is never decisive in the first place for the grant of credits. The creditworthiness of a person is of greater importance, such as the assessment of the ability of performance and profitability."*

151 Hamwijk 2011, p. 626.

152 Schwartz 1989, p. 210.

153 Bebchuk and Fried 1996, p. 922.

154 De Bie 1991, p. 332; Bjerre 1999, p. 305.

155 Wessels 2012, p. 155; Van Buchem-Spapens and Pouw 2008, p. 31.

eral creditors have less unencumbered property to distribute than would be available if there were no such fraudulent act. If the date, when the transfer and the creation of limited property rights take place, can be ascertained reliably, the fraudulent antedating could be avoided. In this respect, the proprietary information of unencumbered property is useful for general creditors.

In sum, general creditors mainly rely on the debtor's overall financial health, in particular the ability of payment. Thus, they pay major attention to such factors as the cash-flow, earning capacity and development prospects of the debtor. The amount of unencumbered property is an indicator of the overall financial health, which, however, has limited importance for general creditors. For general creditors, the proprietary information of unencumbered property is doomed to become outdated after being collected, because the debtor is always disposing of or preparing to dispose of property. For involuntary unsecured creditors, this proprietary information is no use at all, because the legal relationship involved comes into existence against the will of this type of unsecured creditor. However, the possibility of collecting the proprietary information reliably allows general creditors to avert the risk of fraudulent antedating. The limited importance of the proprietary information gives rise to another question concerning the effect of publicity of property rights on general creditors. If, for example, a property right of security is created in the absence of publicity, should this right be effective against general creditors when the debtor falls insolvent? This question is discussed in Chapter 5 (see 5.3.3.2).

2.2.3 Publicity and Proprietary Information

The preceding part has shown that proprietary information is important in different senses for different types of third party. In this part, we discuss how proprietary information is collected. In reality, there are multiple ways in which proprietary information can be collected. Publicity is only one amongst these ways but has certain special aspects.

2.2.3.1 Multiple Ways of Collecting Proprietary Information

In the transfer and creation of property rights, disclosure by counterparties (such as the transferor of ownership and the grantor of limited property rights) and publicity seem to be the two most important ways of collecting proprietary information. In most situations, proprietary information is first provided by counterparties, who can be the seller in the case of sales, the owner in the case of creating a right of usufruct, or the debtor in the case of providing proprietary security. This is not difficult to understand. For example, the seller may guarantee that he or she has full ownership of the thing involved, promising that the purchaser is able to acquire ownership. Moreover, the seller might also provide evidentiary documents to prove that he or she is the owner, such as the contract by virtue of which the thing was acquired or a certificate on which the seller is recorded as the owner.[156] If the thing is in possession by a lessee, the seller will usually demonstrate the legal relationship of lease to show that he or she, though not in possession of the thing, is the real owner.

In general, the proprietary information provided by counterparties may suffer from lack of objectivity. Counterparties usually have a direct stake in disclosing the legal relationships with respect to the object, which implies that they have a strong incentive to cheat.[157] As a result, counterparties may provide incorrect information or remain silent on some relevant matters. For example, in order to persuade the buyer to purchase the commodity in question, the seller might intentionally conceal that the commodity has been pledged to others. Therefore, the information asymmetry faced by third parties might be aggravated rather than alleviated by the disclosure of counterparties.

The disclosure of proprietary information by counterparties is generally regulated by contract law. In the pre-contractual phase, there is a duty of providing information, including proprietary information, prescribed by contract law for negotiators. Failure to fulfill this duty by one party will trigger certain consequences under the law of obligations, such as rescinding the contract by another party on the basis of deception.[158] Apart from this contract law solution, property law also prescribes a solution: publicity.

Publicity is based on the idea that the feature of absoluteness of property rights requires these rights to be made transparent to third parties. In other words, there should be a reliable channel through which third parties can obtain proprietary information.

> *"A legal system that wants to encourage a market in property interests must therefore adopt mechanisms and rules that make it safe for purchasers to assume that apparent owners are absolute owners, or at the very least lessen the risks of a successful challenge to a purchaser's title."*[159]

---

156 Clarke and Kohler 2005, p. 390.

157 Baird and Jackson 1983, p. 179; Pottage 1995, p. 399.

158 For example, A plans to transfer a parcel of land to B, and they have made a contract. After applying for registration of the transfer, B realizes that this parcel of land has been mortgaged to another person. A does not disclose this mortgage to B when they sign the contract of purchase. If B knows this mortgage, he would not agree to buy the land. In this case, B can rescind the contract on the basis of deception by A. In addition, contract law also imposes over the seller a general duty of transferring ownership to the buyer free from any encumbrance (art. 7:15 BW and § 435 BGB). In this hypothetical case, B can choose to require A to remove the mortgage or terminate the contract for monetary compensation on the basis of A's defective performance. See Staudinger/Beckmann 2014, p. 390. The duty of disclosing the existence of proprietary encumbrances to the buyer is implied by the seller's duty of transferring unburdened ownership to the buyer. See Huijgen 2017, p. 43.

159 Clarke and Kohler 2005, p. 388.

> *"Publicity therefore facilitates the search for which property rights are alive, making it possible to reach consent ex ante, purging titles, and reducing information asymmetries between the parties."*[160]

As mentioned above (see 2.1.1.2), there is a difference in the legal effect of publicity between the translative system and the declaratory system (or the consensual system). In the former system, property rights cannot be created or alienated until the requirement of publicity is met. In contrast, the latter system means that the acquisition of property rights is based on parties' consent, and publicity is only a requirement for effect against third parties. Therefore, it can be said that the translative system *forces*, while the declaratory system *encourages*, transacting parties to show the property right to third parties.[161] About this difference, a further discussion is offered in Chapter 5 (see 5.1.4.1). In the next part, we focus on special aspects of publicity as a means of conveying proprietary information to third parties.

2.2.3.2 *Publicity as a Special Source of Proprietary Information*

First of all, publicity is statutory. In principle, publicity cannot be contracted out by individuals. The regime of publicity is stipulated by property law which mainly includes statutory rules.[162] The statutory feature of publicity involves two aspects: the possible forms of publicity and the legal effect of publicity. In principle, property law prescribes a specific form of publicity for every property right according to the nature of the object.[163] Roughly speaking, possession is a form of publicity for corporeal movables, registration is a form of publicity for immovable property and certain intangible things (such as patents and trademarks), and notification to the debtor might be treated as a form of publicity for claims. Individuals are neither allowed to create a new form of publicity nor to replace one form recognized by law with another form. Moreover, the legal effect produced by publicity is also defined by property law without leaving any space for party autonomy. To realize certain proprietary legal consequences, parties have to complete publicity in accordance with property law. For example, delivery of a parcel of land cannot trigger the shift of ownership of this land, when registration is prescribed by property law as the only form of publicity for immovable property and as a condition for the transfer of land ownership.

---

160 Arruñada 2003, p. 411.

161 Here the term "force" is used to mean that transacting parties *must* fulfill the requirement of publicity if they want to create or transfer the property right under the translative system. The declaratory system only "encourages" transacting parties to publicize their property right, because the lack of publicity does not affect the acquisition *per se*. Under the declaratory system, publicity strengthens the legal position of the acquirer in relation to third parties.

162 Snijders and Rank-Berenschot 2017, p. 60.

163 Snijders and Rank-Berenschot 2017, p. 62-63.

Secondly, publicity is in principle singular. The feature of singularity means that, in principle, one object has only one form of publicity. For example, where registration is prescribed as a method of publicity for immovable property, possession should be excluded. Moreover, this feature also means that both the right of ownership and limited property rights on the same object should share the same method of publicity.[164] In other words, all proprietary information with respect to an object should be stored and communicated through the same method of publicity. The singularity can reduce the costs of publicity. This feature avoids the situation that the proprietary information concerning an object can only be fully gained by investigating two or more methods of publicity. However, law might refuse to implement the notion of singularity. In English law, for example, pledge of corporeal movables takes possession as the method of publicity, while the mortgage of corporeal movables granted by companies requires registration as a condition for effect against third parties.[165] Likewise, Article 9 UCC recognizes both possession and registration as an eligible means of publicity for the creation of security interests in corporeal movables.[166] Undoubtedly, the coexistence of multiple methods of publicity for one kind of property not only hampers the reliability of these methods, but also increases the costs of investigation by third parties.[167]

> *"Apart from inflating the cost of credit, treating possession as an alternative to registration has the following other disadvantages. It undermines the reliability of the register as a comprehensive source of information about the potential existence of security rights in the debtor's assets. The subsequent creditors cannot rely on the register to conclude whether the debtor had already created a security in the asset or not."*[168]

For similar reasons, the costs of investigation will also rise when there are different methods of publicity for different kinds of property right created on the same object. For example, if the right of usufruct of land needs to be registered in one register, but the mortgage of land has another register, then third parties have to search these two registers to know whether there are any limited property rights on the land. Undoubtedly, this leads to a heavier burden of investigation that would be unnecessary if the two property rights share the same register.

---

164 This is easy to understand. In E.M. Meijers' viewpoint, creating a limited right amounts to transferring a part of entitlements embodied within the primary right. This is the reason why the rules on the transfer of property are applicable to the creation of limited rights on the same property (art. 3:98 BW). See Snijders and Rank-Berenschot 2017, p. 395-396.

165 Beale, Bridge, Gullifer and Lomnicka 2018, no. 9.06.

166 White and Summers 2012, p. 1207, 1215.

167 Phillips 1979 (2), p. 227.

168 Secured Transactions Law Reform Project 2013, p. 5.

In fact, the statutory feature of publicity is also to save on the costs of publicity. This is easy to understand. If parties are entitled to freely choose a form of publicity for the property right they create, then the purpose of cost-efficiently providing proprietary information would be frustrated. Free choice implies that third parties must be aware of all the possible forms of publicity that might be selected. In this sense, publicity is also subject to a principle of *numerus clausus*.[169]

Thirdly, publicity is objective. As pointed out above, disclosure by counterparties may suffer from a lack of objectivity because counterparties always have an incentive to cheat (see 2.2.3.1). In contrast, publicity can provide proprietary information more reliably because publicity is nearly independent from the influence of interested parties. For example, possession conveys proprietary information through the visible physical proximity between the possessor and the thing possessed, and third parties obtain the information without having to rely on the possessor's disclosure (see 3.2.1.2). In general, whether a person has possession is a question that can be answered with certainty. At least, the answer is, to a large degree, independent from the possessor's internal intention. Registration is also objective. Once property rights are registered or relevant documents are recorded in a register, these rights or documents will become visible to third parties. The interested parties can no longer make any change in the absence of a legal reason. Moreover, they cannot manipulate the registration or the recordation at will.

As an important outcome of the feature of objectivity, publicity is often treated as the "appearance of rights (*Rechtsschein* in German or *schijn van recht* in Dutch)".[170] In general, property rights are an invisible legal relationship, while publicity is an observable fact.[171] The two should be distinguished. For example, the fact that a person is shown to be an owner by a method of publicity does not necessarily mean that this person has ownership. On the other hand, the two are also interconnected in several aspects. Among these aspects, one aspect is that publicity is a means of showing property rights to third parties, and another is the notion of publicity as an outward appearance of rights. This notion lays a foundation for the conclusion of invisible property rights from the observable fact of pub-

169 Reehuis 2004, p. 4. Conventionally, the principle of *numerus clausus* in property law refers to that property rights have "statutory types (*Typenzwang*)" and "fixed content (*Typenfixierung*)". However, it might also be understood in a broader way by including other aspects. For example, "*the way in which these rights can be created, transferred or destroyed*" is also determined by property law. See Van Sjef 2012, p. 65. Publicity can be seen as a part of the way of creating, transferring and destroying property rights, because publicity is necessarily involved. Furthermore, some scholars even interpret the principle of *numerus clausus* mainly from the perspective of publicity: the principle of *numerus clausus* is a "*regulation of the types and degree of notice required to establish different types of property rights*". See Hansmann and Kraakman 2002, p. 374.

170 Füller 2006, p. 247; Nieskens-Isphording and Van der Putt-Lauwers 2002, p. 3-6.

171 Quantz 2005, p. 25.

licity.[172] Concretely speaking, where the proprietary information conveyed by a means of publicity fails to reflect the real legal condition, property law might assume that the information is "correct" for third parties, and their reliance on the information might be protected. By doing so, property law makes publicity become a reliable method of proprietary information for third parties. However, this is only a rough description of the reliability of publicity. In reality, different means of publicity have different degrees of reliability, and whether the reliance of third parties can eventually be protected also depends on other factors.

2.2.4 Conclusion

Proprietary information is information concerning property rights. The third-party effect of property rights makes proprietary information important for third parties. In general, obtaining reliable proprietary information easily is a precondition for efficient utilization of things and the realization of individuals' liberty. Different types of third party have a demand for different proprietary information. Strange interferers only need to know that they cannot act in a certain manner with respect to others' property rights. Subsequent acquirers need to know the details of the property rights created on a specific thing. The proprietary information about unencumbered property owned by the debtor has only limited importance for general creditors. In general, proprietary information can be collected in different ways. Among these ways, publicity, a regime prescribed by property law, has special aspects. It is statutory, singular, objective and reliable. In order to have an efficient regime of publicity, the form and legal effect of publicity should be defined by property law. Moreover, publicity has the merit of objectivity, which allows it to serve as a basis for the protection of the reliance of third parties.

172 Füller 2006, p. 247.

3 Possession and Corporeal Movables

It has been indicated above that possession is often considered to be a method of publicity for corporeal movables. Before the advent of registers, possession was the most important tool of publicity for corporeal things, whether movable or immovable. Nowadays, the effect of publicity of possession is generally confined to the field of corporeal movables. For publicity of immovable property, it is registration that plays the principal role. This chapter examines the rationale of possession as a form of publicity in the field of corporeal movables. The discussion includes a comparative study that involves English law, German law, and Dutch law. For an easier understanding of the study, we also refer to Roman law and the DCFR.

This chapter consists of five sections. The first section presents and clarifies the differences between the selected jurisdictions in the way each jurisdiction defines the concept of possession (see 3.1). It will be found that possession is a concept intended to serve multiple purposes, one of which is publicity. This implies that we cannot fully construe this concept by only focusing on the aspect of publicity. In fact, as we will see, publicity is not a significant concern for legislators in determining how to define the concept of possession. The second section discusses the publicity effect of possession in a general way (see 3.2). In this section, direct possession is argued to be an "abstract" method of publicity, and indirect possession has no publicity effect. By the term "abstract", we mean that direct possession can only indicate that the possessor has a right to the possessed object. To know the detailed content of this right, third parties need to resort to other means. The reason why direct possession is an abstract means of publicity is that it can be associated with a great variety of rights, such as ownership, the right of usufruct, pledge, and lease.

On the basis of this conclusion, the last three sections provide a further discussion about the publicity effect of possession in three different cases: illegal interference (see 3.3), subsequent acquisition (see 3.4), and insolvency (see 3.5). In these sections, we explore the importance of possession for the three types of third parties, namely strange interferers, subsequent acquirers, and unsecured creditors. There, we can find that possession is an important means of publicity for strange interferers, while it fails to convey sufficient proprietary information to subsequent acquirers and to general creditors. Therefore, it can be said that the principle of publicity is no longer tenable by virtue of possession. In general, property rights of corporeal movables are hidden, and the asymmetry of proprietary information is ubiquitous in the field of corporeal movables.

3.1 The Concept of Possession

Possession is a complicated concept.[1] It is used by laymen as well as by lawyers. The two groups of individuals often have different understandings of the concept. Laymen often use the concept to describe factual control by a person over a tangible thing. In their view, possession means a kind of factual control. However, the concept has its special meaning in law, especially in property law. For example, a driver employed by a company might be deemed by laymen as the "possessor" of this company's motor vehicle, but the driver is merely a "possession servant (*Besitzdiener* in German law or *houder* in Dutch law)" in property law.

The above discrepancy can be explained once we realize that law regulates social life in a technical way by virtue of legal concepts. In brief, legal concepts have a function of connecting legislative purposes with social life. When legislators intend certain purposes to be realized, they usually define and use legal concepts in a technical way and attach certain legal consequences to these concepts. In this sense, every legal concept is associated with certain purposes and has its own scope of application: it covers a range of similar facts and links these facts to certain legal consequences.

> *„Damit wird der Zweck und der große Nutzen einer derartigen Begriffsbildung deutlich. Das Gesetz hat diese Aufgabe, eine sehr große Vielzahl mannigfach unterschiedener, in sich höchst komplexer Lebensvorgänge in übersehbarer Weise aufzugliedern, sie durch leicht erkennbare Merkmale zu kennzeichnen und so zu ordnen, dass, soweit sie im Hinblick auf das, was ihre rechtliche Bedeutung ausmacht, ‚gleich' sind, gleiche Rechtsfolgen an sie anknüpft werden können. Um diese Aufgabe zu bewältigen, scheint es der nächstliegende Weg zu sein, Tatbestände aus abstrakten Begriffen zu bilden, unter die alle Lebensvorgange, die Merkmale des Begriffs aufweisen, mühelos subsumiert werden können."*[2]

As will be seen below, the concept of possession is used in different situations and defined to serve multiple purposes. Moreover, different legislators do not always have the same attitude towards these purposes, which further leads them to define the concept in different ways.

In this section, we first provide a brief introduction to the definition of possession in history, under Roman law, Germanic law, and Common law. This helps us to understand how the concept of possession is defined under modern law. As we will see later, the way in which possession is defined is

---

1 Salmond 1947, p. 287.

2 Larenz 1991, p. 441. English translation: *"Therefore, the purpose and great value of such formation of concepts are clear. Law has the task to categorize a large number of completely different and highly complicated social facts, identifying them with easily recognizable features, so that identical legal consequences are linked to the facts that have an 'identical' meaning in law. In order to accomplish this task, the most convenient way seems to be using the abstract concept to describe elements and subsuming social facts under the concept, provided that these facts contain the elements of the concept."*

significantly affected by its history (see 3.1.1.4). The following introduction focuses on *possessio* in Roman law, *Gewere* in Germanic law, and *seisin* in the history of common law.

As we will see, the concept of possession differs significantly between English law, German law and Dutch law. For easier understanding of the analysis of this concept, we introduce the relevant DCFR terminologies as a baseline. The DCFR is an achievement of a comparative study of more than 20 European jurisdictions, including the three jurisdictions selected in this research. It forms a blueprint of the European civil code. The DCFR terms concerning possession are an outcome of the coordination and integration of different concepts used by different jurisdictions. These terms include owner possessor, limited-right possessor, and possession agent. These DCFR terms will be selected as a reference for the conceptual discussion below.

After introducing the history of the concept of possession and the DCFR terms, a comparison of the three jurisdictions selected (English law, German law, and Dutch law) is offered. It will be concluded that different jurisdictions define the concept in different ways because they have different legislative purposes.

3.1.1 An Introduction to the History of the Concept of Possession

3.1.1.1 Roman Law

In Roman law, *possessio* was used to represent the factual situation where a person was in control of an object, forming a distinction from ownership (*dominium*).[3] The distinction is a remarkable feature of Roman law. Possession was regarded as factual control over things, while ownership the "*ultimate entitlement*" to things.[4] The distinction allowed a thief to have possession of the thing stolen "*no less than its owner in actual control*", despite the lack of a lawful basis.[5] It is noteworthy here that there were multiple connections between possession and ownership in Roman law.[6]

In the beginning, possession was only applicable to corporeal things (*res corporales*), and possession of rights was impossible.[7] Due to this requirement, property rights could not be an object of possession. The possessory interdict – the standard remedy of possession under Roman law – was not available for the holder of property rights of use. This type of holder

3 Du Plessis 2015, p. 176; Prichard 1961, p. 164.
4 Du Plessis 2015, p. 176.
5 Thomas 1976, p. 138.
6 In sum, there are three connections: (1) *usucapio*, where the possessor could acquire ownership after a sufficiently long period of possession; (2) *occupatio* and *traditio*, where ownership was acquired by occupation and delivery respectively; and (3) *vindicatio*, where the burden of proof was on the side of the person who had no possession in the case of a dispute of ownership. See Thomas 1976, p. 138.
7 Prichard 1961, p. 164; Du Plessis 2015, p. 177.

was not recognized as a possessor by Roman law. In the late Roman law, a special possessory interdict (*quem usum fructum*) was granted to some users (such as *emphyteuta* and *superficiarius*), and they were treated as having quasi-possession (*quasi-possessio*).[8] It is quasi-possession rather than possession because the object involved is property rights of use.

In addition to the object of possession, another issue concerns the composition of possession. According to Roman lawyer Paul, acquisition of possession required both factual control (*corpus*) and mental intention (*animus*).[9] In brief, the element of *corpus* referred to factual control of the object. In answering whether there was factual control, the nature of the object, the circumstance and common sense should be taken into account.[10] About the element of *corpus*, a more precise guideline is either impossible or useless because of various exceptions.[11] The possessor did not have to exercise factual control in person under Roman law, and the possessor could allow another person to control the object on the former's behalf.[12]

As to the content of the *animus*, fierce debates exist in theory. Some scholars, such as Von Savigny, held that *animus* referred to the intention of holding the thing as one's own (*animus domini*), while others, such as Von Jhering, contested this perception and argued that *animus* merely meant the consciousness of controlling an object (*animus possidendi*).[13] Here we seek to outline the image of *animus* under Roman law, not focusing on the theoretical debate.

According to the criterion of protection, there are different situations where possession is related: (1) persons who were in control as an owner or as if they were an owner, such as in the situation of rightful ownership, theft, and *usucapio*; these persons had *animus domini* and enjoyed possessory protection; (2) persons who were termed as derivative possessors, such as the pledgee in the case of *pignus* and the depositary (*sequester*) in the case of deposition (*depositum*); these persons had no *animus domini* but enjoyed possessory protection; and (3) persons who merely had detention (*detentio*) or natural possession (*possessio naturalis*), such as the borrower, hirer, and lessee; these persons had no *animus domini* and enjoyed no possessory protection.[14] Fourthly, the holder of proprietary rights of use had *quasi*-possession and was entitled to a special possessory interdict.[15]

In relation to the four situations above, six legal terms are used: possession (*possessio*), possession with the possessory interdict (*possessio ad interdicta*), civil possession (*possessio civilis*), possession with the prescriptive acquisition (*possessio ad usucapionem*), quasi-possession (*quasi-possessio*), and

8 Thomas 1976, p. 147; Prichard 1961, p. 169.
9 Digesta 41.2.3.1, cited from Du Plessis 2015, p. 177.
10 Du Plessis 2015, p. 177; Prichard 1961, p. 165; Buckland 1950, p. 199.
11 Du Plessis 2015, p. 178; Prichard 1961, p. 165.
12 Du Plessis 2015, p. 178; Prichard 1961, p. 172.
13 Du Plessis 2015, p. 178; Prichard 1961, p. 171-172.
14 Du Plessis 2015, p. 179.
15 Thomas 1976, p. 147; Du Plessis 2015, p. 180; Prichard 1961, p. 169.

detention or natural possession (*detentio* or *possessio naturalis*).[16] The relationship between these six terms is of great importance for understanding the concept of possession in Roman law. The following discussion clarifies this relationship.

Firstly, *possessio ad interdicta* refers to possession to which possessory interdict is granted for protecting the possessor and is often deemed as an equivalent term of *possessio*.[17] Roman law experts often choose possessory interdict as the criterion in ascertaining whether a person is a possessor under Roman law. In general, the following people were entitled to possessory interdict in Roman law: legal owners, thieves, pledgees, *depositum sequester*, and persons in *usucapio*.

Secondly, *possessio civilis* represents a form of possession that can give rise to acquisition of ownership through *usucapio*. Thus, it is also often called *possessio ad usucapionem*, at least in the post-classical period.[18] However, it should be noted that sometimes *possessio civilis* is used by some scholars as an equivalent term of *possessio*.[19] In Roman law, it embodied two basic elements: a justified cause for possession (*iusta causa possessionis*) and *animus domini*.[20] The cause could be sales, donation and the like.[21] It often existed where *res mancipi* were transferred under *traditio*.[22] In this way, the possessor could acquire ownership after the passage of a sufficiently long period. *Possessio civilis* was a type of *possessio* because possessory interdict was available.[23] However, not every *possessio* had the "ownership-elevating effect". Though some possessors enjoyed possessory protection, they lacked a justified cause or *animus domini*. For example, both pledgees and depositors had no *animus domini*, and they could not claim *usucaptio*;[24] thieves did not have a justified cause, thus they could not acquire ownership through *usscaptio*.[25] In a word, *possessio* (*possessio ad interdicta*) was a broader concept than *possessio civilis* (*possessio ad usucapionem*).[26]

Thirdly, *possessio naturalis* or *detentio* was a contrast to *possessio civilis*, which implied that the former could not lead to the consequence of acquiring ownership.[27] Moreover, *possessio naturalis* was not *possessio* (*possessio*

---

16 Van Zyl 1983, p. 173-174; Mousourakis 2012, p. 158-159; Thomas 1976, p. 147.

17 Mousourakis 2012, p. 158; Buckland 1950, p. 197.

18 Mousourakis 2012, p. 158; Buckland 1950, p. 197; Prichard 1961, p. 168.

19 Lee 1956, p. 179; Buckland 1950, p. 197.

20 Mousourakis 2012, p. 158; Van Zyl 1983, p. 173; Prichard 1961, p. 201-206.

21 It is noteworthy that thieves did not have *possessio civilis* in Roman law. This is because they had no justified cause for factual control and could not acquire ownership on the basis of *usucapio*. However, thieves had possession as the possessory interdict was available for them. See Mousourakis 2012, p. 135.

22 Mousourakis 2012, p. 158.

23 Mousourakis 2012, p. 158.

24 Prichard 1961, p. 201.

25 Mousourakis 2012, p. 135.

26 It is worthwhile reiterating that scholars occasionally use *possessio civilis* in a broader way and equate this concept with *possessio*. See Lee 1956, p. 179; Buckland 1950, p. 197.

27 Prichard 1961, p. 201.

ad interdicta), because the possessory interdict was not granted.[28] Fourthly, *quasi possessio* was not *possessio* because the object involved was incorporeal. As just pointed out, possession could not exist on an intangible object in Roman law. Property rights were an intangible right for which possession was impossible. However, a special possessory interdict was granted to some users, giving rise to *quasi-possessio*.[29] In general, the relationship can be presented using the diagram below:

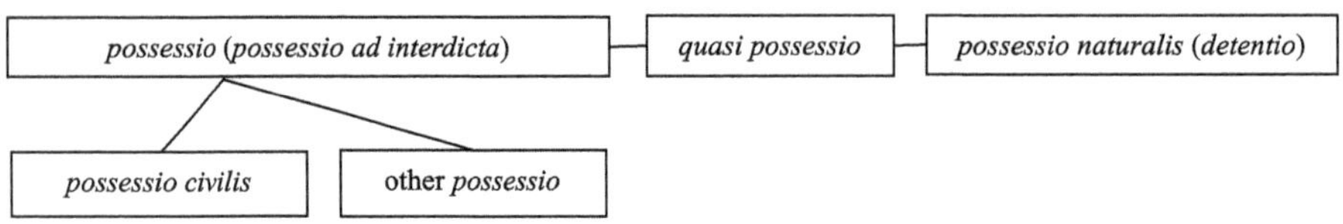

Figure 1

3.1.1.2 *Ancient Germanic Law*

In ancient Germanic law, possession was called *Gewere*, literally referring to "clothing (*Einkleidung*)". This concept is considered as the core of medieval property law. It indicated *"the endeavor to give a tangible embodiment to legal relations that actually exist in the human mind"*.[30] Thus, it can be said that the idea of publicity was already entrenched in medieval property law. In relation to this concept, we should note that ancient Germanic law, unlike Roman law, did not distinguish between possession and ownership.[31]

The concept of *Gewere* was used with differences between movable property and immovable property. For example, possession of movable property required actual control, while possession of land could be direct (physical) and indirect (ideal).[32] In this aspect, Germanic law was different from Roman law, but resembled ancient common law. Roman law had a unitary concept of possession which could be applied to both movable and immovable property. Like Germanic law, ancient common law also recognized a distinction between direct possession and indirect possession of land, but denied the possibility of indirect possession of movable property.[33] Since this research does not concern immovable property, the subsequent discussion will focus on possession of movable property only.

As just mentioned, possession of movable property was only possible when there was actual control under Germanic law.[34] Unlike land, movable property could not be possessed in an indirect way. For example, an owner of a movable thing would lose his possessory position after granting a right

28 Mousourakis 2012, p. 159; Van Zyl 1983, p. 174.
29 Thomas 1976, p. 147.
30 Hübner 1918, p. 184.
31 Emerich 2017, 173.
32 Hübner 1918, p. 404.
33 Pollock and Maitland 1968, p. 38, 152.
34 Hübner 1918, p. 404.

of lease, and it was the lessee who had possession of the movable thing only. Even in the situation where a lawful possessor lost actual control of the movable thing against his will, he no longer had possession.[35] In the Germanic law of movable property, possession was necessarily *"bound up with the corporeal element"*.[36] Multiple layers of possession could not be created on movable property because only one person was able to have actual control.

The notion of publicity and the way of defining *Gewere* were in line with two rules of Germanic law. The first rule is that transfer of movable property required the shift of actual control.[37] Property rights had to be manifested in the form of possession, and transfer of property rights had to be shown to outsiders via delivery. The second rule is known as "hand protects hand (*Hand wahre Hand*)", also a fundamental rule regulating the transfer of movable property in Germanic law.[38] According to this rule, where a conflict took place between the former possessor and the present possessor as a third party, the former possessor was not entitled to restore the thing in question from the latter.

> *"But whoever abandoned possession of a movable renounced the right which found visible expression in his seisin, without which its 'publicital' quality was ineffective; and therefore, also, the power to enforce his right against third persons."*[39]

Under Germanic law, if an original possessor lost possession, whether voluntarily or not, he would only enjoy a claim against the person with whom he had a direct legal relationship. In other words, the original owner's claim did not bind third parties, thereby being personal in nature. For example, A leased a thing to B, and the latter sold it to C, or D stole it from B; in this situation, A could only proceed against B, because the relationship of lease only existed between them; A enjoyed no right against C or D.[40] Over time, this harsh rule was restricted in some situations, and legal protection for former possessors had some third-party effect.[41]

In the end, it is worthwhile mentioning that Germanic law recognized, in a general way, the possibility of "possession of rights (*Rechtsgewere*)", including claims and rights on immovable and movable property.[42] In the medieval period, there was a tendency to assimilate legal rights to things. For example, property rights to land was also a thing, an incorporeal thing,

35 Planitz 1936, p. 124.
36 Hübner 1918, p. 405.
37 Hübner 1918, p. 405.
38 It is often held that the modern rule of *bona fide* acquisition of corporeal movable things finds its historical root from this Germanic law rule. See Wieling 2006, p. 367.
39 Hübner 1918, p. 409.
40 Hübner 1918, p. 408-409.
41 Hübner 1918, p. 416-417.
42 Hübner 1918, p. 209.

under medieval law.[43] As a result, possession of rights was generally recognized, which formed a contrast to Roman law: the latter only permitted quasi-possession of rights in exceptional situations.[44]

3.1.1.3 Ancient Common Law

In understanding the concept of possession in ancient common law, it is inevitable to take into account *seisin*. This term was once used in the situation of land and that of movable property, but it was only used in the law of land later.[45] Literally, *seisin* means *"to seize"* and *"to sit"*, implying the existence of factual control.[46] As has been mentioned, like Germanic law, ancient common law also recognized a distinction between possession of land and possession of movable property. For simplicity, attention will only be given to the ancient English law of movable property here.

Different from possession (*seisin*) of land, possession of movable property could not be hierarchic under ancient English law.[47] In the medieval age, indirect possession was not known in the law of movable property. Only the person who had actual control of movable property enjoyed possession of that property. Where a movable thing was illegally dispossessed, the former possessor would lose possession because he no longer had any actual control. If a movable thing was bailed by the bailor to the bailee on a legal basis such as lease and pledge, the former would lose possession.

> *"In the case of goods we can hardly have any similar phenomenon, and if, as we may be apt to do, we attribute possession to the bailee, we shall have to refuse it to the bailor."*[48]

As only the bailee had possession in the relationship of bailment, the bailor enjoyed no possessory protection in the history of common law.[49] If the movable thing bailed was unlawfully dispossessed from or sold by the bailee, the bailor was not entitled to sue the third party on the basis of larceny or trespass. The problem of such absence of legal protection for the bailor was partially addressed by the absolute liability borne by the bailee to the bailor.[50] In this sense, the bailor's legal position could be seen as personal.

> *"That the bailor has no action against any person other than his bailee, no action against one who takes the thing from his bailee, no action against one to whom the bailee has sold or bailed the thing."*[51]

43 Hübner 1918, p. 161.
44 Hübner 1918, p. 209.
45 Pollock and Maitland 1968, p. 34.
46 Pollock and Maitland 1968, p. 34.
47 Pollock and Maitland 1968, p. 38, 152.
48 Pollock and Maitland 1968, p. 152.
49 Pollock and Maitland 1968, p. 156; Holdsworth 1935, p. 337.
50 Pollock and Maitland 1968, p. 170; Holdsworth 1935, p. 337.
51 Pollock and Maitland 1968, p. 172.

This limitation over the bailor's legal position reminds us of the Germanic law rule of "hand protects hand". According to this rule, the former possessor cannot proceed against third parties, regardless of the way they obtain possession. This has been shown above.

In medieval English law, giving up possession was necessary for the transfer of movable things.[52] In the 13th century, constructive delivery was not recognized, which means that the transferor had to give up actual control of the object involved.[53] This conclusion is in line with the fact that possession of movable property could not be indirect at that time.

In general, it is difficult to conceive of the possession of incorporeal things in ancient English law, due to the impossibility of actual control of them.[54] However, the conception of possession was extended to some incorporeal things in several situations for certain purposes, such as protecting or transferring incorporeal things.[55]

3.1.1.4 A Clue from the History

A clue can be found from the introduction of the history above. This clue is that the concept of possession mainly involves two questions: how to protect the possessor and how to dispose of corporeal movables. For example, Roman law took two functions into account to construct a concept of possession: the protection of possessors through the *interdicta* and the acquisition of ownership through *usucaptio*.

Firstly, possession is closely associated with protection issues: the possessory interdict was generally taken as the sole criterion of *possessio*. However, it is not difficult to find that Roman law was not fully consistent in this aspect. Some persons who had a limited right were recognized as a possessor, while others who had a right of the same nature did not have possession. For example, the lessee was not recognized as a possessor and enjoyed no possessory protection, the usufructuary was entitled to a special possessory interdict and recognized as a quasi-possessor, but the pledgee was a normal possessor who enjoyed possessory protection.

Secondly, it should be noted that ownership was involved in defining the concept of *possessio* in Roman law, in the sense that a particular term, namely *possessio civilis*, was created as a necessary condition for the acquisition of ownership through *usucaptio*. With *possessio civilis*, a special type of *possession*, the possessor could acquire ownership after the passage of a certain period of time. On the other hand, some persons, such as the pledgee, did not have *possessio civilis*, which implied that they could not obtain ownership through *usucaptio*.[56]

---

52 Pollock and Maitland 1968, p. 181; Holdsworth 1935, p. 354.
53 Pollock and Maitland 1968, p. 181.
54 Holdsworth 1935, p. 96.
55 Pollock and Maitland 1968, p. 124-148.
56 Prichard 1961, p. 201

Though both ancient Germanic law and ancient English law were different from Roman law in the way the concept of possession was defined, they also focused on the issue of protection and that of transfer. For example, lessees (and pledgees) were a possessor of the object involved because they had actual control, which further implied that they enjoyed possessory protection against third parties; lessors (and pledgors) only had a personal claim against third parties. Another example is that transfer of movable things required a shift of the actual control under both Germanic law and English law in the medieval period.

3.1.2 Preliminary Comparative Study

3.1.2.1 *The Chosen Terminologies for Comparison*

For easier understanding of the conceptual and comparative analysis of the concept of possession in the three jurisdictions selected, we introduce three DCFR terms concerning possession here. These three terms are owner possessor, limited-right possessor, and possession agent, which are described in the following three model provisions respectively.

> Art. VIII.-1:206 DCFR: "*An 'owner-possessor' is a person who exercises direct or indirect physical control over the goods with the intention of doing so as, or as if, an owner.*"

> Art. VIII.-1:207 (1) DCFR: "*A 'limited-right-possessor' is a person who exercises physical control over the goods either: (a) with the intention of doing so in that person's own interest, and under a specific legal relationship with the owner-possessor which gives the limited-right-possessor the right to possess the goods; or (b) with the intention of doing so to the order of the owner-possessor, and under a specific contractual relationship with the owner-possessor which gives the limited-right-possessor a right to retain the goods until any charges or costs have been paid by the owner-possessor.*"

> Art. VIII.-1:208 (1) DCFR: "*A 'possession-agent' is a person: (a) who exercises direct physical control over the goods on behalf of an owner-possessor or limited-right-possessor without the intention and specific legal relationship required under Article VIII.-1:207 (Possession by limited-right-possessor) paragraph (1); and (b) to whom the owner-possessor or limited-right-possessor may give binding instructions as to the use of the goods in the interest of the owner-possessor or limited-right-possessor.*"

From these three model provisions, we can make three conclusions. Firstly, possession is factual control (*corpus*) plus an intention (*animus*) and in some situations plus a particular legal relationship.[57] Secondly, factual control does not necessarily give rise to possession, because agents who lack

57 Ownership possession includes the intention of "*doing so as, or as if, an owner*", and limited-right possession requires an intention as well as an underlying relationship.

the intention required and the particular relationship are not possessors. Thirdly, possessors include owner possessors and limited-right possessors. These two types differ in the possessory intention and the specific relationship.[58]

In the following discussion, possession by the owner possessor in person or by a possession agent who is acting on behalf of the former is called *ownership possession*, and possession by the limited-right possessor himself or by a possession agent who is acting on behalf of the former is called *limited-right possession*. Here it is worthwhile mentioning that "limited rights (*beperkte rechten*)" are proprietary under Dutch law.[59] In this research, however, the concept of limited right is not confined to proprietary rights. Personal rights are also a type of limited right. Therefore, lessees who have factual control over the object leased are limited-right possessors. As factual control by agents does not constitute possession in the DCFR, it is just called *control by agents*. The subsequent sections compare the three jurisdictions within the conceptual framework provided by the DCFR.

3.1.2.2 English Law

In English property law, possession is a central concept, but subject to much dispute. The concept is used in diverse ways in different contexts, which makes an accurate definition impossible.[60] For simplicity, the subsequent introduction only seeks to highlight the relevant part of the whole picture. Before doing this, it is necessary to bear the following two points in mind.

Firstly, there are several similar terms often used in English law writings, but their precise content is not fixed. These terms include possession, exclusive possession, factual (physical) control, occupation, exclusive occupation, service occupation, custody, actual possession, constructive possession, *de facto* possession, and *de jure* possession. These concepts differ as well as overlap, one may be used with different meanings in different contexts.[61] To know what a concept means, "*careful attention must in every case be paid to the context*".[62] The complexity can be partly ascribed to the lack of legislative definition as a baseline. This creates a chance for English lawyers to use them in a non-unanimous way. Some writings seek to offer a general theory on the concept of possession, but they are proved to be not that successful.[63]

58 In fact, the DCFR adopts a mixed approach which combines the subjective approach (argued by Von Savigny) and the objective approach (argued by Von Jhering). The former takes the possessory intention as the criterion, while the latter focuses on the cause of possession.

59 Snijders and Rank-Berenschot 2017, p. 41-42.

60 Bridge, Gullifer, McMeel and Worthington 2013, p. 55.

61 Hill 2001, p. 24.

62 Pollock and Wright 1888, p. 3.

63 Bridge, Gullifer, McMeel and Worthington 2013, p. 58-59.

Secondly, English property law is based on the dichotomy of land law and the law of movables, and these two branches often do not share the same legal concepts. In this respect, modern English law is not different from the medieval English law. Here, possession is a good example. In the field of corporeal movables, a bailee (e.g., a keeper or pledgee) can have possession, irrespective of the nature of the right he has.[64] However, possession of land is linked to the nature of a right with respect to land: possession can be acquired by a lessee who has a proprietary right, but a licensee who only has a personal right in principle cannot acquire possession.[65] As the theme of this research does not concern immovable property, we do not discuss possession of immovable property.

A General Introduction

In English law, possession is defined as intentional exclusive control of a thing.[66] It is comprised of two elements: factual control (*corpus*) and an intention to possess (*animus possidendi*).

> *"The legal concept of possession has two limbs: there must be factual control exercised over the chattel, coupled with an intention to exclude all others from such control (the animus possidendi)."*[67]

Two points should be mentioned about this definition. One is that possession has an attribute of exclusivity in English law, which implies that possession means a kind of exclusive control.[68] As a result, where a person is exercising control in a way that is subject to others' factual control, there is no possession. The other point is that only an intention to possess suffices, and the possessor does not have to exercise factual control as or as if an owner.[69] This is illustrated by the fact that the bailee has possession in English law.

In the end, possession applies only to tangible things, and incorporeal things (such as claims) cannot be possessed under English law.[70]

B Control by Agents: Custody

In English law, possessors do not have to exercise factual control in person. For example, an employer might require an employee to factually control his or her car. In this situation, it is the employer (rather than the employee) who is treated as the possessor, enjoying possessory interests and bearing liabilities associated with possession.

64 Bridge, Gullifer, McMeel and Worthington 2013, p. 76.
65 Clarke and Kohler 2005, p. 271.
66 Clarke and Kohler 2005, p. 259.
67 Frisby and Jones 2009, p. 21.
68 Clarke and Kohler 2005, p. 271; Bridge 2015, p. 37.
69 Gray 2009, p. 161.
70 Bridge 2015, p. 15.

In general, possession can be maintained through a custodian who acts on behalf of possessors, which leads to a relationship of *custody*.[71] The custodian is not a possessor and enjoys no proprietary interests out of possession. If the custodian's intention changes to be dishonest against the legal possessor, offense of larceny will be committed.[72] Larceny requires dispossession from the owner. If the custodian were deemed as a possessor before he has dishonest intent, it would be difficult to explain the occurrence of larceny.[73] Therefore, the demand for the protection of possession explains why custodians do not have possession in law. Despite being denied recognition as a possessor, custodians are said to have *"factual (physical) control"* or *"custody"* of the movable thing in question.[74]

C Ownership Possession: Insignificance

In English law, possession is an important entitlement embodied within the right of ownership.[75] Therefore, it is not rare that owners have possession. There is no doubt that English law allows owners, precisely the persons having the supreme title, to have possession.[76] However, there is not an individual concept to describe the owners' possession, which is different from German law (*Eigenbesitz*) and Dutch law (*bezit*), as will be seen later. English law does not highlight the importance of having a separate term to describe the situation where the possessor has an intention to exercise factual control for himself (*animus domini*).

In English law, possession by owners may be constructive, which forms a contrast to actual possession. As an outcome of the possibility of constructive possession, a person, despite having no actual control, may still be a possessor.[77] For example, in a relationship of bailment where the bailor gives up possession of corporeal movables to the bailee, the former still enjoys constructive possession.[78] In addition to bailment, the holder of documents to goods (such as a bill of lading) also has constructive possession of the goods involved.[79] In addition, buyers are said to have constructive possession of the goods which are still in the hands of the seller.[80]

71 Clarke and Kohler 2005, p. 265; Bridge, Gullifer, McMeel and Worthington 2013, p. 64.
72 Bridge, Gullifer, McMeel and Worthington 2013, p. 64.
73 Here it should be noted that larceny has been defunct in English law.
74 Frisby and Jones 2009, p. 22; Bridge, Gullifer, McMeel and Worthington 2013, p. 64.
75 Honoré 1987, p. 371.
76 Rostill 2016, p. 286-287.
77 *"The correct use of the term would seem to be coextensive with and limited to those cases where a person entitled to possess is (or was) allowed the same remedies as if he had really been in possession."* See Pollock and Wright 1888, p. 14.
78 Bridge, Gullifer, McMeel and Worthington 2013, p. 59; Acquisition and Loss of Ownership of Goods 2011, p. 387.
79 Bridge, Gullifer, McMeel and Worthington 2013, p. 59, 65; Acquisition and Loss of Ownership of Goods 2011, p. 388.
80 Pearson 2003, p. 159.

D Limited-Right Possession: Bailment

As mentioned above, a possessor does not necessarily have an intention of ownership; only an intention to possess (*animus possidendi*) plus factual control is adequate.[81] As a result, hirers, pledgees and depositories also have possession of the object involved.[82] In general, possession held by other persons than the owner is a central element of bailment in English law.[83]

> *"It is fundamental that there is a delivery or transfer of possession interest from one party to another for bailment to arise."*[84]

Bailment is a concept used to describe legal relationships where possession of corporeal movables is given up to another person for a limited period.[85] For example, where an owner gives up possession of his or her bicycle for the purpose of pledge or lease, there is a legal relationship of bailment between this owner and the pledgee or the lessee.

In the relationship of bailment, the bailee acquires possession on a *"limited or temporary"* basis.[86] By virtue of the possession acquired, a proprietary interest is conferred on the bailee, in the sense that the bailee has a claim against illegal interference.[87] The relationship of custody discussed above does not give rise to a bailment because the custodian does not have possession.

According to the DCFR terms, the bailee is a limited-right possessor. Under the DCFR, the limited-right possessor neither has a right of ownership nor acts as if he were an owner, and there is a proprietary, contractual or statutory relationship between the limited-right possessor and the owner possessor.[88] In general, these two requirements are satisfied in the case of bailment. Therefore, it can be said that the possession held by a bailee is limited-right possession. However, the term limited-right possession does not exist in English law. This reminds us that ownership possession, as opposed to limited-right possession, is not recognized by English law either. In addition, the bailor retains constructive possession after giving up actual possession to the bailee.

In general, the relationship between the concept of possession in the English law of movable property and in the DCFR can be shown in the following table.

81 Clarke and Kohler 2005, p. 266.
82 Acquisition and Loss of Ownership of Goods 2011, p. 388.
83 Bridge, Gullifer, McMeel and Worthington 2013, p. 70-71.
84 Bridge, Gullifer, McMeel and Worthington 2013, p. 76.
85 Palmer 2009, no. 1-001.
86 Bridge, Gullifer, McMeel and Worthington 2013, p. 77.
87 Bridge, Gullifer, McMeel and Worthington 2013, p. 91.
88 Acquisition and Loss of Ownership of Goods 2011, p. 388.

DCFR	Ownership Possession	Limited-Right Possession	Control by Agents
English Law	Possession under English Law		Custody

Figure 2

3.1.2.3 German Law

Unlike English law, German law has a single system of property law. The distinction between the law of movables and land law is alien to German lawyers. As a result, the concept of "possession (*Besitz*)" is applied to both immovable property and movable property without any significant differences. Moreover, German property law is codified as an independent book in the BGB, and this concept has been clearly defined by law. Thus, it is relatively easy to understand this concept.

A General Introduction

According to § 854 BGB, possession refers to "factual control (*tatsächlich Gewalt*)" over "things (*Sachen*)".[89] By understanding this term literally, it is not difficult to find that: (1) possession requires an element of *corpus* and only exists where there is factual control; and (2) possession is available only for tangible things, because the concept of *Sachen* in the BGB is expressly confined to be tangible.[90] To further understand the concept, the following aspects should also be noted.

Firstly, § 854 BGB does not explicitly require any element of intention (*animus*), but the prevailing opinion is that this requirement is indispensable.[91] Based on a systematic interpretation, it can be found that possessory intention is not necessarily *animus domini*, namely an intention to exercise factual control for oneself. However, this does not mean that *animus domini* is entirely irrelevant. § 872 BGB prescribes a distinction between "ownership-possession (*Eigenbesitz*)" and "limited-right possession (*Fremdbesitz*)" according to the possessor's intention.[92] Pursuant to this provision, lessees have limited-right possession because they do not possess the object leased for themselves, while thieves have ownership possession because they possess the object stolen for themselves. These two forms of possession give rise to different legal consequences. Further discussion about this will be provided below.

---

89 § 854 (1) BGB: *„Der Besitz einer Sache wird durch die Erlangung der tatsächlichen Gewalt über die Sache erworben."* English translation: § 854 (1) BGB: *"Possession of a thing is acquired by obtaining factual control of this thing."*

90 § 90 BGB: *„Sachen im Sinne des Gesetzes sind nur körperliche Gegenstände."* English translation: § 90 BGB: *"Only corporeal objects are things as defined by law."*

91 Wolf and Wellenhofer 2011, p. 39; McGuire 2008, p. 42.

92 § 872 BGB: *„Wer eine Sache als ihm gehörend besitzt, ist Eigenbesitzer."* English translation: § 872 BGB: *"A person who possesses a thing as belonging to him is an owner possessor."*

Secondly, possession can exist independently from rights. Possession denotes factual control, and the acquisition of possession does not require any legal right, whether proprietary or personal, as a legal basis. For example, a thief is a possessor, though he has no rightful ownership to the stolen thing.[93]

Thirdly, there is in the BGB an exception to the requirement of tangibility of the object. According to § 1029 BGB, the right of "easement (*Dienstbarkeit*)" can be subject to possession, which is known as "possession of right (*Rechtsbesitz*)".[94] It is noteworthy that this is the only exception in German law.[95] Possession of easement is recognized for the purpose of protection: by allowing the easement to be possessed, the protection for possessors can be extended to the holder of easement. Due to this exception, the conclusion that only tangible things can be possessed is not entirely correct.[96]

B Control by Agents: Besitzdienerschaft

In German law, factual control is not necessarily exercised by the possessor in person. According to § 855, a "possession agent (*Besitzdiener*)" may control the object for the possessor under the instruction from the later, giving rise to an "agency of possession (*Besitzdienerschaft*)".[97] In German law, an employee who acts for his employer is a possession agent.[98] The employee has no possession because he is considered as only a "long arm" of the employer: he is subordinate to the possessor' instructions, as a consequence of the underlying relationship of employment.[99] Moreover, the employee neither has any possessory intention nor enjoys possessory interests. Thus, he does not have to bear liabilities caused by the thing involved. In general, it is the employer who enjoys possessory interests and bears corresponding liabilities. This is in line with the notion that interests and liabilities should

93 Wieling 2006, p. 41; McGuire 2008, p. 43.

94 § 1029 BGB: „*Wird der Besitzer eines Grundstücks in der Ausübung einer für den Eigentümer im Grundbuch eingetragenen Grunddienstbarkeit gestört, so finden die für den Besitzschutz geltenden Vorschriften entsprechende Anwendung, soweit die Dienstbarkeit innerhalb eines Jahres vor der Störung, sei es auch nur einmal, ausgeübt worden ist.*" English translation: § 1029 BGB: "*Where the possessor of a plot of land is disturbed in the use of an easement registered in the land register for the owner, the provisions applying to the protection of possession are applied with the necessary modifications if the easement was used within one year before the interference, even if only once.*"

95 Wieling 2006, p. 81.

96 Baur and Stürner 2009, p. 69.

97 § 855 BGB: „*Übt jemand die tatsächliche Gewalt über eine Sache für einen anderen in dessen Haushalt oder Erwerbsgeschäft oder in einem ähnlichen Verhältnis aus, vermöge dessen er den sich auf die Sache beziehenden Weisungen des anderen Folge zu leisten hat, so ist nur der andere Besitzer.*" English translation: § 855 BGB: "*If a person exercises factual control over a thing for another in the other's household or in the other's trade or business or in a similar relationship, by virtue of which he has to follow instructions from the other that relate to the thing, only the other shall be the possessor.*"

98 Baur and Stürner 2009, p. 82.

99 McGuire 2008, p. 49.

be allocated to the same person. In general, *Besitzdiener* in German law corresponds to possession agent in the DCFR. Both German law and the DCFR refuse to grant a possessory position to the person who merely exercises factual control on behalf of another person and is subordinate to the latter's instructions.

C *Ownership Possession:* Eigenbesitz

The owner possessor is called *Eigenbesitzer* by the BGB. According to § 872 BGB, it is used to describe a person who possesses a thing with the intention of belonging. In other words, *animus domini* is an essential component of "ownership possession (*Eigenbesitz*)". It should be borne in mind that whether the owner possessor has lawful ownership is of no relevance. Here what matters is whether the possessor behaves as an owner.[100] Therefore, a thief is an owner possessor in German law, despite his lack of lawful ownership. The most important legal consequence of ownership possession is that only owner possessors can obtain ownership through prescriptive acquisition.[101] Therefore, it can be found that *Eigenbesitz* in German law amounts to ownership possession in the DCFR. Both require that this kind of possessor must act as, or as if, an owner.

D *Limited-Right Possession:* Fremdbesitz

As just indicated, *animus domini* is not necessary for obtaining possession in German law. Even though a person does not have any intention to control the object for himself, he might still have possession, namely *Fremdbesitz*.[102] Fremdbesitz can arise in the situation where the possessor has no intention to control the object as an owner but has a proprietary limited right, an obligational right or other rights.[103] In general, *Fremdbesitz* amounts to limited-right possession in the DCFR. The main difference between ownership possession and limited-right possession lies in the content of the possessory intention: the limited-right possessor has to acknowledge the legal position of the owner possessor. Briefly speaking, what matters for ascertaining the possessory intention is the factual circumstances. For example, where a person obtains factual control on the basis of a proprietary limited right or an obligational right, this person is only a limited-right possessor.[104] Moreover, where a limited-right possessor changes to hold the object for himself, this

100 Wolf and Wellenhofer 2011, p. 47; McGuire 2008, p. 50.
101 Baur and Stürner 2009, p. 88.
102 Wieling 2006, p. 50; McGuire 2008, p. 50.
103 Baur and Stürner 2009, p. 89.
104 Baur and Stürner 2009, p. 89. In light of the objective theory, the type of the right to possession plays a decisive role in distinguishing ownership possession and limited-right possession. The objective theory is held by a minority of scholars. The prevailing view is the subjective theory according to which the possessor's intention is decisive. Staudinger/Gutzeit 2012, p. 250; MüKoBGB/Joost 2017, § 872, Rn. 3.

possessor does not obtain ownership possession. The change of the intention must be visible to outsiders.[105]

> *„Eigenbesitzer ist [...] wer, eine Sache als ihm gehörend besitzt. Fremdbesitzer ist demnach, wer die Sache nicht mit der Willensrichtung des Eigentümers, sondern mit der des Inhabers eines beschränkten dinglichen, obligatorischen oder sonstigen Rechts besitzt."*[106]

Limited-right possession should be carefully distinguished from factual control by agents. Unlike possession agents who are subordinate to the principal's instructions, limited-right possessors have an independent intention to possess in law. In other words, a limited-right possessor does not have to conform to the instructions of the person from whom he acquires possession. He only needs to control the object according to the underlying relationship, which might be a right of pledge, lease, or deposition. In a word, limited-right possessors can independently enjoy possession within the boundaries stipulated by the underlying relationship, while a possession agent has no possession.

It is necessary to point out that the person from whom a limited-right possessor acquires possession, remains in possession under German law. The possession retained is known as "indirect possession (*mittelbare Besitz*)", as opposed to "direct possession (*unmittelbare Besitz*)".[107] Therefore, where there is a relationship of lease, both the lessor and the lessee have a possessory position: the former has indirect ownership possession, and the latter has direct limited-right possession, provided that the object is not subleased.[108]

In general, the relationship between the German *Besitz* and the DCFR possession can be shown by the following table. It can be found that there is a high level of consistency between the DCFR and the BGB.

105 MüKoBGB/Joost 2017, § 872, Rn. 11; Staudinger/Gutzeit 2012, p. 253. For example, where a borrower wants to retain the book borrowed, he or she does not become an ownership possessor of the book. However, if he writes down his name on the book, he obtains ownership possession. See Westermann 2011, p. 107.

106 Baur and Stürner 2009, p. 89. English translation: *"The owner possessor possesses the thing as it belongs to him. In contrast, the limited-right possessor, who has no intention of ownership, possesses the thing with an intention of being the holder of a proprietary limited right, an obligational right, or another right."*

107 § 868 BGB: *„Besitzt jemand eine Sache als Nießbraucher, Pfandgläubiger, Pächter, Mieter, Verwahrer oder in einem ähnlichen Verhältnis, vermöge dessen er einem anderen gegenüber auf Zeit zum Besitz berechtigt oder verpflichtet ist, so ist auch der andere Besitzer (mittelbarer Besitz)."* English translation: § 868 BGB: *"If a person possesses a thing as a usufructuary, a pledgee, a farmer lessee, a lessee, a depositary or in a similar relationship by virtue of which he is, in relation to another, entitled to possession or obliged to have possession for a period of time, the other person shall also be a possessor (indirect possession)."*

108 Wolf and Wellenhofer 2011, p. 47.

DCFR	Ownership Possession	Limited-Right Possession	Control by Agents
German Law	*Eigenbesitz*	*Fremdbesitz*	*Besitzdienerschaft*

Figure 3

3.1.2.4 *Dutch Law*

Like German law, Dutch property law is also codified and unifies the law of movables and the law of immovable property in one system. As a result, the concept of possession under Dutch law is also less complicated than under English law.

A General Introduction

In Dutch private law, "possession (*bezit*)" is "detention (*houderschap*)" exercised for oneself.[109] This implies that possession includes two ingredients: detention and an intention of "for oneself".[110] The first element is the *corpus* of possession, and the second element is the *animus* of possession.

Detention is not expressly defined by law. However, in light of the prevailing opinion, it means "factual control (*feitelijke macht*)" over things.[111] In determining whether detention exists, direct factual control is not necessary, and what matters is the common opinion and external facts.[112] The second element is an intention to control the object for oneself (*animus domini*). It implies that only the person who holds the object as an owner has possession. The element is a decisive factor in differentiating possession from detention. Pursuant to art. 3:108 BW, whether a person is exercising factual control for himself is determined by the application of relevant rules and the assessment of external facts according to the common opinion.[113] The common opinion plays a decisive role in ascertaining whether *animus domini* exists. As a result, the requirement of *animus* does not refer to a purely subjective intention, but an objectified intention in Dutch law.[114] In addition, it is noteworthy that detention is presumed to be possession unless there is contrary evidence.[115]

---

109 Art. 3:107 (1) BW: "*Bezit is het houden van een goed voor zichzelf.*" English translation: Art. 3:107 (1) BW: "*Possession is the detention of property for oneself.*"

110 Rank-Berenschot 2012, p. 13-14. It is noteworthy that the verb *houden* is not merely used in the situation of detention, while *houder* and *houderschap* are only used in the situation of detention. See Snijders and Rank-Berenschot 2017, p. 97.

111 Salomons 2008 (2), p. 31.

112 Rank-Berenschot 2012, p. 13.

113 Art. 3:108 BW: "*Of iemand een goed houdt en of hij dit voor zichzelf of voor een ander doet, wordt naar verkeersopvatting beoordeeld, met inachtneming van de navolgende regels en overigens op grond van uiterlijke feiten.*" English translation: Art. 3:108 BW: "*Whether somebody holds property and whether he does so for himself or for another, is determined according to common opinion, taking into account the following rules and, otherwise, the facts as they appear.*"

114 Snijders and Rank-Berenschot 2017, p. 99.

115 Art. 3:109 BW: "*Wie een goed houdt, wordt vermoed dit voor zichzelf te houden.*" English translation: Art. 3:109 BW: "*A person is presumed to hold property for him- or herself.*"

In general, both tangible things and patrimonial rights can be the object of possession. Art. 3:107 (1) BW prescribes that "*goed*" can be possessed, and "*goed*" is further defined as an upper concept covering tangible things and patrimonial rights by art. 3:1 BW.[116] This duality of the object of possession leads to an important outcome: a person may have dual positions.

> "*De huurder van een huis of van een auto is houder van die zaak en tegelijkertijd bezitter van (en ook rechthebbende op) het huurrecht. De vruchtgebruiker van een huis of van een auto is houder van die zaak en tegelijkertijd bezitter van (en ook rechthebbende op) het goederenrechtelijke recht van vruchtgebruik.*"[117]

In Dutch property law, there is a distinction between possession and property rights.[118] As a result, thieves have possession of the thing stolen.[119]

B Ownership Possession: Bezit

As discussed in the preceding section, possession (*bezit*) in Dutch law is confined to factual control for oneself, and the possessor must have *animus domini*. Therefore, the concept of *bezit* in Dutch law amounts to ownership possession in the DCFR, at least in terms of the content of the *animus*.

> "*It does not require an inner animus donimi (inner pretension of belonging). In general, however, the requirement may be set of an external pretension that appears to be animus domini (the outwardly apparent pretension of belonging).*"[120]

C Limited-Right Possession and Control by Agents: Houderschap

In Dutch law, both possession agents and persons only having a limited right lack *animus domini*. As a result, they only have detention of the thing involved. For example, both lessees and employees are a detentor, because they do not exercise factual control for themselves, but for the lessor and the employer respectively. However, as just mentioned, lessees have possession of the right of lease, since every patrimonial right can be possessed.

In general, the relationship between the *bezit-houderschap* distinction in Dutch law and the concept of possession in the DCFR can be shown in the following table.

---

116 Art. 3:1 BW: "*Goederen zijn alle zaken en alle vermogensrechten.*" English translation: Art. 3:1 BW: "*Property is comprised of all things and of all proprietary rights and interests.*"

117 Snijders and Rank-Berenschot 2017, p. 97-98. English translation: "*The lessee of a house or a car is a detentor of the thing and at the same time a possessor of (and also the proprietor) of the right of lease. The usufructuary of a house or a car is a detentor of the thing and at the same time a possessor of (and also the proprietor) of the property right of usufruct.*"

118 De Jong 2012, p. 187.

119 Snijders 2014, p. 26.

120 Snijders 2014, p. 26.

DCFR	Ownership Possession	Limited-Right Possession	Control by Agents
Dutch Law	*Bezit*	*Houderschap*	

Figure 4

3.1.3 Further Comparative Study of *Animus*

From the above introduction, it can be found that there are similarities as well as differences in the concept of possession between the three jurisdictions. A major similarity is that possession takes factual control as a constitutive element. The main difference lies in the content of *animus*.[121] This part seeks to provide a further comparative study of the content of *animus* and to find possible reasons for this difference.

3.1.3.1 Differences in Animus

In general, possession includes two elements: *corpus* and *animus*. The element of *corpus* denotes factual control over things, and the element of *animus* refers to the intention of possession.[122] Compared with *corpus*, the content of *animus* is more diverse and complicated in the three jurisdictions. As the chart below shows, each of the three jurisdictions has its specialties in defining the element of *animus*.

<table>
<tr><td rowspan="2">DCFR</td><td colspan="2">Possession</td><td>Control by Agents</td></tr>
<tr><td>Ownership Possession</td><td colspan="2">Limited-Right Possession</td></tr>
<tr><td>English Law</td><td colspan="2">Possession under English Law</td><td>Custody</td></tr>
<tr><td rowspan="2">German Law</td><td colspan="2">Besitz</td><td rowspan="2">Besitzdienerschaft</td></tr>
<tr><td>Eigenbesitz</td><td>Fremdbesitz</td></tr>
<tr><td>Dutch Law</td><td>Bezit</td><td colspan="2">Houderschap</td></tr>
</table>

Figure 5

Taking the DCFR as a baseline, we find that *Besitz* in German law is significantly similar to possession in the DCFR: *Eigenbesitz* corresponds to ownership possession, and *Fremdbesitz* corresponds to limited-right possession. Moreover, *Besitzdienerschaft* is not covered by the concept of *Besitz*. Between Dutch law and the DCFR, it can be found that *bezit* in Dutch law amounts to ownership possession in the DCFR, and *houderschap* covers limited-right possession and control by agents in the DCFR. In the English

121 Of course, the difference in the object of possession is also obvious. For example, only tangible things can be possessed in English law, tangibles and the right of easement can be possessed in German law, while Dutch law generally recognizes possession of both tangibles things and intangible rights.

122 Acquisition and Loss of Ownership of Goods 2011, p. 319.

law of movables, custody amounts to control by agents in the DCFR, and possession resembles the DCFR possession in the sense that *animus domini* is not required. However, English law does not have an individual concept of ownership possession which is different from the DCFR (ownership possession), German law (*Eigenbesitz*), and Dutch law (*bezit*).

In sum, there are three basic divergences between the three jurisdictions: (1) whether ownership possession is separately prescribed; (2) whether there is an individual concept of limited-right possession; and (3) whether control by agents has an independent position. The subsequent three sections discuss these divergences in sequence.

3.1.3.2 Necessity of a Concept of Ownership Possession

A English Law

English law does not have an individual concept of ownership possession. In general, this can be ascribed to the principle of the relativity of title. Under this principle, ownership is not an important concept for judgements, and what matters is the relative strength of two conflicting claims.

> *"These rival titles will each be recognized by law, but they will be of different relative strengths [...]. In order to win, one of them only has to show that he has a better title than the other party to the dispute, not that he has an absolute title."*[123]

The principle is deeply rooted in the common law tradition. Common law is a system mainly based on judicial precedents. It is cases that serve as the fundamental source of law. Common law concentrates more on how to solve specific disputes fairly, rather than how to construct a coherent system of concepts, rules and principles. It enshrines empirical knowledge rather than abstract rationality. Usually, what judges are concerned about is which side (the claimant or the defendant) has superiority and should prevail, rather than who the owner is. The principle of relativity of title fits well with the culture of legal empiricism.

Due to the principle of relativity of title, English property law does not take ownership as a fundamental concept. Instead, possession is more important than ownership and plays a central role in the law of movables as well as land law.[124] Most disputes about a certain thing, whether movable or immovable, are resolved according to the rules of possession. Under the principle of relativity of title, ownership is at most deemed as the *best* right to possession.[125]

---

123 Clarke and Kohler 2005, p. 383.
124 Bridge, Gullifer, McMeel and Worthington 2013, p. 55.
125 Frisby and Jones 2009, p. 21; Bridge, Gullifer, McMeel and Worthington 2013, p. 53.

> *"Although the right to possession is merely one of the rights that make up the concept of 'ownership', and so in this sense is subordinate to it, in everyday practice possession is far more important than 'ownership'."*[126]

As ownership has limited significance, and possession is the basis of the whole system of property law, there are no sufficient reasons to have an independent concept of ownership possession. As will be shown below, the right of ownership plays a central role in German law and Dutch law, which makes a concept of ownership possession necessary.

B German Law and Dutch Law

In this aspect, German law and Dutch law are different from English law: both have a concept of ownership possession. The two jurisdictions are significantly influenced by Roman law. Roman law took ownership (*dominium*) as a central concept, and ownership was unitary, perpetual, independent and comprehensive. In this ownership-dominating context, possession was construed as a concept subordinate to ownership. For example, Roman law created the concept of *possessio civilis* that could be elevated to ownership through *usucaptio*;[127] Von Savigny claimed that the Roman law *possessio* embodied the element of *animus domini*, namely an intention of belonging;[128] Von Jhering contended that the purpose of protecting possession was to protect ownership.[129]

> *"English law gives a possessory remedy to any possessor who is not merely a servant [...]. The Roman law [...] protects the possession of the owner, of the bona fide and mala fide possessor, but not one who holds under a contract as depositary, borrower, mandatory, hirer and so forth."*[130]

This Roman law tradition profoundly affects the modern civil law system. Nowadays, ownership still plays a central role in the civil law system. Despite being eroded to some extent, the unitary feature, perpetuity, principality and comprehensiveness of ownership are generally accepted. In addition, the general doctrines of property law are often clarified by analyzing the right of ownership, the best example of property rights.

> *„Wichtigstes Recht an Sachen ist das Eigentum. Am Beispiel des Eigentums lassen sich am besten für dies Rechte an Sachen charakteristisches Merkmal aufzeigen."*[131]

---

126 Frisby and Jones 2009, p. 21.
127 Mousourakis 2012, p. 158.
128 Bond 1890, p. 271.
129 Bond 1890, p. 261.
130 Lee 1956, p. 179.
131 Wolf and Wellenhofer 2011, p. 2. English translation: *"The most important right with respect to things is ownership. The example of ownership shows in the best way the characteristics of property rights."*

The centrality of ownership partially explains why both German law and Dutch law create an individual term (*Eigenbesitz* and *bezit* respectively) for factual control held by those as or as if an owner.[132] As ownership stands at the center of property law, other institutions (in particular the institution of possession) are inevitably affected by this property right. In general, acquisition (especially prescriptive acquisition), transfer and extinguishment of ownership have a close link with possession, protection of ownership also partly relies on protecting possession, and the right to possess is treated as an important entitlement embodied within ownership. In these situations, ownership possession is an essential concept. If the concept of ownership possession were abolished, the entire system of ownership would malfunction. Moreover, the *animus domini* embodied within ownership possession is necessary for explaining the acquisition, transfer, and protection of ownership.[133]

C Summary

All in all, the reason why English law does not have a concept of ownership possession is that possession *per se* is a more important concept than ownership. Possession is deemed as a root of ownership, and ownership is, at most, treated as the best right to possession. In practice, most disputes are resolved according to the rules of possession, which can be boiled down to the principle of relativity of title. This principle means that the party who has a better right to possession prevails. In contrast, both German law and Dutch law have a Roman law tradition, and ownership is the most important right in property law. Just as English lawyers Buckland and McNair say, "*our Courts deal with rights to possess where the Roman Courts dealt with ownership*".[134] The centrality of ownership makes possession become a concept subordinate to ownership, rather than the opposite. For the system of ownership, an individual concept of ownership possession is essential.

3.1.3.3 Necessity of a Concept of Limited-Right Possession

The chart above (Figure 5) also shows that the three jurisdictions differ in limited-right possession. In German law, *Fremdbesitz* corresponds to limited-right possession, while Dutch law classifies limited-right possession, together with control by agents, under the concept of *houderschap*. In English law, factual control held by a bailee (such as the pledgee) is possession, but an equivalent term to limited-right possession is not used. These differences between the three jurisdictions can be partially accounted for by the legislative policy adopted: what is the fundamental function served by the concept of possession?

132 Van Schaick 2014, p. 5.
133 Emerich 2017, p. 177.
134 Buckland and McNair 1952, p. 68.

A Dutch Law and German Law

In Dutch law, prescriptive acquisition is the fundamental concern in determining how to define the concept of possession. As a result, *bezit* is directly confined to ownership possession, which has been pointed out in the parliamentary explanation of the BW.

> *"In de regeling van het ontwerp daarentegen staat, ten dele in aansluiting met het geldende recht, als gevolg van het bezit de verkrijging voor verjaring en de bescherming van hem, die op weg is door verjaring het goed te verkrijgen, voorop. Mitsdien wordt degene, die een goed voor een ander houdt, niet als bezitter aangemerkt [...]."*[135]

> *"Bij de regeling van het bezit in titel 3.5 hebben de ontwerpers primair de verkrijgende verjaring en, in het verlengde daarvan, de bescherming van hem die bezig is door verjaring te verkrijgen, voor ogen gehad."*[136]

As prescriptive acquisition requires the possessor to have a pretention of belonging (*animus domini*), it is necessary to distinguish possession from detention. Otherwise, it would become difficult to explain how a person having no pretention of belonging can acquire ownership in the way of acquisitive prescription. To put it differently, a detentor cannot claim prescriptive acquisition.[137] A similar policy reason can be found in French law in which possession is also distinguished from detention.[138]

> *"The distinction between possession and detention plays an important role for acquisition of property rights, as the detentor cannot acquire ownership of the object by way of acquisitive prescription."*[139]

From the perspective of legal history, the distinction between possession and detention is partly because of the influence of Roman law.[140] As has been pointed out above, *possessio civilis* was distinguished from *possessio naturalis* (*detentio*) in Roman law (see 3.1.1.1). The biggest difference between them is that the former could give rise to the prescriptive acquisition of ownership, while the latter could not.

---

135 Parlementaire Geschiedenis (3) 1981, p. 424-425. English translation: "*However, the rule in the draft is partially in accordance with the applicable law: prescriptive acquisition and protection of the person who intends to acquire the object through prescription, as a consequence of possession, stand in the fore. Therefore, the one who holds a thing for another person is not treated as a possessor [...].*"

136 Rank-Berenschot 2012, p. 12. English translation: "*With regard to possession in Chapter 3.5, the drafters paid primary attention to prescriptive acquisition and secondly to the protection of the person who aims for acquisition through prescription.*"

137 Vantomme 2018, p. 23-24.

138 Stoljar 1984, p. 1027; Staudinger/Gutzeit 2012, p. 75.

139 Hinteregger 2012, p. 100.

140 Parlementaire Geschiedenis (3) 1981, p. 423.

However, this narrow definition of possession implies that possessory protection is not available for detentors. For example, the protection under art. 3:125 (1) and (2) BW can only be claimed by possessors.[141] As a result, a problem arises: how to protect the legal position of detentors. To address this problem, art. 3:125 (3) BW expressly prescribes that detention is under the protection of the law of torts.[142] This tort law protection can be seen as a complementary scheme.

In contrast to *bezit* in Dutch law, possession (*Besitz*) in German law is defined with a major concern about the issue of protection. As a result, the distinction between possession and detention is not recognized by German law.[143] For German legislators, persons like the lessee should also be provided with possessory protection, even though they exercise factual control in the absence of an intention to be an owner.[144]

> *"In het Duitse en in het Zwitserse Wetboek staat als gevolg van het bezit op de voorgrond: de bescherming tegen eigenrichting. Mitsdien wordt daar zowel aan hem die een goed voor een ander houdt, als aan degene voor wie deze houdt, het bezit toegekend."*[145]

> *„Als problematisch sah man es insbesondere an, dass diese Konzeption nur begrenzt mit der vorgesehenen Ausweitung des Anwendungsbereichs des possessorischen Besitzschutzes harmonierte, der nun auch solche Formen der tatsächlichen Sachherrschaft umfassen sollte, die nach diesem Konzept als bloße Detention einzustufen gewesen waren."*[146]

According to these two excerpts, the main reason why a broader possessory intention (*animus possidendi*) is recognized is to extend possessory protection to the holder of limited rights. This approach enlarges the scope of application of possessory protection, which allows hirers, lessees, pledgees and the

---

141 Snijders and Rank-Berenschot 2017, p. 121.

142 Art. 3:125 (3) BW: *"Het in dit artikel bepaalde laat voor de bezitter, ook nadat het in het eerste lid bedoelde jaar is verstreken, en voor de houder onverlet de mogelijkheid een vordering op grond van onrechtmatige daad in te stellen, indien daartoe gronden zijn."* English translation: Art. 3:125 (3) BW: *"Nothing in this article shall deprive the possessor, even after expiry of the year referred to in paragraph 1, or the detentor, of the possibility, should there be grounds, to institute an action on the basis of the law of torts."*

143 Stoljar 1984, p. 1027; Hinteregger 2012, p. 104.

144 It is worthwhile noting that the first draft of the BGB provided a distinction between *possessio* and *detentio*. However, this was replaced by the distinction between ownership possession and limited-right possession in the second draft. See Wilhelm 2010, p. 212.

145 Parlementaire Geschiedenis (3) 1981, p. 424. English translation: *"In the German Civil Code and the Swish Civil Code, the consequence of possession, namely the protection against interference, has a prominent position. Therefore, those who hold things for another person as well as for themselves are granted with possession."*

146 Müller 2010, p. 39-40. English translation: *"It was seen as particularly problematic that the narrow concept can fit into the policy of expanding the scope of application of possessory protection. The protection should also apply to those kinds of factual control that are, according to this concept, merely categorized as detention."*

like to claim possessory protection. If the concept of *Besitz* were confined to be factual control with an *animus domini*, then the scope of possessory protection would be restricted.

It is noteworthy that the broad concept of *Besitz* also has a historical reason. In defining this concept, both Roman law and ancient Germanic law were taken into account by the drafters of the BGB.[147] As introduced above, possession (*possessio*) in Roman law roughly amounts to ownership possession, and lessees were not a possessor, enjoying no possessory protection (see 3.1.1.1). On the contrary, Germanic law allows lessees to have possession (*Gewere*).[148] To reconcile this divergence between Roman law and Germanic law, the BGB confers indirect ownership possession on lessors, and direct limited-right possession on lessees.[149]

However, the German approach gives rise to a problem: how to coordinate the relationship between possession and ownership? As pointed out above, ownership plays a central role in German property law, and there is demand for a form of possession that is specifically correlated with ownership. In order to solve this problem, the distinction between ownership possession (*Eigenbesitz*) and limited-right possession (*Fremdbesitz*) is recognized. The former must embody *animus domini*, namely an intention of belonging. It is considered an important factor for acquiring, transferring and abandoning ownership.

> *"This distinction plays an important role with regard to provisions, such as the presumption of ownership (Art. 1006) or the preconditions of acquisitive prescription (Art. 937) which now only applies to Eigenbesitz."*[150]

From the preceding discussion, we find that Dutch law and German law define the concept of possession in different ways. However, both focus on the issue of acquisition of ownership and the issue of protection. In the end, no significant differences exist in the legal consequences between the two jurisdictions.

B English Law

In general, *animus domini* is not necessary for acquiring possession in English law, and the distinction between possession and detention is alien to English lawyers. In this respect, English law is akin to German law, but different from Dutch law. However, unlike German law, English law does not have any term equivalent to limited-right possession (*Fremdbesitz*). The following discussion clarifies why English law is special as such.

147 Wilhelm 2010, p. 211.
148 Wilhelm 2010, p. 211-212.
149 Füller 2006, p. 274.
150 Hinteregger 2012, p. 104.

Firstly, English law does not follow Roman law doctrines. Rather, it is rooted in the history of common law. Unlike German law and Dutch law, English law is not heavily influenced by Roman law. As has been shown above (see 3.1.1.1), Roman law differentiates between *possessio*, *possessio civilis* and *detentio* (*possession naturalis*). Scholars of civil law had conducted significant research with respect to these terms in history. The achievement obtained deeply affected later legislation, especially the codification that took place in the 19th century. Neither similar historical studies nor legislative debates take place meaningfully in English law.

Secondly, the principle of relativity of title also explains why limited-right possession does not have an independent position in English law. As pointed out above, English law does not enshrine the concept of ownership, which is at most considered as the *best* right to possession. Under this principle, what matters is the relativity of the strength of competing claims with respect to possession. The legal doctrine not only makes ownership possession dispensable, but also renders limited-right possession unnecessary. The concept of ownership possession and that of limited-right possession exist correlatively, and the lack of the former leads the latter to be redundant.

For example, prescriptive acquisition in civil law is generally equivalent to adverse possession in English law. For the claim of adverse possession, whether adverse possessors have *animus domini* is of no relevance. An adverse possessor can acquire a title to the land involved after the passage of a certain period of time. In light of the principle of relativity of title, the reason why this adverse possessor is protected against the former proprietor is that he has a better title.[151] English law shows no strong interest in the question whether the adverse possessor acquires a title called ownership.

C Summary

In sum, the three jurisdictions have their own characteristics in defining the concept of possession. The English law of possession has its own legal history (ancient English law) and is subject to a special legal principle (relativity of title). Thus, the concept is defined in a distinctive way. In general, Dutch law and German law share the same legal history (Roman law) and focus on two issues (acquisition of ownership and protection of possessors) in defining the concept of possession.[152] However, differences exist between the two jurisdictions.

Dutch law takes prescriptive acquisition as the fundamental function of possession, and *animus domini* is required as an essential element of possession (*bezit*), but this narrow definition restricts the scope of application of possessory protection. To address this problem, Dutch law confers on detentors tort law protection. In contrast, German law treats protection of

151 Vantomme 2018, p. 28-29.
152 In addition, ancient Germanic law (the concept of *Gewere*) also has an influence on the definition of *Besitz* in drafting the BGB, which has been pointed out above.

possessors as the central function of possession, and a large number of persons having no *animus domini* are also treated as a possessor under German law. However, this broad definition gives rise to difficulty in explaining the acquisition of ownership. To address this problem, German law prescribes a distinction between ownership possession and limited-right possession.

> *"At this point, one can conclude that between the two options presented by Caterina, that is, to rely upon a narrow category of possessors and give to all of them the benefits of possession (opening some possessory remedies to non-possessors), or, conversely, to define a wider category of possessors but restricting particular benefits to particular kinds of possession."*[153]

The two jurisdictions choose two different ways to define the concept of possession, but the ultimate legal consequences do not differ substantially.

3.1.3.4 Necessity of a Concept of Factual Control by Agents

In many situations, factual control is not exercised by possessors in person. Instead, it may be a possession agent (such as an employee) who holds the object for the benefit of the possessor (such as an employer). Under the social context of the division of labor, many things are factually controlled by possession agents, which causes a divergence between the right of ownership and factual control. The preceding introduction has shown that possession agents are not recognized as possessor in the three jurisdictions. English law uses the concept of custody, German law uses the term *Besitzdienerschaft*, and Dutch law includes factual control by agents within the concept of *houderschap*. However, a difference also exists between the three jurisdictions. This difference is that Dutch law does not draw a line between possession agents and those who have a limited right (such as the lessee). The following discussion seeks to clarify the similarity as well as the difference.

A Why Are Possession Agents Not a Possessor?

Firstly, possession agents are said to have no possessory intention. In general, possession through an agent requires two elements: a relationship of subordination and the obedience to the possessor's instructions.[154] The first element means that there must be an underlying relationship between the possessor and the possession agent, which requires the latter to hold the thing involved for the former. The underlying relationship can be contractual or statutory.[155] A typical example is employment. The second element means that the possession agent should obey instructions from the

153 Rodriguez 2013, p. 38.
154 Baur and Stürner 2009, p. 81-82; Wilhelm 2010, p. 223.
155 Baur and Stürner 2009, p. 82.

possessor. For example, employers have a right to instruct their employees in managing their property. This power to instruct acts as a decisive criterion in judging who has possession.[156] In this sense, we can say that possession agents are only a "long arm" of the possessor.

Secondly, possession agents do not enjoy benefits or bear liabilities out of possession because they are subordinate to the possessor for whose benefits factual control is exercised. For example, possession agents are not entitled to acquire ownership by factually controlling an ownerless thing (*res nullius*), to gain ownership after the passage of the prescriptive period, or to give up ownership by abandoning possession.[157] Moreover, possession agents cannot be sued as a defendant, when the principal obtains possession in the way of illegal dispossession.[158] These legal consequences are reasonable: they are in line with the principle that benefits and liabilities should be allocated to the same person. In addition, according to the content of the underlying relationship, possession agents usually have no intention to obtain benefits or bear liabilities associated with possession. All in all, for the purpose of properly determining legal consequences out of possession, possession agents should not be recognized as a possessor in law.[159]

B Why Are Possession Agents Not Distinguished?

As pointed out, both limited-right possessors and possession agents are covered by the concept of "detentor (*houder*)" in Dutch law. In this aspect, Dutch law is different from English law and German law. In the latter two jurisdictions, a line is carefully drawn between factual control by agents and that by the holder of limited right. In general, the Dutch law approach seems to be a result of the following two reasons.

The first reason is that Dutch law focuses on prescriptive acquisition in determining how to define the concept of "possession (*bezit*)".[160] As a result, any factual control that cannot generate this legal consequence is strictly excluded from the concept of possession and thus fall under detention. The second reason is that non-possessory factual control has a great variety of variants, and categorizing them is neither easy nor worthwhile. Instead, a practical approach is to regulate this kind of factual control by reference to the underlying relationship between the parties involved.[161] In other words, factual control by the holder of a limited right (such as the lessee) does not seem substantially different from factual control by an agent (such as an employee). The legal consequences of both forms of factual control have to be determined by referring to the underlying relationship.

156 Baur and Stürner 2009, p. 81.
157 Baur and Stürner 2009, p. 83.
158 Wilhelm 2010, p. 223.
159 Füller 2006, p. 281.
160 Rank-Berenschot 2012, p. 12.
161 Van Schaick 2014, p. 47.

3.1.4 Conclusion

The preceding three parts have shown the complexities and divergences surrounding the concept of possession. In general, three factors should be considered to explain these complexities and divergences: historical influence, legal culture, and legislative policy.

Firstly, possession is a concept used to deal with different types of questions, which, in turn, makes this concept difficult to define. It has a connection with, *inter alia*, prescriptive acquisition of ownership, transfer of property rights, protection of possessors, and distribution of liabilities and interests between relevant parties. In general, prescriptive acquisition of ownership requires a narrower definition of possession, while a broader definition is needed for the purpose of protecting owners, pledgees, lessees and the like. For proper allocation of liabilities and interests to relevant parties, factual control by agents for the benefit of another person should be denied as possession. The legislative policy adopted by legislators with respect to these issues largely determines how possession is defined.

As pointed out at the beginning of this chapter, legal concepts are functional and technical, and the meaning of a legal concept is largely determined by legislative purposes.

> *„Die Auswahl der bei der Bildung eines abstrakten Begriffs in seine Definition aufzunehmenden Merkmale wird wesentlich durch den Zweck mitbestimmt, den die betreffende Wissenschaft mit ihrer Begriffsbildung verfolgt. Daher kommt es, dass sich der juristische Begriff, der eine bestimme Klasse von Gegenständen bezeichnet, nicht immer mit dem entsprechenden Begriff einer anderen Wissenschaft oder gar mit dem, was der Sprachgebrauch des Lebens darunter versteht, in vollem Umfange deckt."*[162]

The concept of possession performs multiple functions and is used in a wide range of situations. Therefore, it cannot be fully understood unless we know the functions it is supposed to perform.

> *"Hetgeen in een wet met 'bezit' wordt bedoeld, wordt geheel bepaald door de gevolgen, welke die wet aan het bezit verbindt en de nadere vereisten, welke die wet voor het intreden van die gevolgen stelt."*[163]

Dutch law takes prescriptive acquisition as the primary function. Thus, the possessory intention is confined to *animus domini*, and the possessor needs to act as, or pretend to be, an owner. German law takes protection as the

162 Larenz 1991, p. 440. English translation: *"In defining an abstract concept, the selection of elements is significantly determined by the objective pursued by the academy in defining this concept. Therefore, a legal concept, which can describe a certain category of facts, is not always construed in the same way as the concept correspondingly used in another discipline or daily conversation."*

163 Meijers 1954, p. 230. English translation: *"What 'possession' means in law is totally determined by the consequences attached by law to possession as well as the extra requirements pinned down by law for the occurrence of these consequences."*

primary function. Thus, *animus domini* is not necessary, but it is essential for ownership possession which can lead to prescriptive acquisition. To properly distribute liabilities and interests between relevant parties, both German law and English law refuse to grant possession to possession agents who exercise factual control for the benefit of another person.

Secondly, historical influence is also important. Both German law and Dutch law are, to a lesser or greater degree, influenced by Roman law. As indicated above, the function of acquiring ownership and the function of protection are important for understanding the concept of *possessio* in Roman law (see 3.1.1.1). However, this Roman law concept is not entirely coherent, which triggers fierce debates in theory as well as in legislation, especially the debate concerning the question whether the distinction between possession and detention should be accepted. Compared with German law and Dutch law, English law is less influenced by Roman law; English law has its own history. This partially accounts for why the concept of possession in English law has its own specialties.

Finally, differences in legal culture are also relevant. In general, German law and Dutch law belong to the civil law system. In this system, ownership is a fundamental concept for property law. Thus, there is the need for a concept of ownership possession (*Eigenbesitz* in the BGB and *bezit* in the BW), on account of the tight connection between possession and ownership. In contrast, English law enshrines the principle of relativity of title, a principle that can be seen as a result of legal empiricism. Under this principle, ownership is at most considered as the best title to possession. This explains why a concept of ownership possession does not exist in English law.

3.2 Possession and Publicity

Possession is often treated as a method of publicity for corporeal movables. In this section, we examine how and in what sense possession can convey proprietary information to third parties. We argue that possession is able to convey proprietary information, but only in the sense that it can inform third parties that the possessor has a *right* to the object possessed. The details of the right can only be known through other means. In addition, this section also pays particular attention to indirect possession: can indirect possession be qualified as a method of publicity for corporeal movables? The answer is no.

3.2.1 Possession and the Proprietary Information Conveyed

In this part, we discuss the question whether and in what sense possession can convey proprietary information to third parties. It will be argued that: (1) possession can serve as an outward mark for different kinds of rights; and (2) for this reason, possession merely provides proprietary information in an abstract and thus ambiguous way. With respect to the publicity effect of possession, there are two extreme approaches in theory. One is the ownership approach which holds that possession is an outward appearance of ownership. The other is the non-publicity approach which claims that possession does not have any effect of publicity. These two approaches are examined below.

3.2.1.1 The Field of Application of Possession

A Objects of Possession

A1: Corporeal Movables

In general, possession is of great importance in the law of corporeal movables. At present, there is not any general system of registration for corporeal movables, and possession is treated as the main method of publicity.[164] For corporeal movables, possession is a more suitable method than registration because: (1) corporeal movables usually have low value, while the costs of constructing and maintaining a system of registration are high; (2) corporeal movables are often in frequent circulation, and a requirement of registration would impact on the fluidity of the transaction of corporeal movables; and (3) corporeal movables are often fungible and difficult to be uniquely identified, which makes a registration system nearly impossible.[165] Compared with registration, possession is a much cheaper method of publicity (see 3.2.1.2.A). As a result, possession is considered a "natural" means of publicity for corporeal movables.

In the law of corporeal movables, the fate of property rights is closely related to possession. In general, acquisition, transfer and destruction of property rights are affected, to different degrees, by obtaining, transferring and abandoning possession respectively.[166] This is often explained from the perspective of the publicity effect of possession (see 3.4.1). Moreover, protection of property rights is also related to possession. In many situations, protecting possession implies that the holder of property rights is protected. Moreover, the protection of possession might be explained from the angle of publicity: possession should be respected and protected because possessors have shown their right to third parties via possession (see 3.3.2).[167]

Here it should be noted that securities concerning goods or payment (such as the bill of lading or the bill of exchange) are also a kind of corporeal movable. They can be factually controlled and possessed by the person entitled to the goods or payment.[168] On the other hand, securities are more

164 Snijders and Rank-Berenschot 2017, p. 63; Wolf and Wellenhofer 2011, p. 76.

165 Clarke and Kohler 2005, p. 388.

166 Snijders and Rank-Berenschot 2017, p. 105-106.

167 Baur and Stürner 2009, p. 64.

168 Not all securities have a tangible form. Uncertificated securities are paperless and electronic (see 4.2.1). For this type of securities, possession is not possible.

than a corporeal thing. Securities embody a right, and the disposal of this right is often based on the disposal of securities. Moreover, third parties can obtain proprietary information concerning the right embodied from securities. Due to these two reasons, securities have a function of publicity, which is discussed in Chapter 4 (see 4.2).

A2: Immovable Property

Historically, possession was also a means of publicity for immovable property, but was gradually replaced with registration. The process of this replacement started in the 12th century.[169] At present, most countries have constructed a system of registration for immovable property. More remarkably, even some special movables, such as aircraft and vessels, are publicized by a register.[170] Thanks to registration, proprietary information concerning these things can be recorded and conveyed in a clear, detailed and reliable way.[171] However, since this research concerns only the publicity of corporeal movables and claims, the registration of immovable property and those special movables is outside the scope of this research.

A3: Rights

In some jurisdictions, the object of possession includes not only tangible things, but also rights which are intangible. For example, "possession of easements (*Rechtsbesitz an Dienstbarkeiten*)" is recognized by German law, but only as an exception to the rule that the object of possession is tangible (see 3.1.2.3);[172] Dutch law recognizes possession of patrimonial rights in a general way, which has been pointed out above (see 3.1.2.4).[173]

In this research, we hold that possession of rights has nothing to do with publicity. Rights are intangible. Possession of a right cannot make this right visible to outsiders.[174] In Dutch law, possession of rights just means the enjoyment and exercise of rights. Thus, possession of rights does not have a unitary definition: it depends on the content of the right possessed.[175] Possession of a right of easement is different from possession of a claim of payment, because these rights significantly differ in terms of the content. Therefore, though possession of rights is generally recognized by the BW, Dutch lawyers acknowledge that this kind of possession fails to create a visible outward appearance for the specific right possessed.[176] This is particularly true in the situation of claims.

169 Xie 2011, p. 48.
170 Baird and Jackson 1984, p. 309-310.
171 Hinteregger and Van Vliet 2012, p. 844-902.
172 Wieling 2006, p. 81.
173 Snijders and Rank-Berenschot 2017, p. 97.
174 Emerich 2017, p. 180.
175 Biemans 2007, p. 88; Van Schaick 2014, p. 8.
176 De Jong, Krans and Wissink 2018, p. 289-290.

> *"Vooral het feitelijke element van de machtsuitoefening waarmee bezit gepaard gaat, lijkt moeilijk te verenigen met het ontastbare karakter van vorderingsrechten."*[177]

Possession of rights is recognized for other legislative purposes than publicity. As has been shown above, Roman law recognized possession of rights by providing special protection to certain property rights of use, which gave rise to quasi-possession (see 3.1.1.1).[178] Possession of easements is recognized by modern German law for a similar reason: extending possessory protection to the right of easement.[179] Different from Roman law and German law, Dutch law recognizes possession of rights due to a concern about prescriptive acquisition. Possession of a right is a condition for prescriptive acquisition of this right. Thus, every right susceptible to prescriptive acquisition should be able to be possessed.[180] For example, prescriptive acquisition of claims is generally possible under Dutch law, and this type of acquisition is based on possession; thus, claims can be possessed.[181] Therefore, taking prescriptive acquisition as the principal function (*Hauptfunktion*) determines that the object of *bezit* is not confined to corporeal things.[182]

B Underlying Rights of Possession

In general, possession of corporeal movables can be acquired on different grounds. In most situations, the possessor has a right that underlies the acquisition of possession. This right might be ownership or a right out of pledge, lease, storage, or borrowing. Moreover, the possessor may also obtain possession illegally, such as theft. In this very situation, no underlying right is associated with possession. Here we provide a general view of the underlying right of possession.

B1: Ownership

It is needless to stress that possession can be associated with the right of ownership. As the most comprehensive property right, ownership embodies the entitlement to possess. In general, where an owner loses possession, he is entitled to recover the object unless the present possessor has a legal ground to keep factual control.

> *"The right to possess, viz, to have exclusive physical control of a thing, or to have such control as the nature of the thing admits, is the foundation on which the superstructure of ownership rests."*[183]

---

177 Wibier 2007, p. 261. English translation: *"In particular, it seems difficult to reconcile the element of exercising of control associated with possession, on the one hand, and the invisible feature of claims, on the other hand."*

178 Thomas 1976, p. 147.

179 Westermann 2011, p. 175; Rüfner 2014, p. 173.

180 Parlementaire Geschiedenis (3) 1981, p. 425.

181 Biemans 2007, p. 88.

182 Drobnig 1993, p. 181.

183 Honoré 1987, p. 371.

More importantly, property law is inclined to promote the convergence of possession and ownership, attempting to have ownership and possession held by the same person.[184] To some degree, this inclination can be shown by the following examples: the rule of first possession, the *traditio* rule which requires delivery as a requirement of the transfer of corporeal movables, the rule of *bona fide* acquisition of corporeal movables, the rule of prescriptive acquisition, and the rule of giving up ownership through abandoning possession. The inclination provides a basis for the viewpoint that possession is a method of publicity for ownership of corporeal movables. This viewpoint will be examined later (see 3.2.1.3).

B2: Pledge

Possession can be associated with possessory pledge. In general, the law allows individuals to create a right of pledge through delivery of the collateral to the pledgee to a third party. Possessory pledge is known as *pledge* in English law,[185] *Pfandrecht* in German law (§ 1205 (1) BGB), and *openbaar pandrecht* or *vuistpand* in Dutch law (art. 3:236 (1) BW). In general, there are two different ways to explain the relevance of delivery with the creation of pledge: the positive approach and the negative approach.[186] The former holds that delivery is a method to publicize the right of pledge to third parties. The latter holds that delivery helps address the problem of false appearance of wealth (or ostensible ownership) by preventing pledgors from appearing to have an unencumbered right of ownership.

> *"Deze eis vloeit voort uit het beginsel van publiciteit. Uit de wijziging van de machtsuitoefening blijkt van het bestaan van het pandrecht tegenover derden."*[187]

> *"The debtor's dispossession fulfills two major functions: it makes it more difficult for the debtor to dispose of the pledged goods to a third person; and the debtor can no longer create the misleading impression in the minds of his other creditors of owning the pledged goods which might be available for the satisfaction of their claims."*[188]

It should be noted here that there is a difference between these two approaches. Under the positive approach, possession is treated as a method of publicity for pledge, and delivery is expected to make the pledge transparent to third parties. However, the negative approach implies that possession can indicate the existence of ownership, and retaining possession by pledgors may lead other parties to believe that the collateral is not encumbered with any security interest. Therefore, this approach does not differ

184 Asser/Bartels & Van Mierlo 2013, nr. 114.
185 Goode 2013, p. 32.
186 Füller 2006, p. 296-298.
187 Asser/Van Mierlo 2016, nr. 146. English translation: *"This requirement results from the principle of publicity. Pledge can be shown to third parties through the change of the power of control."*
188 Drobnig 2011, p. 1027.

from the view that possession is an outward appearance of (unencumbered) ownership. This view will be discussed later (see 3.2.1.3).

B3: Intermediary Rights

Apart from ownership and pledge, possession can also be held by a person who has an intermediary right which straddles property law and the law of obligations. A typical case is sales under a clause of reservation of ownership. In this case, possession of the movable in question is given up to the purchaser, but the seller retains the right of ownership usually for a security purpose. In brief, the purchaser acquires a right which can elevate into full ownership upon the fulfillment of the condition agreed, usually the payment of the purchase price.

In German law, this right is known as the "right of expectation (*Anwartschaftsrecht*)", which is partially proprietary.[189] In Dutch law, the buyer obtains a right called "conditional ownership (*voorwaardelijk eigendomsrecht*)".[190] As to the nature of conditional ownership, different opinions exist.[191] It is generally held that the right has a proprietary feature, and the buyer under the clause of reservation of ownership has a proprietary legal position.[192] In English law, what a buyer under the clause of reservation can obtain is more than a personal right, partially because of the acquisition of possession.[193]

Reservation of ownership is a transfer under a suspensive condition. Ownership can also be transferred under a resolutive condition, such as in the situation of transfer of ownership for security purposes. Upon fulfillment of the condition, ownership will be restored to the hands of the transferor. Before the condition is satisfied, the transferor no longer has ownership, but retains possession of the thing involved. In general, as in the case of reservation of ownership, the possession retained by the transferor is also associated with an intermediary right.[194]

B4: Personal Rights

In addition to property rights and intermediary rights, personal rights are also able to serve as a legal basis for the acquisition of possession. A typical example is the right of lease (*hire* in English law, *Miete* in German law, and *huur* in Dutch law). By virtue of this right, the lessee is entitled to acquire possession of the object. The lessee cannot use the object without obtaining possession. It is worthwhile noting that upon obtaining possession by the lessee, the right of lease is no longer a purely personal right under German

189 Baur and Stürner 2009, p. 30; Mincke 1997, p. 209.
190 *Rabobank/Reuser*, HR 3 juni 2016, NJ 2016/290.
191 Nieuwesteeg 2015, p. 168.
192 Schuijling 2017, p. 18.
193 Bridge 2014, p. 123; Pennington 1978, p. 286.
194 Sagaert and Gruyaert 2017, p. 434; Wieling 2007, p. 256.

law and Dutch law.[195] Instead, it begins to have a proprietary feature. In English law, hire of corporeal movables is a kind of bailment, which straddles property law and contract law.[196] As a possessor of the object, the bailee has an intermediary right.

In addition to the right of lease, other personal rights can also serve as a basis on which possession is acquired and maintained. For example, a person may acquire possession on the basis of the relationship of *depositum* (storage in English law, *Verwahrung* in German law, and *bewaarneming* in Dutch law) and *commodatum* (borrowing in English law, *Sachdarlehen* in German law, and *bruikleening* in Dutch law). In these two situations, the depositary and the borrower obtain possession of the thing involved on a contractual basis.

B5: Statutory Legal Relationships

The underlying right of possession is not necessarily a consequence of agreement. Possession can also be obtained as a result of the operation of law. In other words, the underlying right might be statutory. Here one example is lien (*Zurückbehaltung* in German law and *retentie* in Dutch law).[197] A repairman can retain the bicycle he repairs to secure his right to payment of fees. Another example is the finding of lost things. In this situation, the finder acquires possession of the lost thing and bears a duty of care to the owner. Generally speaking, the finder's possession is based on a legal relationship concerning the management, preservation and return of the lost thing.[198]

Moreover, where a contract giving rise to the acquisition of possession is invalid or terminated, the creditor's right to possess out of this contract will come to an end. The creditor has an obligation to return the thing involved to the debtor. Before doing this, however, the creditor remains in possession and has a duty to take care of the thing. This duty is part of the post-contractual relationship, a legal relationship that is often statutory.

B6: Illegal Possession

The way in which possession is obtained appears more diverse, when illegal possession (such as in the situation of robbery and theft) is taken into consideration. Compared with immovable property, corporeal movables are easier to be illegally dispossessed from their owner. In reality, posses-

195 Wolf and Wellenhofer 2011, p. 78; Snijders and Rank-Berenschot 2017, p. 58-59.

196 Bridge, Gullifer, McMeel and Worthington 2013, p. 72.

197 Three things should be noted here. The first is that lien is a complicated term under English law. Lien can be either statutory or contractual. It is impossible to find a legal term equivalent to the English concept of lien in German law and Dutch law. The second is that *Zurückbehaltung* is generally regulated by § 273 BGB, and the possessor's right to *Zurückbehaltung* is specifically regulated by § 1000 BGB. The third is that *retentie* can be either statutory or contractual in Dutch law. However, art. 3:290-295 BW is not applicable to contractual *retentie*.

198 Baur and Stürner 2009, p. 735.

sion of corporeal movables might be obtained through an illegal means. For example, a thief who has factual control of a bicycle stolen is also a possessor, despite his bad faith and lack of a lawful right.[199] The existence of illegal possession is related to the correctness of possession as a method of publicity. Like registration, possession does not always convey correct proprietary information. Nevertheless, this does not disqualify possession from being a method of publicity (see 3.2.1.2.C).

In sum, the preceding discussion shows that possession is connected with a great diversity of underlying legal relationships: (1) it can be acquired in lawful ways as well as in illegal ways; (2) it is not necessarily associated with the right of ownership; (3) it may take both property rights and personal rights as its legal basis; and (4) the underlying relationship of possession can be consensual as well as statutory.

3.2.1.2 Possession as an Abstract Method of Publicity

As possession can be obtained on the basis of different rights and even in an illegal way, two questions arise: (1) what proprietary information can be conveyed by possession to third parties; and (2) whether possession is an eligible method of publicity for corporeal movables. These two questions are discussed in this part.

A Possession and the Information Conveyed

A1: Abstractness

The diversity of underlying rights determines that possession is an abstract method of publicity for corporeal movables. By the term "abstract", we mean that the proprietary information conveyed by possession is merely that the possessor has a right to the thing possessed. To know the specific content of this right, we have to rely on other means, such as inquiring with the possessor or inspecting relevant certificates. Therefore, as a means of publicity, possession has a weakness: it cannot disclose the details of the underlying right enjoyed by the possessor.[200] From possession *per se*, one cannot identify the legal basis on which the possessor obtains possession. In this sense, the information conveyed by possession is ambiguous.[201] However, this does not mean that possession is a useless method of publicity. It does provide outsiders an indication that the possessor has a right to the thing possessed.

199 Wieling 2006, p. 41; Snijders 2014, p. 26.

200 Miceli 1997, p. 127-128.

201 In the viewpoint of some scholars, such as Carol Rose, Raymond Saleilles, and Frédéric Danos, possession has a function of communication. Possession manifests *a right* to third parties or is an outward appearance of this right. However, they often do not specify what the right manifested by possession is. See Emerich 2018, p. 60-61.

"Possession, just like a deed of title recorded in a public registry, is, provided it is 'open and notorious', as the cases on adverse possession say, a way of notifying the world of the existence of a claim."[202]

"Yes, one person can hand over possession to another. But it is very difficult to know from a third-party perspective whether all the rights are being handed over, whether possession is given temporarily, or whether the possessor is giving mere permission to enter (a license). The problems here are so great that possession cannot serve to identify multiple unqualified in rem rights in the same thing."[203]

As has been shown, possession is not necessarily associated with a property right. In practice, the holder of some personal rights is also able to obtain possession. Thus, the information conveyed by possession is not necessarily proprietary information. However, this should not be seen as a reason to refuse to treat possession as a method of publicity in property law. Indeed, the underlying right of possession might be personal, but the right becomes partially proprietary due to possession. For example, the possessory protection granted to the creditor makes this right more than personal (see 3.3.2.4). It can be said that possession lies on the borderline between property law and the law of obligations. In each case, possession with an underlying personal right will make this right partially proprietary.[204] This has been demonstrated by the concept of bailment in English law.[205]

Obviously, the information conveyed by possession is neither as specific nor as clear as that conveyed by registration. By inspecting registers, especially the register for immovable property, searchers can have detailed knowledge concerning the legal relationships of the thing involved. The register usually records the identity of the owner, the existence of property rights of security, the existence of property rights of use, and so forth. This information is much clearer because it is stored and communicated in the form of words. If registration is taken as the bottom standard of publicity, then there will be no doubt that possession does not qualify as a method of publicity. In fact, this is the main argument of the non-publicity approach, which is examined later (see 3.2.1.4). Here it is necessary to mention in advance that this bottom standard is arbitrary.

A2: Cheapness

The feature of abstractness is a downside of possession. On the other hand, it is also an advantage. Possession conveys only simple information to third parties. This allows it to be a much cheaper means of publicity than registration. As pointed out by Smith, the low intensity of information communicated by possession implies that the process of this communication is

202 Posner 2000, p. 561.
203 Smith 2015, p. 86.
204 Snijders and Rank-Berenschot 2017, p. 59; Wolf and Wellenhofer 2011, p. 78; Füller 2006, p. 37-41.
205 Bridge, Gullifer, McMeel and Worthington 2013, p. 72.

cheap.[206] In general, this advantage is reflected in, among other things, three aspects: (1) outsiders can process the information provided by possession rapidly; (2) as a method of publicity, possession is more than a formality; and (3) the shift of possession, namely delivery, can be completed easily.

Firstly, the abstract indication communicated by possession can be rapidly obtained and processed. In general, an outsider can react to possession automatically and immediately, which is rooted in a living custom. This custom is that people take it for granted that the possessor has a right to the thing possessed, and this right should be respected.[207] For example, after seeing a person riding a bicycle, our immediate reaction is that the rider is an owner, at least a person who is entitled. According to recent studies in psychology, this reaction to possession has a biological origin.[208] Instinctively, people presume that the person in factual control of a thing enjoys a right to this thing. This immediate instinctual reaction to possession is described as "*possession heuristic*".[209]

> *"Since the law of property is essentially the law of belongings, its first task is to determine to whom things belong. There are all sorts of complicated inquiries that could be undertaken to figure out and justify an incredible range of answers to this question. Alternatively, there is a simple inquiry that provides a simple answer: a thing belongs to its possessor."*[210]

As the information conveyed by possession can be acquired and processed automatically and instinctively, only a few costs will be incurred. In contrast, when one wants to gain information from a register, he has to search this register which often stores a large amount of data. Moreover, the searcher has to spend time processing the data.

Secondly, possession is more than a means of publicity, a formality. It often merges with use: the user of a thing is usually a possessor of this thing. In legal history, it is often held that enjoyment or use implies possession.[211] This is easy to understand. Use of a thing requires factual control of this thing. Therefore, possession is not purely a burden. Instead, it is often a precondition for making use of a thing. In many situations (such as lease), parties do not deem shifting of possession as a burdensome formality, because acquisition of factual control is necessary for enjoyment or use. In this aspect, possession forms a contrast to registration. The latter is a pure formality, creating inconvenience to transacting parties. Of course, this does not mean that the formality of registration does not bring any benefit to the parties.

206 Smith 2003, p. 1117.
207 Merrill 2015, p. 16.
208 Stake 2004, p. 1763.
209 Krier and Serkin 2015, p. 149.
210 Krier and Serkin 2015, p. 150.
211 Hübner 1918, p. 186; Pollock and Maitland 1968, p. 34.

Thirdly, transfer of possession, namely delivery, requires only handing over the thing involved, which can be completed easily and cheaply. This allows possession to be a means of publicity suitable for corporeal movables, a kind of property which is often in frequent circulation. If delivery were expensive, the circulation of corporeal movables would not be smooth. In this aspect, registration is different: it is expensive to construct a system of registration, and updating this system is also burdensome.[212] This explains why registration is mainly a method of publicity for immovable property and some special movables having high value and a low frequency of transactions.[213]

B Possession and the Possessor's Disclosure

It should be pointed out that the information conveyed by possession should be carefully distinguished from the information provided by the possessor. For example, in the sale of a bicycle, the seller may promise to the purchaser that he has full ownership. This promise embodies a piece of proprietary information. However, it comes from the seller himself rather than from possession. As pointed out above, an important difference between these two sources of information is in the degree of objectivity (see 2.2.3). The seller has an incentive to cheat, and the information provided by the seller is subjective. The fact might be that the bicycle was stolen by the seller. In contrast, the information out of possession is more objective. The purchaser obtains the information from possession on the basis of the observation of the seller's factual control, which is independent of the seller's subjective will. However, we have to acknowledge that possession does not show that the seller has legal ownership, because it is an abstract and ambiguous means of publicity.

The distinction above also exists in the situation where registration is involved. For example, in the course of purchasing a house, the potential buyer will not only make an inquiry with the seller about the legal condition of this house, but also search the corresponding register to check the authenticity of the seller's disclosure and to ensure that the seller has not omitted anything important. The information from the register and that from the seller himself should be distinguished. In general, the principal purpose of registration is to address the problem that the seller might cheat the buyer and disguise or omit relevant information.

C The Issue of Illegal Possession

This part focuses on the situation of illegal possession, namely possession with no lawful underlying right. The existence of illegal possession triggers a question concerning the qualification of possession as a means of publicity. If the possessor may obtain possession in an illegal way, can possession qualify as a method of publicity for corporeal movables?

212 Rose 1985, p. 84.
213 Clarke and Kohler 2005, p. 388.

Before discussing this question, it is necessary to first distinguish the right *based on* possession from the right *indicated by* possession.[214] This distinction is important because publicity is supposed to show rights to outsiders. Publicity itself does not create rights. For example, in creating a right of hypothec, the entry of this right in the register is only to provide an access to third parties, allowing them to know about the existence of this property right. Indeed, registration might be constitutive for creating the right of hypothec in some jurisdictions. However, this neither means that the property right is a result of registration alone, nor that registration has any other ultimate purposes than showing the right to third parties in private law. In fact, the purpose of treating registration as a constitutive requirement is just to ensure that the property right is visible to third parties upon the creation of that right.

Different from registration, possession has a dual relationship with rights. Firstly, possession can give rise to rights and duties in law, irrespective of whether the way of acquisition is lawful. For example, thieves are entitled to enforce and protect their possession of the thing against other persons, except for those who have a better right (such as the legal owner). This is a legal consequence of possession. In this sense, possession itself creates rights. Secondly, possession is also a method of publicity. It can show the underlying right to outsiders, though in an abstract way. This determines that possession, like registration, is also a tool of communicating information. In the situation of theft, thieves have no legal right that needs to be publicized to third parties because possession is obtained in the absence of any right. Truly, the thief-possessor enjoys some rights on the basis of possession. However, these rights are not what possession, as a method of publicity, is expected to show to third parties. The thief-possessor only has an outward appearance, which makes him or her appear to be the holder of a right. In this situation, possession fails to publicize the true legal state and conveys an incorrect indication. It indicates that the illegal possessor has a right, which the possessor in fact does not have, to the thing possessed.

Nevertheless, this does not mean that possession does not qualify as a method of publicity. In fact, not only possession but also registration might be proven to be mistaken. It happens that information from a register proves to be false. However, this never forms a sufficient reason for denying registration as a method of publicity. Errors in the register can be rectified by those who are entitled to do so. Likewise, law allows lawful proprietors to recover the thing involved from illegal possessors, which can also be seen as a scheme of rectification.[215] This scheme ensures that possession can be

214 In the viewpoint of Bell, there is a differentiation between "*de jure* rights" and "*de facto* possessory rights" in the situation of unlawful possession. A thief-possessor enjoys *de facto* possessory rights on the basis of his possession, but the real owner has *de jure* rights. See Bell 2015, p. 328. In this research, *de facto* possessory rights are rights based on possession and *de jure* rights are rights that are expected to be made visible by possession.

215 Van Schaick 2014, p. 43.

held by legal possessors. Moreover, illegal possession does not exist ubiquitously in reality. Most corporeal movables are factually controlled by those who do have a legal right, such as the owner, lessee, pledgee, and borrower. This general association of possession with a legal right guarantees that possession is an eligible method of publicity for corporeal movables.

> "外观之表象和实质之内容通常八九不离十，社会之现状大抵亦复如此。占有乃是权利存在之外观，占有存在时，通常均有实质或真实之权利为基础。" [216]

In a nutshell, just like other methods of publicity, possession also provides incorrect information in some situations.

3.2.1.3 *The Ownership Approach: Does Possession Indicate Ownership?*

Traditionally, possession is treated as an outward appearance of ownership in the law of corporeal movables. This ownership approach finds its basis in several legal rules, among which *bona fide* acquisition and the presumption of ownership are the most important. In this part, we argue that the ownership approach is not as plausible as it appears.

A *Main Problems of the Ownership Approach*

In general, the ownership approach is no longer commonly accepted at present. It fails to take into account the simple fact that possession can be associated with different underlying rights (see 3.2.1.1). The diversity of the underlying rights determines that possession is not necessarily an outward mark of ownership.[217] Instead, it is merely an abstract and thus ambiguous method of publicity. It might be true that ownership and possession were usually held by the same person in the past when transactions were neither frequent nor complex. In modern society, however, possession diverges from ownership in many situations, such as lease, pledge, reservation of ownership, security transfer of ownership, financial lease, and sale and leaseback.[218] Under this context, it is no longer plausible to say that possession is an outward mark of ownership.

B Bona Fide *Acquisition*

Bona fide acquisition of corporeal movables is often used to demonstrate the ownership approach.[219] According to this approach, a transferee in good faith is entitled to acquire ownership from the unauthorized transferor,

---

216 Xie 2011, p. 1174. English translation: "*Generally speaking, it is a social fact that the outward appearance is often consistent with the internal substance. Possession provides an indication of the existence of a right. Where there is possession, there is a real or substantive right as its legal basis.*"

217 Staudinger/Gutzeit 2012, p. 74.

218 Xie 2011, p. 273.

219 *Bona fide* acquisition of corporeal movables will be further discussed later on the basis of a comparative study (see 3.4.3). Therefore, the discussion here is brief.

because the latter's possession indicates the existence of ownership. Possession is an outward appearance of ownership. The transferee's reliance on this appearance deserves protection.[220]

> *"For decades, law students have been taught that the acquirer of a movable deserves protection because he should be able to rely upon the actual possession of the transferor: this actual possession legitimizes the transferor as the owner [...] or possession of the transferor 'creates an image of ownership'."*[221]

> *"Het bezit legitimeert den bezitter als eigenaar; wie door zijn bezit eigenaar schijnt te zijn, wordt voor eigenaar gehouden, en ieder die daarop voortbouwt is veilig."*[222]

Moreover, proponents of this approach often compare possession of corporeal movables with registration of immovable property. In their viewpoint, *bona fide* acquisition of corporeal movables and that of immovable property share the same ground, namely the reliability of publicity.[223] Some proponents add that there is a difference in the degree of reliability between these two methods of publicity.

> *„Die Legitimation des Veräußerers liegt hier im Besitz; deshalb sind ja alle Übertragungsformen, mit Ausnahme der in § 931 geregelten, an den Besitz des Veräußerers gebunden. Aber eine sichere Garantie für das Eigentum gibt der Besitz nicht, und deshalb können hier eher als beim Grundeigentum, bei dem das Grundbuch eine weitgehende Sicherheit für seiner Richtigkeit gewährt, praktische Falle vorkommen, in denen ein Erwerb vom Nichteigentümer stattfinden."*[224]

On a closer look, however, the ownership approach is not plausible. Generally speaking, this approach does not correctly interpret the importance of possession in justifying *bona fide* acquisition of corporeal movables, overstating the accuracy and clarity of possession. Moreover, it fails to consider other relevant rationales behind *bona fide* acquisition.

---

220 Mattei 2000, p. 108.

221 Salomons 2008 (1), p. 11.

222 Asser/Scholten, Zakenrecht, 1905, p. 65, cited from Salomons 2000, p. 905. English translation: "*Possession legitimizes the possessor as an owner; the person who appears to be an owner due to his possession is assumed as the owner, and everyone who relies on that is secure.*"

223 Wilhelm 2010, p. 19.

224 Schwab and Prütting 2020, Rn. 423. English translation: "*The legitimation of transferors lies in possession; therefore, all forms of transfer are, subject to the exception under § 931, related to the transferor's possession. However, possession cannot provide a safe guarantee for ownership. Thus, the acquisition from the unauthorized here is more difficult than that in the situation of land ownership, where the land register provides extensive security for its correctness.*"

Firstly, possession is merely an abstract method of publicity, as has been argued above. It does not inform third parties that the possessor is an owner. This is the main reason why the ownership approach is seen as *"unrealistic"*.[225]

> *„Anders ist die Lage im Mobiliarsachenrecht; hier ist es eine Erfahrungstatsache, dass Eigentum und unmittelbare Besitz häufig auseinanderfallen."*[226]

Secondly, the ownership approach fails to consider that indirect possession has no publicity effect, which will be argued later (see 3.2.2). The unauthorized transferor is not necessarily in direct possession of the object. Rather, the transferor might be an indirect possessor only. As indirect possession has no publicity effect, *bona fide* acquisition cannot be explained from the angle of publicity, let alone under the ownership approach.[227]

Thirdly, *bona fide* acquisition is not based on possession alone. It also involves other requirements that cannot be explained from the perspective of publicity. In brief, *bona fide* acquisition also concerns, among other things, whether the acquirer is in good faith, whether the transfer is gratuitous, and whether the object involved is a stolen or lost thing. These aspects are closely related to legal policy: (1) *bona fide* acquisition is not applicable to gratuitous transfer because this acquisition is to promote the fluidity of transactions; (2) the original owner loses ownership to the third party in good faith because the former contributes to the disparity between ownership and possession, which may require that lost or stolen things are not susceptible to *bona fide* acquisition; and (3) a transferee who already knows the defect of the transferor's power of disposal cannot acquire ownership because *bona fide* acquisition is to protect the reliance of third parties in good faith.

> *"It is argued quite often that there is a practical or economic need of protecting commerce, as it would be too burdensome, costly and insecure if each acquirer was forced to undertake detailed investigations as to the asset's origin. Not having a good faith acquisition rule would create considerable legal uncertainty, even in numerous cases where the transferor was, in fact, entitled to transfer ownership. Thus, good faith acquisition would also serve the aim of promoting legal certainty."*[228]

In a nutshell, two conclusions can be made here. The first one is that possession is only a necessary but insufficient condition for *bona fide* acquisition, and this acquisition cannot be explained from the angle of the publicity of possession alone. The second one is that ownership cannot be inferred from possession because possession is only an abstract means of publicity.

225 Acquisition and Loss of Ownership 2011, p. 898.
226 Baur and Stürner 2009, p. 662. English translation: *"In the property law of movables, the situation is different; here it is an empirical fact that ownership and direct possession often diverge from each other."*
227 Füller 2006, p. 324.
228 DCFR 2009, p. 4827.

C Presumption of Ownership

Another example which appears consistent with the ownership approach is the rule of the presumption of ownership: possessors are presumed to be the owner of the object possessed. This rule is generally accepted in the civil law system, such as art. 3:119 (1) BW and § 1006 (1) BGB. In light of the ownership approach, if a possessor is presumed to be an owner, then possession should be treated as an outward mark of ownership.

> *„Eine zweite Folge der Publizitätsfunktion des Besitzes ergibt sich aus § 1006. Aus dem Umstand, dass der Besitz üblicherweise das Bestehen von Rechten an der Sache dokumentiert, sieht das Gesetz die Konsequenz, indem es zugunsten des Besitzers die Vermutung ausstellt, dass er Eigentümer der Sache sei."*[229]

> *"Op zijn beurt wordt de bezitter krachtens art. 3:119 vermoed de eigenaar te zijn [...]. Bij dit vermoeden sluit art. 3:86 lid 1 als het waar aan. De derde die te goede trouw afgaat op de legitimatie van eigenaar die is verbonden aan het in de macht hebben van de zaak door de vervreemder, krijgt bescherming indienen blijkt dat de laatstgenoemd niet beschikkingsbevoegd was."*[230]

Moreover, proponents of the ownership approach often compare possession with registration in this respect. This presumption for corporeal movables is akin to the presumption of correctness of registration for immovable property.

> *„Die Eintragung im Grundbuch hat für die Begründung, Übertragung und Aufhebung von Grundstücks-rechten eine ähnliche Wirkung wie die Besitzübertragung bei entsprechenden bewegliche Sachen betreffenden Rechtsvorgängen. Daraus erklärt sich die dem § 1006 verwandte Vermutung des § 891."*[231]

The largest problem of the ownership approach is that it fails to distinguish the presumption from publicity. The rule of presumption (such as § 1006 (1) BGB and art. 3:119 (1) BW) concerns how to distribute a burden of proof. According to this rule, the person who holds possession enjoys an advantage in proceedings: the party who has no possession needs to prove that

229 Wolf and Wellenhofer 2011, p. 41. English translation: "*The second consequence of the publicity function of possession results from § 1006. Under this circumstance, possession often shows the existence of a right to the object; thus, law prescribes, for the benefit of the possessor, a presumption that the possessor is the owner of the object.*"

230 Reehuis 2015, p. 82. English translation: "*In turn, the owner is, according to art. 119, presumed to be an owner [...]. This presumption is related to paragraph 1 art. 3:86, as if it is true. A third party, who is in good faith with respect to the owner's legitimation which is related to the transferor's factual control of the thing, receives protection when the latter has no authority to dispose.*"

231 Baur and Stürner 2009, p. 107. English translation: "*For creation, transfer and extinguishment of land rights, the entry into land registers has a similar effect as the transfer of possession for the transfer of rights on movables. This explains the presumption under § 891, which is akin to § 1006.*"

the possessor is not the real owner. The rule does not apply until the facts concerning a dispute are unascertainable.[232] Therefore, the main function of this presumption is procedural and has nothing to do with the publicity effect of possession.

> *"In my view, such rules serve solely the procedural purpose of evidence for the protection of the entitled party. Since in practice the asset will remain most of the time in the physical possession of the entitled party, that party deserves the benefit of procedural advantage should anyone contest its right."*[233]

> *„So gesteht die herrschende Meinung einmütig zu, dass eine Rechtszustandsvermutung aus § 1006 das Beweisbelasten überfordere: Dieser musste in diesem Fall generell den fehlenden Eigentumserwerb des Besitzers nachweisen […]. Hinter der These von der Erwerbsvermutung vergibt sich daher eine grundsätzliche Skepsis an Einigung des Besitzes als Publizitätsträger."*[234]

Moreover, if there is sufficient evidence contrary to the presumption, then the presumption will be overturned. In practice, most limited-right possessors and illegal possessors can be proven as having no ownership. This means that the presumption is incorrect in most situations. Therefore, if possession is taken as a method of publicity for ownership of corporeal movables, then it will be doomed to being incorrect in most situations.[235] In other words, once being treated as an outward mark of ownership, possession will be generally unreliable. Thirdly, even if we acknowledge that the presumption is based on the publicity effect of possession, the ownership approach is still problematic. This is because this presumption can be applied by analogy in other situations. A possessor might be presumed to be the holder of another right than ownership.

> *„Nach § 1006 Abs. 1 S. 1 wird zugunsten des Besitzers einer beweglichen Sache vermutet, dass er seit Beginn seines Besitzes Eigentümer der Sache sei. In § 1065 wird dir Vermutung auf den Nießbrauch, in § 1227 auf das Pfandrecht ausgedehnt […]. Daraus folgt: die Vermutung streitet nur für denjenigen, der die Sache als Eigenbesitzer oder als Nießbrauchs- bzw. als Pfandbesitzer besitzt."*[236]

---

232 Rosenberg, Schwab and Gottwald 2010, p. 644.

233 Hamwijk 2012, p. 309.

234 Füller 2006, p. 291. English translation: *"The predominating view is that the presumption of the state of rights reverses the burden of proof: he has to prove that the acquisition of ownership by the possessor is flaw […]. Under the thesis of the presumption of acquisition, a fundamental doubt exists to the equation of possession as a means of publicity."*

235 Füller 2006, p. 324.

236 Baur and Stürner 2009, p. 105. English translation: *"Pursuant to the first sentence of paragraph 1 § 1006, the possessor of a movable thing is beneficially presumed to be the owner of the thing since the beginning of possession. The presumption is extended to the usufruct in § 1065 and pledge in § 1227 […]. Therefore, the presumption only benefits those who possess a thing as an ownership possessor or as a usufruct- or pledge-possessor."*

"Ook bezitters van vorderingen op naam, waardepapieren, quoteringsrechten, intellectuele-eigendomsrechten en ander vermogensrechten, worden tot op het tegenbewijs vermoed rechthebbende van dat recht te zijn."[237]

The Taiwanese Civil Code includes a rule of presumption, which only stipulates that possessors are presumed to have a right that embodies possession as a component.[238] Therefore, possessors are not necessarily presumed to be an owner.

"例如，占有人于占有物上行使所有权时，即推定其有所有权，于占有物形式租赁权时，即推定其有租赁权。惟不以占有为内容之权利，则不再推定之范围内。" [239]

Fourthly, the presumption of ownership is applied only to ownership possession, namely *Eigenbesitz* in German law and *bezit* in Dutch law.[240] As a result, the application of this presumption involves a subjective requirement: the possessor must have an intention of belonging (*animus domini*). This requirement also requires us to distinguish the presumption of ownership from publicity. The former involves a subjective element, which is at odds with the feature of objectivity of publicity (see 2.2.3.2).

„Der Eigenbesitz entwertet gleichwohl die Publizitätswirkung des Besitzes, da nicht mehr rein sei es auch noch so verschwommen erkennbares Faktum die Vermutungsbasis darstellt, sondern ein unsichtbarer Wille des Besitzers."[241]

In a nutshell, the presumption of ownership concerns how to allocate the burden of proof. It should not be confused with the publicity of possession. Moreover, the application of this presumption involves a subjective requirement. Even if the presumption is seen as related to the publicity of possession, we need to note that this presumption is applied by analogy to other rights than ownership.

---

237 Van Schaick 2014, p. 84. English translation: *"The possessor of claims to a named debtor, securities, quotation rights, intellectual property rights and other patrimonial rights will also be deemed to be the holder of these rights, unless there is contrary evidence."*

238 《台湾民法典》第943条："占有人于占有物上行使之权利，推定其适法有此权利"。English translation: Art. 943 Taiwanese Civil Code: *"Where a right exercised by the possessor in relation to the possessed thing, it is presumed that the possessor has this right."*

239 Xie 2011, p. 1075. English translation: *"For example, when the possessor exercises ownership in relation to the possessed object, he is presumed to be an owner; when the possessor exercises a right of lease, he is presumed to be a lessee. The possessor should not be presumed to have a right which does not have possession as a component."*

240 Baur and Stürner 2009, p. 105; Sdu Commentaar/Jacobs & Ter Horst 2019, art. 119.

241 Füller 2006, p. 291. English translation: *"Ownership possession also depreciates the publicity effect of possession, because the basis of presumption is no longer neither a pure nor a clear visible fact, but the possessor's invisible will."*

3.2.1.4 The Non-Publicity Approach: Possession Indicates Nothing?

Contrary to the ownership approach, the non-publicity approach is pessimistic to the publicity of possession for corporeal movables. According to the non-publicity approach, possession is too ambiguous to provide any useful information to third parties.

> *"Since physical possession can signify many legal relationships with respect to an asset, it in fact tells the viewer nothing [...]. It does not render possession a viable means to provide information in respect of the question i) who holds an interest, ii) what kind of interest, iii) in what asset and iv) in what capacity."*[242]

From this excerpt, we can find that the main reason why this approach denies possession as a method of publicity lies in the diversity of underlying rights of possession. As possession can be obtained and kept on the basis of a great diversity of rights, it tells third parties nothing.

Usually, proponents of the non-publicity approach compare possession with registration. Possession is not as clear as registration. Thus, it should not be treated as a method of publicity. Implicitly, this approach considers registration as the bottom criterion of publicity.

> *„Nach dem Grunddenken des Publizitätsprinzips kann der Besitz nur als Publizitätsträger deinen, wenn er dazu geeignet ist, unsichtbar Rechtsverhältnisse wahrnehmbar zu gestalten. Der Vergleich mit dem Grundbuch zeigt, dass der Besitz, verstanden als tatsächliches Faktum, keine derart eindeutigen Rückschlüsse auf die Rechtslage ermöglicht."*[243]

In general, the problem of the non-publicity approach can be summarized as follows: (1) it arbitrarily takes registration as the bottom criterion for the method of publicity; (2) it neglects the fact that there are different types of registration conveying information of different degrees of clarity; and (3) it fails to note that possession does provide some information.

Firstly, there are no adequate reasons to treat registration as the bottom criterion of publicity. Indeed, possession does not convey information as clearly as registration (especially the land register). From possession, one cannot know the details of the right enjoyed by possessors. As an abstract means of publicity, it only indicates that the possessor has a right to the thing possessed. In contrast, registers allow searchers to know details of the proprietary relationship with respect to the thing registered. More impor-

242 Hamwijk 2012, p. 310-311.

243 Füller 2006, p. 247-248. English translation: *"According to the rationale of publicity, possession can only function as a means of publicity when it can make invisible legal relationships transparent. The comparison between possession and registration indicates that the former, which is understood as a fact, does not lead to any clear conclusion on the condition of rights."*

tantly, all information from registers is communicated in the form of words, which means that registration usually causes no misunderstandings.

However, this difference between possession and registration is not a sufficient reason to deny possession as a method of publicity. The opinion that all methods of publicity in property law must be as clear as registration is arbitrary. With respect to the difference, we can take another view: there are different methods of publicity in property law, and these methods convey information with different degrees of clarity. Possession qualifies as a method of publicity for corporeal movables, despite the fact that it is not clear as registration. There is a continuum of methods of publicity in the law of property: one side of this continuum is registration, and the other side can be possession.

Secondly, there are different types of registration, and the information conveyed by them varies in the degree of clarity. In general, the information provided by the land register seems to be the clearest. However, other registers are less clear than the register for land. For example, Article 9 UCC and the Cape Town Convention on International Interests in Mobile Equipment creates a system of registration, and this system provides only a simple notice (or warning) about the existence of property rights to third parties.[244] Compared with the registration of land, this notice embodies only a small amount of information.

> *"The Article 9 filing system should be distinguished from registries familiar to virtually all legal systems such as those covering real property. Those are, in many cases, the source of real rights [...]. In those registries, original substantive documents [...] are placed in full on the record."*[245]

The system of registration is supposed to provide the *"minimalist"* information or *"a minimum amount of information"*, so that the fluidity of transactions will not be hampered.[246] Inevitably, it is ambiguous to some extent. Here, we will take the register of Article 9 UCC, a system for security interests in movables, as an example. In this system, a financing statement needs to be filed. However, this statement cannot make security interests fully clear to third parties. To know about the security interest, searchers have to make further inquiries with relevant parties, such as the security provider.[247] At least, the statement is ambiguous in two aspects: (1) it suffices that the movable collateral involved is ascertainable by a description with sufficient

---

244 Article 9 UCC creates a system of registration for security interests of movables. The function of this system, briefly speaking, is to warn that the secured creditor may have a security interest with respect to certain collaterals owned by the debtor. The Cape Town Convention on International Interests in Mobile Equipment constructs a similar system. This system records *"the international interest"* established on certain *"mobile equipment"*.

245 Sigman 2004, p. 78.

246 Van Erp 2004, p. 97; Sigman 2004, p. 76.

247 Uniform Commercial Code Committee 2008, p. 518.

accuracy, which implies that the searcher cannot ascertain which specific assets are involved by only inspecting the system;[248] and (2) the amount of the secured obligation is not required to be fixed by the statement, which means that the searcher cannot know how many encumbrances will be finalized in the end.[249]

Thirdly, the non-publicity approach straightforwardly asserts that possession communicates nothing because possession is ambiguous.[250] This amounts to equating "ambiguity" with "nothing", which seems inappropriate. Possession can be associated with different rights, but this does not mean that it conveys nothing useful for third parties. At least, third parties can from possession know that the possessor has a right to the object possessed.

3.2.2 Publicity Effect of Indirect Possession

After arguing possession as an abstract means of publicity, we now turn to a special form of possession: indirect possession (*constructive possession* in English law, *mittelbare Besitz* in German law, and *middellijk bezit* in Dutch law). In this part, we discuss the question of whether indirect possession is qualified as a method of publicity for corporeal movables. In general, the crucial difference between direct possession and indirect possession is whether the possessor has actual or physical control over the thing. In this part, we argue that indirect possession is invisible due to the absence of physical control by the indirect possessor, which makes it unable to be a means of publicity. In general, the concept of indirect possession is recognized for other reasons than publicity.

3.2.2.1 The Essence of Indirect Possession

A The Composition of Indirect Possession

Indirect possession exists where a person (such as the lessor) gives up his actual control to another person (such as the lessee). In this situation, the former remains in possession through the latter who acts as an intermediary. According to the German legal theory, the relationship of indirect possession includes three components: an intermediary who has actual control, an intermediary relationship, and a right of recovery by the indirect possessor.[251]

Firstly, indirect possession takes the existence of direct possession as a condition. As its name indicates, "indirect" possession is held in an indirect way. There must be an intermediary person, the direct possessor, who exercises actual control on behalf of the indirect possessor. For example, a

248 Hamwijk 2014, p. 198.
249 Von Wilmowsky 1996, p. 160-161.
250 Hamwijk 2012, p. 310.
251 Baur and Stürner 2009, p. 75-76.

lessor retains his possessory legal position after giving up actual control to the lessee. Therefore, indirect possession is possession without physical domination over the thing.[252]

Secondly, indirect possessors should have an underlying relationship with direct possessors. This relationship is known as the intermediary relationship of possession (*Besitzmittlungsverhältnis* in German law).[253] It can take various forms. On the basis of the intermediary relationship, direct possessors acquire and preserve actual control of the object, and indirect possessors give up actual control.[254] For example, lease can be seen as an intermediary relationship on the basis of which the lessee and the lessor have direct possession and indirect possession respectively. The intermediary relationship serves as a channel between indirect possessors and direct possessors. Thus, it is considered as the most important component of indirect possession.[255]

Thirdly, indirect possessors should have a right to recover the object from direct possessors when the intermediary relationship comes to an end.[256] This right of recovery implies that indirect possession exists only for a limited period, and the direct possessor cannot keep actual control forever.[257] The right of recovery is often considered as the central element of the intermediary relationship.[258] However, the right can exist without being affected by the invalidity of this relationship.[259]

From the introduction above, we can find that indirect possession is no more than a relationship between the indirect possessor and the direct possessor.[260] This relationship concerns actual control: the indirect possessor gives up actual control to the direct possessor and will reobtain it after a certain period. However, the relationship itself is not actual control. The core of indirect possession is that the indirect possessor has a right of recovery, a right to reobtain actual control from the direct possessor.

> „*Das Besitzmittlungsverhältnis ist ein Rechtsverhältnis, so dass im Ergebnis dies drauf hinausläuft, aus einem rechtlichen Verhältnis auf die Sachherrschaft und damit auf eine Tatsache zu schließen. Den Kern des Publizitätsprinzips stellt ein solches Vorgehen geradezu auf den Kopf. Ebenso wenig überzeugt auch der oft gegebene Hinweise, dass der mittelbare Besitzer ja nur eine zeitlich begrenzte Sachherrschaft habe: Sie äußere sich deswegen, da der mittelbare Besitzer eine Herausgabeanspruch gegenüber dem Besitz-*

252 Westermann 2011, p. 128.
253 Brehm and Berger 2014, p. 47.
254 Baur and Stürner 2009, p. 75; Van Schaick 2014, p. 10.
255 Brehm and Berger 2014, p. 47.
256 Where possession is differentiated from detention, the right of recovery is treated as the crucial criterion for this differentiation. See Vantomme 2018, p. 19-20.
257 Baur and Stürner 2009, p. 76.
258 Brehm and Berger 2014, p. 47.
259 Brehm and Berger 2014, p. 47.
260 MüKoBGB/Joost 2017, § 868, Rn. 5.

> *mittler habe. Jedoch widerlegt sich dieses Argument selbst. Wenn der mittelbare Besitzer eine tatsächliche Sachherrschaft haben soll, stellt sich die Frage, warum er dann noch eines Herausgabeanspruches bedarf."*[261]

In English law, indirect possession (constructive possession) is often treated as a right to possess. This implies that the essence of indirect possession is no more than a right or a legal relationship.

> *"Right to possess, when separated from possession, is often called 'constructive possession'. The correct use of the term would seem to be coextensive with and limited to those cases where a person entitled to possess is (or was) allowed the same remedies as if he had really been in possession."*[262]

> *"Falling short of actual possession, a person may have constructive possession of property if he has the right to take actual possession."*[263]

The preceding argument is also illustrated by the bailor's legal position in English law. Bailors are often said to have constructive possession. However, as we will show later, they are not allowed to sue on the basis of trespass, a kind of illegal interference with possession *per se* (see 3.3.3.1). In English law, bailors have a right known as reversionary interest, namely an interest of obtaining actual possession when the bailee's actual possession comes to an end.[264] The reversionary interest is a future interest. If this interest is infringed, bailors are be entitled to claim protection under tort law.[265] This also implies that indirect possession amounts to a right of recovery.

B The Change of Indirect Possession

In general, acquisition, transfer, and destruction of indirect possession are largely dependent on the intermediary relationship between the direct possessor and the indirect possessor. Firstly, the existence of an intermediary relationship is necessary for acquiring indirect possession.[266] As just pointed out, this relationship forms the most important element of indirect possession. One cannot become an indirect possessor when there is no intermediary relationship with the holder of actual control.

---

261 Füller 2006, p. 284. English translation: *"The intermediary relationship of possession is a legal relationship; thus, it amounts to a legal relationship with respect to factual control, namely with respect to a fact. The core of the principle of publicity makes this approach chaotic. Likewise, the often-cited view that the indirect possessor has temporal and limited factual control is not convincing: this view says so because the indirect possessor enjoys a claim of recovery against the intermediary of possession. It stultifies itself. If the indirect possessor has factual control, then the question will arise of why the indirect possessor still needs a right of recovery."*

262 Pollock and Wright 1888, p. 28.

263 Gardiner 2008, p. 181.

264 Clarke and Kohler 2005, p. 298.

265 Palmer 2009, no. 2-004,4-066.

266 Brehm and Berger 2014, p. 47-48.

Secondly, the transfer of indirect possession is based on the assignment of the right of recovery or a change of the intermediary relationship.[267] The transfer of indirect possession is known as non-factual delivery. It is non-factual because it does not involve any shift of actual control, and what matters fundamentally is the parties' consent.[268] As pointed out by Rank-Berenschot in the following excerpt, *traditio per constitutum possessorium* is contractualized because mere agreement suffices for this way of transferring indirect possession.

> *"De erkenning van de mogelijkheid tot bezitsoverdracht door enkele tweezijdige verklaring brengt mee dat het corporele element steeds minder betekenis krijgt. Men kan in dit verband spreken van 'contractualisering' van de bezitsverschaffing."*[269]

Thirdly, indirect possessors lose indirect possession when the intermediary relationship comes to an end.[270] In general, this relationship can extinguish in two situations. One situation is that the direct possessor loses direct possession, whether voluntarily or involuntarily.[271] For example, the lessee, as a direct possessor of the thing leased, disposes of and gives up factual control of the thing to a third party. The second situation is that the right of recovery ceases to exist.[272] For example, the lessor transfers ownership of the thing involved to the lessee.

---

267 In general, the way how indirect possession is transferred is different between German law, Dutch law and English law. Here, we take the situation where the direct possessor is a third party as an example. Under German law, just assignment of the claim of recovery against the direct possessor suffices for the transfer of indirect possession. Neither notifying the direct possessor nor obtaining approval of the direct possessor is necessary. The direct possessor does not have to be involved. There is no doubt that this simplifies the course of delivery (*traditio longa manu*). See Brehm and Berger 2014, p. 51-52; MüKoBGB/Oechsler 2017, § 931, Rn. 1. According to Dutch law, indirect possession is transferred via "mutual declaration (*tweezijdige verklaring*)" by the transferor and the transferee. However, just a mutual declaration is insufficient. The direct possessor, i.e. the "detentor (*houder*)" in Dutch law, has to be informed of the transfer or acknowledge that the object will be held for the transferee. In the viewpoint of some Dutch scholars, where the direct possessor is not aware of the transfer, it is difficult to say that the transferee obtains any factual control of the object. Due to this extra requirement, the course of delivery might be burdensome, especially when the transfer involves a large number of corporeal movables that are under the factual control by different third parties. See Rank-Berenschot 2012, p. 67. However, upon transfer of indirect possession, the claim of recovery is assigned, and the intermediary relationship is changed. Under English law, indirect possession is obtained through attornment. For the acquisition of indirect possession, it is necessary that the direct possessor expressly attorns to the transferee. Neither assigning the claim of recovery nor providing a notification to the direct possessor suffices. See Bridge 2015, p. 75-76.

268 Reehuis 2004, p. 49; Westermann 2011, p. 140.

269 Rank-Berenschot 2012, p. 61. English translation: "*The recognition of the possibility of transferring possession only through a two-sided declaration means that the corporeal element has less significance. In this situation, we can say 'contractualization' of the provision of possession.*"

270 Brehm and Berger 2014, p. 49.

271 Baur and Stürner 2009, p. 80.

272 Baur and Stürner 2009, p. 80.

3.2.2.2 *Indirect Possession Has No Publicity Effect*

After discussing the essence of indirect possession, we will demonstrate that indirect possession cannot convey any information to third parties due to the lack of actual control.

A Indirect Possession: A Hidden Relationship
Indirect possession is a legal relationship with respect to actual control. Actual control is visible, but this relationship *per se* is hidden to third parties. The purpose of publicity is to make invisible property rights transparent to third parties. Registration realizes this purpose by conveying information in the form of words. Possession realizes this purpose through actual control, which can give rise to physical proximity between the possessor and the thing possessed. This physical proximity can be observed by third parties.

Indirect possession does not let third parties observe its existence. Different from direct possession, indirect possession lacks actual control and thus is hidden to third parties.[273] As a result, no information is provided by indirect possession. This is the reason why indirect possession is often called "mental possession".[274]

> *„Diese abgeschwächte Beziehung zur Sache hat man dadurch zu charakterisieren versucht, dass man den mittelbaren Besitz als ‚vergeistigte' Sachherrschaft im Gegensatz zur tatsächlichen Sachherrschaft des unmittelbaren Besitzes gekennzeichnet hat."*[275]

In fact, indirect possession is hidden, and whether it really exists is always a problem for third parties. In order to know whether one has indirect possession, we have to conduct an investigation. To a large extent, this investigation is no more than an inquiry concerning the underlying right enjoyed by the indirect possessor. Is the indirect possessor, for example, a lessor or pledgor who has ownership? Therefore, indirect possession is an object of publicity, rather than a means of publicity. If the main purpose of publicity is to make invisible legal relationships transparent, then indirect possession is one of these legal relationships. Indirect possession *per se* is a legal relationship that needs to be publicized to third parties.

B An Illustration: Traditio per Constitutum Possessorium
Typically, the disqualification of indirect possession as a method of publicity can be illustrated by *traditio per constitutum possessorium*, a form of fictional delivery (*traditio ficta*). This delivery occurs where the transferor remains

273 Quantz 2005, p. 41-42; Chang 2015, p. 120.
274 Westermann 2011, p. 128.
275 Wolf and Wellenhofer 2011, p. 82. English translation: "*The weakened relationship with the thing leads us to characterize indirect possession as 'mental' control, which forms a contrast to the actual control of direct possession.*"

in actual control of the thing involved but agrees to hold this thing for the transferee. As a result of this delivery, the transferee becomes an indirect possessor, and the transferor retains direct possession.

In German law, *traditio per constitutum possessorium* is known as *Besitzkonstitut*. It gives rise to an intermediary relationship, and the indirect possessor obtains a right of recovery. As pointed out by some German lawyers, *Besitzkonstitut* is a change of the possessory intention only: the "ownership possessor (*Eigenbesitzer*)" becomes a "limited-right possessor (*Fremdbesitzer*)".[276] In Dutch law which distinguishes possession and detention, *traditio per constitutum possessorium* is also no more than a change of the parties' intention: the "possessor (*bezitter*)" becomes a "detentor (*houder*)".[277] This change is termed the "statement of detention (*houderschapsverklaring*)".[278] In English law, *traditio per constitutum possessorium* is known as attornment by transferors to transferees.[279] It only allows the latter to obtain constructive possession. The attornment consists of any overt or positive acknowledgment by the direct possessor and can arise in the absence of any change of actual control.[280] It has no effect of publicity. For example, where a pledge is created by attornment by the pledgor, this pledge is hidden and has no "*outward sign*".[281]

As *traditio per constitutum possessorium* is merely a change of the possessory intention, the entire process is hidden to third parties. For example, where a bicycle is sold and leased back, the seller does not lose the actual control, nor does the purchaser acquire actual control. In this situation, what changes is only the legal identity of both parties: the original owner becomes a lessee, and the purchaser becomes an owner. For third parties, the process of this sale and leaseback is in secrecy. Therefore, *traditio per constitutum possessorium* fails to perform any function of publicity.

> "*Aangezien een levering constituto possessorio zich slechts tussen partijen afspeelt, blijft de vervreemder in staat tegenover anderen te doen alsof niets is veranderd. Aldus is het voor derden niet kenbaar dat en controleerbaar of het bezit is overgegaan. Was de vervreemder bezitter, dan kan hij zich tegenover anderen nog steeds als bezitter gedragen.*"[282]

276 Füller 2006, p. 319; Schwab and Prütting 2020, Rn. 379.
277 Rank-Berenschot 2012, p. 62.
278 Reehuis 2004, p. 48.
279 Bridge 2015, p. 76.
280 Palm 1991, p. 1368.
281 Beale, Bridge, Gullifer and Lomnicka 2018, no. 5.27-5.28.
282 Reehuis 2004, p. 48. English translation: "*On account of the fact that traditio per constitutum possessorium only exists between the parties, the transferor remains in the state against others, as if nothing occurs. Therefore, whether possession shifts is invisible to third parties. If the transferor is a possessor, he can still behave as a possessor in relation to others.*"

3.2.2.3 Functions of Indirect Possession

Indirect possession has no publicity effect, but this does not mean that this legal concept is useless or should be abandoned. This is because indirect possession has other functions.

Firstly, indirect possession provides a conceptual basis for conferring possessory protection on a particular group of persons, namely indirect possessors. This function can be explained in the following way: (1) the law protects possessors from illegal interference; and (2) to provide such protection for lessors, pledgors, depositors and the like, it is necessary to recognize them as an indirect possessor. By virtue of indirect possession, indirect possessors are entitled to act, like a direct possessor, against illegal interference. This consideration of protection is an important reason why indirect possession is recognized by German law.

> *„Wie die historische Analyse zeigt, diente der Begriff des mittelbaren Besitzes dazu, dem Vermieter und vergleichbaren Personen einen Besitzschutz einzuräumen und somit die Vorschrift des § 869 zu rechtfertigen. Als einfachster Weg erschien dem Gesetzgeber, die als schutzbedürftig erkannten Personen auch als Besitzer zu bezeichnen. Der mittelbare Besitzer dient als rechtliches Versatzstück dazu, einem Besitzer ohne Sachherrschaft Besitzschutzrechte einzuräumen."*[283]

The function of protection becomes more important where the indirect possessor has no legal ownership and can only claim protection on the basis of indirect possession.[284] For example, a thief leases the stolen things to another person and becomes an illegal indirect possessor.

Secondly, indirect possession is an important concept for prescriptive acquisition. Briefly speaking, prescriptive acquisition means that a possessor who continuously controls a thing for himself for a sufficiently long period is entitled to acquire ownership of this thing. When the possessor gives up actual control to another person, the question arises whether such prescriptive acquisition is still possible. In general, the law provides a positive answer on the basis of the concept of indirect possession.

For example, when a thief leases a bicycle he had stolen to another person, the thief can still claim prescriptive acquisition of this bicycle. Despite the loss of actual control, his possession is considered to be continuous, with a change from direct possession to indirect possession only. In this sense, indirect possession is conceptually useful for explaining this continuity of possession. In the absence of this concept, it becomes difficult to explain

283 Füller 2006, p. 285. English translation: *"As the historical analysis shows, the concept of indirect possession is to protect lessees and the like, which justifies art. 869. It seems that the simplest way for the legislator is categorizing those who deserve protection as a possessor. The term indirect possessor acts as a legal means to provide possessory protection to those who have no actual control."*

284 Van Schaick 2014, p. 76.

why the thief still enjoys the right to acquire ownership after he gives up actual control to the lessee.

The preceding consideration is salient in Dutch law. As has been indicated above, Dutch law defines the concept of "possession (*bezit*)" by first focusing on prescriptive acquisition (see 3.1.3.3). According to art. 3:107 (2) BW, when the possessor allows another person to control the object without giving up the pretention of belonging, the former might simply become an indirect possessor.[285] As a result, the possessor's right to prescriptive acquisition is not affected.[286]

Thirdly, the concept of indirect possession helps to explain fictional delivery in theory.[287] In general, delivery requires a transfer of possession. Typically, it involves the handover of actual control, forming the actual delivery. However, delivery does not involve this handover in many situations, which leads to fictional delivery, including *traditio brevi manu*, *traditio longa manu*, and *traditio per constitutum possessorium*. In general, these three forms of fictional delivery involve transfer or provision of indirect possession.[288] Without the concept of indirect possession, the question will arise how to explain that non-factual or fictional delivery is also delivery.

3.2.3 Conclusion

In modern society, possession still qualifies as a method of publicity for corporeal movables. As possession can be obtained and preserved on the basis of a great variety of rights, it is an abstract and thus ambiguous method of publicity. Possession only indicates that the possessor has a *right* to the thing possessed. The details of this right cannot be shown by possession. To know the details, we need to make use of other means, such as making inquiries with the possessor. As an abstract means of publicity, possession is not an outward mark of ownership.

That the possessor has actual control is necessary for the function of publicity. Actual control can give rise to physical proximity between the possessor and the thing possessed, which is visible to third parties. This implies that indirect possession, as a hidden legal relationship between the direct possessor and the indirect possessor, cannot provide any indication to third parties. Moreover, whether indirect possession really exists is always

---

285 Snijders and Rank-Berenschot 2017, p. 98.

286 However, it seems that the concept of indirect possession is dispensable where the distinction between possession and detention (*detentio*) is recognized. For example, in the case of leasing a bicycle stolen, the lessor is the possessor, and the lessee has detention. On the basis of this distinction, acquisitive prescription by the lessor can be explained without any conceptual difficulty. French law distinguishes possession from detention, but the differentiation between direct possession and indirect possession is not recognized. See Stoljar 1984, p. 1027.

287 Brehm and Berger 2014, p. 51-52.

288 Staudinger/Gutzeit 2012, p. 222.

a question for third parties. The concept of indirect possession is recognized due to considerations of possessory protection, prescriptive acquisition, and fictional delivery. In creating this concept, publicity is not taken into account by legislators.

3.3 Possession and Third-Party Effect: Strange Interferers

Now we will examine the importance possession, as a means of publicity, has for third parties. As has been pointed out in Chapter 2, third parties bear a liability to respect property rights. In general, third parties are of three types: strange interferers, subsequent acquirers, and general creditors. The following three sections discuss the relevance of possession to the effect against these three types of third party. The main aim of this discussion is to reveal whether and in what sense possession lays a foundation for the effect of property right against third parties. In this section, we focus on possession and strange interferers. Possession and the other two types of third party are discussed later.

In this section, we first provide an introduction to the legal protection of possession. After that, an explanation of this protection is provided from the perspective of publicity. It will be argued that possessors deserve protection because they have shown their right to third parties though actual control over the thing possessed. At the end of this section, we also explain why legal protection is also available for those whose rights are infringed but do not have direct possession as an outward appearance.

3.3.1 The Concept of Possessory Protection

In this research, possessory protection means legal protection enjoyed by possessors. It is distinguished from the protection of underlying rights. The purpose of possessory protection is to maintain the state of possession *per se*: it is not relevant whether the possessor has a legal underlying right, or whether the right is personal or proprietary in nature. For example, thieves are entitled to possessory protection despite their lack of legal ownership of the thing stolen; lessees can also claim possessory protection despite the fact that their right to use is originally personal.

In general, the term possessory protection covers four different remedies enjoyed by possessors. The first is the right to use self-help. With this right, the possessor is entitled to a quick self-remedy when judicial measures cannot be reasonably expected. The self-help measure taken by the possessor should be immediate and proportionate.[289] The second is the right to recover, which means that the possessor can repossess the object

289 DCFR 2009, p. 4340.

when it has been illegally dispossessed by another person. It only happens in the situation where the possessor entirely loses possession.[290] The third remedy is to address other kinds of interference than illegal dispossession. It allows the possessor to require the interferer to remove imminent interference or suspend existing interference.[291] The final remedy is the right to claim damages or pecuniary compensation. This remedy is only possible when the possessor suffers loss due to illegal interference.

In terms of the way of protecting possession, there are two different systems: one is the civil law system, and the other is the common law system. The former has a dualist regime of protection, while the latter a single regime. Under the civil law system, possession is protected by property law as well as by the law of obligations (mainly on the basis of torts and unjust enrichment). This gives rise to a distinction between real protection and personal protection: the first means protection under property law, and the second refers to protection under the law of obligations.[292] In general, personal protection is subject to more restrictions than real protection, especially in the aspect of the burden of proof.[293] This distinction is alien to common law lawyers. In common law, possession is unitarily protected by tort law.[294] In this research, the term possessory protection covers all legal remedies that can be claimed to protect possession. The nature (personal or real) and the legal basis (property law or the law of obligations) of these remedies are deemed as irrelevant to our discussion. Therefore, details concerning the possessory protection itself are not provided here.

To avoid misunderstandings, it is necessary to mention in the end that possessory protection also includes the legal protection granted to those who only have a limited right, such as the lessee. As has been shown above, there is a distinction between "possession (*bezit*)" and "detention (*houderschap*)" in Dutch law (see 3.1.2.4). The following discussion includes the legal protection available for the detentor, as we will see later (see 3.3.2.4).

3.3.2 Possession, Protection and Publicity

After introducing the concept of possessory protection, we now turn to the relationship between this protection and the publicity of possession. In this part, we attempt to justify possessory protection from the angle of publicity.

290 DCFR 2009, p. 4346.
291 DCFR 2009, p. 4347.
292 Westermann 2011, p. 151; Reehuis and Heisterkamp 2019, p. 383.
293 Van Schaick 2014, p. 72. For example, personal protection is, in principle, available when the illegal interferer has fault, while real protection is not subject to this requirement. Therefore, if the possessor cannot prove that the interferer has fault, the possessor cannot claim remedies on the basis of the law of obligations.
294 Hinteregger 2012, p. 161.

Before starting our discussion, it is necessary to mention that scholars also justify possessory possession from other perspectives.[295]

3.3.2.1 *Possessory Protection and Publicity Effect*

A Normal Case: Protection of Underlying Rights

Possession has a function of publicity and a function of protection. These two functions are often considered as separate issues.[296] In fact, they are closely related: the function of publicity justifies the function of protection.[297] Every right should be respected, and possession indicates to outsiders that the possessor has a right to the thing possessed (see 3.2.1.2). Therefore, possession should be respected by outsiders. Possession indicates the existence of a right, thus every person is expected to not interfere with this right.[298] Protecting possession is an outcome of the necessity of protecting the right that is made visible by possession.

> *„Bei näherer Betrachtung entspringen diese Funktionen freilich einer einheitlichen Wurzel. Diese ist die Erkenntnis, dass der Besitz in aller Regel Ausdruck bestimmter Rechte oder Interessen ist; daher werden mit ihm die, hinter ihm liegenden Interessen geschützt."*[299]

In fact, the connection between publicity of possession and protection of possession can be traced to the notion of *Gewere* in ancient Germanic law. As has been shown above, *Gewere* literally refers to the "clothing" of rights (see 3.1.1.2).[300] According to this notion, a person could show his or her

295 As summarized by German scholar Müller, there are different approaches: (1) protecting possession is to protect the personality of the possessor (*Besitzschutz als Persönlichkeitsschutz*); (2) protecting possession is to protect the continuity of the relationship of economic life (*Kontinuitätstheorie*); (3) protecting possession is to protect the public peace (*Besitzschutz als Friedensschutz*); (4) protecting possession is to protect the right of ownership (*Besitzschutz als Eigentumsschutz*); (5) protecting possession allows the owner to enjoy protection without having to prove his or her right of ownership (*Beweislastverteilung*); and (6) protecting possession has the function of protecting personal rights associated with possession, thereby making these rights partially proprietary (*Verdinglichung*). In addition to these six approaches, protection of possession is also analyzed from an economic perspective. For example, some scholars argue that protecting possession is to protect the right to use (*wertbasierter Ansatz*), and others contend that it is a result of the fact that possession is a means of publicity (*informationsbasierte Ansatz*). See Müller 2010, p. 225-244. Among these approaches, the last one, namely the information-based approach, is a justification from the perspective of publicity.

296 Wolf and Wellenhofer 2011, p. 76; Salomons 2008 (2), p. 36-40.

297 Emerich 2014, p. 30.

298 Müller 2010, p. 240-241.

299 Baur and Stürner 2009, p. 64. English translation: "*On closer inspection, however, these functions share the same root. Possession is recognized as an expression of a certain right or interest in ordinary situations; therefore, the interest behind possession is also protected.*"

300 Hübner 1918, p. 186.

right through factual control and economic use of the thing involved, and the right should be respected because it has been shown by *Gewere* to the public.

> *"The actual circumstances of possession were regarded as 'prima facie' evidence of a legal right. It was therefore forbidden to disturb such possession by force, i.e. otherwise than by way of judicial action."*[301]

Through actual control, possessors can show to outsiders that they have a right to the thing possessed. Those who receive this signal should respect possession. Truly, the details of this right are not shown by possession, an abstract means of publicity. However, these details are not relevant. For outsiders, just knowing that the possessor has a certain right to the thing possessed suffices (see 2.2.2.2.A). Any illegal interferer cannot be exempted from liabilities by claiming that he or she does not know which right is enjoyed by the possessor.[302]

Law might not only distinguish possession from rights, but also provide a distinction between the protection of possession and the protection of the underlying right. For example, the right of ownership has its own rules of protection.[303] However, this never means that the former protection has nothing to do with the latter protection. Instead, this distinction facilitates the protection of underlying rights. To claim possessory protection, the possessor does not have to prove that he or she has any legal right to keep possession, which alleviates the possessor's burden of proof.[304] In general, what the possessor needs to demonstrate is that he or she has possession previously, and possession is interfered with in the absence of his or her approval. In the situation where the right of ownership is interfered with, the owner may choose to claim possessory protection to avoid the burden of proving his or her right of ownership.[305]

B Exceptional Case: Protection of Convergence

The preceding argument from the perspective of publicity appears problematic in the situation of illegal possession. For example, why is a thief-possessor also protected from illegal interference by others? According to the publicity argument, the thief has no legal right to acquire and maintain factual control of the thing stolen, thus he or she should not be protected.

301 Hübner 1918, p. 193.

302 Hansmann and Kraakman 2002, p. 411; Smith and Merrill 2007, p. 1853-1854.

303 This is quite clear in Dutch law and German law. In particular, the owner is entitled to *rei vindicatio*, a remedy that allows the owner to repossess the object (art. 5:2 BW and § 985 BGB). See Reehuis and Heisterkamp 2019, p. 428-429; Brehm and Berger 2014, p. 120.

304 Müller 2010, p. 235-236; Emerich 2018, p. 77.

305 Müller 2010, p. 235-236; Van Oven 1905, p. 10.

However, this conclusion contradicts the fact that possessory protection is generally available. In law, a general rule is that possession is protected irrespective of whether the possessor has a lawful underlying right.[306] Interference with possession is actionable *per se*.

In fact, the protection granted to illegal possessors can also be justified from the perspective of publicity. Every possessor is presumed to have a right to maintain his or her possession. This presumption is generally in line with the reality: the possessor has a legal right to the thing possessed in most situations. Inevitably, illegal possessors benefit from the presumption. Just as German lawyer Von Jhering pointed out, granting possessory protection to thieves was a price of the presumption.[307] If a person obtains actual control, an outward appearance of rights, then he or she will be protected by law, irrespective of whether this acquisition is illegal. To third parties, the illegal possessor has conveyed an indication that he has a right to the thing possessed.

Though this indication is incorrect, not every person is entitled to sue the illegal possessor. Law only allows those who have a justifiable basis (such as the owner) to recover possession from the illegal possessor. In general, these persons know about the divergence of possession from underlying rights. Vesting a right of recovery in them can eliminate this divergence. As has been pointed out above, possession is a method of publicity that might be incorrect, and the legal protection of possession can be seen as a regime of rectification (see 3.2.1.2.C). This protection guarantees that possession will be held by those who really have a legal right to the thing involved.

In the situation of theft, even if the possessor's identity has been known by a third party, this third party cannot dispossess the thief, unless he or she has a legal right to do so. For example, a robber cannot defend his criminal act by claiming that the person he robbed is a thief. In principle, possession can only shift when there is a lawful basis, such as the transfer of ownership or the creation of a right of pledge. Possession remains unaffected in the absence of a lawful contrary cause. This is of great importance for maintaining the general convergence of underlying rights and possession, an outward mark. As has been shown, this general convergence is a precondition for the qualification of possession as a means of publicity (see 3.2.1.2). If people, in the absence of any lawful basis, were allowed to dispossess illegal possessors, then illegal dispossession would be encouraged. In the long run, the order of possession would be threatened, and the general convergence of possession and underlying rights would be hampered.[308]

---

306 Hinteregger 2012, p. 99; Clerk and Lindsell 2014, p. 1251.

307 Von Jhering, Über den Grund des Besitzschutzes, p. 55, cited from Müller 2010, p. 234.

308 In justifying the protection of possession, an important approach is that possession, including possession held by a person who has no lawful right to the thing possessed, is protected to maintain the public peace or the social order of possession. See Van Oven 1905, p. 37; Emerich 2018, p. 77. In general, the order of possession provides a social basis for the convergence between possession and underlying rights.

3.3.2.2 Possession as a System of Navigation

The preceding discussion concerns how the publicity effect of possession justifies possessory protection in a normal case and in an exceptional case. In this part, we view possession as a method of publicity under a broader context. Humans live in a world full of things owned, used and enjoyed by others. Everyone has a statutory duty to respect others' rights. In relation to this duty, a problem arises of how a person can avert infringing others' rights. To put it differently, how can a person know the boundary between his and others' sphere of free activities?

In general, possession can address this problem. Possession can give rise to physical proximity between the possessor and the thing possessed. From this physical proximity, outsiders can know that the possessor has a right to the thing and then adjust their acts. In this sense, the indication provided by possession helps outsiders avoid becoming illegal interferers.

> *"The concept of possession is a vital tool that allows people to navigate through the every-day world without interfering in the interest of others. Each person continually observes the things around him and can tell at a glance based on physical cues whether they are possessed or not."*[309]

The information-communicating process is mutual: when a person informs others of his right to a thing through his actual control of this thing, this person also acquires similar indications from the actual control by others. Through this mutual process, every person is able to live in harmony with others. In reality, possession takes various specific forms, such as fencing a plot of land, storing commodities in a warehouse, locking a bicycle, or holding a book. The common feature of these forms is that they can be easily observed by outsiders.

As has been pointed out, possession is an abstract method of publicity (see 3.2.1.2). The information conveyed by possession is inadequate for subsequent acquirers (see 3.2.1.3) and general creditors (see 3.2.1.4). However, possession is a sufficient method of publicity for strange interferers, and the abstract indication provided by possession "happens" to be adequate for this type of third party to avoid interfering with others' property. Once a person knows that someone is in possession of a thing, he or she is required to respect the latter's possession of this thing, unless there is a lawful contrary reason. In general, the specific legal identity of the possessor is unimportant for strange interferers, because they do not enjoy or plan to obtain a specific proprietary interest in the thing.

309 Merrill 2015, p. 32.

3.3.2.3 *Possessory Protection, Publicity Effect, and Proprietary Effect*

The preceding two parts have explained possessory protection from the perspective of publicity and shown that possession can act as a system of navigation for humans. In this part, we argue that in the aspect of protection, the boundary between property rights and personal rights is made obscure by possession.

Property rights and personal rights are different in the aspect of the effect on third parties. This difference is shown by the way of protection. In general, property rights can be enforced against strange interferers, while personal rights cannot.[310] For creditors, the principal remedy is requiring the defaulting debtor to bear certain liabilities. Tort law protection is, in general, unavailable to personal rights (see 2.1.3.2).[311] This is in line with the fact that personal rights are a legal relationship *inter partes*.

It has been shown that possession is not necessarily associated with property rights (see 3.2.1.1). Various personal rights and intermediary rights can also be a legal basis of acquiring and maintaining possession. Where a person acquires possession on the basis of a personal right, this person is entitled to claim possessory protection against illegal interference with his or her possession. That is to say the personal right is enforced against strange interferers. In this sense, possession bestows a proprietary effect on the personal right, making the right partially proprietary.[312] Therefore, possession can make the boundary between property rights and personal rights obscure in terms of legal protection.

In general, this consequence can also be explained from the perspective of the publicity of possession. As has just been shown, possession can give outsiders an indication that the possessor has a right; thus, possession should be respected by outsiders. If a personal right embodies an element of possession, then this personal right will be made visible to outsiders. From the perspective of publicity, there is no reason to disallow the creditor claiming possessory protection against when his or her possession is illegally interfered with. After all, the personal right is made transparent by possession, and outsiders can easily know the existence of this right.

In civil law, possession is not treated as an important factor in pinning down the boundary between property rights and personal rights. In general, whether a right is associated with possession seems to be of little relevance to the nature of this right. This can be partially ascribed to the principle of *numerus clausus* and the distinction between possession and property rights.[313] The type of property rights is determined by property

310 Canaris 1978, p. 373.

311 Reehuis 2015, p. 358; Rank-Berenschot 1992, p. 133; Wolf and Neuner 2012, p. 227.

312 Müller 2010, p. 237.

313 The distinction between possession and property rights can be traced to Roman law: property rights have nothing in common with possession (*nihil commune habet proprietas cum possession*). See Wieling 2006, p. 126.

law by providing a closed list. Moreover, whether a right is proprietary is independent of possession, and property rights, especially the right of ownership, and possession represent legal domination and factual domination respectively.[314] In the closed list, some property rights embody the element of possession (e.g., *superficie*), while some property rights do not (e.g., easement). In addition, not all rights embodying possession are included in the closed list. As a result, a number of personal rights can also give rise to acquisition of possession. Lease is a typical example. In constructing the system of property rights, the failure to pay sufficient attention to possession gives rise to two results: one is that non-possessory property rights do not involve factual domination over things, and the other is that the existence of possessory personal rights obscures the boundary between property rights and personal rights, at least in terms of protection.[315]

In contrast, the distinction between property rights and possession does not play a fundamental role in common law.[316] Possession is not completely distinguished from property rights. Instead, possession is a source of proprietary effect.[317] For example, bailment, a legal relationship which takes possession as an essential element, straddles contract law and property law.[318] Another example is that lease of immovable property is, due to the lessee's possession, a typical property right in common law.[319] It is said that common law, like civil law, also has a closed list of property rights.[320] However, possession has great importance in creating the closed list by common law, while civil law treats property rights and possession as two separate issues.[321] As indicated by the common law maxim "*possession is nine tenths of the law*", possession plays a fundamental role in the common law of property.

3.3.2.4 *Lease as an Illustration*

Now we use lease as an example to show how personal rights are made partially proprietary by possession. To avoid misunderstandings, some conceptual divergences between the three jurisdictions (English law, Dutch law, and German law) are presented first. In English law, there is a dichotomy between the law of movables and land law. Lease can be used in both movable property and immovable property, and lease of movable property is

314 Wolf and Wellenhofer 2011, p. 39; Brehm and Berger 2014, p. 35. However, possession is never only a fact. It can give rise to certain legal consequences. As a result, possession is also considered as a right. See Snijders and Rank-Berenschot 2017, p. 110-111; Asser/Bartels & Van Mierlo 2013, nr. 104.

315 Füller 2006, p. 37-41.

316 Tay 1964, p. 480-481.

317 Bridge, Gullifer, McMeel and Worthington 2013, p. 60.

318 Bridge, Gullifer, McMeel and Worthington 2013, p. 72.

319 Cheshire and Burn 2011, p. 185.

320 Swadling 2013, p. 181-182; Merrill and Smith 2000, p. 3.

321 Müller 2010, p. 237.

also known as "hire" in English law.[322] Both German law and Dutch law use the same term (*Miete* and *huur* respectively) to describe the lease of movable property and the lease of immovable property. Moreover, both jurisdictions treat lease as a personal right and regulate it under the law of obligations.[323] As this chapter concerns only the publicity of corporeal movables, the following discussion will confine itself to the lease of corporeal movables.

A English Law

In English law, hire of corporeal movables is a type of bailment for which possession is essential. The bailor has to give up possession to the hirer (bailee). As a type of bailment, hire straddles property law and contract law and has a proprietary as well as a contractual dimension.[324] There is no doubt that the hirer enjoys possessory protection under tort law. Moreover, in principle, law only allows the hirer to sue interferers who illegally intervene in the peaceful enjoyment of possession, and the bailor is only entitled to do so when the interest of reversion is damaged.[325]

Due to the hirer being permitted to claim tort law protection, it is generally held that the relationship of hire is proprietary.

> *"Whilst some doubt has been expressed about the proprietary character of a lease or hire of goods, the better view is that all bailees with a right of possession have a right of a proprietary character, which carries with it the right to sue third parties who wrongfully interfere with the goods."*[326]

English lawyers have doubts with respect to the proprietary qualification of the hirer's right, but these doubts mainly exist in the situation where the corporeal movable hired is disposed of to third parties or the bailor falls into insolvency.[327] In other words, the doubts concern whether and to what extent the hirer's legal position has binding force over subsequent acquirers and general creditors. It is never problematic that the hirer enjoys possessory protection against strange interferers.

B German Law

In German law, possession can take property rights and personal rights as its legal basis.[328] As a result, possession is not necessarily associated with the property right, and the holder of a personal right may also have pos-

322 Clarke and Kohler 2005, p. 609.
323 *Miete* is in Section 2 of Chapter 8 in the second book in the BGB, and *huur* is regulated in Chapter 4 and 5 in the seventh book in the BW.
324 Bridge, Gullifer, McMeel and Worthington 2013, p. 116-124.
325 Bridge, Gullifer, McMeel and Worthington 2013, p. 120.
326 Bridge, Gullifer, McMeel and Worthington 2013, p. 91.
327 Bridge, Gullifer, McMeel and Worthington 2013, p. 117.
328 Baur and Stürner 2009, p. 89; Akkermans 2008, p. 239.

session. The association of personal rights with possession is thoroughly discussed by German lawyers. According to the prevailing view, a personal right will be reinforced by possession to become partially proprietary.[329]

> *„In der Tat genießt das durch Besitzüberlassung verstärkte obligatorische Recht zum Besitz in vielem einen quasidinglichen Schutz."*[330]

This view is based on the fact that the creditor, who is in possession of the thing involved, is entitled to claim possessory protection against illegal interference. In other words, the creditor has an independent legal position to sue illegal interferers. Here the contractual privity is eroded: the creditor does not have to rely on his counterparty.[331] German lawyers call the effect of possessory protection "function of preservation (*Erhaltungsfunktion*)".[332] Among the personal rights associated with possession, a typical one is the right of lease.

Lease is a specific contract prescribed in the book of obligations in the BGB (§ 535 BGB). It is commonly held that the right of lease, though owning some proprietary attributes, is a personal right, namely a contractual relationship between the lessee and the lessor. The content of lease is largely decided by the agreement made by the two parties (§ 535 (1) BGB). However, after acquiring possession, lessees are entitled to claim possessory protection when the thing leased is interfered with by an outsider.

> *„Der Mieter [...] kann nach Besitzeinräumung die Beachtung seines Besitzes gemäß §§ 861, 862 von jedermann, auch vom Vermieter, verlangen."*[333]

In general, all remedies of possession are available to lessees. Therefore, the lessee can according to § 861 BGB recover the thing leased from those who conduct illegal dispossession, and § 862 BGB allows the lessee to suspend existing interference and to remove imminent interference. In addition, the lessee, when as a direct and limited-right possessor, is also entitled to use self-help according to § 859 BGB. The remedies provided by these three provisions are real protection, which should be distinguished from personal protection on the basis of the law of obligations. As a possessor, the lessee is also allowed to protect his right to use under tort law and the law of unjust enrichment.[334]

---

329 Wolf and Wellenhofer 2011, p. 78.

330 Baur and Stürner 2009, p. 66. English translation: "*In fact, the obligational right to possession is reinforced due to the transfer of possession and enjoys quasi-proprietary protection.*"

331 Müller 2010, p. 237.

332 Baur and Stürner 2009, p. 65; Wolf and Wellenhofer 2011, p. 76.

333 Wolf and Wellenhofer 2011, p. 78. English translation: "*The lessee [...] can according to § 861 and § 862 request recovery of possession from everyone, including the lessor.*"

334 Baur and Stürner 2009, p. 100-103.

C Dutch Law

Lease (*huur*) is a relationship of personal right regulated in Book 7 of the BW. The right of lease is configured as a result of the contract of lease, a contract that is subject to the principle of privity.[335] As to the content of the relationship, what counts is the contract. Before exploring whether and in what way possessory protection is available for the lessee, two points need to be mentioned first.

One point is that Dutch law distinguishes "possession (*bezit*)", which is equivalent to ownership possession, from "detention (*houderschap*)". As a result, the lessee is only a detentor of the thing leased: the lessee is subject to the contract of lease and controls the thing for the lessor.[336] On the other hand, the lessee is also a possessor of the right of lease *per se*, because both patrimonial rights and tangible things can be the object of possession in Dutch law.[337] The other point is that Dutch law, like many other civil law jurisdictions, has a dualist system of protection. Protection of possession can be real as well as personal: the possessor is entitled to take actions on the basis of both property law and the law of obligations.[338]

Due to the lack of "possession (*bezit*)", lessees cannot invoke art. 3:125 (1) and (2) BW.[339] These two paragraphs provide legal protection only to possessors, while lessees are merely a detentor of the thing leased.[340] However, it does not mean that the lessee enjoys no legal protection in Dutch law. Art. 3:125 (3) BW expressly provides that the detentor is entitled to claim protection under tort law. Permitting this tort law protection makes the right of lease partially proprietary, in the sense that the right also has some strength of exclusivity.

335 Akkermans 2008, p. 300.

336 Salomons 2008 (2), p. 32.

337 Snijders and Rank-Berenschot 2017, p. 97-98.

338 Art. 3:125 (3) BW: "*Het in dit artikel bepaalde laat voor de bezitter, ook nadat het in het eerste lid bedoelde jaar is verstreken, en voor de houder onverlet de mogelijkheid een vordering op grond van onrechtmatige daad in te stellen, indien daartoe gronden zijn.*" English translation: Art. 3:125 (3) BW: "*Nothing in this article shall deprive the possessor, even after expiry of the year referred to in paragraph 1, or the detentor, of the possibility, should there be grounds, to institute an action on the basis of the law of torts.*"

339 Snijders and Rank-Berenschot 2017, p. 121.

340 This restrictive approach is criticized. See Van Schaick 2014, p. 81. Here, it should be noted that the lessee has two legal positions in Dutch law: the detentor of the thing leased and the possessor of the right of lease. The dual positions are a result of the possibility of possession of rights. It is unclear whether the lessee can, in the name of a possessor of the right of lease, invoke art. 3:125 (1) and (2) BW. It seems that particular attention is not paid to this question by Dutch lawyers. It is worthwhile mentioning here that "*possession of an incorporeal right can only be protected by the possessory remedies where it is coupled with physical control over a corporeal thing*" in Austrian law. See Rüfner 2014, p. 173. Under South African law, possessory protection is available to the lessee's possession of the right to use. See Kleyn 2014, p. 195.

> *"Een zekere exclusiviteit kan men niet aan het huur- en pachtrecht ontzeggen en wel in die zin dat huurder en pachter kunnen ageren tegen derden die hen zodanig storen dat zij uit dien hoofde aansprakelijk zijn uit onrechtmatige daad."*[341]

Therefore, the lessee enjoys legal protection against third parties under Dutch law. However, unlike German law, Dutch law does not entitle the lessee to claim real protection, and only remedies on the basis of tort law are possible.

D Conclusion

In a word, the possibility of possessory protection for the personal right of lease makes this right partially proprietary in the three jurisdictions, giving rise to a phenomenon of "propertization (*Verdinglichung* in German law or *verzakelijking* in Dutch law)".[342] In general, this phenomenon is not without ground. It can be justified by the publicity effect of possession. Once the lessee obtains possession, the personal right to use will be made visible to outsiders, beginning to have an outward appearance.

3.3.3 Protection in the Absence of Actual Possession

It has been argued in the preceding discussion that one ground of possessory possession is that (direct) possession can convey an indication to third parties. As a result, a right associated with possession should not be interfered with, regardless of whether this right is initially proprietary or personal. However, this argument does not mean that protection will be denied where direct possession is absent. In law, property rights are also protected, even though they are not associated with direct possession. For example, an owner has a right of recovery against illegal dispossessors by virtue of his or her ownership, and an indirect possessor enjoys possessory protection despite the fact that indirect possession has no effect of publicity (see 3.2.2). These two examples appear to be at odds with our preceding argument. However, this is not true when we note that the perception that direct possession should, due to its publicity effect, be respected does not mean that a right dissociated from direct possession deserves no protection.

3.3.3.1 Protection of Indirect Possession

The concept of indirect possession is recognized by English law (constructive possession), German law (*mittelbare Besitz*), and Dutch law (*middellijk bezit*). In general, these three jurisdictions differ in the aspect of protecting

---

341 Snijders and Rank-Berenschot 2017, p. 59. English translation: *"It cannot be denied that certain exclusivity is enjoyed by the tenant and the farming tenant, in the sense that the tenant and the farming tenant may act against third parties who are liable for their illegal acts."*

342 Gray 2009, p. 163; Baur and Stürner 2009, p. 66; Snijders and Rank-Berenschot 2017, p. 59.

indirect possession, especially between English law and the other two civil law jurisdictions.

In German law, protective measures which can be taken by direct possessors are also available for indirect possessors. Thus, the indirect possessor has a right of recovery, a right to suspend and remove disturbance, and even a right to use self-help.[343] Dutch law protects indirect possessors and direct possessors in the same way: art. 3:125 (1) BW is identically applied to direct possession and indirect possession. As a result, the possessor, whether direct or indirect, is entitled to restore possession and to remove and suspend disturbance.[344]

Different from both German law and Dutch law, English law restricts constructive possessors taking actions in the situation of illegal interference with possession. For example, in the case of bailment only the bailee, who holds actual possession, has a right to sue on the basis of trespass.[345] In English law, the bailor's constructive possession is not a form of possession that is intended to be protected from trespass. However, exceptions exist: bailors can sue when they have an immediate right to possession out of the revocable bailment or when their reversionary interest is harmed.[346] For constructive possessors (bailors), possessory protection is in principle not available.[347] In general, what the bailor enjoys is no more than a reversionary interest, a right to reobtain actual possession in the future. This interest is protected by tort law as far as it is damaged, such as when the thing involved is destroyed by or sold to others.[348] The restrictive approach adopted by English law implies that constructive possession is, in essence, a right of recovery, which has been shown above (see 3.2.2.1).

Indirect possession cannot perform the function of publicity or give any indication to third parties (see 3.2.2). Due to the lack of publicity effect, it appears that indirect possessors should not be entitled to possessory protection, unless their right of recovery is damaged or threatened. This conclusion is in line with English law. As just shown, English law generally disallows indirect possessors to claim possessory protection. However, the conclusion contradicts both German law and Dutch law. In these two jurisdictions, possessory protection is generally available to indirect possessors. The following discussion presents that the main reason for this difference lies in legislative policy.

---

343 Wolf and Wellenhofer 2011, p. 51. However, as to whether indirect possessors have a right to use force against illegal interferers, different opinions exist. See Wilhelm 2010, p. 241-242.

344 Here, it is worthwhile noting that Dutch law prohibits possessors from using force to defend possession against illegal interference. Possessors are supposed to initiate a judicial proceeding. See Van Schaick 2014, p. 71.

345 Bridge, Gullifer, McMeel and Worthington 2013, p. 120.

346 Winfield and Jolowicz 2010, p. 823; Palmer 2009, no. 4-065-4-075.

347 Bridge 2015, p. 84-86.

348 Palmer 2009, no. 4-068.

In general, indirect possession can be explained from the perspective of possessory protection in German law. As has been shown above, possession is defined broadly for the purpose of providing possessory protection to such persons as the lessee (see 3.1.3.3).[349] Due to this concern, German legislators draw a distinction between direct possessors (such as the lessee) and indirect possessors (such as the lessor).[350] In Roman law, there was a tradition that owners had *possessio* and enjoyed possessory protection, regardless of whether they exercise actual control in person. German law follows this tradition. Truly, the owner can sue the interferer by virtue of the right of ownership. However, this does not make possessory protection on the basis of the owner's legal position as an indirect possessor useless. Possessory protection is advantageous to the owner in terms of the burden of proof, which has been pointed out above (see 3.3.2.1). In addition, it is worthwhile noting that not every indirect possessor has a legal right. For example, a thief leases the stolen bicycle, thus becoming an indirect possessor. In this very situation, legal protection on the basis of an underlying right is impossible for the thief, and only possessory protection is available.[351]

In English law, one reason why indirect possessors cannot claim possessory protection is doctrinal: in essence, indirect possessors have no possession.[352] In terms of protection, indirect possession is no more than a reversionary interest. Another more important reason is that English law has a deep concern about double liability which is prejudicial to defendants.[353] The denial of possessory protection to indirect possessors can avoid the following situation: the same interferer is sued twice by the direct possessor and the indirect possessor. The concern about double liability helps us to understand s. 8 (1) Torts (Interference with Goods) Act 1977.[354] According to this paragraph, the defendant is entitled to refute the plaintiff's claim by proving that a third party has a better right than the plaintiff.[355] However, the denial of possessory protection does not trigger a large problem to indirect possessors for two reasons. Firstly, the direct possessor (bailee) bears a strict liability to the indirect possessor (bailor), which can encourage the former to take positive measures against illegal interference from third parties.[356] Secondly, the reversionary interest enjoyed by the

349 Füller 2006, p. 285.
350 Staudinger/Gutzeit 2012, p. 217-218.
351 Van Schaick 2014, p. 76.
352 Palmer 2009, no. 4-008; Clerk and Lindsell 2014, p. 1349.
353 Bridge 2015, p. 103-104.
354 S. 8 (1) Torts (Interference with Goods) Act: "*The defendant in an action for wrongful interference shall be entitled to show, in accordance with rules of court, that a third party has a better right than the plaintiff as respects all or any part of the interest claimed by the plaintiff, or in right of which he sues, and any rule of law (sometimes called jus tertii) to the contrary is abolished.*"
355 Bridge, Gullifer, McMeel and Worthington 2013, p. 140.
356 Bridge 2015, p. 103.

indirect possessor is protected under tort law.[357] Thus, the legal position of indirect possessors has been well protected, despite the lack of possessory protection.

Therefore, the difference of English law from German law and Dutch law is principally a consequence of legislative policy. Both German law and Dutch law are concerned more about the protection of possessors against illegal interference. Both direct possessors and indirect possessors are entitled to take protective measures. As a result, the indirect possessor does not have to rely on the direct possessor: the former has an independent legal position to sue for unlawful interference. In contrast, English law is concerned more about the problem of double liability which is unjust to unlawful interferers. To address this problem, only direct possessors are allowed to claim protection. The indirect possessor cannot sue unless the reversionary interest is damaged.

3.3.3.2 Protection of Non-Possessory Property Rights

In reality, some property rights are not associated with direct possession or indirect possession, thus becoming non-possessory. Nevertheless, this does not mean that these non-possessory property rights are not protected by law. In other words, even though possession is absent, property rights *per se* are still protected.

For example, an easement usually does not vest possession in the owner of the dominant land, but law entitles this owner to sue when this property right is interfered with; the creditor who has a right of mortgage (hypothec) is not in possession of the collateral, but legal protection is available for this proprietor. Property law not only protects possession and possessory rights, but also non-possessory rights. In fact, with respect to one specific thing, there are often multiple legal relationships, among which only one can be made visible to third parties by possession. For example, A is an owner of a bicycle, he leases this bicycle to B and pledges it to his creditor C. In this situation, only B has direct possession, and his right of lease is made visible. Both A and C have no actual control, which means that the right of ownership and the right of pledge are not made visible to third parties.

Non-possessory property rights should be respected. In general, every property right constitutes a part of the proprietor's patrimony and represents an interest enjoyed by the proprietor. Therefore, every property right should be protected, irrespective of whether it embodies the element of possession. Possession deserves protection because it indicates the existence of a right. However, this does not mean that a property right in the absence of possession should be disrespected. In fact, possession should be respected because it usually has a certain underlying right, and it is the necessity of protecting this right that justifies the protection of possession (see 3.3.2.1).

357 Bridge 2015, p. 103; Clerk and Lindsell 2014, p. 1349.

If we acknowledge this, then the absence of possession should never be deemed as a sufficient reason for denying protecting property rights.

3.3.3.3 *A Possible Explanation*

The preceding discussion has shown that: (1) possession should be respected, because it makes the underlying right visible, and the necessity of protecting this right provides a basis for the protection of possession; and (2) indirect possession and non-possessory property rights are also protected from illegal interference, despite the fact that they are invisible to third parties. Therefore, possession should be protected because of the effect of publicity, but this does not mean that only property rights made visible by possession can be enforced against illegal interferers. These two conclusions appear contradictory. In this part, we provide an explanation by viewing the effect of publicity of (direct) possession under a more general context.

Indeed, indirect possession and non-possessory property rights are not visible to strange interferers. However, this does not mean that strange interferers face a problem of information asymmetry. This is because where indirect possession and a non-possessory right are involved, correlative direct possession has communicated an indication to strange interferers. In other words, if there is an actual possessor who physically controls the thing involved, then strange interferers are able to know from this physical control that a certain right exists and to gain sufficient information to adjust their acts. If they fail to adjust their acts, then it seems unproblematic to allow the indirect possessor or the holder of the non-possessory right to sue. Therefore, the grant of protection to indirect possessors and the holder of non-possessory property rights does not make strange interferers fall into a worse situation.[358]

In the preceding case concerning the bicycle, owner A gives up actual possession to lessee B, and both ownership and pledge are invisible. However, the hidden ownership and pledge do not cause any problem of information to strange interferers, because strange interferers have obtained an indication from the actual control by lessee B. The bicycle has already been possessed by B, and strange interferers are able to navigate their acts according to the B's actual control. As has been argued above, possession can convey an abstract indication, and the possessor's specific legal identity is not important for strange interferers (see 3.3.2.1). Therefore, it suffices for strange interferers that the lessee exercises actual control over the bicycle.

358 Here it should be noted that this does not involve the problem of double liability, which concerns English lawyers deeply. It only means that the protection does not create an extra burden in terms of the collection of proprietary information by strange interferers.

3.3.4 Conclusion

From the preceding discussion, it can be seen that possession has a function of protection and a function of publicity. These two functions are closely related. Specifically speaking, possession should be protected because it is an outward symbol of underlying rights that need to be respected. The underlying right justifies the protection of possession. Three points merit special emphasis about this conclusion.

Firstly, possession indicates that the possessor has a certain right to the thing possessed, and thus third parties should respect possession. This indication is communicated through the physical proximity between the thing and the possessor. Instinctively, third parties can immediately react to this physical proximity and adjust their behaviors to avoid conducting illegal interference. Otherwise, they will incur liabilities. In everyday life, people rely on possession to navigate their behaviors. In this sense, possession can be seen as a system of navigation that can provide information to third parties cheaply and efficiently.

Secondly, possession does not always have an underlying right. For example, thieves have possession of the thing stolen. From the perspective of publicity, the possessory protection granted to illegal possessors can facilitate the general convergence of underlying rights and the outward mark (possession). Excluding illegal possessors from possessory protection in a general way is tantamount to encouraging unlawful interference, which will, in the long run, threaten the order of possession and hamper the general convergence of underlying rights and possession. Of course, those who have a lawful ground are entitled to recover the thing involved from illegal possessors. Illegal possession causes a divergence between possession and the underlying right. The claim of recovery can rectify such divergence.

Thirdly, the two preceding points only concern why (direct) possession should be protected. They do not touch upon the issue of the protection of indirect possession and non-possessory property rights. In reality, not all property rights are made visible through direct possession. Some property rights are only associated with indirect possession, and some do not include any possession. Though these rights are hidden to third parties, they still should be protected from illegal interference. In general, there is an "indirect" connection between this protection and publicity of possession: these invisible property rights (such as the lessor's right of ownership) are often associated with actual possession held by another person (such as the lessee's actual possession), and third parties are always able to navigate their behaviors according to this actual possession.

3.4 Possession and Third-Party Effect: Subsequent Acquirers

After demonstrating the importance of possession for strange interferers, we now turn to the relationship between possession and another type of third party, namely subsequent acquirers. As argued above, possession is an abstract method of publicity (see 3.2.1.2). This determines that possession is not an adequate method of publicity for subsequent acquirers who demand detailed proprietary information. In this section, we first present that possession cannot satisfy the demand for proprietary information by subsequent acquirers (see 3.4.1). After that, we discuss the role played by possession, as a means of publicity, in two specific situations: transfer of ownership (see 3.4.2) and *bona fide* acquisition (see 3.4.3). This discussion includes a comparative study of the three jurisdictions: English law, German law, and Dutch law.

3.4.1 Possession and Subsequent Acquirers

Unlike the strange interferer, subsequent acquirers have or intend to have a property right with respect to a specific thing. Subsequent acquirers include the transferee who intends to acquire ownership, the usufructuary who aims to have a proprietary right of use, and the secured creditor who seeks to have a prior right of enforcement. Subsequent acquirers are "subsequent" in the sense that they are a latecomer: before the acquisition, other parties already have a property right with respect to the thing involved. As a result of the rule of *prior tempore*, subsequent acquirers have a legal position inferior to those who have an "older" property right.

Because of this inferior legal position, subsequent acquirers require proprietary information concerning the existing property rights. Compared with strange interferers for whom an abstract indication suffices, subsequent acquirers need more detailed proprietary information. Before obtaining a property right with respect to a certain thing, subsequent acquirers will usually investigate the property rights that already exist on this thing. By this investigation, they want to avoid running into a conflict with other proprietors. In general, the investigation involves, among other things, the date of the creation of these property rights, the content of these rights, and whether and how these rights will affect the property right they intend to acquire.

In many sources, possession is considered as a means of publicity that can satisfy the demand for proprietary information by subsequent acquirers.[359] In fact, however, possession is almost of no use to subsequent acquirers. As emphasized many times, possession is only an abstract method of publicity. It can only give third parties an indication that the possessor has a right to the thing possessed. The details of this right cannot be shown by possession. In this sense, possession is ambiguous. This ambiguity implies that possession is far from being a method of publicity sufficient for subsequent acquirers. Subsequent acquirers need to know the details of the existing property rights with respect to the thing involved. The problem of

359 Clarke and Kohler 2005, p. 389-390; Wolf and Wellenhofer 2011, p. 76; Snijders and Rank-Berenschot 2017, p. 63.

information asymmetry for subsequent acquirers cannot be addressed by possession.

In general, the failure of possession to address the problem of information asymmetry is related to two facts: (1) the publicity effect of possession has been made dispensable to a large extent in the law of corporeal movables, and property rights can be acquired without involving (direct) possession in many situations; and (2) the publicity effect of possession is never decisive for the acquisition of property rights, and many other factors have to be taken into consideration. In other words, publicity is neither always necessary nor sufficient for acquiring property rights of corporeal movables. Here we briefly explain these two facts.

The first fact is that (direct) possession is not necessarily involved in the creation and transfer of property rights in many situations. In other words, property rights might be acquired invisibly. For example, the time when ownership of goods passes to the transferee is decided by transacting parties under the consensual system. Transfer or provision of possession is not necessary. Under the translative system, delivery is essential for the transfer of ownership. However, this delivery does not necessarily require the shift of direct possession. It can take other forms, such as *traditio brevi manu*, *traditio per constitutum possessorium*, and *traditio longa manu*. These three forms of delivery allow the thing involved to remain physically where it is. As a result, the transfer occurs invisibly, and for this reason, they are termed as "invisible delivery" in this research.[360] Correspondingly, delivery involving the change of physical control of the object is called "visible delivery" in this research.[361]

Moreover, transacting parties are also entitled to decide the date on which ownership passes under the translative system. The relationship between possession and the transfer of ownership is further discussed below (see 3.4.2). In the situation where corporeal movables are used as collateral, possession is not necessarily involved. For example, a non-possessory security device, such as mortgage and non-possessory pledge, might be created on corporeal movables (see 3.5.3.1). On the basis of this non-possessory security device, the security provider can continue having actual control of the collateral. As a result, possession fails to make the security device visible.

In general, the law allows the actual control of corporeal movables to remain unaffected by the disposal of corporeal movables. The reason is that transacting parties have an individual right to decide the person who will enjoy direct possession. Truly, (direct) possession is a method of publicity,

360 Generally speaking, the term invisible delivery is equivalent to the concept of constructive delivery, as opposed to actual delivery, in English law, as will be seen in 3.4.2.1.C. Moreover, invisible delivery is also called "fictional delivery (*traditio ficta*)" in some writings (see 3.4.2.4.A).

361 In general, visible delivery is known as actual delivery in English law (see 3.4.2.1.C) and "true delivery (*traditio vera*)" in some writings.

and visible delivery can show the disposal of corporeal movables in an abstract way. However, possession is also essential for making use of things in many situations. It embodies the interest of use. Sometimes, possession is defined by referring to using an object or excluding others from the enjoyment or use of this object.[362] Usually, possessing a thing is necessary for making use of or enjoying this thing. Transacting parties should be entitled to decide the person who can use the thing involved by obtaining and preserving actual control of the thing. For example, a seller can transfer ownership of a bicycle he has and retain possession of this bicycle by leasing it back. In this situation, the transfer is completely invisible to third parties.

The second fact is that (direct) possession alone does not suffice for the creation and transfer of property rights of corporeal movables. Possession is an abstract and thus ambiguous method of publicity. In the situation where possession is expected to give rise to certain proprietary consequences, such as *bona fide* acquisition, law always requires the fulfillment of other conditions. For example, possession cannot indicate the existence of ownership, thus third parties are required to be prudent when transacting with the possessor. Third parties should not believe that the possessor has legal ownership just because the latter is in actual control of the thing involved. Instead, they should be sufficiently attentive to ascertaining the possessor's true legal identity and conduct some investigations. If they fail to do so, their purpose of acquisition might be frustrated. Whether third parties are sufficiently prudent is often a question in the situation of *bona fide* acquisition. About the relationship between possession and *bona fide* acquisition, further discussion will be provided below (see 3.4.3).

3.4.2 Transfer of Ownership of Corporeal Movables

This part focuses on the role of possession and its publicity effect under the context of the transfer of corporeal movables. We will first introduce the role of possession under English law, German law and Dutch law and then provide a comparative and conclusive analysis. In this part, it will be concluded that: (1) for each jurisdiction, the starting point is that parties are entitled to decide the time when ownership passes as well as the person who will hold direct possession; and (2) invisible delivery has no effect of publicity, and visible delivery has the publicity effect only in an abstract sense.

3.4.2.1 English Law

In this part, we provide an introduction to the role possession plays in the transfer of corporeal movables in English law. This introduction concerns

362 Emerich 2018, p. 51. In ancient Germanic law and common law, the concept of possession was often defined on the basis of use or enjoyment. A possessor was a person who enjoyed or made use of the thing. See Gray 2009, p. 151; Hübner 1918, p. 186.

two requirements for a valid transfer: one is that the parties have a valid consent of the transfer, and the other is that the thing involved has to be specified. For the sake of simplicity, the following discussion concentrates only on the transfer of corporeal movables in the situation of the sales.

A A Consensual System

According to s. 17 (1) Sale of Goods Act (SGA), ownership of corporeal movables passes at the time decided by parties, provided that the thing involved is specific.[363] If individuals do not decide any specific moment, then the default rule is that ownership passes to the transferee when the contract takes effect. This default rule is set forth in s. 18 (1) SGA.

> S. 18 (1) SGA: "*Where there is an unconditional contract for the sale of specific goods in a deliverable state the property in the goods passes to the buyer when the contract is made, and it is immaterial whether the time of payment or the time of delivery, or both, is postponed.*"

In this sense, the SGA creates a consensual system, and delivery is not a prerequisite for the transfer of ownership.[364]

Where ownership passes to the transferee in the absence of delivery, there is a divergence between ownership and possession. This divergence will undermine the strength of the ownership acquired by the purchaser. Pursuant to s. 24 SGA, a third party in good faith is entitled to acquire ownership from "*the seller in possession*", provided that all relevant requirements are met. In this sense, we can say that the ownership acquired by the purchaser is relative in the absence of delivery. S. 24 SGA is a rule of *bona fide* acquisition that is further discussed below (see 3.4.3).

In understanding the SGA, it is necessary to note that the term "*agreement to sell*" is distinguished from "*sale*". S. 2 (4) SGA provides that "*Where under a contract of sale the property in the goods is transferred from the seller to the buyer the contract is called a sale*". S. 2 (5) SGA stipulates that "*Where under a contract of sale the transfer of the property in the goods is to take place at a future time or subject to some condition later to be fulfilled the contract is called an agreement to sell*". According to these two paragraphs, a difference between the two terms lies in whether ownership is acquired by the buyer.[365] This difference further implies that the "*agreement to sell*" and the "*sale*" are treated differently in the following aspects: the protection against illegal interference, the power of further disposal to third parties, the right of separation in the situation of insolvency, and the allocation of fruits and risks.[366] Therefore, it

363 S. 17 (1) SGA: "*Where there is a contract for the sale of specific or ascertained goods the property in them is transferred to the buyer at such time as the parties to the contract intend it to be transferred.*"

364 Van Vliet 2000, p. 91.

365 Bridge, Gullifer, McMeel and Worthington 2013, p. 42.

366 Bridge, Gullifer, McMeel and Worthington 2013, p. 43-44.

can be said that the SGA draws a distinction between, in the jargon of German legal theory, the proprietary contract and the obligational contract.[367]

B The Requirement of Specificity

As just mentioned, a condition for the transfer of ownership in the absence of delivery is that the subject matter should be specific and ascertained.[368] According to s. 61 SGA, a good is specific when it can be "*identified and agreed on at the time a contract of sale is made*". The requirement of specificity is defined by s. 16 SGA. According to this provision, ownership of unspecific goods cannot pass until the goods have been ascertained.[369] This requirement is easy to understand. Ownership is a property right and can be enforced against general third parties. Thus, this right must exist on a specific object. Otherwise, third parties would be exposed to an excessive risk of uncertainty.[370]

However, English law recognizes an exception to the requirement of specificity: the "*sale of goods forming part of a bulk*" or "*quasi-specific goods*".[371] Typically, this exception arises in the following situation and the like: five tons of oil are sold out of ten tons of oil stored in a specific tank, but the oil sold is not yet appropriated. This situation was once regulated by s. 16 SGA. As a result, the buyer cannot acquire ownership of five tons of oil because the subject matter is not specified. If the buyer has paid the price in advance, then the buyer will fall into a disadvantageous position if the seller becomes insolvent. To address this problem, the Law Commission and the Scottish Law Commission conducted a reform and introduced the rule of bulk ownership: Sale of Goods Forming Part of a Bulk. This rule is embodied in s. 20A and 20B of the SGA.[372] The central consequence of this rule is that the buyer can temporarily acquire a share of the whole bulk

367 In German legal theory, proprietary contract refers to the contract that can give rise to proprietary legal consequences, while obligational contract can only give rise to a legal relationship of personal rights. These two contracts are distinguished from each other. For acquisition of property rights, a proprietary contract is essential. The obligational contract only provides an obligational basis for the proprietary contract. See Wolf and Wellenhofer 2011, p. 68-71.

368 S. 16 SGA: "*Where there is a contract for the sale of unascertained goods no property in the goods is transferred to the buyer unless and until the goods are ascertained.*"

369 Where there is a contract for the sale of unascertained goods, no ownership is transferred to the buyer until the goods are ascertained.

370 Clarke and Kohler 2005, p. 156.

371 Bridge, Gullifer, McMeel and Worthington 2013, p. 273; Van Vliet 2000, p. 93.

372 S. 20A SGA: "(1) *This section applies to a contract for the sale of a specified quantity of unascertained goods if the following conditions are met—(a) the goods or some of them form part of a bulk which is identified either in the contract or by subsequent agreement between the parties; and (b) the buyer has paid the price for some or all of the goods which are the subject of the contract and which form part of the bulk.* (2) *Where this section applies, then (unless the parties agree otherwise), as soon as the conditions specified in paragraphs (a) and (b) of subsection (1) above are met or at such later time as the parties may agree—(a) property in an undivided share in the bulk is transferred to the buyer, and (b) the buyer becomes an owner in common of the bulk.*"

in proportion to the price paid. In other words, the buyer becomes a joint owner of the specific bulk.[373]

The rule of bulk ownership tempers the harshness of the requirement of specificity. In practice, this rule is very meaningful if the seller goes bankrupt, or if the bulk involved is distrained by a creditor of the seller. With joint ownership, the buyer can release the share from the bankruptcy or the seizure.[374] As indicated by the final report issued by the Law Commission and the Scottish Law Commission, the principal purpose of the reform is to protect the buyer, who has paid the purchase price in advance, from the risk of the seller's insolvency.[375]

To acquire a specified share of the entire bulk, two requirements must be met: a specific quantity and a specific bulk. The bulk should be sufficiently specific. Otherwise, the share cannot be determined even though the quantity agreed is specific.[376] By the same token, the specifically-agreed quantity will become nonsense if the whole bulk cannot be ascertained.[377] In a nutshell, the rule requires that both the quantity sold and the bulk involved should be specific. Due to these two requirements, we can say that the rule of bulk ownership does not completely dispense with the principle of specificity.

The rule of bulk ownership gives rise to joint ownership. However, this joint ownership is interim and different from ordinary co-ownership. Upon the delivery or the appropriation of the corporeal movables sold out of the bulk, the joint ownership will come to an end, and ownership of the thing delivered passes to the buyer.[378] About this appropriation, s. 20B SGA prescribes the "*deemed consent*" of all joint owners. This means that, in the absence of consent of joint owners, the seller has the right of delivery and a right to perform the contractual duty of transferring ownership.[379] When the seller delivers a thing out of the bulk to a buyer, the latter will acquire ownership of this thing. In the situation of overselling where multiple buyers are a co-owner, the seller's delivery to one buyer may cause a

373 Bridge, Gullifer, McMeel and Worthington 2013, p. 302.

374 Clarke and Kohler 2005, p. 485.

375 The Law Commission 1993, p. 2.

376 S. 61 (1) F1 SGA: "*'bulk' means a mass or collection of goods of the same kind which—(a) is contained in a defined space or area; and (b) is such that any goods in the bulk are interchangeable with any other goods therein of the same number or quantity.*"

377 According to s. 20A (2) SGA, another requirement is that "*the buyer has paid the price for some or all of the goods which are the subject of the contract and which form part of the bulk.*" This requirement is a result of the balance between conflicting interests, thus it is irrelevant to the definition *per se*.

378 See s. 20A (4) SGA; Bridge, Gullifer, McMeel and Worthington 2013, p. 302.

379 S. 20B (1) SGA: "*A person who has become an owner in common of a bulk by virtue of section 20A above shall be deemed to have consented to—(a) any delivery of goods out of the bulk to any other owner in common of the bulk, being goods which are due to him under his contract; (b) any dealing with or removal, delivery or disposal of goods in the bulk by any other person who is an owner in common of the bulk in so far as the goods fall within that co-owner's undivided share in the bulk at the time of the dealing, removal, delivery or disposal.*"

shrinkage of the other buyers' share.[380] Nevertheless, these other buyers are not entitled to complain about the shrinkage.[381] Therefore, the buyer who gains possession earlier will have a superior position, and the buyer does not have to bear any liability to the other buyers whose shares shrink. This *"first delivery first ownership"* rule is also applicable in the situation of the seller's insolvency.[382]

C Actual Delivery and Constructive Delivery

Under the English consensual system, corporeal movables can be transferred independently from delivery. However, this does not mean that delivery is not important. As will be seen later, the formality of delivery largely determines whether the ownership acquired is effective against third parties in good faith (see 3.4.3.1). For this reason, we now introduce the concept of delivery in English law.

The SGA defines delivery as *"voluntary transfer of possession from one person to another"* in s. 61 (1). In general, delivery can be actual as well as constructive, depending on whether actual control is handed over.[383] Roughly speaking, actual delivery is equivalent to visible delivery, and constructive delivery to invisible delivery. By actual delivery, the acquirer can obtain actual possession, while constructive delivery does not involve any change of actual control and the subject matter remains where it is.[384] Actual delivery involves handing over actual control. This is a bilateral process between the transferor who surrenders actual control and the transferee who receives actual control.[385] It is worthwhile noting that handing over the key to the premise where the corporeal movables involved are stored is actual delivery in English law.[386] However, different opinions exist.[387]

Constructive delivery can occur in different situations, and a common aspect of these situations is that the transferee does not obtain actual control. In general, constructive delivery includes attornment, delivery to a third party, and symbolic delivery. Attornment can take place in three situations: (1) the transferor attorns to the transferee and retains actual control (*traditio per constitutum possessorium*); (2) a third party holding actual control of the object attorns to the transferee (*traditio longa manu*); and (3) the transferee who has obtained possession begins to hold the object for his

380 Overselling means that the seller disposes of more goods than the total amount of the bulk. In this situation, the last buyer can also acquire joint ownership according to s. 24 (the seller in possession). As a result, the other buyers' share will shrink proportionally.
381 Bridge, Gullifer, McMeel and Worthington 2013, p. 306.
382 The Law Commission 1993, p. 33-36.
383 Benjamin 2014, p. 424.
384 Frisby and Jones 2009, p. 26.
385 Frisby and Jones 2009, p. 26.
386 Frisby and Jones 2009, p. 26-27; Bridge 2015, p. 75.
387 In the viewpoint of some scholars, handing over the key is a kind of "symbolic or constructive delivery", just like the delivery of bills of lading. See Benjamin 2014, p. 427.

or her own account (*traditio brevi manu*).[388] In the first case, the transferor is said to remain in possession *"in the capacity of bailee"*.[389] In fact, possession does not shift, and only a relationship of bailment comes into existence. As pointed out by some scholars, *"possession and delivery go their separate ways"* in this case.[390]

Under the second attornment, a third party who attorns to the transferor before the transfer changes to attorn to the transferee after the transfer. This third party is known as bailee in English law. The second attornment can take place in the situation where delivery orders, warrants, wharfingers' certificates, warehousemen's certificates or the like are involved.[391] To accomplish this attornment, it is necessary to obtain an acknowledgment from the third party. This means that, for example, if a warehouseman refuses to hold the object for the transferee, then attornment will not be completed. In the absence of communicating the fact of transfer to and having an acknowledgment from the warehouseman, modification of the warehouse certificate alone does not suffice.[392] Even if the warehouseman has promised, in advance, to attorn to the person who holds the certificate, constructive delivery does not complete either.[393] A bill of lading is a special document that can directly give rise to constructive delivery upon negotiation of the bill of lading, even when the carrier does not express any acknowledgment. It forms a contrast to delivery warrants: the latter requires warehousemen's specific attornment, regardless of whether they contain the warehousemen's undertaking in advance.[394] Because of this difference between the bill of lading and the other documents concerning goods, the former is a document of title to goods in common law and sometimes treated as a document which can trigger symbolic delivery.[395]

Constructive delivery may also take place when the object is delivered to a third party who holds it for the benefit of the transferee.[396] For example, where a seller directly delivers a bicycle to the buyer's borrower, constructive delivery arises. The borrower possesses this bicycle for the buyer. However, if the third party is an employee or a servant of the transferee, then actual delivery will take place. Possession cannot be acquired by employees or servants under English law.[397]

On the basis of the introduction above, the concept of delivery in English law can be shown in the following diagram (Figure 6).

388 Bridge, Gullifer, McMeel and Worthington 2013, p.122.
389 Bridge 2015, p. 75; Benjamin 2014, p. 427.
390 Bridge 2015, p. 75.
391 Benjamin 2014, p. 429.
392 Bridge, Gullifer, McMeel and Worthington 2013, p. 133.
393 Bridge 2015, p. 77.
394 Bridge 2015, p. 77-78; Benjamin 2014, p. 429.
395 Benjamin 2014, p. 427. The bill of lading is the only document of title to goods in the common law sense, as we will show later (see 4.2.2.1).
396 Bridge 2015, p. 75-76.
397 Bridge 2015, p. 76.

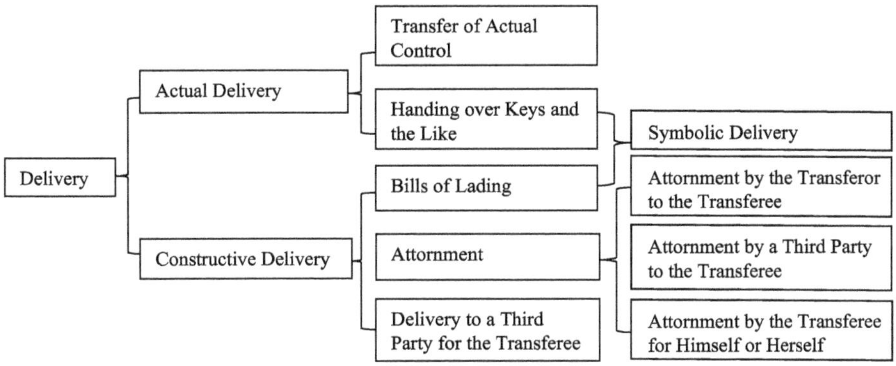

Figure 6

3.4.2.2 German Law

A A Traditio *System*

German law constructs a *traditio* system for the transfer of ownership of corporeal movables. Under this system, "delivery (*Übergabe*)" is a condition for valid transfer of ownership and thus has constitutive effect. Pursuant to § 929 BGB, a complete transfer includes two elements: consent and delivery.[398] It should be noted that the consent refers to "proprietary agreement (*dingliche Einigung*)", as opposed to "obligational agreement (*schuldrechtliche Einigung*)".[399] Under the principle of separation, transfer of ownership of corporeal movables is an outcome of the proprietary agreement, and an obligational agreement only allows the creditor to require the debtor to transfer the object. Consent is a basis for the transfer, and delivery performs the function of showing the consent to third parties.[400] Therefore, delivery has a function to make the proprietary agreement visible.[401]

Originally, delivery refers to the shift of actual control.[402] One purpose of the requirement of delivery is to guarantee "*the conformity of possession and ownership*" and to deter unauthorized dispositions.[403]

---

398 § 929 BGB: „*Zur Übertragung des Eigentums an einer beweglichen Sache ist erforderlich, dass der Eigentümer die Sache dem Erwerber übergibt und beide darüber einig sind, dass das Eigentum übergehen soll […].*" English translation: § 929 BGB: "*For the transfer of ownership of a movable thing, it is necessary that the owner delivers this thing to the acquirer, and both agree on the transfer of ownership […].*"

399 Brehm and Berger 2014, p. 11-12.

400 Wolf and Wellenhofer 2011, p. 76.

401 Wieling 2006, p. 41.

402 Wolf and Wellenhofer 2011, p. 79; McGuire 2008, p. 96.

403 McGuire 2008, p. 97.

„Die Funktion dieser Übergabe sah der Gesetzgeber darin, Besitz und Recht deckungsgleich zu halten: ‚Wie im Immobiliarrecht das Eintragungsprinzip der Richtigerhaltung des Grundbuchs dient, so dient im Mobiliarrecht das Traditionsprinzip ähnlichen Zweck, indem es ein Auseinanderfallen von Besitz und Recht verhütet […]'."[404]

It is noteworthy that the element of consent under § 929 BGB has a special meaning. German law insists on the "principle of distinction (*Trennungsprinzip*)", which differentiates between the obligational legal act (including obligational contracts) and the proprietary legal act (including proprietary contracts).[405] The consent in this provision refers to a proprietary agreement.[406] In most situations, this proprietary agreement is implicit.[407] Where there is not any express proprietary agreement, an interpretation on the basis of the circumstances involved is necessary.[408] In general, when the obligational contract has taken effect, delivery usually implies that there is a proprietary agreement concerning the transfer of ownership.[409] The proprietary agreement must be made with respect to a specific object, which is required by the principle of specificity.

„Die Bestimmtheit muss im Zeitpunkt der Einigung gegeben sein […] und so beschaffen sein, dass jeder mit den Vereinbarungen vertraute Dritte als objektiver Betrachter dies übereignete Sache ohne Schwierigkeiten von anderen unterscheiden kann [...]."[410]

The requirement of specificity finds its root in the nature of ownership. As a kind of property right, ownership can only exist on a specific thing. It is impossible to transfer the ownership of unidentified things. However, this requirement is never an obstacle to the valid creation of obligational contracts.

B Special Cases

The requirement of delivery is tempered by three special forms of invisible delivery in German law: *traditio brevi manu* (sentence 2 of § 929 BGB), *traditio per constitutum possessorium* (§ 930 BGB), and *traditio longa manu* (§ 931 BGB).[411] These three forms of invisible delivery constitute an exception to

404 Füller 2006, p. 299. English translation: "*Legislators think that delivery has a function to guarantee that rights and possession are obtained concurrently: 'In the law of immovable property, the principle of registration guarantees the correctness of the land register, and the traditio principle in the law of movable property serves for a similar purpose by preventing the divergence between possession and rights […]'.*"

405 Wolf and Wellenhofer 2011, p. 19.

406 Wolf and Wellenhofer 2011, p. 77.

407 Van Vliet 2000, p. 31.

408 Wolf and Wellenhofer 2011, p. 77; Van Vliet 2000, p. 31.

409 Baur and Stürner 2009, p. 639.

410 Wolf and Wellenhofer 2011, p. 78. English translation: "*The specificity must be realized at the time of the agreement [...] and should be such that every third party knowing the agreement can, as an objective observer, distinguish without difficulty the object from other objects […].*"

411 Baur and Stürner 2009, p. 651.

the requirement of delivery, once this requirement is interpreted strictly.[412] For comprehensiveness, this part also discusses another special case: "*Geheißerwerb* (acquisition at the behest)".

B1: Traditio Brevi Manu

Traditio brevi manu occurs where the transferee has already acquired possession of the object.[413] In this situation, ownership passes to the possessor (buyer) when the contract of transfer comes into effect.[414] Due to this delivery, the transferee turns from a "limited-right possessor (*Fremdbesitzer*)" to be an "ownership possessor (*Eigenbesitzer*)".[415] In this sense, this delivery is, in essence, a change of the possessory intention: from the limited-right purpose to the ownership purpose. At the same time, the transferor loses indirect possession, because the transferee no longer has an intention to control the object for the transferor.[416] However, it should be noted that *traditio brevi manu* does not necessarily involve a shift of indirect possession. The transferor may completely lose possession. For instance, an owner transfers his bicycle stolen by a thief to this thief. In this very situation, the owner does not have any possession to alienate.

In general, *traditio brevi manu* is often treated as an exception to the requirement of delivery in the German literature.[417] Law recognizes this delivery for the purpose of simplification: since the process of publicity precedes the alienation of ownership, there is neither need nor possibility to carry out visible delivery.[418] In essence, *traditio brevi manu* is a method to transfer ownership merely on the ground of the parties' consent, thereby falling under the consensual system.[419] It does not produce any effect of publicity, and third parties are not made aware of the transfer.

> „*Die verbreitete Gegenansicht deutet den Eigentumswechsel nach § 929 Satz 2 als reinen Konsensualakt, der für dritte nicht erkennbar sei.*"[420]

412 Baur and Stürner 2009, p. 637.

413 McGuire 2008, p. 100.

414 § 929 BGB: „*[...] Ist der Erwerber im Besitz der Sache, so genügt die Einigung über den Übergang des Eigentums.*" English translation: § 929 BGB:" *[...] If the acquirer is in possession of the thing, agreement on the transfer of the ownership suffices.*"

415 Baur and Stürner 2009, p. 644; Füller 2006, p. 317.

416 Baur and Stürner 2009, p. 80.

417 Brehm and Berger 2014, p. 434.

418 Baur and Stürner 2009, p. 644.

419 Füller 2006, p. 302; McGuire 2008, p. 100.

420 Füller 2006, p. 317. English translation: "*The widespread opposite view holds that the transfer of ownership according to sentence 2 of § 929 is a purely consensual deed, which is not observable to third parties.*"

To add a word, this delivery rectifies, to some extent, the existing divergence between possession and ownership. This is because it is often associated with the outcome that the direct possessor acquires ownership. However, *traditio brevi manu* cannot indicate when ownership is transferred.[421]

B2: Traditio per Constitutum Possessorium

Traditio per constitutum possessorium takes place in the situation where the transferor remains in possession of the subject matter but agrees to hold it for the transferee.[422] This delivery is provided for in § 930 BGB.[423] It is the converse to *traditio brevi manu*. In practice, *traditio per constitutum possessorium* often occurs in the "security transfer (*Sicherungsübereignung*)".[424] It usually allows the seller to retain direct possession by only transferring indirect possession to the buyer.[425] Therefore, the concept of indirect possession is deemed as necessary for *traditio per constitutum possessorium*.[426] However, this delivery can also arise in the situation where the transferor only has indirect possession: it suffices that the transferor has indirect possession and agrees to hold the object for the transferee.[427] In this very situation, direct possession is held by a third party, the transferee acquires an upper indirect possession, and the transferor retains a lower indirect possession. This leads to multilayer indirect possession.[428]

However, indirect possession is in essence a legal relationship between the direct possessor and the indirect possessor. The shift of indirect possession does not make the transfer of ownership visible. Like *traditio brevi manu*, this delivery is also a change of the possessory intention: the transferor turns from an "ownership possessor (*Eigenbesitzer*)" to be a "limited-right possessor (*Fremdbesitzer*)".[429] Therefore, *traditio per constitutum possessorium* falls short of the principle of publicity and has no difference from the consensual system in the aspect of publicity.[430] Moreover, different from *traditio brevi manu*, this form of delivery usually causes a divergence of ownership from direct possession.

421 Quantz 2005, p. 54.
422 McGuire 2008, p. 101.
423 § 930 BGB: „*Ist der Eigentümer im Besitz der Sache, so kann die Übergabe dadurch ersetzt werden, dass zwischen ihm und dem Erwerber ein Rechtsverhältnis vereinbart wird, vermöge dessen der Erwerber den mittelbaren Besitz erlangt.*" English translation: § 930 BGB: "*If the owner is in possession of the thing, the delivery may be replaced by a legal relationship being agreed between the owner and the acquirer by which the acquirer obtains indirect possession.*"
424 Brehm and Berger 2014, p. 436.
425 McGuire 2008, p. 101.
426 Baur and Stürner 2009, p. 74.
427 Brehm and Berger 2014, p. 435.
428 Brehm and Berger 2014, p. 50.
429 Füller 2006, p. 319.
430 McGuire 2008, p. 104; Füller 2006, p. 319; Quantz 2005, p. 56.

B3: Traditio Longa Manu

In the case of *traditio longa manu*, visible delivery is substituted by an assignment of the transferor's claim of recovery.[431] This form of invisible delivery is recognized by § 931 BGB.[432] This often occurs in the situation where a third party is in actual possession of the object for the transferor, and the transferor only has indirect possession. To transfer ownership, indirect possession has to be given up to the buyer by assigning the claim of recovery.[433] If the transferor entirely loses possession, such as in the case of a stolen or lost bicycle, just assignment of the claim of recovery suffices.[434]

Like the two forms of invisible delivery discussed above, *traditio longa manu* also fails to make the process of transfer visible to third parties.

> *„Nicht nur in diesem eher exotischen Fall, sondern auch im Regelfall, bei dem ein Anspruch aus dem Besitzmittlungsverhältnis abgetreten wird, ist der Eigentumswechsel nicht erkennbar."*[435]

This delivery involves a change of the direct possessor's possessory intention: from holding the object for the transferor to holding the object for the transferee. The transferor does not have direct possession as an outward mark. In essence, *traditio longa manu* amounts to the assignment of a right, namely the claim of recovery against the direct possessor. The assignment cannot make the transfer of corporeal movables visible.[436] In the process of transfer, it is the direct possessor who holds actual possession. In this sense, *traditio longa manu* has nothing different from the consensual system in the aspect of publicity.[437]

B4: Geheißerwerb

In brief, *Geheißerwerb* refers to *"acquisition at the behest"*.[438] This usually occurs in the situation where the transferor does not have possession yet. For example, A lost his bicycle which is found by B, and A transfers this bicycle to C and requests B to deliver it to C, and B does so. In this situation, A has neither direct possession nor indirect possession, and C acquires

---

431 McGuire 2008, p. 104.

432 § 931 BGB: *„Ist ein Dritter im Besitz der Sache, so kann die Übergabe dadurch ersetzt werden, dass der Eigentümer dem Erwerber den Anspruch auf Herausgabe der Sache abtritt."* English translation: § 931 BGB: *"If a third party is in possession of the thing, delivery may be replaced by the owner assigning to the acquirer the claim to delivery of the thing."*

433 Wolf and Wellenhofer 2011, p. 91.

434 McGuire 2008, p. 104.

435 Füller 2006, p. 322. English translation: *"Not only in rare cases, but also in ordinary cases, the change of ownership cannot be made visible by an assignment of the claim out of the intermediary relationship of possession."*

436 Quantz 2005, p. 54.

437 Füller 2006, p. 321.

438 McGuire 2008, p. 111.

ownership and possession from A and B respectively.[439] *Geheißerwerb* can also arise in the situation known as the "chain transfer". For example, A sells a bicycle to B, and B immediately sells this bicycle to C and asks A to deliver it to C. In this situation, B never acquires possession, and C obtains ownership and possession from B and A respectively.[440]

In general, it is held that *Geheißerwerb* is regulated under § 929 BGB because it leads to the outcome that the transferee obtains actual possession, though not from the transferor.[441] However, *Geheißerwerb* has a feature: possession and ownership are not acquired from the same person. The transferee acquires ownership from the transferor, while possession is obtained from a third party. *Geheißerwerb* should not be confused with *traditio longa manu*. In the former situation, the transferor has no intermediary relationship with the possessor, a third party who abides by the transferor's instruction and gives up possession to the transferee designated.[442] With respect to *Geheißerwerb*, a question arises as to whether this acquisition satisfies the requirement of delivery. It is not, because there is no intermediary relationship between the transferor and the direct possessor (the possessory intermediary).[443] However, opponents claim that *Geheißerwerb* is able to show the intention of transferring ownership, thereby fulfilling the requirement of delivery.[444] This theoretical debate does not have much practical significance, however. The BGH has recognized *Geheißerwerb* as an adequate cause for the transfer of ownership for the sake of commercial convenience.[445]

3.4.2.3 Dutch Law

A A Traditio *System*

In Dutch law, "delivery (*levering*)" is necessary for the transfer of property.[446] According to the prevailing opinion, delivery is a legal act comprised of two elements: the "proprietary agreement (*goederenrechtlijke overeenkomst*)" and the "act of delivery (*leveringshandeling*)".[447] The latter manifests

439 Baur and Stürner 2009, p. 642.
440 Baur and Stürner 2009, p. 642-643; Brehm and Berger 2014, p. 429.
441 Brehm and Berger 2014, p. 428.
442 Brehm and Berger 2014, p. 428. In the case of the transfer of a lost bicycle, if the owner only transfers the claim of recovery to the transferee, then *traditio longa manu* takes place. However, if the owner asks the finder to give up the bicycle to the transferee, and the finder does so, then *Geheißerwerb* occurs.
443 Baur and Stürner 2009, p. 643.
444 Brehm and Berger 2014, p. 432.
445 Wolf and Wellenhofer 2011, p. 96-97.
446 Art. 3:84 (1) BW: "*Voor overdracht van een goed wordt vereist een levering krachtens geldige titel, verricht door hem die bevoegd is over het goed te beschikken.*" English translation: Art. 3:84 (1) BW: "*Transfer of property requires delivery pursuant to a valid title by the person who has the right to dispose of the property.*"
447 Snijders and Rank-Berenschot 2017, p. 288; Salomons 2008 (2), p. 60.

the proprietary agreement.[448] Like German law, Dutch law recognizes a distinction between obligational contracts and proprietary contracts.[449] In general, the form of delivery varies from one kind of property to another kind of property.

> *"In de tweede plaats moet deze wilsovereenstemming blijken uit een leveringshandeling waarvoor de wet verschillende vormen voorschrijft al naar gelang de aard van het over te dragen goed (de leveringsformaliteit)."*[450]

For the transfer of corporeal movables, Dutch law has a requirement of delivery. In principle, ownership of a corporeal movable does not pass to the acquirer until delivery occurs. As pointed out by Dutch lawyers, there is an inclination of having possession (*bezit*) and ownership held in the hands of the same person in Dutch law.[451] Art. 3:90 BW stipulates that delivery of movable things requires "provision of possession (*bezitsverschaffing*)".[452] Here, it is worthwhile noting that "transfer of possession (*overdracht van bezit*)" should be distinguished from the provision of possession: the former only arises in the situation where the transferor has possession, while the latter can even take place when the transferor is only a "detentor (*houder*)" having no possession.[453] This distinction is an outcome of the differentiation between possession and detention in Dutch law.

Moreover, Dutch law accepts the principle of specificity, which means that ownership of unidentified corporeal movables cannot be transferred.[454] This requirement is satisfied through delivery. Thus, delivery has a function of individualization.[455] Because of the principle of specificity, the rule of bulk ownership, which has been accepted by English law (see 3.4.2.1.B), is difficult to reconcile with Dutch law.[456]

In most situations, provision of possession requires a shift of "actual control (*feitelijke macht*)" from the transferor to the transferee. This delivery is treated as *traditio* in the strict sense (*traditio vera*),[457] which has been

---

448 Suijling 1940, p. 278; Reehuis 2004, p. 1.

449 Van Vliet 2000, p. 141.

450 Asser/Bartels & Van Mierlo 2013, nr. 219. English translation: *"In the second place, the consensus of will should be shown by the act of delivery, and law prescribes different types of delivery according to the nature of the property (the formality of delivery)."*

451 Asser/Bartels & Van Mierlo 2013, nr. 114.

452 Art. 90 (1) BW: *"De levering vereist voor de overdracht van roerende zaken, niet-registergoederen, die in de macht van de vervreemder zijn, geschiedt door aan de verkrijger het bezit der zaak te verschaffen."* English translation: Art. 90 (1) BW: *"Delivery required for the transfer of movable things which are non-registerable property and which are under the control of the alienator is made by giving possession of the thing to the acquirer."*

453 Snijders and Rank-Berenschot 2017, p. 114.

454 Van Vliet 2000, p. 139.

455 Snijders and Rank-Berenschot 2017, p. 120.

456 Van Vliet 2010, p. 272.

457 Van Vliet 2010, p. 141.

prescribed by art. 3:114 BW.[458] It should be noted that this provision covers handing over the key to the house where the subject matter is stored.[459] In addition to the provision of actual control, there are three forms of invisible delivery: *traditio per constitutum possessorium*, *traditio brevi manu*, and *traditio longa manu*.[460] Pursuant to art. 3:115 BW, these three forms of invisible delivery are in essence a "mutual declaration (*tweezijdige verklaring*)" which does not involve any change of control.[461] As a result, what is decisive for delivery is not provision of actual control, but "provision of a right to actual control (*verschaffen van recht op heerschappij*)".[462]

B Special Cases

Before further introducing these forms of invisible delivery, it is necessary to mention that the distinction between "possession (*bezit*)" and "detention (*houderschap*)" is important for understanding delivery in Dutch law. In general, this distinction implies two things: (1) shift of actual control does not necessarily trigger the transfer of possession, and this shift might lead to acquisition of detention only; and (2) with respect to the question whether possession is acquired, the decisive factor is whether the transacting parties have an intention to transfer or provide possession.[463]

B1: Traditio per Constitutum Possessorium

Traditio per constitutum possessorium occurs where the transferor agrees to hold the subject matter for the transferee.[464] Under this delivery, actual control is still in the hands of the transferor, and what changes is merely the transferor's intention: changing from a possessor to be a detentor.[465] This is the reason why *traditio per constitutum possessorium* is often called the "declaration of detention (*houderschapsverklaring*)".[466]

Since the change of the transferor's intention is invisible to third parties, *traditio per constitutum possessorium* is unable to show the process of transfer to third parties.

---

458 Art. 3:114 BW: "*Een bezitter draagt zijn bezit over door de verkrijger in staat te stellen die macht uit te oefenen, die hij zelf over het goed kon uitoefenen.*" English translation: Art. 3:114 BW: "*A possessor transfers his possession by enabling the acquirer to exercise such control over the property as he himself was able to exercise over it.*"

459 Snijders and Rank-Berenschot 2017, p. 115.

460 Reehuis 2004, p. 47-53.

461 Art. 3:115 BW: "*Voor de overdracht van het bezit is een tweezijdige verklaring zonder feitelijke handeling voldoende [...].*" English translation: Art. 3:115 BW: "*A bilateral declaration without further action is sufficient for the transfer of possession [...].*"

462 Mijnssen and Schut 1991, p. 88.

463 Rank-Berenschot 2012, p. 55; Nieuwenhuis 1980, p. 30-32.

464 Art. 3:115 (a) BW: "*[...] wanneer de vervreemder de zaak bezit en hij haar krachtens een bij de levering gemaakt beding voortaan voor de verkrijger houdt [...].*" English translation: Art. 3:115 (a) BW: "*[...] where the alienator possesses the thing and henceforth holds it for the acquirer by virtue of a stipulation made at the time of delivery [...].*"

465 Rank-Berenschot 2012, p. 62.

466 Reehuis 2004, p. 48.

> *"Aangezien een levering constituto possessorio zich slechts tussen partijen afspeelt, blijft de vervreemder in staat tegenover anderen te doen alsof niets is veranderd. Aldus is het voor derden niet kenbaar dat en controleerbaar of het bezit is overgegaan. Was de vervreemder bezitter, dan kan hij zich tegenover anderen nog steeds als bezitter gedragen."*[467]

As a result, transfer of ownership in the way of *traditio per constitutum possessorium* has no difference from the consensual system in the aspect of publicity.[468] This transfer might mislead creditors of the transferor.[469]

B2: Traditio Brevi Manu

Traditio brevi manu occurs where the transferee already controls the object.[470] As the transferee is in actual control of the object, there is neither need nor possibility of visible delivery. In essence, *traditio brevi manu* is a bilateral declaration between the transferor and the transferee. It causes a change of the former's intention: changing from a detentor to be a possessor.[471]

> *"Deze wijze van overdracht vormt het spiegelbeeld van de overdracht per constitutum possessorium. Wordt in dat geval de bezitter tot houder, bij traditio brevi manu geldt kort samengevat het omgekeerde: de houder wordt bezitter."*[472]

Therefore, this delivery cannot make the process of transfer visible to third parties. Nevertheless, some Dutch scholars say that *traditio brevi manu* has a stronger publicity effect than *traditio per constitutum possessorium*.[473] This is because the consequence of *traditio brevi manu* is usually that ownership and possession are in the hands of the same person (namely the transferee), and ownership begins to have an outward mark.[474] However, the transferee does not necessarily acquire direct possession. The transferee may be an indirect detentor before the completion of *traditio brevi manu*, and it is a third party who is in actual control of the object.[475] In this very case, it is still

467 Reehuis 2004, p. 48. English translation: "*On account of the fact that constitutum possessorium only occurs between the parties, there seem to be no changes to the state of transferor in relation to others. Therefore, whether possession shifts is invisible to third parties. If the transferor is a possessor, then he can still behave as a possessor in relation to others.*"

468 Pitlo and Bolweg 1972, p. 79.

469 Pitlo and Bolweg 1972, p. 79; Snijders and Rank-Berenschot 2017, p. 294.

470 Art. 3:115 (b) BW: "*[...] wanneer de verkrijger houder van de zaak voor de vervreemder was [...].*" English translation: Art. 3:115 (b) BW: "*[...] where the acquirer was detentor of the thing for the alienator [...].*"

471 Snijders and Rank-Berenschot 2017, p. 116; Mijnssen and Schut 1991, p. 96.

472 Rank-Berenschot 2012, p. 64. English translation: "*This method of transferring possession forms a reflection to constitutum possessorium. In the latter situation, the possessor becomes a detentor, while traditio brevi manu gives rise to an opposite consequence: the detentor becomes a possessor.*"

473 Reehuis 2004, p. 52.

474 Pitlo and Bolweg 1972, p. 78.

475 Rank-Berenschot 2012, p. 65.

difficult to say that *traditio brevi manu* has a stronger effect of publicity than *traditio per constitutum possessorium.*

B3: Traditio Longa Manu

Traditio longa manu is a form of delivery used when the object is in the actual control of a third party.[476] As the object is controlled by a third party, this invisible delivery is also no more than a mutual declaration. However, different from the other two forms of invisible delivery, *traditio longa manu* does not complete until the third party acknowledges the transfer or obtains a notification from the transacting parties, as prescribed by art. 3:115 (c) BW. In the absence of any notification or acknowledgment, it is difficult to say that the transferee obtains factual control of the thing involved.[477]

However, this does not change the fact that *traditio longa manu* only means the third party, who initially holds the object for the transferor, changes to hold the object for the transferee.[478] In this sense, this delivery is also only a change of the intention.

> *"Kort samengevat: de houder voor A (vervreemder) wordt houder voor B (verkrijger). Men denke aan een veem dat goederen voor de vervreemder en, na de overdracht, voor de verkrijger in bewaring heeft."*[479]

In general, as an invisible change of the third party's intention, *traditio longa manu* cannot make the transfer visible. However, some scholars claim that this delivery has a stronger publicity effect than *traditio per constitutum possessorium.*[480] Different from visible delivery, the simplest and the most robust way to show the intention of transferring ownership, *traditio longa manu* realizes the effect of publicity through the actual control by a third party.

> *"Die legitimatie is uiteraard het eenvoudigste en het sterkst bij direct bezit, wanneer de rechthebbende de zaak feitelijk onder zich heft [...]. In die gevallen is de verkrijger voor zijn legitimatie afhankelijk van de medewerking van [...] de derde-houder."*[481]

---

476 Art. 3:115 (c) BW: "*[...] wanneer een derde voor de vervreemder de zaak hield, en haar na de overdracht voor de ontvanger houdt. In dit geval gaat het bezit niet over voordat de derde de overdracht heeft erkend, dan wel de vervreemder of de verkrijger de overdracht aan hem heeft medegedeeld.*" English translation: Art. 3:115 (c) BW: "*[...] where a third party held the thing for the alienator and holds it for the recipient after the transfer. In this event possession does not pass until the third party has acknowledged the transfer or has been notified of it by the alienator or acquirer.*"

477 Rank-Berenschot 2012, p. 67.

478 Pitlo and Bolweg 1972, p. 80-81; Mijnssen and Schut 1991, p. 102.

479 Rank-Berenschot 2012, p. 66. English translation: "*Briefly speaking, the detentor for A (transferor) becomes a detentor for B (acquirer). For example, a warehouseman who keeps the goods for the transferor begins to keep the goods for the acquirer after the transfer.*"

480 Reehuis 2004, p. 53.

481 Rank-Berenschot 2012, p. 57. English translation: "*The legitimation is for sure the simplest and strongest in the case of direct possession, where the entitled controls factually the thing [...]. In these cases, the acquirer's legitimation is dependent on the co-operation of [...] the detentor as a third party.*"

B4: Levering bij Akte

In addition to the three forms of invisible delivery, we also need to be cognizant of art. 3:95 BW.[482] This provision applies where the transferor has neither direct possession nor indirect possession. For example, the corporeal movable transferred by the owner is a lost thing or a thing stolen by others. As the owner has legal ownership, there is no reason to prohibit this person from disposing of the thing. According to art. 3:95 BW, the owner can deliver the thing through a "deed (*akte*)" which is known as "delivery by deed (*levering bij akte*)".[483] Because of the principle of specificity, the deed has to specify the object which is intended to be transferred.[484]

In essence, as an exception to the requirement of delivery, delivery by deed is either an agreement bilaterally made by the transacting parties or a declaration unilaterally made by the transferor.[485] In Dutch law, it is an independent method of transfer, being distinguished from *traditio longa manu*.[486] In this aspect, Dutch law and German law differ. In German law, *traditio longa manu* (§ 931 BGB) can apply to the situation where the transferor does not have any possession and only alienates the claim of recovery to the transferee.

3.4.2.4 *Comparative and Conclusive Analysis*

Based on the preceding introduction, it is easy to find that there is a general distinction between the consensual system (English law) and the translative system (German law and Dutch law). Under the consensual system, delivery is not necessary for the transfer of ownership. In contrast, the translative system includes a requirement of delivery, which means that ownership will not be alienated until delivery takes place. However, this distinction should not be overstated on account of the recognition of various forms of invisible delivery. In this part, we also discuss the question whether the principle of publicity is, on the basis of delivery, tenable for the transfer of corporeal movables.

A Significant Similarities

In general, both systems allow parties to transfer ownership without affecting actual possession. In English law, the fundamental rule is that parties can decide the moment when ownership of corporeal movables passes.[487]

482 Art. 3:95 BW: "*Buiten de in de artikelen 89-94 geregelde gevallen en behoudens het in de artikelen 96 en 98 bepaalde, worden goederen geleverd door een daartoe bestemde akte.*" English translation: Art. 3:95 BW: "*In cases other than those provided for in Articles 89-94 and without prejudice to Articles 96 and 98, property is delivered by an appropriate deed.*"

483 Asser/Bartels & Van Mierlo 2013, nr. 227; Brahn 1992, p. 26.

484 Reehuis 2004, p. 105.

485 Van Vliet 2000, p. 144; Reehuis 2004, p. 105.

486 Van Vliet 2000, p. 142-143.

487 S. 17 (1) SGA: "*Where there is a contract for the sale of specific or ascertained goods the property in them is transferred to the buyer at such time as the parties to the contract intend it to be transferred.*"

In German law and Dutch law, a similar consequence can be realized by invisible delivery, especially *traditio per constitutum possessorium* and *traditio brevi manu*. Under *traditio brevi manu*, visible delivery precedes the transfer of ownership. This delivery often occurs in the situation of reservation of ownership, where the transferee acquires actual possession in advance and gains ownership when the condition agreed is satisfied. By *traditio per constitutum possessorium*, the transfer of ownership can precede the shift of actual control. This form of invisible delivery often occurs in the situation of the security transfer of ownership. Because of these two forms of delivery, direct possession can be obtained by the transferee before or after the transfer of ownership. In sum, just as under the consensual system, it is also possible to determine the fate of possession and that of ownership separately under the *traditio* system.

As has been argued, indirect possession is merely a legal relationship between the indirect possessor and the direct possessor (see 3.2.2). Invisible delivery is no more than a bilateral declaration involving a change of the possessory intention (see 3.4.2.2.B and 3.4.2.3.B) and does not affect direct possession. In this aspect, invisible delivery and the consensual system do not differ substantially.[488] In fact, recognition of invisible delivery is only to maintain the *traditio* system in a formal sense, which has been shown above (see 3.2.2.3). Invisible delivery is also known as "fictional delivery (*traditio ficta*)" by some scholars.

> *"In the case of* traditio ficta *the transfer of ownership is brought about by mere agreement without any physical act being needed, a striking similarity between the consensual and tradition system."*[489]

In the line of this viewpoint, invisible delivery is a fiction (*ficta*).[490] Regardless of whether the viewpoint is correct, the recognition of invisible delivery is of great importance for commercial transactions under a *traditio* system.[491]

488 In the preceding introduction, we have shown that Dutch law prescribes "delivery by deed (*levering bij akte*)" as an independent way of the transfer of ownership. This special delivery is not covered by *traditio longa manu* in Dutch law, because the transferor has neither direct possession nor indirect possession. In contrast, German law includes *levering bij akte* in *traditio longa manu* and regulates both forms of delivery in the same provision (§ 931 BGB). As a result, *traditio longa manu* perhaps involves no transfer of indirect possession in German law. This unitary treatment implies that the transfer of indirect possession is no more than the consent concerning the transfer of a claim of recovery.

489 Van Vliet 2010, p. 201.

490 In the viewpoint of some scholars, fictional delivery is a "substitute (*surrogaat*)" for delivery. It is not delivery but can substitute delivery. See Pitlo and Bolweg 1972, p. 78; Brehm and Berger 2014, p. 435.

491 Nieuwenhuis 1980, p. 31.

> *"The general opinion remains as before—that normal or proper traditio involves physical act but that, by a fiction, other acts can have the same effect, or the same effect can be realized without the intervention of any physical act at all."*[492]

Even under German law and Dutch law which construct a *traditio* system, it is the parties' autonomy that constitutes the starting point. The requirement of delivery never precludes parties from determining the date on which ownership passes to the transferee. Therefore, the real difference between the *traditio* system and the consensual system lies in the default rule: whether delivery is necessary when parties are silent on the date of transfer of ownership. Delivery is not necessary under English law, while it is essential under both German law and Dutch law.[493]

B Publicity Effect of Delivery

In general, the principle of publicity is marginalized in the transfer of corporeal movables.[494] The transfer is not clearly shown to third parties. This fact can be explained from two aspects: one is that invisible delivery has no publicity effect, and the other is that visible delivery only has an abstract effect of publicity.

Invisible delivery cannot make the transfer of ownership visible for third parties. Usually, invisible delivery involves a shift of indirect possession, and direct possession remains in the hands of the transferor or a third party. Indirect possession is a hidden relationship between the direct possessor and the indirect possessor. This determines that invisible delivery has no effect of publicity.[495] Invisible delivery is treated as a "bilateral declaration (*tweezijdige verklaring*)" in Dutch law (art. 3:115 BW). In Roman law, both *traditio brevi manu* and *traditio per constitutum possessorium* imply that "bare will (*nuda voluntas*)" suffices for transferring ownership.[496] It only involves a change of the possessory intention, which is invisible to third parties. Publicity is to provide proprietary information to third parties, addressing the problem of information asymmetry. However, invisible delivery is a hidden process. Thus, it cannot convey any proprietary information to third parties. This is one reason why invisible delivery, in essence, has nothing different from the consensual system in the aspect of publicity.

492 Gordon 1970, p. 179.

493 On the other hand, some scholars choose to understand the significant similarities from an opposite angle: construing the consensual system as a "hidden" *traditio* system. In their opinions, an agreement concerning transfer of ownership implies that possession is given up to the transferee. In other words, *traditio per constitutum possessorium* occurs on the basis of the implied consent of the two parties. See Sagaert 2014, p. 715.

494 Spath 2010, p. 334.

495 Van Vliet 2000, p. 201.

496 Mousourakis 2012, p. 133.

Different from invisible delivery, visible delivery has an effect of publicity. Direct possession can give rise to physical proximity between the possessor and the thing possessed. Visible delivery is able to alter this physical proximity. For example, if A sells a bicycle to B and directly hands over this bicycle to B, then B becomes the person who has physical proximity with the bicycle. Commonly, delivery is usually completed within a very short period of time and cannot be observed by outsiders. However, the outcome of delivery, namely B's actual control of the bicycle, is visible for outsiders. In this sense, we can say that visible delivery shows the transfer of ownership to third parties. In general, visible delivery ensures that ownership passes together with its outward mark.

However, the publicity effect of visible delivery is abstract and thus ambiguous. This is because direct possession is an abstract and thus ambiguous method of publicity: it only indicates that the possessor has a right to the object possessed (see 3.2.1). Possession is not necessarily associated with the right of ownership.[497] Visible delivery can take place in various situations, and transfer of ownership is merely one amongst these situations. For example, visible delivery might be made to create a right of pledge or to establish a relationship of lease. Therefore, we can only say that visible delivery indicates that the new actual possessor acquires a certain right to the object delivered. To know the details of this right, we have to investigate the underlying relationship, namely the reason why visible delivery occurs.

The recognition of invisible delivery implies that the rationale behind the requirement of delivery is not the effect of publicity.[498] If we hold that the purpose of delivery is to publicize the transfer of corporeal movables, how can we justify invisible delivery?[499] In theory, there is another approach justifying the requirement of delivery. According to this approach, the act of delivery implies that the transferor and transferee have a serious intention to transfer the object.[500] Delivery is a "manifestation of the will of transfer (*Ausdruck des Übereignungswillens*)".[501] With respect to this approach, two points should be noted. One point is that the manifestation only concerns whether the transacting parties do have a will of transfer, while publicity of this will to third parties is another issue.[502] The existence of a will of transfer does not mean that this will is made visible to third parties by possession. The other point is that whether invisible delivery, especially *traditio per constitutum possessorium*, is able to manifest the will of transfer is always a problem. As argued above, invisible delivery is no more than an agreement of transfer and falls short of the principle of publicity.

497 Staudinger/Gutzeit 2012, p. 74.
498 Staudinger/Wiegand 2017, p. 184.
499 Staudinger/Wiegand 2017, p. 184; MüKoBGB/Oechsler 2017, § 929, Rn. 3.
500 Staudinger/Wiegand 2017, p. 184; McFarlane 2008, p. 172.
501 MüKoBGB/Oechsler 2017, § 929, Rn. 3.
502 Füller 2006, p. 303.

3.4.3 *Bona Fide* Acquisition of Corporeal Movables

Traditionally, *bona fide* acquisition is treated as an example that is strongly connected with the publicity effect of possession. Compared with the transfer of ownership discussed above, *bona fide* acquisition more markedly illustrates this effect: the former concerns the acquisition of ownership from the transferor who has the authority to dispose, while the latter means that a third party acquires ownership from the transferor who has no authority of disposal. *Bona fide* acquisition implies that the third party's reliance on possession prevails over the legal position of the original owner. Before starting our discussion, it should be mentioned that *bona fide* acquisition is not confined to the acquisition of ownership of corporeal movables. Other property rights, such as the right of pledge, can also be acquired in this way. However, for the sake of simplicity, the following discussion concerns only *bona fide* acquisition of ownership. The subsequent three parts will introduce English law, German law, and Dutch law respectively. After that, there will be a comparative and concluding analysis. This analysis focuses on the role possession plays in *bona fide* acquisition of ownership.

3.4.3.1 English Law

In English law, the starting point of the system of transfer is the *nemo dat* rule: nobody can transfer more than he or she has.[503] However, there is a list of exceptions in English law. Unlike civil law which usually has a unified system of *bona fide* acquisition, English law has a patchy system consisting of different exceptions to the *nemo dat* rule.[504] These exceptions can be found in both statutory law and case law. Each has a special field of application. With respect to this patchy system, some scholars think that a "*recodification in a statute*" is desirable.[505]

In general, there are five exceptions to the *nemo dat* rule. In this part, we introduce these exceptions. It will be found that *bona fide* acquisition and apparent agency are occasionally mixed in English law. Apparent agency arises in the situation where the principal gives his or her agent an appearance of agency relationship and fails to deny the agent's appearance of authority.[506] Like *bona fide* acquisition, it is also a regime that can provide protection to third parties in good faith. In German law and Dutch law, apparent agency is known as *Anscheinsvollmacht* and *schijnvolmacht* respec-

503 Bridge, Gullifer, McMeel and Worthington 2013, p. 333.
504 Salomons 2011 (2), p. 1066.
505 Bridge, Gullifer, McMeel and Worthington 2013, p. 333.
506 Munday 2010, p. 88-89.

tively.[507] However, English lawyers distinguish apparent agency from *bona fide* acquisition in theory.[508]

A Apparent Authority

Apparent authority is derived from the case law and forms an exception to the *nemo dat* rule. It is used to describe the following situation: "*an owner has by some act indicated to a third party that another is acting with authority on his behalf, or has allowed another to appear as the true owner while dealing with a third party then he will be estopped from denying the title of the third party transferee*".[509] The rule of apparent authority has been absorbed in s. 21 (1) SGA.

> S. 21 (1) SGA: "*Subject to this Act, where goods are sold by a person who is not their owner, and who does not sell them under the authority or with the consent of the owner, the buyer acquires no better title to the goods than the seller had, unless the owner of the goods is by his conduct precluded from denying the seller's authority to sell.*"

In general, s. 21 (1) SGA can apply to two different situations: the apparent authority to be an agent and the apparent authority to be an owner.[510] In the first situation, the seller disposes of the object in the name of and on behalf of the principal, thereby acting as an agent. Therefore, this situation, in fact, concerns apparent agency.[511] In contrast, the seller in the second situation transfers the object in his or her own name, thereby acting as a transferor or an owner. Therefore, the second situation concerns apparent ownership and *bona fide* acquisition. [512] In this research, *bona fide* acquisition is a term confined to the situation of unauthorized disposals: the person who intends to conduct a disposal lacks the authority to dispose. In general, unauthorized disposal and unauthorized agency differ in two aspects. One concerns the name in which the object is disposed of, and the other concerns the person for whose benefit the object is disposed of. For example, where a transferor alienates the object in his own name and for his own benefit, but lacks the authority to transfer, there is an unauthorized disposal; if this transferor alienates the object in another person's name and for the latter's benefit, but lacks the authority to represent the latter, then there is an unauthorized agency. The SGA regulates these two different issues in one provision. Since this part only concerns *bona fide* acquisition, we will

507 Wolf and Neuner 2012, p. 628; Tai 2003, p. 290.

508 Apparent agency is a form of "apparent authority" to be an agent, and *bona fide* acquisition is known as "apparent ownership". In the latter situation, an owner allows another party to appear to have ownership to his property. See Munday 2010, p. 273-274.

509 *Eastern Distributors Ltd v. Goldring* [1957] 2 QB 600, cited from Frisby and Jones 2009, p. 120.

510 Bridge, Gullifer, McMeel and Worthington 2013, p. 354; Bridge 2014, p. 205; Goode 2010, p. 457.

511 Bridge 2014, p. 205.

512 Benjamin 2014, p. 361; Goode 2010, p. 457.

focus on the issue of unauthorized disposal, and unauthorized agency falls outside our discussion.

In the situation of unauthorized disposal, s. 21 (1) SGA is applied restrictively: only giving up possession to the buyer does not give rise to a valid apparent authority.[513] The legal owner must give the buyer an indication on the basis of which the seller can be reasonably treated as having ownership.[514] The form of this indication (such as words or conduct) is immaterial, but the indication must be clear and unequivocal.[515] In practice, apparent authority by an indication of conduct rarely takes place. The legal owner's disconnection with possession alone does not suffice.[516] In other words, the legal owner has to do something more than giving up possession, which can mislead the buyer into the belief that the seller has ownership of the object. The reason why just giving up possession to the seller is not sufficient is that "*possession is consistent with a range of transactions from bailment to outright sale*".[517]

Moreover, giving up possession to the seller is not necessary in some situations. Even though the seller does not have possession in the transaction, the buyer might also be able to acquire ownership of the object. This has been upheld by a landmark judgement. In this case, the buyer successfully acquired ownership due to his reliance on the legal owner's express statement that the seller had ownership.[518] In sum, the seller's possession is neither sufficient nor necessary for the application of the rule of apparent authority.[519]

B Voidable Title

Voidable title refers to the property right acquired on the basis of a voidable contract, a contract that can be rescinded by the transferor.[520] In English law, voidable title remains valid before rescission of the contract. Therefore, title does not return to the transferor in the meantime, and the transferee is entitled to transfer it. [521] When the second transfer takes place prior to the annulment of the first contract, the sub-transferee (as a third party) can acquire the title, provided that he or she acts in good faith with respect to the flaw in the first contract.[522] Transfer of a voidable title often happens in

513 Frisby and Jones 2009, p. 120.
514 Bridge, Gullifer, McMeel and Worthington 2013, p. 356.
515 Bridge, Gullifer, McMeel and Worthington 2013, p. 356-357.
516 Benjamin 2014, p. 362.
517 Bridge 2014, p. 207.
518 *Eastern Distributors Ltd v. Goldring* [1957] 2 QB 600.
519 Benjamin 2014, p. 361.
520 Title is a term having different meanings in property law. It can refer to the legal ground, such as contracts, on which property rights are acquired. On the other hand, this term is also used to mean the property right *per se*, such as voidable title and relativity of title. See Van Erp 2012, p. 47.
521 Bridge, Gullifer, McMeel and Worthington 2013, p. 351.
522 Frisby and Jones 2009, p. 121.

the case of chain contracts. The rule of voidable title has been recognized by the SGA to preclude avoidance of the first contract from affecting subsequent disposals.

> S. 23 SGA: "*When the seller of goods has a voidable title to them, but his title has not been avoided at the time of the sale, the buyer acquires a good title to the goods, provided he buys them in good faith and without notice of the seller's defect of title.*"

Strictly speaking, the voidable title rule falls outside the sphere of *bona fide* acquisition. This is because the transferor in the second transfer has already acquired a legal title from the original owner, though subject to the latter's equitable right of recovery under equity law. The second transfer does not constitute typical unauthorized disposal: firstly, the transferor has a legal title; and secondly, the third party can obtain a voidable title, regardless of whether this party acts in good faith.[523]

For acquiring a fully valid title from the transferor who only has a voidable title, neither possession nor delivery is necessary. The transferor perhaps has no possession of the object in the second transaction. This is because the transferor might acquire a voidable title without obtaining any possession in the first voidable transaction under the consensual system. In principle, parties are entitled to determine the time when ownership passes in English law (see 3.4.2.1). For the same reason, the sub-transferee (as a third party) can acquire a fully valid title despite obtaining no possession.[524] However, the third party must be in good faith. Therefore, this acquisition is a result of the doctrine that equitable title, namely the title owned by the original seller, cannot bind *bona fide* third parties. It has nothing to do with the protection of the third parties' reliance on possession.

> "*It should be noted that s. 23 has no requirement of transfer of possession in relation to either transaction [...]. This is because it is merely an example of the rule that a bona fide purchaser for value takes free of equitable interests, for which there is no requirement of entrustment or transfer of possession.*"[525]

C Mercantile Agency

Mercantile agent is a term used in the Factors Act (1889) (FA). It refers to the person who in the customary course of business has authority "*to sell goods, to consign goods for the purpose of sale, to buy goods or to raise money on the security of goods*".[526] The mercantile agent conducts activities for the

---

523 Bridge, Gullifer, McMeel and Worthington 2013, p. 353.

524 Bridge 2014, p. 198.

525 Bridge, Gullifer, McMeel and Worthington 2013, p. 354.

526 S. 1 (1) FA: "*The expression 'mercantile agent' shall mean a mercantile agent having in the customary course of his business as such agent authority either to sell goods, or to consign goods for the purpose of sale, or to buy goods, or to raise money on the security of goods.*" It is noteworthy that this definition excludes "*servants and employees, carriers, repairers and warehousemen*". See Bridge 2014, p. 217.

benefit of the principal and is subject to the instruction from the principal. In practice, the agent may violate the principal's instructions or exceed the authority. S. 2 (1) FA was enacted to protect the reliance of third parties in this situation.

> S. 2 (1) FA: "*Where a mercantile agent is, with the consent of the owner, in possession of goods or of the documents of title to goods, any sale pledge, or other disposition of the goods, made by him when acting in the ordinary course of business of a mercantile agent, shall, subject to the provisions of this Act, be as valid as if he were expressly authorised by the owner of the goods to make the same; provided that the person taking under the disposition acts in good faith, and has not at the same time of the disposition notice that the person making the disposition has no authority to make the same.*"

This provision may not be invoked unless the following conditions are satisfied. The first condition is that the agent must be in possession of the corporeal movables or the documents of title. Secondly, the agent acquires possession with the consent of the principal, which suggests that stolen things are excluded.[527] Usually, this consent is presumed in the absence of contrary evidence.[528] Thirdly, the transaction happens in the ordinary course of business of a mercantile agent. This means that the disposal must be made "*within business hours, at a proper place of business, and in other respects in the ordinary way in which a mercantile agent would act.*"[529] Lastly, the transferee must act in good faith.

Mercantile agents may transact in their own name or in the name of their principal. Thus, it is irrelevant whether or not their counterparty (the transferee) realizes that they are an owner or an agent.[530] Like the rule of apparent authority, the rule of mercantile agency also includes two different situations: the unauthorized disposal (in the name of the transferor himself) and the unauthorized agency (in the name of the principal). In both situations, it is necessary that the agent is in possession of the object with the principal's consent. S. 2 (1) FA does not mention any requirement of delivery. Thus, it is irrelevant whether the transferee acquires possession of the object.[531] However, the absence of delivery might "color" the conditions mentioned above, in particular the "*ordinary course of business*" and "*good faith*".[532] In other words, delivery of the object is not necessary but is import.

From the preceding introduction, it can be deduced that the rationale behind the rule of mercantile agency is not just about the publicity of possession. Rather, it is an outcome of a comprehensive consideration of various factors.

---

527 Bridge, Gullifer, McMeel and Worthington 2013, p. 361.
528 Benjamin 2014, p. 378.
529 *Oppenheimer v. Attenborough* [1908] 1 KB 221, cited from Bridge, Gullifer, McMeel and Worthington 2013, p. 362.
530 Benjamin 2014, p. 382.
531 Bridge 2014, p. 225.
532 Bridge 2014, p. 225.

"The goods must be entrusted to the mercantile agent in that capacity because the law does not penalise the owner merely because of appearances [...]. Thus, the exception emanated from and extended the existing position of a mercantile agent acting with apparent authority: once the principal entrusted goods to a mercantile agent the law deemed him to have authority to sell or pledge goods in the ordinary course of business and attributed the dispositive act of the agent to the owner of the goods."[533]

D Seller in Possession

As shown above, English law allows ownership to be transferred in the absence of delivery. Therefore, ownership and possession might be held by the transferee and the transferor respectively, which gives rise to a situation known as the seller in possession. Possession retained creates a chance for the seller to dispose of the same corporeal movable to a third party. This might cause a clash between the lawful owner (the transferee) and this third party. This conflict is regulated by s. 24 SGA, a provision prescribing an exception to the *nemo dat* rule.

S. 24 SGA: *"Where a person having sold goods continues or is in possession of the goods, or of the documents of title to the goods, the delivery or transfer by that person, or by a mercantile agent acting for him, of the goods or documents of title under any sale, pledge, or other disposition thereof, to any person receiving the same in good faith and without notice of the previous sale, has the same effect as if the person making the delivery or transfer were expressly authorised by the owner of the goods to make the same."*

According to this provision, the third party in good faith can only acquire ownership when the following requirements are fulfilled. Firstly, s. 24 SGA applies only to the situation where the seller transfers ownership but retains possession. Possession retained by the seller can be actual as well as constructive.[534] The seller does not have to possess the object in person. It suffices that a bailee controls the object for the benefit of the seller. This has been upheld in case law and is generally approved in theory.[535] In practice, a large number of corporeal movables are managed by bailees, which makes it unrealistic to require the seller to possess the object in person.[536] Moreover, s. 1 (2) FA expressly stipulates that constructive possession is also possession.[537] However, some scholars hold that including constructive possession within s. 24 SGA is not totally consistent with the understanding of this provision by the Privy Council: The Privy Council asserts that the

533 Merrett 2008, p. 380.

534 Benjamin 2014, p. 389; Bridge 2014, p. 235.

535 *City Fur Manufacturing Co Ltd v. Fureenbond (Brokers) London Ltd* [1937] 1 All E. R. 937, cited from Benjamin 2014, p. 389.

536 Bridge 2014, p. 235.

537 S. 1 (2) FA: *"Where a mercantile agent has, with the consent of the owner, been in possession of goods or of the documents of title to goods, any sale, pledge, or other disposition, which would have been valid if the consent had continued, shall be valid notwithstanding the determination of the consent: provided that the person taking under the disposition has not at the time thereof notice that the consent has been determined."*

purpose of this provision is to protect the "*innocent purchaser who is deceived by the vendor's physical possession of goods or documents and who is inevitably unaware of legal rights which fetter the apparent power to dispose.*"[538]

Secondly, the object has been delivered to the transferee. In relation to this requirement, the traditional opinion is that there must be a change of direct possession, and constructive delivery is not sufficient.[539] In other words, there should be either "*actual delivery*" of the object or "*actual delivery*" of the documents of title.[540] The latter delivery can make the object deliverable to the transferee. However, this traditional opinion is challenged in a recent case involving double sale and leaseback.[541] In this case, the seller sold and leased back a machine from the purchaser, and the seller remained in possession of this machine, which was not disputable.[542] Afterwards, the seller disposed of the machine to a third party in the same way, namely selling it and then leasing it back. The court held that constructive delivery (i.e. attornment by the transferor to the transferee) was sufficient, and the second buyer could acquire ownership of the machine. According to this judgement, constructive delivery has the same legal effect as actual delivery.[543] This judgement has invoked a fierce debate among English lawyers.[544]

In a word, possession is closely related to the application of s. 24 SGA in two aspects: (1) the seller must be in (actual or constructive) possession of the object; and (2) the object has to be delivered (in an actual or constructive way). However, this does not mean that the rationale behind s. 24 SGA is just protecting the reliance of third parties on possession, nor does it mean that possession is an appearance of ownership. As introduced directly above, both the seller's possession and the way of delivery can be constructive, while constructive possession (indirect possession) and constructive delivery (invisible delivery) have no effect of publicity.

> "*Although section 24 is not based on agency or holding out and thus may not require entrusting of the goods to the seller in the same way, it is clear that the exceptions are based on the conduct of the first buyer rather than simply the expectations of the third party. The conduct of the first buyer on which section 24 is based, is his failure to take delivery of the goods. Because he has not completed his sale he is at risk if the seller makes a completed sale to a second buyer.*"[545]

---

538 *Pacific Motor Auctions Ltd v. Motor Credits Ltd* [1965] A. C. 867, cited from Bridge 2014, p. 235.

539 Benjamin 2014, p. 392.

540 Benjamin 2014, p. 391.

541 *Michael Gerson (Leasing) Ltd v. Wilkinson and State Securities Ltd*, 31 July 2000 [2001] Q. B. 514.

542 McKay 2000, p. 283.

543 McKay 2000, p. 283.

544 McKay 2000, p. 282; Benjamin 2014, p. 392; Bridge 2014, p. 240-241.

545 Merrett 2008, p. 387.

E Buyer in Possession

In English law, individuals have extensive autonomy in deciding the fate of ownership and possession. Thus, a seller may give up possession of the object but reserve the right of ownership. In this situation, there is a divergence between possession and ownership, which might trigger a conflict between the seller (the owner) and third parties. This conflict is regulated by s. 25 SGA (buyer in possession). If the buyer disposes of the object to a third party, then s. 25 (1) SGA can under certain conditions be applied in favor of this third party.

> S. 25 (1) SGA: "*Where a person having bought or agreed to buy good obtains, with the consent of the seller, possession of the goods or the documents of title to the goods, the delivery or transfer by that person, or by a mercantile agent acting for him, of the goods or documents of title, under any sale, pledge, or other disposition thereof, to any person receiving the same in good faith and without notice of any lien or other right of the original seller in respect of the goods, has the same effect as if the person making the delivery or transfer were a mercantile agent in possession of the goods or documents of title with the consent of the owner.*"

This provision has the same legislative purpose as s. 24 SGA (seller in possession): protecting the reliance of third parties in good faith and promoting the certainty of transactions. It can be easily observed that the two provisions regulate two similar divergences between possession and ownership: s. 24 SGA applies where ownership is transferred in the absence of delivery, while s. 25 SGA applies where possession is transferred in the absence of alienation of ownership. As these two provisions apply to similar situations, they have similar requirements.

First of all, the transferor, who is a buyer in the previous sale, must be in possession of the object. The transferor's possession is often actual but can be constructive. It suffices that a bailee controls the object for the transferor, and the transferee only acquires constructive possession through attornment.[546] The second requirement is delivery of the object. In relation to this requirement, a question is whether delivery can be constructive. The traditional opinion is that the delivery under s. 25 SGA must be actual.[547] However, recent judgements, including the judgement mentioned above concerning double sale and leaseback, have shown that constructive delivery is also adequate.[548] With respect to this judicial attitude towards constructive delivery, some scholars provide an explanation based on the

546 *Four Point Garage Ltd v. Carter* [1985] 3 All E. R. 12, cited from Benjamin 2014, p. 398.

547 *Gamer's Motor Centre (Newcastle) Pty Ltd v. Natwest Wholesale Australia Pty Ltd* [1987] 163 C.L.R. 236, cited from Benjamin 2014, p. 401-402; Bridge, Gullifer, McMeel and Worthington 2013, p. 365.

548 *Michael Gerson (Leasing) Ltd v. Wilkinson and State Securities Ltd*, 31 July 2000 [2001] Q. B. 514; *Forsythe International (UK) Ltd v. Silver Shipping Co Ltd* [1993] 2 Lloyd's Rep. 268, cited from Benjamin 2014, p. 402.

theory of risk: the owner who entrusts possession to another person should bear the risk of losing ownership to a third party acting in good faith.[549]

F Summary: A Mixed and Patchy System

In sum, there is not any general rule of *bona fide* acquisition in English law. English law has only a mixed and patchy system of exceptions to the *nemo dat* rule. It is mixed because more than one type of issues is regulated under the same provision, such as the rule of apparent authority and the rule of mercantile agency. Not only can these two rules apply to the situation of unauthorized disposal, but also to that of unauthorized agency. This mixture cannot be found in the other exceptional rules. For example, neither the seller in possession nor the buyer in possession is an agent because they dispose of the object in their own name. As to the rule of voidable title, it should be noted that transfer of a voidable title is not a typical unauthorized disposal. In some sense, it is an authorized disposal because the transferor has legal title (ownership), at least in statutory law. As has been mentioned, voidable title only means that the title is subject to an equitable right in equity law (see 3.4.3.1.B).

This system is also patchy because the five exceptional rules can be divided into three categories: apparent agency, *bona fide* acquisition, and authorized disposal. These five rules are applied in different situations and under different conditions. For example, mercantile agency only exists in the situation of commercial agency in the ordinary course of business, seller in possession and buyer in possession only exist where there is a previous transaction, and voidable title requires the existence of a voidable contract. In addition, these five rules also differ in whether and how possession is related. Possession and delivery are neither sufficient nor necessary for the rule of apparent authority and of voidable title. These two elements are partially relevant to the rule of mercantile agency: the agent has to be in possession with the consent of the principal. Possession and delivery have significant importance for the rule of the buyer in possession and that of the seller in possession: the transferor must have possession and then transfer it to the transferee.

3.4.3.2 German Law

Unlike English law, German law has a general system of *bona fide* acquisition of corporeal movables. This system is considered as an outcome of the tradeoff between "the certainty of transactions (*Verkehrssicherheit*)" and the preservation of ownership.[550] For *bona fide* acquisition of corporeal movables, "possession (*Besitz*)" is an important concept. It is usually held that *bona fide* acquisition is rooted in the rationale of possession as an outward

549 Benjamin 2014, p. 401.
550 Baur and Stürner 2009, p. 665; Wieling 2007, p. 117.

appearance of ownership.[551] The discussion below first introduces the conditions under which third parties can acquire ownership from the unauthorized transferor. A further examination of the relevance of possession to this acquisition then follows.

A *General Requirements of* Bona Fide *Acquisition*

Firstly, *bona fide* acquisition cannot be claimed by a third party to obtain stolen or missing things, as expressly stipulated by § 935 (1) BGB.[552] This restriction can be explained from the following perspective: only when the owner voluntarily entrusts possession to another person, can the former be expected to assess the latter's trustworthiness and to bear the associated risk out of *bona fide* acquisition.[553] In the situation of missing and stolen things, the owner loses possession in a way contrary to his or her will. The owner does not contribute to the unauthorized transferor's acquisition of ownership, the appearance of ownership.[554] Thus, the owner's interest in preserving these things needs to be protected in priority.[555] However, it is worthwhile noting that, pursuant to § 935 (2), this restriction does not apply when the missing or stolen thing is money or bearer securities, or when the third party acquires this thing through public auction.[556] The "*interest of society and fluency of legal transactions*" should prevail in these special situations.[557]

Secondly, there must be a legal ground for acquisition. The transferor and the third party must reach a valid agreement but for the lack of the authority to dispose.[558] This agreement has to be a trade transaction because the rules of *bona fide* acquisition are used to facilitate the fluency and security of transactions.[559] Where the third party lacks a legal ground, there is no need to protect the reliance of this person. Therefore, gratuitous acquisition

---

551 Weber 2012, p. 127; Wolf and Wellenhofer 2011, p. 97; Westermann 2011, p. 406.

552 § 935 (1) BGB: *„Der Erwerb des Eigentums auf Grund der §§ 932 bis 934 tritt nicht ein, wenn die Sache dem Eigentümer gestohlen worden, verloren gegangen oder sonst abhandengekommen war. Das Gleiche gilt, falls der Eigentümer nur mittelbarer Besitzer war, dann, wenn die Sache dem Besitzer abhandengekommen war."* English translation: § 935 (1) BGB: "*The acquisition of ownership based on §§ 932 to 934 does not take place, if the thing has been stolen from the owner, became missing or otherwise lost. The same applies, where the owner was only indirect possessor, if the thing was lost by the possessor.*"

553 McGuire 2008, p. 133.

554 Weber 2012, p. 144; Westermann 2011, p. 411.

555 Baur and Stürner 2009, p. 679.

556 § 935 (2) BGB: *„Diese Vorschriften finden keine Anwendung auf Geld oder Inhaberpapiere sowie auf Sachen, die im Wege öffentlicher Versteigerung oder in einer Versteigerung nach § 979 Absatz 1a veräußert werden."* English translation: § 935 (2) BGB: "*These provisions do not apply to money or bearer instruments or to things that are alienated by way of public auction or in an auction pursuant to section 979 (1a).*"

557 McGuire 2008, p. 139.

558 McGuire 2008, p. 141; Baur and Stürner 2009, p. 677.

559 McGuire 2008, p. 140; Baur and Stürner 2009, p. 663.

is excluded: a donee is not entitled to acquire ownership from an unauthorized donor. This requirement is a result of the rules of unjust enrichment (§ 816 BGB).[560]

Thirdly, the transferor is in possession of the object. *Bona fide* acquisition is partially based on possession as an "appearance of rights (*Rechtsschein*)": this appearance misleads the third party to believe that the transferor has lawful ownership.[561] If there is not any outward appearance, then third parties will lose the possibility of acquisition. The transferor's possession can be direct as well as indirect. This is why German lawyers often think that, just like direct possession, indirect possession is also an eligible outward appearance.[562]

Fourthly, the object must be delivered to the third party. It is not disputable that delivery can take the form of visible delivery and *traditio brevi manu*.[563] In the situation of *traditio brevi manu*, the third party must obtain possession from the transferor himself in advance. This extra requirement is to guarantee that the transferor has possession as an outward appearance, and the third party has legitimate reliance on possession.[564] According to § 933 BGB, *traditio per constitutum possessorium* is not a qualified form of delivery here.[565] In other words, only reliance on the transferor's possession does not suffice, and the third party has to acquire complete possession from the transferor.[566] It is possible to acquire ownership from unauthor-

560 McGuire 2008, p. 137. § 816 (1) BGB: *„Trifft ein Nichtberechtigter über einen Gegenstand eine Verfügung, die dem Berechtigten gegenüber wirksam ist, so ist er dem Berechtigten zur Herausgabe des durch die Verfügung Erlangten verpflichtet. Erfolgt die Verfügung unentgeltlich, so trifft die gleiche Verpflichtung denjenigen, welcher auf Grund der Verfügung unmittelbar einen rechtlichen Vorteil erlangt."* English translation: § 816 (1) BGB: *"If an unauthorized person disposes of an object and the decision is effective against the authorized person, then he is obliged to make restitution to the authorized person of what he gains by the disposal. If the disposition is gratuitous, then the same duty applies to a person who as a result of the disposition directly gains a legal advantage."*

561 Baur and Stürner 2009, p. 662; Weber 2012, p. 127.

562 Baur and Stürner 2009, p. 670; Westermann 2011, p. 438.

563 § 932 (1) BGB: *„Durch eine nach § 929 erfolgte Veräußerung wird der Erwerber auch dann Eigentümer, wenn die Sache nicht dem Veräußerer gehört, es sei denn, dass er zu der Zeit, zu der er nach diesen Vorschriften das Eigentum erwerben würde, nicht in gutem Glauben ist. In dem Falle des § 929 Satz 2 gilt dies jedoch nur dann, wenn der Erwerber den Besitz von dem Veräußerer erlangt hatte."* English translation: § 932 (1) BGB: *"As a result of a disposal carried out under section 929, the acquirer becomes the owner even if the thing does not belong to the alienator, unless the acquirer is not in good faith at the time when under these provisions he would acquire ownership. In the case of section 929 sentence 2, however, this applies only if the acquirer had obtained possession from the alienator."*

564 McGuire 2008, p. 144.

565 § 933 BGB: *„Gehört eine nach § 930 veräußerte Sache nicht dem Veräußerer, so wird der Erwerber Eigentümer, wenn ihm die Sache von dem Veräußerer übergeben wird, es sei denn, dass er zu dieser Zeit nicht in gutem Glauben ist."* English translation: § 933 BGB: *"Where a thing alienated under section 930 does not belong to the alienator, the acquirer becomes the owner if the thing is delivered to him by the alienator, unless he is not in good faith at this time."*

566 Baur and Stürner 2009, p. 668.

ized transferors through *traditio longa manu*, provided that the transferor has indirect possession (sentence 1 of § 934 BGB).[567] Therefore, where the transferor completely loses possession and lacks the outward appearance, only an assignment of the claim of recovery is not adequate. In this situation, the third party cannot acquire ownership until he or she obtains possession of the object (sentence 2 of § 934 BGB).[568] In the opinion of some scholars, § 934 BGB implies that indirect possession is a qualified outward appearance of rights and can justify *bona fide* acquisition.[569]

Lastly, the third party must be in good faith: this person does not know that the transferor has no authority to dispose. The state of acting in good faith has to continue throughout the whole process of the transaction.[570] Pursuant to § 932 (2) BGB, if third parties do not know about the defect concerning the authority of disposal because of gross negligence, then they are not acting in good faith.[571] The requirement is an outcome of the purpose of *bona fide* acquisition: protecting the reliance of third parties. This reliance does not exist when third parties know or should have known about the lack of the authority to dispose.

B Possession and Bona Fide *Acquisition*

In general, the importance of possession for *bona fide* acquisition lies in two aspects under German law. The first is that the transferor must have possession as an outward appearance. The other is that the transferee acquires possession from the transferor, and the latter cannot retain any possession. We further clarify these two aspects below.

B1: Possession of the Transferor

The transferor must have possession at the time of delivery. The main justification of this requirement is that the transferor's possession is an outward appearance of ownership, which has been pointed out by the BGH.

567 § 934 BGB: „*Gehört eine nach § 931 veräußerte Sache nicht dem Veräußerer, so wird der Erwerber, wenn der Veräußerer mittelbarer Besitzer der Sache ist, mit der Abtretung des Anspruchs [...].*" English translation: § 934 BGB: "*Where a thing alienated under section 931 does not belong to the alienator, the acquirer becomes owner, if the alienator is the indirect possessor of the thing, on the assignment of the claim [...].*"

568 § 934 BGB: „*[...] anderenfalls dann Eigentümer, wenn er den Besitz der Sache von dem Dritten erlangt, es sei denn, dass er zur Zeit der Abtretung oder des Besitzerwerbs nicht in gutem Glauben ist.*" English translation: § 934 BGB: "*[...] or otherwise when the acquirer obtains the possession of the thing from the third party, unless at the time of the assignment or the acquisition of possession he is not in good faith.*"

569 Baur and Stürner 2009, p. 670; Weber 2012, p. 132.

570 McGuire 2008, p. 149.

571 § 932 (2) BGB: „*Der Erwerber ist nicht in gutem Glauben, wenn ihm bekannt oder infolge grober Fahrlässigkeit unbekannt ist, dass die Sache nicht dem Veräußerer gehört.*" English translation: § 932 (2) BGB: "*The acquirer is not in good faith if he is aware, or as a result of gross negligence he is not aware, that the thing does not belong to the alienator.*"

> *"Voraussetzung für den gutgläubigen Erwerb des Eigentums an einer beweglichen Sache ist neben dem guten Gläubigen der auf dem Besitz beruhende Rechtsschein."*[572]

The reliance of third parties will become groundless if the unauthorized transferor has no possession. This is said to be a reason why sentence 2 of § 934 BGB stipulates that when the transferor has no possession and only assigns a claim of recovery, the third party cannot acquire ownership until he or she obtains possession.[573]

> *"As the transferor lacks any kind of legitimizing appearance, neither transfer by means of assignment of the (non-existent) claim for recovery nor by mere agreement will suffice to protect the transferee."*[574]

The transferor's possession can be indirect since *traditio longa manu* is an eligible form of delivery. Pursuant to sentence 1 of § 934 BGB, *bona fide* acquisition is possible when the unauthorized transferor provides the transferee with indirect possession by assigning a claim of recovery. As a result, when the object is directly held by a third party (a limited-right possessor), the transferor's indirect possession can also be treated as an eligible outward appearance.[575]

B2: Delivery to the Transferee

Delivery must be conducted: the transferor has to provide possession of the corporeal movable to the transferee in good faith. According to German lawyers, *bona fide* acquisition is not only rooted in possession as an outward appearance of ownership, but also in the transferor's "ability to provide possession (*Besitzverschaffungsmacht*)".[576]

However, nor every form of delivery is eligible.[577] As shown above, delivery can be actual and fictional (*traditio brevi manu* and *traditio longa manu*), but *traditio per constitutum possessorium* is excluded (§ 933 BGB). In relation to this exclusion, one explanation is that the law does not permit the transferor to retain any possession.[578] With the former three forms of delivery, the transferor completely gives up possession to the transferee. In contrast, *traditio per constitutum possessorium* allows the transferor to retain possession, usually direct possession of the object. Another explanation is

---

572 BGHZ 10, 81, cited from Baur and Stürner 2009, p. 662. English translation: "*In addition to good faith, another requirement of bona fide acquisition of ownership of a movable thing is the outward appearance of rights on the basis of possession.*"

573 MüKoBGB/Oechsler 2017, § 932, Rn. 6.

574 McGuire 2008, p. 148.

575 Baur and Stürner 2009, p. 670; Weber 2012, p. 132.

576 Staudinger/Wiegand 2017, p. 393.

577 Staudinger/Wiegand 2017, p. 393.

578 Staudinger/Wiegand 2017, p. 394; Baur and Stürner 2009, p. 668.

that *traditio per constitutum possessorium* is not different from the consensual system in the aspect of publicity, and § 933 BGB emphasizes the requirement of delivery in strict sense (§ 929 BGB) by excluding this form of delivery.[579] In the absence of visible delivery, the transferee should be suspect of the seriousness of the transferor's intention to dispose of the object.[580] In the 19th century, the transfer of ownership in the absence of abandoning direct possession was treated as a fraudulent transaction, which deserved special attention from the transferee.[581] Moreover, the exclusion of *traditio per constitutum possessorium* also implies that *bona fide* acquisition has to be visible.[582]

The exclusion gives rise to an inconsistency between § 933 BGB (the prohibition of *bona fide* acquisition by *traditio per constitutum possessorium*) and § 934 BGB (the possibility of *bona fide* acquisition by *traditio longa manu*). These two provisions grant different legal consequences to indirect possession, thereby causing a "contradiction of value (*Wertungswiderspruch*)".[583] According to § 933 BGB, a third party in good faith cannot acquire ownership when he obtains indirect possession but allows the transferor to retain direct possession. However, § 934 BGB permits third parties to acquire ownership, though they merely obtain indirect possession and allow a fourth person to hold direct possession.[584] The third parties obtain indirect possession in these two situations. The only difference lies in the person who directly holds the object: the transferor in the first situation (§ 933 BGB), while a fourth person in the second situation (§ 934 BGB).

This inconsistency creates a possibility for parties to elude the exclusion under § 933 BGB.[585] For example, the unauthorized transferor can first deposit the object in the place of a fourth party and then transfer this object to the third party. In a landmark judgement, the BGH held that the inconsistency should be accepted due to the express legislative intent.[586] In that case, the plaintiff sold a machine to H. KG under a clause of reservation of ownership, and then H. KG transferred this machine for a security purpose to C who sold it to the defendant. Even though C did not acquire ownership due to the statutory exclusion of *traditio per constitutum possessorium* (§ 933 BGB), the defendant could acquire ownership through *traditio longa manu* (§ 934 BGB).

579 MüKoBGB/Oechsler 2017, § 933, Rn. 2; Füller 2006, p. 335.
580 MüKoBGB/Oechsler 2017, § 933, Rn. 2.
581 Brehm and Berger 2014, p. 442.
582 Quantz 2005, p. 202.
583 Füller 2006, p. 336.
584 Baur and Stürner 2009, p. 671.
585 Füller 2006, p. 336.
586 Füller 2006, p. 336-337.

3.4.3.3 *Dutch Law*

Like German law, Dutch law also has a general system of *bona fide* acquisition of corporeal movables, which is governed by art. 3:86 BW.[587] The purpose of this provision is to promote business and trade and to balance interests between the acquirer and the original owner.[588] In this part, we first introduce the conditions of *bona fide* acquisition and then examine the relevance of "possession (*bezit*)" to this acquisition.

A General Requirements of Bona Fide *Acquisition*

Firstly, only corporeal movables (i.e. corporeal and unregistered things) are regulated by art. 3:86 BW. This is because possession can only be treated as an outward appearance of the authority to dispose of corporeal movables.[589] In general, stolen things are not susceptible to *bona fide* acquisition, but they can be acquired under certain restrictive conditions (art. 3:86 (3) BW).[590] However, *bona fide* acquisition can apply to stolen money and securities made payable to bearer or order. Lost things are regulated differently from stolen things: the rule of *bona fide* acquisition can apply to lost things.[591] The rationale behind the application of this rule to lost things is that owners are usually to blame, to some degree, for the loss of the thing.[592]

587 Art. 3:86 (1) BW: "*Ondanks onbevoegdheid van de vervreemder is een overdracht overeenkomstig artikel 90, 91 of 93 van een roerende zaak, niet-registergoed, of een recht aan toonder of order geldig, indien de overdracht anders dan om niet geschiedt en de verkrijger te goeder trouw is.*" English translation: Art. 3:86 (1) BW: "*Although an alienator lacks the right to dispose of the property, a transfer pursuant to Article 90, 91 or 93 of a movable object, unregistered property, or a right to bearer or order is valid, if the transfer is not by gratuitous title and the acquirer acts in good faith.*"

588 Salomons 2008 (2), p. 108.

589 Snijders and Rank-Berenschot 2017, p. 315.

590 Art. 3:86 (3) BW: "*Niettemin kan de eigenaar van een roerende zaak, die het bezit daarvan door diefstal heeft verloren, deze gedurende drie jaren, te rekenen van de dag van de diefstal af, als zijn eigendom opeisen, tenzij: (a) de zaak door een natuurlijke persoon die niet in de uitoefening van een beroep of bedrijf handelde, is verkregen van een vervreemder die van het verhandelen aan het publiek van soortgelijke zaken anders dan als veilinghouder zijn bedrijf maakt in een daartoe bestemde bedrijfsruimte, zijnde een gebouwde onroerende zaak of een gedeelte daarvan met de bij het een en ander behorende grond, en in de normale uitoefening van dat bedrijf handelde; of (b) het geld dan wel toonder- of orderpapier betreft.*" English translation: Art. 3:86 (3) BW: "*Nevertheless, the owner of a movable object, who has lost its possession through theft, may recover it during a period of three years from the day of theft, unless: (a) the object was acquired by a natural person, not acting in the conduct of a profession or business, from an alienator whose business it is to deal with the public in similar objects, otherwise than as an auctioneer in business premises for such purpose, being an immovable structure or part thereof with the land belonging thereto, and provided that the alienator acted in the ordinary course of his business; or (b) in the case of money or paper payable to bearer or order.*"

591 Brahn 1992, p. 61-62.

592 Salomons 2008 (2), p. 110.

Secondly, only acquisition for value is permitted.[593] In other words, a donee is not allowed to obtain the corporeal movable donated to him in the way of *bona fide* acquisition. This requirement is a result of the following legislative purposes: (1) donees should be less protected than those who bear a liability to provide counter-performance; and (2) the purpose of art. 3:86 BW is to facilitate the security of commercial transactions.[594]

Thirdly, possession must be given up to the transferee in good faith. This requirement of delivery is not directly mentioned in art. 3:86 BW. It is a result of a reference to three other provisions, namely art. 3:90, 3:91 and 3:93 BW.[595] Pursuant to these three provisions, visible delivery, *traditio brevi manu* and *traditio longa manu* are eligible forms of delivery for *bona fide* acquisition. Both *traditio per constitutum possessorium* and "delivery by deed (*levering bij akte*)" are excluded.[596] The possible reasons for this exclusion are be presented below.

Lastly, the third party must act in good faith. Pursuant to art. 3:11 BW, the third party will not be in good faith if he or she knows or should have known about the fact of unauthorized disposal.[597] This implies that the law imposes a duty on the third party to inquire into the transferor's authority to dispose.[598] If the third party has a reason to doubt the transferor's authority of disposal, he or she will not act in good faith, regardless of whether an inquiry is possible.[599] The requirement of good faith is easy to understand: the purpose of art. 3:86 BW is to protect the reliance of third parties acting in good faith.

B *Possession and* Bona Fide *Acquisition*

B1: Possession of the Transferor

In theory, there are two approaches to justify the Dutch rule of *bona fide* acquisition: the "doctrine of legitimation (*legitimatieleer*)" and the "doctrine of ownership (*eigendomsleer*)".[600] Under the former approach, possession has an effect of legitimizing the transferor as an owner, and possession is a crucial element for *bona fide* acquisition.[601] Possession is treated as an outward appearance of ownership, which establishes a basis for the reliance of third parties in good faith.[602]

593 Snijders and Rank-Berenschot 2017, p. 317-318.
594 Salomons 2008 (2), p. 108.
595 Snijders and Rank-Berenschot 2017, p. 316-317.
596 Brahn 1992, p. 66-71.
597 Snijders and Rank-Berenschot 2017, p. 318.
598 Salomons 2008 (2), p. 112.
599 Snijders and Rank-Berenschot 2017, p. 318; Salomons 2008 (2), p. 112.
600 Snijders and Rank-Berenschot 2017, p. 313.
601 Salomons 2008 (2), p. 109.
602 Salomons 2000, p. 904.

> *"De ratio van beide bepalingen is dezelfde: bescherming van de derde te goeder trouw die verkregen heeft van een persoon met feitelijke macht, feitelijke macht die de schijn wekt van beschikkingsbevoegdheid en de vervreemder als zodanig legitimeert."*[603]

According to the doctrine of ownership, possession acquired by a third party in good faith should be directly treated as ownership.[604] *Bona fide* possession amounts to ownership.[605] Between these two doctrines, there are some differences. For example, according to the doctrine of legitimation, the third party in good faith must have a valid legal basis, usually a valid contract, for acquisition, while the doctrine of ownership does not have such restriction.[606] In general, the doctrine of legitimation underlies art. 3:86 BW, which means that only obtaining possession in good faith does not suffice for *bona fide* acquisition of ownership.[607]

As to the question whether the transferor must have direct possession, an answer in the negative is provided by Dutch law.[608] Indirect possession can also be a basis for the reliance of third parties.[609] For example, *traditio longa manu* is an eligible form of delivery for *bona fide* acquisition, albeit that this form of invisible delivery only leads to the provision of indirect possession. Moreover, it is difficult for acquirers to ascertain whether the transferor has actual control under the context of electronic commerce.[610] Though direct possession is not necessary, the transferor must have indirect possession. This can be inferred from the fact that "delivery by deed" is excluded.[611] If the transferor does not have any possession, and the outward appearance does not exist, then there is no ground to entitle third parties to *bona fide* acquisition.[612]

---

603 Snijders and Rank-Berenschot 2017, p. 313. English translation: *"The ratio of both provisions is identical: the protection of third parties in good faith who obtained from a person actual control, which serves as an outward appearance of the authority to dispose and legitimizes the alienator as such."*

604 Snijders and Rank-Berenschot 2017, p. 313.

605 Pitlo and Bolweg 1972, p. 113.

606 Snijders and Rank-Berenschot 2017, p. 313; Pitlo and Bolweg 1972, p. 114.

607 In fact, the doctrine of legitimation has been accepted by the Hoge Raad by applying art. 2014 of the old Dutch Civil Code in the landmark case "*Damhof/Staat*" in 1951. In this case, the Hoge Raad clearly stated that the rule of *bona fide* acquisition is an exception of the requirement of eligible authority of disposal, and other requirements for successful transfer, such as a valid underlying contract, have to be satisfied. See Schut 1976, p. 42-44.

608 Salomons 2008 (2), p. 109-110.

609 Brahn 1985, p. 341; Reehuis and Heisterkamp 2019, p. 150.

610 Salomons 2000, p. 905.

611 Asser/Bartels & Van Mierlo 2013, nr. 364.

612 Brahn 1992, p. 70.

B2: Delivery to the Transferee

As just pointed out, delivery, i.e. provision of possession, is necessary for *bona fide* acquisition. This requirement of delivery implies that the rationale behind art. 3:86 BW is the doctrine of legitimation.[613] As indicated above, however, not every form of delivery is eligible.

Visible delivery or provision of direct possession is certainly eligible. In addition, *traditio brevi manu* and *traditio longa manu* are also an eligible form of delivery for *bona fide* acquisition. Under these two forms of invisible delivery, indirect possession passes to the transferee in good faith.[614] As a result of art. 3:111 and art. 3:90 (2) BW, *traditio per constitutum possessorium* is not qualified.[615]

According to the former provision, the "detentor (*houder*)" cannot change his or her intention of holding the object for the "possessor (*bezitter*)", unless the possessor allows or requires the detentor to do so, or the detentor has a good reason to do so.[616] In the situation of unauthorized disposal, *traditio per constitutum possessorium* triggers a change of the detentor's intention: from holding the object for the possessor to holding the object for the third party. Therefore, this invisible delivery cannot be validly made under art. 3:111 BW.[617]

> *"Een beschikkingsonbevoegde houder kan door middel van constitutum possessorium het bezit niet verschaffen. Op grond van artikel 3:111 BW kan een houder zich niet van houder voor de een buiten de wil van de ene om, tot houder van de ander maken (het interversieverbod)."*[618]

In addition, art. 3:90 (2) BW also creates a legal obstacle to *bona fide* acquisition. Pursuant to this provision, an acquirer under *traditio per constitutum possessorium* cannot enforce what he gains against an "older" property right. The relative effect is ascribed to the failure to make the transfer of ownership visible by *traditio per constitutum possessorium*.[619] In the situation of unauthorized disposal, the original ownership is such an older property right, and this right cannot be defeated by the third party in good faith.[620] However, this does not mean that the third party obtains nothing. Instead, the third party in good faith can acquire "relative ownership" in this situation.

---

613 Snijders and Rank-Berenschot 2017, p. 316; Reehuis and Heisterkamp 2019, p. 150.

614 Brahn 1992, p. 86.

615 Snijders and Rank-Berenschot 2017, p. 316.

616 Snijders and Rank-Berenschot 2017, p. 103.

617 Brahn 1992, p. 67.

618 Sdu Commentaar/Van Peski 2019, art. 90, nr. C.3. English translation: "*The unauthorized detentor cannot provide possession through constitutum possessorium. On the ground of art. 3:111 BW, a detentor for one person cannot hold the object for another person, in the absence of the former's approval (the prohibition of intervention).*"

619 Parlementaire Geschiedenis (3) 1981, p. 384-385; Reehuis and Heisterkamp 2019, p. 218.

620 Salomons 2008 (2), p. 110.

> *"De eigendom echter, die de verkrijger aldus verwerft, is naar luidt van artikel 3:90 lid 2 een slechts relatief werkende, een eigendom die geldt jegens derden, niet echter jegens de ouder, de oorspronkelijke, gerechtigde die een ouder recht op het goed heeft dan dat hetwelk de derde uit handen van de beschikkingsonbevoegde bezitter heeft verkregen."*[621]

In other words, ownership obtained by the third party is, in general, effective against third parties, but restricted by "older" property rights. For example, if the original owner transfers ownership to another person after *traditio per constitutum possessorium* takes place between the unauthorized transferor and the third party, then what this another person acquires is younger than what the third party acquires; as a result, the third party can acquire ownership securely.[622]

Apart from *traditio per constitutum possessorium*, "delivery by deed (*levering bij akte*)" is also excluded by Dutch law for *bona fide* acquisition of corporeal movables.[623] As has been shown above, this delivery is introduced to allow for the possibility of transfer of ownership where the transferor has neither direct possession nor indirect possession (see 3.4.2.3.B).[624] If the transferor has neither ownership nor possession, then there is no justification for the third party to acquire ownership at the sacrifice of the original owner's interest.[625] For example, where a finder loses the bicycle found by him, a third party cannot acquire ownership of this bicycle from the finder via "delivery by deed", regardless of whether this third party is in good faith.

3.4.3.4 Comparative and Conclusive Analysis

Traditionally, *bona fide* acquisition is justified under the approach of publicity. Possession is an outward appearance of ownership. Therefore, third parties in good faith can safely rely on this appearance and should be protected.[626] However, this possession-oriented theory is "*unrealistic*" nowadays,[627] and most scholars are not in favor of this theory.[628] Sometimes, the focus is laid on delivery. Under this delivery-oriented theory, the ability to provide possession can justify the reliance of third parties and *bona fide* acquisition of corporeal movables.[629] The two theories are introduced and examined below.

---

621 Brahn 1992, p. 67. English translation: "*However, according to paragraph 2 art. 3:90, ownership obtained by the acquirer is a right of ownership that can be enforced against third parties, except the older, the original, owner who has an older right with respect to the object than what is obtained by the third party from the unauthorized possessor.*"

622 Snijders and Rank-Berenschot 2017, p. 317.

623 Brahn 1992, p. 70.

624 Brahn 1992, p. 70.

625 Brahn 1992, p. 71; Reehuis and Heisterkamp 2019, p. 150.

626 Karner 2006, p. 160.

627 Acquisition and Loss of Ownership 2011, p. 889.

628 Karner 2006, p. 173.

629 Karner 2006, p. 179-180.

A The Possession-Oriented Theory

According to the possession-oriented theory, possession is an outward mark of ownership and has the effect of legitimizing unauthorized transferors as an owner.[630] Therefore, third parties in good faith can rely on the transferor's possession, and such reliance is protected. This theory originates from the notion of *Gewere* in ancient Germanic law.[631] As has been shown above, possession was in Germanic law known as *Gewere*, which literally referred to the "clothing" of rights (see 3.1.1.2).

> *"If [...] a legal system pursued to the same degree a policy of facilitating transactions [...], it would maintain that a transferee acting in good faith could trust in the appearance of ownership created by possession of goods in the hands of the transferor."*[632]

> *"Het bezit legitimeert den bezitter als eigenaar; wie door zijn bezit eigenaar schijnt te zijn, wordt voor eigenaar gehouden, en ieder die daarop voortbouwt is veilig."*[633]

In general, this theory can explain the following fact: the unauthorized transferor must have possession of the object. If the unauthorized transferor has no possession, *bona fide* acquisition is impossible for the transferee. As has been shown above, "delivery by deed" is not an eligible form of delivery for *bona fide* acquisition under Dutch law, and assigning the claim of recovery by the transferor who has no indirect possession cannot give rise to *bona fide* acquisition in German law. In both situations, the unauthorized transferor lacks possession as an outward appearance. Therefore, according to the possession-oriented theory, the ground of the third party's reliance is absent.

However, the possession-oriented theory is problematic in explaining *bona fide* acquisition. As has been argued above, possession is an abstract and thus ambiguous means of publicity for corporeal movables (see 3.2.1), and indirect possession does not have any publicity effect (see 3.2.2). This means that the possession-oriented theory is problematic in explaining *bona fide* acquisition by viewing possession as an outward appearance of ownership. This is why this theory is no longer held by most scholars.[634]

In general, direct possession means that the possessor has actual control, which gives rise to visible physical proximity between the possessor and the object. This physical proximity informs third parties that the possessor has a right to the object. However, the details of this right cannot be shown by possession. Therefore, possession is an abstract and thus ambiguous means

630 Pollock and Wright 1888, p. 4; Baur and Stürner 2009, p. 662; Salomons 2008 (2), p. 109.

631 Karner 2006, p. 167-168; Von Gierke 1928, p. 59.

632 Bridge 2014, p. 196.

633 Asser/Scholten, Zakenrecht, 1905, p. 65, cited from Salomons 2000, p. 905. English translation: "*Possession legitimizes the possessor as an owner; the person who appears to be an owner due to his possession is assumed as the owner, and everyone who relies on that is secure.*"

634 Karner 2006, p. 173.

of publicity. Due to the ambiguity of possession, it is not convincing to treat possession as an outward mark of ownership (see 3.2.1.3).[635] Moreover, law either provides a consensual system or recognizes invisible delivery under a *traditio* system. As a result, direct possession and ownership often fall apart in modern transactions (see 3.4.2.4). This ubiquitous divergence between direct possession and ownership further makes the view of possession as an outward appearance of ownership groundless.[636] Moreover, even the possessor does have ownership, he or she might lose the authority to dispose because of judicial seizure or insolvency.[637]

In reality, individuals might have an inclination to deem that possessors are an owner, but this reaction to possession is emotional and unreliable.[638] Truly, the instinctive reaction can guide one person to avert illegally interfering with another's property (see 3.3.2.2). However, it does not provide a sufficient basis for *bona fide* acquisition of ownership from an unauthorized transferor. Before entering into a transaction with the potential transferor, the potential transferee needs to identify whether the former really has ownership. The fact that the transferor has possession only means that this person might be an owner. The transferee has to carry out investigations to identify whether the transferor is really the owner. If the transferee fails to do so, then the requirement of acting in good faith will not be fulfilled, which further implies that *bona fide* acquisition is impossible.

As has been shown above, indirect possession is also recognized as an outward appearance of ownership to justify *bona fide* acquisition of corporeal movables under the possession-oriented theory. In English law, *bona fide* acquisition is possible where the unauthorized transferor's possession is indirect. In German law and Dutch law, *traditio longa manu* is an eligible form of delivery, which implies that it suffices that the unauthorized transferor has indirect possession. Moreover, the publicity effect of indirect possession is also indicated by the following fact: *bona fide* acquisition is impossible where the unauthorized transferor is not an indirect possessor and only has a claim of recovery. Proponents of the possession-oriented theory often hold that indirect possession has publicity effect, though this effect is weaker than the publicity effect of direct possession.[639]

Here, we contend that it seems problematic to say that indirect possession can generate any effect of publicity. As has been argued, indirect possession is, in essence, a legal relationship that is invisible to third parties (see 3.2.2). It cannot be said that indirect possession can serve as an outward appearance of rights, let alone the right of ownership.[640] A successful claim

635 Baur and Stürner 2009, p. 665; Ernst 1993, p. 101.
636 Baur and Stürner 2009, p. 662; Kindl 1999, p. 315; Hager 1990, p. 240.
637 Hager 1990, p. 240.
638 Füller 2006, p. 323.
639 Van Vliet 2010, p. 284.
640 Ernst 1993, p. 104.

of *bona fide* acquisition is dependent on the enjoyment of indirect possession by the unauthorized transferor.[641] However, whether the transferor really has indirect possession is an unclear question to the transferee.[642] The transferee has to investigate this question. This investigation amounts to investigating the legal relationship between the direct possessor and the indirect possessor. Therefore, we can say that the relationship of indirect possession is an object of publicity, rather than a means of publicity.

Nevertheless, the present law recognizes that the holding of indirect possession by unauthorized transferors suffices. In our opinion, this recognition has nothing to do with the publicity effect that indirect possession lacks. Perhaps it is a result of the following practical consideration: if indirect possession were denied, then *bona fide* acquisition would become impossible for corporeal movables for which a document of title (such as the bill of lading) is created.[643]

> *"Goederen plegen immers veelvuldig te worden verhandeld terwijl zij in pakhuizen of elders zijn opgeslagen en te verwachten valt dat zij daar gedurende langere tijd opgeslagen zullen blijven. Het is in het belang van het handelsverkeer dat dergelijke goederen kunnen worden overgedragen op een wijze waarbij de bescherming van de verkrijger tegen een mogelijke beschikkingsonbevoegdheid tot haar recht kan komen zonder dat de zaken behoeven te worden verplaatst."*[644]

In the end, the possession-oriented theory cannot explain why *traditio per constitutum possessorium* is excluded in *bona fide* acquisition by German law and Dutch law. If possession is an appearance of ownership and can be relied on by the transferee, then the transferee's reliance should also be protected in the situation where the transferor retains possession. As has been shown, direct possession can be transferred independently from ownership under present law due to the recognition of invisible delivery (see 3.4.2.4). In modern transactions, the transferor often retains direct possession when alienating ownership to the transferee. For example, sale and leaseback is an ordinary transaction in modern society. Where an unauthorized transferor sells a machine and then leases this machine back, there is no reason to say that the transferee's reliance, if he or she has it, disappears or weakens because of the retention of direct possession by the transferor. This kind of transaction is so commonplace that the transferee in good faith should

641 Wieling 2006, p. 390.
642 Füller 2006, p. 324; Hager 1990, p. 241.
643 Bridge 2014, p. 235.
644 Rank-Berenschot 2012, p. 84. English translation: "*After all, things tend to be transferred frequently, but they are stored in warehouses or elsewhere and are expected to remain there for a long period of time. For the benefit of commerce, these things can be transferred in such a way that the purpose of protecting the transferee against the lack of authority to dispose can be realized without having to relocate the things.*"

not be expected to be suspicious of the retention of direct possession.[645] Therefore, the prejudice against *traditio per constitutum possessorium* in the situation of *bona fide* acquisition is groundless, at least from the perspective of the transferee's reliance on possession.[646]

B The Delivery-Oriented Theory

As *bona fide* acquisition cannot be successfully explained by focusing on possession, some scholars turn to focusing on delivery or the provision of possession. According to this delivery-oriented theory, possession cannot be a basis of reliance, and what matters is that possession is provided to the transferee in good faith.[647] This ability implies that the transferor has the authority to dispose.

> *„Der Grund für das Vertrauen des Erwerbers in das Eigentum des Veräußerers liegt also darin, dass der Veräußerer den Besitz an der Sache an den Erwerber oder eine von diesem eingeschaltete Geheißperson transferieren kann. Aus der Besitzverschaffungsmacht des Veräußerers resultiert daher auch der den gutgläubigen Erwerb rechtfertigende Rechtsschein."*[648]

This theory avoids the following difficulty: indirect possession is invisible and cannot be a basis of reliance, and *bona fide* acquisition is only possible when the transferee does obtain indirect possession.[649]

The delivery-orientated theory is based on the following fact: the unauthorized transferor has to provide possession to the transferee. As has been shown, delivery is necessary for *bona fide* acquisition in the three jurisdictions. In general, visible delivery, *traditio brevi manu* and *traditio longa manu* are eligible forms of delivery. If actual control of the object is acquired by the transferee, then the requirement of delivery can be satisfied. This occurs in the situation of visible delivery and that of *traditio brevi manu*. It also suffices that the transferor provides indirect possession to the transferee when the object is controlled by a third party (*traditio longa manu*). Under German law, if the transferor has no possession and only assigns a claim of recovery,

---

645 In the 19th century, where the transferor retained direct possession, the transfer would be treated as a fictitious transaction, and legislators and judges would take a discriminatory attitude towards this transfer. See Brehm and Berger 2014, p. 442. However, this discrimination has become groundless at present. Retention of direct possession by the transferor is not only possible in law, but also really occurs in many situations.

646 This is a reason why the English judgement concerning double sale and leaseback holds that the third party in good faith could acquire ownership through *traditio per constitutum possessorium*. See McKay 2000, p. 283.

647 Karner 2006, p. 179-180.

648 MüKoBGB/Oechsler 2017, § 932, Rn. 6. English translation: "*The ground of the acquirer's reliance on the transferor's ownership is that the transferor can transfer possession of the thing to the transferee or a person designated by the transferee. The appearance of rights justifying bona fide acquisition also results from the transferor's ability to provide possession.*"

649 Karner 2006, p. 183.

bona fide acquisition is only possible when the transferee obtains possession (§ 934 BGB). This also illustrates that provision of possession, instead of possession, lays the basis of *bona fide* acquisition.[650]

However, the delivery-oriented theory fails to successfully explain *bona fide* acquisition for three reasons. The first reason is that the ability to provide possession cannot be seen as a basis of reliance of third parties in good faith, and *bona fide* acquisition cannot be justified by focusing on delivery. Providing possession by the transferor does not mean that he or she has ownership of the object.[651] There are various reasons why the transferor obtains and enjoys factual control of the object. For example, the transferor might be a lessee who obtains factual control of the object on the basis of a contract of lease. The transferee should not believe that the transferor is the owner just because possession is provided. Therefore, the delivery-oriented theory has the same problem as the possession-oriented theory in explaining *bona fide* acquisition.

The second reason is that property law does not stipulate a different meaning for delivery in *bona fide* acquisition from that in the acquisition from the authorized.[652] For the former acquisition, the requirement of delivery is prescribed by referring to the provisions regarding the latter acquisition. In German law, § 932 and § 934 BGB refer to § 929 and § 931 BGB respectively. In Dutch law, art. 3:86 BW refers to art. 3:90, art. 3:91 and art. 3:93 BW. The reference indicates that delivery does not play different roles in the situation of *bona fide* acquisition and that of the acquisition from the authorized. If the transferee does have any reliance, such reliance comes into existence before the provision of possession.[653] Otherwise, the transferee would not agree to make a contract of transfer with the transferor. Therefore, the delivery-oriented theory cannot explain how the reliance comes into existence before providing possession by the transferor.[654] Delivery is a result of the performance of this contract by the transferor.[655] The provision of possession just implies that the transferor fulfills his or her promise to deliver and transfer the object.[656] Therefore, viewing the provision of possession as a basis of reliance is not correct.

The third reason is that the delivery-oriented theory cannot explain the exclusion of *traditio per constitutum possessorium* by German law (§ 933 BGB) and Dutch law (art. 3:111 and art. 3:90 (2) BW). According to German lawyers, the unauthorized transferor has to provide complete possession to the transferee without retaining any possession.[657] However, why is retain-

650 Staudinger/Wiegand 2017, p. 394.
651 Hager 1990, p. 247.
652 Füller 2006, p. 326; Hager 1990, p. 246.
653 Hager 1990, p. 248; Ernst 1993, p. 112.
654 Rusch 2010, p. 220.
655 Füller 2006, p. 325.
656 Füller 2006, p. 324.
657 Baur and Stürner 2009, p. 668.

ing no possession necessary for *bona fide* acquisition? The delivery-oriented theory cannot provide a convincing answer to this question. In the situation of *traditio longa manu*, indirect possession is obtained by the transferee, and thus *bona fide* acquisition is possible. Indirect possession can also be provided to the transferee through *traditio per constitutum possessorium*, but *bona fide* acquisition is not available to the transferee. Like the possession-oriented theory, the delivery-oriented theory cannot explain this difference in the treatment of *traditio longa manu* and *traditio per constitutum possessorium* either.

C The Role of Legal Policy

C1: Legal Policy, Possession and Delivery

From the preceding introduction, it can be seen that possession and delivery are highly relevant to *bona fide* acquisition of corporeal movables. In English law, the mercantile agent, the seller in possession, and the buyer in possession must have possession (whether direct or indirect), and delivery (whether actual or fictional) is required in the latter two situations. In German law and Dutch law, the unauthorized transferor must have possession (whether direct or indirect). Moreover, this possession must be given up to the transferee through visible or invisible delivery, but *traditio per constitutum possessorium* is excluded. Because of this high relevance, there are two theories justifying *bona fide* acquisition from the perspective of publicity: the possession-oriented theory and the delivery-oriented theory. As has been shown, both theories are problematic. Here we examine the role played by legal policy in *bona fide* acquisition.

Bona fide acquisition is just an outcome of legal policy. This policy is that where a third party obtains possession in a certain way, this party is able to acquire ownership, even though the transferor has no ownership. Correspondingly, the original owner loses the right of ownership.

> *„Der gutgläubige Erwerb und der mit ihm verbundene Rechtsverlust des Eigentümers sind, wenn man so will, durch die rechtspolitische Entscheidung legitimiert, dass, wer bona fide eine Sache gegen Entgelt erwirbt, dieselbe auch dann soll behalten dürfen, wenn der Veräußerer nicht der Eigentümer war."*[658]

Possession and delivery are two factors taken into consideration in answering the following question: are there sufficient grounds for the acquisition by the third party and for the loss of ownership of the original owner.[659]

---

658 Ernst 1993, p. 114. English translation: "*The bona fide acquisition and the associated loss of the right of the owner are, if you will, justified by the legal-political decision that the person who acquires a thing for consideration in good faith can preserve this thing, even though the transferor was not the owner.*"

659 Ernst 1993, p. 114.

The main function of possession and delivery is to resolve the conflict between the interests of the original owner and the third party fairly. Therefore, possession and delivery are two factors that lay a basis for balancing the interests of the original owner and the third party. To illustrate this, we will discuss the exclusion of *traditio per constitutum possessorium* below.

As has been shown above, *traditio per constitutum possessorium* is excluded in *bona fide* acquisition in Dutch law and German law. From this exclusion, we can find that where the original owner and a third party situate in the "same" position, namely that neither has direct possession, legislators tend to favor the original owner. In other words, if the third party's position is no better than the actual owner's, the former's position will not be favored by sacrificing the latter's ownership. This preference of protecting the original owner has nothing to do with publicity of possession or reliance on possession. It is mainly an outcome of legal policy.[660]

Here, we take double sale and leaseback as an example: if a person sells and leases back a machine to two different buyers, which buyer should be protected? According to a recent judgement in English law, the second buyer can acquire ownership, albeit that the seller retains direct possession.[661] However, this judgement has encountered fierce criticism, which includes why the second buyer can enjoy more protection than the first buyer who in fact has the same position as the former.[662] The conduct of these two buyers is exactly the same.

In German law, the first buyer will prevail under § 933 BGB. In theory, this provision is explained by the view that neither the transferor nor the original owner can have any "residual (*Rest*)" of possession.[663] In the double sale and leaseback case, the first buyer, i.e. the true owner, has a claim of recovery against the transferor, at least on the basis of the agreement of lease.[664] Though the true owner is no longer an indirect possessor because of the lessee's change of the possessory intention, the true owner still has "little residual of factual control (*geringer Rest von tatsächlicher Gewalt*)".[665] It is this "residual of factual control" that makes the true owner able to prevail the third party (namely the second buyer in this case), despite the fact that the latter has obtained indirect possession.[666] However, why can the residual of factual control be a sufficient reason to exclude the third party's acquisition? This question is not answered. In our opinion, the legal policy of protecting the true owner in priority underlies § 933 BGB.

660 Ernst 1993, p. 119-120.
661 *Michael Gerson (Leasing) Ltd v. Wilkinson and State Securities Ltd*, 31 July 2000 [2001] Q. B. 514.
662 Merrett 2008, p. 392.
663 Staudinger/Wiegand 2017, p. 462-463; Baur and Stürner 2009, p. 668.
664 Hager 1990, p. 342-344.
665 Ernst 1993, p. 119.
666 Hager 1990, p. 344.

In Dutch law, the legal policy is implemented by art. 3:111 BW, a provision concerning the "prohibition of intervention (*interversieverbod*)".[667] Pursuant to this provision, a detentor is prohibited from holding the object for himself or a third party in the absence of the possessor's permission or a legal ground. In the situation of unauthorized disposal, *traditio per constitutum possessorium* involves a change of the intention of the detentor (the unauthorized transferor), which is prohibited by art. 3:111 BW. Therefore, the third party in good faith cannot validly acquire possession under this provision, which further makes *bona fide* acquisition impossible.[668] Therefore, Dutch law and German law use different rules to implement the same legal policy presented above.[669]

C2: Legal Policy and Other Requirements

The preceding introduction has shown that, in addition to these two requirements, some other conditions also have to be fulfilled. These conditions concern whether the transferee is in good faith, whether the transfer is gratuitous, whether the object is a stolen or lost thing, and other circumstances under which the transfer takes place. In general, these conditions cannot be explained from the perspective of publicity of possession. Instead, they are outcomes of legal policy.

Firstly, the rule of *bona fide* acquisition is recognized to promote the security of commercial transactions concerning corporeal movables.[670] Promoting the security of transactions is a legal policy that is in tension with the legal policy of protecting ownership.[671] Thus, this rule is not applied to gratuitous transfer, even though the donee has reliance on the donor's possession of the object.[672] In addition, exclusion of *bona fide* acquisition for a donee in good faith usually does not make him or her suffer any significant disadvantages.[673] Therefore, the original owner should be protected in priority. This implies that the legal policy of balancing the interests of the original owner and the third party in good faith also matters.

---

667 Art. 3:111 BW: "*Wanneer men heeft aangevangen krachtens een rechtsverhouding voor een ander te houden, gaat men daarmede onder dezelfde titel voort, zolang niet blijkt dat hierin verandering is gebracht, hetzij ten gevolge van een handeling van hem voor wie men houdt, hetzij ten gevolge van een tegenspraak van diens recht.*" English translation: Art. 3:111 BW: "*A person who commences detention for another pursuant to a juridical relationship shall continue to do so under the same title, so long as no change is apparent in his title, resulting either from an act by the person for whom he holds or from the latter's right having been contested.*"

668 Brahn 1992, p. 67.

669 Here is should be noted that the first draft of the BGB accepted the distinction between possession and detention. On the basis of this distinction, the detentor cannot provide possession to a third party in the way of *traditio per constitutum possessorium*. However, the second draft gave up the distinction. As a result, § 933 BGB was made. See MüKo-BGB/Oechsler 2017, § 933, Rn. 1; Staudinger/Wiegand 2017, p. 462.

670 Staudinger/Wiegand 2017, p. 391; Acquisition and Loss of Ownership 2011, p. 890.

671 Karner 2006, p. 122.

672 Acquisition and Loss of Ownership 2011, p. 892.

673 Acquisition and Loss of Ownership 2011, p. 892.

Secondly, the original owner loses ownership because this person intentionally contributes to the disparity between ownership and possession.[674] The original owner often obtains benefits by giving up possession and thus needs to bear the associated risk arising out of *bona fide* acquisition by a third party acting in good faith. This is known as the "principle of ascription (*Veranlassungsprinzip* in German law and *toedoenbeginsel* in Dutch law)".[675] The principle explains why stolen things and lost things are not susceptible to *bona fide* acquisition in German law (see 3.4.3.2). However, with respect to lost things, there is an opposite legal policy: where the owner loses possession accidentally, the rule of *bona fide* acquisition is also applicable because the owner's negligence contributes to the loss of possession.[676] This consideration is accepted by Dutch law (see 3.4.3.3). To guarantee the safe circulation of money and securities, the rule of *bona fide* acquisition is applicable to these two types of corporeal movable. This implies that the legal policy of promoting the security of transactions prevails. Moreover, art. 3:86 (3) (a) BW provides special protection to consumers by entitling this type of third parties to *bona fide* acquisition of stolen things. In general, this is a result of the legal policy of "consumer protection (*consumentenbescherming*)".[677]

Thirdly, *bona fide* acquisition requires that the third party to be in good faith: this person neither knows nor should have known about the defect of the authority to dispose. Because of this requirement, the third party should be prudent and bears a duty to investigate in the transaction.[678] The requirement of good faith implies that the third party needs to respect the original owner when he knows or should have known about the defect. Undoubtedly, the requirement is not only important for balancing the interests of the original owner and that of the third party, but also for the smooth operation of transactions.[679] If courts take a strict attitude towards the satisfaction of this requirement, then the original owner will enjoy more protection, and the possibility of acquisition by the third party will become lower. Moreover, this further means that the third party needs to take more measures to investigate the transferor's authority of disposal and bear more costs.

In sum, the importance of legal policy implies that possession and delivery are not sufficient for *bona fide* acquisition, and the traditional approach of publicity cannot fully explain why third parties in good faith can prevail over the original owner. In general, *bona fide* acquisition is a rule based on a tradeoff between the protection of ownership and the security of transactions.[680] More requirements (restrictions) of this acquisition imply stronger protection for the original owner. If possession and delivery could

674 Karner 2006, p. 250; Snijders and Rank-Berenschot 2017, p. 320.
675 Snijders and Rank-Berenschot 2017, p. 320.
676 Salomons 2008 (2), p. 110.
677 Snijders and Rank-Berenschot 2017, p. 321.
678 Wolf and Wellenhofer 2011, p. 107; Snijders and Rank-Berenschot 2017, p. 318.
679 Karner 2006, p. 387-388; Acquisition and Loss of Ownership 2011, p. 895.
680 Bridge 2014, p. 196.

sufficiently give rise to *bona fide* acquisition, then the protection of original owners would become deficient.[681] Obviously, ownership also deserves protection: like the interest of third parties in acquiring property, the interest of original owners in preserving their property is also important. From the perspective of law and economics, if possession and delivery are sufficient, then owners would be discouraged from giving up possession to others, which would eventually inhibit the utilization of property to the largest extent.[682] Moreover, third parties would be discouraged from investigating whether the transferor really has lawful authority to dispose.[683]

3.4.4 Conclusion

In the preceding discussion, we have examined whether possession can be a sufficient means of publicity for subsequent acquirers in two situations: transfer of ownership of corporeal movables and *bona fide* acquisition of ownership of corporeal movables. In conclusion, possession cannot provide sufficient proprietary information to subsequent acquirers because direct possession is an abstract method of publicity, and indirect possession has no effect of publicity.

In the situation of transfer of ownership, the publicity effect of delivery cannot be overstated. Firstly, visible delivery only shows to third parties that the transferee acquires a certain right. From visible delivery, a third party cannot necessarily know that a right of ownership is transferred to the acquirer. We can only say that ownership is transferred in an abstractly visible way. Secondly, invisible delivery is invisible, thereby conveying no information to third parties. As a result, where invisible delivery is made, the transfer of ownership is completely invisible to third parties. In general, under the consensual system or the *traditio* system, individual parties are allowed to decide the time when ownership passes as well as the person who holds direct possession of the object. Law allows ownership to be transferred independently from direct possession, and there is a ubiquitous disparity between ownership and possession in reality.

In the situation of *bona fide* acquisition of ownership, the publicity effect of possession cannot be overstated either. Firstly, possession is never an outward appearance of ownership. This is because direct possession of the unauthorized transferor only indicates that this person has a right, which is not necessarily ownership. Another reason is that indirect possession has no effect of publicity. Indirect possession is invisible, and whether the unau-

681 In history, there were two extremes concerning this tradeoff: one is Roman law that, in principle, only protected original owners (*nemo dat quod non habet*), and the other is ancient Germanic law that provided very extensive protection to third parties (*Hand wahre Hand*). See Salomons 2008 (1), p. 143-144; Von Gierke 1928, p. 59.

682 Salomons 2011 (2), p. 1077-1078.

683 Salomons 2011 (2), p. 1077-1078.

thorized transferor really has indirect possession is unclear to third parties. Secondly, provision of possession cannot lay a sufficient basis for the third party's reliance either. In general, giving up possession of the object to the third party is an outcome of performing the obligation of delivery. Moreover, if the third party in good faith has any reliance, this reliance will come into existence before the provision of possession. Thirdly, various types of legal policy play an important role in justifying *bona fide* acquisition of corporeal movables. For example, the exclusion of *traditio per constitutum possessorium* is an outcome of the following legal policy: where the original owner and the transferee in good faith have the same position, the former prevails. In addition to possession and delivery, some other requirements also need to be fulfilled. For example, the third party has to act in good faith, the acquisition by the third party is not gratuitous, and the original owner does not contribute to the disparity between possession and ownership. In general, these requirements are a result of legal policy.

3.5 Possession and Third-Party Effect: General Creditors

In the preceding two sections, the publicity effect of possession for strange interferers and that for subsequent acquirers have been discussed. In this section, we turn to another type of third party, namely general creditors. The focus of our discussion is whether possession can provide any useful information to general creditors. In 3.5.1, we introduced general creditors and the proprietary information demanded by them. In the situation of the debtor's insolvency, general creditors can only distribute assets owned by the insolvent debtor but not encumbered with any security interests. Therefore, general creditors have an interest in knowing the answers to two questions: (1) which assets are owned by the insolvent debtor, and (2) which assets have been mortgaged or pledged.

Since the entire Chapter 3 addresses only the publicity effect of possession for corporeal movables, the following discussion is confined to possession of corporeal movables, a kind of assets owned by the debtor. Correspondingly, we adapt the questions which are discussed below: (1) can possession indicate how many corporeal movables are owned by the debtor; and (2) can possession indicate how much proprietary encumbrance has been created over the debtor's corporeal movables? These two questions are discussed in 3.5.2 and 3.5.3 respectively. In the end, a conclusion is provided.

3.5.1 General Creditors and the Desired Information

3.5.1.1 Two Types of Proprietary Information

In Chapter 2, we introduced the legal status of general creditors and the information they demand (see 2.2.2.2.C). Here, some of the most salient points are reiterated. General creditors have unsecured personal rights. In general, these personal rights are guaranteed by the total unencumbered assets owned by the debtor. Unlike general creditors, secured creditors have a preferential right with respect to specific collateral. In practice, there are many reasons why a creditor might be willing to be an unsecured creditor. For example, this creditor believes that the debtor has the ability to pay, the costs of creating a proprietary security right might be too high, the creditor's bargaining power is not equal as the debtor's, and the creditor might choose other measures to counter the risk of underpayment.[684]

In Chapter 2, we have also shown that the overall financial health of the debtor is the most important for general creditors, and the unencumbered assets the debtor has are of very limited importance (see 2.2.2.2.C). In practice, general creditors are mainly concerned about the debtor's cashflow, earning ability, and development prospects.[685] The information concerning these factors is not proprietary information since these factors are unrelated to property rights. Therefore, they fall outside the scope of this research. In this section, we focus only on whether possession can provide information concerning the unencumbered assets owned by the debtor, despite this proprietary information having very limited value for general creditors. As has been shown in Chapter 2, the proprietary information concerning unencumbered assets involves two aspects: how many assets belong to the debtor (the information of ownership), and how much proprietary encumbrance is created over the debtor's assets (the information of proprietary encumbrance).

A The Information of Ownership

The total asset owned by a debtor usually consists of corporeal movables, immovable property and incorporeal property. Immovable property takes registration as the method of publicity. In general, a creditor is able to know the immovable property owned by the creditor from the land register. Here, a question is whether a creditor can know the corporeal movables owned by the debtor on the basis of possession. This question can be described in another way: does possession of more corporeal movables mean that the possessor owns more corporeal movables and is wealthier?

In many articles and discussions, an answer in the affirmative is argued. Possession is treated as an indication of ownership, and the divergence of possession from ownership causes a problem of "*ostensible ownership*" or "*false appearance of wealth*".[686] If a debtor who lacks ownership holds possession, then he will look like an owner and thus appear wealthier than he really is. To tackle this problem, a system of registration should be introduced to demonstrate the divergence.[687] Usually, this opinion can be found

684 Finch 1999, p. 638; Mann 1997, p. 658-663.
685 Von Wilmowsky 1996, p. 162.
686 Baird and Jackson 1983, p. 175; Gullifer 2016, p. 3.
687 Baird and Jackson 1983, p. 200.

in the discussion concerning the publicity of non-possessory security interests of movables (see 5.4). Moreover, some scholars recommend having a general system of registration for all property rights of corporeal movables, rather than security interests alone.

> *"We think that, as a general rule, the party wishing to take or retain a nonpossessory property interest should bear the burden of curing the ostensible ownership problem, regardless of the type of relationship that party has with the party in possession of the collateral."*[688]

In general, we think that general creditors do not rely on possession to ascertain the assets owned by the debtor because possession is an abstract method of publicity. The divergence between possession and ownership does not trigger the problem of ostensible ownership. About these two arguments, a detailed discussion is provided below (see 3.5.2).

B The Information of Proprietary Encumbrance

Even if a general creditor has ascertained the assets owned by the debtor, this creditor still does not know how much performance he can expect if the debtor becomes bankrupt. This is because his unsecured claim is subordinate to property rights of security. The amount of proprietary encumbrance also affects the extent to which the unsecured obligation will be performed in the event of the debtor's bankruptcy. Therefore, the general creditor also has an interest in knowing how much proprietary encumbrance exists over the assets owned by the debtor. One question here is whether possession can convey the information concerning proprietary encumbrance to general creditors.

There are two relevant approaches to this question: the positive approach and the negative approach.[689] According to the positive approach, possession can show the existence of proprietary encumbrance over corporeal movables (such as possessory pledge): the creation of this encumbrance has been indicated through delivery of the corporeal movable collateral.[690] The negative approach justifies delivery of the collateral from a different angle: delivery can preclude the debtor from appearing falsely wealthy.[691] According to the negative approach, where a property right of security is created in the absence of delivery of the collateral, there will be the problem of ostensible ownership, and general creditors will be misled to believe that the collateral belongs to insolvency assets.

As argued later, these two approaches are not convincing. Again, the main reason is that possession is an abstract and thus ambiguous method of publicity. Delivery cannot indicate the existence of any proprietary encum-

688 Baird and Jackson 1983, p. 189.
689 Füller 2006, p. 296-298; Hamwijk 2012, p. 315.
690 Hamwijk 2012, p. 308.
691 Drobnig 2011, p. 1027.

brance, and possession does not make the possessor falsely wealthy. For example, delivery cannot inform general creditors that a possessory pledge has been created on the thing delivered. The positive approach ignores the simple fact that delivery can be made due to various legal grounds. Later we provide a detailed discussion of the positive approach (see 3.5.3). In light of the negative approach, delivery can avoid the problem of ostensible ownership. In essence, this approach treats possession as an outward appearance of unencumbered ownership. Thus, it is discussed in a separate part (see 3.5.2).

3.5.1.2 Reiteration of Two Caveats

For the sake of clarity, two caveats need to be reiterated before starting our further discussion. Firstly, the discussion focuses only on whether possession can provide proprietary information concerning unencumbered assets to general creditors. As has been emphasized above, this information has very limited importance for general creditors (see 2.2.2.2.C). In practice, what unsecured creditors are mainly concerned about is the debtor's overall financial health of the debtor.

Secondly, the following discussion is confined to corporeal movables. Therefore, the question discussed is whether possession can indicate the corporeal movables owned by the debtor and the proprietary encumbrance created over the debtor's corporeal movables. The debtor usually owns different types of assets, among which corporeal movables are only one type. Therefore, for a general creditor who wants to ascertain the total unencumbered assets owned by the debtor, giving attention to only corporeal movables is obviously insufficient.

3.5.2 Possession and the Information of Ownership of Corporeal Movables

3.5.2.1 Is Possession an Indicator of Ownership?

In this part, the central question discussed is whether possession can indicate how many corporeal movables are owned by the debtor. In general, the answer is in the negative for two reasons: (1) direct possession is an abstract and thus ambiguous method of publicity for corporeal movables (see 3.2.1); and (2) indirect possession has no effect of publicity (see 3.2.2). The second reason is easy to understand. Indirect possession held by the debtor is hidden to general creditors. Thus, indirect possession cannot convey any information to general creditors. The following discussion concerns the first reason.

As an abstract method of publicity, direct possession is not necessarily associated with the right of ownership. In modern society, direct possession and ownership diverge from each other extensively in the field of corporeal movables (see 3.4.2.4). A corporeal movable directly possessed by a debtor does not necessarily belong to this debtor. For example, the debtor might be just a lessee. Indeed, possession of a thing indicates that the possessor has a certain right to this thing. However, this abstract and ambiguous indication is not sufficient for general creditors because what they are concerned about is whether the thing can be distributed if the debtor becomes bankrupt. In principle, for the thing to be able to be distributed among general creditors, a condition is that the bankrupt debtor is the owner. Therefore, direct possession conveys no useful information to general creditors, and general creditors cannot rely on direct possession to ascertain the assets owned by the debtor.

The failure of possession to be an indicator of the debtor's ownership can also be ascribed to another fact: a debtor might have ownership of a corporeal movable thing, despite this thing not being directly possessed by the debtor. As just mentioned, ownership and direct possession are often held by different persons in reality. It is common that an insolvent debtor (such as the lessor) enjoys ownership of a corporeal movable, while this movable is directly possessed by another person (such as the lessee). If direct possession is treated as an outward mark of ownership, then two incorrect results ensue: the amount of the bankrupt debtor's assets is underestimated, and the amount of the possessor's assets is overestimated. Therefore, the question whether a corporeal movable is susceptible to distribution among general creditors is never determined by direct possession.

3.5.2.2 Is Possession a Cause of Ostensible Ownership?

The preceding part presented the main reason why possession cannot show how many assets are owned by the debtor. In this part, we turn to the problem of ostensible ownership, a problem often seen as an outcome of the divergence between possession and ownership. However, we are of the opinion that this problem does not exist for general creditors. Here, more grounds will be provided to demonstrate that general creditors neither treat possession as an indicator of ownership nor are misled by possession.

A Introduction of the Problem

As mentioned above, it is often held that the separation between ownership and possession causes the problem of ostensible ownership: possession makes the possessor appear wealthier than he or she really is. In general, the problem of ostensible ownership can arise in two different situations. One situation is that the possessor, such as a lessor, does not have ownership. The other situation is that the possessor, such as a mortgagor, is an owner but has granted a limited property right to another person. In other words, the possessor only has encumbered ownership.

In the first situation, the possessor who has no ownership appears to be the owner of the thing possessed. To avoid this situation, possession must be held by the owner. This opinion can be found in an ancient English case, the *Twyne's Case*.[692] In that case, a farmer sold his sheep to another person

692 Baird 1983, p. 53.

but retained possession. Due to the retention of possession, this transaction was ruled as fraudulent and thus void. The transaction was carried out in the way of *traditio per constitutum possessorium*. In history, this form of invisible delivery was treated as a fraudulent activity.[693] In general, this discrimination against *traditio per constitutum possessorium* can be ascribed to the concern about the problem of ostensible ownership.

> *"Separation of ownership and possession has been viewed as a source of mischief toward third parties and, for that reason, as fraudulent."*[694]

> *"One reason for a better right for the seller's creditors could be that they should be entitled to believe that everything in the possession of the seller belongs to him."*[695]

In the English case above, the seller remained in possession of the sheep and continued appearing to be the owner, which was inconsistent with the fact that ownership had been alienated to the purchaser. For the seller's creditors, the seller appeared wealthier than he really is. With respect to *traditio per constitutum possessorium*, the concern about the problem of ostensible ownership can still be found in current law and theory.[696]

> *"Dit houdt verband met de publiciteitseis voor goederenrechtelijke rechten: de vervreemder c. p. wekt na de overdracht toch nog de indruk rechthebbende te zijn en wekt daarmee de valse schijn van kredietwaardigheid."*[697]

The problem also exists in situations other than transfer of ownership. According to some scholars, every bailment, which is based on the separation of ownership and possession, can cause the problem of ostensible ownership.[698] For example, where a relationship of lease is created, the lessee acquires possession by virtue of a right of use, but possession makes the lessee appear to have ownership. To tackle this problem, a system of registration should be constructed to allow third parties to know whether the possessor really has ownership.[699]

---

693 Brehm and Berger 2014, p. 442.

694 Baird and Jackson 1983, p. 180.

695 Hästad 2006, p. 40.

696 In Swedish law, where transfer is made in the way of *traditio per constitutum possessorium*, the transferee does not have a right to separate the object from the transferor's insolvency assets. If the transferor remains in possession, the transferee will have a position equal to other general creditors, except that the transferee is a customer or has registered the transfer. The rationale behind this rule is that *traditio per constitutum possessorium* triggers the problem of "*false wealthy*" and forms a sham transaction. See Lilja 2011, p. 59-62.

697 Snijders and Rank-Berenschot 2017, p. 116. English translation: "*It has a connection with the requirement of publicity of property rights: the transferor remains as a proprietor in the situation of constitutum possessorium, which gives rise to a false appearance of creditability.*"

698 Baird and Jackson 1983, p. 186.

699 Baird and Jackson 1983, p. 200.

In the second situation, the possessor, who has granted a limited property right, appears to enjoy unencumbered ownership. To avert this situation, possession needs to be given up by the owner. This opinion is often met in the course of justifying the requirement of delivery for possessory pledge and the construction of a registration system for non-possessory pledge: (1) delivery of the movable collateral by the pledgor avoids this person being falsely wealthy; and (2) where the pledgor retains possession of the movable collateral, registration of this non-possessory pledge can avoid general creditors being misled. In general, the rationale behind these concerns is that possession retained by the pledgor induces general creditors to overestimate the pledgor's creditability.[700]

> *"The debtor's dispossession fulfills two major functions: it makes it more difficult for the debtor to dispose of the pledged goods to a third person; the debtor can no longer create the misleading impression in the minds of his other creditors of owning the pledged goods which might be available for the satisfaction of their claims."*[701]

This rationale once underlay art. 38 of the English Bankruptcy Act (1914), a provision which defines the scope of insolvency assets according to possession.[702] This provision was abolished in 1985.[703] At present, the problem of ostensible ownership still exists, but this problem should be addressed by registration, rather than delivery of the collateral. Putting aside the question of whether a system of registration is desirable, we discuss only the question of whether the problem really exists for general creditors.

B Non-Existence of the Problem

The problem of ostensible ownership does not exist in practice. The separation of ownership and possession does not make the possessor falsely wealthy to general creditors. As has been argued, the first and foremost reason is that possession does not indicate that the possessor has ownership (see 3.5.2.1).[704] Obviously, general creditors cannot evaluate the debtor's creditability according to the amount of the corporeal movables possessed by the debtor. Possession only indicates that the debtor has a certain right, which is not necessarily ownership.

Secondly, the amount of corporeal movables possessed by a debtor is largely contingent on the business content of this debtor. For example,

---

700 Hamwijk 2012, p. 302.

701 Drobnig 2011, p. 1027.

702 Pursuant to art. 38 (c) of the Bankruptcy Act (1914), the insolvency asset includes "*All goods being, at the commencement of the bankruptcy, in the possession, order or disposition of the bankrupt, in his trade or business, by the consent and permission of the true owner, under such circumstances that he is the reputed owner thereof; provided that things in action other than debts due or growing due to the bankrupt in the course of his trade or business shall not be deemed goods within the meaning of this section*".

703 Beale, Bridge, Gullifer and Lomnicka 2018, no. 9.05.

704 Corral 2013, p. 414.

a warehousing enterprise is often in possession of a large amount of corporeal movables, which, however, neither means that this enterprise has ownership of these things, nor implies that it has good creditability. The reason is simple: the central business content of the enterprise is "possessing" and managing corporeal movables for others. At most, the amount of corporeal movables possessed indicates that the enterprise is running well. In contrast, an IT company might have good creditability, even though only a small amount of corporeal movables is possessed by this company. The reason is also simple: the major wealth of this company is incorporeal.

Thirdly, general creditors do not investigate the debtor's possession of corporeal movables because the cost of investigations is usually high. It is high for several reasons. Possession can take different forms and is exercised in different places. Possession can be indirect and hidden. Thus, general creditors cannot easily find out how many corporeal movables are in the debtor's indirect possession. The debtor often has more than one premises, which may be located in different cities, even foreign countries. Obviously, it is costly to go to each of the premises and ascertain the amount of corporeal movables. Another reason is that corporeal movables possessed by the debtor are always changing, which also makes the investigation difficult and expensive. For example, a manufacturing enterprise is always obtaining possession of materials and giving up possession of finished products. Moreover, the fluctuations in the object of possession also imply that the information collected is only useful for a short period.

Fourthly, delivery cannot avert the problem of ostensible ownership. Instead, it might be a cause of this problem. For example, once the pledgor delivers the movable collateral to the pledgee, the pledgee will appear to have ownership, which in fact he does not.[705] General creditors of the pledgee will be misled to believe that the pledgee enjoys ownership of the movable collateral.

> *"Strictly speaking, pledges of chattels, which were recognized at common law, created ostensible ownership problems as well, because the creditor holding pledged property would appear to own property that in fact belonged to another."*[706]

As delivery cannot solve the problem of ostensible ownership, there is no reason to expect that general creditors will rely on possession.

Lastly, general creditors commonly know that a thing possessed by the debtor does not necessarily belong to the debtor. Even if this thing does belong to the debtor, general creditors know that the thing is very likely to be mortgaged or pledged. Possession and ownership often diverge from each other in many situations, such as the security transfer, reservation of ownership, and sale and leaseback. In practice, professional businesspeople know that, for example, goods are often sold under a clause of reservation

705 Hamwijk 2012, p. 313.
706 Baird 1983, p. 54.

of ownership, and equipment is often mortgaged to the bank or rented from a financial lessor.[707] Businesspeople's common knowledge also implies that possession will not make the possessor falsely wealthy.

> *"With the increasing use of ownership-based, non-possessory security interests (retention of title with various extensions, security transfer of ownership) the question arises of whether purchasers today can still believe that movables which they find in the possession of the seller are in fact owned by the latter. In 1980, the BGH decided that in those business sectors where practically all goods are sold under retention of title, purchasers can no longer trust that the goods which the seller possesses are in fact his property."*[708]

For the reasons discussed above, possession cannot be considered as an indicator of ownership, and separation of possession from ownership does not cause the problem of ostensible ownership.

3.5.3 Possession and the Information of Proprietary Encumbrance over Corporeal Movables

As mentioned above, general creditors are not only affected by how many assets the debtor has in the event of the debtor's insolvency, but also by the amount of proprietary encumbrance over the assets. In this part, we turn to the latter aspect: whether possession can provide information about proprietary encumbrance over corporeal movables to general creditors.

It has been pointed out that there are two approaches in justifying the importance of delivery for general creditors: the positive approach and the negative approach (see 3.5.1.1). According to the positive approach, delivery can show possessory security interests to third parties. Under the negative approach, delivery is seen as a method to preclude the debtor from being falsely wealth and to avoid misleading third parties into the belief that the debtor has unencumbered ownership. The negative approach has just been discussed. In this part, we address only the positive approach.

This part begins with an introduction of both possessory security interests and non-possessory security interests in the three jurisdictions: English law, German law, and Dutch law. It can be found that these jurisdictions have a similar rule concerning possessory pledge, but differ in the non-possessory security interest. After that, a conclusive analysis is provided. There, we point out that the most commonly used security device in practice is non-possessory. Even if the possessory security interest is created with delivery, delivery cannot show this interest to third parties. As a result, possession cannot indicate the existence of proprietary encumbrance over corporeal movables to general creditors.

707 Snijders and Rank-Berenschot 2017, p. 427.
708 Kieninger 2007, p. 653.

3.5.3.1 *Introduction of Security Interests*

A English Law

In English law, apart from liens which are usually statutory, there are three types of consensual security right on movable things: pledge, mortgage, and charge.[709] The following discussion focuses on the relationship between these security rights and possession.

A1: Pledge

Pledge is a traditional security right in English law. Pledge is a possessory security right. To establish a right of pledge on a movable thing, the pledgor has to deliver this thing to the pledgee.[710] Mere agreement of creation is not adequate.[711] The prominent case is that the pledgor gives up actual possession to the pledgee, which is known as visible delivery. Visible delivery also takes place in the situation where the means of control, such as the key to the house in which the collateral is stored, is given up to the pledgee.[712] Delivery can be constructive in English law.

If the pledgee is already in possession of the collateral, "*a change in the nature of possession*" suffices.[713] This constitutes *traditio brevi manu*. If the movable collateral is possessed by a third party, the pledge also comes into existence when the third party attorns to the pledgee.[714] This attornment is equivalent to *traditio longa manu*. It should be specially mentioned that pledge can also be created via attornment by the pledgor to the pledgee, namely *traditio per constitutum possessorium*.[715] In other words, the pledgor can retain actual possession by only acknowledging holding the movable collateral for the pledgee. However, it is held by some writers that pledge created in this way is hidden and should be recharacterized as a charge.[716]

The prevailing opinion about the possibility of equitable pledge, a contract of pledge in the absence of any actual or constructive delivery is that equitable pledge is conceptually impossible.[717] Pledge is necessarily possessory. Equity law does not recognize "equitable possession", which implies that equitable pledge is not possible.[718] Moreover, where a pledge is allegedly created by parties in the absence of delivery, it is highly likely that this pledge will be re-characterized as a charge.[719]

---

709 Goode 2013, p. 32-35.
710 Goode 2013, p. 32.
711 Beale, Bridge, Gullifer and Lomnicka 2018, no. 5.23.
712 Beale, Bridge, Gullifer and Lomnicka 2018, no. 5.24.
713 Beale, Bridge, Gullifer and Lomnicka 2018, no. 5.88.
714 Beale, Bridge, Gullifer and Lomnicka 2018, no. 5.26.
715 *Dubin City Distillery v. Doherty*, [1914] A.C. 828, p. 852.
716 Beale, Bridge, Gullifer and Lomnicka 2018, no. 5.28.
717 Beale, Bridge, Gullifer and Lomnicka 2018, no. 5.60.
718 Bridge, Gullifer, McMeel and Worthington 2013, p. 157.
719 Beale, Bridge, Gullifer and Lomnicka 2018, no. 5.60.

A2: Mortgage

In English law, mortgage is an instrument of security on the basis of transfer of ownership, or precisely speaking, transfer of title.

> *"A mortgage is a non-possessory security whereby the mortgagor transfers ownership to the mortgagee subject to an obligation to retransfer ownership on satisfaction of the underlying obligation."*[720]

Mortgage requires a transfer of ownership. The corporeal movable mortgaged is not required to be delivered to the mortgagee, whether in an invisible or visible way.[721] In this aspect, mortgage and pledge differ. If the mortgagor defaults, the mortgagee has a right, either expressly-agreed or readily-implied, to possess and sell the collateral.[722] After performing the secured obligation, any surplus of the proceeds out of the sale will be held by the mortgagee for the mortgagor, forming a constructive trust.[723] In this sense, mortgage has a function of security, but this function is not reflected in the legal form of this transaction.[724] Besides the remedy of sale, the mortgagee is also entitled to request an order of foreclosure from the court. If the request is approved, then the collateral will be absolutely vested in the mortgagee, and the mortgagor will lose the collateral. Moreover, a successful foreclosure means that the mortgagee has no duty to return the surplus.[725] Foreclosure is rarely requested and approved nowadays.[726]

The mortgagor has the right to redeem, a right to recover ownership of the collateral. This right can be legal (when there is an express agreement) as well as equitable (when there is no express agreement).[727] If the mortgagor fulfills the secured obligation, then the legal ground on which ownership is transferred, will come to an end. As a result, ownership of the collateral will return to the mortgagor immediately.

For the creation of a mortgage, it suffices that the mortgagee acquires ownership of the movable collateral. Under the consensual system of English law, delivery is not necessary (see 3.4.2.1). However, since mortgage brings a risk to third parties, including general creditors, registration is required to make this security interest transparent.[728] If the mortgage is provided by a company, it should be registered under the Companies Act.[729]

720 Beale, Bridge, Gullifer and Lomnicka 2018, no. 6.01.
721 Goode 2013, p. 35.
722 Beale, Bridge, Gullifer and Lomnicka 2018, no. 6.06.
723 Bridge, Gullifer, McMeel and Worthington 2013, p. 174.
724 Beale, Bridge, Gullifer and Lomnicka 2018, no. 6.01.
725 Bridge, Gullifer, McMeel and Worthington 2013, p. 174.
726 Beale, Bridge, Gullifer and Lomnicka 2018, no. 18.19.
727 Beale, Bridge, Gullifer and Lomnicka 2018, no. 6.02.
728 Sealy and Hooley 2009, p. 1139.
729 Sealy and Hooley 2009, p. 1139.

If the mortgage is given by an individual in written form, it should be registered as a bill of sale under the Bills of Sale Acts.[730] However, it should be noted that the registration as a bill of sale is not open to the public, which means that the mortgage is still hidden.[731] In general, registration is only a requirement for "perfecting" mortgage. The lack of registration does not affect the creation. Moreover, mortgage can take effect in equity law: where there is a valid contract of creation, there is an equitable mortgage.[732]

A3: Charge

Charge is another security right in English law. Charge is introduced by equity, thus it is in principle equitable.[733] It neither requires the chargor to give up possession, nor requires the chargor to transfer ownership to the chargee. Charge is a limited encumbrance over the collateral.[734] Therefore, charge is different from pledge as well as mortgages.

> *"A charge is a non-possessory security whereby the charged property is appropriated to the discharge of an obligation without the transfer of ownership."*[735]

In terms of the execution, charge and mortgage also have some differences. For example, where there is a specific agreement, the chargee can claim certain judicial remedies, such as the order of sale and the appointment of a receiver. The mortgage is different: the mortgagee has a right of possession and can apply for foreclosure.[736] On the other hand, charge has a close relationship with mortgage. In many situations, these two terms are used interchangeably.[737]

B German Law

German law also recognizes possessory as well as non-possessory security interests. The subsequent discussion focuses on two types of security interest: one is the "pledge (*Pfandrecht*)" which is possessory, and the other is the "security transfer (*Sicherungsübereignung*)" which is non-possessory.

---

730 Sealy and Hooley 2009, p. 1139.
731 Beale 2016, p. 5.
732 Beale, Bridge, Gullifer and Lomnicka 2018, no. 6.07.
733 Clarke and Kohler 2005, p. 664.
734 Goode 2013, p. 36.
735 Beale, Bridge, Gullifer and Lomnicka 2018, no. 6.17.
736 Bridge, Gullifer, McMeel and Worthington 2013, p. 187.
737 Beale, Bridge, Gullifer and Lomnicka 2018, no. 6.54.

B1: Pledge

Pledge is a traditional security right, which has been prescribed by the BGB (§ 1204).[738] It requires dispossession and thus applies mainly to corporeal movables.[739] Pledge can also exist on certain incorporeal property, such as shares in limited liability companies, intellectual property and bank accounts.[740] In addition, "securities (*Wertpapieren*)" can also be an object of pledge since they can be possessed like a corporeal movable.[741] Upon default of the debtor, the pledgee has a right to sell the collateral and use the proceeds out of the sale to discharge the secured debt.[742] Moreover, pledge can be enforced against unsecured creditors in the situation of the pledgor's bankruptcy.[743]

For establishing the pledge, delivery is necessary as a means of publicity. Visible delivery suffices because it requires the pledgor to give up direct possession to the pledgee. As to invisible delivery, German legislators take a stricter attitude to the creation of pledge than to the transfer of ownership. Firstly, *traditio per constitutum possessorium* is prohibited, and the pledgor cannot retain direct possession of the movable collateral.[744] Secondly, *traditio longa manu* is not validly completed until notification is given to the third party who is in direct possession of the collateral.[745] It is worthwhile noting that such notification is not necessary for transferring ownership.

> § 1205 BGB: „*(1) Zur Bestellung des Pfandrechts ist erforderlich, dass der Eigentümer die Sache dem Gläubiger übergibt und beide darüber einig sind, dass dem Gläubiger das Pfandrecht zustehen soll. Ist der Gläubiger im Besitz der Sache, so genügt die Einigung über die Entstehung des Pfandrechts. (2) Die Übergabe einer im mittelbaren Besitz des Eigentümers befindlichen Sache kann dadurch ersetzt werden, dass der Eigentümer den mittelbaren Besitz auf den Pfandgläubiger überträgt und die Verpfändung dem Besitzer anzeigt.*"[746]

The requirement of delivery gives rise to significant inconvenience in practice, which partially accounts for the security transfer of ownership being commonly used.[747]

---

738 In German law, pledge can be consensual as well as statutory. The statutory pledge is an outcome of the operation of law, while the consensual pledge is a result of the parties' agreement. This part concerns only the consensual pledge.

739 Akkermans 2008, p. 225.

740 Rakob 2007, p. 68.

741 See § 1292 and § 1293 BGB; Baur and Stürner 2009, p. 754.

742 Baur and Stürner 2009, p. 747.

743 Baur and Stürner 2009, p. 747.

744 Baur and Stürner 2009, p. 750.

745 Baur and Stürner 2009, p. 750.

746 English translation: § 1205 BGB: "*(1) To create a pledge, it is necessary for the owner to deliver the thing to the creditor and for both to agree that the creditor is to be entitled to the pledge. If the creditor is in possession of the thing, agreement on the creation of the pledge suffices. (2) The delivery of possession of a thing in the indirect possession of the owner may be replaced by the owner transferring indirect possession to the pledgee and notifying the possessor of the pledging.*"

747 Baur and Stürner 2009, p. 750.

B2: Security Transfer of Ownership

Because of the stringent requirement of delivery in creating the pledge, individual parties turn to an ownership-based security device: the security transfer of ownership.[748] This device is not expressly provided by law. It is a result of commercial necessity and judicial creation.[749] Under this device, the purpose of security is realized by transferring ownership of corporeal movables to the creditor in the way of *traditio per constitutum possessorium*.[750] As a result, the creditor acquires ownership to secure the claim, and the debtor can continue using the collateral by retaining direct possession. The security transfer of ownership tempers the requirement of delivery, thus averting the inconvenience caused by this requirement. In terms of enforcement, the creditor can, by analogy with the rules of pledge, sell the collateral if the debtor defaults.[751] However, the creditor bears a liability of liquidation to return the surplus to the debtor.

For the security transfer, an "intermediate relationship of possession (*Besitzmittlungsverhältnis*)" is necessary.[752] Under this relationship, the debtor agrees to possess the movable collateral for the creditor, namely the security owner. Any other requirement of publicity is not necessary. Therefore, the security transfer of ownership is a hidden security device.[753]

C Dutch Law

In Dutch law, "pledge (*pand*)" is a security device that can be established on corporeal movables. Pledge can be "possessory (*vuistpand*)" and "non-possessory (*vuistloos pand*)".[754] Security transfer of ownership has been prohibited since the new BW, and the non-possessory pledge is recognized as an equivalent.[755] The following discussion focuses on these two types of pledge.

C1: Possessory Pledge

To create a possessory pledge, the pledgee has to obtain factual control. However, the pledgee does not have to directly control the collateral in person, and it also suffices that the pledgee indirectly controls the collateral through a third party.[756] In the latter situation, the third party has to hold

748 In German law, this security device is applicable to both corporeal movables and incorporeal things, such as claims. The discussion here concerns only the former, and the security assignment of claims is discussed in 4.1.4.2. Immovable property cannot be transferred for the purpose of security.

749 Rakob 2007, p. 69.

750 Baur and Stürner 2009, p. 785.

751 Akkermans 2008, p. 190.

752 Baur and Stürner 2009, p. 789.

753 Brinkmann 2016, p. 340.

754 See art. 3:236 BW and art. 3:237 BW.

755 Veder 2007, p. 193.

756 Steneker 2012, p. 91.

the collateral for the pledgee rather than the pledgor.[757] Moreover, a notification should be given to the third party, so that this party will hold the collateral for the pledgee.[758] Pursuant to art. 3:236 BW, the pledgor cannot retain any factual control. If the pledgor does not give up factual control to the pledgee, the possessory pledge does not come into existence. Therefore, the pledge cannot be created in the way of *traditio per constitutum possessorium*.[759] If the pledgor regains factual control of the collateral, then the pledge will cease to exist.[760] It is noteworthy that "possession (*bezit*)" is always held by the pledgor due to the distinction between possession and "detention (*houderschap*)". As to the formality of the contract of creation, there is not any special requirement.[761]

Possessory pledge requires the pledgee to obtain factual control of the collateral, and *traditio per constitutum possessorium* is not recognized. This prevents the pledgor from continuing making use of the collateral. As a result, this security device is seldom used in practice.[762] The purpose of security is often realized through the non-possessory pledge.

C2: Non-Possessory Pledge

In contrast to the possessory pledge, non-possessory pledge does not require placing the collateral under the factual control by the pledgee or a third party. For this reason, the latter is also known as "silent pledge".[763] Non-possessory pledge is treated as an alternative to the security transfer of ownership, which has been prohibited by the new BW (art. 3:84 (3)). In general, non-possessory pledge can be established in two ways. One is notarizing the deed of creation, and the other is registering the deed in the tax authorities. However, this registration is not open to the public, and outsiders cannot search the system.[764] The main purpose of the registration is to prevent antedating, and this purpose can be realized by notarization as well.[765] In a word, the non-possessory pledge requires neither delivery nor public registration, thus this security device is completely hidden.

If the debtor fails to perform the secured debt or there is a good reason for the creditor to believe that the debtor will not perform the debt,

757 Steneker 2012, p. 91.
758 Snijders and Rank-Berenschot 2017, p. 462; Reehuis and Heisterkamp 2019, p. 628.
759 Snijders and Rank-Berenschot 2017, p. 462; Reehuis and Heisterkamp 2019, p. 628.
760 Veder 2007, p. 195.
761 Veder 2007, p. 193.
762 Steneker 2012, p. 92.
763 Akkermans 2008, p. 290.
764 Veder 2007, p. 196.
765 Van Erp 2003, p. 6.

the pledgee is entitled to take control of the movable collateral.[766] Consequently, the non-possessory pledge becomes a possessory pledge. As a form of proprietary right of security, the non-possessory pledgee has a superior legal position over general creditors in the situation of the debtor's bankruptcy.[767]

D *Comparative Analysis*

From the introduction above, it is evident that there are two lines to compare security interests in corporeal movables. One is whether the security interest is possessory, and the other is whether the non-possessory interest is ownership-based. In the three jurisdictions, the pledge in English law, the "pledge (*Pfandrecht*)" in German law and the "possessory pledge (*vuistpand*)" in Dutch law are a possessory security interest. The non-possessory security interest includes the mortgage and charge in English law, the "security transfer (*Sicherungseigenung*)" in German law, and the "non-possessory pledge (*vuistloos pand*)" in Dutch law. Among these non-possessory interests, the mortgage under English law and the security transfer of ownership under German law are ownership-based, while the charge and the non-possessory pledge are a limited proprietary encumbrance.

The security transfer of ownership and the English-law mortgage take the transfer of ownership as their legal form.[768] However, they perform an economic function of security. In English law, mortgage and charge are often used interchangeably in theory, judicial practice and legislation.[769] In German law, the security transfer of ownership is treated as a pledge-like device.[770] In the economic essence, what the acquirer (the creditor) gains is a proprietary interest of preference.

---

766 Art. 3:237 (3) BW: "*Wanneer de pandgever of de schuldenaar in zijn verplichtingen jegens de pandhouder tekortschiet of hem goede grond geeft te vrezen dat in die verplichtingen zal worden tekortgeschoten, is deze bevoegd te vorderen dat de zaak of het toonderpapier in zijn macht of in die van een derde wordt gebracht. Rusten op het goed meer pandrechten, dan kan iedere pandhouder jegens wie de pandgever of de schuldenaar tekortschiet, deze bevoegdheid uitoefenen, met dien verstande dat een andere dan de hoogst gerangschikte slechts afgifte kan vorderen aan een tussen de gezamenlijke pandhouders overeengekomen of door de rechter aan te wijzen pandhouder of derde.*"
English translation: Art. 3:237 (3) BW: "*Where the pledgor or the obligor fails to perform his obligations as regards the pledgee, or gives him good cause for concern that there will be such a failure, the pledgee is entitled to demand that the thing or the paper to bearer be brought under his control or that of a third person. Where there are several rights of pledge over the property, each pledgee as regards whom the pledgor or the obligor fails to perform his obligations, can exercise this right, in which case no pledgee, other than the most senior in rank, may demand surrender to a pledgee or to a third person, if so agreed by the pledgees jointly, or to a pledgee or third person to be appointed by the court.*"

767 Hamwijk 2014, p. 83.

768 Beale, Bridge, Gullifer and Lomnicka 2018, no. 6.01.

769 Beale, Bridge, Gullifer and Lomnicka 2018, no. 6.54.

770 Akkermans 2008, p. 190.

„Wirtschaftlich betrachtet ist aber der Sicherungsnehmer nur Pfandgläubiger, der Schuldner (=Sicherungsgeber) ist ‚Eigentümer' geblieben; Dies kommt auch rechtlich darin zum Ausdruck, dass die zur Sicherheit übereignete Sache nach Tilgung der gescherten Forderung an den Schuldner zurückfallen soll."[771]

Security transfer of ownership was once recognized in judicial practice in the Netherlands. However, the new BW expressly prohibits this transfer under art. 3:84 (3) BW. The principal reason is that the purpose of the security transfer can be equivalently realized by the non-possessory pledge, and what the creditor should obtain is no more than a right of pledge.[772] This also illustrates that the security transfer of ownership is akin to the non-possessory pledge.

Different from the non-possessory security device, the possessory security device takes the same legal form: (possessory) pledge. In the three jurisdictions, the pledge is a limited property right, which does not involve any transfer of ownership. However, a difference exists between these jurisdictions. In both German law and Dutch law, *traditio per constitutum possessorium* cannot be used to create the possessory pledge: the pledgor is not allowed to retain actual control. In contrast, the possessory pledge can be created by *traditio per constitutum possessorium* in English law, albeit that the existence of mortgage and charge makes this unnecessary. As has been demonstrated above, pledge can also be created through attornment by the pledgor to the pledgee under English law (see 3.5.3.1.A).[773] In this way, the pledgor is able to retain factual control of the collateral, just like in the situation of creating a charge or mortgage. It is noteworthy that the possessory pledgee does not necessarily obtain direct possession of the movable collateral in the three jurisdictions. It might be a third party who is in actual control of the collateral. In this situation, the possessory pledge is created in the way of *traditio longa manu*. Moreover, the third party should be notified of the pledge.

3.5.3.2 Is Possession an Indicator of Proprietary Encumbrance?

On the basis of the discussion above, we find that possession cannot provide any information of proprietary encumbrance to general creditors for two reasons: (1) the ubiquitous existence of non-possessory security interests, and (2) possession is an abstract method of publicity.

771 Baur and Stürner 2009, p. 787. English translation: *"However, in the economic sense, the security acquirer is only a pledgee, and the debtor (namely the security provider) remains as the 'owner'. This is also correct on account of the fact that the object transferred for security will return to the debtor upon performance of the secured obligation."*

772 Akkermans 2008, p. 267.

773 *Dubin City Distillery v. Doherty*, [1914] A.C. 828, p. 852.

A The Ubiquitous Existence of Non-Possessory Security Interests

Even if we assume that possession can indicate the existence of proprietary encumbrance, the popularity of non-possessory security interests implies that general creditors cannot obtain information of proprietary encumbrance from possession. As most encumbered corporeal movables are still under the actual control by the debtors, how can a third party know about the proprietary encumbrance via possession?

It is worthwhile noting here that though the movable collateral is still possessed by the debtor when a non-possessory security right is created, the problem of ostensible ownership does not arise (see 3.5.2.2). Possession is not an outward mark of ownership, let alone that of unencumbered ownership. Moreover, prudent businesspeople know that there is a ubiquitous divergence between ownership and possession, and they will not be misled by the retention of possession by the debtor.

B The Abstract Publicity Effect of Possession

Traditionally, it is generally held that the possessory pledge should be made visible by delivery of the movable collateral to the pledgee. Moreover, *traditio per constitutum possessorium* cannot be used to create the pledge, because this invisible delivery does not have any effect of publicity.

> *"This is usually rationalized on the basis that possession is sufficient notice of the interest and so registration is not necessary."*[774]

> *"Het object van het pandrecht moet in de macht van de pandhouder of die derde worden gebracht om te bewerkstelligen dat de pandgever niet over het object van het pandrecht kan beschikken. Deze eis vloeit voort uit het beginsel van publiciteit. Uit de wijziging van de machtsuitoefening blijkt van het bestaan van het pandrecht tegenover derden."*[775]

> *„Eine Pfandrechtsbestellung durch Besitzkonstitut scheidet aus, weil die Pfandrechtsbestellung durch eine Änderung der Besitzverhältnisse für andere Gläubiger äußerlich erkennbar sein soll, woran es § 930 in fehlt."*[776]

In general, the opinion above is in line with the conventional view that possession is a means of publicity for corporeal movables. However, this opinion is not convincing. It is problematic to say that possession is able to make general creditors aware of the existence of a pledge on the movable collateral under the pledgee's control.

---

774 Goode 2013, p. 82.

775 Asser/Van Mierlo 2016, nr. 146. English translation: *"The object of the pledge must be under the control by the pledgee or a third party to make sure that the pledgor is not able to dispose of the object of the pledge. This requirement results from the principle of publicity. The pledge can be shown to third parties through the change of the power of control."*

776 Wolf and Wellenhofer 2011, p. 219. English translation: *"The creation of pledge though constitutum possessorium is excluded, because the creation of pledge must be made visible to other creditors by changing the relationship of possession, which does not take place under art. 930."*

Firstly, direct possession is only an abstract means of publicity for corporeal movables. Due to the great diversity of the legal basis on which direct possession can be obtained, possession cannot clearly indicate the specific right enjoyed by the possessor.[777]

> *"After all, possession by the pledge-holder cannot alone indicate that a lien over the item exists. The pledge-holder could also be the owner, lessee or custodian of the item."*[778]

For general creditors, it is completely impossible to infer the existence of pledge from the pledgee's direct possession. Direct possession only indicates that the possessor has a right to the thing possessed.

Secondly, indirect possession has no effect of publicity. As has been shown above, the possessory pledge can be created by allowing a third party to hold the collateral for the pledgee in the three jurisdictions. In this situation, the pledgee has indirect possession. As indirect possession is hidden to general creditors, it cannot provide any information.

> *"Where possession is transferred to the creditor by attornment rather than by an actual transfer of possession, it is hard to see that the creditor's possession constitutes very effective public notice."*[779]

In sum, there is no reason to believe that possession is an eligible means of publicity for the possessory pledge of corporeal movables. Therefore, general creditors cannot know from possession the existence of possessory pledge.

3.5.4 Conclusion

This section focuses on the importance of possession for general creditors. The central question discussed is whether possession can indicate how many corporeal movables are owned by the debtor (the information of ownership) and how much proprietary encumbrance is created over the corporeal movables owned by the debtor (the information of proprietary encumbrance).

In the second part of this section (3.5.2), we argue that possession cannot provide the information of ownership of corporeal movables to general creditors. The reason is simple: direct possession is an abstract and thus ambiguous method of publicity, and indirect possession has no effect of publicity. Moreover, it is difficult, costly and inappropriate to ascertain the corporeal movables owned by the debtor through possession. In practice,

777 Hamwijk 2012, p. 307.
778 Lukas 2004, p. 99.
779 Goode 2013, p. 82.

creditors know that a corporeal movable possessed by the debtor might belong to another person, while a corporeal movable not possessed by the debtor might belong to the debtor. Therefore, the divergence between ownership and possession does not give rise to the problem of ostensible ownership.

In the second part of this section (3.5.3), we argue that possession cannot provide the information of proprietary encumbrance over corporeal movables to general creditors. The main reason is that most proprietary security interests are non-possessory in practice. Possession is completely useless for ascertaining the existence of non-possessory security interests. Even if a possessory security right is created, this proprietary encumbrance cannot be made transparent by possession obtained by the creditor. The reason is simple: direct possession is only an abstract and thus ambiguous method of publicity, and indirect possession has no effect of publicity.

4 Notification, Documental Recordation, and Claims

Traditionally, notification and documental recordation are the two methods of publicity for claims. For example, if a seller assigns a claim for the payment of purchase price against a buyer to a third party, this seller usually notifies the buyer who will then pay the purchase price to the assignee. The notification is often said to perform a function of publicity.[1] If the purchase price has been paid by the buyer using a negotiable document (such as a check), then the seller can assign the claim embodied within this document by delivering and endorsing the document. The document is often treated as the method of publicity for the claim embodied, and transfer of the document can make disposal of the claim embodied effective against third parties.[2] In this chapter, we will discuss these two methods of publicity. In addition to these two traditional methods of publicity, the following discussion also devotes attention to "private registration", a formality of assignment and pledge of claims in Dutch law (art. 3:94 (3) and 3:239 (1) BW).

Chapter 4 is divided into three sections. The first two sections focus on notification to debtors (see 4.1) and documental recordation (see 4.2) respectively. In each section, English law, German law and Dutch law are selected for a comparative study. Moreover, Chapter 4 follows the framework of the discussion in Chapter 3: section 4.1 and 4.2 examine the importance of the two methods of publicity for the three types of third parties, namely strange interferers, subsequent acquirers, and general creditors. In these two sections, the focus of our discussion is whether the two methods of publicity convey sufficient information to subsequent acquirers.

4.1 Notification to Debtors

Nowadays, claims (or personal rights), especially monetary claims (receivables), form an important asset. Like corporeal movables, claims can also be transferred by the creditor, pledged for the purpose of security, and even taken as an object of proprietary usufruct. In these situations, a notification concerning the disposal is often given to the debtor. However, the legal effect of this notification varies from one jurisdiction to another. The notification might be a prerequisite of the disposal, a method which can make the disposal effective against third parties, or a factor which is only

1 DCFR 2009, p. 1076; Proprietary Security in Movable Assets 2014, p. 447.
2 DCFR 2009, p. 4553; Proprietary Security in Movable Assets 2014, p. 418.

relevant to the issue of the debtor's performance. In section 4.1, we examine the rationale of notification to debtors.

4.1.1 Notification and Personal Rights

4.1.1.1 The Dual Characteristics of Personal Rights

In general, personal rights have two aspects in law: personal rights as a means to acquire property and personal rights as a type of wealth.[3] The first aspect means that personal rights are a legal basis for the acquisition of things, which usually occurs between two particular parties. On the other hand, personal rights also constitute a type of property, which means that they can be disposed of like a thing.

> *"De Schuldvordering heeft een dubbel karakter, een persoonlijk en een zakelijk; enerzijds is zij ene persoonlijke betrekking tussen den schuldeiser en den schuldenaar, anderzijds is zij ene onlichamelijke zaak, een vermogensobject."*[4]

A Publicity and Personal Rights as a Means of Acquisition

Personal rights are personal (*in personam*) in nature because they only denote that the creditor is entitled to a certain performance by the debtor. In essence, a personal right is a legal relationship between the creditor and the debtor. As shown in Chapter 2, personal rights and property rights mainly differ in the breadth of enforceability (see 2.1.3). In general, personal rights cannot bind third parties and are subject to the principle of *paritas creditorum* and the principle of privity. The former principle means that personal rights are treated equally in the event of the debtor's insolvency, and the latter principle means that personal rights only bind particular parties under contract law. As a result, this type of right does not cause any problem of information asymmetry to third parties. Third parties can transact with a creditor or a debtor without having to fear being bound by the latter's relationship of personal rights.[5]

---

3 Radbruch 1929, p. 78.

4 Wiarda 1937, p. 84. English translation: *"The personal claim has a dual character, one personal and one proprietary; on the one hand it is a personal relationship between the creditor and the debtor, and on the other hand it is an incorporeal thing, a patrimonial object."*

5 For example, where A sells a bicycle to B, but ownership of this bicycle does not shift to B due to a certain reason, such as the lack of delivery, then C, as a third party, can transact with A with respect to the bicycle. In principle, the relationship of the sale between A and B cannot affect C's acquisition of ownership. Moreover, because B's personal claim against A is only an internal relationship between the two parties, this claim is difficult to be interfered with. Only when C intentionally induces A to breach the first contract with a purpose of damaging B, is he liable for the tort to B. In this hypothetical case, the personal right arising out of the contract is a means to acquire ownership of the bicycle. The difficulty in damaging the personal right in law is closely related to the legal policy of free competition. If B's personal right could generally bind C, then the free circulation of the bicycle would be hampered. See Honoré 1960, p. 468.

As a means of acquisition, personal rights are, in principle, a legal relationship *inter partes*, yielding no effect on third parties. The principle of publicity is alien to personal rights. In the law of obligations, the starting point is that individuals can create an obligation free from any formality, let alone publicity.[6] In principle, the relationship of obligations concerns personal affairs of the creditor and the debtor involved. Thus, there is no reason to require this relationship to be shown to third parties.

In some special situations, for the purpose of secure acquisition, personal rights might be allowed to be registered, so that they are effective against certain parties. For example, the right to acquire immovable property may enter the land register, which is known as preemptive registration (*Vormerkung*).[7] After being registered, the transferee is able to acquire the immovable property without being affected by subsequent disposal by the transferor. In the situation of preemptive registration, the claim of acquisition is strengthened to be partially proprietary, and the claim serves an acquisition purpose.

B Publicity and Personal Rights as a Part of Wealth

Though personal rights are not proprietary in legal nature, they occupy a large proportion of our wealth in modern society.[8] Personal rights are not only a means of acquisition, but also an important part of wealth.

> *„Macht- und Zinsgenuss von Forderungsrecht ist jetzt das Ziel alles Wirtschaftens, das Forderungsrecht nicht mehr Mittel, zum Sachenrecht und zum Sachgenuss zu gelangen, sondern selber Ziel des Rechtslebens.“*[9]

Here bank accounts serve as a good example: individuals usually deposit their incomes in a bank account and use a bank card to pay for daily consumption. The depositing of fund can give rise to a personal right against the depositing bank. The payment involves debiting the payor's account and crediting the payee's account.[10] In general, the payment involves a combination of multiple acts made by the parties involved, such as the payor, the payee, and the bank(s) entrusted with these acts by the payor and the payee.[11]

> *"Aldus werd het mogelijk om de schuldvordering, die voor de schuldeiser een recht op een prestatie van zijn schuldenaar inhoudt, over te dragen aan een derde en ook te beschouwen als een op geld waardeerbaar, actief bestanddeel van het vermogen van de*

---

6 Hijma, Van Dam, Valk and Van Schendel 2016, p. 14.

7 See art. 7:3 BW and § 1094 BGB.

8 Pound 1999, p. 225.

9 Radbruch 1929, p. 79. English translation: "*The enjoyment of power and interests out of claims is nowadays the purpose of all economic activities, and claims are no longer a means to acquire property rights or enjoyment of property, but the purpose of the economic life.*"

10 Mijnssen 2017, p. 53.

11 Mijnssen 2017, p. 54.

> *schuldeiser. Het is in en door haar hoedanigheid van vermogensrecht en dus van vermogensbestanddeel, dat de schuldvordering tot voorwerp van het eigendomsrecht of een daarvan afgeleid goederenrechtelijk recht kan worden gemaakt."*[12]

In legal history, the aspect of personal rights as a part of wealth was overlooked. The personal right was considered as a means of acquisition which could lead to a legal bond (*iuris vinculum*) between the creditor and the debtor in Roman law.[13] Assignment would make the personal right lose its identity and thus was prohibited.[14] However, some scholars, such as Windscheid and Delbrück, argued that the fact that personal rights were a relationship between particular persons should not be an obstacle to their qualification as a transferable asset.[15] French scholars and Dutch scholars thought that personal rights contained both a personal aspect and a proprietary aspect: the former means that personal rights are a legal relationship between two parties, and the latter means that personal rights are an incorporeal asset that can be transferred.[16] At present, personal rights are, in principle, transferable. The disposal of personal rights, especially receivables, has constituted an important part of commercial transactions, as indicated by securitization, factoring, and the pledge of receivables.[17] According to some scholars, this leads to a phenomenon of "objectification (*objectivering*)" and "propetization (*verzakelijking*)" of personal rights.

> *"In de geschetste voorbeelden en in het dagelijkse handelsverkeer in het algemeen worden schuldvorderingen niet louter geconcipieerd als een rechtsband die bestaat tussen minstens een schuldeiser en een schuldenaar, maar bovendien geobjectiveerd of gedepersonaliseerd als een object dat een op geld waardeerbaar bestanddeel van het vermogen van de schuldeiser uitmaakt. Schuldvorderingen worden als het ware 'verzakelijkt'."*[18]

In a nutshell, personal rights are not only a means of acquisition, a legal relationship between the creditor and the debtor, but also a type of wealth susceptible to disposals.[19] This is a reason why the Dutch legislature includes personal rights within the concept of "property (*goed*)" and pro-

---

12 Lebon 2010, p. 157. English translation: "*Therefore, it becomes possible to transfer to third parties a personal claim which includes the creditor's right with respect to the performance by the debtor, and to treat this right as a monetary asset of the creditor's patrimony. Due to its capacity as a patrimonial right and a patrimonial component, the claim can be an object of both ownership and a property right derived therefrom.*"

13 Wiarda 1937, p. 75.

14 Wiarda 1937, p. 75-76.

15 Wiarda 1937, p. 79-80.

16 Wiarda 1937, p. 82-83.

17 Verhagen 2002, p. 241.

18 Lebon 2010, p. 2. English translation: "*In general, in the examples outlined and the ordinary business transaction, personal rights are not only conceived as a legal relationship between the creditor and the debtor, but are objectified or depersonalized as an object that constitutes a valuable part of the creditor's patrimony. In this sense, personal rights are 'propertized'.*"

19 Eggens 1960, p. 198-199.

vides in patrimonial law for a general part which treats tangible property and intangible property equally in the BW.[20] Truly, there are different views on the status of personal rights in the law of property, but the debate is mainly theoretical.[21]

As a type of property, personal rights can be an object of different forms of disposal, such as transfer, pledge and creation of a property right of use. This means that there might be a conflict between two or more forms of disposal of the same personal right. For example, a creditor might transfer his personal right to two different persons, which causes a problem of double assignments; the creditor may pledge the right twice, which leads to a conflict between two pledgees; it is also likely that the creditor creates two rights of usufruct on the personal right. In general, every conflict that can arise in the disposal of corporeal movables might also take place in the disposal of personal rights. Therefore, once personal rights are included in transactions, a problem of information asymmetry arises to third parties. As mentioned above, notification to debtors is often seen as a method of publicity for the disposal of personal rights. However, this viewpoint is subject to heavy criticism.[22] In the following discussion, we focus on the question whether notification to debtors can qualify as a method of publicity.

C *The Scope of the Following Discussion*

As just shown above, a personal right is a legal relationship between a debtor and the creditor. Therefore, the consequence of the assignment of personal rights is that the assignee, i.e. the new creditor, is entitled to request the debtor to perform the debt. However, this does not mean that the debtor is necessarily obliged to provide performance, nor that the creditor can obtain performance. In principle, the debtor can claim the defenses he or she has against the original creditor also against the new creditor (art. 6:145 BW[23] and § 404 BGB[24]). The debtor of a claim should never be disadvantaged due to the disposal of this claim by the creditor.

For example, if a person acquires a personal right out of a contract against the debtor and then assigns this right, the debtor is, in principle, able to refuse to offer performance to the assignee by claiming, for example, that the contract is created on the basis of fraud or that the original creditor failed to provide counter performance appropriately.[25] As a result, the claim

20 Meijers 1954, p. 159-160.

21 Lebon 2012, p. 367-375.

22 Rongen 2012, p. 497-499; Von Wilmowsky 1996, p. 392-393.

23 Art. 6:145 BW: "*Overgang van een vordering laat de verweermiddelen van de schuldenaar onverlet.*" English translation: Art. 6:145 BW: "*Assignment of a claim does not affect the obligor's defences.*"

24 § 404 BGB: „*Der Schuldner kann dem neuen Gläubiger die Einwendungen entgegensetzen, die zur Zeit der Abtretung der Forderung gegen den bisherigen Gläubiger begründet waren.*" English translation: § 404 BGB: "*The debtor may raise against the new creditor the objections that he was entitled to raise against the previous creditor at the time of assignment.*"

25 Nörr, Scheyhing and Pöggeler 1999, p. 41; Rongen 2002, p. 288-289.

acquired by the assignee might turn out to be "valueless". In general, this also applies, *mutatis mutandis*, to a pledge of a personal right.[26]

The question whether the debtor can claim defenses against the assignee or the pledgee is beyond the scope of the following discussion. In general, we focus only on the disposal of the claim *per se* and thus the proprietary aspect of the claim. The possibility of claiming defenses by the debtor is a problem of performance regulated by the law of obligations, thereby concerning the obligational aspect.[27]

4.1.1.2 *The Rationale of Notification*

A *Notification and Two Functions*

Notification to debtors refers to notifying the debtor involved of the disposal.[28] A valid notification has to fulfill several requirements which involve, for example, the person who provides the notification, the way in which the notification should be made, and the content the notification needs to indicate. These requirements might be regulated by different laws in different ways.[29] In the following discussion, we focus only on the function of notification.

In general, notification to debtors serves two functions. One function is that notification helps debtors to know the person to whom they need to perform the obligation.[30] The other function is that notification to debtors can make the assignment of claims transparent to third parties.[31] If the debtor is not notified of the assignment, then two consequences might arise: (1) the debtor is entitled to be discharged from performing the obligation to the assignor (the original creditor), as if the assignment never occurred; and (2) the assignee might end up in a disadvantageous position, if the same claim is assigned to a third party who notifies the debtor earlier. These two functions, known as the function of performance and the function of publicity in this research, were disputed in legal history.

---

26 Verdaas 2008, p. 313.

27 Van Empel and Huizink 1991, p. 50-52.

28 In German legal theory, notification is a "quasi-legal act (*geschäftsähnliche Handlung*)", which means that it is neither a "legal act (*Rechtsgeschäft*)" nor a "factual act (*Realakt*)". See Medicus 2010, p. 89.

29 In the situation of assignment, notification to the debtor might be given by the assignor or assignee, which is often decided by the parties to the assignment. As to the formality of notification, law may require a written form, but oral notification or even constructive notification through acts might also be recognized. The notification is important for the debtor to ascertain the person to whom the debtor has to perform the debt. Thus, law usually requires the notification to be sufficiently precise and clear. In general, it needs to indicate the assignee, the claim assigned, the amount assigned, and the date of assignment. See Snijders and Rank-Berenschot 2017, p. 303; Medicus and Lorenz 2015, p. 375-376.

30 Parlementaire Geschiedenis (3) 1981, p. 392; Schlechtriem 2003, p. 304-305.

31 Parlementaire Geschiedenis (3) 1981, p. 392.

> *"Al in het klassieke en na-klassieke Romeinse recht was de precieze functie van de mededeling onduidelijk. Dient de mededeling slechts om aan de debiteur aan te geven aan wie hij moet betalen, of is zij een constitutief vereiste voor de overdracht van de vordering."*[32]

As we will see later, the controversy still exists in present private law. The function of publicity is denied in some jurisdictions, such as German law, while it is a reason for the legal effect against third parties in French law.[33]

In the viewpoint of Dutch scholar Rongen, both functions concern publicity: the function of performance is "direct publicity with respect to the debtor (*directe publiciteit ten opzichte van de schuldenaar*)", and the function of publicity is "indirect publicity with respect to third parties (*indirecte publiciteit ten opzichte van derden*)".[34] The term "indirect" means that third parties can only obtain information indirectly, namely making inquiries with the debtor about the claim involved.

The first function only concerns how to identify the person to whom performance has to be carried out by the debtor. The debtor is entitled to perform the obligation to the assignor (the original creditor) when the debtor does not obtain any notification concerning the assignment. Therefore, the first function is a result of the demand for protecting the debtor in good faith. It has nothing to do with the assignment *per se*. The fact that the debtor in good faith is discharged from performing the obligation to the assignor does not mean that the assignment fails: the assignee, the actual creditor, can require the assignor to disgorge the performance on the ground of, for example, unjust enrichment.[35] For this reason, the first function is not included within the concept of publicity in this research. Even Rongen acknowledges that the "direct publicity with respect to the debtor" only has "obligational significance (*verbintenisrechtelijke betekenis*)".[36]

The second function implies the legal effect of notification on third parties. For determining the priority between competing interests with respect to the same claim, notification might play an important role. Therefore, the second function falls under the concept of publicity in this research and will be examined in this Chapter. According to Rongen's viewpoint, "indirect publicity with respect to third parties" has the following effects: determining whether and when the assignment arises; addressing the problem of *"false appearance of wealth"*; avoiding the risk of multiple assignments; protecting the subsequent acquisition against earlier disposal; setting up a

32 Verhagen 1997, p. 165. English translation: *"In the classic and post-classic Roman law, the precise function of notification was not clear: it served to inform the debtor of the person to whom he has to perform or was a constitutive requirement for the assignment of the claim."*

33 Lebon 2012, p. 388-392.

34 Rongen 2012, p. 484-489.

35 Schlechtriem 2003, p. 304; Reehuis and Heisterkamp 2019, p. 254-255.

36 Rongen 2012, p. 484.

barrier against the assignment of future claims.[37] In general, these aspects can be divided into two categories: the function of determining the date of assignment and the function of providing information.

B Notification and the Function of Publicity: Introduction

Firstly, it is often held that notification to the debtor is helpful for determining the priority of competing disposals of the same claim. The notification has a function of countering fraudulent assignments: once notification is stipulated as a prerequisite of assignment, then the problem of antedating can be addressed to some extent.

> *"To some extent and at least in some respects, notification can be understood as being functionally similar to publicity by registration, since a notification requirement can to some degree achieve common objectives such as the prevention of antedating."*[38]

The function of preventing antedating can be illustrated by a hypothetical case concerning double assignment (Figure 7): A is a creditor of B, and A first assigns his claim to C and then assigns the same claim to D.

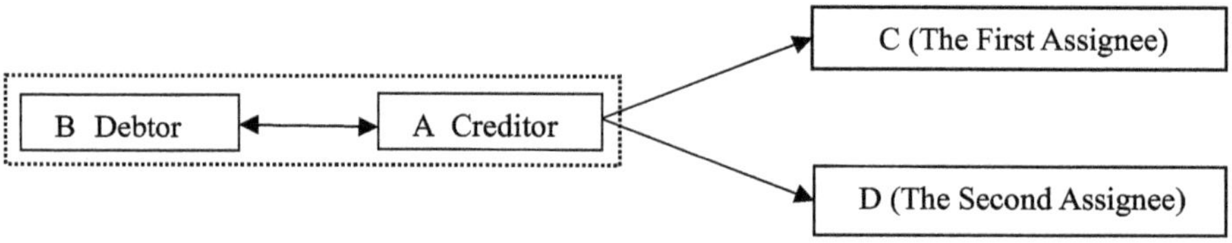

Figure 7

If notification is not a condition for valid assignment, and both assignments are unknown to B, then C will have a preferential position over D. This is because the assignment to C occurs earlier (the *nemo dat* rule). However, D might attempt to avert this disadvantage by conspiring with A and fraudulently antedating the second assignment. This activity can be prevented or inhibited by notification. If the law requires notification as a condition for valid assignment, which forces C and D to notify the debtor (B), then B, as a witness, can prove before the court the actual date of the two assignments.

In addition to the situation of double assignment, the function of determining the date of assignment is also useful for the assignor's creditors in the event of the assignor's bankruptcy.[39] This function was taken into consideration by Dutch legislators (art. 3:94 (1) BW).

37 Rongen 2012, p. 489.
38 Proprietary Security in Movable Assets 2014, p. 447.
39 Parlementaire Geschiedenis (3) 1981, p. 396.

> *"Bij zijn beslissing om dit stelsel in het gewijzigd ontwerp te handhaven heeft voor de ondergetekende de doorslag gegeven de grotere rechtszekerheid die het biedt ten aanzien van de vraag of een vordering al dan niet overgedragen is [...]. Nagenoeg gelijke rechtszekerheid is op andere wijze niet te verkrijgen."*[40]

Secondly, it is often said that notification to debtors also has a function of providing information to third parties. As has been shown above, the main purpose of publicity is to provide information to third parties, so that they do not have to only rely on their counterparties who have a motive to cheat (see 2.2.3). Notification is often treated as a way to realize this purpose.[41] For example, in order to know whether the assignor has disposed of the claim involved, potential assignees can ask the debtor about the claim.

> *"The second is that an intending assignee, before giving value, can ask the debtor whether the debtor has received any prior notice of assignment. If the first assignee has failed to give such a notice the second assignee should be entitled to assume that there is no earlier assignment, unless the second assignee has acquired knowledge of the earlier assignment in some other way or ought to have known of the earlier assignment, e.g. because it had been registered in a public register."*[42]

> *„Dritte konnten von der Abtretung Kenntnis erlangen, indem sie sich an den Schuldner der abgetretenen Forderung wenden; es erscheine naheliegend dass sie sich an ihn wenden, um Auskünfte einzuholen."*[43]

The two excerpts above show that assignees are expected to inquire with the debtor about the claim. If an assignee fails to do so, then he has to bear the risk of being subordinated to an earlier assignment. On the ground of this concern, some jurisdictions adopt a first-to-notify rule, which is also accepted by the DCFR.[44] Moreover, the DCFR drafters also think that notification is "*the closest equivalent to the acquiring of possession in good faith, which is a recognized method of obtaining priority in the case of corporeal movables*".[45]

In sum, notification to debtors is often treated as a method of publicity for the disposal of claims. Thus, there is always the notion that an advantageous position should be granted to assignees or pledgees who notify the debtor involved earlier.[46] In the following discussion, we argue that notification does not qualify as a method of publicity for claims.

---

40 Parlementaire Geschiedenis (3) 1981, p. 396. English translation: "*By determining to maintain this system in the modified draft, greater legal certainty, as to whether or not a claim has been transferred, can be provided to the undersigned. Similar legal certainty cannot be given in other ways.*"

41 Snijders and Rank-Berenschot 2017, p. 302.

42 DCFR 2009, p. 1076.

43 Von Wilmowsky 1996, p. 392. English translation: "*Third parties can gain knowledge of the assignment by making an inquiry with the debtor of the claim assigned; it seems obvious that they should turn to the debtor for information.*"

44 DCFR 2009, p. 1075.

45 DCFR 2009, p. 1076.

46 *Dearle v. Hall* (1828) 3 Russ 1; Parlementaire Geschiedenis (3) 1981, p. 396.

C Notification and the Function of Publicity: Questioning

C1: Notification and the Prevention of Antedating

As just demonstrated, notification can alleviate or prevent the problem of fraudulent antedating. It can be used to determine the actual date of competing disposals.[47] However, this function is not the central aim of publicity, nor does it allow notification to be an eligible method of publicity.

The main reason why (public) registration qualifies as a method of publicity is that the register is open to the public. Registration provides information to third parties who can then predict their legal position, especially the possibility of acquiring the right and the ranking of the right acquired. Publicity is rooted in the notion of preventive justice: preventing the occurrence of conflicts *ex ante*, instead of solving conflicts *ex post*.

> *"Preventive justice is an essential element of the European legal systems. As part of it, government authorities support citizens in carrying out important legal acts. Especially in the area of title transaction German law provides a high standard of transaction security through the concept of preventive justice. This concept focuses on the means by which the state provides preventive protective mechanisms designed to avoid the need to resolve disputes ex post facto. The idea is to avoid the inefficiency and social cost of court proceedings to the greatest extent possible by means of measures to clarify and to rationalize high value transactions. In particular, public registers such as the Land Register and the Commercial Register are designed to provide a high level of certainty in real estate title and corporate capacity matters."*[48]

The distinctive feature of every method of publicity is that this method is open to third parties. Otherwise, conflicts cannot be prevented in advance. Certainly, once a property right is registered, the date of creation of this right will become fixed. In this sense, the prevention of antedating is merely a subordinate outcome of publicity.

Truly, notification is helpful for addressing the problem of antedating and facilitating the legal certainty of transactions. However, notification cannot make the assignment visible to third parties. As will be discussed later, though a creditor transfers his claim, and the debtor is informed of the transfer, third parties cannot easily know about the transfer. This means that the problem of information asymmetry to third parties still exits, and the purpose of preventing the occurrence of conflicts is not realized. In fact, the prevention of antedating by notification falls, to a large extent, within the *ex-post* approach: when two competing assignments have taken place, notification is helpful in ascertaining the actual date of each assignment.

Secondly, the effect of preventing antedating can also be achieved in other ways than notification. For example, notarization and private registration can determine the date of assignment, which lays a basis for the intro-

---

47 Rongen 2012, p. 486.
48 Limmer 2013, p. 329-330.

duction of the undisclosed or silent assignment in 2004 in the Netherlands (art. 3:94 (3) BW).[49] The problem of antedating can be addressed through these two ways: once the contract of assignment is made before a notary or deposited in the tax authorities, the date of assignment can be safely fixed.[50] Nevertheless, these two ways should not be treated as a method of publicity. The assignment, though notarized or privately registered, remains hidden to third parties.[51] The register administrated by the tax authorities is not accessible for third parties, and the problem of information asymmetry cannot be addressed by the registration. The purpose of preventing conflicts is not realized. According to some Dutch lawyers, notarization and private registration perform a "function of evidence (*bewijsfunctie*)" only: these two formalities demonstrate the time of assignment, thereby addressing the problem of antedating.[52]

Finally, whether notification is able to prevent antedating is still open to doubts. As mentioned above, notification addresses the problem of antedating indirectly: inquiring with the debtor involved. If antedating arises, then the debtor is expected to point out the fraudulent act. However, this way meets multiple challenges in practice. For example, the debtor may also participate in the fraudulent activity.[53] In most situations, it may be the subsequent assignees who induce the debtor to antedate their notification of the assignment. However, the debtor might also be an interested party in the disposal of claims, which means that the debtor perhaps cheats for his or her own benefit.[54] Therefore, notification cannot address the problem of antedating better than notarization or private registration does. Moreover, if the notification is made orally, then the debtor will have a chance to knowingly lie about the date of notification.

C2: Notification and the Provision of Information

In addition to the prevention of antedating, another argument for notification as a method of publicity is that third parties can obtain some information about the claim in question by inquiring with the debtor.[55] This function of publicity is considered by Dutch law and German law, which will be shown in the subsequent comparative study.[56] However, notification does not make claims, which are intangible *per se*, visible to third parties.

49 Rongen 2012, p. 481-482.
50 Rongen 2012, p. 486.
51 Struycken 2009, p. 140.
52 Struycken 2009, p. 140.
53 Rank 1992, p. 14.
54 For example, if assignment has a legal effect of interrupting the period of extinctive prescription, the debtor might claim that the assignment occurs later than the date asserted by the assignee.
55 Rongen 2012, p. 487.
56 Von Wilmowsky 1996, p. 392; Parlementaire Geschiedenis (3) 1981, p. 396.

> *"Publicity by notice to a contract obligator is of little efficacy as being transparent and obvious because other creditors cannot see the intangible, let alone see whether the notice has been given to the debtor of the issuer."*[57]

At most, we can say that notification creates a possibility for third parties to obtain information from the debtor notified. No information is conveyed by the notification itself. In other words, information is communicated indirectly. Unlike notification, possession and registration directly convey information to third parties. The specialty of how information is communicated determines that notification to debtors does not qualify as a method of publicity.

Firstly, the law does not prescribe any obligation of disclosure to debtors.[58] In general, assignees and pledgees can have some benefits from notification, which encourages them to inform the debtor of the assignment or pledge. However, this does not mean that the debtor notified will honestly disclose the disposal that has already occurred to third parties, because the debtor is not required to do so by law. The absence of a legal duty of disclosure is understandable. The disclosure is not without costs, especially when the debtor has a large number of creditors, and the claim involved has been disposed of many times. If the debtor does not plan to cooperate and refuses to provide any information, it is unclear whether the inquirer can sue the debtor.

Secondly, even if the debtor is willing to cooperate, the information provided might be incomplete or incorrect.[59] The debtor might tell the inquirer what he or she knows, but some information may be missed. The claim might be assigned and pledged many times, and the debtor perhaps does not keep a full record of all the disposals. The debtor might only disclose some of the transactions to third parties, negligently omitting the other transactions. After all, the debtor has no duty of disclosure under law. A worse situation is that the debtor conspires with the creditor or other parties and intentionally misleads the inquirer by providing incorrect information.

> *"Zijn administratie kan onbetrouwbaar zijn, zodat hij niet meer op de hoogte is van de eerdere cessie. Hij kan zelfs op frauduleuze wijze samenspannen met de cedent. Dit laatste geldt ook bij mogelijke 'schijncessies', bedoeld om de crediteren van de cedent te benadelen."*[60]

In these situations, the inquirer is unable to obtain complete or correct proprietary information concerning the claim.

57 Wood 2019, no. 9-014.

58 Von Wilmowsky 1996, p. 392; Rongen 2012, p. 488; Beale, Bridge, Gullifer and Lomnicka 2018, no. 14.10.

59 Von Wilmowsky 1996, p. 392-393; Rank 1992, p. 14; Beale, Bridge, Gullifer and Lomnicka 2018, no. 14.10.

60 Verhagen 1997, p. 175. English translation: "*His administration can be unreliable so that he fails to be aware of the previous assignment. He can even fraudulently conspire with the assignor. He might also declare 'fake assignment', with an intention to compromise the creditability of the assignor.*"

Thirdly, due to the unreliability of the information provided by the debtor, *bona fide* acquisition is not generally recognized. In principle, property law does not provide legal protection to the inquirer's reliance on the debtor's disclosure.[61] In the above hypothetical case, A alienates a claim to C, and the debtor B is notified of the assignment; after that A assigns the same claim to D who inquires about this claim with B, but B does not disclose the first assignment, either negligently or intentionally.

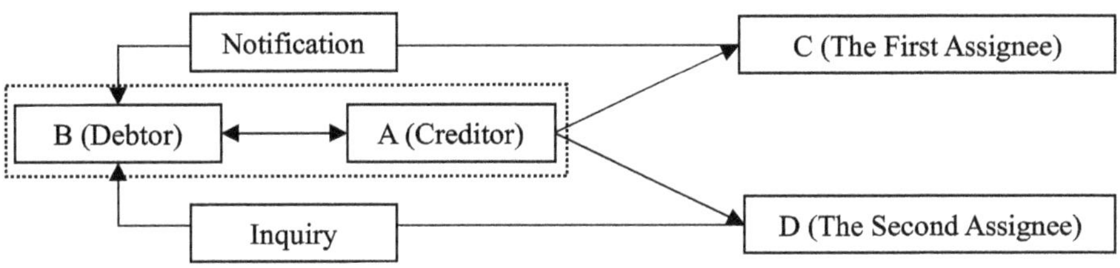

Figure 8

In this case, it is highly possible that D will rely on B's disclosure. Nevertheless, D is not entitled to acquire the claim. In principle, *bona fide* acquisition of claims is not recognized by law, and it is the *nemo dat* rule that regulates the disposal of claims. Notification is not an outward appearance which can trigger the legal protection of reliance of third parties.

> *„Anders als das Sachenrecht [...] kennt also das Zessionsrecht grundsätzlich keinen gutgläubigen Erwerb einer nichtexistenten oder gläubigerfremden Forderung [...]. Das erklärt sich daraus, dass es anders als bei Sachen, wo Grundbucheintrag bzw. Besitz der Sache einen Rechtsschein der Inhaberschaft eines nichtberechtigt Verfügenden erzeugen können, ein solcher Rechtsscheinträger bei Forderung nicht existiert."*[62]

> *"Vanwege de gebrekkige publiciteit die de mededeling ten opzichte van derden aan de overdracht toekent, kan er mee worden ingestemd dat naar huidig recht de mededeling geen absoluut constitutief vereiste is voor de geldige levering van een vordering op naam. Ook verdient het geen aanbeveling de mededeling een functie te laten vervullen in het kader van een nieuw ontwerpen derden beschermingsbepaling voor het geval van een meervoudige beschikking over een vordering op naam."*[63]

---

61 Von Wilmowsky 1996, p. 392.

62 Medicus and Lorenz 2015, p. 365. English translation: *"Different from property law, the law of assignments does not generally recognize bona fide acquisition of non-existent claims or claims belonging to others [...]. This is explained by the fact that, contrary to the situation where an entry in the land register or possession of the property can create a legitimate appearance of ownership of unauthorized disponers, a similar legitimate appearance does not exist in the situation of claims."*

63 Rongen 2012, p. 498. English translation: *"Due to the fact that notification only provides defective publicity to third parties, it is commonly held that notification should not be an absolute constitutive requirement for the valid delivery of a named claim under the current law. It is also advisable that notification should not fulfill the function under the context of introducing a new provision for protecting third parties in the situation of multiple disposals of a named claim."*

In addition to the above-mentioned defects of notification as a method of communicating information, notification also has some practical drawbacks.

If the assignment or pledge involves many claims, then the assignee or the pledgee needs to inquire about each claim with the debtor, which is costly and hampers the fluidity of transactions.[64] Moreover, where future claims are involved, the debtor's identity might not be ascertained.[65] In this situation, transacting parties are unable to notify the debtor, nor third parties are able to make inquiries with the debtor.[66] Inevitably, the disposal of future claims has to be restricted, as Dutch law did before 2004.[67] In reality, creditors often do not want their debtors to know that the claim against the debtor has been assigned or pledged to another person.[68] This resistance also casts doubt on the desirability of adopting notification as a method of publicity for claims.

The above-mentioned practical difficulties imply that notification is not an appropriate method of publicity. If the law imposes a duty of disclosure on the debtor and grants protection to the inquirer's reliance on the debtor's disclosure, then the smooth operation of transactions would be significantly affected. In general, a method of publicity should not cause significant inconvenience to concluding transactions. Otherwise, it should be replaced by another method or abolished.[69]

In a nutshell, notification to debtors does not qualify as a method of publicity for claims. Truly, notification can address the problem of antedating and creates an opportunity for third parties to acquire some information by inquiring with the debtor notified. However, it fails to make the assignment of or the proprietary encumbrance over claims visible to third parties. The aim of preventing the occurrence of conflicts cannot be realized. Moreover, the likelihood that the information provided by the debtor is incomplete or incorrect is high. As a result, *bona fide* acquisition by third parties is not generally recognized by law. Lastly, notification is not an appropriate method of publicity because it causes many inconveniences to transactions.

---

64 Von Wilmowsky 1996, p. 393; Akseli 2013, p. 212.
65 Beale, Bridge, Gullifer and Lomnicka 2018, no. 14.10.
66 Von Wilmowsky 1996, p. 393; Akseli 2013, p. 212.
67 Rongen 2012, p. 497.
68 Verhagen 1997, p. 164.
69 Here, the recognition of the undisclosed assignment by Dutch law in 2004 is an example. By doing so, individuals can avert the burden of notification by turning to notarization or private registration. See Rongen 2012, p. 481-482. Another example is possession. As has been shown above, the requirement of actual delivery under the *traditio* rule hampers the smooth operation of transactions. However, this problem can be addressed by recognizing indirect possession and fictional delivery (*traditio ficta*), which amounts to abandoning the requirement of publicity. Unlike possession, however, notification cannot be carried out in a fictional way, and the term "indirect notification" is never used.

4.1.2 Notification and Third-Party Effect: Strange Interferers

After arguing that notification is not an eligible method of publicity for claims, we move on to discuss the question of whether notification is useful for different types of third party: strange interferers, subsequent acquirers, and general creditors. As has been shown above, these three types of third party demand different proprietary information (see 2.2.2.2).

In this part, we argue that notification is, in principle, of no importance for strange interferers. Moreover, notification provides no proprietary information for general creditors (see 4.1.5). In some of the literature, the function of publicity of notification for subsequent acquirers is discussed under the context of the assignment and pledge of claims, instead of the protection of claims. For this reason, a detailed and comparative discussion concerning the importance of notification for subsequent acquirers will be provided later in 4.1.3 and 4.1.4. To the issue of protection of claims, the formality of notification is not relevant.

In principle, personal rights are difficult to be unlawfully interfered with (see 2.1.3.2). Personal rights are a legal relationship between two or more particular parties. The core of this relationship is that the creditor is entitled to request the debtor to do or not to do something. In other words, the object of personal rights is the performance by the debtor, rather than the thing or service the creditor intends to obtain.[70] Therefore, despite the proprietary aspect of claims as a type of wealth, the legal nature of claims determines that they are not generally susceptible to unlawful interference. As a legal relationship *inter partes*, personal rights are mainly protected by imposing a liability on the particular debtor. Creditors rarely enjoy protection under tort law. One exception here is where third parties cause damage to the creditor by intentionally inducing the debtor to breach the contract.[71]

The way of protecting personal rights corresponds to the failure of notification to convey any indication to strange interferers. In general, notification is only related to the assignment and pledge of personal rights: when a personal right is transferred or pledged by the creditor to another person, it is better for the transferee or the pledgee to notify the debtor. However, the personal right does not become visible to third parties because of the notification. In this aspect, direct possession differs from notification. Direct possession can convey an abstract indication by the physical proximity between the possessor and the thing possessed. In the viewpoint of some scholars, possession of personal rights is possible in the case of assignment. Possession of a personal right refers to the factual enjoyment of this right

70 For example, A plans to buy a bicycle from B, and they have created a contract; before ownership of this bicycle passes to A, he merely has a right to request transfer, a right which is personal in nature. If the bicycle is destroyed by a third party, A has no right to sue this third party. The reason is simple: A's personal right, as a legal relationship with respect to performance between A and B, is not interfered with.

71 Non-Contractual Liability Arising out of Damage Caused to Another, p. 546-555.

and the exercise of the entitlements of this right.[72] However, according to this viewpoint, possession of personal rights does not give rise to any physical proximity, and this kind of possession is only mental.

> *"Wat de onlichamelijke schuldvorderingen betreft, kan er geen fysieke band met de bezitter bestaan; een onmiddellijke machtsverhouding van de schuldeiser ten aanzien van zijn schuldvordering is enkel intellectueel te vatten."*[73]

In sum, notification to debtors is useless for strange interferers for two reasons. One reason is that personal rights are difficult to be interfered with because they are a legal relationship *inter partes*. Even in exceptional situations where personal rights are damaged, notification has nothing to do with the protection of personal rights. The other reason is that notification is only relevant to the disposal of personal rights. Even if the debtor is notified of the disposal, the personal right involved does not become visible to strange interferers.

4.1.3 Notification and Third-Party Effect: Subsequent Acquirers in Outright Assignment

In general, the disposal of claims is a *quasi*-proprietary problem, which has been pointed out above (see 4.1.1.1). For the disposal of claims, there is an issue of how to determine the priority between competing interests with respect to the same claim. Usually, this conflict occurs between subsequent acquirers. To examine the importance or non-importance of notification for subsequent acquirers, we will select two types of disposal for the following comparative discussion. These two types are outright assignment of claims and pledge of claims. Here, outright assignment means that the assignment does not have any purpose of providing security, forming a contrast to the security assignment. The comparative discussion includes English law, German law, and Dutch law. For simplicity, the discussion focuses on receivables.[74] Receivables are a personal right (claim) for monetary payment: the object of performance is a certain amount of money.

---

72 Lebon 2010, p. 173.

73 Lebon 2010, p. 171. English translation: "*Where an intangible personal right is involved, no physical proximity exists with the possessor; the creditor's direct relationship of domination with respect to the claim is only mental.*"

74 In practice, other claims might also be able to be assigned or pledged. For example, where a buyer obtains a claim for transferring ownership of a bicycle against the seller, this buyer can assign or pledge this claim. However, the assignment of this claim often occurs in the situation where the bicycle, a future thing for the buyer, is intended to be transferred. Therefore, the assignment needs to be discussed under the context of the disposal of future things, which is a complicated issue. The pledge of the claim is closely related to the pledge of the bicycle. According to the rule of substitution, the bicycle will be pledged when the buyer obtains ownership of the bicycle. Therefore, the assignment and pledge of the claim are often a temporary pre-stage for transferring and pledging the bicycle. See Schuijling 2016, p. 355.

In this part, we discuss the outright assignment of receivables. It first provides an introduction to English law, German law, and Dutch law. After that, there is a comparative and conclusive analysis concerning the role notification plays in the assignment. As to pledge of receivables, a comparative and conclusive discussion will be offered in another part (see 4.1.4). In that part, we also devote attention to the security assignment of receivables, a kind of assignment for the purpose of providing security.

4.1.3.1 English Law

The rule of assignment of receivables is in English law complicated, mainly due to the dichotomy between common law and equity law, the distinction between outright assignments and security assignments (mortgages), and the difference in the treatment of companies and individuals. In practice, it is not always easy to distinguish an outright assignment of receivables from a security assignment.[75] However, these two types differ in some aspects, especially the possibility of registration: the security assignment is registerable, while the outright assignment, such as a factoring agreement, is not registerable.[76] Here, we only deal with the outright assignment, and the security assignment and pledge of receivables are discussed later (see 4.1.4).

S. 136 of the Law of Property Act (LPA) is a general provision for "*absolute assignment*", including both outright and security assignments.[77] According to this provision, a valid assignment has to fulfill two requirements, regardless of whether the assignor is a company or an individual: (1) the contract of assignment should be in writing and signed by the assignor; and (2) a written notification should be given to the debtor involved. If one of these two conditions is not satisfied, the assignment will not take effect between the assignor and the assignee.

However, this strict provision is somewhat relaxed by equity law, which makes a distinction between legal (or statutory) assignment and equitable assignment. The latter can be made by "*purely informal means*": neither the requirement of a written contract nor the requirement of a written notification is necessary in equity law.[78] In other words, an equitable assignment can take effect on the basis of an oral agreement. Equitable assignment can yield some proprietary effects and give rise to a fiduciary relationship between the assignor and the assignee.[79] For example, the debtor

---

75 Goode 2013, p. 98.

76 Bridge 2009, p. 166.

77 S. 136 (1) LPA (1925): "*Any absolute assignment by writing under the hand of the assignor (not purporting to be by way of charge only) of any debt or other legal thing in action, of which express notice in writing has been given to the debtor, trustee or other person from whom the assignor would have been entitled to claim such debt or thing in action, is effectual in law (subject to equities having priority over the right of the assignee) to pass and transfer from the date of such notice […].*"

78 Bridge 2009, p. 136.

79 Tolhurst 2016, p. 67.

can discharge himself by performing the obligation to the assignor when the debtor is not notified, but the money paid is *"treated as the assignee's and (provided it remains traceable) it may be claimed by the assignee even if the assignor is insolvent"*.[80] More importantly, an equitable assignment prevails over the subsequent disposal of the same claim, provided that the subsequent acquirer does not act in good faith. This consequence is in line with the conventional doctrine of notice in equity law: only the *bona fide* acquirers are free from the binding force of equitable interests.[81]

However, the law of equity does not mean that notification to debtors is not of no relevance. In general, notification plays a fundamental role in determining the priority between competing assignments.[82] Before clarifying this role, it should be first mentioned that under equity law notification can be made free from any formality, which means that it does not have to be in writing.[83]

If a claim is assigned by the creditor two times, then the assignee who notifies the debtor earlier will usually have a superior position. In this situation, notification averts the risk that equitable assignees might be defeated by a competing assignee who obtains legal title to the claim in good faith.

> *"A notice compliant with the requirements of equitable assignment ought to suffice for the purpose of establishing the order of priority between competing assignments, since, whether the assignment is an equitable or a statutory one, the rule of priority is the same."*[84]

This effect of priority of notification can be traced to the landmark case *Dearle v. Hall* (1828). This case pinned down an exception to the *nemo dat* rule, a rule which regulates competing equitable interests according to the date of creation.[85] In light of this case, where there are two equitable assignments with respect to the same claim, the assignee who notifies the debtor earlier will earn a superior position.[86]

> *"The equitable interest of the assignee is also liable to be defeated by a subsequent assignee who acquires the legal interest in the receivables for value and without notice of the prior equitable interest."*[87]

In justifying the notification-first rule, there are four approaches: (1) the first assignor who fails to notify the debtor is guilty of *"gross negligence"* and thus should be responsible for this foreseeable consequence; (2) the first

80 Kötz 2010, p. 1299.
81 Gray 2009, p. 1093.
82 Tolhurst 2016, p. 77.
83 Guest and Liew 2018, no. 3-63.
84 Bridge 2009, p. 170.
85 Smith and Leslie 2018, no. 27.44.
86 Smith and Leslie 2018, no. 27.49.
87 Parsons 2008, p. 149.

assignment is not complete until a notification is made; (3) notification can convert the legal creditor, namely the assignor, to be a trustee for the second assignee; and (4) notification can preclude fraudulence by creating a chance to inquire with the debtor.[88] It is held that, among these approaches, only the last seems convincing.[89] The function of preventing fraudulence is also articulated by Chadwick in the case of *United Bank of Kuwait v. Sahib*.[90]

> *"The rule is based upon the inequity of allowing an assignee, who has taken no step (by giving notice to trustees to whom inquiry might be made) to protect subsequent assignees against the possibility of fraud on the part of the assignor, from setting up his prior assignment against those who have been deceived."*[91]

In a nutshell, notification to debtors leads to effectiveness against *bona fide* third parties in the situation of outright assignment in English law. If there are two competing assignments with respect to the same claim, then the assignee who notifies the debtor earlier will usually prevail. If it is the second assignee who notifies the debtor earlier, then this assignee can be protected from the first assignment when that assignee is in good faith. In this sense, we can say that *bona fide* acquisition of receivables is recognized by English law.

4.1.3.2 German Law

In German law, receivables can be validly transferred without having to satisfy any formalities (§ 398 BGB). The transfer takes effect upon the creation of a contract of transfer, and this contract does not have to be in writing. Notification is not a prerequisite of assignment. It is only related to the problem of performance. If the debtor of the claim assigned is not notified, then the obligation can be performed to the assignor, namely the original creditor. If there are two competing assignments, then the failure to notify the debtor of the first assignment will not place the first assignee in an inferior position.[92]

> *„Es möge G seine Forderung gegen S zunächst (wirksam) an A abgetreten haben und sie später noch einmal an B abtreten. Dann ist diese zweite Abtretung – weil von einem nichtgläubiger vorgenommen – unwirksam; Gläubiger des S ist also A."*[93]

---

88 Guest and Liew 2018, no. 6-03-6-06.
89 Guest and Liew 2018, no. 6-06.
90 Guest and Liew 2018, no. 6-06.
91 *United Bank of Kuwait v. Sahib* [1997] Ch 107 at 119 (ChD), cited from Smith and Leslie 2018, no. 27.61.
92 Kötz 2010, p. 1296.
93 Medicus 2004, p. 365. English translation: *"G first assigns his claim against S (validly) to A and then assigns this claim to B. The second assignment is ineffective, because it is done by a non-creditor. As a result, the creditor of S is A."*

In this sense, we can say that German law applies the *nemo dat* rule to resolve the conflict between conflicting assignments. In general, this rule has no exceptions: *bona fide* acquisition of receivables is impossible under German law.[94] Moreover, notification to debtors is irrelevant in determining the priority. According to § 408 BGB, if a claim is assigned twice and the debtor is only informed of the second assignment, then the debtor can perform the obligation to the second assignee, despite the fact that the second assignee is not a legal creditor.[95] This provision is only to protect the debtor's reliance in respect of performance. It has nothing to do with the assignment *per se*. In this situation, the second assignee obtains performance in the absence of any legal basis. Thus, the first assignee (the actual creditor) is entitled to require the second assignee to disgorge the performance on the basis of unjust enrichment (§ 816 BGB).[96]

In a nutshell, German law takes a formality-free approach to the assignment of receivables. Notification is related only to the issue of performance by the debtor. In the situation of conflicting assignments, what matters is the date of assignment, rather than the time of notifying the debtor. As a result of this approach, the process of the assignment is totally invisible to third parties, and there is a problem of fraudulent antedating in practice.

> *„Aufgrund der Formlosigkeit der Zession und dem gleichzeitigen gesetzgeberischen Verzicht auf ihre Anzeige (Denunziation) besteht die Gefahr eines betrügerischen Zurückdatierens von Abtretungsverträgen. Und in der Tat kommt sie vor."*[97]

German law has its own special way of constructing the legal structure of assignments. In Chapter 3, we have shown that German property law has the "principle of separation (*Trennungsprinzip*)" and the "principle of abstraction (*Abstraktionsprinzip*)" (see 3.4.2.2). These two principles are also applicable to the assignment of claims.[98]

> *„Der Abtretungsvertrag bedeutet eine Verfügung über die Forderung. Er muss daher unterschieden werden von dem Kausalgeschäft […]. Nach dem Abstraktionsprinzip ist die Wirksamkeit der Abtretung grundsätzlich unabhängig von der Wirksamkeit des Kausalgeschäfts. So kann die Abtretung wirksam sein, wenn der zugrundeliegende Kauf unwirksam ist […]."*[99]

94 Bülow 2012, Rn. 636.
95 Rakob 2009, p. 115.
96 Schlechtriem 2003, p. 304.
97 Nörr, Scheyhing and Pöggeler 1999, p. 150. English translation: "*Due to the informality of assignments and the legislative renunciation of notification (denunciation), there is a risk of fraudulent antedating of assignments. In practice, it happens.*"
98 Medicus 2004, p. 365.
99 Medicus and Lorenz 2015, p. 365. English translation: "*The agreement of assignment refers to a disposal of the claim. Here, it must be distinguished from the causal legal act […]. According to the principle of abstraction, the validity of the assignment is independent of the validity of the causal legal act. Therefore, the assignment can still be effective when the underlying contract of sale is invalid […].*"

The principle of abstraction leads to an important legal consequence to third parties in the situation of successive transactions. For example, A sells due to a deception a claim to B, and B further assigns the claim to C. The legal relationships between the parties in this case can be summarized as follows: (1) the underlying relationship between A and B is voidable; (2) the assignment from A to B is in general not affected by the defect of the underlying relationship due to the principle of abstraction, which implies that B acquires the claim;[100] (3) the assignment between B and C is valid, and there is not any defect in B's authority of disposal; and (4) C can obtain the claim, irrespective of whether C is in good faith. This hypothetical case indicates that the principle of abstraction has a function of protecting third parties and facilitating the certainty of subsequent transactions.

In German law, an assignment might be made for the purpose of acquisition or the purpose of security, which gives rise to a distinction between outright assignment and security assignment. The absence of a requirement of notification provides significant convenience for creditors who want to use receivables as collateral.[101] As shown later, a security assignment is a popular alternative to the pledge of receivables which requires notification in German law (see 4.1.4.2).

4.1.3.3 Dutch Law

Under Dutch law, the assignment of receivables is, in principle, only possible in the outright sense: the security assignment is expressly prohibited (art. 3:84 (3) BW).[102] Dutch legislators use "undisclosed pledge (*stil pand*)" as an alternative. This pledge is discussed later (see 4.1.4.3).

In general, receivables can be assigned under Dutch law in two ways: "disclosed assignment (*openbare cessie*)" and "undisclosed assignment (*stille cessie*)".[103] The difference between these two ways is whether a notification is given to the debtor. Disclosed assignments are regulated by art. 3:94 (1) BW.[104] According to this paragraph, valid transfer of receivables does not take place until two requirements are fulfilled: a private deed is reached, and notification is made by the assignor or the assignee to the debtor involved. A private deed does not have to be authenticated, which causes a

---

100 Schlechtriem 2003, p. 291.
101 Rakob 2009, p. 92.
102 Timmermann and Veder 2009, p. 185.
103 Snijders and Rank-Berenschot 2017, p. 302.
104 Art. 3:94 (1) BW: "*Buiten de in het vorige artikel geregelde gevallen worden tegen een of meer bepaalde personen uit te oefenen rechten geleverd door een daartoe bestemde akte, en mededeling daarvan aan die personen door de vervreemder of verkrijger.*" English translation: Art. 3:94 (1) BW: "*In cases other than those provided for in the preceding article, rights to be exercised against one or more specific persons are delivered by means of an appropriate instrument and notice thereof given by the alienator or acquirer to those persons.*"

risk of antedating. To avert this risk, this paragraph stipulates notification be made.[105]

The undisclosed assignment, as its name indicates, does not require notifying the debtor (art. 3:94 (3) BW). In the discussion above, we have mentioned that this form of assignment was recognized in 2004 to avoid the practical inconvenience caused by the requirement of notification. There are two methods to carry out an undisclosed assignment: one is authenticating the deed of assignment, and the other is registering the private deed at an office of the tax authorities.[106] An authentic deed is usually made before a notary. It should be noted that the register is not open to the public because the principal purpose of registration is to prevent "*backdating*".[107] This is the reason why registration does not produce any legal effect different from notarization: where the deed of assignment is notarized, the risk of fraudulent antedating can also be averted. Notarization and registration are often said to perform a function of publicity similar to notification, at least in preventing antedating.

> "*Voor de stille cessie eist de wet echter een authentieke of geregistreerde onderhandse akte, dit ter compensatie van het gebrek aan publiciteit van deze leveringsvorm bij gebrek van een eis van mededeling aan de debitor cessus.*"[108]

In the situation of double assignment, the *nemo dat* rule will be applied. The assignment completed first will prevail because the assignor loses the authority of disposal afterwards. Depending on the type of the two assignments (disclosed or undisclosed) chosen, different requirements have to be satisfied. Notification is not always a source of priority: (1) if the two assignments are carried out as disclosed assignments, then the earlier notification implies a superior legal position; (2) if there are two undisclosed assignments, then notification is totally irrelevant; (3) if a conflict exists between a disclosed assignment and an undisclosed assignment, then notification can lead to priority only when it occurs before the completion of authentication or registration.[109] In other words, if a claim has been validly alienated in an undisclosed way, then any later disclosed assignment of this claim will not succeed, even though the debtor receives notification of the later assignment.

---

105 Snijders and Rank-Berenschot 2017, p. 302.
106 Timmermann and Veder 2009, p. 183.
107 Timmermann and Veder 2009, p. 210.
108 Snijders and Rank-Berenschot 2017, p. 302. English translation: "*However, law requires an authentic or privately-registered deed for the undisclosed assignment, which can compensate the lack of publicity of this form of assignment due to the absence of any notification to the debtor involved.*"
109 Snijders and Rank-Berenschot 2017, p. 303.

In principle, protection against unauthorized disposals is not possible, except for art. 3:88 BW.[110] Art. 3:86 BW, a provision concerning the *bona fide* acquisition of corporeal movables, does not include claims, because claims do not have any outward appearance that can legitimize the assignor's authority of disposal.[111]

The provision of art. 3:88 BW can be applied to the case of successive disposals: A assigns a claim to B who later assigns this claim to C. If the A-B assignment proves to be invalid not due to A's lack of the authority of disposal, then C is still able to acquire the claim when he is in good faith at the moment of notifying the debtor involved, despite the fact that B has no authority to dispose.[112] The main function of this provision is to facilitate security of transactions by preventing the principle of causation from affecting subsequent acquirers: "*een rem op al te rigoureuze consequenties van het causale stelsel voor derden*".[113] To apply art. 3:88 BW, one requirement is that the assignee acts in good faith when the debtor involved is notified in the situation of undisclosed assignments (art. 3:94 (3) BW). The requirement of good faith up to the moment of notification implies a difference between a disclosed assignment and undisclosed assignment. The assignee of disclosed assignments can claim legal protection under art. 3:88 BW, while the assignee of undisclosed assignments is only able to do so after notifying the debtor.[114] In the aspect of this *bona fide* acquisition, undisclosed assignments are "discriminated against": the two formalities associated with the undisclosed assignment, notarization and private registration, cannot give rise to *bona fide* acquisition of claims. Notification is necessary for the application of art. 3:88 BW in the assignment of claims.

4.1.3.4 *Comparative and Conclusive Analysis*

A Differences and Similarities

From the introduction above, we find that notification has different legal effects in the three jurisdictions. In general, notification is involved in two situations: (1) one is double assignment, where the creditor assigns the same

---

110 Art. 3:88 (1) BW: "*Ondanks onbevoegdheid van de vervreemder is een overdracht van een registergoed, van een recht op naam, of van een ander goed waarop artikel 86 niet van toepassing is, geldig, indien de verkrijger te goeder trouw is en de onbevoegdheid voortvloeit uit de ongeldigheid van een vroegere overdracht, die niet het gevolg was van onbevoegdheid van de toenmalige vervreemder.*" English translation: Art. 3:88 (1) BW: "*Although an alienator lacks the right to dispose of property, the transfer of registered property, a personal right or other property to which Article 86 does not apply, is valid if the acquirer is in good faith and if the lack of the right to dispose results from the invalidity of a previous transfer, which itself did not result from the alienator's lack of the right to dispose at that time.*"

111 Snijders and Rank-Berenschot 2017, p. 315.

112 Reehuis and Heisterkamp 2019, p. 266.

113 Snijders and Rank-Berenschot 2017, p. 329. English translation: "*[...] a brake against the extensive consequences of the principle of causation to third parties.*"

114 Asser/Bartels & Van Mierlo 2013, nr. 461.

receivable twice to different persons; and (2) the other is successive assignments, where a creditor (the first hand) assigns a receivable on the basis of an invalid or voidable contract to another person (the second hand) who later alienates the claim to a third party (the third hand). As to whether the second assignee can obtain the claim in these two situations, notification plays different roles in the three jurisdictions.

In English law, notification has an effect of *bona fide* acquisition in the situation of double assignment: the second assignee in good faith might prevail over the first assignee by notifying the debtor earlier. A rationale behind this notification-first rule is publicity and self-responsibility: "*As the first assignee has enabled a fraud to be committed on the second assignee, it is only fair that he should be postponed*".[115] A similar consideration can be found in the rule of "seller in possession" (s. 24 SGA): where a purchaser allows the seller to remain in possession of the corporeal movable, this purchaser might be defeated by a third party in good faith because he fails to complete the purchase and exposes himself to the risk.[116] The comparison of these two rules indicates that the role notification plays in the assignment of claims resembles the role played by delivery in the transfer of corporeal movables.

However, the notification-first rule is only applied to double assignment ("A-B and A-C" transactions), and successive assignments ("A-B-C" transactions) fall outside the scope of application. In the latter situation, if the A-B assignment is void, then this assignment will be treated as having never happened: it does not "*create any rights or obligations at all*" *ab initio*.[117] Furthermore, the third party (C) cannot obtain the claim from B. This is a result of the *nemo dat* rule. If the assignment is voidable, then a different consequence will occur.[118] In general, a voidable transaction does not affect the acquisition, because the transaction is valid under statutory law before being rescinded. However, the acquisition is subject to an equitable interest. Therefore, before the rescission, the assignee can give a good title to "*a sub-purchaser who buys without notice of the buyer's defective title and in good faith*".[119] If B (as the second hand) acquires the claim on the basis of a voidable contract, then there is the possibility that C (as the third hand) can obtain the claim.[120]

In Dutch law, the starting point is that notification is not necessarily relevant because of the recognition of the undisclosed assignment, and it is the *nemo dat* rule that regulates the conflict of double assignment ("A-B and A-C" transactions). Where a claim is assigned twice to different persons,

115 Smith and Leslie 2018, no. 27.61.
116 Merrett 2008, p. 387.
117 Cartwright 2016, p. 161.
118 In Chapter 3, we have introduced that voidable title is an exception to the *nemo dat* rule in the English law of corporeal movables (see 3.4.3.1).
119 Bridge, Gullifer, McMeel and Worthington 2013, p. 231.
120 Bridge, Gullifer, McMeel and Worthington 2013, p. 101.

the assignment completed earlier will prevail. Therefore, notification is not necessarily decisive: a later disclosed assignment does not prevail over an earlier undisclosed assignment.[121] Notification is different from possession: the former does not lead to any factual control which can legitimize the assignor's authority to dispose.[122] The later disclosed assignment cannot succeed, regardless of whether the assignee is in good faith.

However, notification has an effect of *bona fide* acquisition in the context of art. 3:88 BW. In successive assignments ("A-B-C" transactions), the second assignee might be protected from defects (except the defect in the authority to dispose) of the previous assignment, provided that this assignee is in good faith at the moment of notifying the debtor. It should be noted that the purpose of art. 3:88 BW is to preclude the adverse effect of the principle of causation over the security of transactions, rather than the publicity effect of notification.[123] This is easy to understand. The previous assignment (between A and B) might be carried out as an undisclosed assignment. Therefore, we cannot say that the third party (C) in the later assignment (between B and C) has any reliance over notification. Notification may never occur in the previous assignment. Moreover, art. 3:88 BW does not require third parties to continue being in good faith after notifying the debtor, and it suffices that they are in good faith at the moment of notification.[124] In other words, if the debtor tells third parties that the previous assignment is defective, they can still obtain the claim.

Therefore, Dutch law differs from English law in the aspect of protecting third parties. Notification is necessary for legal protection in the case of successive assignments ("A-B-C" transaction) in Dutch law, while it only triggers an effect of priority in the case of double assignment ("A-B and A-C" transaction) in English law. In this aspect, German law resembles Dutch law, but these two jurisdictions take different approaches.

In principle, *bona fide* acquisition of claims is not recognized by German law as well as Dutch law in the situation of double assignment. This is because claims differ from property rights: the former lack an outward appearance to legitimize the assignor's authority to dispose.[125] However, these two jurisdictions differ in the legal effect of notification. Where a claim is assigned twice, the assignment which takes effect earlier will prevail in German law. In German law, notification has nothing to do with the assignment *per se*, and it is only related to the issue of performance by the debtor. Unlike German law, Dutch law takes notification as a prerequisite for disclosed assignment.

121 Reehuis and Heisterkamp 2019, p. 236-237.
122 Snijders and Rank-Berenschot 2017, p. 315.
123 Snijders and Rank-Berenschot 2017, p. 329.
124 Asser/Bartels & Van Mierlo 2013, nr. 461.
125 Medicus and Lorenz 2015, p. 365; Snijders and Rank-Berenschot 2017, p. 315.

In the situation of successive assignments, German law differs partially from English law, but resembles Dutch law significantly. Due to the principle of abstraction, a defect of the underlying relationship usually does not affect the transfer of the claim. This principle facilitates the security of transactions and averts the undesirable chain of influence over later transactions. Dutch law does not recognize the principle of abstraction. However, the aim of transactional security is honored under art. 3:88 in the BW. As a scheme to break the chain, this provision is made to inhibit the chain effect over third parties. Therefore, German law and Dutch law have different rules but reach a similar outcome in terms of the protection of third parties.[126]

In general, the preceding observation can be shown in the following table (Figure 9).

	Double Assignment (A-B & A-C)	Successive Assignment (A-B-C)
English Law	The *Dearle v. Hall* rule: C enjoys *bona fide* acquisition by earlier notification.	The *nemo dat* rule: C enjoys no *bona fide* acquisition except in the situation of voidable title.
German Law	The *nemo dat* rule: C enjoys no *bona fide* acquisition regardless of earlier notification.	The principle of abstraction: C enjoys protection regardless of good faith.
Dutch Law	The *nemo dat* rule: C enjoys no *bona fide* acquisition.	The rule of art. 3:88 BW: C enjoys *bona fide* acquisition after notification.

Figure 9

B Notification, Publicity, and Assignment

As has been shown above, there is a consideration of preventing fraudulence behind the English judgement in *Dearle v. Hall* (see 4.1.3.1). This consideration can also be found from the distinction between a disclosed assignment and an undisclosed assignment in Dutch law (see 4.1.3.3). In general, the consideration is not groundless. Notification is helpful for addressing the problem of antedating and provides a chance for potential assignees to obtain some information from the debtor. If a claim has been assigned or pledged, and the debtor has been notified, then the debtor might disclose the assignment or pledge to potential assignees. According to some scholars, a prudent assignee is expected to inquire with the debtor about the claim assigned.[127]

However, notification cannot completely prevent fraudulent antedating, as has been pointed out above (see 4.1.1.2.C). More remarkably, the possibility of inquiry and disclosure cannot make notification qualify as a method

126 Here, an important difference should be noted. To claim the legal protection under art. 3:88 BW, the third party has to be innocent before notifying the debtor involved. However, this requirement of good faith does not exist in German law. Under the principle of abstraction, the third party is entitled to acquisition, regardless of whether this party is in good faith.

127 Smith and Leslie 2018, no. 27.83.

of publicity, which has also been argued above (see 4.1.1.2.C). Among the reasons given above, the most important two are: (1) the debtor bears no legal duty to provide complete and correct information to third parties; and (2) the reliance of third parties on the information obtained from the debtor is not generally protected.[128] As notification is not an eligible outward appearance for claims, it fails to provide a firm basis for allowing the assignee in good faith to prevail over the actual creditor. As pointed out by some English lawyers, the notification-first rule produces *"at least as much injustice as it has prevented"*.[129]

As also has been shown, German law and Dutch law provide legal protection to third parties in the situation of successive assignments. However, this protection cannot be explained on the basis of publicity that notification does not have. Art. 3:88 BW is mainly a result of legal policy: facilitating the transactional security by restricting the application of the principle of causation. This provision does not indicate that notification leads third parties to have any reliance. The reason is simple: third parties do not have to continue being in good faith after notifying the debtor, and it suffices that they are in good faith at the moment of notification.[130] In German law, notification is entirely irrelevant. The second assignee as a third party is entitled to acquire the claim by virtue of a valid contract of assignment only. Moreover, under the principle of abstraction, the second assignment does not have any defect in the assignor's authority to dispose. This implies that the third party does not even have to be in good faith. This further implies that protection has nothing to do with publicity and the third party's reliance.

4.1.4 Notification and Third-Party Effect: Subsequent Acquirers in Pledge and Security Assignment

Receivables are an important form of collateral. In general, receivables can be used to secure the performance of obligations in two ways: security assignment and pledge. The former involves an assignment for the purpose of security. The latter creates a limited property right of pledge over receivables. In this part, we first introduce English law, German law, and Dutch law. After that, a comparative and conclusive analysis is provided. It can be found that the notification to debtors plays different roles and produces different legal effects in these three different jurisdictions.

---

128 Guest and Liew 2018, no. 6-06; Verhagen 2002, p. 249.

129 Guest and Liew 2018, no. 6-07.

130 Asser/Bartels & Van Mierlo 2013, nr. 461.

4.1.4.1 *English Law*

In English law, receivables can be used as collateral in two ways: security assignment (mortgage) and charge.[131] It is noteworthy that a pledge can only exist on corporeal movables because this security device is necessarily associated with possession.[132] Mortgage refers to a security assignment, which can take two forms: statutory assignment and equitable assignment. This distinction concerns whether the requirements under s. 136 of the Law of Property Act (LPA) are fulfilled.[133] According to this statutory rule, statutory assignment requires a written contract and a written notification. In contrast, assignment can occur under equity law due to a valid agreement, which is known as equitable assignment. For this form of assignment, notification is irrelevant.

Charge, a limited proprietary interest, neither exists in common law nor in the LPA (1925). It is an equitable security interest. Charge can be either fixed or floating, depending on whether the collateral has been fixed at the moment of creation.[134] Charge and mortgage differ obviously in terms of the legal form: the former is a limited property right, while the latter involves an assignment. However, the difference between charge and mortgage is not as obvious as it appears. These two terms are often used interchangeably in legal theory, judicial practice and legislation.[135] For example, s. 859A Companies Act (2006) expressly stipulates that charge includes mortgages.

For creating a charge or mortgage, two steps are involved: attachment and perfection. Roughly speaking, attachment implies that the security interest comes into existence, and perfection means that the security interest can be effective against third parties.[136] In general, registration is the method of perfection.[137] Registration can grant some substantial benefits to the secured creditor: it makes the charge or mortgage enforceable against

---

131 Bridge 2009, p. 150.

132 Bridge 2009, p. 150.

133 Bridge, Gullifer, McMeel and Worthington 2013, p. 417.

134 *Illingworth v. Houldsworth*, [1904] A. C. 355 at 358.

135 Beale, Bridge, Gullifer and Lomnicka 2018, no. 6.54.

136 About the meaning of the two terms, we can see the following two excerpts. "*Attachment is a term to describe the process whereby the chargee acquires a particular kind of proprietary interest in a specific asset. The effects of attachment are that first, the charge can be enforced on that property without any further act on the part of the chargee, second, the chargor cannot dispose of that property or any interest therein free of the charge without the consent of the charge, and third, that the chargee has priority over any other interests arising after the date of the agreement for the charge under the nemo dat (first in time) rule, unless an exception applies.*" See Beale, Bridge, Gullifer and Lomnicka 2018, no. 6.72. "*The expression 'perfection' is a useful way to describe any steps that a secured creditor has to take in order to be able to make the security effective against other secured creditors, trustees in bankruptcy and company liquidators or administrators.*" See Beale, Bridge, Gullifer and Lomnicka 2018, no. 9.01.

137 In present English law, companies and individuals do not share the same register. Moreover, the register for the mortgage created by individuals is not open to the public. See Beale 2016, p. 5.

other secured creditors and bankruptcy administrators. In many situations, registration of a charge or mortgage leads to constructive knowledge of the existence of this charge or mortgage.[138] For example, a fixed charge which is registered can defeat a later assignment, albeit that the assignee first notifies the debtor. This is because registration leads to "*constructive notice*", and the assignee can no longer claim that he or she is in good faith.[139] Therefore, registration restricts the application of the notification-first rule: where a mortgage or charge has been registered, subsequent assignees are assumed to know this encumbrance exists.[140]

However, perfection by registration does not completely dispense with the importance of notification.[141] An important reason is that there is a 21-day gap between attachment and perfection. Upon valid attachment, the charge or mortgage can be perfected by registration within 21 days. If the receivables are assigned during this blind period, then there will be a conflict between this assignment and the registered mortgage or charge. This conflict needs to be resolved according to the *nemo dat* rule and the notification-first rule.[142] Another reason is that an outright assignment does not have to be registered. If a receivable is assigned but not for the purpose of security, and later the assignor mortgages or charges this claim, there will be a conflict between the two disposals. Here, this conflict needs to be resolved under the notification-first rule. If the assignee fails to notify the debtor, while the mortgagee or chargee sends a notification, then the mortgagee or chargee will prevail, provided that he or she is in good faith.[143]

In sum, English law uses registration as a means of publicity for the mortgage and charge of receivables. This narrows the scope where notification matters for determining the priority between competing proprietary interests. However, notification is not completely irrelevant. It is important in the situation where registration plays no role, such as the 21-day blind period and un-registerable outright assignment.

4.1.4.2 German law

In German law, receivables can be used as collateral in two ways: pledge and security assignment. These two ways differ in terms of notification.

According to § 1280 BGB, notification to debtors is necessary for a valid pledge over receivables.[144] As a result, if a creditor pledges his claim twice

---

138 Guest and Liew 2018, no. 6-48.

139 Guest and Liew 2018, no. 6-59.

140 Goode 2013, p. 179; Beale, Bridge, Gullifer and Lomnicka 2018, no. 14.10.

141 Goode 2013, p. 109-110.

142 Bridge 2009, p. 166-167.

143 Beale, Bridge, Gullifer and Lomnicka 2018, no. 14.14.

144 § 1280 BGB: *„Die Verpfändung einer Forderung, zu deren Übertragung der Abtretungsvertrag genügt, ist nur wirksam, wenn der Gläubiger sie dem Schuldner anzeigt."* English translation: § 1280 BGB: *"The pledging of a claim, for which a contract of assignment suffices, is effective only if the creditor gives notice thereof to the debtor."*

to different persons, then the pledge communicated to the debtor first will prevail, regardless of whether the pledgee knows about the other pledge. Pledge of receivables is governed by the first-to-notification rule: notification is decisive for determining the priority between competing pledges.[145] It is often held that the requirement of notification is based on the consideration of publicity.[146] Notification plays a delivery-like role.[147] In addition to the effect of priority, notification is also related to the debtor's performance. In the absence of an agreement to the contrary, the debtor of the claim pledged has to offer payment to the pledgor and the pledgee jointly, when the claim becomes due.[148]

In addition to pledge, "security assignment (*Sicherungsabtretung*)" is also a method to provide security. The security assignment is a pledge-like device: both pledgees and security assignees enjoy a preferential position and are entitled to release the receivable involved from the insolvency assets. However, the security assignment is different from pledge in the aspect of notification. Like the outright assignment, security assignment does not require notifying the debtor. The decisive factor for determining the priority between two competing security assignments is the date of occurrence, rather than the time of notification.

> *"If there is more than one assignment of security of the same receivable, the first assignment takes precedence (so-called 'priority principle' (Prioritätsprinzip)). Unlike in the case of a pledge, the second assignment does not create a lower ranking security right."*[149]

About the security assignment of receivables, particular attention needs to be paid to "global assignment (*Globalzession*)". It arises where the debtor assigns all present and future receivables to the secured creditor, and the future receivables are automatically acquired by the secured creditor as soon as they come into existence.[150] The global assignment has a problem concerning the specificity of the collateral. Under the principle of specificity, individuals are required to identify the receivables assigned with sufficient accuracy. In German law, *"all trade receivables"* is a description which can meet this requirement, and individuals do not have to describe the receivables involved by indicating any specific information.[151] Under a global assignment, the assignee can become the new creditor without having to

---

145 Haag and Peglow 2008, p. 214.
146 Herrmann 2003, p. 154; Mincke 1997, p. 204.
147 Augustin and Kregel 1996, § 1280, p. 132; MüKoBGB/Damrau 2017, § 1280, Rn. 1.
148 § 1285 (1) BGB: *„Hat die Leistung an den Pfandgläubiger und den Gläubiger gemeinschaftlich zu erfolgen, so sind beide einander verpflichtet, zur Einziehung mitzuwirken, wenn die Forderung fällig ist."* English translation: § 1285 (1) BGB: *"Where performance is to be made to the pledgee and the creditor jointly, they are reciprocally obliged to cooperate in the collection if the claim is due."*
149 Haag and Peglow 2008, p. 214.
150 Haag and Peglow 2008, p. 214.
151 Rakob 2009, p. 98.

do any extra act when future receivables come into existence. The assignee often needs, only for practical purposes, more information about the receivables, such as the debtors' name and the amount of these claims.[152] Moreover, the insolvency administrator cannot avoid the global assignment by claiming the hardening period, a period of three months within which the insolvent debtor is not able to dispose of its assets.[153]

German law treats pledge and security assignment differently in terms of notification, despite both devices performing the same function. Due to the irrelevance of notification to the security assignment, this device is much more popular than pledge.[154] It seems difficult to say whether this different treatment causes any systematic incoherence. After all, both assignment and pledge are a disposal of receivables. If notification is required for pledge due to the consideration of publicity, then there is no reason to dispense with this requirement for assignment.[155]

As demonstrated above, German law does not recognize *bona fide* acquisition of claims (see 4.1.3.2). In general, *bona fide* acquisition is not possible in the situation of pledge or security assignment either. If the pledgor does not have the authority to dispose, then a pledge cannot be created validly, irrespective of whether the debtor has been notified, or whether the pledgee is in good faith. The reason is simple: claims lack an outward appearance to legitimize the pledgor's authority of disposal.[156] However, the principle of abstraction can offer some protection to third parties, whether in good faith or not, in the situation of successive transactions. Due to this principle, where the pledgor obtains a claim on the basis of a defective contract, this pledgor might still have the authority to dispose of this claim. As a result, the pledge can be validly created, regardless of whether the pledgee is in good faith.

4.1.4.3 Dutch Law

As has been pointed out above, security assignment is prohibited by Dutch law (art. 3:84 (3) BW), and pledge is the only device of security. Like outright assignment, pledge also includes "disclosed pledge (*openbaar pand*)" and "undisclosed pledge (*stil pand*)", depending on how the pledge is created.

According to art. 3:236 (2) BW and art. 94 (1) BW, a disclosed pledge has to fulfill two conditions: one is making a valid deed of pledge, and the other is sending a notification to the debtor.[157] As we have shown above, notification may cause significant inconveniences (see 4.1.1.2.C). For this reason, Dutch law introduced the undisclosed pledge in 2004. Like the undisclosed

152 Rakob 2009, p. 98.
153 Rakob 2009, p. 96-102.
154 Haag and Peglow 2008, p. 213.
155 Meijers 1954, p. 222.
156 Bülow 2012, Rn. 636.
157 Rank 2008, p. 25.09.

assignment, undisclosed pledge can also be created in two ways: authentication and private registration. Individuals may create a pledge by making a deed of pledge before a notary, and the pledge takes effect upon the completion of the deed being notarized. If the transacting parties do not want to involve a notary, they are allowed to conclude a private deed and then register this deed with an office of the tax authorities. The register is not open to the public. As mentioned above, the main purpose of notarization and registration is to address the problem of fraudulent antedating.[158]

In general, the priority between competing pledges of the same receivable is determined by applying the *nemo dat* rule. According to art. 3:246 (3) BW, the pledge which is successfully created earlier will prevail.[159]

> *"The order of priority among various rights of pledges over the same collateral is, in principle, determined by the moment at which the pledges were created, the general rule being that the earlier pledge prevails ('first in time, first in right')."*[160]

Since whether a pledge is validly created depends on how the pledge is created, notification is not the sole factor that should be taken into consideration. Therefore, a later disclosed pledge has a lower rank than an earlier undisclosed pledge, regardless of whether the disclosed pledgee is in good faith.[161] Notification given by a pledgee who has a lower rank cannot increase its ranking.[162]

> *"Zou men een pandhouder die zijn recht nog niet heeft medegedeeld een zwakkere positie geven dan degene die het wel (reeds) heeft gedaan, dan zou dit licht tot ongerechtvaardigde rangwisselingen kunnen leiden en bij het ontstaan van twijfel aan de soliditeit van de pandgever zouden pandhouders zich haasten tot mededeling over te gaan, daardoor wellicht een onnodige deconfiture uitlokkende."*[163]

In general, notification only leads to priority in two situations: (1) where there are two competing disclosed pledges, the pledge of which the debtor is notified earlier will prevail; (2) where there is a conflict between a disclosed pledge and an undisclosed pledge, the former only prevails when the

158 Timmermann and Veder 2009, p. 210.

159 Art. 3:246 (3) BW: "*Rust op de vordering meer dan één pandrecht, dan komen de in de vorige leden aan de pandhouder toegekende bevoegdheden alleen aan de hoogst gerangschikte pandhouder toe.*" English translation: Art. 3:246 (3) BW: "*Where more than one right of pledge encumbers a claim, the powers granted to the pledgee in the preceding paragraphs can only be exercised by the most senior ranking pledgee.*"

160 Rank 2008, p. 25, 28.

161 Rank 2008, p. 25, 28.

162 Asser/Bartels & Van Mierlo 2013, nr. 226.

163 Parlementaire Geschiedenis (3) 1981, p. 764. English translation: "*If a pledgee, who has not yet notified the debtor of his right, has a legal position inferior to those who have done that, then there would be an unjustified interchange of rankings; pledgors would hurry for notification when the pledgor's solvency is doubted, which might cause an unnecessary collapse.*"

notification is given to the debtor before the completion of the authentication or private registration of the latter. In these two situations, the pledge created earlier has a higher ranking.

Bona fide acquisition of pledge is not recognized by Dutch law. The pledgor must have the authority to dispose. Otherwise, the right of pledge cannot be validly created, irrespective of whether the pledgee is in good faith, or whether the debtor has been notified.[164] The reason is simple: claims do not have any outward appearance to legitimize the pledgor's authority to dispose.[165] However, according to art. 3:239 (4) BW, art. 3:88 BW should be applied in favor of third parties acting in good faith in the situation of successive transactions.[166] Under art. 3:88 BW, where a pledgor acquires the claim pledged on the basis a defective contract, the pledgee may still be able to obtain a right of pledge. As a result, art. 3:88 BW restricts the influence of previous transactions over later transactions. It should be noted that, according to art. 3:239 (4) BW, this provision is only applied if the pledgee acted in good faith at the moment of notification. As a result, art. 3:88 BW does not apply to the pledge made in the undisclosed way through an authentic deed or private registration. Notification is necessary for *bona fide* acquisition of pledge of claims.

4.1.4.4 *Comparative and Conclusive Analysis of Notification*

A *Differences and Similarities*

From the introduction above, we find that similarities and differences exist between the three jurisdictions in the use of receivables as collateral. For example, security assignment is prohibited by Dutch law, but German law and English law recognize this type of security device. In the following discussion, we concentrate on the role played by notification to debtors.

Firstly, notification is necessary for creating a right of pledge in German law and disclosed pledge in Dutch law, but it is often irrelevant to mortgage and charge in English law. In general, it is registration that serves as the method of perfection in English law. Mortgage and charge of receivables can be made enforceable against third parties by registration. The scope of application of the notification-first rule has been significantly narrowed by registration. However, notification still has some importance in the situation where registration plays no role, such as an outright assignment and the 21-day blind period.

---

164 Asser/Bartels & Van Mierlo 2013, nr. 225.

165 Snijders and Rank-Berenschot 2017, p. 315.

166 Art. 3:239 (4) BW: "*Artikel 88 geldt slechts voor de pandhouder wiens recht overeenkomstig lid 1 is gevestigd, indien hij te goeder trouw is op het tijdstip van de in lid 3 bedoelde mededeling.*" English translation: Art. 3:239 (4) BW: "*Article 3:88 only applies to the pledgee whose right has been established according to paragraph 1, if he acted in good faith at the moment of notification as meant in paragraph 3.*"

Secondly, each of the three jurisdictions recognizes a device of security which can be created without involving notification, because notification causes much inconvenience. In German law, this device is the security assignment. It is the undisclosed pledge in Dutch law. An important difference exists between undisclosed pledge and security assignment: the former requires notarization or private registration, while the latter is not subject to any formality. In English law, mortgage and charge take registration as the method of perfection. Therefore, notification does not create a significant issue for legal practice. Here, we note that registration under English law differs from registration under Dutch law: the former is open to the public when the pledgor is a company, while the latter cannot be inspected by third parties.[167]

Thirdly, where notification is made, third parties in good faith cannot be protected on the basis of this notification against the defect of the security provider's authority to dispose. As shown above, German law and Dutch law do not recognize *bona fide* acquisition of the right of pledge over claims. Even though legislators of both jurisdictions hold that notification has some publicity effect,[168] they refuse to treat notification as an outward appearance. The security provider's authority to dispose is not legitimized. In English law, registration has significantly narrowed the scope of application of notification. Nevertheless, notification can still give rise to *bona fide* acquisition in some situations. For example, where a receivable is assigned and then mortgaged, the person who notifies the debtor earlier will win.[169] Here, we can find an interesting difference: notification is initially treated as a method of publicity in German law and Dutch law, but the effect of *bona fide* acquisition is denied; notification has an effect of *bona fide* protection in some situations under English law, though it has been generally replaced by registration in the field of secured transactions.

Lastly, the outright assignment and the secured transaction (including pledge and the security assignment) might be treated differently in the aspect of notification, despite the fact that both form a disposal. In principle, property rights on an object should share the same method of publicity: the method of publicity for ownership should not be different from that for limited property rights (see 2.2.3.2). However, the disposal of claims has a patchy system of publicity. English law has introduced registration to the mortgage and charge of claims, but outright assignment is not registerable. German law requires notification as a condition for pledge of claims, but assignment (whether outright or security) does not need notification. Dutch law has a different problem here. Truly, Dutch law treats assignment and pledge of claims equally: both can be either disclosed or undisclosed.

167 In English law, the register for the mortgage (and charge) provided by individuals is not open to the public either.

168 Meijers 1954, p. 222; Snijders and Rank-Berenschot 2017, p. 302; Herrmann 2003, p. 154; Mincke 1997, p. 204; Augustin and Kregel 1996, § 1280, p. 132.

169 Beale, Bridge, Gullifer and Lomnicka 2018, no. 14.14.

However, there are three ways of "publicity": notification, notarization, and private registration. If a claim is first disposed of in one way and then disposed of in another way, then discrepancy will arise. For example, where a claim is first pledged on the basis of a notarized deed and then pledged by notifying the debtor involved, this debtor cannot be expected to disclose that the claim was already pledged. In principle, one kind of property should only have one method of publicity, which has been pointed out above (see 2.2.3.2).

In general, the preceding discussion and comparison can be shown in the following table (Figure 10).

	Irrelevance of Notification	Relevance of Notification
English Law	Mortgage and Charge: Registration	Mortgage and Charge: Notification in the Blind Period
German Law	Security Assignment: No Publicity	Pledge: Notification
Dutch Law	Undisclosed Pledge: Notarization and Private Registration	Disclosed Pledge: Notification

Figure 10

B *Notification, Publicity, and Pledge*

As we have argued above, notification does not qualify as a method of publicity for the outright assignment of claims (see 4.1.3.4.B). Therefore, there is no reason to say that notification can be a method of publicity for a security assignment. In this part, we focus on notification and pledge of claims from the perspective of publicity.

There is a strong inclination to treat notification as a method of publicity for the pledge of claims. For example, German law allows claims to be assigned in the absence of any notification, but requires notification as a condition for the valid pledge of claims. In general, there are three explanations for the requirement of notification for the pledge of claims. The first explanation is that notification creates a possibility for third parties to know about the existence of this proprietary encumbrance.[170] The second is that notification prevents the pledgor from disposing of the claim, thus avoiding the problem of "*false appearance of wealth*".[171] The third explanation is that notification precludes fraudulent antedating by fixing the date of creation.[172]

In general, the former two explanations are not convincing, and the third explanation does not mean that notification qualifies as a method of publicity for claims. As has been argued, notification only creates a possibility for third parties to know about the disposal of claims, but it is too defective to be a method of publicity (see 4.1.1.2.C). The debtor involved

170 MüKoBGB/Damrau 2017, § 1280, Rn. 1.
171 Beale, Bridge, Gullifer and Lomnicka 2018, no. 14.10.
172 Timmermann and Veder 2009, p. 210.

bears no duty to provide information, and the reliance of third parties on the information provided by the debtor is not protected by law. Therefore, pledge of claims is not necessarily made transparent to third parties. Moreover, notification causes much inconvenience, which makes it inappropriate to be a method of publicity. This is why claims can be used as collateral in the absence of notification in the three jurisdictions.

Due to similar reasons, there is a problem of "*false appearance of wealth*", and this problem cannot be addressed by notification. Even after notifying the debtor involved, reliable information cannot be necessarily obtained by third parties (see 4.1.1.2.C). In fact, this problem does not exist in reality, because pledge and security assignment of claims often occur without involving any notification. The debtor is not notified of the secured transaction. As a result, third parties will not inquire with the debtor. For third parties, there is no reason to believe that no secured transaction exists simply because the debtor declares that no relevant notification needs to be given.

As to the third explanation, we have argued that the function of preventing antedating does not make notification qualify as a method of publicity (see 4.1.1.2.C). After all, preventing antedating is not preventing the occurrence of conflicts.

4.1.5 Notification and Third-Party Effect: General Creditors

In principle, general creditors can only get paid on the basis of the debtor's unencumbered assets in the event of the debtor's insolvency. Therefore, general creditors have an interest in knowing which assets belong to the debtor and how much encumbrance exists over these assets (see 2.2.2.2.C). The insolvent debtor's personal rights form a part of these assets, provided that they are not pledged or assigned. For this reason, publicity of pledge and assignment of personal rights is often said as important for general creditors. Moreover, notification is often treated as a method of publicity for claims. If a personal right is assigned or pledged in the absence of a notification of the debtor, the problem of "*false appearance of wealth*" will arise.[173] This consideration is held by E.M. Meijers during the recodification of the BW.[174] A similar consideration also exists in German law. As has been shown, pledge of claims requires notifying the debtor under German law (see 4.1.4.2). Just like the delivery of corporeal movables, this requirement is also stipulated to serve a purpose of publicity.[175]

However, we hold that, like possession of corporeal movables, notification is not useful for general creditors. Firstly, notification cannot perform the function of publicity in the situation of assignment and pledge, which

173 Rongen 2012, p. 474.
174 Meijers 1954, p. 222.
175 Augustin and Kregel 1996, § 1280, p. 132.

has been argued above (see 4.1.1.2). Notification cannot make the assignment or pledge of claims transparent to subsequent acquirers, let alone general creditors. Truly, notification provides an opportunity for third parties to obtain some information from the debtor. However, it is too defective to qualify as a method of publicity.

Secondly, a creditor might have many debtors, and it is difficult and costly to inquire all debtors to know whether these claims have been pledged. For this reason, the general creditor rarely inquires all the debtors of his or her debtor in reality. Even if general creditors carry out a costly investigation, the information obtained will become outdated after a short period. This is because the claims owned by the debtor are always in fluctuation, and the debtor is entitled to pledge his or her claims after the investigation. Moreover, it is imaginable that the debtor is often unwilling to disclose his or her debtors to the general creditor, because this information is an important commercial secret.

Thirdly, valid disposal of claims can take place independently from notification. In principle, general creditors can only distribute the claims owned by the insolvent debtor and encumbered with no proprietary security. However, whether a personal right belongs to the insolvent debtor is a question affected by multiple factors. Notification is never a decisive factor nor a reliable indicator. As has been shown, law generally recognizes that assignment or pledge of claims can successfully occur in the absence of notification, for the purpose of the smooth operation of transactions (see 4.1.3 and 4.1.4). In practice, the disposal of claims in the absence of notification is ordinary, such as securitization, factoring, and the pledge of bulk receivables. Therefore, general creditors cannot obtain reliable information by inquiring the debtor notified.

Fourthly, general creditors will not pay particular attention to the claims owned by the debtor. As has been argued above, general creditors are mainly concerned about the overall financial health of the debtor (see 2.2.2.2.C). Even if we assume that the proprietary information concerning claims can be obtained reliably through inquiring the debtor, this information is not important to potential creditors. The reason is simple: the information cannot indicate the overall financial health of the debtor. In contrast, financial reports include more comprehensive information and thus more useful for general creditors.[176] Moreover, notification is of no value for involuntary creditors, such as tort victims. This kind of general creditor has no chance to decide whether to have a claim of compensation.[177]

On the basis of the preceding reasons, we can conclude that notification fails to allow general creditors to obtain any useful information. However, this does not mean that notification has no value to general creditors. Notification helps to determine the date of assignment and pledge, addressing the

176 Van den Boezem and Goosmann 2010, p. 61.
177 LoPucki 1994, p. 1893.

problem of fraudulent antedating to some extent. However, we have argued above that the function of preventing antedating should not be exaggerated (see 4.1.1.2.C). Notification has some defects in tackling the problem of antedating, and there are better solutions, such as notarization and private registration. Moreover, this function only concerns how to resolve conflicts, rather than how to prevent the occurrence of conflicts.

4.1.6 Conclusion

Personal rights (claims) are a legal relationship *inter partes* and not subject to the principle of publicity. However, as a type of wealth, personal rights can be assigned, pledged and distributed by creditors in the situation of the debtor's insolvency. In this sense, personal rights have a proprietary aspect. Due to this reason, personal rights may also involve a problem of publicity. Notification is often treated as a method of publicity for this type of wealth. In the preceding discussion, we have examined the question whether notification can convey any useful information to third parties.

In general, notification conveys no useful information to strange interferers. The protection of creditors is mainly based on the rule concerning default by debtors, which has nothing to do with notification. Notification is not useful for general creditors. This is because notification can neither indicate how many claims the insolvent debtor has, nor show whether these claims have been pledged or assigned for the purpose of security. More importantly, general creditors are mainly concerned about the general financial health of the debtor, rather than how many unencumbered claims are owned by the debtor.

In terms of the role played by notification in the situation of disposal of claims (assignment and pledge), it has been shown that many divergences exist between the three jurisdictions. It is a controversial issue whether notification should be treated as relevant in determining the priority between competing disposals. This issue is closely related to the question whether notification has any effect of publicity. About this question, a negative answer has been argued by this research on the ground of two important reasons.

The first reason is that notification only creates a possibility to inquire the debtor involved. It does not guarantee that subsequent acquirers can obtain reliable information. The debtor has no duty to provide information, and the information provided might be incomplete or incorrect. As a result, notification cannot be used to realize the purpose of preventing conflicts. The second reason is that notification cannot be an appropriate method of publicity. Notifying and inquiring the debtor is costly, especially when a large number of claims are involved. Moreover, the requirement of notification implies that the disposal of future claims might become impossible. Due to these reasons, notification cannot be seen as a method of publicity for claims. In the preceding discussion, we have shown that English law introduces registration for charge and mortgage of claims. However, the outright assignment remains hidden in English law.[178]

Due to the absence of a method of publicity, individuals cannot obtain reliable information in the field of the transaction of claims. Property rights existing on claims remain in a hidden state ubiquitously. This implies a high possibility of conflicts between different transactions. In general, the conflict is regulated by the *nemo dat* rule: the person who obtains a property right with respect to the in-question claim earlier has a better position. Undoubtedly, this rule is disadvantageous to subsequent acquirers: they have to be cautious about earlier but hidden property rights. Potential acquirers have to bear a heavy burden of investigation, which further affects the liquidity of personal claims. In the viewpoint of some scholars, protection against unauthorized disposal should be granted to subsequent acquirers in good faith to make claims as transferable as corporeal things.[179]

Obviously, claims have played an important part in current transactions and should have as high negotiability as corporeal things. However, claims neither have an abstract outward appearance (namely possession of corporeal movables), nor a clear and reliable means of publicity (registration of immovable property). There is not any proper fulcrum to introduce a general rule of *bona fide* acquisition of claims. Therefore, the insufficient protection of subsequent acquirers in good faith is not a result of legal policy, but a result of the lack of a reliable method of publicity. In English law, the notification-first rule grants protection to subsequent acquirers in good faith. However, as notification does not qualify as a means of publicity, this rule produces "*at least as much injustice as it has prevented*".[180]

4.2 Documental Recordation

In the preceding section, we have discussed claims and notification to debtors. In practice, some claims are embodied within a document (security), such as the bill of exchange and the warehouse receipt. This document record details of the claim embodied, which allows outsiders to know this claim. Moreover, the disposal of the claim usually does not require any notification to debtors, but cannot validly take place without involving the document.[181] For example, the assignment of the claim often requires the document to be delivered to the assignee. Claims of this kind are known as "*documentary intangibles*" in English writings.[182] In this research, they are termed "documental rights" or "documental claims".

178 Akseli 2013, p. 211.
179 Verhagen 2002, p. 256.
180 Guest and Liew 2018, no. 6-07.
181 Goode 2010, p. 52.
182 Goode 2010, p. 52.

In this section, particular attention is paid to documental rights and documental recordation. At first, there is a general introduction of securities (documents). After that, we discuss two types of securities: securities to goods (see 4.2.2) and securities of payment (see 4.2.3). The discussion focuses on how these two types of securities function as a method of publicity for documental claims. Just like the last section, this section also includes a comparative study of English law, German law and Dutch law.

4.2.1 Introduction of Securities

4.2.1.1 Categories of Securities

In this research, the concept of securities is used to describe documents which embody a personal right, such as the right of payment or the right of recovery of goods. This concept is an academic term in German law (*Wertpapier*) and in Dutch law (*waardepapier*).[183] It is equivalent to "document of title", the document containing a title to payment or goods, in English law.[184] In addition to "document of title", English law also has another relevant term: negotiable instrument. Negotiable instrument mainly refers to securities to payment.[185]

According to the content of the right embodied and the field of application, securities can be roughly categorized into three groups.[186] The first group is securities of payment, which include bills of exchange, cheques and promissory notes.[187] As these securities involve the payment of a certain amount of money, they are also called monetary documents. The second group is securities to goods, including warehouse receipts and bills of lading.[188] The last group is capital securities or investment securities, which

183 Zöllner 1978, p. 1; Reehuis and Heisterkamp 2019, p. 233.
184 Bridge, Gullifer, McMeel and Worthington 2013, p. 637.
185 Bridge, Gullifer, McMeel and Worthington 2013, p. 640; James 1991, p. 17-23.
186 Bridge, Gullifer, McMeel and Worthington 2013, p. 12.
187 This type of securities is known as "negotiable instrument" in English law, "*Wertpapiere des Zahlungs- und Kreditverkehrs*" in German law, and *mutanis mutandis* "*schuldvorderingspapieren*" in Dutch law. See Zöllner 1978, p. 3-4; Reehuis and Heisterkamp 2019, p. 233.
188 This type of securities is known as "document of title to goods" in English law, "*Wertpapiere des Güterumlaufs*" in German law, and *mutanis mutandis* "*zakenrechtelijk papier*" in Dutch law. See Zöllner 1978, p. 4-5; Reehuis and Heisterkamp 2019, p. 233. However, it should be noted that the Dutch term "*zakenrechtelijk papier*" is in German legal theory a kind of "*forderungsrechtliches Wertpapier*", as opposed to "*sachenrechtliches Wertpapier*" which only includes *Hypotheken-, Grundschuld-* and *Rentenschuldbrief*. This is because securities to goods do not embody the right of ownership of the goods involved, but only a personal claim of delivery of the goods. See Zöllner 1978, p. 8-9. Just as Dutch scholar Mulder points out, the "*zakenrechtlijk papier*" embodies a personal right. See Mulder 1948, p. 11.

mainly refer to shares (stocks) and bonds (debenture).[189] The categorization indicates that securities play an important role in different sections of the market economy, such as the transaction of goods, payment, and the capital market. In general, securities not only evidence but also embody a right.[190] Disposal of the right embodied is largely realized by disposing of the securities, a kind of corporeal movable. As a result, the right embodied can be disposed of like a tangible and movable thing. For this reason, the right is often said to be "objectified (*verkörpert*)",[191] thereby having a "*somewhat hybrid nature*".[192]

According to the way in which securities are issued and transferred, there is a distinction between bearer securities, order securities, and named securities. Bearer securities are a document which does not specify the name of the entitled.[193] This type of document is alienated just like a corporeal movable: delivery of the document is necessary.[194] In general, the holder of the document is assumed to be the person who enjoys the right embodied.[195] In contrast, order securities need to specify the name of the entitled by including a clause like "to X or order".[196] Disposal of this type of document not only requires delivery of the document, but also usually involves endorsement.[197] In general, the last endorsee is the person who enjoys the right embodied. Like order securities, named securities also specify the name of the entitled.[198] However, named securities do not "embody" a right. The entitled cannot dispose of the right by disposing of the named document, and the right can, in principle, be validly disposed of without involving the document.[199] As a result, the entitled is not necessarily the person whose name is indicated by the document. In the viewpoint of some scholars, the main purpose of the named document is to prove the existence of the right involved.[200] In the following discussion, named securities are excluded.

---

189 This type of security is known as "*Wertpapier des Kapitalmarkts*" in German legal theory. See Zöllner 1978, p. 2. It is broader than the concept of "*lidmaatschapspapier*" in Dutch legal theory, because bonds (debentures) are not a kind of "*lidmaatschapspapier*". See Reehuis and Heisterkamp 2019, p. 233. German legal theory has a particular term, namely "*Mitgliedschaftspapier*", equivalent to the Dutch term "*lidmaatschapspapier*". This particular term mainly refers to shares. See Zöllner 1978, p. 8.

190 Bridge, Gullifer, McMeel and Worthington 2013, p. 638.

191 Hueck and Canaris 1986, p. 2; Brox and Henssler 2009, p. 259.

192 Zöllner 1978, p. 17; Bridge, Gullifer, McMeel and Worthington 2013, p. 11.

193 This type of document is called "*Inhaberpapiere*" in German law and "*toonderpapier*" in Dutch law. See Zöllner 1978, p. 9-11; Zevenbergen 1951, p. 329.

194 Zevenbergen 1951, p. 336; Hueck and Canaris 1986, p. 24.

195 Zevenbergen 1951, p. 329; Hueck and Canaris 1986, p. 24.

196 This type of document is known as "*Orderpapier*" in German law and "*orderpapier*" in Dutch law. See Zöllner 1978, p. 12-14; Scheltema 1993, p. 84; Zevenbergen 1951, p. 63.

197 Zöllner 1978, p. 13.

198 This type of document is known as "*Rektapapier*" or "*Namenspapier*" in German legal theory and "*rektapapier*" in Dutch legal theory. See Zöllner 1978, p. 11-12; Scheltema 1993, p. 86; Zevenbergen 1951, p. 52.

199 Zöllner 1978, p. 11; Hueck and Canaris 1986, p. 22.

200 Scheltema 1993, p. 86. However, different opinions exist. See Zevenbergen 1951, p. 52-57.

4.2.1.2 Challenges to Securities

In the last several decades, securities experienced a significant challenge. This challenge is that the traditional paper-based securities, especially capital securities, have been dematerialized to a large extent due to the development of technology.[201] Capital securities have experienced a significant dematerialization: most certificated securities have become uncertificated. Many countries have built an electronic central system for the transfer and settlement of capital securities. Investors are provided with an electronic account of securities linked to this system. Most capital securities are stored in an electronic account and transferred through the electronic central system, and only a few capital securities still have a tangible form.[202] As a result, possession and delivery of certificates are not involved in the transaction of most capital securities. Due to this reason, capital securities are not included in the following discussion.

Dematerialization also occurs in the field of securities to goods and securities of payment under the context of electronic commerce.[203] The transaction of securities of payment has become partially paperless, such as the emergence of electronic cheques.[204] However, electronic monetary securities are not common yet due to the concern about safety, especially the integrity and reliability of the electronic information.[205] In fact, the biggest challenge against the traditional monetary securities comes from new means of payment, especially the payment card.[206] Nevertheless, paper-based securities of payment are still used in practice.[207] As to securities to goods, some of them, such as warehouse receipts, might have taken an electronic form and are used in commercial practice.[208] However, strong resistance exists in the progress of the digitalization.[209] For example, businessmen still show reluctance to electronic bills of lading due to the concern about the safety of electronic information.[210] For bills of lading, widespread digitalization does not occur yet.[211]

201 Haentjens 2007, p. 33.
202 Rogers 2012, p. 50.
203 UNCITRAL Yearbook 2003, p. 283.
204 Geva 2007, p. 689; Geva 2015, p. 96.
205 Botchway 2004, p. 525; Zwitser 2006, p. 2; Guest 2016, no. 5-004.
206 Rogers 2012, p. 4-5. Payment cards are issued by financial institutions, such as the bank, to a customer. With a payment card, the cardholder can access the funds in the customer's designated bank accounts and make payments by the transfer of electronic funds.
207 For example, around "*70 billion checks are written and processed each year in the United States. All of these checks are written on paper, and some of them are transported in physical form for long distances within the U.S. banking system—a process that requires airplane and truck fuel.*" See Clarkson, Miller and Cross 2017, p. 480.
208 UNCITRAL Yearbook 2003, p. 287-288; Winn and Wright 2019, p. 9.36-9.37.
209 Salomons 2008 (2), p. 76.
210 Van Maanen and Claringbould 2017, p. 9; Aikens, Lord and Bools 2016, no. 2.123.
211 Goode, Kronke and Mckendrick 2015, p. 291; Aikens, Lord and Bools 2016, no. 2.124.

"Shippers, consignees, carriers, and intermediaries all incur expenses due to the delays caused by the handling and transmittal of paper documents. Paper documents are also, in some ways, less secure than electronic transmissions. However, many participants in the process harbor concern about security and about how the controlling functions of the bill of lading can be retained in the electronic version."[212]

In a nutshell, traditional paper-based securities have been dematerialized to a large extent, but they still play a role in commercial transactions. Therefore, the following discussion concerning traditional securities is not totally useless.

4.2.1.3 The Scope of the Following Discussion

This research focuses on the principle of publicity in the law of movables. In revealing the publicity effect of securities for the personal right embodied, we only pay attention to securities to goods and securities of payment. These two types of securities will be discussed in separation because they differ in legal consequences as well as the field of application. The transfer of securities of payment means the transfer of the monetary claim embodied (see 4.2.3). This type of document is mainly used in the field of payment. The transfer of securities to goods means that the claim of recovery of the goods, rather than the right of ownership of the goods, is alienated.[213] The transfer is also closely related to the disposal of the goods. As will be seen later, transfer of securities to goods has an effect of delivery of the goods (see 4.2.2). Securities to goods are mainly used in the commercial transaction of goods. Capital securities are not included in the following discussion. This is because they have been dematerialized to a very large extent, as just mentioned. Moreover, the typical kind of capital securities, i.e. shares, embodies a right of membership,[214] while Chapter 4 mainly focuses on claims.

In the following discussion, we do not pay attention to the issue of the debtor's defense: can the debtor refuse to perform the debt to the new creditor by claiming that he or she has a defense against the original creditor? In the preceding discussion of notification to debtors, this issue is also excluded (see 4.1.1.1.C). As has been pointed out there, the debtor's defense against the assignee concerns the performance of obligations and thus the obligational aspect of the claim.[215] The issue of the debtor's defense should be carefully distinguished from the acquisition of claims: acquiring a claim does not necessarily mean that the acquirer can require the debtor to provide the performance.[216] In general, the issue of acquisition concerns

212 Beecher 2006, p. 627.
213 Goode 2010, p. 52.
214 Reehuis and Heisterkamp 2019, p. 233.
215 Van Empel and Huizink 1991, p. 50-52.
216 Stranz and Stranz 1952, p. 108; Tiedtke 1985, p. 241.

who the owner of the document is and who the creditor is. Only after ascertaining the creditor can we answer whether and to what extent the creditor can request the debtor to perform the obligation. In this sense, the issue of acquisition is a "preliminary question (*Vorfrage*)" to the issue of the debtor's defense.[217] In the following discussion, we only focus on this preliminary question. As to whether the debtor can refuse performance on the ground of a defense against the original creditor, providing a brief answer here seems sufficient.

It has been pointed out that the debtor can, in principle, claim his or her defenses without being affected by the disposal of the claim (see 4.1.1.1.C). However, securities to goods and securities of payment are differently treated in this aspect in favor of the new creditor. Roughly speaking, the debtor of a document is not allowed to refuse to provide performance to the new creditor by claiming that he or she has a defense out of the legal relationship with the original creditor.[218] This is known as the exclusion of "personal defenses (*persönliche Einwendungen* in German law and *persoonlijke verweermiddelen* in Dutch law)".[219] Here we take the bill of exchange as an example. The holder of a bill of exchange has this bill accepted by a bank by fraud and then transfers the bill to a third party who is in good faith with respect to this defective acceptance. In this case, the third party is able to require the acceptor (the bank) to pay, and the latter cannot refuse on the ground of the original holder's fraud.

4.2.2 Securities to Goods

In the literature concerning securities to goods, this type of document is often treated as an "appearance of rights (*Rechtsschein*)"[220] or an "appearance of the authority of disposal (*schijn van beschikkingsbevoegdheid*)".[221] In particular, this appearance lays a basis for *bona fide* acquisition of the goods involved by third parties in good faith.[222]

> *"Die den Erwerber legitimierende Übertragung des Traditionspapiers schafft den dafür erforderlichen und ausreichenden Publizitätsakt, ohne daß es überhaupt auf den Besitzmittlungswillen des Papierschuldners ankommt. Wie der besitzende Veräußerer durch*

---

217 Stranz and Stranz 1952, p. 109.

218 The exclusion of personal defenses is pinned down by art. 6:146 BW, for bills of exchange by art. 116 WvK, and for bills of lading by art. 8:414 and art.8:441 (2) BW in Dutch law. In German law, the corresponding provision is art. 17 WG for bills of exchange and § 364 (2) HGB for securities to goods. In English law, s. 29 BEA excludes personal defenses for bills of exchange.

219 Goode 2010, p. 533; Zöllner 1978, p. 130; Hueck and Canaris 1986, p. 102; Hammerstein 1998, p. 43; Scheltema 1993, p. 128.

220 Hueck and Canaris 1986, p. 203; Schnauder 1991, p. 1648.

221 Scheltema 1993, p. 96-99; Vriesendorp 1994, p. 242.

222 Zevenbergen 1951, p. 68.

den unsichtbaren Rechtsschein des mittelbaren Besitzes, so wird der nicht-besitzende Veräußerer durch den Rechtsschein des Papiers legitimiert. Das muß als Grundlage für den gutgläubigen Erwerb genügen."[223]

To reveal the function of publicity of securities to goods, we need to focus on two aspects: (1) the effect of publicity for the claim of recovery embodied within this type of document; and (2) the effect of publicity for the goods involved. As we will see, securities to goods embody a personal right of recovery against the direct possessor of the goods, usually the issuer of the document. Usually, this personal right is disposed of by disposing of the document. On the other hand, securities to goods are closely related to the disposal of the goods involved. For example, transfer of the document can yield an effect of delivery, which means that the goods involved are delivered to the acquirer of the document. This effect is important for the disposal of the goods, especially when the disposal occurs under the *traditio* system that requires delivery for the disposal of corporeal movables.

In disclosing the function of publicity of securities to goods, we discuss two issues: (1) the legal effect of this type of securities in the disposal of the goods; and (2) the blocking effect of this type of securities in the disposal of goods.[224] The first issue concerns the legal effect yielded by securities to goods. For example, what legal consequences can be given rise to by transferring securities to goods? The second issue mainly concerns whether the goods under a document can be disposed of without involving this document. For example, can the goods under a document be transferred in the way of *traditio longa manu* but independently from this document? As we will see later, this issue is directly related to the reliability of securities to goods as a method of publicity for goods.

Here, English law, German law and Dutch law are selected for the comparative study of the two issues. An introduction to securities to goods in these three jurisdictions is first provided (see 4.2.2.1-4.2.2.3). After this

223 Schnauder 1991, p. 1648. English translation: "*The legitimized transfer of the traditio document provides the acquirer with necessary and sufficient publicity, which is nearly independent from the possessory intention of the document debtor. Like the possessing vendor who is legitimized by the invisible appearance of rights of indirect possession, the non-possessing vendor is legitimized by the appearance of rights of the document. This suffices for being a basis for the bona fide acquisition.*"

224 In fact, the function of publicity of securities to goods is also indicated by the following aspect: the reliance of third parties on the document is protected against the debtor's defense on the ground of the personal legal relationship with the original creditor. In general, the debtor of the document is not entitled to refuse performance to the new creditor in good faith by claiming that there is a defect in his or her personal legal relationship with the original creditor. The restriction over the debtor's means of defense is often explained by the "theory of appearance of rights (*Rechtsscheintheorie*)": third parties can safely assume that they can enforce the right obtained just as the document shows. See Staub/Canaris 2004, § 364, Rn. 26; Brox and Henssler 2009, p. 263-264; Zwitser 2012, p. 39; Van Empel and Huizink 1991, p. 85. In general, the protection of third parties against personal defenses is an issue in the law of obligations. Therefore, it is not discussed here. See Van Empel and Huizink 1991, p. 50-52.

introduction, there is a comparative discussion (see 4.2.2.4). On the basis of this comparative discussion, we reveal the rationale of publicity of securities to goods (see 2.2.2.5-4.2.2.6).

4.2.2.1 *English Law*

A *The Legal Effect of Securities to Goods*

As mentioned above, securities to goods are known as the "document of title to goods" in English law. This term is used in two senses: the common law sense and the statutory law sense.[225] The crucial difference between these two senses lies in whether transfer of the document can lead to a shift of possession of the goods concerned.[226] In the common law sense, documents of title to goods represent indirect possession (constructive possession) of the goods, thus the transfer of these documents can allow the acquirer to become an indirect possessor.[227] In this process, any attornment by the direct possessor of the goods is not necessary.

In English law, bills of lading are the only document of title to goods in the common law sense: the transfer of bills of lading has an effect of delivery. Transfer of the other documents concerning goods (such as delivery orders, warrants and warehouse certificates) have no effect of delivery.[228] The principal function of these other documents is to provide *"proof of the possession or control of goods"*.[229] However, these other documents are called by English lawyers as *"a document of title in the statutory sense"*.[230] This is because s. 1 (4) of the Factors Act (1898) expressly includes these documents, together with the bill of lading, under the concept of *"document of title"*.[231] Moreover, this paragraph also applies for the purpose of the SGA (1979).[232] As a result, transfer of these other documents can yield an effect of delivery under some statutory rules, such as s. 24 and s. 25 SGA (see 3.4.3.1). The distinction between the document of title to goods in common law and that in statutory law reminds us that possession is a vague concept in English law. In understanding this concept, the context under which it is used is important: *"a person might have possession (control) for the purposes of one legal rule but not for another"*.[233]

---

225 Benjamin 2014, p. 1168.
226 Benjamin 2014, p. 1168, 1394.
227 Benjamin 2014, p. 1168-1169.
228 Bridge 2014, p. 429.
229 Benjamin 2014, p. 1171.
230 Benjamin 2014, p. 1398.
231 S. 1 (4) FA (1898): *"The expression 'document of title' shall include any bill of lading, dock warrant, warehouse-keeper's certificate, and warrant or order for the delivery of goods, and any other document used in the ordinary course of business as proof of the possession or control of goods, or authorising or purporting to authorise, either by endorsement or by delivery, the possessor of the document to transfer or receive goods thereby represented [...]."*
232 S. 61 (1) SGA (1979): *"'document of title to goods' has the same meaning as it has in the Factors Acts [...]."*
233 Rostill 2016, p. 21.

In common law, other documents than the bill of lading might not lead to the acquisition of indirect possession. Indirect possession has to be obtained via ordinary methods, namely attornment. In other words, individuals can obtain indirect possession only when the direct possessor acknowledges that the goods are held on their behalf.[234] In general, attornment is a separate act, which cannot be inferred from the transfer of these documents. To understand this, we take two different types of document as an example: delivery orders and delivery warrants. Delivery orders are issued by sellers to require the direct possessor (such as a warehouseman) to deliver the goods to buyers. Delivery orders do not have any effect of delivery in common law. The direct possessor who fails to respond to the delivery order held by a buyer only owes an obligation to the seller.[235] Delivery warrants are made by the direct possessor (such as a warehouseman) who undertakes to deliver the goods. Despite this acknowledgment in advance, indirect possession of the goods does not pass to the acquirer of delivery warrants until the direct possessor attorns to the acquirer separately.[236]

In terms of the effect of delivery of securities to goods, English law seems to stick to a principle of *numerus clausus*: whether a document has the effect of delivery cannot be decided by individual parties, but by commercial custom.

> *"At common law, a document can become a 'negotiable' (i.e. transferable) document of title only by virtue of a mercantile custom to this effect; and it follows from the reasoning on which this submission is based that a document cannot acquire the characteristic of this kind of transferability merely by virtue of the intention of the parties to it, or of one, as expressed in its terms."*[237]

On the other hand, the list is also open, because commercial custom determines whether a document is qualified as a document of title and has the effect of delivery.[238] It is imaginable that once a document is commonly deemed as a document of title in commercial transactions, there is no reason to refuse to add this document into the closed list.[239]

Here, it is worthwhile noting that the lack of the effect of delivery of most documents (except the bill of lading) does not impede the transaction of goods. This is because English law insists on the consensual principle: ownership can be transferred independently from delivery (see 3.4.2.1). Just as pointed out by English lawyers, the transfer of ownership and the transfer of possession (delivery) are two separate matters: the requirement of attornment by the actual possessor never affects the transfer of owner-

---

234 Benjamin 2014, p. 1394.
235 Bridge 2015, p. 77.
236 Bridge 2015, p. 77.
237 Benjamin 2014, p. 1395.
238 Bridge, Gullifer, McMeel and Worthington 2013, p. 659.
239 Goode 2010, p. 53; Zwitser 2006, p. 10.

ship.[240] Moreover, transfer of bills of lading has an effect of delivery, but this does not necessarily give rise to the "*passing of property in the goods to the buyer*", because what matters is the parties' intention.[241] However, it should be noted that where a document other than the bill of lading is issued for certain goods, these goods cannot be pledged through pledging this document.[242]

It is not completely correct to say that other securities to goods than the bill of lading do not have any effect of delivery. These securities can be a document of title to goods in statutory law. For example, transfer of these documents is stipulated as an equivalent to delivery of the goods in the situation of *bona fide* acquisition.[243] Under s. 24 SGA (seller in possession after sale) and s. 25 SGA (buyer in possession after sale), the transfer of documents of title to goods, which includes warehouse receipts and delivery orders, can satisfy the requirement of delivery.[244] In this situation, the attornment by the actual possessor is unnecessary.[245]

If possession is treated as an outward appearance of ownership of the goods involved, and delivery is necessary for *bona fide* acquisition, then a document of title (in the statutory law sense) can also be seen as an outward appearance, and the transfer of this document has the effect of delivery. In the situation of *bona fide* acquisition, the unauthorized transferor's control of the document represents possession of the goods,[246] and the transfer of the document to the transferee in good faith amounts to delivery of the goods.[247] Therefore, though a document to goods might fail to lead to delivery in the situation of authorized disposals, this document can make delivery of the goods involved dispensable in the situation of *bona fide* acquisition (s. 24 and s. 25 SGA).

B *The Blocking Effect of Securities to Goods*

As just shown, English law draws a distinction between the document of title in the common law sense and that in the statutory law sense. Under common law, only the bill of lading is a document of title and has the effect of delivery. In practice, however, the buyer might not obtain the bill of lading after having acquired ownership of the goods involved. For example,

240 Benjamin 2014, p. 1397.
241 Bridge 2014, p. 300; Peel 2002, p. 141-142.
242 Beale, Bridge, Gullifer and Lomnicka 2018, no. 5.41.
243 Benjamin 2014, p. 1399.
244 S. 24 SGA (1979): "*Where a person having sold goods continues or is in possession of the goods, or of the documents of title to the goods, the delivery or transfer by that person, or by a mercantile agent acting for him, of the goods or documents of title under any sale, pledge, or other disposition thereof, to any person receiving the same in good faith and without notice of the previous sale, has the same effect as if the person making the delivery or transfer were expressly authorised by the owner of the goods to make the same.*"
245 Benjamin 2014, p. 1399.
246 Bridge 2014, p. 235.
247 Bridge 2014, p. 241.

the ship arrives before the bill of lading, and the buyer cannot present the bill of lading to the carrier.[248] In this very situation, the carrier bears no obligation to deliver the goods to the buyer, according to the predominant opinion.[249] In principle, the carrier is obliged to deliver the goods to the person who holds the bill of lading. Otherwise, the carrier will expose him- or herself to the risk of misdelivery.

Here it is noteworthy that transfer of ownership of the goods under a bill of lading is not dependent on this bill in English law. The main reason is that English law sees the transfer of ownership and delivery of the goods as two separate issues: whether and when ownership is transferred is contingent on the individuals' intention (see 3.4.2.1). In the case of pledge, the goods can be pledged without involving the bill of lading under equity law.[250] However, before delivering, and when necessary endorsing, the bill of lading to the pledgee, the pledge created cannot be enforced against third parties in good faith, such as another pledgee who obtains possession of the bill.[251] Therefore, the pledge is not perfected until the bill of lading is properly involved.[252]

As has been shown above, the transfer of other documents than the bill of lading cannot give rise to an effect of delivery in common law, and the transferee cannot obtain indirect possession until the direct possessor attorns to him or her. This implies that these other documents might be held by another person than the indirect possessor of the goods involved. For example, a warehouseman acknowledges holding the goods stored on behalf of the transferee when the transferor remains in control of the warehouse receipt. As also has been shown above, what matters for the transfer of goods is the parties' intention in English law. This implies that these other documents might be held by another person than the owner of the goods. For example, the owner transfers ownership of the goods under a warehouse receipt to the transferee but retains this warehouse receipt. In sum, other documents than the bill of lading are not necessarily held by the owner of the goods.

The above-shown divergence between securities to goods and ownership triggers a risk. This risk is that the owner first transfers ownership of the goods to one person by retaining the document, and then uses this document to mislead another person. In this very situation, the latter person is able to claim *bona fide* acquisition under some conditions. Among these conditions, one is that this person obtains the document from the previous

---

248 Goode 2010, p. 1158.

249 Aikens, Lord and Bools 2016, no. 5.3-5.10. However, the carrier might also agree to deliver the goods to the buyer who does not receive the bill yet. Usually, the buyer needs to offer a letter of indemnity to dispel the carrier's fear about the risk of misdelivery. See Aikens, Lord and Bools 2016, no. 5.66-5.68.

250 Zwitser 2005 (1), p. 170.

251 Zwitser 2005 (1), p. 170.

252 Curwen 2007, p. 162; Beale, Bridge, Gullifer and Lomnicka 2018, no. 5.37.

owner (see s. 24 and s. 25 SGA).[253] Here there are still two questions: (1) if the former person obtains the document, can the latter person successfully claim *bona fide* acquisition; and (2) if the former person does not obtain the document but has acquired indirect possession of the goods in the way of attornment, can the latter person successfully claim *bona fide* acquisition after obtaining the document? In the following discussion, we analyze these two particular questions in a hypothetical case involving a warehouse receipt.

In this hypothetical case, A stores his goods in the place of B (the warehouseman) and transfers the goods together with the warehouse receipt to C. After this transfer, A pledges the goods to D who obtains indirect possession of the goods from B: B acknowledges holding the collateral for D. Is D able to acquire a property right of pledge?

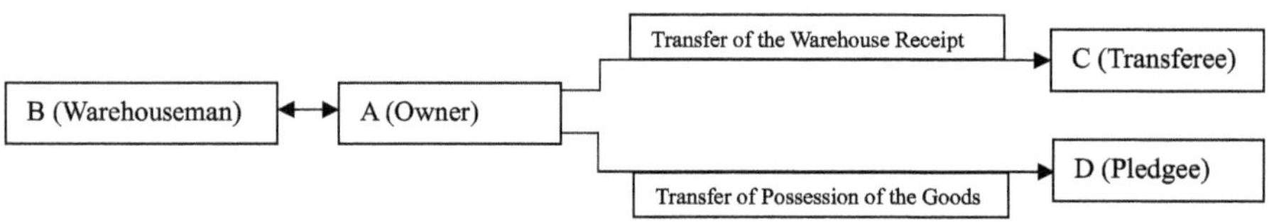

Figure 11

According to a landmark precedent ("*City Fur v. Fureenbond*"), D can acquire the right on the ground of s. 24 SGA (seller in possession after sale), a provision of *bona fide* acquisition.[254] As warehouse receipts are not a document of title under common law (see 4.2.2.1.A), the transfer of the warehouse receipt neither deprives A of his indirect possession, nor allows C to obtain indirect possession of the goods. A is still in possession of the goods after the transfer, despite the fact that he is neither in actual control of the goods nor the warehouse receipt.[255] However, if A or C has notified B of the transfer, and B immediately agrees to hold the goods on behalf of the new owner C, then D will lose the chance to obtain the right of pledge. B's attornment to C means that A loses his possession completely on the one hand, and C obtains indirect possession of the goods on the other hand. After the attornment, the possibility of *bona fide* acquisition by D will be excluded.

The analysis above indicates that the transferee who merely obtains the document of title involved is not absolutely safe. The risk of *bona fide* acquisition by third parties still exists before the direct possessor attorns to the transferee. About the hypothetical case, one doubt is whether D should be expected to be aware of the abnormality of the secured transaction. As the collateral is warehoused goods, should D pay particular attention to A's failure to present the warehouse receipt? If the answer is positive, then it

---

253 Bridge, Gullifer, McMeel and Worthington 2013, p. 363-366.

254 *City Fur Manufacturing Co Ltd v. Fureenbond (Brokers) London Ltd* [1937] 1 All E. R. 937, see Bridge 2014, p. 235-236.

255 Bridge 2014, p. 236.

seems difficult to say that D is in good faith with respect to A's authority to dispose.[256]

Now let us reverse the way of transferring the right of ownership and the way of creating the right of pledge. A transfers ownership of the goods to C, and C obtains B's attornment and thus becomes an indirect possessor. After this transfer, A pledges the goods to D by giving up the warehouse receipt. Is D able to obtain a property right of pledge?

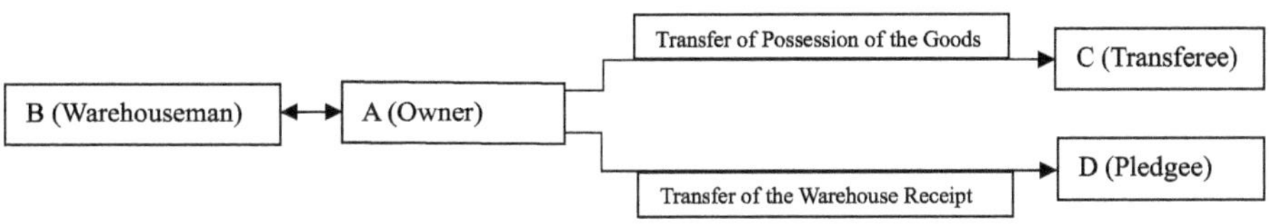

Figure 12

On the basis of a literal understanding of s. 24 SGA, D seems able to acquire a right of pledge: A is in direct possession of the document and delivers it to D.[257] For the application of this provision, what matters is the seller's possession of the document and the delivery of this document to third parties in good faith. It is irrelevant whether the seller remains in possession of the goods involved. Therefore, the buyer who allows the seller to retain the document to goods involved will run a risk out of s. 24 SGA: a third party in good faith might prevail after obtaining this document.

In sum, the transfer of securities to goods is neither a condition for acquisition of ownership of the goods, nor a condition for acquisition of possession of the goods. However, securities to goods are treated as a cause for the reliance of third parties in good faith. As a result, to entirely preclude the risk of *bona fide* acquisition by third parties, the transferee not only needs to obtain attornment by the direct possessor, but also acquire the document from the transferor.

4.2.2.2 German Law

Securities to goods are known as *Güterpapiere* in German law.[258] The concept of *Wertpapiere* (literally the document of value) is broad and includes other securities than securities to goods, such as shares, bonds, cheques and bills

---

256 *"Depending on the circumstances, a potential transferee may expect from the third party's type of business that this person will usually issue documents. If so, and goods are offered without related documents being presented, the buyer may have reason to be suspicious and may wish to check with the third party before proceeding further."* See Acquisition and Loss of Ownership of Goods 2011, p. 611.

257 This way of understanding is in line with the rule that the unpaid seller cannot enforce his or her right of lien or right of stoppage against *bona fide* third parties who obtain the document of title to the goods. See Bridge, Gullifer, McMeel and Worthington 2013, p. 380.

258 Staub/Canaris 2004, § 363, Rn. 52.

of exchange. Generally speaking, German law has a closed list of securities.[259] Individuals are not entitled to create a new type of document to goods as they wish. In general, there are four types of document to goods: the "bill of lading (*Konnossement*)", the "shipping note (*Ladeschein*)", the "warehouse receipt (*Lagerschein*)", and the "delivery order (*Lieferschein*)".[260] The former two types are a freight document. The biggest difference between the delivery order and the warehouse receipt is that the former is made by depositors, while the latter is issued by warehousemen.[261] In this part, we focus on two issues: one is the legal effect of securities to goods, and the other is the blocking effect of securities to goods.

A The Legal Effect of Securities to Goods

In general, securities to goods are a document embodying a personal right, thereby being treated as a kind of "obligational document".[262] This personal right is a claim of recovery against the direct possessor of the goods, usually the issuer of the document.[263] It is often held that securities to goods "objectify" the claim of recovery, so that the claim can be disposed of just like a corporeal movable.[264] Disposal of the document implies that the claim embodied is disposed of. For example, transfer of a document to goods allows the transferee to obtain the claim of recovery embodied within this document,[265] and pledge of the claim can be realized by pledging the document (§ 1292 BGB).[266] In addition, objectification of the claim of recovery by the document lays a basis for *bona fide* acquisition of the claim: third parties in good faith can acquire the claim by *bona fide* acquisition of the document, even when the document is stolen by the transferor (§ 935 BGB).[267]

---

259 Hueck and Canaris 1986, p. 196; Zöllner 1978, p. 25.
260 Hueck and Canaris 1986, p. 194-196.
261 Staub/Canaris 2004, § 363, Rn. 37.
262 Zöllner 1978, p. 8-9.
263 Hueck and Canaris 1986, p. 193; MüKoHGB/Langenbucher 2018, § 363, Rn. 45.
264 Hueck and Canaris 1986, p. 199; Staub/Canaris 2004, § 363, Rn. 55.
265 Zöllner 1978, p. 153; MüKoHGB/Langenbucher 2018, § 364, Rn. 7.
266 Here the pledge of the claim of recovery by pledging the document should be carefully distinguished from the pledge of the goods *per se*. The object of the former pledge is the claim of recovery, while the object of the latter pledge is the goods under the document. On the other hand, these two pledges are closely related in two aspects. The first aspect is that if it is uncertain whether the claim of recovery or the goods *per se* are pledged when the document is delivered for the purpose of pledge, it will be assumed that the goods *per se* are pledged, provided that the document involves ascertainable goods. See MüKoBGB/Damrau 2017, § 1292, Rn. 3. The second aspect is that when the claim of recovery pledged is realized, the pledge of the claim "continues" existing on the goods delivered by the debtor of the document due to the rule of "real substitution (*dingliche surrogation*)" (§ 1287 BGB). In fact, the outcome of this rule is that a new pledge comes into existence on the goods, which is known as "pledge on substitutes (*Surrogationspfrandrecht*)". See Staub/Canaris 2004, § 364, Rn. 13; Heymann/Horn 2005, § 364, Rn. 5.
267 Heymann/Horn 2005, § 363, Rn. 27. However, *bona fide* acquisition of the claim does not mean that *bona fide* acquisition of the lost goods is possible, as will be seen later.

In terms of the way of disposing of the document, there is a distinction of bearer securities and order securities. If the document is made out to bearer, then the document needs to be delivered to the transferee in the case of transfer or the pledgee in the case of pledge.[268] If the document is made out to a particular person or his or her order, both delivery and endorsement are required (§ 364 HGB).[269] In the situation of transfer, the transferor records the transferee's name on the back of the document. Delivery is not confined to be actual, and *traditio per constitutum possessorium* also suffices.[270] In the situation of pledge, the endorsement usually includes a mark of pledge, such as "*zur Verpfändung* (for pledge)" or "*zur Sicherheit* (for security)". However, the endorsement for pledge may not include such mark, which is known as "concealed endorsement for pledge (*verdeckte Pfandindossament*)".[271] The absence of a mark of pledge does not affect that a pledge is validly created between the pledgor and the pledgee.[272] It is noteworthy that the pledgor needs to deliver the document in the way prescribed by § 1205 and 1206 BGB.[273] Therefore, *traditio per constitutum possessorium* is excluded when the document is under direct possession of the pledgor.[274] If the document is under indirect possession of the pledgor, then the pledgor needs to provide indirect possession and notify the direct possessor.[275]

As a personal right, the claim of recovery embodied within order securities to goods can also be disposed of according to civil law rules (the BGB) without involving endorsement. This concerns the blocking effect of the document and will be discussed later.

Securities to goods are not only related to the disposal of the claim of recovery, but also to the disposal of the goods *per se*.[276] In general, "transfer (*Übertragung*)" of securities to goods recognized by law has an "effect of delivery (*Traditionswirkung*)" of the goods.[277] For this reason, securities to goods are termed "*traditio* document (*Traditionspapiere*)".[278] As has been shown above, German law has a *traditio* system for the disposal of corporeal movables (see 3.4.2.2). The effect of delivery implies that the transfer of a document to goods allows the goods under this document to remain where they are. Upon the transfer of the document, the transferee obtains

268 Tiedtke 1985, p. 286.

269 Staub/Canaris 2004, § 364, Rn. 1; Heymann/Horn 2005, § 364, Rn. 1.

270 Staub/Canaris 2004, § 364, Rn. 1; Heymann/Horn 2005, § 364, Rn. 1.

271 MüKoHGB/Langenbucher 2018, § 364, Rn. 18.

272 MüKoHGB/Langenbucher 2018, § 364, Rn. 18.

273 MüKoBGB/Damrau 2017, § 1292, Rn. 3; Westermann 2011, p. 1206-1207.

274 Brehm and Berger 2014, p. 528.

275 Brehm and Berger 2014, p. 528.

276 MüKoHGB/Langenbucher 2018, § 363, Rn. 59.

277 Hueck and Canaris 1986, p. 199. Here, it should be noted that just delivering the document is not sufficient, the ownership of the document must be transferred. The new law deliberately requires transfer of the document, rather than mere delivery of the document. See MüKoHGB/Herber 2018, § 524, Rn. 14.

278 Wieling 2006, p. 351.

(indirect) possession of the goods involved, and the requirement of delivery is fulfilled.[279] The effect of delivery is confirmed by § 448,[280] § 475g,[281] and § 524 HGB.[282] The effect also implies that mere transfer of the document does not suffice for transferring or pledging the goods.[283] Other requirements, especially the power of disposal and valid agreement of the transfer or pledge, also have to be satisfied.[284]

As to the way of understanding the effect of delivery, there are controversies. The "absolute theory (*absolute Theorie*)" treats § 448, § 475g and § 524 HGB as three provisions independent from the BGB.[285] In contrast, the effect of delivery should be understood under the BGB according to the "relative theory (*relative Theorie*)". The document to goods embodies a claim of recovery. Transfer of the document implies the transfer of the claim, which suffices for *traditio longa manu* under § 931 BGB.[286] According to this provision, indirect possession of the goods can be provided by assigning the claim of recovery.[287] The predominant viewpoint is a third theory: the "representation theory (*Repräsentationstheorie*)". According to this theory, the document represents indirect possession of the goods, and transfer of the document can represent delivery of the goods.[288] The effect

279 McGuire 2008, p. 107.

280 § 448 HGB: "*Die Begebung des Ladescheins an den darin benannten Empfänger hat, sofern der Frachtführer das Gut im Besitz hat, für den Erwerb von Rechten an dem Gut dieselben Wirkungen wie die Übergabe des Gutes. Gleiches gilt für die Übertragung des Ladescheins an Dritte.*" English translation: § 448 HGB: "*The issuance of the shipping note to the consignee named therein has the same effect as the delivery of the goods for the acquisition of rights to the goods, provided that the carrier is in possession of the goods. The same applies to the transfer of the shipping note to third parties.*"

281 § 475g HGB: "*Die Begebung des Lagerscheins an denjenigen, der darin als der zum Empfang des Gutes Berechtigte benannt ist, hat, sofern der Lagerhalter das Gut im Besitz hat, für den Erwerb von Rechten an dem Gut dieselben Wirkungen wie die Übergabe des Gutes. Gleiches gilt für die Übertragung des Lagerscheins an Dritte.*" English translation: § 475g HGB: "*The issuance of the warehouse receipt to the person, who is named therein and entitled to receive the goods, has the same effect as the delivery of the goods for the acquisition of rights to the goods, provided that the warehouseman is in possession of the goods. The same applies to the transfer of the warehouse receipt to third parties.*"

282 § 524 HGB: "*Die Begebung des Konnossements an den darin benannten Empfänger hat, sofern der Verfrachter das Gut im Besitz hat, für den Erwerb von Rechten an dem Gut dieselben Wirkungen wie die Übergabe des Gutes. Gleiches gilt für die Übertragung des Konnossements an Dritte.*" English translation: § 524 HGB: "*The issuance of the bill of lading to the person, who is named therein and entitled to receive the goods, has the same effect as the delivery of the goods for the acquisition of rights to the goods, provided that the shipper is in possession of the goods. The same applies to the transfer of the bill of lading to third parties.*"

283 Hueck and Canaris 1986, p. 200.

284 Zöllner 1978, p. 150.

285 Hueck and Canaris 1986, p. 200; Wieling 2006, p. 353.

286 Hueck and Canaris 1986, p. 199; Wieling 2006, p. 353.

287 § 931 BGB: "*Ist ein Dritter im Besitz der Sache, so kann die Übergabe dadurch ersetzt werden, dass der Eigentümer dem Erwerber den Anspruch auf Herausgabe der Sache abtritt.*" English translation: § 931 BGB: "*If a third party is in possession of the thing, then delivery may be replaced by assigning the claim of recovery of the thing to the acquirer by the owner.*"

288 Hueck and Canaris 1986, p. 200; Wieling 2006, p. 353.

of delivery falls under § 929 BGB, a provision concerning actual delivery, instead of § 931 BGB.[289] The three theories do not differ substantially in legal consequences.[290]

Furthermore, transfer of the document can also make delivery of the goods *per se* unnecessary for *bona fide* acquisition of the goods. According to the representation theory, the *bona fide* acquisition occurs under § 932 BGB, a provision concerning *bona fide* acquisition in the way of actual delivery and *traditio brevi manu*.[291] In contrast, the relative theory explains *bona fide* acquisition under § 934 BGB, a provision concerning *bona fide* acquisition in the way of *traditio longa manu*.[292] In general, it is immaterial which provision is applied.[293] In addition to delivery, the other requirements of *bona fide* acquisition also have to be fulfilled. For example, the third party must be in good faith with respect to the transferor's defective authority of disposal and pay a reasonable price.

As to *bona fide* acquisition in the situation involving a document to goods, particular attention should be paid to § 935 BGB. According to this provision, *bona fide* acquisition is not applicable to lost, missing or stolen things, except currency and bearer securities. Therefore, ownership of lost or stolen bearer securities to goods might be acquired by a third party from an unauthorized transferor. Here two points should be noted. The first point is that *bona fide* acquisition of a bearer document to goods does not necessarily mean that the goods under this document are acquired. If the goods *per se* are lost or stolen contrary to the owner's will, *bona fide* acquisition of the goods remains impossible.[294] In other words, *bona fide* acquisition of lost or stolen documents cannot make *bona fide* of lost or stolen corporeal movables possible. The second point is that *bona fide* acquisition of the bearer document to goods implies that the claim of recovery embodied is acquired. This forms an exception to the rule that *bona fide* acquisition of personal rights is generally impossible in German law (see 4.1.3.2). § 935 BGB is a rule applicable to the *bona fide* acquisition of bearer securities to goods.

---

289 Hueck and Canaris 1986, p. 200; Wieling 2006, p. 353.

290 The three theories differ in the following issue: whether the document debtor needs to have possession of the goods. For example, in light of the absolute theory, the holder of a warehouse receipt can deliver the goods by transferring this receipt, even though the warehouseman does not have possession of the goods. However, according to the relative theory, the goods cannot be successfully delivered by transferring the receipt when the warehouseman is not possession of the goods. Under the representation theory, a precondition for the effect of delivery is that the debtor of the document has possession of the goods. In other respects, the representation theory does not have substantial differences from the relative theory either. This is why some German scholars think that it does not matter which approach is adopted. See Staub/Canaris 2004, § 363, Rn. 102; Hueck and Canaris 1986, p. 200; Zöllner 1978, p. 153-154; Brox and Henssler 2009, p. 334.

291 Zöllner 1978, p. 154.

292 Hueck and Canaris 1986, p. 201-202.

293 Zöllner 1978, p. 154.

294 Zöllner 1978, p. 155; Tiedtke 1985, p. 281.

To the acquisition of order securities to goods from an unauthorized transferor, another rule is applicable.[295]

B The Blocking Effect of Securities to Goods

In German law, the existence of securities to goods does not mean that civil law rules (the BGB) are inapplicable. In general, where a document to goods is made out for certain goods, both the claim of recovery embodied and these goods can be disposed of under the BGB.

For example, the claim of recovery can be transferred in the way of "assignment (*Zession*)" according to § 398 BGB.[296] Endorsement is unnecessary for the assignment, and § 364 HGB is not relevant. However, as an extra requirement, the assignor has to deliver the document to the assignee.[297] Here *traditio per constitutum possessorium* suffices for satisfying this requirement.[298] This implies that the new creditor does not necessarily obtain actual control of the document. If the claim is transferred in the way of assignment, *bona fide* acquisition is impossible.[299] Moreover, the claim of recovery can be pledged under § 1274 BGB, a provision concerning the pledge of rights. Just like in the situation of assignment, there is an extra requirement: the document needs to be delivered to the pledgee.[300] Due to this extra requirement, notifying the debtor, usually the direct possessor who bears the duty to deliver the goods, is unnecessary.[301] Pursuant to § 1280 BGB, pledge of an ordinary claim requires notifying the debtor of this claim (see 4.1.4.2).

In addition to the claim of recovery, the goods under a document can also be transferred according to the civil law (the BGB), especially the rules concerning the acquisition of corporeal movables in the way of *traditio longa manu* (§ 931 BGB).[302] Securities to goods are usually issued by the direct possessor of the goods, such as a warehouseman or carrier, who acknowledges holding possession for and owes a right of recovery to the holder of the document. The holder has indirect possession as well as a claim of recovery against the direct possessor. For this reason, German law allows the holder to dispose of the goods in the way of *traditio longa manu* by directly assigning the right of recovery to the transferee.

---

295 According to § 365 (1) HGB, art. 16 (2) WG, a paragraph concerning the *bona fide* acquisition of bills of exchange, is also applicable to securities to goods. About this paragraph, a detailed discussion will be provided later (see 4.2.3.2.B).

296 MüKoHGB/Langenbucher 2018, § 364, Rn. 9; Staub/Canaris 2004, § 364, Rn. 18.

297 MüKoHGB/Langenbucher 2018, § 364, Rn. 9; Staub/Canaris 2004, § 364, Rn. 18.

298 MüKoHGB/Langenbucher 2018, § 364, Rn. 9; Staub/Canaris 2004, § 364, Rn. 18.

299 MüKoHGB/Langenbucher 2018, § 364, Rn. 10; Staub/Canaris 2004, § 364, Rn. 24.

300 MüKoBGB/Damrau 2017, § 1292, Rn. 17; Staub/Canaris 2004, § 364, Rn. 23.

301 MüKoBGB/Damrau 2017, § 1292, Rn. 17; Staub/Canaris 2004, § 364, Rn. 23.

302 MüKoHGB/Langenbucher 2018, § 363, Rn. 73.

However, transfer of the goods in the way of *traditio longa manu* only takes effect when, as an extra requirement, the document is delivered to the transferee. This requirement is an outcome of judicial precedents.[303] For fulfilling the requirement, delivery of the document suffices. The document does not have to be transferred. This means that endorsement is unnecessary when the document is made out to order.[304] The rationale behind the extra requirement is that the document should be in the hands of the real owner, so that the transferor is precluded from using the document to mislead others.[305]

> *"Da der Anspruch auf Herausgabe der Ware im Papier verkörpert ist, bleibt er untrennbar mit der Urkunde verbunden und kann deshalb auch nicht gesondert von ihr geltend gemacht werden. Infolgedessen können Güter, über die ein Traditionspapier ausgestellt ist, durch Einigung und Abtretung des Herausgabeanspruchs nur übereignet werden, wenn gleichzeitig auch das Papier übergeben wird. Das verbriefte Recht auf Herausgabe soll nicht vom Besitz am Papier getrennt werden."*[306]

Before the document is given up to the transferee, the right of recovery cannot be validly assigned. Not only does this imply that delivery of the goods is not completed, but also that ownership of the goods does not pass to the transferee.[307] To add a word, even though the transferee is not aware of the existence of the document, the goods cannot be acquired until the document is handed over.[308] Thus, a risk of acquiring no ownership due to the fraudulent retention of the document by the transferor exists for the transferee.[309] This concerns the problem of the invisibility of securities to goods, which will be discussed later (see 4.2.2.5.C).

The extra requirement averts the divergence between possession of the document and ownership of the goods to a large extent. Nevertheless, the divergence might still occur. This is because both *traditio per constitutum possessorium* and *traditio longa manu* are an eligible method to deliver the document to the transferee.[310] In these two situations, the transferee does not obtain actual control of the document. In general, where the document

303 Hueck and Canaris 1986, p. 205.
304 Staub/Canaris 2004, § 363, Rn. 142.
305 Staub/Canaris 2004, § 363, Rn. 142; Hueck and Canaris 1986, p. 205; Tiedtke 1985, p. 285-286.
306 NJW 1968, p. 591, cited from Schnauder 1991, p. 1648. English translation: "*Since the claim to recover the goods is embodied within the document, the claim remains inseparably related to the document and thus cannot be enforced independently from the document. As a result, the goods, for which a traditio document is issued, can only be transferred by agreement and assignment of the claim to recover when this document is handed over at the same time. The documentalized right to recover should not be separated from possession of the document.*"
307 Staub/Canaris 2004, § 363, Rn. 143.
308 Hueck and Canaris 1986, p. 205.
309 MüKoHGB/Frantzioch 2018, § 475g, Rn. 73.
310 Staub/Canaris 2004, § 363, Rn. 142; MüKoHGB/Langenbucher 2018, § 363, Rn. 73.

is still controlled by the transferor, there is a possibility that the document is used by the transferor to mislead third parties. Furthermore, there is a need to protect third parties in good faith.[311]

A question regarding the blocking effect can arise in the following hypothetical case: A transfers his goods stored at the place of a warehouseman to B via transferring the warehouse receipt, then A pledges the same goods to innocent C through assigning the claim of recovery and notifying the warehouseman. In this situation, B can safeguard his ownership against C, because C cannot claim *bona fide* acquisition due to the defect in delivery. After transferring ownership of the goods and the document to B, A loses ownership of the goods as well as the claim of recovery against the warehouseman. As *bona fide* acquisition of claims is generally impossible in German law, C is not able to acquire the claim of recovery from C. As a result, delivery through assigning the claim is impossible. According to the German legal theory, what § 934 BGB can cure is the "defect of ownership (*Mangel des Eigentums*)", rather than the defect of delivery.[312] Even if C obtains actual control of the goods later, he cannot acquire a pledge due to the absence of valid delivery, regardless of whether he is in good faith. In general, German law is different from English law (s. 24 SGA and "*City Fur Manufacturing Co Ltd v. Fureenbond (Brokers) London Ltd*") here: under English law, C is able to obtain indirect possession and acquires the pledge.

The existence of a document to goods does not prevent the goods from being able to be pledged according to § 1205 (2) BGB, a paragraph concerning the pledge of corporeal movables.[313] For this way of pledge, endorsement is not necessary when the document is made out to order. However, an extra requirement is that the document needs to be delivered to the pledgee. Pursuant to § 1205 (2) BGB, when the corporeal movable collateral is under factual control by a third person, notifying this person is necessary. The extra requirement of delivery of the document to the pledgee makes such notification dispensable.[314] It is unclear whether this extra requirement can be fulfilled by *traditio per constitutum possessorium*. It seems that the answer is negative. As has been shown above, in the situation of pledge of the document *per se*, *traditio per constitutum possessorium* is excluded when the document is under direct possession of the pledgor.[315]

311 In fact, the extra requirement of delivery of the document has been doubted by some scholars. Where this requirement is completely abolished, it suffices that third parties in good faith can be protected by entitling them to *bona fide* acquisition when the original owner uses the document retained to mislead them. See Staub/Canaris 2004, § 363, Rn. 144.

312 Staub/Canaris 2004, § 363, Rn. 143-144.

313 Schnauder 1991, p. 1648.

314 Schnauder 1991, p. 1648.

315 MüKoBGB/Damrau 2017, § 1292, Rn. 3; Westermann 2011, p. 1206-1207; Brehm and Berger 2014, p. 528.

4.2.2.3 Dutch Law

In Dutch law, securities to goods are known as "proprietary securities (*goederenrechtelijk waardepapier*)". However, this term is misleading: securities to goods do not represent ownership or any limited property right of the goods, but only a personal claim of recovery.[316] The right embodied within a bearer and order document is termed "right to bearer and order (*recht aan toonder en order*)" respectively in the BW (art. 3:93 BW). In general, Dutch law has an open system of bearer and order securities.[317] This open system is confirmed in the landmark case "*Zürich/Lebosch*".[318] There are three typical securities to goods: the "warehouse receipt (*ceel*)", the "bill of lading (*cognossement*)", and the so-called "CT-document" (the combined transport document).[319]

A The Legal Effect of Securities to Goods

As just mentioned, the right embodied within securities to goods is a claim of recovery of the goods. Due to the existence of the document, this claim can be disposed of like a corporeal movable.[320] For example, the claim can be transferred and pledged by transferring and pledging the document respectively.[321] If the document is made out to bearer, then delivery of the document is necessary for the transfer and pledge of the document (art. 3:93 and 3:236 (1) BW). If the document is made out to order, then both delivery and endorsement are required (art. 3:93 and 3:236 (1) BW). In the situation of pledging an order document, the endorsement usually includes a mark of pledge, such as "*ter verpanding* (for pledge)".[322] As to the question whether the endorsement for pledge can be made in a "concealed (*geheime*)" manner,

316 Mulder 1948, p.11; Van Maanen and Claringbould 2017, p. 2.
317 Van der Lely 1996, p. 71.
318 Zwitser 2006, p. 9.
319 Van der Lely 1996, p. 70-71; Reehuis 2004, p. 54.
320 Reehuis and Heisterkamp 2019, p. 233.
321 Here, it should be noted that where a document to goods is pledged, the object of the pledge is, in essence, the right of recovery of the goods, rather than the goods themselves. In general, whether the goods are pledged is a question depending on the bilateral agreement between the pledgor and the pledgee. See Van Maanen and Claringbould 2017, p. 4. However, the pledgee of the document, namely pledge of the claim of recovery, is often also a pledgee of the goods involved. Where the document is given up for the purpose of pledge, parties have an intention to pledge the goods involved in normal situations. As a result, pledge of the document is pledge of the goods. See Logmans, p. 262. However, it is not always so. For example, if ownership of the goods is not acquired by the pledgor when the document is pledged, then only the claim of recovery can be pledged. See Zwitser 2006, p. 227. However, on the basis of the rule of "substitution (*zaakvervanging*)", the pledge of the claim can "continue" existing on the goods delivered by the debtor of the document. See Steneker 2012, p. 131.
322 Zwitser 2012, p. 223.

the predominant opinion is in favor of a positive answer.[323] Therefore, the lack of a mark of pledge does not affect the valid creation of pledge.

As the claim of recovery is embodied within a document, *bona fide* acquisition of the claim is possible for third parties by acquiring this document in good faith.[324] In Dutch law, *bona fide* acquisition of rights to bearer and order and that of corporeal movables are regulated in the same provision, namely art. 3:86 BW.

Securities to goods are closely related to the disposal of the goods. As has been shown above, Dutch law has a *traditio* system for the disposal of corporeal movables (see 3.4.2.3). Where a document is issued for certain goods, "transfer (*levering*)" of this document can yield an effect of delivery of the goods.[325] This legal effect is affirmed by art. 6:607 (1) BW, a paragraph concerning the warehouse receipt,[326] as well as art. 8:417 and 8:924 BW, two provisions concerning the bill of lading.[327] Due to the effect of delivery, securities to goods are called "*traditio* documents (*Traditionspapieren*)".[328] In understanding the effect, two points should be noted.

The first point concerns the way to understand the effect of delivery. The predominant opinion seems to be that the effect occurs in the sense of *traditio longa manu*.[329] As shown above, a claim of recovery is embodied within the document to goods. According to Van der Lely, transfer of the document leads to the assignment of the claim of recovery, which suffices for providing possession of the goods.[330] However, delivery through assigning the claim of recovery is not explicitly recognized by the BW. Pursuant to art. 3:115 (c) BW, *traditio longa manu* requires either acknowledgment by or notification to the person who is in factual control of the goods.[331] In

323 Zwitser 2006, p. 223-224; Asser/Van Mierlo 2016, nr. 149; Van Maanen and Claringbould 2017, p. 4.

324 Reehuis and Heisterkamp 2019, p. 235.

325 Asser/Van Mierlo 2016, nr. 159.

326 Art. 7:607 (1) BW: "*Indien ter zake van een bewaarneming een ceel of een ander stuk aan toonder of order is afgegeven, geldt levering daarvan vóór de aflevering van de daarin aangeduide zaken als levering van die zaken.*" English translation: Art. 7:607 (1) BW: "*If a warehouse receipt or another document to order or to bearer has been made for the sake of custody, then delivery of this receipt or document, before delivery of the goods, is treated as delivery of the goods.*"

327 Art. 8:417 BW: "*Levering van het cognossement vóór de aflevering van de daarin vermelde zaken door de vervoerder geldt als levering van die zaken.*" English translation: Art. 8:417 BW: "*Before delivering the goods mentioned in the bill of lading by the shipper, delivery of the bill of lading is treated as delivery of the goods.*"

328 Zevenbergen 1951, p. 59.

329 Snijders and Rank-Berenschot 2017, p. 117; Zwitser 2005 (1), p. 169; Van der Lely 1993, p. 115-118; Mijnssen and Schut 1991, p. 108-109; Scheltema 1993, p. 33.

330 Van der Lely 1996, p. 96-97.

331 In this aspect, art. 3:115 (c) BW is different from § 931 BGB. The latter only requires assignment of the claim of recovery for *traditio longa manu*. However, the former requires that the third party who is in factual control of the goods has to acknowledge holding the goods for the transferee or, at least, the third party is notified of the transfer. In the viewpoint of Dutch legislators, this extra requirement is necessary for the transferee's acquisition of factual control of the goods. See Rank-Berenschot 2012, p. 67.

contrast, the satisfaction of this requirement is unnecessary for securities to goods to yield an effect of delivery. For this reason, some Dutch scholars see the transfer of the document as a special or independent form of delivery, though they recognize that this form of delivery is closely connected to *traditio longa manu*.[332] However, it is possible to argue that the issuer of the document, i.e. the person who is in factual control of the goods, has expressed an acknowledgment in advance when making out the document.[333] According to this argument, the legal effect of delivery falls under *traditio longa manu*.

The second point is that only transfer of the document does not suffice for acquiring ownership of the goods. Except the requirement of delivery, the other requirements for the valid transfer of the goods also have to be fulfilled. Therefore, the transferor needs to have authority to dispose, and there must be a valid legal ground (usually a contract) for the transfer.

The effect of delivery might also occur in the situation of *bona fide* acquisition of the goods (art. 3:86 BW). In practice, the transferor may neither have legal ownership of the goods nor be a legal holder of the document.[334] For example, the unauthorized transferor is a thief of the document. In this very situation, the transferee is still able to acquire ownership of the goods when certain conditions are satisfied. Among these conditions, one is that possession of the goods is provided to the transferee. According to Van der Lely, possession of the goods is provided in the following way: the innocent transferee obtains ownership of the document from the illegal holder (art. 3:86 (3) BW), which further allows the transferee to acquire the claim of recovery (art. 3:86 (1) BW) and indirect possession of the goods.[335] In sum, three *bona fide* acquisitions occur: one is *bona fide* acquisition of the document, another is *bona fide* acquisition of the right of recovery, and the third is *bona fide* acquisition of ownership of the goods.[336]

B The Blocking Effect of Securities to Goods

Now let us turn to the issue of the blocking effect of securities to goods in Dutch law. Here one question is whether the claim embodied in a document to goods can be transferred in a different way from that prescribed by art. 3:93 BW. In general, this question is answered in the negative. For the sake of legal certainty, the way of transferring property is pinned down

332 Reehuis 2015, p. 101; Zevenbergen 1951, p. 323.

333 Zwitser 2005 (1), p. 169; Van Maanen and Claringbould 2017, p. 8.

334 Van der Lely 1996, p. 127.

335 Van der Lely 1996, p. 125.

336 Here it should be mentioned that *traditio per constitutum possessorium* of a document is in principle not an eligible method for *bona fide* acquisition ownership of the document, which further means that the right of recovery cannot be obtained in good faith (art. 3:90 (2) and 3:111 BW). As a result, possession of the goods cannot be provided when the unauthorized transferor retains factual control of the document, and *bona fide* acquisition of the goods is impossible. See Van der Lely 1996, p. 126.

by law, and individuals cannot choose a way not recognized by the BW.[337] As a result, the right to bearer or order has to be transferred according to art. 3:93 BW, a provision which requires delivery of and, when necessary, endorsement of the document.[338] Individuals are not allowed to transfer the claim embodied according to art. 3:94 BW, a provision regulating the assignment of "claims to the named (*vorderingen op naam*)". Moreover, the claim of recovery has to be pledged according to art. 3:236 (1) and 3:237 (1) BW, instead of art. 3:236 (2) in combination with art. 3:94 (1) and art. 3:239 (1) BW. In other words, the claim cannot be pledged independently from the document by notifying the debtor, and non-possessory pledge (*vuistloos pand*) cannot be created on the claim embodied within an order document.[339]

In the viewpoint of Dutch legislators, the blocking effect is recognized to avoid the divergence between the document and the claim embodied.[340] If the claim is assigned without involving the document, and the document remains in factual control of the assignor, then the assignee would not obtain the claim. However, an exception exists. The claim embodied within a document can be assigned under art. 3:94 BW, if the transferor loses factual control of this document.[341] This exception is implied by the "under the control of the transferor (*in de macht van de vervreemder*)" in art. 3:93 BW.

Another question is whether the goods under a document can be disposed of without involving this document. In particular, can the goods be delivered according to art. 3:115 (c) BW, a paragraph concerning *traditio longa manu*? With respect to this question, the Hoge Raad provided a negative answer in the landmark case "*Bosman/Condorcamp*".[342] In this case, the Hoge Raad held that the possessory pledge (*vuistpand*) over the shipped goods could not be created independently from the order bill of lading at the expense of the holder of the bill, despite the fact that the creditor had obtained factual control of the goods.[343] According to some Dutch scholars,

337 Reehuis 2004, p. 4.

338 Zwitser 2012, p. 34. Art. 3:93 BW: "*De levering, vereist voor de overdracht van een recht aan toonder waarvan het toonderpapier in de macht van de vervreemder is, geschiedt door de levering van dit papier op de wijze en met de gevolgen als aangegeven in de artikelen 90, 91 en 92. Voor overdracht van een recht aan order, waarvan het orderpapier in de macht van de vervreemder is, geldt hetzelfde, met dien verstande dat voor de levering tevens endossement vereist is.*" English translation: Art. 3:93 BW: "*Delivery required for the transfer of rights to bearer, the bearer paper of which is under the control of the alienator, is made by delivery of the paper in the manner and with the consequences specified in articles 90, 91 and 92. The same applies to the transfer of rights to order, the order paper of which is under the control of the alienator, provided endorsement is required for delivery.*"

339 Vriesendorp 1994, 247; Scheltema 1993, p. 107.

340 Parlementaire Geschiedenis (3) 1981, p. 391.

341 Reehuis 2004, p. 75.

342 *Bosman/Condorcamp*, HR, 26-11-1993, NJ 1995, 446.

343 Van der Lely 1996, p. 132-133.

the judgement implies that the goods under a document cannot be pledged in the way of *traditio longa manu* by circumventing this document.[344]

> *"Geformuleerd volgens de hier gebruikte begrippen: door het in het leven roepen van een zakenrechtelijke waardepapier wordt de bevoegdheid de zaak 'longa manu' te verpanden opgeschort. Een recht van vuistpand op de zaak dient voortaan door middel van verpanding van het recht op afgifte aan toonder of order te worden gevestigd. Dit pandrecht komt tot stand door het waardepapier uit de macht van de pandgever te brengen."*[345]

In the viewpoint of Vriesendorp, delivery of the goods independently from the document is impossible, because the direct possessor (detentor in Dutch law) of the goods is only liable to deliver the goods to the legal holder of the document.[346] The only exception is that the owner loses factual control of the document.[347] In this very situation, the goods can be delivered according to art. 3:115 BW, especially in the way of *traditio longa manu*. However, opposite opinions exist.[348]

In another landmark case ("*EWL/Fortis*"),[349] the Hoge Raad held that non-possessory pledge created over the goods under an order bill of lading was not enforceable against the shipper and the holder of the bill of lading.[350] The bill of lading plays a decisive role in the transaction of the goods shipped, and the principle of publicity requires that the property right of the goods must be mentioned by the bill of lading.[351] For the goods under a bill of lading, non-possessory pledge cannot be created according to art. 3:237 BW at the expense of the holder of this document. This judgement is criticized by some scholars.[352]

However, the necessary involvement of the document does not mean that the document will be necessarily given up by the owner. For example, in the situation of transfer of the goods, the requirement of transferring the document might be satisfied in the way of *traditio per constitutum possessorium* (art. 3:90 and 3:115 (b) BW).[353] Here the transferor acknowledges hold-

---

344 Vriesendorp 1994, 246; Zwitser 2005 (2), p. 189-190.

345 Van der Lely 1996, p. 133. English translation: "*According to the terminologies used here: where a proprietary document is created, the authority to pledge the goods in the way of 'longa manu' will be excluded. A possessory pledge over the goods needs to be created by pledging the claim of recovery to order or bearer. The latter pledge comes into existence by depriving the pledgor of the control of the document.*"

346 Vriesendorp 1994, 246.

347 Van der Lely 1996, p. 105.

348 Van Maanen and Claringbould 2017, p. 8. According to Zwitser, the viewpoint of the Hoge Raad amounts to restricting the owner's authority to dispose. It neither conforms to the general principles of Dutch property law nor be in line with English law and German law. See Zwitser 2005 (2), p. 189-190.

349 *EWL/Fortis*, HR, 17-10-2003, NJ 2004, 52.

350 Zwitser 2005 (1), p. 168.

351 Zwitser 2005 (1), p. 168.

352 Zwitser 2005 (1), p. 169-170.

353 Van der Lely 1996, p. 104; Reehuis 2004, p. 74.

ing the document on behalf of the transferee, thereby becoming a detentor of the document.[354] However, the transferor remains in factual control of the document, and there is a divergence between the document and the ownership of the goods.[355] The transferor may use the document retained to mislead others.[356] Correspondingly, the transferee is exposed to the risk of *bona fide* acquisition by a third party. According to art. 3:86 BW, where the document is still held by the transferor, third parties are entitled to acquire ownership of the goods when obtaining the document in other ways than *traditio per constitutum possessorium*, provided that the other requirements are also fulfilled.[357]

In the situation of pledge of the goods under an order document, the basic rule is that this document cannot be circumvented. According to the viewpoints of the Hoge Raad in "*Bosman/Condorcamp*" and "*EWL/Fortis*", two conclusions can be made: (1) possessory pledge by directly controlling the goods is only enforceable against the holder of the document when the pledge is indicated by the document;[358] and (2) non-possessory pledge created directly on the goods is unenforceable against the holder of the document.[359] Therefore, the order document to goods has a strong blocking effect in terms of pledging the goods: to enforce the pledge against the holder of the document, the document has to be involved in such a way that the holder is able to be aware of the existence of the pledge.

4.2.2.4 *Comparative Analysis*

A *The Legal Effect of Securities to Goods*

From the preceding introduction of English law, German law and Dutch law, it can be found that similarities and differences exist between these jurisdictions. Securities to goods are a *traditio* document in Dutch law and German law, because transfer of this type of document has an effect of delivery of the goods. This effect might be construed as a special way of delivery or a form of *traditio longa manu*. Moreover, securities to goods embody a claim of recovery of the goods in German law and Dutch law. Disposal of this claim can be realized by disposing of the document. In contrast,

---

354 Here it should be noted that art. 3:90 (2) BW stipulates a relative legal effect for *traditio per constitutum possessorium*. According to this paragraph, the transferee cannot enforce the right embodied in the document against an older right, which further implies that the transferee cannot enforce ownership of the goods against an older right with respect to the same goods. See Van der Lely 1996, p. 104.

355 Here, there is also a divergence between the claim of recovery and possession of the document: when the document is transferred in the way of *traditio per constitutum possessorium*, the claim is also transferred to the acquirer. As a result, the original creditor continues holding the document.

356 Snijders and Rank-Berenschot 2017, p. 298.

357 Van der Lely 1996, p. 104-105.

358 Zwitser 2005 (2), p. 189.

359 Zwitser 2005 (1), p. 168.

English law has a dual system: only bills of lading are a *traditio* document under common law, and the other types of securities to goods only produce the *traditio* effect under statutory law, especially in the situation of *bona fide* acquisition of corporeal movables (s. 24 and s. 25 SGA). As a result, where a document to goods, except the bill of lading, is transferred, the direct possessor bears no liability to deliver the goods to the transferee of the document.

This difference of German law and Dutch law from English law cannot be fully understood until we note the difference between these jurisdictions in the transfer of ownership of corporeal movables. As has been stressed above, English law has a consensual system: the transfer of ownership has nothing to do with possession, and what matters is the parties' intention. Under this consensual system, there is no need to see the transfer of warehouse receipts and the like as a way of delivery, at least in the situation of authorized disposals. On the contrary, both Dutch law and German law accepts the *traditio* rule, which implies that ownership of corporeal movables cannot pass in the absence of delivery. To coordinate securities to goods and the *traditio* rule, it is necessary to treat the transfer of securities to goods as a means of delivery. Otherwise, the goods could not be disposed of smoothly on the basis of the document.

The restrictive approach adopted by the English common law with respect to other securities to goods than the bill of lading has been tempered by statutory law, especially in the situation of *bona fide* acquisition of goods. For example, according to s. 24 and s. 25 SGA, the transfer of securities to goods amounts to delivery of the goods. With respect to these two provisions, some English scholars hold that the transfer of the document is, in essence, a form of fictional delivery.[360] Therefore, there is a divide in the system of English law. From a systematic perspective, there is no reason to grant no effect of delivery to the transfer of securities to goods in the situation of authorized disposals, but equate the transfer with fictional delivery in the situation of *bona fide* acquisition. English lawyers often explain this differential treatment on the basis of commercial custom. In commercial practice, participants commonly deem that the transfer of a bill of lading entitles indirect possession to the transferee, while the transfer of other securities to goods does not have such effect.[361]

B The Blocking Effect of Securities to Goods

In general, the blocking effect might occur in two situations: disposal of the claim of recovery embodied and disposal of the goods involved. Here, the first question is whether the claim of recovery can be disposed of without involving the document. In German law, the claim of recovery can, just like an ordinary claim, be disposed of according to civil law. For example, the claim can be transferred in the way of "assignment (*Zession*)" (§ 398 BGB).

---

360 Bridge 2014, p. 241.
361 Benjamin 2014, p. 1395.

This means that endorsement is not necessary when the claim is embodied within an order document. However, an extra requirement is that the document has to be delivered to the assignee. For fulfilling this requirement, *traditio per constitutum possessorium* suffices. In Dutch law, the claim cannot be disposed of without involving the document, except when the creditor loses factual control of the document. For example, "assignment (*cessie*)" (art. 3:94 BW) is in principle not applicable to the claim embodied within a bearer document or an order document. To transfer the claim, the creditor has to transfer the document, including in the way of *traditio per constitutum possessorium*. To pledge the claim, the document has to be controlled by the pledgee (art. 3: 236 (1) BW), except when the document is made out to bearer and pledged in the non-possessory way (art. 3:236 (1) BW).

The second question is whether the goods under a document can be disposed of independently from this document. In general, where a document of title is issued for certain goods, there might be a conflict between the holder of this document and the possessor of these goods. For example, ten bicycles are stored at the place of a warehouseman, and the owner disposes of these bicycles to two persons: one person obtains the warehouse receipt, while the other obtains possession of the bicycles *per se*. In general, this kind of conflict occurs due to one of the following two reasons: (1) the goods are allowed to be disposed of without involving the document; and (2) the document has to be transferred or delivered, but parties are entitled to transfer and deliver the document in the way of *traditio per constitutum possessorium*. Due to these two reasons, the previous owner has a chance to use the document retained to mislead third parties. On account of this, should law prevent the divergence between the document and the goods, and how to prevent? In this aspect, the three jurisdictions differ.

English law takes the most lenient approach. In general, ownership of the goods is transferred at the moment decided by the transacting parties. Neither transfer of the document nor delivery of the goods is necessary.[362] In principle, delivery is a separate issue from the transfer of ownership, and transfer of a document to goods cannot yield an effect of delivery in common law, except when this document is a bill of lading. For the transferee, the main benefit of acquiring the document is that the risk of *bona fide* acquisition by a third party can be averted. As has been shown above, third parties in good faith might prevail over the transferee by obtaining the document (see 4.2.2.1.B). Therefore, we can say that English law encourages but never requires parties to obtain the document to goods. Undoubtedly, this lenient approach implies that the legal owner of the goods may not be the person who holds the document.

362 English judges tend to treat the transfer of the bill of ladings as an indication of the bilateral consent on the transfer of ownership of the goods involved. See Aikens, Lord and Bools 2016, no. 6.30; Zwitser 2005 (2), p. 191.

German law is more restrictive than English law in this aspect. Due to the *traditio* rule, parties usually transfer the document to goods to satisfy the statutory requirement of delivery. However, German law allows parties to dispose of the goods in the absence of transferring the document. For example, the goods can be validly transferred in the way of *traditio longa manu*, which requires the transferor to assigns the claim of recovery against the direct possessor to the transferee. In this very situation, however, an extra requirement is that the document has to be delivered (either actually or fictionally) to the transferee. The purpose of this requirement is to guarantee that the new owner of the goods controls the document, so that the original owner cannot use the document to mislead third parties. In general, the goods can also be pledged in a similar way under the extra condition that the document is delivered to the pledgee.

Different from German law, Dutch law does not allow individuals to circumvent the document by directly resorting to *traditio longa manu*, at least when the document is under the transferor's control. Due to this restriction, the divergence between ownership of the goods and factual control of the document is alleviated to a large extent. However, the difference between German law and Dutch law is not as significant as it appears. Firstly, the additional requirement of delivering the document in German law can lead to a similar outcome: the transferee obtains factual control of the document. Secondly, both Dutch law and German law allow the document to be delivered in a fictional way. For example, *traditio per constitutum possessorium* suffices for delivering the document to the transferee, which means that the document might remain in factual control by the transferor.

In principle, pledge of the goods under an order document relies on this document in Dutch law: (1) possessory pledge cannot be created by directly controlling the goods by the pledgee, unless the pledge is indicated by the document ("*Bosman/Condorcamp*"); and (2) non-possessory pledge of the goods themselves is unenforceable against the holder of the document ("*EWL/Fortis*"). In this aspect, German law has differences and similarities. In German law, the goods can be pledged in the way of *traditio longa manu* under the extra condition that the document is delivered to the pledgee. The extra condition guarantees that the pledgee possesses the document. To use the goods as a collateral, the owner can also transfer ownership of the goods for the purpose of security.[363] Therefore, it is possible that the owner transfers the ownership in the way of *traditio longa manu* and satisfies the extra requirement of delivery though *traditio per constitutum possessorium*. In this situation, the original owner might use the document retained to mislead others, and there is a need to protect those who are in good faith and obtain the document from the original owner.

363 In general, the security transfer of ownership in German law resembles the non-possessory pledge in Dutch law: both are a non-possessory device of security (see 3.5.3.1).

4.2.2.5 *The Function of Publicity of Securities to Goods: Two Rights*

To reveal the function of publicity of securities to goods, we need to pay attention to two aspects: the personal right embodied within this type of document and the property right of goods for which the document is issued. Securities to goods not only embody a claim of recovery, but are also closely related to the disposal of the goods. For example, transfer of securities to goods has an effect of delivery. Due to this effect, securities to goods can be used to simplify the delivery of the goods.[364] To reveal the function of publicity of securities to goods, we also need to consider the distinction between order securities and bearer securities. This distinction has been introduced above (see 4.2.1.1). As will be shown later, these two types of document differ in terms of publicity.

A *The Function of Publicity and the Right Embodied*

A1: General Introduction

In general, the right embodied by a document to goods is neither ownership nor any other property right with respect to the goods, but a personal claim of recovery of the goods. This is why securities to goods are an obligational document.[365] Under Dutch law, possession of the document to goods means possession of the right of recovery embodied.[366] According to German lawyers, securities to goods is a tool with which the legal holder enjoys a right of recovery against, for example, the warehouseman, the shipper or the carrier.[367] Moreover, securities to goods are an outward appearance of the claim of recovery: holding this type of document generally implies enjoying a right to require the debtor to deliver the goods. This lays a basis for *bona fide* acquisition of the right of recovery.[368] As has been pointed out above, personal rights lack an outward mark, and *bona fide* acquisition of personal rights is not generally recognized (see 4.1.3). The right of recovery embodied within a bearer or order document to goods is special: the right is "objectified (*verkörpert*)" by this document and has an outward appearance.[369] By holding the document, the holder informs third parties that he or she enjoys the claim of recovery. In exceptional situations, such as stolen, lost or forged documents, the holder does not enjoy the claim of recovery in law.

In general, the embodied right of recovery can, just like a corporeal movable, be acquired by third parties in good faith. It is often held that *bona fide* acquisition of the embodied right shares the same rationale with

364 Hueck and Canaris 1986, p. 200-201; Zöllner 1978, p. 153.
365 Zöllner 1978, p. 9; Mulder 1948, p. 11.
366 Van der Lely 1996, p. 82.
367 Zöllner 1978, p. 5. In English law, only the bill of lading is a document of title to goods in the common law sense. The acquirer of a bill of lading obtains the claim of recovery against the carrier, thereby becoming an indirect possessor of the goods shipped.
368 Brox and Henssler 2009, p. 263-264.
369 Hueck and Canaris 1986, p. 2.

that of corporeal movables: both *bona fide* acquisitions are based on the possessor's factual control.[370] In the situation of *bona fide* acquisition of the right of recovery embodied within a document to goods, the third party is misled by the document to believe that the holder is the true creditor. In the situation of *bona fide* acquisition of a corporeal movable, the third party is said to believe that the possessor is the true owner.[371] For this reason, Dutch law regulates *bona fide* acquisition of corporeal movables and that of the right embodied within bearer documents or order documents by the same provision, namely art. 3:86 BW.

A2: Bearer Securities to Goods

As has been pointed out above, securities to goods can be made out to order or bearer (see 4.2.1.1). Bearer securities to goods do not specify the name of the creditor, i.e. the person who is entitled to request the debtor to deliver the goods involved. This type of document is alienated just as a corporeal movable: delivery of the document is necessary.[372] In general, the holder of the document is assumed to be the person who enjoys the claim of recovery.[373] Where a bearer document is issued for certain goods, the holder of this document is assumed to be entitled to require the direct possessor of the goods, usually the issuer of the document, to deliver these goods. On the basis of this assumption, *bona fide* acquisition of the claim of recovery is granted to third parties in good faith. In understanding the function of publicity of bearer securities, three aspects need to be noted.

Firstly, bearer securities to goods do not specify the creditor's name, let alone the holder's legal position, thus this type of document can neither indicate whether the holder is a legal holder having ownership of the document, nor whether the holder really enjoys the claim of recovery embodied. For example, the holder might obtain the document in an illegal way, such as theft. In this very situation, the illegal holder neither has ownership of the document, nor enjoys the claim embodied.[374] Incorrect information is communicated: the illegal holder appears to have ownership of the document and enjoy the claim embodied.

Secondly, the holder might only have indirect possession of the document. The communication of information by bearer securities is based on the factual control exercised by the holder over the document. The factual control must be visible to third parties. In the situation where the holder is only in indirect possession of the document, third parties cannot be made aware of the holder's legal position by such indirect possession. This is because, as has been argued above, indirect possession *per se* is invisible (see 3.2.2.1).

---

370 Snijders and Rank-Berenschot 2017, p. 315; Reehuis and Heisterkamp 2019, p. 235.
371 However, *bona fide* acquisition of corporeal movables cannot be fully explained on the basis of the unauthorized transferor's possession. This has been stated above (see 3.4.3.4).
372 Zevenbergen 1951, p. 336; Hueck and Canaris 1986, p. 24.
373 Zevenbergen 1951, p. 329; Hueck and Canaris 1986, p. 24.
374 Hueck and Canaris 1986, p. 24.

Thirdly, bearer securities to goods are disposed of under the requirement of delivery, and the specific legal ground on which the document is delivered cannot be shown to third parties. In general, there are various legal reasons for which the document can be delivered. For example, the document might be delivered to transfer the claim, pledge the claim, or create a right of usufruct over the claim.[375] The specific legal ground is not made visible through delivery of the document. In this sense, we can say that bearer securities to goods are an ambiguous method of publicity for the claim of recovery. Moreover, the document might be delivered in the way of *traditio per constitutum possessorium*, which means that the transferor retains factual control of the document. In essence, this way of delivery is invisible, and no indication can be conveyed to third parties (see 3.2.2.2.B).

In sum, bearer securities to goods are a defective means of publicity for the claim of recovery embodied. The holder shows his or her legal position with respect to the claim through possession of the document. Therefore, our observations concerning possession (a method of publicity for corporeal movables) in Chapter 3 are, in general, also applicable to bearer securities (a method of publicity for the claim of recovery embodied).

A3: Order Securities to Goods

Apart from bearer securities, law also recognizes a better means of publicity for the claim of recovery: order securities to goods. Order securities to goods specify the name of the creditor who is entitled to further transfer the document. Moreover, the order document is transferred in a different way from the bearer document: the former not only needs delivery, but also endorsement.[376] In general, endorsement makes the order document more informative and reliable than the bearer document: the legal position of the endorsee might be shown by the endorsement.

> *"Tegenover derden wordt de positie van den geëndosseerde beheerst door den inhoud van het endossement, door hetgeen het endossement aan hen kenbaar maakt."*[377]

For example, when an order document to goods is pledged, endorsement of this document often contains a mark of "for pledge", "for security" or the like.[378] From the perspective of publicity, this mark is important for third parties: it shows the legal position of the endorsee. The mark makes the right of pledge visible and allows third parties to know whether there is any

375 Zevenbergen 1951, p. 27-28.

376 Zevenbergen 1951, p. 69; Hueck and Canaris 1986, p. 23.

377 Zevenbergen 1951, p. 70. English translation: *"The position of the endorsee against third parties is determined by the content of the endorsement, which has been made visible to them by the endorsement."*

378 Zevenbergen 1951, p. 320; Heymann/Horn 2005, § 364, Rn. 5. In addition to the endorsement for pledge, the document might also be endorsed for the purpose of collection, which can indicate that the endorsee is merely an agent of the endorser. See Zevenbergen 1951, p. 320; Staub/Canaris 2004, § 364, Rn. 10.

proprietary encumbrance existing on the claim.[379] However, endorsement might fail to guarantee that the relationship of pledge is made visible for two reasons.

Firstly, the pledge of an order document to goods requires endorsement of this document in German law and Dutch law, but failure to include a mark of pledge does not affect the valid creation of the pledge.[380] In other words, the endorsement for pledge can be made in a "concealed" way.

> *"Wordt een vordering aan order verpand zonder dat dit uit het endossement blijkt, dan is de verpanding overigens geldig. De houder is dan jegens derden als volledig rechthebbende gelegitimeerd. In zijn verhouding tot de pandgever zal hij zijn recht echter slechts als pandhouder mogen uitoefenen."*[381]

In general, where an order document is endorsed to the pledgee in the absence a mark of pledge, the pledgee will, in relation to third parties, be legitimized as the person who fully enjoys the claim of recovery.[382] As a result, the endorser exposes him- or herself to the risk out of *bona fide* acquisition by third parties in good faith. If the pledgee transfers the document to a third party, this party might be able to acquire the document and the claim embodied at the expense of the pledgor. In general, however, this outcome is not unfair to the pledgor. The pledgor could easily avoid the risk of *bona fide* acquisition by showing the true legal position of the pledgee by endorsing the document with a mark of pledge.

Secondly, the requirement of endorsement might be circumvented by disposing of the claim of recovery embodied as an ordinary claim. As has been shown above, German law allows the claim to be assigned and pledged according to the BGB (see 4.2.2.2.B). For this way of disposal, endorsement is unnecessary. As an extra requirement, the document has to be delivered to the assignee or pledgee, but this requirement cannot make the disposal visible to third parties. The reason is simple: there are various reasons for which the document might be delivered.[383] Moreover, the extra requirement might fail to avert the possibility that the assignor uses the document to mislead third parties, because *traditio per constitutum possessorium* is not excluded. If this occurs, there is a need to protect third parties in good faith. In general, this protection is not unfair to the new

---

379 Zevenbergen 1951, p. 71.

380 Zwitser 2006, p. 84; MüKoHGB/Langenbucher 2018, § 364, Rn. 18. An opposite opinion exists. According to this opinion, the requirement of publicity and the nature of the document to order require that the endorsement must indicate the existence of the pledge. See Scheltema 1993, p. 107.

381 Asser/Van Mierlo 2016, nr. 149. English translation: *"If the pledge of a claim to order is not shown by the endorsement, then the pledge is still valid. The holder is legitimized as fully entitled against third parties. In his relationship with the pledgor, he can only enforce his right as a pledgee."*

382 Zevenbergen 1951, p. 70.

383 In the case of pledge, the pledgee cannot use the order document delivered to him or her to mislead third parties. This is because the pledgee is not an endorsee of the document.

creditor: the new creditor could avoid this situation by obtaining factual control of the document or recording him- or herself as the last endorsee on the document.

B The Function of Publicity and the Goods Involved

B1: General Introduction

Though as a document only embodying a claim of recovery, securities to goods also play an important role in the disposal of the goods involved. In general, disposal of the goods is usually associated with the disposal of the document. The legal position of the holder with respect to the document is often decisive for the holder's legal position with respect to the goods involved.[384] For example, pledge of a document to goods not only means that the claim of recovery embodied is pledged, but also that the goods are pledged in most situations.[385] From the pledge of the document, it can be inferred that the parties also have an intention to pledge the goods involved. Transfer of a document to goods often means transfer of ownership of the goods. However, exceptions exist.[386] For example, the seller might reserve ownership of the goods but unconditionally transfer the document to the buyer; the document might also be transferred to an agent for the purpose of collecting the goods.[387] In these two situations, the buyer and the agent do not obtain ownership of the goods but are made to look like the owner of the goods. For this reason, we need to discuss the function of publicity of securities to goods for the goods involved.

In general, securities to goods imply that the goods are now under the factual control of the issuer (debtor) of the document and will be delivered to the holder (creditor) of the document. The document does not represent ownership of the goods, and transfer of the document does not necessarily mean that ownership of the goods passes to the transferee.[388] The reason is simple: there are different grounds on which a document to goods is under the holder's control.

> *"Es gibt daher nach geltendem Recht keinen strikten Parallelismus zwischen dem Eigentum am Traditionspapier und dem Eigentum an den Gütern. Vielmehr können mit Hilfe eines Traditionspapiers keine weitergehenden Rechtsfolgen erzielt werden als durch die Übergabe der Güter. Daraus folgt ohne weiteres, dass es zur Übereignung der Güter außer der Übertragung des Traditionspapiers zusätzlich einer Einigung bezüglich der Güter bedarf. Diese ist im Übrigen auch aus praktischen Gründen unterläßlich;*

384 Zevenbergen 1951, p. 321.
385 Zevenbergen 1951, p. 321; MüKoBGB/Damrau 2017, § 1292, Rn. 3; Van Maanen and Claringbould 2017, p. 4; Zwitser 2006, p. 227. In English law, s. 3 FA (1889) expressly provides that "*pledge of the document of title to goods shall be deemed to be a pledge of the goods*".
386 Claringbould 1998, p. 24.
387 Claringbould 1998, p. 24-25.
388 Zevenbergen 1951, p. 321-322; Tiedtke 1985, p. 281.

insbesondere läßt sich erst aus ihr und nicht schon aus der Einigung bezüglich der Papierübertragung entnehmen, ob die Güter übereignet, verpfändet oder mit einem Nießbrauch belastet werden sollen."[389]

Holding a document to goods only implies that the holder has indirect possession of and is entitled to acquire direct possession of the goods by virtue of this document. In general, the document represents indirect possession of the goods or functions as a means to possess the goods.[390] The agreement on the disposal of the document should be separated from the agreement on the disposal of the goods themselves.[391]

However, this does not mean that, in terms of publicity, securities to goods have no difference from indirect possession, an invisible legal relationship which does not qualify as a method of publicity (see 3.2.2). In general, third parties are able to collect some proprietary information concerning the goods from this type of document. To understand this, we need to consider the distinction between bearer securities to goods and order securities to goods.

B2: Bearer Securities to Goods

It has been shown that bearer securities to goods are an ambiguous and defective means of publicity for the claim of recovery embodied (see 4.2.2.5.A). In general, a similar conclusion can be made for bearer securities to goods as a means of publicity for the goods involved. This becomes obvious when we realize that the core of indirect possession is the claim of recovery (see 3.2.2.1).

Firstly, bearer securities to goods can, at most, indicate the existence of indirect possession of the goods. This type of document does not specify the creditor's name, let alone the holder's specific legal position with respect to the goods. It is impossible to know from the bearer document whether the holder has any property right with respect to the goods. In general, factual control of a bearer document to goods only indicates that the holder has indirect possession of the goods.[392] Indirect possession is an invisible legal relationship between the indirect possessor and the direct possessor (see 3.2.2.1). The bearer document to goods can make this legal relation-

389 Hueck and Canaris 1986, p. 20. English translation: *"Therefore, there is no strict parallel between ownership of the traditio document and ownership of the goods under the current law. Rather, with the help of a traditio document no more legal consequences can be caused than delivery of the goods. As a result, the transfer of goods also requires an agreement concerning the goods, apart from the transfer of the traditio document. Moreover, this is also a necessary result of practical reasons; in particular, only from this agreement rather than the agreement regarding the transfer of the document, it is possible to know whether the goods are transferred, pledged or encumbered with a usufruct."*

390 Tiedtke 1985, p. 284; Zevenbergen 1951, p. 323.

391 Zevenbergen 1951, p. 321-322; Staub/Canaris 2004, § 363, Rn. 105.

392 In English law, other documents to goods than the bill of lading do not allow the holder to enjoy indirect possession or a claim of recovery against the direct possessor (see 4.2.2.1.A).

ship visible to third parties, indicating that the holder of the document, as an indirect possessor of the goods, has a certain right with respect to the goods. However, the bearer document cannot show the content of this right to third parties. In this sense, we can say that bearer securities to goods are an abstract and thus ambiguous method of publicity for the goods involved.

Secondly, bearer documents to goods are transferred under the requirement of delivery, but the legal ground on which the document is delivered is not made visible to third parties. The document might be delivered for the purpose of transferring ownership of the goods, pledging the goods, or creating a right of usufruct on the goods. In general, the specific agreement concerning the disposal of the goods cannot be shown by the delivery of the document.

Thirdly, the holder may only have indirect possession of the bearer document, and delivery of the document does not necessarily allow the receiver to obtain actual control of the document. Indirect possession is invisible (see 3.2.2). As a result, where the holder is only in indirect possession of the document, his or her legal position with respect to the goods is completely hidden to third parties. In addition, the bearer document can be delivered in the way of *traditio per constitutum possessorium*, which allows the transferor to retain factual control of the document. As a result, the transferor appears to have indirect possession of the goods involved, and the transferee's legal position with respect to the goods is completely invisible.

B3: Order Securities to Goods

Apart from bearer securities, individuals can also choose a better information-communicating method: order securities to goods. Order securities need to specify the creditor, and transfer of this type of document not only requires delivery, but also endorsement. This makes the order document more informative and reliable than the bearer document: the legal position of the endorsee with respect to the goods might be shown by the order document.

For example, when the goods under an order document are pledged, this document might be endorsed to the pledgee by recording a mark of "for pledge", "for security" or the like.[393] From the perspective of publicity, this mark is important: it indicates that an encumbrance of pledge exists on the goods involved. Not only does the mark allow third parties (in particular the potential acquirer of the goods) to know the existence of the encumbrance, but also prevent the pledgee from using the document to mislead this parties.[394] Moreover, the mark also brings benefits to the pledgor: his or her legal position is shown by the document to third parties. However, the endorsement for pledge might fail to indicate the existence of the pledge in several situations.

393 Zevenbergen 1951, p. 320; Heymann/Horn 2005, § 364, Rn. 5.

394 Zevenbergen 1951, p. 71.

The first situation is that the endorsement for pledge is made in a "concealed" way. As has been shown above, pledge of an order document to goods requires endorsement in Dutch law and German law, but failure to include a mark of pledge does not affect the valid creation of the pledge.[395] In the absence of such a mark, the right of pledge is invisible to third parties. The "concealed" endorsement for pledge legitimizes, in the relationship to third parties, the pledgee as the legal owner of the goods involved.[396] As a result, if the pledgee transfers the goods to a third party, this party is able to acquire ownership of the goods on the basis of the rule of *bona fide* acquisition. In general, this outcome is not unfair to the pledgor, the true owner of the goods. The pledgor could endorse the document by including a mark of pledge to show that the endorsee is only a pledgee.[397]

The second situation is that the goods are pledged in the absence of endorsement. As has been shown above, German law allows the goods to be disposed of in the way of *traditio longa manu* by assigning the claim of recovery (see 4.2.2.2.B). For pledging the goods in this way, an extra requirement is that the document must be delivered to the pledgee. Despite this extra requirement, the property right of pledge remains invisible to third parties. The reason is simple: there are various legal grounds on which the document might be delivered. In general, the pledgee cannot use the order document delivered to him or her to mislead third parties. This is because the last endorsee of the document is still the pledgor, rather than the pledgee. However, a risk here is that the pledgee might forge an endorsement to make him or her appear to be the owner. This concerns the defect of securities to goods as a means of publicity, which will be discussed immediately.

C Two Defects of Securities to Goods as a Method of Publicity

As a means of publicity, securities to goods have two defects. The first one is that they have a risk of unsafety. As has been mentioned above, securities to goods might be held by an illegal possessor, such as a thief who obtains possession of the document in an unlawful way. Moreover, it is possible that securities to goods are forged by the holder. In these situations, the holder, who is neither the true creditor nor the owner of the goods involved, appears to enjoy the claim of recovery and even ownership of the goods.

The requirement of specifying the creditor makes the order securities to goods more secure than the bearer document.[398] For the illegal possessor of

395 MüKoHGB/Langenbucher 2018, § 364, Rn. 18; Asser/Van Mierlo 2016, nr. 149.
396 MüKoHGB/Langenbucher 2018, § 364, Rn. 18; Asser/Van Mierlo 2016, nr. 149.
397 Therefore, as a means of publicity for corporeal movables, securities to goods are different from possession. As has been shown, delivery of the movable collateral for the purpose of pledge might make the pledgee look like the owner of the collateral, which means that the pledgor is exposed to the risk of *bona fide* acquisition by third parties when the pledgee illegally disposes of the collateral (see 3.5.2.2.B). With a document to goods, not only is the pledgor able to pledge the goods, but also to avoid the risk of *bona fide* acquisition.
398 Goode 2010, p. 528.

the order document, it is more difficult to use the document to mislead others: the illegal possessor has to forge document to make him or her appear to be a legal holder of the document.

> *"Seine Funktion liegt vor allem darin, dass im Gegensatz zum Inhaberpapier dem Berechtigten einen gewissen Schutz vor den Gefahren des gutgläubigen Erwerbs bietet; den na der Berechtigte namentlich im Papier benannt ist, bedarf es bei dessen Übertragung durch einen Nichtberechtigen einer Unterschriftenfälschung, und darin liegt eine nicht zu unterschätzende praktische und psychologisches Barriere."*[399]

In general, when a bearer document is made out or obtained, it can be assumed that the parties are aware of and thus willing to accept the higher risk of safety.

The risk of safety does not mean that bearer securities to goods are not qualified as a means of publicity. There are two reasons to say so. These two reasons have been shown in discussing possession as a means of publicity for corporeal movables (see 3.2.1.2.C). One reason is that the holder of securities to goods is usually the legal creditor and has a right with respect to the goods involved in reality. The other reason is that law grants certain remedies to the legal creditor when the document is controlled by a person who incorrectly appears to enjoy the claim of recovery. For example, the legal creditor can recover, on the basis of the right of ownership, the document from illegal possessors. Where there is a forgery of the document, this forgery can be rectified.

The second defect is that securities to goods *per se* have a problem of invisibility: the existence of securities to goods is not necessarily known.[400] For example, in the transfer of the goods for which a document is made out, the transferee might be unaware of the existence of this document, especially when the transferor conceals the document on purpose. This might cause two undesirable outcomes: (1) the transferor retains and uses the document to mislead third parties after the transaction; and (2) the possible proprietary encumbrance over the goods cannot be shown by the document to the transferee. However, the problem of invisibility should not be overstated.[401]

In most situations, the acquirer of the goods under a document is aware of the existence of the document, because the transferor shows and delivers the document. It seems rare that the transferor attempts to retain the document by fraudulently keeping silent on or denying the existence of the

---

399 Hueck and Canaris 1986, p. 23. English translation: "*Unlike bearer documents, the primary function of the order document is to provide the entitled with certain protection against the risk of bona fide acquisition. In particular, when the entitled is named in a document, transfer of this document by an unauthorized person requires forgery of the signature, which is a practical and psychological barrier that should not be underestimated.*"

400 Quantz 2005, p. 56.

401 Acquisition and Loss of Ownership of Goods 2011, p. 611.

document. Where the goods are in direct possession by a warehouseman, shipper or carrier, it is abnormal that transferor does not show the document to the transferee. It can be expected that the transferee, usually as a professional businessman, will be suspicious about the absence of the document and further check with the direct possessor.[402] Nevertheless, whether the transferee really knows the existence of the document in a specific situation is a question depending on the circumstances involved. If the transferee is unaware of and fails to obtain the document, and the transferor uses the document to mislead third parties, then *bona fide* acquisition by third parties might occur at the expense of the transferee.[403]

4.2.2.6 The Function of Publicity of Securities to Goods: Three Third Parties

In the preceding discussion, we have shown the legal position of third parties with respect to securities to goods. In general, there are three types of third party: strange interferers, subsequent acquirers, and general creditors (see 2.2.2.2). Third parties in the preceding discussion of securities to goods only refer to subsequent acquirers. Securities to goods are a method of publicity mainly important for subsequent acquirers and convey no useful information to the other two types of third party. This is implied by the fact that securities to goods are used for the transaction of the goods involved.

A Securities to Goods and Strange Interferers

The claim of recovery embodied within securities to goods is a personal right which is, in principle, difficult to be interfered with (see 2.1.3.2). Obviously, securities to goods, as a kind of corporeal movable, are susceptible to illegal interference. The owner and possessor of the document are entitled to certain remedies against the illegal interferer on the basis of ownership and possession of the document respectively. However, illegal interference with the document is another issue that should be distinguished from the interference with the claim of recovery embodied.

The goods for which a document is made out might be illegally interfered with. However, this document is irrelevant to the illegal interference with the goods: it provides no useful information to strange interferers. Instead, it is often direct possession of the goods *per se* (namely factual control exercised by the debtor of the document) that conveys a useful indication to strange interferers, who in return can adjust their behaviors (see 3.3.2.2). To avoid misunderstandings, it should be noted that this does not mean that the holder of the document, as an indirect possessor of the goods, enjoys no legal protection against illegal interference with the goods (see 3.3.3).

---

402 Acquisition and Loss of Ownership of Goods 2011, p. 611.
403 MüKoHGB/Frantzioch 2018, § 475g, Rn. 73.

B Securities to Goods and General Creditors

In general, securities to goods are useless for general creditors. The principal reason is that general creditors are mainly concerned about the overall financial health of the debtor, and knowing about the proprietary relationships concerning one or more specific assets is useless for them because the information will become outdated after a certain period (see 2.2.2.2.C).

Bearer securities to goods are an ambiguous method of publicity which is of no importance for general creditors. This type of document can, at most, show that the holder has indirect possession of the goods involved. However, as has been argued above, possession conveys no useful information to general creditors (see 3.5). Truly, order securities to goods are able to convey clear information, such as the existence of pledge on the goods. However, the pledgor and the pledgee are entitled to pledge the goods without recording any mark of pledge on the document. Moreover, the goods might be pledged in the absence of any endorsement in some jurisdictions. In these situations, the pledge is validly created with binding force over general creditors.[404] For this reason, order securities to goods are not reliable for general creditors.

It is worthwhile noting that securities to goods cannot address the problem of fraudulent antedating (see 2.2.2.2.C). Bearer securities to goods are disposed of under the formality of delivery. Delivery, especially *traditio per constitutum possessorium*, is not an appropriate method to fix the date of the disposal. Even in the situation which involves an order document, the problem cannot be addressed properly for two reasons. One reason is that the goods under this document might be disposed of in the absence of endorsement. The other reason is that recording the date of the disposal on the document is not necessary for valid endorsement.[405] As a result, the date of disposal cannot be ascertained on the basis of the document *per se*.

C Securities to Goods and Subsequent Acquirers

Securities to goods are an important means of publicity for subsequent acquirers, such as the transferee and pledgee of the goods. In the preceding comparative and conclusive discussions, we have shown the importance of securities to goods for and the legal protection granted to subsequent acquirers. Here, a brief reiteration suffices.

In general, this type of document is treated as an outward appearance of the claim embodied and the goods involved. For a person who intends to obtain a property right with respect to the goods under a document, this

---

404 The lack of this binding force might be beneficial for general creditors. For example, where the document is pledged with a concealed endorsement, the pledgee can only claim that he or she has a property right of pledge, rather than ownership of the goods. This means that the surplus after enforcement of the pledge can be distributed to general creditors. For subsequent acquirers who obtains the document from the pledgee, *bona fide* acquisition is available.

405 Zevenbergen 1951, p. 144; Schnauder and Müller-Christmann 1991, p. 72-73.

person can safely assume that the holder of the document enjoys the claim of recovery and ownership of the goods, unless the document contains a contrary indication. For example, if the document includes a mark of pledge, indicating that the holder is a pledgee, then there is no reason to entitle the person to *bona fide* acquisition of the goods from the holder.

4.2.2.7 Conclusion

Securities to goods are a method of publicity with two defects for the claim of recovery embodied and the goods involved. In principle, disposal of the claim and the goods involves the document. Moreover, the document acts as an outward appearance and lays a basis for *bona fide* acquisition of the claim and the goods by third parties.

Order securities to goods can be used to provide clear proprietary information concerning the claim embodied and the goods involved. For example, when the claim or the goods are pledged, a mark of pledge can be recorded on the document. Truly, the endorsement for pledge might be made in a "concealed" way, and the pledgee has a chance to use the document to mislead third parties; the pledgor and the pledgee might choose to pledge the goods without any endorsement, and the pledgee perhaps uses the document to mislead third parties. However, this does not give rise to an unjust outcome. On the one hand, third parties in good faith are protected at the expense of the pledgor on the basis of the rule of *bona fide* acquisition; on the other hand, the pledgor can avert such *bona fide* acquisition by recording a mark of pledge on the document. If the pledgor fails to do so, then it can be assumed that he or she is willing to accept the risk of *bona fide* acquisition by third parties.

Bearer securities to goods are an ambiguous method of publicity, because this type of document conveys information via factual control of the document. Unlike order securities, bearer securities do not record any mark that can indicate the existence of, for example, the property right of pledge. As a result, it is impossible for third parties to know from a bearer document the specific legal position of the holder of this document. To address this problem, the law grants legal protection to third parties in good faith by the rule of *bona fide* acquisition, when the holder of the bearer document is not the true creditor (or owner). In general, the *bona fide* acquisition is not unfair to the original creditor (or owner). The creditor (or owner) could request an order document and then record his or her legal position on this document. If the creditor (or owner) fails to do so and agrees to just have a bearer document, then it can be assumed that he or she is aware of and willing to bear the risk out of *bona fide* acquisition by third parties.

Both order securities to goods and bearer securities to goods run a risk of unsafety and have a problem of visibility. The risk of safety does not make these two type of document unqualified as a means of publicity for two reasons: (1) the document is controlled by the true creditor (or owner) in most situations; and (2) where the holder of a document does not have any legal ground to keep this document, there is a scheme of rectification. The problem of invisibility exists but should not be overstated. In practice, the document is usually shown and delivered by the owner in the disposal of the goods. Even if the owner may attempt to conceal the document, the counterparty will be usually suspicious about the absence of a document and will further check with the direct possessor.

As a means of publicity, securities to goods are useful and important for subsequent acquirers. In general, they convey no useful information to general creditors and strange interferers. The problem of fraudulent antedating cannot be addressed by securities to goods (see 4.2.2.6.B.).

4.2.3 Securities of Payment

In this part, we focus on another type of document: securities of payment or monetary securities. This type of document known as "*Wertpapieren des Zahlungs*" in German law and "*betalingspapieren*" in Dutch law. Roughly speaking, securities of payment correspond to negotiable instruments in English law.[406] Securities of payment mainly include the bill of exchange ("*gezogene Wechsel*" in German law and "*wissel*" in Dutch law), the promissory note ("*eigen Wechsel*" in German law and "*promesse*" in Dutch law), and the cheque ("*Scheck*" in German law and "*cheque*" in Dutch law). Bills of exchange are different from promissory notes in the person who bears the liability to pay: the debt of bills of exchange is mainly performed by a third party (the drawee or acceptor), while the promissory note requires the maker to pay the sum. Cheque is a special bill of exchange. Like bills of exchange, cheque also requires a third party (i.e. the bank of which the maker is a customer) to provide payment. However, unlike bills of exchange, cheque is not or not intended to be accepted by the maker's bank because the maker has sufficient funds in the bank.[407]

The three types of instrument of payment are monetary securities which differ from securities to goods discussed above. Monetary securities concern the payment of a certain amount of money, while the latter involves the delivery of certain goods. However, the nature of the right embodied by the two types of securities has no difference: both embody a personal right. As a means of publicity, monetary securities and securities to goods are also different in the subject matter of publicity. The former are only related to the claim of payment embodied, while the latter not only concern the claim of delivery embodied, but also the goods involved (see 4.2.2.5).

The rationale of publicity of monetary securities only concerns how to show the embodied right of payment to third parties. For the sake of simplicity, the following discussion mainly focuses on bills of exchange to

406 However, the concept of negotiable instrument might be used more broadly by including the bill of lading by some English lawyers. See Sealy and Hooley 2009, p. 525.

407 Guest 2016, no. 13-003.

reveal this rationale of publicity. The bill of exchange *"epitomizes"* the use of monetary securities in transactions, and the observations about the bill of exchange are generally applicable to the other types of instrument of payment.[408] The following discussion involves two issues: (1) the transfer of pledge of bills of exchange; and (2) the protection of third parties in good faith.[409] Transfer and pledge are two representative forms of disposal of the claim embodied within bills of exchange. For this reason, we first show how the bill of exchange is involved as a method of publicity in the situation of transfer and pledge. The second issue concerns whether and how third parties are protected due to their reliance on the bill of exchange. To reveal the function of publicity of the bill of exchange, discussing the second issue is inevitable.

In this part, an introduction of English law, German law and Dutch law is provided first (see 4.2.3.1-4.2.3.3). Following this introduction, there is a comparative discussion (see 4.2.3.4). In the end, we attempt to reveal the function of publicity of securities of payment (see 2.2.3.5-4.2.3.6).

4.2.3.1 English Law

A The Transfer and Pledge of Bills of Exchange

English law recognizes a number of negotiable instruments of payment, among which the most important one is the bill of exchange. It is regulated by the Bills of Exchange Act (1882) (hereafter abbreviated as BEA). This act is also applicable to, with necessary modifications, cheques and promissory notes.[410] In brief, the bill of exchange is a negotiable document drawn by one person (the drawer) to request another person (the drawee or acceptor) to pay a certain amount of money to a third person (the payee) at a certain moment. It embodies a personal claim, and the creditor enjoys a right to require the debtor to pay. However, the claim is special in two aspects: the

---

408 Goode 2010, p. 521.

409 In fact, the function of publicity of securities of payment is also shown by the legal exclusion of "personal defenses (*persönliche Einwendungen* in German and *persoonlijke verweermiddelen* in Dutch)". Where a claim embodied is transferred, the debtor cannot refuse payment to the new creditor by claiming that there is a defect in his or her personal legal relationship with the original creditor (art. 17 WG, art. 6:146 (1) BW, and art. 116 WvK). The legal exclusion of personal defenses is often explained by the notion of "appearance of rights (*Rechtsschein*)": the new creditor can safely rely on the content of the document. See Goode 2010, p. 533; Hueck and Canaris 1986, p. 104; Zöllner 1978, p. 133-134; Hammerstein 1998, p. 43-44; Zevenbergen 1951, p. 34. In general, the legal protection of third parties against personal defenses is an issue falling under the law of obligations. Therefore, it is not discussed here. See Van Empel and Huizink 1991, p. 50-52.

410 S. 73 BEA: *"A cheque is a bill of exchange drawn on a banker payable on demand. Except as otherwise provided in this Part, the provisions of this Act applicable to a bill of exchange payable on demand apply to a cheque."* S. 89 (1) BEA: *"Subject to the provisions in this part, and except as by this section provided, the provisions of this Act relating to bills of exchange apply, with the necessary modifications, to promissory notes."*

way of disposal and the protection of third parties under the rule of *"the holder in due course"*. The second aspect will be dealt with later.

Roughly speaking, the method of transferring and pledging a bill of exchange is dependent on the type of this bill. If the bill of exchange is made payable to bearer, then the debtor has to perform the obligation of payment to the person who holds the bill of exchange. Both pledge and transfer of the bill require delivery, namely the shift of possession of the bill.[411] If the bill of exchange is made payable to order, then the debtor has to pay to the last endorsee who is often also the possessor of the bill of exchange. Order bills of exchange need to be disposed of through endorsement plus delivery.[412] Therefore, for the disposal of both bearer and order bills of exchange, delivery is necessary. According to s. 2 BEA, the concept of delivery includes both actual delivery and constructive delivery.[413] For example, the transferor's acknowledgment of controlling the bill for the transferee suffices for fulfilling the requirement of delivery.[414] In theory, the bill of exchange can also be pledged by the pledgor attorning to the pledgee, which means that factual control of the document is retained by the pledgor.[415] As a result, the requirement of delivery cannot guarantee that the document is always controlled by the transferee or the pledgee.

In the situation of pledging order bills of exchange, it is unclear whether a mark of pledge has to be recorded on the document.[416] The BEA includes no specific provision with respect to the endorsement for pledge. It seems that the rules concerning the endorsement of collection, a kind of "restrictive endorsement", as opposed to "full endorsement", will apply to the pledge of bills of exchange.[417] Therefore, the endorsee/pledgee is entitled to receive the payment, but cannot transfer the bill of exchange.[418] It can be imagined that if the existence of the pledge is not indicated by the bill of exchange, which implies that the endorsee/pledgee appears to be a full creditor, then third parties in good faith will be protected.[419]

As has been indicated above, the bill of exchange embodies a personal right of payment. Therefore, it is also possible that the creditor transfers this personal right in the way of assignment.[420] To assign the right, the conditions required for the assignment of ordinary claims have to be fulfilled. However, the assignee's legal position may be overridden by the legal posi-

411 S. 31 (2) BEA: *"A bill payable to bearer is negotiated by delivery."*
412 S. 31 (3) BEA: *"A bill payable to order is negotiated by the indorsement of the holder completed by delivery."*
413 S. 2 BEA: *"'Delivery' means transfer of possession, actual or constructive, from one person to another."*
414 Hedley and Hedley 2001, p. 46.
415 Beale, Bridge, Gullifer and Lomnicka 2018, no. 5.27.
416 UNCITRAL Yearbook 1971, p. 124.
417 UNCITRAL Yearbook 1971, p. 124; Chalmers 1919, p. 166; Guest 2016, no. 5-032.
418 Guest 2016, no. 5-034; Goode 2010, p. 565-566.
419 Ashcroft and Ashcroft 2013, p. 273.
420 Guest 2016, no. 5-067; Chalmers 1919, p. 150.

tion of a subsequent party who acquires the same claim from the creditor in the way of endorsement.[421] Moreover, *bona fide* acquisition is not available to the assignee: the assignee cannot obtain a better title than the assignor.[422] In sum, the bill of exchange does not have blocking effect in English law. The existence of the bill of exchange does not mean that the creditor cannot assign the claim embodied without involving the document.

B The Holder in Due Course

Bills of exchange have the feature of negotiability. In general, this feature includes two aspects: (1) the right embodied within bills of exchange can be disposed of like a corporeal movable; and (2) *bona fide* transferees for value are able to acquire a better title than the transferor.[423] The first aspect has been discussed above. Now we turn to the second aspect.

The second aspect is based on the rule of "*the holder in due course*" (s. 29 BEA).[424] According to this rule, a holder in due course can acquire the bill of exchange free from any defects of the earlier parties' title, including the personal defenses an earlier party has against another earlier party.[425] In general, the rule of "*the holder in due course*" can give rise to two important outcomes: (1) *bona fide* acquisition of the claim embodied; and (2) legal protection against personal defenses raised by the debtor. As has been mentioned above, the second outcome will not be discussed (see 4.2.1.3).

> *"The bolder in due course is in a powerful position. He can acquire a good title from or through a thief. He is not affected by the fact that any predecessor obtained the bill by fraud or pursuant to a fraudulent or otherwise illegal purpose, or that the consideration given for the bill by a predecessor has wholly failed, as where the original holder took the bill as payment for goods which he failed to deliver or which were lawfully rejected. [...] The only limitation on the right of the holder in due course is that, where a signature on the bill has been forged or is otherwise of no legal effect, he has no rights against those who were parties to the bill prior to the ineffective signature, for vis-a-vis those parties he is not a holder at all."*[426]

---

421 Guest 2016, no. 5-067; Chalmers 1919, p. 151.

422 Guest 2016, no. 5-007.

423 Sealy and Hooley 2009, p. 526; Furmston and Chuah 2013, p. 343.

424 S. 29 BEA: "(1) *A holder in due course is a holder who has taken a bill, complete and regular on the face of it, under the following conditions; namely, (a) That he became the holder of it before it was overdue, and without notice that it had been previously dishonoured, if such was the fact: (b) That he took the bill in good faith and for value, and that at the time the bill was negotiated to him he had no notice of any defect in the title of the person who negotiated it.* (2) *In particular the title of a person who negotiates a bill is defective within the meaning of this Act when he obtained the bill, or the acceptance thereof, by fraud, duress, or force and fear, or other unlawful means, or an illegal consideration, or when he negotiates it in breach of faith, or under such circumstances as amount to a fraud.*"

425 Furmston and Chuah 2013, p. 353.

426 Goode 2010, p. 533.

As an exception to the *nemo dat* rule, *bona fide* acquisition of bills of exchange (precisely speaking, *bona fide* acquisition of the right embodied) can arise in two types of situations: (1) the transferor is not the creditor and has no title to the bill of exchange; and (2) the transferor is the creditor and has defective title to the bill of exchange.[427]

For example, where a bill of exchange is stolen by a thief who then transfers this bill to a third party, this third party is able to acquire the bill and the claim embodied under certain conditions.[428] In this situation, the thief has no title to the bill of exchange. Nevertheless, the legal creditor from whom the bill of exchange is stolen might lose the right to recover the bill from the third party. The possibility of *bona fide* acquisition by the third party only exists when the bill of exchange is payable to bearer.[429] If the stolen bill is payable to order, which means that endorsement is necessary, then the thief has to forge the signature of the legal creditor. Pursuant to a provision concerning forged and unauthorized signatures (s. 24 BEA),[430] the third party, whether in good faith or not, cannot acquire the bill of exchange against the previous parties including the legal creditor.[431] The third party has "*no rights against those who were parties to the bill prior to the ineffective signature*" and is only entitled to request the thief/forger to pay.[432] This amounts to excluding the possibility of *bona fide* acquisition by the third party.[433]

The rule of "*the holder in due course*" is also applicable to the situation where the transferor only has a defective title. For example, the transferor obtained the bill of exchange from the original creditor by fraud. In this very situation, the transferor might only have a voidable title to the bill of exchange: the original creditor is entitled to make this title void, which is "*a matter of the general law*".[434] It seems that the original creditor has an equitable title to the bill of exchange in equity law.[435] Nevertheless, the transferee, as a third party, is able to acquire from the transferor the bill of exchange

427 Guest 2016, no. 4-062.
428 Guest 2016, no. 4-066.
429 Guest 2016, no. 4-062.
430 S. 24 BEA: "*Subject to the provisions of this Act, where a signature on a bill is forged or placed thereon without the authority of the person whose signature it purports to be, the forged or unauthorised signature is wholly inoperative, and no right to retain the bill or to give a discharge therefor or to enforce payment thereof against any party thereto can be acquired through or under that signature, unless the party against whom it is sought to retain or enforce payment of the bill is precluded from setting up the forgery or want of authority.*"
431 Guest 2016, no. 3-006; Byles 2002, p. 218.
432 Goode 2010, p. 533.
433 In the case of forgery, however, an exception is estoppel. Briefly speaking, where the legal creditor has admitted the signature or would have avoided the forgery of his or her signature, the rule of estoppel may require the legal creditor to pay the third party. See Guest 2016, no. 3-079; Byles 2002, p. 278.
434 Byles 2002, p. 230.
435 The term "*defects of title*" refers to matters which were known as "*equities attaching to the bill*" before the enactment of the BEA. See Guest 2016, no. 4-062.

free from the binding force of the equitable title of the original creditor.[436] In this case, the original creditor's signature is not forged by the transferor, thus the provision concerning forged and unauthorized signatures (s. 24 BEA) is not applicable.

According to s. 29 BEA, certain conditions have to be satisfied for obtaining the legal position of *"the holder in due course"*. One condition is that the holder must be in good faith and has no notice of the defect in the title of the person who negotiates the bill of exchange.[437] Another condition is that *"the holder should himself furnish value, so that he could not rely on value provided by the predecessors"*.[438] This condition precludes a donee from acquiring a better title than the title the donor has. A third condition is that the bill of exchange must be *"complete and regular on its face"*.[439] If the bill has conveyed a warning to the transferee, then the transferee can no longer obtain a better title than the title of the transferor. For example, where the endorsement is irregular, the third party will not be a holder in due course.[440] In the end, to be a holder in due course, the third party has to qualify as a "holder" of the bill of exchange.[441] For being a holder, it is necessary that the third party must have possession of the bill, whether direct or indirect.[442] As indirect possession suffices, it seems that *bona fide* acquisition is not excluded where the bill of exchange is delivered in the way of *traditio per constitutum possessorium*.[443]

4.2.3.2 German Law

In German law, there are two kinds of monetary securities: (1) one is the *Wechsel*, including *eigener Wechsel* and *gezogener Wechsel*; and (2) the other is the "cheque (*Scheck*)". In general, *eigener Wechsel* is promissory note: the drawer him- or herself bears a duty to pay a certain amount of money.[444] *Gezogener Wechsel* is equivalent to the English term "bill of exchange": a third party, instead of the drawer, is required to pay a certain amount of money.[445] For the purpose of convenience, we use the term "bill of exchange" to represent *Gezogener Wechsel*, and our following discussion only focuses on this type of monetary document. Bills of exchange are regulated by the *Wechselgesetz* (1933) (abbreviated as WG).

---

436 Guest 2016, no. 4-0623. The relationship between *bona fide* acquisition and voidable title has also been discussed in the situation of corporeal movables (see 3.4.3.1.B).

437 Byles 2002, p. 220.

438 Goode 2010, p. 535.

439 Guest 2016, no. 4-052.

440 Byles 2002, p. 219.

441 Byles 2002, p. 219; Guest 2016, no. 4-051.

442 Byles 2002, p. 93; Guest 2016, no. 1-021.

443 As to *bona fide* acquisition and *traditio per constitutum possessorium* in the situation of ordinary corporeal movables, a detailed discussion has been provided (see 3.4.3.1.D).

444 Zöllner 1978, p. 51; Moshenskiĭ 2008, p. 7.

445 Zöllner 1978, p. 51.

A The Transfer and Pledge of Bills of Exchange

Different from English law, German law does not allow a bill of exchange to be drawn to bearer. The bill of exchange must indicate the payee's name. Otherwise, the issuance will be incomplete.[446] In principle, once a bill of exchange is validly made out, this bill can be disposed of in the way of endorsement. This way of disposal is laid down by art. 11 (1) WG.[447] For a valid endorsement, the endorser has to declare the transfer by indicating the name of the transferee on the back of the bill of exchange.[448] In addition, the bill of exchange also needs to be delivered to the endorsee, including in the way of *traditio per constitutum possessorium*.[449]

The claim embodied can also be pledged in the way of endorsement (§ 1292 BGB).[450] According to art. 19 (1) WG, valid endorsement for pledge requires a mark of pledge, such as "value for security (*Wert zur Sicherheit*)" or "value for pledge (*Wert zum Pfand*)". There is no doubt that the mark has a function of publicity: third parties can be informed that an encumbrance of pledge exists on the claim embodied.[451] If the pledgor does not record such mark, however, a right of pledge still exists between the pledgor and the pledgee.[452] This is known as "concealed endorsement for pledge (*verdeckte Pfandindossament*)".[453] In this case, the pledgee appears to be the full creditor for third parties, which creates a possibility of *bona fide* acquisition when the pledgee disposes of the bill of exchange.[454] To pledge bills of exchange, the pledgor also needs to deliver the document to the pledgee in the way prescribed by § 1205 and 1206 BGB.[455] As a result, *traditio per constitutum possessorium* is excluded when the document is under actual possession by the pledgor. If the bill of exchange is indirectly possessed by the pledgor, then the pledgor not only has to transfer indirect possession to the pledgee, but also notify the direct possessor.

The claim embodied in a bill of exchange can also be disposed of in another way than the way of endorsement. As a personal right, the claim can be transferred in the way of "assignment (*Zession*)" under the BGB.[456]

---

446 Zöllner 1978, p. 70; Hueck and Canaris 1986, p. 64-65.

447 Art. 11 (1) WG: "*Jeder Wechsel kann durch Indossament übertragen werden, auch wenn er nicht ausdrücklich an Order lautet.*" English translation: Art. 11 (1) WG: "*Each bill of exchange can be transferred by endorsement, even when it is not expressly declared as payable to order.*"

448 Zöllner 1978, p. 13.

449 Schnauder and Müller-Christmann 1991, p. 72.

450 § 1292 BGB: "*Zur Verpfändung eines Wechsels oder eines anderen Papiers, das durch Indossament übertragen werden kann, genügt die Einigung des Gläubigers und des Pfandgläubigers und die Übergabe des indossierten Papiers.*" English translation: § 1292 BGB: "*For pledging a bill of exchange or any other instrument that may be transferred by endorsement, agreement between the creditor and the pledgee and the delivery of the instrument endorsed suffice.*"

451 Zöllner 1978, p. 105.

452 Schnauder and Müller-Christmann 1991, p. 86.

453 Zöllner 1978, p. 105.

454 Schnauder and Müller-Christmann 1991, p. 86; Tiedtke 1985, p. 265.

455 MüKoBGB/Damrau 2017, § 1292, Rn. 3; Westermann 2011, p. 1206-1207.

456 Hueck and Canaris 1986, p. 81; Schnauder and Müller-Christmann 1991, p. 69.

This reminds us that the claim embodied within securities to goods can be disposed of in both the way of endorsement and that of assignment in German law (see 4.2.2.2.B). According to § 398 BGB, a claim can be assigned on the basis of an agreement, and notifying the debtor involved is not necessary.[457] As an extra requirement, the assigner has to deliver the document to the assignee to make the "state of the right (*Rechtszuständigkeit*)" and the "appearance of the right (*Rechtsschein*)" consistent with each other.[458] To fulfill this extra requirement, the assignor does not have to give up actual control of the document to the assignee. For example, *traditio per constitutum possessorium* also suffices.[459] This can, more or less, be explained by the following viewpoint: there is no reason to treat bills of exchange differently from other corporeal movables.[460] If the claim embodied is transferred in the way of assignment, then the possibility of *bona fide* acquisition of the claim will be excluded due to the lack of endorsement.[461]

The claim embodied within bills of exchange can be pledged in another way than endorsement. As a personal right, the claim can be pledged according to the general rules of civil law (§ 1274 BGB).[462] For this way of pledge, delivery of the document to the pledgee is necessary.[463] However, due to this extra requirement, notifying the debtor is unnecessary.[464] According to § 1280 BGB, providing notification to the debtor is essential for creating a property right of pledge on ordinary claims (see 4.1.4.2). If the claim is pledged in the civil-law way under the extra condition of delivery of the document, then *bona fide* acquisition will not be available to the pledgee.[465]

B The Function of Negotiation

In general, endorsement of bills of exchange has a "function of negotiation (*Transportfunktion*)" in German law.[466] This function involves three aspects: (1) the claim embodied can be transferred by transferring the bill of ex-

---

457 § 398 BGB: "*Eine Forderung kann von dem Gläubiger durch Vertrag mit einem anderen auf diesen übertragen werden (Abtretung). Mit dem Abschluss des Vertrags tritt der neue Gläubiger an die Stelle des bisherigen Gläubigers.*" English translation: § 398 BGB: "*A claim may be transferred by the creditor to another person by agreement with that person (assignment). When the agreement takes effect, the new creditor steps into the shoes of the previous creditor.*"

458 Hueck and Canaris 1986, p. 82; Schnauder and Müller-Christmann 1991, p. 69-70.

459 Hueck and Canaris 1986, p. 81; Schnauder and Müller-Christmann 1991, p. 70.

460 Hueck and Canaris 1986, p. 82-83. As we have pointed out above, ownership of corporeal movables can be transferred in the way of *traditio per constitutum possessorium* in German law (see 3.4.2.2.B).

461 Hueck and Canaris 1986, p. 83.

462 MüKoBGB/Damrau 2017, § 1292, Rn. 17.

463 MüKoBGB/Damrau 2017, § 1292, Rn. 17.

464 MüKoBGB/Damrau 2017, § 1292, Rn. 17.

465 Schnauder and Müller-Christmann 1991, p. 86.

466 Hueck and Canaris 1986, p. 88; Zöllner 1978, p. 92. In addition to this function, endorsement also has a "function of legitimization (*Legitimationsfunktion*)" and a "function of guarantee (*Garantiefunktion*)". The former function implies that the endorsee is legitimized as the entitled, and the latter function means that every endorser is responsible for the payment. See Zöllner 1978, p. 91-93; Hueck and Canaris 1986, p. 87-93.

change; (2) the claim can be acquired from an unauthorized transferor by third parties in good faith on the basis of *bona fide* acquisition of the bill of exchange; and (3) personal defenses of previous debtors are restricted for the benefit of the endorsee.[467] The first aspect has been just discussed, and the third aspect will not be discussed here (see 4.2.1.3).

In general, *bona fide* acquisition of the claim embodied within a bill of exchange is possible by *bona fide* acquisition of ownership of this bill of exchange.[468] This possibility is recognized by art. 16 (2) WG.[469] This paragraph is not only applicable to the situation where the original creditor loses factual control of the bill of exchange contrary to his or her will, but also to the situation where the original creditor voluntarily gives up factual control of the bill.[470] In the former situation, the bill of exchange might be stolen from the original creditor and then transferred by the thief to a third party.[471] In the latter situation, the bill of exchange might be deposited by the original creditor and then transferred by the custodian to a third party.[472] The rule of *bona fide* acquisition is also applicable when the transferor obtains the factual control of the bill of exchange on the basis of a defective consent made by the original creditor.[473]

In the situation where the transferor obtains factual control of the bill of exchange contrary to the original creditor's will, forgery of signatures might arise. For example, A draws a bill of exchange to B who later endorses this bill to C, D steals the bill from C and then transfers it to E who is in good faith. The endorsement appears consistent because the thief D forges an endorsement by C to D. In this case, E is able to acquire the bill of exchange and the claim embodied on the basis of art. 16 (2) WG, provided that all

467 Hueck and Canaris 1986, p. 88-91.

468 Hueck and Canaris 1986, p. 89; Tiedtke 1985, p. 240.

469 Art. 16 (2) WG: "*Ist der Wechsel einem früheren Inhaber irgendwie abhanden gekommen, so ist der neue Inhaber, der sein Recht nach den Vorschriften des vorstehenden Absatzes nachweist, zur Herausgabe des Wechsels nur verpflichtet, wenn er ihn in bösem Glauben erworben hat oder ihm beim Erwerb eine grobe Fahrlässigkeit zur Last fällt.*" English translation: Art. 16 (2) WG: "*If the bill of exchange has somehow been lost to the original holder, the new holder, who proves his or her right according to the rule of the preceding paragraph, is only obliged to give up the bill if he or she acquired it in bad faith or was grossly negligent in acquiring the bill.*"

470 Bülow 2004, p. 100.

471 Bülow 2004, p. 100.

472 Zöllner 1978, p. 95; Schnauder and Müller-Christmann 1991, p. 77.

473 Bülow 2004, p. 100; Stranz and Stranz 1952, p. 109; Schnauder and Müller-Christmann 1991, p. 77. Here, it is necessary to mention the relationship between the principle of abstraction and the validity of the bill of exchange. The German law of bills of exchange accepts the principle of abstraction. Under this principle, the underlying legal relationship of obligations does not affect the bill of exchange itself. However, the principle cannot guarantee that the bill of exchange is necessarily valid, because the validity of bills of exchange is determined by some factors, such as the legal capacity of the parties involved, the authority of the agent, and the validity of the "declaration of intent (*Willenserklärung*)". See Zöllner 1978, p. 36. For example, where a bill of exchange is endorsed and delivered because of fraud, the endorsement *per se* is voidable, and the endorsee lacks a valid basis to keep the bill of exchange. If the fraudulent endorsee further transfers the bill to a third party, then *bona fide* acquisition is possible to this third party.

relevant conditions are satisfied. As a result, E can require A (the drawer) or B (a previous endorser) to provide the payment.[474] In principle, C bears no duty of payment to E.[475]

According to art. 16 (2) WG, the third party must be in good faith or, precisely speaking, with no gross negligence.[476] Moreover, the endorsement must be consistent without any break, which implies that the transferor must be the last endorsee or a regular holder.[477] The third party in good faith is not expressly required by art. 16 (2) WG to offer consideration, but § 816 BGB imposes an obligation of return over the third party who acquires the bill gratuitously.[478]

Here, a question is whether the bill of exchange has to be delivered to the third party in good faith. Though the WG does not directly provide an answer, the "return of bills of exchange (*Herausgabe des Wechsels*)" implies the requirement of delivery: the third party has to obtain possession of the bill of exchange.[479] As to whether *traditio per constitutum possessorium* suffices for satisfying this requirement, the prevailing opinion is in favor of a positive answer.[480] Therefore, *bona fide* acquisition of bills of exchange is different from *bona fide* acquisition of ordinary corporeal movables in the requirement of delivery.[481] In the case of bills of exchange, the reliance of third parties on the endorsement matters, and whether direct possession of the document is given up to third parties is irrelevant.[482]

4.2.3.3 Dutch Law

In Dutch law, the most important three types of securities of payment are "bills of exchange (*wissel*)", "promissory note (*promesse* or *orderbriefje*)" and "cheques (*cheque*)".[483] These securities of payment are regulated by the BW

---

474 Schnauder and Müller-Christmann 1991, p. 80; Zöllner 1978, p. 98.

475 The principle of abstraction is not applicable to the question whether C bears a duty of payment to E. The principle only insulates the bill of exchange from the underlying legal relationship. However, the validity of the bill itself is affected by some factors. In this case, C does not express any valid consent to the endorsement forged by D, thus the endorsement is invalid. In general, the question needs to be answered by applying the rationale of "appearance of rights". See Zöllner 1978, p. 98-99; Hueck and Canaris 1986, p. 112-113; Bülow 2004, p. 282. According to this rationale, the person, whose signature is forged, is only liable for the payment when the forgery is attributable to his or her act or omission. Usually, forgery of the signature of a person cannot be attributed to this person, which means that he or she does not bear any duty of payment to the third party (E in this case). See Bülow 2004, p. 282.

476 Zöllner 1978, p. 94.

477 Bülow 2004, p. 99; Tiedtke 1985, p. 242.

478 Baumbach, Hefermehl and Casper 2008, p. 193.

479 Hueck and Canaris 1986, p. 89; Bülow 2004, p. 99.

480 Hueck and Canaris 1986, p. 89; Zöllner 1974, p. 238.

481 As we have shown above, *traditio per constitutum possessorium* is not an eligible form of delivery for *bona fide* acquisition of ordinary corporeal movables (see 3.4.3.4.B).

482 Hueck and Canaris 1986, p. 89.

483 Hammerstein 1998, p. 6-7; Mees 1980, p. 5.

and the *Wetboek van Koophandel* (1838) (abbreviated as WvK). As will be seen later, the BW, which took effect since 1992, includes some modifications to the WvK.[484] In this part, we focus on the bill of exchange.

A The Transfer and Pledge of Bills of Exchange

In general, the way of transferring the right embodied within securities, including the bill of exchange, is determined by art. 3:93 BW. According to this provision, the right embodied within a bearer document is transferred by delivering this document, and a right embodied within an order document is transferred by delivery plus endorsement of this document.[485] According to art. 100 WvK, the bill of exchange can only be made payable to order.[486] Therefore, endorsement is necessary for transferring bills of exchange.[487] As has been shown above, the way of transfer is statutory in Dutch law and cannot be contracted out for the sake of legal certainty (see 4.2.2.3.B).[488] The creditor of the bill of exchange is not allowed to transfer the claim in the way of "assignment (*cessie*)" under art. 3:94 BW.[489] This would lead to a divergence between the document and the claim, as pointed out by Dutch legislators.

> *"Het zou niet raadzaam zijn daarnaast de mogelijkheid van cessie toe te laten. Deze zou er gemakkelijk toe kunnen leiden dat wel het recht overgaat, maar het toonder- of orderpapier niet in handen van de verkrijger komt."*[490]

484 Scheltema 1993, p. 100-102.

485 Art. 3:93 BW: *"De levering, vereist voor de overdracht van een recht aan toonder waarvan het toonderpapier in de macht van de vervreemder is, geschiedt door de levering van dit papier op de wijze en met de gevolgen als aangegeven in de artikelen 90, 91 en 92. Voor overdracht van een recht aan order, waarvan het orderpapier in de macht van de vervreemder is, geldt hetzelfde, met dien verstande dat voor de levering tevens endossement vereist is."* English translation: Art. 3:93 BW: *"Delivery required for the transfer of rights to bearer, the bearer document of which is under the control of the alienator, is made by the delivery of the document in the manner and with the consequences specified in articles 90, 91, and 92. The same applies to the transfer of rights to order, the order document of which is under the control of the alienator, under the condition that endorsement is required for delivery."*

486 Hammerstein 1998, p. 16. However, bill of exchange does not have to include an order clause. According to art. 110 WvK, the bill which is not clearly indicated to be payable to order can also be transferred in the way of endorsement. If a bill of exchange lacks an order clause, this bill will also be assumed to be an order bill of exchange. See Zevenbergen 1951, p. 103; Mees 1980, p. 39.

487 Art. 110 (1) WvK: *"Elke wisselbrief, ook die welke niet uitdrukkelijk aan order luidt, kan door middel van endossement worden overgedragen."* English translation: Art. 110 (1) WvK: *"Each bill of exchange, including those which are not expressely declared as payable to order, can be transferred through endorsement."*

488 Reehuis 2004, p. 4.

489 This has been confirmed by the Hoge Raad (see 4.2.2.3.B). However, some scholars hold the opposite opinion. See Van Empel 2002, p. 57.

490 Parlementaire Geschiedenis (3) 1981, p. 391. English translation: *"Moreover, it is not advisable to recognize the possibility of assignment. This could easily lead to the situation that the right passes while the order or bearer document remains in the hands of the transferor."*

However, if the creditor loses factual control of the bill of exchange, and endorsement is impossible, then assignment is permitted.[491] In this very situation, there is no reason to deny the creditor's right to dispose.

To transfer the claim embodied in the way of endorsement, the transferor needs to deliver the bill of exchange to the transferee.[492] This requirement of delivery does not mean that the transferor has to give up actual control of the bill of exchange to the transferee, because *traditio per constitutum possessorium* is permitted.[493] When the transferor agrees to hold the document for the acquirer, the claim embodied can also pass to the latter, provided that the other conditions are fulfilled. However, there is a risk associated with *traditio per constitutum possessorium*. This form of delivery only yields relative effect: the acquisition is subject to the property right existing on the claim earlier (art. 3:90 (2) BW).[494]

The claim embodied within bills of exchange can be pledged in the way of endorsement. According to art. 3:236 (1) BW, pledge of the claim not only requires endorsement of the bill of exchange, but also factual control of the document by the pledgee.[495] Pursuant to art. 118 WvK, the endorsement must contain a mark of pledge, such as "value for security (*waarde tot zekerheid*)" or "value for pledge (*waarde tot pand*)", to show the existence of the pledge. Undoubtedly, from the perspective of publicity, this mark is important for third parties. Here, there are two questions that have direct connection with the function of publicity of the endorsement for pledge. The first question is whether "concealed endorsement for pledge (*geheim pandendosement*)" is permitted.[496] In general, most lawyers are in favor of a positive answer.[497] In their view, the absence of a mark of pledge does not affect the valid creation of the pledge between the pledgor and the pledgee, and the pledgee is, in relation to third parties, legitimized as the creditor of the bill of exchange.[498] The second question is whether it is possible to create a silent pledge over bills of exchange payable to order. The prevailing

491 Parlementaire Geschiedenis (3) 1981, p. 391; Snijders and Rank-Berenschot 2017, p. 298.

492 Scheltema 1993, p. 92; Zevenbergen 1951, p. 139.

493 Reehuis 2004, p. 74; Snijders and Rank-Berenschot 2017, p. 298.

494 Reehuis 2004, p. 74.

495 Art. 3:236 (1) BW: "*Pandrecht op een roerende zaak, op een recht aan toonder of order, of op het vruchtgebruik van een zodanige zaak of recht, wordt gevestigd door de zaak of het toonder- of orderpapier te brengen in de macht van de pandhouder of van een derde omtrent wie partijen zijn overeengekomen. De vestiging van een pandrecht op een recht aan order of op het vruchtgebruik daarvan vereist tevens endossement.*" English translation: Art. 3:236 (1) BW: "*The right of pledge on a corporeal movable, on a right payable to bearer or order, or on the usufruct of such a thing or right, is established by bringing the thing or the document to bearer or order under the control of the pledgee or of a third person agreed upon by the parties. Furthermore, endorsement is required for the establishment of a right of pledge on a right payable to order or on the usufruct thereof.*"

496 Hammerstein 1998, p. 37.

497 Zwitser 2006, p. 83-84; Zevenbergen 1951, p. 154; Asser/Van Mierlo 2016, nr. 149. However, opposite opinions exist. See Scheltema 1993, p. 106.

498 Zevenbergen 1951, p. 155; Asser/Van Mierlo 2016, nr. 149.

view is that, according to art. 3:237 BW, it is impossible to create a silent pledge on an order bill of exchange.[499] As a result, both endorsement and delivery of the document are necessary for pledging bills of exchange.

B Protection of Reliance

In general, bills of exchange are a "reliable document (*betrouwbaar waardepapier*)" for third parties.[500] In general, the protection of the reliance of third parties includes two aspects: one is *bona fide* acquisition of the bill of exchange and the claim embodied, and the other is the limitation of personal defenses of the debtor.[501] The second aspect is not discussed here (see 4.2.1.3).

As has been shown above, *bona fide* acquisition of ordinary claims is not generally recognized by Dutch law (see 4.1.3.3). However, according to art. 3:86 (1) BW, the right embodied within bearer or order securities can be acquired, just like a corporeal movable, from the unauthorized transferor.[502] If the document is stolen by the transferor, then art. 3:86 (3) BW is applicable.[503] According to this paragraph, the transferee is able to acquire the document and the right embodied without having to wait for three years. The legal protection granted to third parties in good faith is also recognized by art. 115 (2) WvK.[504] In general, the rationale behind the legal protection is that the document creates an "appearance of rights (*schijn van recht*)" for third parties.[505]

If the order bill of exchange was obtained by the unauthorized transferor from the original creditor through an illegal means, such as theft, then

---

499 Scheltema 1993, p. 107; Steneker 2012, p. 94; Snijders and Rank-Berenschot 2017, p. 466. However, opposite opinions exist. See Zwitser 2006, p. 83-84.

500 Mees 1980, p. 26; Van Empel and Huizink 1991, p. 48.

501 Mees 1980, p. 26.

502 Art. 3:86 (1) BW: "*Ondanks onbevoegdheid van de vervreemder is een overdracht overeenkomstig artikel 90, 91 of 93 van een roerende zaak, niet-registergoed, of een recht aan toonder of order geldig, indien de overdracht anders dan om niet geschiedt en de verkrijger te goeder trouw is.*" English translation: Art. 3:86 (1) BW: "*Although the transferor lacks the right to dispose, the transfer pursuant to articles 90, 91 or 93 of a movable object, unregistered property, or a right to bearer or order is valid, if the transfer does not have a gratuitous basis and the acquirer acts in good faith.*"

503 Art. 3:86 (3) BW: "*Niettemin kan de eigenaar van een roerende zaak, die het bezit daarvan door diefstal heeft verloren, deze gedurende drie jaren, te rekenen van de dag van de diefstal af, als zijn eigendom opeisen, tenzij [...] het geld dan wel toonder- of orderpapier betreft.*" English translation: Art. 3:86 (3) BW: "*Nevertheless, the owner of a corporeal movable, who has lost its possession due to theft, may recover it during a period of three years from the day of theft, except for [...] in the case of money or paper payable to bearer or order.*"

504 Art. 115 (2) WvK: "*Indien iemand, op welke wijze dan ook, het bezit van den wisselbrief heeft verloren, is de houder, die van zijn recht doet blijken op de wijze, bij het voorgaande lid aangegeven, niet verplicht den wisselbrief af te geven, indien hij deze te goeder trouw heeft verkregen.*" English translation: Art. 115 (2) WvK: "*If someone lost possession of the bill of exchange in any way whatsoever, then the holder is not obliged to return the bill of exchange when he or she proves the right according to the preceding paragraph and obtains the right in good faith.*"

505 Zevenbergen 1951, p. 28; Mees 1980, p. 26.

bona fide acquisition usually involves a forgery of the original creditor's signature. To make the endorsement appear consistent, the unauthorized transferor needs to forge the endorsement by the original creditor. For example, A draws a bill of exchange to B, C steals this bill from B and then transfers it to D; C forges the endorsement by B to C; D is in good faith. In this situation, D is able to acquire ownership of the bill of exchange and the claim embodied, provided that relevant conditions are fulfilled.[506] After *bona fide* acquisition, D can require A to pay. The issuance of the bill by A is valid and independent from C's forgery (art. 106 WvK).[507] Moreover, B is, in principle, not liable for the payment.[508]

For *bona fide* acquisition of the bill of exchange, certain requirements have to be satisfied. The first requirement is that the unauthorized transferor appears to be the legal creditor, which means that he or she must be formally legitimized as a regular holder of the document.[509] For example, the endorsement of the bill of exchange has to be consistent without any break. The second requirement is that the third party must be in good faith with respect to the defect in the transferor's authority to dispose.[510] The third requirement is that the third party offers consideration to the transferor.[511] In addition, possession of the bill of exchange is provided to the third party in good faith in a way other than *traditio per constitutum possessorium*.[512] In the aspect of delivery, *bona fide* acquisition of bills of exchange and that of ordinary corporeal movables do not differ.

4.2.3.4 Comparative Analysis

From the preceding introduction, we can find that the bill of exchange plays an important role in the disposal of the claim embodied in English law, German law and Dutch law: (1) the claim can be deposed of by disposing of the bill of exchange; and (2) the reliance of third parties in good faith on the bill of exchange is extensively protected. However, the three jurisdictions differ in whether the claim embodied within bills of exchange can be disposed of without involving the document. Moreover, they also have some differences in *bona fide* acquisition of the bill of exchange and the claim embodied.

---

506 Zevenbergen 1951, p. 155-156; Hammerstein 1998, p. 39.

507 Zevenbergen 1951, p. 93-94; Van Empel and Huizink 1991, p. 67.

508 The question whether B bears a duty of payment to D needs to be answered according to art. 6:147 BW. Pursuant to this provision, B might bear the obligation of payment to D when the forgery is attributable to B's act or omission. In general, the possibility of such attribution is low in the situation of forgery of signatures. See Van Empel and Huizink 1991, p. 68.

509 Hammerstein 1998, p. 39; Scheltema 1993, p. 100.

510 According to the old rule of art. 115 (2) WvK, having no gross negligence suffices. However, art. 3:86 BW modifies this rule. See Hammerstein 1998, p. 39.

511 The old rule of art. 115 (2) WvK does not includes such requirement. However, art. 3:86 BW requires the third party in good faith to provide counter performance, thereby excluding the possibility of *bona fide* acquisition by a donee. See Scheltema 1993, p. 102.

512 Snijders and Rank-Berenschot 2017, p. 317; Scheltema 1993, p. 98.

A The Blocking Effect of Bills of Exchange

Briefly speaking, blocking effect means that the existence of a bill of exchange excludes the possibility of disposing of the claim embodied without involving this bill. Typically, the effect concerns the question whether the claim embodied can be transferred, just as an ordinary personal right, in the way of assignment. With respect to this question, English law, German law and Dutch law have different rules.

In English law, the bill of exchange does not have blocking effect. As a personal right, the claim embodied within bills of exchange can be transferred in the way of assignment. For the assignment, neither endorsement nor delivery of the bill is necessary. However, the assignee, namely the new creditor, cannot benefit from the rule of "*the holder in due course*". In other words, the assignee is not allowed to claim *bona fide* acquisition and cannot obtain a better title than the assignor's title. Moreover, the assignee's legal position might be prevailed over by the legal position of a third party in good faith to whom the original creditor transfers the same claim in the way of endorsement.

Like English law, German law also permits the claim embodied within bills of exchange to be transferred in the way of assignment according to the BGB. However, an extra requirement is that the document has to be delivered to the assignee. This requirement is to avoid the divergence between the claim embodied and the outward appearance (i.e. the bill of exchange). However, the divergence cannot be completely averted because *traditio per constitutum possessorium* suffices for satisfying the requirement of delivery. In German law, when the claim embodied is transferred in the way of assignment, the assignee cannot claim *bona fide* acquisition. Moreover, if the assignor retains factual control of the bill of exchange and further disposes of the bill to a third party, then this third party might be entitled to *bona fide* acquisition at the expense of the assignee's interests. Therefore, English law and German law have no substantial differences in terms of the legal consequences of the assignment.

Unlike English law and German law, Dutch law recognizes the blocking effect of bills of exchange. In Dutch law, the creditor of a bill of exchange has to dispose of the claim embodied in the way of endorsement, at least when the creditor has factual control of the document. In the viewpoint of Dutch legislators, the recognition of the blocking effect is to guarantee that the claim and the document can be transferred simultaneously from one person to another.[513] As mentioned above, however, this legislative target cannot be completely realized due to the possibility of *traditio per constitutum possessorium*: the transferor can alienate the bill of exchange but retains factual control of the document.[514] In the case of bearer bills of exchange, the transferor has a chance to use the document retained to mislead third parties. In the case of bills of exchange payable to order, the transferor usually does

513 Parlementaire Geschiedenis (3) 1981, p. 391.
514 Snijders and Rank-Berenschot 2017, p. 298.

not have such chance. Though the bill is retained by the transferor, the last endorsee of the document is the transferee, the new creditor. As a result, the transferor cannot use the bill retained to mislead third parties, unless he or she erases the endorsement or forges an endorsement to him- or herself.

In general, there seem to be no sufficient reasons to prohibit the assignment of the claim embodied within bills of exchange, even when endorsement is possible.[515] For the transacting parties, the way how the claim is transferred belong to their own affairs. For third parties, what matters is that their reliance will be protected.[516] In principle, when the transferee acquires the claim embodied in a way that allows the transferor to retain the bill and appear to be the true creditor, *bona fide* acquisition by a third party in good faith is not unfair to the transferee. This way of transfer is chosen, at least approved, by the transferee. It can be assumed that the transferee is aware of and thus is willing to accept the risk out of *bona fide* acquisition by the third party.[517]

B Bona Fide *Acquisition of Bills of Exchange*

From the preceding introduction, it can be found that *bona fide* acquisition of bills of exchange and the claim embodied is recognized in the three jurisdictions. In general, *bona fide* acquisition is not only possible when the original creditor loses factual control of the document contrary to his or her will, but also when the original creditor voluntarily gives up factual control of the document. However, an important difference exists in the situation where *bona fide* acquisition is associated with forgery of signatures by the unauthorized transferor. Here, we use a hypothetical case to show this difference between the three jurisdictions. In this case, A draws a bill of exchange to B, C steals this bill from B and transfers it to D; C forges the endorsement by B to him- or herself; D is in good faith and obtains the bill of exchange.

In principle, both A and B do not have to pay D under English law. This is because B's signature is forged by C and thus ineffective, and D has "*no rights against those who were parties to the bill prior to the ineffective signature*".[518] As a result, D can only require C to pay. However, according to German law and Dutch law, A bears a duty to pay, and B, in principle, does not have to pay D. The endorsement by B to C is an outcome of forgery, thus B bears no duty to D. Under the "principle of the independence of the declaration of bills of exchange", the validity of A's signature and undertaking of payment is not affected by the forgery.[519] In general, it can be said that

515 Zwitser 2006, p. 83-84; Van Empel and Huizink 1991, p. 56-57.
516 Staub/Canaris 2004, § 363, Rn. 144.
517 In essence, the blocking effect of bills of exchange concerns the legal effect of publicity. About the legal effect of publicity, a general discussion is provided in Chapter 5 (see 5.1.4).
518 Goode 2010, p. 533.
519 This principle is known as the "*Prinzip der Selbständigkeit der Wechselerklärungen*" in German law (art. 7 WG) and the "*beginsel van zelfstandigheid der wisselverklaringen*" in Dutch law respectively. See Hueck and Canaris 1986, p. 60; Zevenbergen 1951, p. 93-94.

German law and Dutch law are in favor of third parties in good faith, while English law is in favor of the party whose signature is forged.

The requirements of *bona fide* acquisition of bills of exchange are only slightly different between the three jurisdictions. For example, the third party has to be in good faith and furnish value, and the unauthorized transferor has to appear to be a regular holder. Here a difference which deserves our attention concerns the possibility of *bona fide* acquisition in the situation of *traditio per constitutum possessorium*. If the bill of exchange is delivered to the third party in the way which allows the transferor to retain factual control of the document, can the third party claim *bona fide* acquisition? It seems that a positive answer can be found from German law and English law, while Dutch law clearly provides a negative answer.[520]

4.2.3.5 *The Function of Publicity of Securities of Payment: The Claim of Payment*

After the comparative discussion of bills of exchange, a representative type of securities of payment, we now turn to the function of publicity of securities of payment. In general, the function of publicity of this type of document is rooted in the notion of "objectification (*Verkörperung*)": the claim of payment is embodied within and thus made visible by the corporeal document.[521] The notion has been mentioned in discussing the function of publicity of securities to goods (see 4.2.2.5). Unlike securities to goods which are not only related to the claim of recovery embodied but also to the goods involved, securities of payment only concern the claim of payment embodied. Here, we focus on the publicity of the claim of payment by securities of payment. As will be seen later, bearer documents and order documents differ in this aspect.

In general, securities of payment can provide proprietary information concerning the claim embodied to third parties. For a person who intends to acquire a claim, it is always necessary to ascertain, for example, the "owner" of and the proprietary encumbrance over this claim. Securities of payment are useful in this aspect. In principle, it can be assumed that the holder of securities of payment is the creditor when the document includes no contrary indication or warning. Even if the assumption is overturned in the end, the third party can still, under certain conditions, acquire document and the claim embodied on the basis of the rule of *bona fide* acquisition.[522]

520 Here it should be noted that the exclusion of the possibility might find its legal basis from different rules in Dutch law. For example, if it a pledgee who transfers the bill of exchange to a third party in the way of *traditio per constitutum possessorium*, both art. 3:111 and art. 90 (2) BW will exclude *bona fide* acquisition. If it is a thief who transfers the bill of exchange to a third party in the way of *traditio per constitutum possessorium*, then only art. 90 (2) BW can be applied to exclude *bona fide* acquisition. The two provisions, *traditio per constitutum possessorium* and *bona fide* acquisition of ordinary corporeal movables have been discussed above (see 3.4.3.4.B).

521 Zöllner 1978, p. 15; Van Lier 1937, p. 13.

522 Tiedtke 1985, p. 242.

Therefore, securities of payment provide the claim of payment an "external state (äußerer tatbestand)" on which third parties can rely.[523]

According to whether the creditor's name is specified by the document and how the document is transferred, there is a distinction between bearer securities and order securities (see 4.2.1.1). In the above, we have discussed the function of publicity of securities to goods on the basis of this distinction (see 4.2.2.5). Here we discuss the function of publicity of securities of payment also on the basis of this distinction. In general, order securities of payment are different from bearer securities of payment in publicity: the former can convey clearer and more detailed information than the latter. Moreover, it will be shown that, just like securities to goods, securities of payment also have a risk of unsafety and a problem of invisibility.

A Bearer Securities of Payment

Bearer securities of payment do not specify the creditor's name. Therefore, the creditor cannot be ascertained on the basis of the recordation of the document. The claim embodied within a bearer document of payment has a close link with the factual control of this document. The holder of the document shows his or her legal position with respect to the document and thus the claim by factual control of the document. To understand this, two aspects should be noted.

The first aspect is that only the person who directly possesses the document can show his or her legal position to third parties. Indirect possessors of the document cannot make their legal position visible to third parties. This is because indirect possession is invisible to third parties (see 3.2.2). As a result, where a bearer document is transferred in the way of *traditio per constitutum possessorium*, third parties cannot be made aware of the transfer.

The second aspect is that the direct possessor of the document is neither necessarily the owner of the document, nor the true creditor. There are various grounds on which direct possession of the document can be obtained. The direct possessor might be the owner of the document and thus the true creditor. However, the direct possessor might also be an agent holding the document for the creditor, a pledgee having a property right of pledge on the claim, a finder, or even a thief who has no legal interest with respect to the claim. In general, direct possession of the document cannot show the specific legal ground on which the document is under factual control by the possessor. This reminds us that direct possession is merely an abstract and thus ambiguous method of publicity for corporeal movables (see 3.2.1.2).

B Order Securities of Payment

Compared with bearer securities of payment, securities payable to order can convey clear and more detailed information concerning the claim embodied. This is not only because order securities of payment specify the

523 Hueck and Canaris 1986, p. 23.

creditor's name, but also because they are usually transferred in the way of endorsement. To make out an order document, the drawer has to indicate the creditor's name clearly. In doing so, the true creditor can be ascertained not only on the basis of possession of the document, but also on the basis of the recordation by the document. If the creditor intends to transfer the document and the claim embodied, the new creditor's name is usually recorded on the document: the new creditor replaces the original creditor and becomes the last endorsee.[524] If the order document is endorsed for the purpose of pledge or agency, the document often records a mark of pledge or agency. From the perspective of publicity, this mark is important for third parties: not only is the specific legal position of the endorsee with respect to the claim made visible, but also is the true creditor shown to third parties. However, order securities of payment might fail to perform a function of publicity in the following two situations.

The first situation concerns the blocking effect of securities of payment. The claim might be disposed of in a way involving no endorsement. As has been shown above, English law allows, under no extra condition, the creditor to assign the claim embodied just as an ordinary claim; German law allows, under the extra condition of delivering the document to the assignee or pledgee, the claim to be assigned and pledged according to the BGB. The unconditional or conditional denial of blocking effect implies two outcomes: (1) the document cannot show the transfer or pledge of the claim; and (2) the assignor or pledgor might retain the order document and use it to mislead third parties. As has been argued above, where the claim embodied can be disposed of independently from the document, there is a need to protect *bona fide* third parties who rely on the document (see 4.2.3.4.B). In essence, the issue of blocking effect concerns whether delivery and endorsement of securities of payment, a means of publicity, are a necessary requirement for the disposal of the claim embodied. Is this means of publicity a condition for acquisition of the claim or merely a condition for the legal effect of enforceability against third parties in good faith? The issue of blocking effect has nothing to do with whether order securities of payment can be qualified as a means of publicity.

The second situation is that the endorsement for pledge and agency might be made in a "concealed" way: the document does not record a mark of pledge or agency. As a result, the legal relationship of pledge or agency is not visible to third parties, and the endorsee appears to be the owner of the document as well as the true creditor. If the pledgee or agent disposes of the document to a third party in good faith, then this third party will often be protected at the expense of the true creditor's interests. In general, this

524 Here it is necessary to mention that the new creditor's name is not recorded on the document in the situation of blank endorsement: the endorser only puts his or her name on the document without naming the endorsee. In general, blank endorsement is not prohibited and can make the order document become a bearer document. See Goode 2010, p. 528; Hueck and Canaris 1986, p. 97; Mees 1980, p. 20.

protection of the third party is not unfair to the true creditor. This is because the true creditor allows the pledgee or agent to appear as the person who enjoys the claim embodied. It can be assumed that the true creditor is aware of and is willing to accept the risk out of *bona fide* acquisition by the third party. In essence, the issue of "concealed" endorsement only concerns whether parties are allowed to decide not to show their legal relationship to third parties clearly. The recognition of "concealed" endorsement does not mean that securities of payment cannot qualify as a means of publicity.

C Two Defects of Securities of Payment as a Means of Publicity

In general, securities of payment have two defects as a means of publicity for the claim of payment embodied. The two defects, which also exist for securities to goods, have been discussed above (see 4.2.2.5.C). One defect is that securities of payment have a risk of unsafety: the holder might obtain the document through an illegal means or forge the content of the document. The other defect is that securities of payment have a problem of invisibility: the existence of the document is not necessarily known by third parties.

As we have argued when discussing securities to goods, the risk of safety is not a sufficient reason to completely deny that securities of payment, especially order securities, are a means of publicity (see 4.2.2.5.C). This is because the document is usually controlled by a legal holder, and there is a scheme of rectification.[525] The problem of invisibility should not be exaggerated. If the holder of a bill of exchange wants to pay the purchase price to the seller by this bill, then delivering the bill to the seller is necessary for making him or her accept this means of payment. If the holder of the bill of exchange attempts to conceal the bill by transferring the claim embodied in the way of assignment, the assignee can often know about the existence of the bill by consulting the debtor.

4.2.3.6 The Function of Publicity of Securities of Payment: Three Types of Third Parties

In the above, we have discussed the function of publicity of securities to goods for the three types of third parties: strange interferers, subsequent acquirers, and general creditors (see 4.2.2.6). It has been argued there that securities to goods are, as a means of publicity, only important for subsequent acquirers and of no use for strange interferers or general creditors. In general, this conclusion is also applicable to securities of payment.

525 For example, the legal holder can recover the document from the hands of illegal possessors. See Bülow 2004, p. 320; Byles 2002, p. 445. In German law, the legal creditor who loses the document can initiate a proceeding of annulment (i.e. *Aufgebotsverfahren*) to nullify the document. See Bülow 2004, p. 320. If the document includes a forgery, then this forgery can be rectified. See Byles 2002, p. 277.

Firstly, the claim of recovery embodied within securities of payment is a personal right which is, in principle, difficult to be illegally interfered with (see 2.1.3.2). Therefore, there is no reason to say that this method of publicity is useful for strange interferers in avoiding conducting illegal interferences. To avoid misunderstandings, it is necessary to note that illegal interference with securities of payment *per se* is another issue and should be distinguished from the illegal interference with the claim of payment embodied. As a corporeal movable, securities of payment *per se* might be damaged.

Secondly, securities of payment are, in general, useless for general creditors. The principal reason is that general creditors are mainly concerned about the overall financial health of the debtor, and knowing about the proprietary relationships of one or more specific assets is meaningless for general creditors (see 2.2.2.2.C). Moreover, securities of payment cannot address the problem of fraudulent antedating (see 4.2.2.6.B). Even in the situation of the order document which usually involves endorsement, the date of the disposal of the claim embodied does not have to be recorded on the document when the document is transferred or pledged.[526] As a result, the date when the claim is disposed of cannot be ascertained on the basis of the document *per se*.

Thirdly, securities of payment are an important means of publicity for subsequent acquirers, such as the acquirer and pledgee of the claim. In general, this type of document is treated as an outward appearance of the claim embodied. For a person who intends to obtain a property right with respect to the claim embodied within securities of payment, this person can safely assume that the holder enjoys the claim just as the document shows. Moreover, *bona fide* acquisition is, in principle, possible for the person when the holder's authority to dispose proves to be defective, unless he or she knows or should know the defect. For example, if the document includes a mark of pledge, indicating that the holder is only a pledgee who cannot dispose of the claim, then there is no reason to entitle the person to *bona fide* acquisition of the claim.

4.2.3.7 Conclusion

Securities of payment are a method of publicity with two defects for the claim of payment embodied. In principle, the disposal of the claim involves the document. Moreover, the document acts as an outward appearance of the claim and lays a basis for *bona fide* acquisition of the claim by third parties in good faith. The two defects are that securities of payment have a risk of unsafety and a problem of visibility. The risk of safety does not make these two types of document unqualified as a means of publicity. The problem of invisibility exists but should not be overstated.

526 Zevenbergen 1951, p. 144; Schnauder and Müller-Christmann 1991, p. 72-73.

Order securities of payment can be used to provide clear proprietary information concerning the claim embodied. For example, when the claim is pledged, a mark of pledge can be recorded on the document. Truly, the endorsement for pledge might be made in a "concealed" way, and the pledgor and pledgee might choose to pledge the claim in the absence of any endorsement. In both situations, the pledgee perhaps uses the document to mislead third parties. However, this does not give rise to an unfair outcome to the parties involved. On the one hand, third parties in good faith are protected at the expense of the pledgor under the rule of *bona fide* acquisition; on the other hand, the pledgor can avert such *bona fide* acquisition by recording a mark of pledge on the document. If the pledgor fails to do so, then it can be assumed that he or she is willing to accept the risk of *bona fide* acquisition by third parties.

Bearer securities of payment are an ambiguous method of publicity, because this type of document conveys information via factual control of the document. Bearer securities do not record any mark that can indicate the existence of, for example, the right of pledge. As a result, it is impossible for third parties to know from a bearer document the specific legal position of the holder. Fortunately, legal protection is granted to third parties in good faith by the rule of *bona fide* acquisition, when the holder who disposes of the document is, for example, just a pledgee. In general, such *bona fide* acquisition is not unfair to the true creditor, i.e. the pledgor. The true creditor could request an order document and then record his or her legal position on this document. If the true creditor does not do so and agrees to just have a bearer document, then it can be assumed that he or she is aware of and willing to bear the risk out of *bona fide* acquisition by third parties.

As a means of publicity, securities of payment are useful and important for subsequent acquirers. In general, they convey no useful information to general creditors and strange interferers. Securities of payment is not an appropriate way to address the problem of fraudulent antedating. This is because the date when the claim is disposed of does not have to be recorded on the document.

5 Meeting the Requirement of Publicity by Registration

The previous two chapters have dealt with three forms of publicity in the law of property: possession (Chapter 3), notification to debtors (Chapter 4), and documental recordation (Chapter 4). Possession is an abstract and thus ambiguous means of publicity for corporeal movables. It cannot completely solve the problem of information asymmetry in a transaction concerning corporeal movables. In some special fields, such as goods warehoused, possession is substituted by securities to goods, a type of document having the legal effect of delivery. In general, securities to goods can provide more reliable and clear proprietary information concerning the goods than possession. Moreover, the reliance of third parties on securities to goods is generally protected by law.

In the transaction of claims, especially receivables, a method of publicity is notification to the debtor. As has been shown in Chapter 4, it is often held that this method creates a chance for third parties to obtain proprietary information concerning the claim. This is why notification is in some jurisdictions treated as a basis of priority in favor of third parties, including subsequent acquirers and general creditors.[1] However, this research contends that notification does not qualify as a means of publicity for claims because it rarely conveys any useful information to third parties. The priority on the basis of the formality of notification lacks a sufficient ground. Moreover, notification is not an outward appearance of claims. General protection is not provided to third parties who act in good faith and might rely on the notification. Unlike notification to debtors, securities can function as a means of publicity for the claim embodied. In Chapter 4, we demonstrated that monetary securities can "tangiblize" the claim of payment, and securities to goods can "tangiblize" the claim of recovery. As a result, these two types of claim obtain an outward appearance, and third parties can safely rely on the information conveyed by securities.

It can be concluded from Chapter 3 and Chapter 4 that property rights of corporeal movables and claims are often in a hidden or semi-hidden state. This *status quo* is distant from the notion that property rights should be transparent to third parties. In the viewpoint of many lawyers, it is desirable to make these (semi-)hidden property rights visible to third parties

---

1 Dutch law provides an example here, see 4.1.2.3 and 4.1.3.3. In the case of double assignment, the assignee who notifies the debtor earlier has a stronger position under English law, which is discussed in 4.1.3.1.

through registration.[2] Registration, traditionally a method of publicity for immovable property, should be introduced in the law of corporeal movables and claims. It is time to deny possession and notification as a qualified means of publicity. However, there is fierce resistance to this move because registration has various side effects.[3] Moreover, the system of registration constructed for corporeal movables will be different from that for immovable property in many aspects.[4] Nowadays, the debate mainly arises in the field of secured transactions of movables.[5]

On the basis of the preceding discussions, Chapter 5 provides a further and conclusive analysis of the rationale of publicity in the law of corporeal movables and claims. In this Chapter, we first discuss the rationale of publicity from a general perspective (see 5.1). After that, we point out that hidden property rights exist ubiquitously in the law of corporeal movables and claims and argue it is desirable to have a system of registration (see 5.2). Section 5.3 focuses on the question of how to construct a system of registration for corporeal movables and claims. After dealing with this question, we discuss three specific topics: publicity of secured transactions of corporeal movables and claims (see 5.4), publicity of the trust of corporeal movables and claims (see 5.5), and publicity of motor vehicles (see 5.6).

5.1 The Rationale of Publicity

5.1.1 Merits and Disadvantages of Publicity

5.1.1.1 Publicity as a Formality

Patricia Critchley in her article on legal formalities begins with the distinction between "substance" and "form". Formalities are defined as *"a requirement that matters of substance must be put into a particular form (in order to have a specified effect)"*.[6] In her opinion, the relationship of a property right is treated as the substance, and publicity can be seen as a formality of this right. If the property right fails to satisfy the formality of publicity, then it will either fail to be validly created in law or will be recognized as partially enforceable. This is illustrated by the distinction between the translative system and the consensual system (see 5.1.4.1). Under the former system

2 Baird and Jackson 1983, p. 200; Bridge, Macdonald, Simmonds and Walsh 1999, p. 567.
3 Baird and Jackson 1984, p. 299; Bridge, Macdonald, Simmonds and Walsh 1999, p. 567.
4 Sigman 2008, p. 156; Von Wilmowsky 1996, p. 160-162. For some special corporeal movables, such as aircraft and vessels, it is possible to construct a land-register-like system.
5 About the arguments for a system of registration, see Struycken 2009, p. 115; Hausmann 1996, p. 427. As to the objections against a system of registration, see Van den Boezem and Goosmann 2010, p. 43; Lwowski 2008, p. 174; Stürner 2008, p. 166.
6 Critchley 1998, p. 508.

contrary to the latter, the formality of publicity is required as a constitutive requirement for the creation and transfer of property rights.[7]

After defining formality, Critchley concludes that formalities have importance for four groups of persons and entities: parties to the transaction, third parties, courts, and states. A formality creates a chance for transacting parties to "*stop and think*", protects them "*against outside pressures, such as influence or duress*", provide them with "*a beneficial protective effect*" where legal professionals have to present, helps them to "*clarify the terms of the transaction*", "*educates the parties as to the precise effects of their transaction*", and serves as a source of "*evidence it secures*".[8] Some types of formalities have a function of publicity for third parties, letting them know about the existence and the terms of a transaction and offering some protection "*when publicity is not forthcoming*".[9] The importance of formalities for courts mainly lies in "*evidence*": judges can use formalities to determine the facts of a transaction in dispute before making a judgement.[10] In the end, Critchley also points out that formalities are useful for the state which, for example, can collect data from the land register for the purpose of taxation.[11] These observations on the advantages and disadvantages of formalities are also demonstrated by Ben McFarlane in his book *The Structure of Property Law*.[12]

The concept of formality is broader than the theme of this research, namely publicity. This concept includes all external requirements concerning how transactions have to be carried out by individuals.[13] The concept also contains, in addition to publicity, the written form of contracts, the attendance of notaries, and so forth. There is no doubt that the statutory requirement of written form is a formality in making contracts, but it is by no means a method of publicity for third parties. The central feature of all methods of publicity is that a transaction must be verifiable or transparent for third parties, so that these parties have a chance to know about the occurrence and the content of transactions (see 2.2.3.2). The written form of contracts cannot make contractual relationships visible to third parties. In this research, we do not address those formalities that are not a means of publicity.

Moreover, the beneficiaries of the formalities mentioned above are broader than what this research focuses on. As just shown, formalities are not only useful for third parties and transacting parties, but also for courts and the state. Undoubtedly, this extensive inspection inspires us to view the principle of publicity in a broader context and guides our attention not only to civil law, but also to civil procedural law and even public administration.

---

7 Snijders and Rank-Berenschot 2017, p. 276-278; Sagaert 2008, p. 18.
8 Critchley 1998, p. 513-516.
9 Critchley 1998, p. 516-517.
10 Critchley 1998, p. 517.
11 Critchley 1998, p. 518.
12 McFarlane 2008, p. 101-109.
13 McFarlane 2008, p. 101.

The extensive inspection also reminds us of the fact that the French land register was introduced by Napoleon for the purpose of taxation.[14] However, since this research focuses only on publicity in the area of property law, we do not examine the latter two beneficiaries (courts and states) and discuss only the importance of publicity for transacting parties and third parties.

5.1.1.2 The Merits of Publicity

A The Function of Evidence for Transacting Parties

In general, every method of publicity has an evidentiary function for transacting parties. It can be used to prove whether and in which way a transaction is carried out between the particular transacting parties. However, one method of publicity differs from another in this respect. As has been argued above, notification to debtors does not qualify as a means of publicity (see 4.1.1.2). For this reason, this formality is not included in the following discussion, despite the fact that it is a source of evidence.

Possession can be seen as a clue for the occurrence of a transaction or the enjoyment of a right by the possessor. This is reflected by the rule of presumption: the possessor is presumed to be the owner of the object possessed (§ 1006 (1) BGB and art. 3:119 (1) BW). In essence, the rule of presumption concerns the allocation of the burden of proof, as has been indicated above (see 3.2.1.3.C).[15] It applies when the facts of a dispute are unclear.[16] For example, when the owner of a bicycle is sued by another person who claims that this bicycle belongs to him or her, the owner can take possession as a means of defense. In this case, if the facts concerning ownership of the bicycle are unclear, namely that the opponent fails to provide sufficient contrary evidence, then the judge will presume that the possessor has ownership. In this sense, possession is *prima facie* evidence of ownership, which may be refuted by contrary evidence. All in all, possessors have an advantageous position in disputes concerning ownership of the object possessed.

The function of supplying evidence has diminished in modern times. This is because proprietary legal relationships are often indicated by written documents, such as written contracts, certificates, receipts and the like.[17] In earlier times, it was expedient to prove property rights, and the person who had possession enjoyed a great advantage in judicial proceedings. Nowadays, refuting the legal presumption by the real owner has become much easier by presenting contrary documents.

The function of evidence of securities is obvious. Securities embody rights that are assumed to be validly existent. This is the reason why they are a type of document of evidence (*Beweisurkunde* in German law and

14 Dekker 2005, p. 237.
15 Füller 2006, p. 291; Brehm and Berger 2014, p. 135; Van Schaick 2014, p. 83.
16 Rosenberg, Schwab and Gottwald 2010, p. 644.
17 Bond 1890, p. 278.

schriftelijk bewijsstuk in Dutch law).[18] In general, the holder of securities enjoys a substantial advantage in proving his or her legal position with respect to the embodied right.[19] For example, a holder of a bill of exchange is *prima facie* deemed to be a holder in due course, and it is the person aiming to refute the presumption who has to bear the burden of proof.[20]

Registration is a means of publicity for immovable property. This method of publicity also has a function of preserving evidence. To understand this function, we need to note two aspects. The first aspect is that the contract concerning transactions is preserved by a registry. This excludes the risk that the contract might be forged or destroyed later. From the history of land registers, it can be found that the register is initially constructed for the purpose of preserving written contracts.[21] The second aspect is that registration might be presumed to be correct, which implies that it has a function to distribute the burden of proof (§ 891 BGB).[22] As a result, the opponent has to provide sufficient evidence contrary to the facts registered.

Before turning to the function of publicity for third parties, it should be mentioned that the function of evidence only relates to the issue of allocating the burden of proof in civil proceedings.[23] If there is no dispute, then the effect of presumption will not be invoked. The problem of proof in civil proceedings only arises between two particular parties (i.e. the plaintiff and the defendant), thereby having nothing to do with the collection of proprietary information by third parties. Preservation of evidence is at most a subordinate function of publicity. As McFarlane argues, "*if evidence [...] is the key concern, signed writing may be enough; although if there is a pressing need for strong evidence, it may also be sensible to require a witness or two*".[24] Therefore, publicity is not the only method of preserving evidence; there are a number of other methods, such as written deeds, the statements of witnesses, and the presence of legal professionals. These formalities do not have the effect of publicity, but they are important sources of evidence.

B The Function of Publicity for Third Parties

In general, publicity can convey proprietary information to third parties, and their reliance on the information obtained from publicity is often protected. In this way, publicity can address the problem of information

---

18 Bridge, Gullifer, McMeel and Worthington 2013, p. 638; Zevenbergen 1951, p. 10; Meyer-Cording 1990, p. 2.

19 Mulder 1948, p. 16.

20 Guest 2016, no. 4-081.

21 Simpson 1986, p. 121; Ellickson and Thorland 1995, p. 386.

22 § 891 BGB: "*(1) Ist im Grundbuch für jemand ein Recht eingetragen, so wird vermutet, dass ihm das Recht zustehe. (2) Ist im Grundbuch ein eingetragenes Recht gelöscht, so wird vermutet, dass das Recht nicht bestehe.*" English translation: § 891 BGB: "*(1) If a right has been entered in the Land Register for a person, it is presumed that the person is entitled to this right. (2) If a right entered in the Land Register is deleted, it is presumed that the right does not exist.*"

23 Brehm and Berger 2014, p. 135.

24 McFarlane 2008, p. 106.

asymmetry and facilitate the security of transactions.[25] If a property right enforceable against third parties is invisible because of the lack of a reliable means of publicity, two undesirable outcomes will ensue.

The first outcome is that third parties have to make use of "informal" methods to collect the proprietary information. Informal methods might be more costly than publicity. Publicity is a "formal" channel through which information concerning property rights is communicated. It is formal because it is provided for by property law (see 2.2.3.2). In principle, to know about the property rights existing on a certain thing, third parties only need to search the method of publicity provided for by property law for this thing. In principle, attention does not have to be given to other resources of information. On the contrary, there are various kinds of informal methods, and proprietary information is often conveyed by informal methods in a dispersed manner. For example, the third party can inquire with relevant parties, especially his or her counterparty, and independent and professional intermediaries may also be able to provide some proprietary information. Inquiry with these parties or intermediaries and collecting information via other information methods are not without costs, though. In many situations, the costs associated with informal methods are higher than those associated with the formal method, publicity.

The second outcome is that the information collected by third parties via costly informal methods might prove to be incorrect or incomplete. Publicity is an objective method of communicating proprietary information. Moreover, this method is presumed to be singular: all proprietary information concerning an object is conveyed through the same method (see 2.2.3.2). As a result, publicity can convey reliable and complete proprietary information. In contrast, informal methods are not as objective as publicity and often unable to provide complete information. This implies a high possibility of conflicts between the actual proprietor and the third party. Conflicts are undesirable. While a conflict implies that one of the competing interests or rights has to be subordinated to the other, and resolving the conflict triggers costs.[26]

Because of these two undesirable outcomes, the smooth circulation of property will be influenced (see 2.2.1.2.C). This is not difficult to understand. Where there is not sufficient proprietary information or where it is too costly to collect sufficient reliable proprietary information, third parties might choose to take no action because of the fear of conflicts. For example, if a person is interested in a bicycle but finds it difficult to ascertain whether the possessor is the actual owner, this person may, for the sake of security, decide not to purchase it. This simple example illustrates how important the possibility of obtaining reliable information cheaply is for the transac-

25 Arruñada 2014, p. 59.

26 In general, the costs triggered by resolving conflicts not only include the resources spent by the litigants ("*private costs*"), such as the fee paid to the lawyer, but also the judicial resources borne by the court ("*public costs*"). See Bayles 1987, p. 22.

tion of property. Smooth circulation is necessary for letting the asset flow to the person who can make the most of it, so that the asset can be utilized to the maximum. Thus, the lack of a reliable means of publicity influences the smooth circulation of property, which will further affect the maximum utilization of property.[27]

In general, an eligible system of publicity can avert two undesirable outcomes by making property rights visible (the principle of publication) and protecting the reliance of third parties (the principle of "public reliance (*öffentliche Glaube*)").[28] Firstly, publicity takes *"preventive justice"* as its fundamental notion: preventing the occurrence of conflicts by providing sufficient proprietary information.[29] Secondly, publicity also serves as a basis of *bona fide* acquisition. The purpose of publicity is not only to make property rights visible but also to protect third parties acting in good faith, so that they can rely on publicity without having to worry that the information conveyed is incorrect or incomplete.[30] In general, a system of publicity which cannot provide *bona fide* protection to third parties is doomed to fail because third parties will not generally use this unreliable system.

However, as we will see later, different methods of publicity differ significantly in their function as publicity (see 5.1.2). For example, possession is an abstract and thus ambiguous means of publicity, and possession is never a sufficient basis for *bona fide* acquisition of corporeal movables, while registration is much more reliable and associated with extensive protection.

5.1.1.3 The Disadvantages of Publicity

Apart from the merits presented above, publicity also has some disadvantages. According to Patricia Critchley, formalities have four downsides: the costs of compliance, the failure of informal transactions, the unfairness or injustice caused, and the detriment to other legal policy aims.[31] Publicity also has these downsides. In the following discussion, we focus on three main disadvantages of publicity: the increase of the cost of transactions,

---

27 The rule of *bona fide* acquisition may allow the buyer to obtain the bicycle when the seller is proved to be not the actual owner of the bicycle. In this sense, the rule facilitates the security of transactions. However, the protection granted to the buyer does not necessarily guarantee that the bicycle will be utilized more efficiently. This is because the bicycle might be more valuable for the actual owner than for the buyer. For example, the bicycle may be worth € 1,000 for the actual owner and only € 900 for the buyer. The price agreed by the seller and the buyer is € 800. This price is appealing to the buyer, and this is why the buyer agrees to purchase the bicycle. However, the price is not acceptable for the actual owner. As a result, *bona fide* acquisition by the buyer cannot lead to an economically efficient outcome.

28 The principle of public reliance is also known as the "effect of good faith (*Guteglaubenswirkung*)". See Baur and Stürner 2009, p. 39. This principle requires that the means of publicity should be reliable, so that third parties acting in good faith can safely rely on it.

29 Lurger 2006, p. 50.

30 Füller 2006, p. 247.

31 Critchley 1998, p. 520-527.

the failure to balance the interests of relevant parties, and the restriction on the parties' autonomy. The fourth disadvantage, i.e. the detriment to other legal policy aims, will be passed over since it falls outside the scope of this research.

A Increase in Transaction Costs

Publicity requires certain positive acts, such as handing over the object involved in the situation of corporeal movables, applying for registration in the registry in the situation of immovable property, or delivering and/ or endorsing the document in the situation of securities. These acts are not without costs. Therefore, where publicity is involved, it increases the total costs of the transaction.

In general, different methods of publicity are costly to different degrees, as we demonstrate later (see 5.1.2). For example, possession and delivery are a cheap method of publicity for corporeal movables, especially on account of the possibility of fictional delivery (*traditio ficta*), while registration is a more costly means of publicity.

B Failure in Fairness

The requirement of publicity might cause unfairness in some situations. In essence, publicity is a legal formality, forming a contrast to the substance of parties' will. McFarlane expressly asserts that rules concerning formality are "*obstacles – annoying hurdles [...] before the parties' intentions*".[32] This is not difficult to understand. Publicity gives rise to technical complexities. It is not easy for all transacting parties to understand the legal consequences of publicity fully and correctly. As a result, the requirement of publicity may frustrate the parties' expectations and even cause some moral difficulties.

For example, a buyer of a bicycle mistakenly believes that mere agreement is sufficient for the acquisition of this bicycle and then pays the purchase price in advance, but the seller becomes bankrupt after the payment. Under the *traditio* rule, the lack of delivery prevents the buyer from acquiring ownership and obtaining a safe legal position against the seller's bankruptcy. The buyer's claim, which is personal in nature, is subject to the principle of equality of creditors (*paritas creditorum*). On the other hand, the money paid by the buyer become a bankruptcy asset under the rule of mingling (*confusio*) and cannot be recovered by the buyer.[33] To address this unfair outcome, some scholars propose a solution: "vindication of monetary value (*Geldwertvindikation*)".[34]

In another situation, a conflict might also arise with our sense of fairness. For example, a buyer reaches an agreement with the seller and pays the purchase price, but the required publicity is not completed. After that, the seller disposes of the same object to another buyer who knows about the

32 McFarlane 2008, p. 100.
33 Zwalve 1996, p. 85.
34 Van Vliet 2000, p. 26-27; Zwalve 1996, p. 91.

first sale, and the requirement of publicity is fulfilled in the second sale. If publicity is necessary for the transfer of the object, the second buyer might prevail, despite the fact that he or she does not act in good faith. To address this unfair outcome, a solution on the basis of tort law might be applied to prevent the second buyer acting in bad faith from acquiring the bicycle. However, we note that the requirements of this tort-law solution are comparatively strict.[35]

The preceding two examples require us to deal with the following question: in order to achieve a fair outcome between the relevant parties, should and how the failure to satisfy the requirement of publicity affect the acquirer's legal position? This question concerns the model of the acquisition of property rights and will be discussed in detail later (see 5.1.4).

C Restriction on Parties' Autonomy

As just mentioned above, publicity, as a kind of formality, forms a regulation of or an obstacle to parties' autonomy. In brief, parties' autonomy means that individuals are entitled to manage their own affairs as they think fit. One aspect of this principle is the "freedom from formalities (*vormvrijheid*)": in principle, parties should be allowed to determine the formality of transactions they carry out.[36] In some situations, the law may require a formality to be satisfied for some reason. As a result, the parties' purpose cannot be realized until this formality is fulfilled. In this sense, the formality forms a restriction on the parties' autonomy.

> *"Formality is something which is added to the basic requirements of the law in relation to a particular transaction. It therefore creates a separate obstacle which must be surmounted if we are to enter the transaction."*[37]

It is always a question of whether publicity forms a justifiable restriction over the principle of autonomy in private law. For example, registration, as the prominent means of publicity for immovable property, might be treated as a "*public intervention on private contracts*".[38] This reminds us of the reason why French law constructs a consensual system in the field of land transactions: the freedom of parties would be improperly restricted if registration is necessary for the transfer of land ownership.

> *"Any system which subordinated the efficacy of such an agreement to the formality of registration was seen as contrary to the freedom of parties [...]. The system of publicity [of land transactions] prevents families from keeping secret their affairs [...] this secret has always been regarded as one of the principal aspects of individual freedom."*[39]

35 Faber 2012, p. 336.
36 Hijma, Van Dam, Valk and Van Schendel 2013, p. 14.
37 Critchley 1998, p. 520.
38 Arruñada 2014, p. 58.
39 Bell, Boynton and Whittaker 2008, p. 281.

In addition to registration, the *traditio* rule is also deemed by some writers as "*unduly restrictive and inconsistent with contractual autonomy*".[40] According to this rule, delivery is necessary for acquiring property rights of corporeal movables. However, modern property law either straightforwardly dispenses with this rule or tempers this rule by recognizing various forms of fictional delivery. Consequently, parties are able to conduct proprietary transactions without affecting the state of actual control of the subject matter. In essence, as we have pointed out above, it is parties' autonomy that is treated as the starting point for the transfer of corporeal movables, whether under the translative system or the consensual system (see 3.4.2.4).

5.1.1.4 Conclusion

As a type of formality, publicity has its merits and downsides. It has a function of evidence for the transacting parties and a function of publicity for third parties. An eligible means of publicity not only allows third parties to obtain proprietary information, but also lays a basis of *bona fide* protection. On the other hand, publicity has several disadvantages. It gives rise to extra costs, might cause an unfair outcome between relevant parties, and forms a restriction on parties' autonomy. For this reason, it is necessary to determine the legal consequences of publicity carefully.

5.1.2 Comparison of Different Methods of Publicity

After examining the merits and downsides of publicity from a general perspective, we further compare different methods of publicity here. The main purpose of the comparison is to show the advantages and disadvantages of each method of publicity in the communication of proprietary information. The methods compared include possession, documental recordation, and registration. In general, the comparison is conducted on the basis of four aspects: clarity, comprehensiveness, conclusiveness, and operational costs.

5.1.2.1 Clarity

The aspect of clarity concerns whether and to what extent a method of publicity can show the content of proprietary relationships and convey proprietary information to third parties clearly. In general, registration is able to show the content of property rights registered clearly, and searchers can understand the information entered in the register easily. This method of publicity carries proprietary information in the form of words. In general, as a tool to communicate information, words are clear. Although words are

40 Parish 2009, p. 11.

necessarily vague,[41] there will usually be a need to interpret the information from the register.[42] However, the vagueness is limited and should not be exaggerated. In many situations, information can be communicated via words clearly, especially when the context in which the words are used is fixed. In this aspect, registration differs from possession.

Possession is merely an abstract and thus ambiguous method of publicity: possession cannot show the legal identity of the possessor accurately (see 3.2.1.2).[43] Possession can be acquired on the basis of different legal relationships, such as ownership, pledge, lease, and borrowing. However, it only makes these underlying relationships visible through physical proximity between the possessor and the object possessed. As a result, the details of the legal relationship cannot be presented by possession clearly. This is why possession is a weaker "indicator" than registration.[44]

It should be noted here that one type of registration might differ from another type in respect of clarity. For example, the notice-filing system constructed for secured transactions of movables simply conveys a "warning" of the existence of security interests, and third parties have to conduct further inquiries to know about the details (see 3.2.1.4). The system provides only "minimum information".[45] In contrast, the land register provides much more detailed proprietary information concerning immovable property.[46] Usually, the information collected from the land register is adequate for a person to make a decision with respect to the land.

Documental recordation, especially in the situation of order securities, resembles registration in the aspect of clarity. As a method of publicity, securities can also convey proprietary information concerning the right embodied in the form of words. The relationship of the right embodied is defined by the document visibly. The holder's identity, the sum payable or the goods involved, the due date, and even the encumbrance of a pledge can be known after glancing at the document, provided that the document is made to order. Compared with order securities, bearer securities convey information less clearly. Bearer securities are closely connected to possession of the document. The ambiguity of possession, as a means of publicity, determines that bearer securities are also ambiguous to some extent. For example, the holder's identity cannot be indicated by bearer securities, and the proprietary encumbrance over the right embodied cannot be known by glancing at the document.

41 Keefe 2000, p. 6.
42 Veenstra 2009, p. 47.
43 Lipson 2005, p. 433.
44 Lurger 2006, p. 47.
45 Van Erp 2004, p. 97.
46 Sigman 2010, p. 508.

5.1.2.2 *Comprehensiveness*

Comprehensiveness refers to the sphere to which a method of publicity can be applied. Registration is comprehensive. In principle, all details of every right can be presented in the form of words and recorded by the register. However, whether and how a right will be registered is contingent on legal policy in practice, being a question of "registerability". In general, for the purpose of simplicity and smooth operation of the register, law restricts the information that can be stored in the system. Otherwise, the register would be disorderly, which would cause a problem of overload and impose a heavy burden of searching on third parties.[47] In this sense, it is argued that the principle of *numerus clausus* of property rights facilitates the smooth operation of the system of registration.[48] The principle restricts the type and content of property rights and thus excludes personal rights from the register. However, it should be noted that, as an exception, some personal rights might be allowed to be entered in the system.[49]

Possession is also a comprehensive method of publicity. It can exist in different situations: (1) property rights and personal rights; and (2) consensual relationships and statutory relationships. In principle, where factual control of the object is involved, there might be possession. However, we note that only direct possession has the effect of publicity, and indirect possession does not qualify as a means of publicity (see 3.2.2). As a result, possession can only show a single legal relationship. If actual control is given up by the lessor to the lessee, making the lessee's right to use visible, then the lessor's right of ownership is doomed to be invisible. Registration is different in this respect: this means of publicity is able to publicize two or more property rights concurrently.[50] For example, where a parcel of land is encumbered with a property right of usufruct, both the usufructuary and the owner can be seen from the register.

In terms of publicity, securities are primarily used to show the ownership of the goods concerned or the claim embodied. Usually, the person who holds the document enjoys the right embodied or the goods concerned. However, there are exceptions. For example, where a bearer document is pledged, the pledgee holds the document but enjoys a right of pledge only. Different from bearer securities, order securities can indicate the existence of the encumbrance by recording a mark of pledge on the surface of the document. As a result, both the pledgor and the pledgee can be shown by the order document. In theory, it can be said that securities can record as much information as the parties desire. However, there is a problem of "recordability": the information which can be recorded by securities, even

47 Smith 2003, p. 1167-1173.

48 Smith 2003, p. 1172.

49 Brehm and Berger 2014, p. 224; Snijders and Rank-Berenschot 2017, p. 84-85.

50 Arruñada 2014, p. 215.

securities made to order, is limited by law. For example, the clause of reservation of ownership cannot be recorded on warehouse receipts, a form of security to goods.

Moreover, securities are only used in special situations, usually commercial transactions, and there is a principle of *numerus clausus* of securities in some jurisdictions.[51] For example, securities to goods are mainly used in the situation of the goods warehoused or transported. It seems impossible to have a document for all types of corporeal movables.

5.1.2.3 *Conclusiveness*

The term conclusiveness involves whether and to what degree a method of publicity is reliable. It amounts to reliability. A conclusive system of publicity implies that third parties do not have to pay attention to the other resources of information.[52] If third parties can rely on the information conveyed by a method of publicity, it can be said that this method is reliable or has public reliance.[53] Conclusiveness is an important attribute of publicity. It assures third parties that the information conveyed is reliable and their reliance on publicity will be protected.

In general, registers can be a conclusive source of proprietary information, and transactions made on the basis of the information entered in the register will be protected. If the registration is proven to be incorrect or incomplete later, the protection usually means that the actual proprietor's legal position will be subordinated. The degree of conclusiveness of a register is, in essence, a matter concerning legal policy and affected by multiple factors. The reliability of a system of publicity might vary from one jurisdiction to another. For example, there is a continuum from the positive system to the negative system of registration in land law, and the reliance of third parties is protected to different degrees in different jurisdictions.[54]

Possession is not a conclusive source of proprietary information in the situation of corporeal movables. A third party acting in good faith cannot be protected merely because of his reliance on possession. In principle, the third party has to pay reasonable attention to and use reasonable efforts to investigate the authority of disposal. As a result, gross negligence is often an obstacle to *bona fide* acquisition of corporeal movables. Moreover, where possession is commonly separated from the right of ownership, the claim of *bona fide* acquisition of corporeal movables will usually be rejected by

---

51 Benjamin 2014, p. 1395; Hueck and Canaris 1986, p. 25; Zwitser 2006, p. 83-84. Under Dutch law, securities are not subject to the principle of *numerus clausus*. See Zwitser 2006, p. 9-10.

52 The Law Commission 2001, p. 18.

53 Raff 1999, p. 427.

54 Here an example is that the German *Grundbuch* is a positive system, the French *publicité foncière* is negative, while the Dutch *Openbare Registers* are somewhere in between, being semi-positive. See Snijders and Rank-Berenschot 2017, p. 82-83.

courts.[55] In this situation, the third party is expected to be suspicious of the possessor's authority of disposal. In other words, the third party cannot just rely on the possessor's factual control. Instead, a third party needs to use other means to investigate the possessor's authority to dispose. In general, the unreliability or limited reliability of possession can be accounted for by the fact that possession is an ambiguous means of publicity for corporeal movables.

In principle, securities, especially securities of payment, is a conclusive and reliable source of information. The reliance of third parties on the documental recordation will be protected. The legal relationship indicated by securities cannot be denied or modified against third parties because of facts outside of the document. However, the strength of protection varies slightly between different jurisdictions (see 4.2.3.4.B). Generally speaking, extensive protection of third parties is necessary because smooth negotiations are the main function of securities.

5.1.2.4 *Operational Costs*

Operational costs refer to the resources that must be invested or consumed during the operation of a system of publicity. In general, possession is a very cheap method of publicity (see 3.2.1.2.A). The physical proximity between the possessor and the object possessed can be processed by third parties quickly. The function of publicity of possession is rooted in human nature and our daily customs. The abstract indication from possession can be immediately obtained by third parties once they observe the physical proximity. Moreover, delivery is cheap, especially because of the possibility of fictional delivery. For example, delivery can be realized through consent (such as *traditio per constitutum possessorium* and *traditio brevi manu*), assignment of the claim of recovery (such as *traditio longa manu* under § 931 BGB), notification to or acknowledgment by a third party (such as *traditio longa manu* under art. 3:115 (c) BW), and delivery of the document representing the goods (such as bills of lading). Unlike ancient Germanic law which confined delivery to be actual in the field of corporeal movables, modern private law recognizes various forms of fictional delivery. As we have pointed out above, modern private law has removed the obstacle of delivery to the transaction of corporeal movables (see 3.4.2.4).[56]

Compared with possession, registration is a more expensive method of publicity (see 3.2.1.2.A). The expense of registration results from several aspects, such as constructing and maintaining the system, recording new transactions in the system, and updating and when necessary rectifying the system. The high costs determine that, from the perspective of efficiency, registration should not be treated as a master key to the problem

55 Kieninger 2007, p. 653; Snijders and Rank-Berenschot 2017, p. 416-417.
56 Parish 2009, p. 12.

of information asymmetry in every situation. Before introducing a system of registration, it is necessary to weigh carefully the benefits this system will create and the costs it will bring. This is the theme of the subsequent discussion (see 5.3).

Compared with registration, documental recordation is also a cheaper method of publicity. For example, valid issuance only requires making a document and delivering this document to the creditor, and transfer of the document simply requires delivery of the document and, if necessary, endorsement. For transacting parties, the main burden is that the document must be issued and transferred in the way strictly stipulated by law. If one of the statutory requirements is not satisfied, the disposal might be unsuccessful. Moreover, securities have a risk of safety, and preserving the document is not without costs (see 4.2.2.5.C). Nevertheless, it can be generally said that securities are a relatively cheap means of publicity.

5.1.3 Publicity and Third Parties

Property rights should be made visible to third parties. This is known as the principle of publicity. However, this description of the principle is quite vague. It neither indicates which method of publicity is important for third parties and in what sense, nor does it clarify what information is desired by each type of third parties. In this part, we examine the importance of different methods of publicity for different categories of third parties: strange interferers, subsequent acquirers, and general creditors. To understand this, it is necessary to bear in mind the demand for proprietary information by the three types of third parties, as has been described above (see 2.2.2.2).

5.1.3.1 Publicity and Strange Interferers

As has been shown (see 2.1.3.2.A), strange interferers are a special type of third parties: they only need to know the boundaries between their free activities and the domain of others' property rights. Before knowing about the boundaries, a person cannot navigate his behavior without interfering with others' property. However, to avoid conducting illegal interference, it is unnecessary for strange interferers to know about the details of the proprietary legal relationships.

In general, possession is a navigating system for strange interferers and can satisfy their demand for knowing about the boundaries (see 3.3.2.2). Though an abstract and thus ambiguous method of publicity, possession can indicate the boundaries of corporeal things. In daily life, people can easily adjust their behaviors according to the abstract indication conveyed by possession. This, in turn, explains why the possessor's right should not be interfered with illegally. In this world crowded with tangible things, people are able to live in harmony with each other by relying on possession, forming the order of possession.

In principle, the problem of boundaries does not arise with respect to claims. The main reason is that claims are relative, and it is difficult for third parties to interfere with claims. The nature of relativity also explains why personal claims are allowed to be invisible. It also explains why the failure of notification to perform a publicity function does not cause a problem to strange interferers (see 4.1.2). Some scholars hold that every patrimonial right is "absolute" and claims are also enforceable against every person.[57] Truly, tort law protection is available to claims, and in this sense we can say that claims are also "absolute". However, this does not alter the fact that illegal infringement of claims only arises in rare cases, and the starting point is that claims are not generally protected under tort law.[58] This general denial of tort law protection can find its doctrinal justification from the notion that personal rights are a legal relationship between particular parties, i.e. the creditor and the debtor.

5.1.3.2 Publicity and General Creditors

In general, publicity is of limited value for general creditors who are mainly concerned about the debtor's overall financial health (see 2.2.2.2.C). This type of third party knows that the unsecured claim will not be realized in full if the debtor is declared bankrupt. Nevertheless, general creditors do not request the debtor to provide proprietary security, mainly because they believe that the debtor is able to pay and can offset the risk of underpayment through other means, such as increasing the loan rate or the selling price.[59] In addition, involuntary creditors, such as tort victims, are unable to require the debtor to provide proprietary security before the occurrence of the obligation.[60]

Even though there is a system of publicity for property rights, general creditors cannot know from the system whether the debtor will become bankrupt or to what extent their unsecured claim will be realized for at least two reasons. One reason is that the debtor's unencumbered assets are always in fluctuation, and the information general creditors obtain from the system of publicity will become outdated after a short period of time. The other reason is that the total amount of debts borne by the debtor cannot be shown by the system of publicity. In practice, general creditors usually evaluate the risk of underpayment on the basis of other factors, especially the debtor's reputation and (semi-)annual financial reports.[61]

Possession is not able to show which corporeal movables can be distributed among general creditors in the event of the debtor's bankruptcy. This is because some corporeal movables possessed by the bankrupt debtor do

57 Rank-Berenschot 1992, p. 328-329; Honoré 1960, p. 459.
58 Reehuis 2015, p. 358; Wolf and Neuner 2012, p. 227.
59 LoPucki 1994, p. 1941.
60 Bebchuk and Fried 1996, p. 882-891.
61 Sigman 2008, p. 151.

not belong to him or her, while corporeal movables not possessed by the debtor might belong to him or her (see 3.5.2).[62] Notification to debtors can neither indicate how many claims the debtor enjoys, nor does this formality indicates the total amount of encumbrances over the debtor's claims. The reason is simple: notification does not qualify as a means of publicity (see 4.1.1.2) and has very limited value to general creditors (see 4.1.5). For the same reasons, securities to goods and securities of payment do not provide useful information concerning the claim embodied to general creditors (see 4.2.2.6.B and 4.2.3.6).

5.1.3.3 Publicity and Subsequent Acquirers

It has been shown that possession, a means of publicity for corporeal movables, is important for strange interferers, and publicity is of little value for general creditors. However, this does not lead to the disappointing conclusion that publicity is dispensable in property law, because publicity is significantly important for subsequent acquirers, such as transferees, proprietary users, and secured creditors. These subsequent acquirers take publicity as an important source of proprietary information (see 2.2.2.2.B). In practice, most disputes about the third-party effect of property rights concern whether subsequent acquirers should be bound by a proprietary legal relationship that came into existence earlier.

Possession is highly relevant to subsequent acquisitions, such as the transfer and pledge of corporeal movables. Firstly, delivery is necessary for disposing of corporeal movables under the *traditio* rule. Secondly, possession is indispensable for *bona fide* acquisition by subsequent acquirers. However, this does not mean that possession qualifies as an outward appearance of ownership. This is because possession is an abstract and thus ambiguous means of publicity. This means of publicity cannot indicate the specific right the possessor has. Moreover, possession is not sufficient for *bona fide* acquisition, and even the indispensability of possession for *bona fide* acquisition of corporeal movables is mainly an outcome of legal policy (see 3.4.3.4.C). Therefore, publicity is important for subsequent acquirers of corporeal movables, but possession cannot satisfy the demand for proprietary information by this type of third party.

As has been argued above, notification to debtors does not qualify as a method of publicity for claims, and this is why *bona fide* acquisition of claims is in general impossible. Some scholars hold that notification implies a kind of factual control over the claim in question.[63] However, this formality can never make claims or the disposal of claims visible to subsequent acquirers. Moreover, it is not an appropriate method of publicity, especially in the situation of assigning or pledging a large number of claims (see

62 Lipson 2005, p. 431-432.
63 Fesevur 2005, p. 109.

4.1.1.2). Therefore, publicity is important for subsequent acquirers of claims, but notification cannot satisfy the demand for proprietary information by this type of third party.

Securities are different from notification to debtors. The former, especially securities made payable to order, is a means of publicity that can indicate the claim embodied, allowing subsequent acquirers to know about the proprietary legal relationships existing on the claim. In general, securities are important for subsequent acquirers in the following aspect: *bona fide* acquisition of the claim embodied. For subsequent acquirers, securities are a generally reliable means of publicity (see 4.2.2.5 and 4.2.3.5).

5.1.4 Publicity and the Model of Acquisition

The model of acquisition is linked with publicity in two aspects: (1) whether publicity is a condition for valid acquisition of property rights; and (2) whether publicity should be treated as an argument for the abstraction principle. According to this principle, any defect in the underlying contract does not affect the acquisition of property rights. In this section, we discuss the relationship between publicity and the model of acquiring property rights.

5.1.4.1 Publicity and the Consensual/Translative System

In this section, we examine the question of whether publicity should be a necessary condition for the acquisition of property rights. There is a distinction made here between the consensual system and the translative system. In some jurisdictions, such as German law and Dutch law, alteration of property rights must take publicity as a condition (the translative system).[64] In contrast, publicity has legal effect against third parties acting in good faith under English law (the consensual system).[65]

For the purpose of convenience, we use a hypothetical case involving four different parties (Figure 13). A *seller* intends to transfer ownership of an object to the *buyer*, but the requirement of publicity is not fulfilled yet. Before the fulfillment, a strange *interferer* illegally damages the object, and the seller becomes bankrupt. There is a *general creditor*. Moreover, the seller transfers the same object to another person, a *subsequent acquirer*. Here we examine, from the angle of publicity, the relationship between the first buyer with these three third parties: the acquirer (the second buyer), the strange interferer, and the general creditor. Before this, we first examine the legal relationship between the seller and the first buyer.

64 Wieling 2006, p. 40-41; Snijders and Rank-Berenschot 2017, p. 62.
65 Sagaert 2009, p. 10.

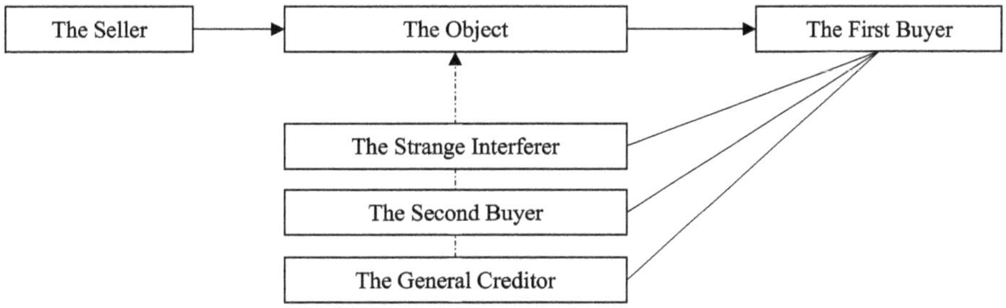

Figure 13

A The Transacting Parties

In the preceding case, the seller has validly reached an agreement of transfer with the first buyer. If the parties have an intention to transfer ownership, then there seems to be no reason to deny the first buyer's acquisition of the object, despite the lack of publicity. In general, the consensual principle is better in line with the rationale of publicity. In other words, publicity should not affect the acquisition of ownership *inter partes*. Of course, if the parties have no intention to transfer ownership, there is no reason that acquisition can take place.

In general, the principal value of publicity is making property rights visible to third parties, in particular subsequent acquirers. The two transacting parties (the seller and the first buyer) in the hypothetical case have known about the transfer of ownership, which means that there is no information asymmetry concerning ownership (see 2.2.2.1). For this reason, publicity is not relevant to the transfer between the two parties.

Private law enshrines the principle of parties' autonomy. Individual parties should be left to arrange their own affairs. Of course, a precondition of parties' autonomy is that no adverse effect is imposed on others, including third parties. Just as Mill argued in *On Liberty*, "*the only purpose for which power can be rightfully exercised over any member of a civilized community, against his will, is to prevent harm to others*".[66] For the legal relationship of transfer *inter partes*, there is no sufficient reason to set up a barrier of publicity. This is why individual parties are allowed to decide the time of the transfer of ownership of corporeal movables (see 3.4.2.4).

In 5.1.1, we have demonstrated that publicity is a formality that has merits and downsides. In balancing these two aspects, the principle of proportionality should be observed: the imposition of a requirement of a formality is only justifiable when this formality is really necessary, suitable

66 Mill 1859, p. 26.

and reasonable.[67] For the acquisition *inter partes*, the requirement of publicity seems unnecessary and violates the principle of proportionality.

In examining publicity under the principle of proportionality, it is necessary to note that publicity is not of no value. Firstly, publicity has a function of preserving evidence for the transacting parties and making them more prudent with respect to the transaction. Nevertheless, these two functions are insufficient for treating publicity as a condition of acquisition. Other types of formality, such as the written contract, also have these two functions.[68] Moreover, possession, as a method of publicity, is not as effective as written contracts in preserving evidence. Possession is abstract and ambiguous, and delivery can occur for different reasons. Therefore, the two functions of publicity are not sufficient for treating it as a condition of acquisition *inter partes* without violating the principle of proportionality.

Secondly, publicity is, to varying degrees and in different senses, important for third parties. For this reason, publicity is often treated as constitutive for the acquisition of property rights. Implicitly, in the view of third parties, the value of publicity for third parties allows it to not violate the principle of proportionality. In the following discussion, we examine the value of publicity for third parties.

B The Strange Interferer

In general, allowing the buyer to acquire ownership independently from publicity does not give rise to any injustice to the strange interferer. For the tortfeasor who illegally interferes with the object, it is irrelevant whether the object is owned by the seller or the first buyer. The interferer is always able to navigate its acts on the basis of possession. For the interferer, it suffices that it knows that the object should not be interfered with because it is owned by others and not a *res nullius*. The failure to publicize the transfer should not be treated as a reason to restrict the first buyer's right to sue the interferer.

Therefore, the legal position of strange interferers does not have to be taken into consideration in answering the question of whether publicity should be treated as a prerequisite of acquisition of ownership. Even though the new owner is unknown to the interferer, the new owner should still be

67 The "principle of proportionality (*Verhältnismäßigkeitsprinzip*)" existed in public law only, serving as a scheme to restrict the power of administrative authorities. It includes three sub-principles, namely the principle of "necessity (*Erfordlichkeit*)", the principle of "suitability (*Geeignetheit*)", and the principle of balance (*Angemessenheit*)". The third sub-principle is also known as the principle of proportionality in strict sense. Nowadays, the principle has crept into the area of private law in the context of constitutionalization of private law. It has taken on a constitutional law feature. According to the principle, both the legislature and court have to abide by the three sub-principles in the event of restricting the right and freedom of individuals. The principle now forms a fence against the legislative and judicial power. See Medicus 1992, p. 35-70.

68 McFarlane 2008, p. 106.

entitled to protect its ownership from any illegal interference. In English law, a buyer, after acquiring ownership of the goods in the absence of delivery, begins to have *"an immediate right to possession"* on the basis of which this buyer is entitled to sue interferers.[69]

C The General Creditor

The requirement of publicity can also not be explained by the legal position of general creditors. As has been argued above, general creditors do not rely on publicity to decide whether they will enter into a transaction without requiring any proprietary security (see 2.2.2.2.C). Truly, publicity might be able to address the problem of fraudulent antedating, which is beneficial to general creditors in the event of the debtor's bankruptcy.[70] However, this does not mean that general creditors have any reliance on publicity: general creditors rarely pay attention to publicity because the proprietary information obtained will become outdated within a period of time (see 2.2.2.2.C).[71]

In the hypothetical case introduced above (Figure 13), the general creditor will benefit from the treatment of publicity as a condition of the transfer of ownership: the object can be distributed to this general creditor. This is at odds with the fact that he has no reliance on publicity. Moreover, the benefit he obtains is at the sacrifice of the first buyer's interests. In contrast, under the consensual principle, the first buyer can acquire the object in the absence of publicity. This outcome causes no injustice to the general creditor. The general creditor does not suffer any unfair loss because the first buyer has to pay the purchase price to the insolvency administrator.[72] In other words, the first buyer's failure to acquire the object because of publicity implies that the general creditor will obtain double benefits (i.e. the sum paid by the first buyer and the object), which is obviously unfair.[73]

D The Subsequent Acquirer

Now let us turn to the value of publicity for subsequent acquirers. In the preceding hypothetical case, there is a conflict between the two buyers. This conflict can be regulated in two different ways: (1) the translative system; and (2) the consensual system plus the rule of *bona fide* acquisition. In the following discussion, we argue that the latter is more in line with the rationale of publicity.

---

69 Bridge, Gullifer, McMeel and Worthington 2013, p. 266; Winfield and Jolowicz 2010, p. 823.

70 Possession, an abstract means of publicity, notification to debtors (see 4.1.1.2.C) and securities (see 4.2.2.6.B and 4.2.3.6) cannot address this problem.

71 Von Wilmowsky 1996, p. 162; Hamwijk 2011, p. 619.

72 Even if the purchase price has not been paid, the general creditor will not suffer any loss unfairly. This because the insolvency administrator is entitled to cancel the contract and refuse delivery of the object. Therefore, different parties cannot be treated fairly only according to publicity in the event of the debtor's bankruptcy.

73 Wood 2019, no. 9-008.

Under the first approach, publicity is a prerequisite of acquisition, and the first buyer cannot acquire the object until the condition of publicity is fulfilled. This leads to two important consequences for the second buyer. The first consequence is that the seller still has the authority of disposal, which implies that the second buyer can acquire the object. The second consequence is that the time when the two buyers fulfill the requirement of publicity is decisive. As a result, if the second buyer completes publicity earlier, he can acquire the object, even though he does not act in good faith.[74]

Under the second approach, the second buyer has an opportunity to acquire the object at the cost of the first buyer's ownership only when he acts in good faith. In general, the rule of *bona fide* acquisition is justifiable in determining which of the two buyers will prevail. This is because publicity is important for subsequent acquirers. If the first buyer does not complete publicity, making his ownership visible to third parties, then he has to bear the risk of losing the right of ownership to a subsequent acquirer. Under the consensual system plus the rule of *bona fide* acquisition, the parties' autonomy is well balanced with the protection of subsequent acquirers acting in good faith. The function of publicity, namely providing reliable information to third parties, is implemented by the rule.

From the introduction above, we find that there is a crucial difference between the two approaches. Under the translative system, the second buyer bears no duty of investigation, and good faith is not relevant. In contrast, under the rule of *bona fide* acquisition, the second buyer has to investigate the transferor's authority of disposal, and good faith is an indispensable condition. Therefore, the translative system grants stronger protection to the second buyer than the rule of *bona fide* acquisition. However, this stronger protection is open to doubt.

Firstly, why can the second buyer enjoy this protection even when he does not act in good faith? If the second buyer has known that the seller no longer has ownership, and the first buyer is the true owner, then he is expected to give up the transaction. In this situation, the problem of information asymmetry, that publicity seeks to address, does not exist. The second buyer knows about the first transaction. It cannot be said that the second buyer has any reliance on publicity that deserves preferential protection.

---

74 If both buyers fail to accomplish publicity, each of them enjoys a personal claim against the seller. The two claims are equal, as a result of the principle of equality of personal rights. However, exception might be recognized by law. For example, according to art. 3:298 BW, the first buyer is entitled to acquisition in priority to the second buyer under certain conditions. Art. 3:298 BW: "*Vervolgen twee of meer schuldeisers ten aanzien van één goed met elkaar botsende rechten op levering, dan gaat in hun onderlinge verhouding het oudste recht op levering voor, tenzij uit de wet, uit de aard van hun rechten, of uit de eisen van redelijkheid en billijkheid anders voortvloeit.*" English translation: Art. 3:298 BW: "*Where two or more creditors enjoy conflicting claims for the delivery of the same thing, the oldest claim has priority in their mutual relation, unless the law, the nature of their claims, or the requirement of reasonableness and fairness requires otherwise.*"

There is no sufficient reason to sacrifice the first buyer's ownership. If the object is fungible, the second buyer can choose another thing of the same kind. If the object is not fungible, the second buyer can negotiate with the first buyer, trying to obtain the object from the true owner.[75]

Secondly, the target of easing the burden of investigation of the second buyer can also be realized by adjusting the criterion of good faith. In general, the requirement of good faith implies a burden of investigation to the second buyer. This might affect the smooth operation of transactions. However, if it is really desirable to reduce the burden of investigation, then we can lower the standard of good faith, for example, by recognizing that the second buyer acts in good faith unless he has acted with gross negligence.[76]

In sum, the translative system goes too far in protecting subsequent acquirers.[77] The drafters of the DCFR realize this.[78] As a result, even though the DCFR accepts the *traditio* rule as the default rule in the transfer of corporeal movables,[79] it rejects the acquisition by subsequent acquirers not acting in good faith in the situation of multiple transfers.

> Art. VIII.-2:301 DCFR: "(1) *Where there are several purported transfers of the same goods by the transferor, ownership is acquired by the transferee who first fulfils all the requirements of Section 1 and, in the case of a later transferee, who neither knew nor could reasonably be expected to know of the earlier entitlement of the other transferee.* (2) *A later transferee who first fulfils all the requirements of Section 1 but is not in good faith in the sense of paragraph (1) must restore the goods to the transferor. The transferor's entitlement to recovery of the goods from that transferee may also be exercised by the first transferee.*"

According to this provision, if the later transferee obtains possession earlier but acts in bad faith, he or she cannot acquire ownership in priority to the earlier transferee.[80] Therefore, this model rule diverges from the translative system (the *traditio* rule), the starting point of the transfer of corporeal movables in the DCFR, by treating the element of good faith as relevant to the regulation of double transfers.[81]

---

75 Carlson 1986, p. 223.

76 Füller 2006, p. 128.

77 It is possible that the second buyer acting in bad faith bears an obligation of compensation to the first buyer under tort law or the law of unjust enrichment. However, this obligation law solution is a "detour" in relation to the property law solution, namely disallowing the second buyer to obtain ownership by including the requirement of good faith. See DCFR 2009, p. 4117; Acquisition and Loss of Ownership of Goods 2011, p. 793.

78 DCFR 2009, p. 4117.

79 Art. VIII.-2:101 (1) DCFR: "*The transfer of ownership of goods under this Chapter requires that: [...] (e) there is an agreement as to the time ownership is to pass and the conditions of this agreement are met, or, in the absence of such agreement, delivery or an equivalent to delivery.*"

80 The PEL follows the same approach. See Acquisition and Loss of Ownership of Goods 2011, p. 793.

81 DCFR 2009, p. 4115; Acquisition and Loss of Ownership of Goods 2011, p. 793.

E Conclusion: Publicity, Declaratory Effect, and Public Reliance

The preceding discussion indicates that to reconcile parties' autonomy and the protection of third parties, the formality of publicity should only yield declaratory effect, the legal effect against third parties acting in good faith. In general, the reasons can be summarized as follows.

Firstly, the declaratory effect is more in line with the rationale of publicity. Publicity is to address the problem of information asymmetry. However, this problem does not exist between the transacting parties, thus publicity should not be treated as relevant to the acquisition *inter partes*. Publicity is only important for third parties. In the absence of publicity, the alteration of property rights between the transacting parties cannot bind third parties (specifically speaking, subsequent acquirers only). If a third party has known the alteration, acting in bad faith, this party deserves no preferential protection. This is because the problem of information asymmetry does not exist to the third party acting in bad faith.

Secondly, the declaratory effect is required by the principle of proportionality. For strange interferers, who has ownership is not important. Publicity is of little importance for general creditors who are mainly concerned about the debtor's overall financial health. Therefore, failing to complete publicity should not be treated as a sufficient reason to restrict the acquirer's right against these two types of third party. If acquisition of property rights is denied because of the absence of publicity under the translative system, the acquirer cannot sue the interferer, nor can he or she reclaim the object from the transferor's bankruptcy assets. The basic function of publicity is to guarantee that property rights are visible to third parties. However, the transacting parties are not third parties, third parties acting in bad faith have known about the property right, and both strange interferers and general creditors do not have interest in the publicity of property rights. Therefore, the consequence of publicity should be confined to the legal effect against third parties acting in good faith. Under this restrictive approach, it can be said that publicity is proportional to the purpose it serves.

Thirdly, the constitutive effect of publicity or the translative system causes a problem of unfairness, which has to be addressed by other measures. For example, some jurisdictions provide for an obligation law solution: the first buyer is entitled to recover the object or obtain compensation from the second buyer acting in bad faith, provided that certain conditions are fulfilled.[82] To some extent, this obligation law solution addresses the problem of unfairness. Nevertheless, the first buyer still suffers the risk that the second buyer becomes bankrupt.[83] Moreover, "*solving the conflicts within*

82 Lurger 2012, p. 54; Faber 2012, p. 336.

83 DCFR 2009, p. 4119; Acquisition and Loss of Ownership of Goods 2011, p. 793.

property law itself may, as such, be considered advantageous as compared to making a 'detour' to the rules on noncontractual liability for damage", as pointed out by the DCFR.[84]

In sum, publicity has its merits as well as detriments. Law should carefully make a balance and confine the legal effect of publicity when necessary. If an acquirer fails to complete publicity, then he should bear the corresponding risk, namely the possibility of *bona fide* acquisition by a subsequent acquirer acting in good faith. In general, this is in line with the "principle of ascription (*toedoenbeginsel* or *Veranlassungsprinzip*)": where an acquirer tolerates the divergence between the actual state of property rights and the outward appearance, he has to bear the associated risk.[85] However, failure to complete publicity does not prevent the property right acquired from being effective against other types of third parties. By defining the legal effect of publicity in this way we can say that the restriction on parties' autonomy is necessary and reasonable.

5.1.4.2 Publicity and the Causation/Abstraction Principle

Publicity is also relevant in the situation where the underlying contract of a proprietary transaction is defective. For this situation, there is a distinction between the causation principle and the abstraction principle. Under the causation principle, a defect in the underlying legal relationship will affect the acquisition of property rights. In contrast, the abstraction principle means that the acquisition of property rights is independent of the underlying relationship, thus any defect of the relationship does not affect the acquisition *per se*. In the literature, it is often held that the abstraction principle makes the system of publicity, such as the land register, more reliable than the causation principle.

> *"Der Unterschied zwischen dem Kausal- und dem Abstraktionsprinzip beschränkt sich auf die in Betracht kommende Rechtsgrundlage. Zweifelsohne wird unter der Geltung des Abstraktionsprinzips das Grundbuch in mehr Fallen formal richtig sein, als bei einem Kausalprinzip."*[86]

The excerpt above concerns the law of immovable property, and similar viewpoints can also be found in the law of corporeal movables: the abstraction principle allows property rights of corporeal movables to be held by the possessor even in the situation where the underlying contract is defective.

84 DCFR 2009, p. 4117; Acquisition and Loss of Ownership of Goods 2011, p. 793.

85 Nieskens-Isphording and Van der Putt-Lauwers 2002, p. 3-4; Wieling 2006, p. 368.

86 Füller 2006, p. 240. English translation: *"The distinction between the causation principle and the abstraction principle is limited to the legal rationale. Undoubtedly, the abstraction principle can make the land register correct in more situations, compared with the causation principle."*

> *"Since, under an abstraction principle, avoidance of a contract only creates an obligation to re-transfer but the transferee for the time being (usually until delivery) remains the owner, this approach obviously fits better to the idea of publicity than a causal approach, under which ownership retroactively reverts to the transferor. This may speak in favour of the abstract transfer approach."*[87]

In this part, we argue that the causation principle plus the rule of *bona fide* acquisition is more justifiable, and the abstraction principle is not a necessary condition for granting protection to third parties having reliance on publicity.

The following discussion starts with a hypothetical case (Figure 14). In this case, a *seller* sells and transfers an object to another party, the *buyer*, but the sale contract is made due to the buyer's duress. After the completion of the transaction, an *interferer* illegally damages the object, and the buyer becomes bankrupt. There is a *general creditor*. Moreover, the buyer further transfers the object to a third party, a successive buyer.

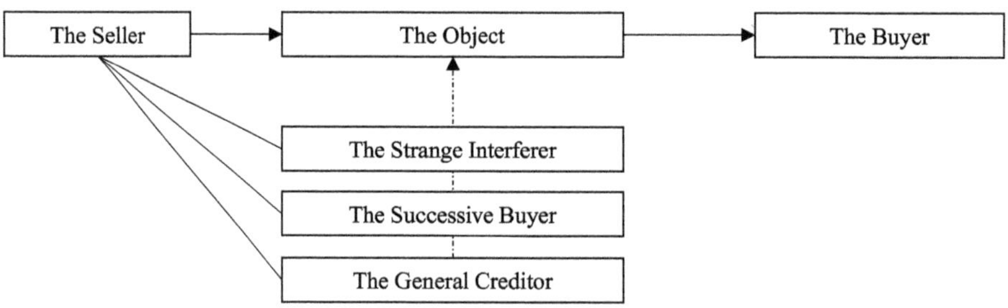

Figure 14

In this case, should the seller be entitled to sue the interferer and to separate the object from the buyer's insolvency assets? The following discussion will not touch upon the doctrinal debate on whether there is a distinction between the obligational act and the proprietary act or whether the latter should be independent of the former. Instead, what we are mainly concerned with is how the correlative relationship between these parties should be arranged from the perspective of publicity.

A The Transacting Parties

Even though the buyer has completed publicity, obtaining the outward mark of the right of ownership, there is no reason to deny an automatic recovery of ownership to the seller. This is because, according to the rationale of publicity, the problem of information asymmetry often does not exist for the transacting parties. It can be imagined that the buyer is, from the outset, aware of the duress and that the seller does not truly have the will

87 Acquisition and Loss of Ownership of Goods 2011, p. 454.

to transfer.[88] Even if the buyer does not know about the duress at the beginning, he will be made aware of the defect when the seller requests to rescind the transaction. In general, whether the buyer knows about the defect has nothing to do with publicity. The completion of publicity is an outcome of performing the defective underlying contract. Publicity *per se* cannot inform the buyer that the underlying contract is voidable on the basis of the duress.

Between the transacting parties, publicity is not relevant to determining the legal consequences of a defect in the underlying legal relationship.[89] In the situation where there is a defect in the underlying contract, the main task is how to rectify the defect and determine the legal consequences between the transacting parties. Truly, in the hypothetical case, the buyer has completed publicity and obtained the outward mark of ownership. However, this should not be taken into consideration in determining the legal consequences *inter partes*. Publicity cannot be a reason to deny automatic recovery of the object to the seller.

In some jurisdictions, such as German law, an abstraction principle is implemented, but under various exceptions.[90] According to this principle, only a personal claim of recovery is granted to the seller on the basis of the rule of unjust enrichment. The hypothetical case of duress falls under the "identity of defect (*Fehleridentität*)", a cause of exception to the abstraction principle.[91] Therefore, the object is also automatically restored to the seller under German law. Sometimes, it is held that the abstraction principle *"fits better to the idea of publicity than a causal approach"*.[92] This view is problematic. Indeed, the buyer has completed publicity and obtained the outward mark of ownership. As has just been argued, however, the buyer knows or will know about the defect, and the main task is how to determine the legal consequences between the seller and the buyer properly. Thus, publicity is completely irrelevant.

88 Even if it is a third party who compels the transferor to transfer the object, it is conceivable that the buyer might also know about the coercion. If the buyer neither knows nor should know about the coercion by this third party, the seller's right of revocation might be restricted. This is accepted by the DCFR. Art. II.-7:208 DCFR: "(1) *Where a third person for whose acts a party is responsible or who with a party's assent is involved in the making of a contract:* (a) *causes a mistake, or knows of or could reasonably be expected to know of a mistake; or* (b) *is guilty of fraud, coercion, threats or unfair exploitation, remedies under this Section are available as if the behaviour or knowledge had been that of the party.* (2) *Where a third person for whose acts a party is not responsible and who does not have the party's assent to be involved in the making of a contract is guilty of fraud, coercion, threats or unfair exploitation, remedies under this Section are available if the party knew or could reasonably be expected to have known of the relevant facts, or at the time of avoidance has not acted in reliance on the contract.*"

89 Acquisition and Loss of Ownership of Goods 2011, p. 454.

90 Baur and Stürner 2009, p. 59-61.

91 Füller 2006, p. 134.

92 Acquisition and Loss of Ownership of Goods 2011, p. 454.

B The Strange Interferer

We have argued that automatic recovery of ownership should be available to the seller where the contract of sale is declared invalid. Following this, one question is whether automatic recovery can be effective against the interferer. Our answer to this question is in the positive.

The reason is simple. The imposition of liabilities on the interferer is not relevant to the following question: who (the seller or the buyer) is the owner in law and can sue the interferer by virtue of ownership? The specific identity of the owner is an immaterial question to strange interferers, as has been argued above (see 2.2.2.2.A). This type of third parties only desires to know the boundaries of their free acts, and an abstract indication conveyed by (actual) possession suffices for them. It makes no difference which party will claim remedies on the basis of ownership. Moreover, the fact that the owner is not in actual possession of the object does not affect his or her right to sue the interferer, which has been demonstrated above (see 3.3.3). Therefore, automatic recovery of ownership and the associated remedies against the strange interferer should not be denied to the seller just for the reason that the seller has no possession.

C The General Creditor

General creditors are a type of third party who is not concerned about publicity, which has been shown above (see 2.2.2.2.C and 5.1.4.2.C). General creditors have no reliance on publicity. In the hypothetical case, though the buyer has obtained the outward appearance of ownership, the general creditor will not be misled by it. Therefore, the buyer's general creditor should not be entitled to include the object in the bankruptcy assets just for the reason that the buyer preserves the outward appearance of ownership. Otherwise, the seller's interest would be threatened, especially when the purchase price is not paid by the buyer. Under the abstraction principle, the seller only has a general claim for the purchase price, which is subject to the principle of equality of obligations (*paritas creditorum*) and might give rise to an unfair outcome. This outcome is that both the sum to be paid by the buyer and the object are available to the general creditor.[93]

> *"Since avoidance cases are rooted in special defects affecting the validity of the contract, the appropriate policy is considered to be that the transferee's creditors should step into their debtor's shoes. This policy is considered to be a causal approach."*[94]

In sum, publicity is not a decisive factor in determining whether a thing belongs to the bankruptcy assets. As has been mentioned above, although possession once acted as a criterion to determine the scope of the bank-

93 McGuire 2008, p. 114.
94 Acquisition and Loss of Ownership of Goods 2011, p. 454.

ruptcy asset by the English Bankruptcy Act, this approach has been given up (see 3.5.2.2).[95]

D The Subsequent Acquirer

If the buyer disposes of the object to another third party, a subsequent acquirer, then the question of who holds the outward mark of ownership becomes relevant. In the hypothetical case, the successive (subsequent) acquirer is a third party who not only has a specific interest in the buyer's authority of disposal, but also reliance on the publicity. If the successive acquirer acts in good faith with respect to the defect of the earlier sale, then there is a reason to protect him from the defect.

Under the causation principle, the buyer does not obtain ownership from the outset. Therefore, the buyer lacks authority to dispose in the successive transfer. However, based on the rule of *bona fide* acquisition, the successive acquirer is able to acquire the object, and the security of the successive transaction can be guaranteed.[96] To successfully apply the rule, certain requirements, such as the acquirer's acting in good faith, must be satisfied. In this way, the divergence between the actual state of and the outward appearance of ownership, which the causation principle gives rise to, does not cause any unfair disadvantage to the successive acquirer acting in good faith.

In contrast to the causation principle, the abstraction principle allows the buyer to obtain ownership without being affected by the duress. As a result, the successive acquirer is able to obtain the object from the buyer independently of the defect. In this way, the security of the successive transaction is safeguarded. However, a problem caused by the abstraction principle is that the successive acquirer can obtain the object even when he acts in bad faith. In general, this outcome collides with our sense of fairness. As a way of facilitating the security of transactions, the abstraction principle goes too far.[97] Moreover, the problem of information asymmetry, which publicity is intended to address, does not exist since the successive acquirer knows about the defect in the previous sale. Therefore, it can be said that the abstraction principle, under which protection is available to *mala fide* successive acquirers, is not in line with the rationale of publicity.

Obviously, there is a slight difference between the rule of *bona fide* acquisition and the abstraction principle in terms of the duty of investigation. In general, the principle imposes no duty of investigation on the successive acquirer and thus facilitates the security of transactions to a larger degree. The factor of good faith is not relevant in applying this principle. In contrast, the rule of *bona fide* acquisition includes a requirement of good faith, which implies that the successive acquirer bears a duty of investigation.

95 Beale, Bridge, Gullifer and Lomnicka 2018, no. 9.05.
96 Faber 2012, p. 328.
97 Van Vliet 2000, p. 34; Faber 2012, p. 328.

However, this difference in protecting the security of transactions can be moderated by adjusting the standard of good faith. For example, the law can lower the standard of good faith by denying *bona fide* acquisition only when the successive acquirer acts with gross negligence. In this way, the burden of investigation can be alleviated, and the transaction can operate more smoothly.[98]

E Conclusion: Publicity, the Causation Principle and Public Reliance

From the preceding analysis of the hypothetical case introduced above (Figure 14), it can be concluded that the causation principle plus the rule of *bona fide* acquisition is more in line with the rationale of publicity. From the perspective of publicity, at least, it is not justifiable to deny the automatic recovery of ownership in the situation of a defective transaction. In general, publicity is completely irrelevant in answering the following question: should the original owner be protected against strange interferers and general creditors by recognizing the automatic recovery of ownership? These two types of third party have no reliance on publicity. Thus, there is no sufficient reason to deny protection of the original owner before he or she re-obtains the outward appearance. Otherwise, the principle of proportionality would be breached.[99]

Along this line of reasoning, a subsequent acquirer who knows about the defect in the underlying legal relationship should not be entitled to acquire ownership either. Where the subsequent acquirer has been aware of the defect, the problem of information asymmetry does not arise for him or her. Individuals bear a general duty to respect others' property right. Protecting a person who acts in bad faith in priority is at odds with our sense of fairness. If the object is fungible, this person can choose another thing of the same kind. If the object is not fungible, and the person does need the object, he can negotiate with the actual owner.

Truly, unlike the causation principle, the abstraction principle allows publicity to remain consistent with the state of property rights by excluding the influence of defects in the underlying contract on the proprietary acquisition. Under the causation principle, a defect in the underlying contract may reverse the acquisition automatically, which will cause a temporary discrepancy between the actual state of property rights and publicity, provided that the publicity has been completed.[100] As a result, the subsequent acquirer might be misled. However, this should never be treated as an adequate reason to deny the causation principle. In general, the subsequent acquirer can be protected via the rule of *bona fide* acquisition.[101] In terms of facilitating the security of transactions, the abstraction principle does

98 Füller 2006, p. 128.
99 About this principle, see 5.2.2.
100 Dubarry 2016, p. 625.
101 Füller 2006, p. 241.

not differ significantly from the causation principle plus a rule *bona fide* acquisition.[102]

It could be said that publicity under the causation principle is not as reliable as that under the abstraction principle. According to the causation principle, a defect in the underlying legal relationship will affect the correctness of publicity. It is expected that the subsequent acquirer is aware of this, and *bona fide* acquisition should be denied. However, this view is problematic. In general, the abstraction principle is not a premise of the protection of the subsequent acquirer from the defect in the previous transaction. In the hypothetical case, who should be protected in priority between the seller and the successive acquirer? This question is, in essence, an issue concerning legal policy.[103] Both the seller and the third party are blameless.[104]

5.1.4.3 The Phenomenon of Relativity of Property Rights

The consensual principle implies that ownership acquired in the absence of publicity is, in essence, relative. In light of the discussion above, the ownership acquired should be effective against the strange interferer, the general creditor, and the subsequent acquirer acting in bad faith, despite the lack of publicity. However, the ownership is unenforceable against the subsequent acquirer acting in good faith. In this sense, we can say that the ownership acquired in the absence of publicity is not fully absolute: it is restricted by the rule of *bona fide* acquisition.

A similar observation can also be found from the discussion of the causation principle. Where the underlying legal relationship is defective, ownership should be restored to the transferor automatically. In general, the ownership recovered should be enforceable against every type of third party, except the subsequent acquirer acting in good faith.

Therefore, there is a phenomenon of the relativity of property rights under both the consensual principle and the causation principle. This phenomenon is a result of protecting the reliance of third parties on publicity. In reality, the phenomenon is common because there is a great variety of reasons why publicity fails to show the relationship of property rights correctly. As Ulph says, we are in a world where ownership is *"relative rather*

---

102 Intangible things, such as claims, may lack a means of publicity. As has been argued above, notification to debtors cannot serve as a method of publicity for claims. Consequently, *bona fide* acquisition of claims lacks a proper basis. For this type of intangible property, the abstraction principle can block the influence of the defective previous transaction on subsequent transactions. See Hästad 2006, p. 43.

103 In fact, the abstraction principle is also often explained by legal policy, namely facilitating the security of transactions. See Acquisition and Loss of Ownership of Goods 2011, p. 453.

104 In this aspect, the seller in this case and the first buyer in the situation of double sale are different. Where the same object is transferred twice, and the first buyer fails to complete the publicity, allowing ownership and publicity to diverge from each other, he or she is "blameable" in the sense that the divergence can be ascribed to him or her.

than absolute".[105] For example, where the owner is not in actual possession of the object, his or her ownership will become relative in the sense that there is a possibility of *bona fide* acquisition by a third party. This implies that the phenomenon of relativity of property rights may also exist under a translative system. If a party obtains ownership of a bicycle in the way of *traditio per constitutum possessorium*, this person runs the risk of *bona fide* acquisition when the transferor disposes of the bicycle to a third party.

> *"Eigendom van een roerende zaak is echter in zoverre 'relatief' dat het onder omstandigheden 'gevolg' mist [...]. Wie een roerende zaak kwijtraakt, kan zijn eigendomsrecht soms niet vervolgen onder een derde die de zaak te goeder trouw verkreeg (zie art. 3:86)."*[106]

In German law, this is known as the "relative proprietary right (*Relative dingliche Rechte*)", a term used to describe those property rights that can be enforced against everyone except the party who enjoys a better position.[107] In Dutch legal theory, the rule of *bona fide* acquisition is also deemed to be a cause of the "relativization of property rights (*relativering van goederenrechtelijke rechten*)".[108]

This phenomenon is not difficult to explain. The starting point of property rights is that they are exclusive against everyone. However, the effect of exclusivity might be restricted for other purposes, especially protecting subsequent acquirers acting in good faith. Notably, the phenomenon does not mean that a property right without an outward appearance will deteriorate to be purely personal. To know the precise extent to which this property right will be restricted for the protection of third parties, it is necessary to know the function of publicity. As we have argued above, publicity is mainly important for subsequent acquirers, allowing this type of third party to obtain proprietary information safely and easily. In principle, general creditors and strange interferers do not rely on publicity. For this reason, the effect of an invisible property right should not be restricted in relation to these two types of third party.

5.2 Meeting the Requirement of Publicity by Registration

5.2.1 Ubiquitous Existence of Hidden Property Rights

From Chapter 3 and Chapter 4, we can conclude, somewhat disappointingly, that hidden property rights are common in the law of corporeal movables and claims. Possession is, at most, an abstract means of publicity for

105 Ulph 1998, p. 405.

106 Nieuwenhuis 2015, p. 9. English translation: "*The ownership of movables is 'relative' in the sense that it might miss the effect of 'following' [...]. The person who acquires a movable thing cannot follow the object to the place of a third party who succeeds in good faith acquisition (see art. 3:86).*"

107 Wieling 2006, p. 670.

108 Snijders and Rank-Berenschot 2017, p. 55.

corporeal movables and can only communicate an ambiguous indication. The direct possessor's right is made visible to third parties through actual control ambiguously (see 3.2.1). The right enjoyed by indirect possessors is entirely invisible to third parties, and indirect possession does not qualify as a means of publicity (see 3.2.2). As a result, possession cannot be treated as an eligible means of publicity for corporeal movables. In evaluating the importance of delivery for the transfer of ownership of corporeal movables, the drafters of the DCFR acknowledge that *"the value of this aspect of publicity is heavily eroded"*.[109]

Securities to goods can, more or less, address the problem of publicity (see 4.2.2.5). Securities to goods have the effect of *traditio*, implying that they can publicize the relationship of (indirect) possession. The holder of a document to goods can show his or her indirect possession to third parties. In this sense, it can be said that the document "tangiblizes" indirect possession. Moreover, securities to goods are able to show the legal identity of the holder, who might be an owner, a pledgee or an agent, provided that they are made to order. In showing the holder's legal identity, bearer securities to goods convey less information than order securities.

Notification to debtors does not qualify as a method of publicity for claims. "Ownership" of and the possible encumbrance over a claim cannot be made visible to third parties through notifying the debtor involved (see 4.1.1.2). This implies a higher possibility of multiple assignments and the conflict between different security interests. Similar to corporeal movables, the answer to the question of how to avoid conflicts and facilitate the transactional certainty is also a problem for claims, an important type of asset in modern transactions.[110] At present, *bona fide* acquisition is not generally applicable to claims, because of the lack of an appropriate means of publicity. As a result, it is the *nemo dat* rule that will apply when conflicts arise. This implies that third parties often run a risk of uncertainty, even though they act in good faith (see 4.1.3 and 4.1.4).

In general, no problem of publicity will arise for claims embodied within a document. The right embodied mainly includes two types: one is the claim of recovery embodied within securities to goods (see 4.2.2.5), and the other is the claim of payment embodied within securities to payment (see 4.2.3.5). From the document, third parties can obtain certain proprietary information concerning the claim embodied, especially when the document is made payable to order. Moreover, protection is granted to third parties acting in good faith at the sacrifice of the actual creditor. As a result, securities are a reliable means of publicity for third parties. Because of the general protection of third parties, claims embodied within securities have higher negotiability than ordinary claims.

109 Acquisition and Loss of Ownership of Goods 2011, p. 432.
110 The Scottish Law Commission 2011, p. 93.

In modern society, the importance of immovable property has somewhat declined, while movable assets have become increasingly important.[111] Nevertheless, nearly every jurisdiction has a strong principle of publicity for immovable property, while a different attitude is taken with respect to the publicity of corporeal movables and claims.[112] The ubiquitous existence of hidden property rights has given rise to a severe hindrance to transactions concerning movable assets, especially in financial practice.

Property rights have binding force against third parties. Hidden property rights bring about a heavy burden of information to third parties.

> *"Property rights thus face a trade-off with positive and negative effects [...]. Their survival after conveyance of the asset or any other transformation of rights requires costly institutions and resources in order to organize the process of searching, bargaining and contracting for consent. In particular, the possibility of hidden property rights increases the information asymmetry between the conveying parties: the seller knows better than the acquirer about hidden property rights."*[113]

Due to the lack of a reliable means of publicity for corporeal movables and claims, it is difficult for third parties, especially subsequent acquirers, to obtain reliable proprietary information. This gives rise to two undesirable outcomes, which has been pointed out above (see 5.2.1). The first outcome is that third parties have to make use of "informal" methods to collect proprietary information, which might be more costly. The second outcome is that the information collected by third parties via costly informal methods might be proven to be incorrect or incomplete, which gives rise to conflicts between different parties, especially the actual proprietor and third parties. Because of these two undesirable outcomes, the smooth circulation of property will be influenced.

At present, there is a sophisticated system of rules developed to address the conflicts that have arisen in the law of corporeal movables and claims. Among these rules, a typical one is the *bona fide* acquisition of corporeal movables. However, this rule is, in essence, an *ex-post* approach. The rule inevitably faces the following dilemma: a choice has to be made between the actual owner and the third party acting in good faith.[114] If the actual owner is entitled to preferential protection, then the third party acting in good faith cannot acquire the corporeal movable. If the third party is protected in priority, the actual owner will lose his or her right of ownership. As we have argued above, the rule of *bona fide* acquisition of corporeal movables cannot be justified by the publicity effect of possession (see 3.4.3.4). Possession is an ambiguous means of publicity, and the reliance of the third party on possession lacks a sufficient ground. The frequent occurrence of

111 Gilmore 1999, p. 25; Huijgen 1995, p. 5.
112 Mincke 1997, p. 205; The Scottish Law Commission 2011, p. 94.
113 Arruñada 2011, p. 237.
114 Karner 2006, p. 57.

bona fide acquisition implies that possession cannot avert conflicts concerning corporeal movables. The rule is to resolve, rather than to prevent, the conflict between the actual owner and the third party acting in good faith.

5.2.2 Meeting the Requirement of Publicity by Registration

To facilitate smooth transactions concerning corporeal movables and claims, it is desirable to adopt an *ex-ante* approach by having a reliable method of publicity. With a reliable method of publicity, individuals can obtain the proprietary information they want easily. They do not have to resort to informal resources of information. More importantly, a reliable method of publicity enables third parties to make decisions with security on the basis of the information obtained. For the actual proprietor, it is possible to show his or her property rights through publicity, without having to worry about the loss of the right to any third party.

In general, (public) registration is an appropriate method of publicity that can be used to prevent conflicts in the law of corporeal movables and claims. This method has been demonstrated to be effective in the field of immovable property. Nowadays, registration has been extended to patents, trademarks, and some special corporeal movables, such as ships and aircraft. In many jurisdictions, it is also introduced in the field of secured transactions concerning corporeal movables and claims (see 5.4). Moreover, registration, as a means of publicity, plays an important role in the transactions concerning some new types of property, such as emission rights and agricultural products quota.[115] Apart from registration, there seems to be no other proper means of publicity that can be used to address the problem of publicity in the law of corporeal movables and claims: possession is ambiguous, notification to debtors has no effect of publicity, and securities have a very limited field of application. Thus, we will shift our attention to how to build a system of registration for corporeal movables and claims.

5.3 The Introduction of Registration: A General Discussion

From the preceding discussion, it can be concluded that registration has merits and drawbacks, not only as a formality (see 5.1.1) but also as a special method of publicity (see 5.1.2). The question which then follows this conclusion is whether and to what extent registration should also be employed to address the problem of information asymmetry in transactions concerning corporeal movables and claims. This question is discussed in 5.3. The subsequent discussion seeks to provide some general guidelines

115 Cole 2016, p. 10; Snijders and Rank-Berenschot 2017, p. 44; Cardwell 2000, p. 168.

concerning the way of constructing a system of registration, the scope of application of this system, and the legal effect of registration.

The subsequent discussion takes the system of registration for secured transactions concerning movable property as an important model. In general, there are two reasons to do so. One reason is that registration has been introduced in the field of secured transactions in many jurisdictions and proposed at the international level, such as the UNCITRAL Model Law on Secured Transactions. The other reason, also the most important reason, is that a register for corporeal movables and claims is mainly needed in the practice of secured transactions. Only a few transactions, such as the outright assignment of claims, actual lease, and the trust for management (*fiducia cum amico*), fall outside the secured transaction. Thus, the system of registration for the secured transaction qualifies as representative. The system can be taken as a basis on which a "general" register for corporeal movables and claims will be constructed. Here the term "general" means that the register proposed in this research is not only applicable to secured transactions, but also to those transactions having no function of security.

To make this research more concrete and useful for practice, we provide some proposals after the discussion of each aspect of the system of registration. Compared with the recommendations provided by the UNCITRAL Legislative Guide on Secured Transactions, the proposals made in this research are less comprehensive. Some issues, which are necessarily involved in constructing a system of registration, are not included in this research. For example, rules concerning the modification and cancellation of registration are indispensable for a register to operate well. However, this issue falls outside the scope of this research.

5.3.1 The Construction of the System

5.3.1.1 A Subject-Based System

To construct a system of registration, it is necessary to find an index according to which the system can be established. Compared with immovable property, it is more difficult to find a proper index for corporeal movables and claims. Because of the cadastral survey, land has been partitioned off with a unique identifier, leading to the "*invisible line*", which lays a foundation for the present system of land registration.[116] In contrast, most corporeal movables are either infungible (such as new refrigerators of a certain brand and crude oil of a certain quality) or difficult to distinguish by referring to a unique feature (such as a particular used refrigerator). Nevertheless, it is still possible to construct a system of registration. Before understanding this possibility, it is necessary to have a general view of the format of registers.

---

116 Dekker 2003, p. 177.

In general, there are two types of registers according to the criterion of format: the object-based system (*Realfolium*) and the subject-based system (*Personalfolium*).[117] The former is constructed on the basis of the identity of the object of property rights, and the latter is built according to the identity of the parties involved. For example, the German land register (*Grundbuch*) is an object-based system, and a particular folio is attributed to every specific parcel of land.[118] Traditionally, the French land register was established according to the name of the landowner. In 1955, a land-based system of registration was introduced.[119] The format of a system is important for searchers to find the right folio. Every system of registration must have a unique criterion according to which searchers can distinguish the targeted folio from the other folios. As it is usually either impossible or difficult to find a unique identifier for corporeal movables, an object-based register is, practically speaking, not possible.

> *"Another problem is that, in the case of tangible things, registration cannot work unless each individual thing is easily distinguishable from every other like thing. This means that registration is ruled out for all types of tangible property except those where each individual item is unique (such as pieces of land, or works of art, or racehorses) or can be made so by fixing on an identification mark or name plate (so, for example, it would be feasible to set up a system for registration of car ownership, although we have not yet done so in this country)."*[120]

Claims, a type of movable property, are often unique: they arise between specific creditors and debtors and have different content, and the date of creation is often different. Nevertheless, it is not easy to identify claims and have an object-based system. If an individual folio is attributed to a claim, then this claim has to be described with sufficient accuracy by indicating the parties, the date of creation and even the content. The description is burdensome. More importantly, the folio of the claim can only be found by entering the information recorded, which is costly and might lead to mistakes. Moreover, the relationship of the claim might change for various reasons, which means that the description has to be updated to maintain its accuracy. As a consequence, it is unrealistic to have a system of registration organized by reference to claims.

In general, it is only possible to have a subject-based system for corporeal movables and claims. The system would have to be constructed according to the index of the identity of the parties. Correspondingly, third parties can search the system by entering the information concerning the party's identity. How can the party be identified, and what is the party's identifier? In general, the party's name is an identifier. However, only the

---

117 Schmid, Hertel and Wicke 2005, p. 32.
118 Hinteregger and Van Vliet 2012, p. 857.
119 Hinteregger and Van Vliet 2012, p. 892.
120 Clarke and Kohler 2005, p. 388.

name is sometimes insufficient since different parties perhaps have the same name, especially when the party is a natural person. For this reason, additional information about the party, such as the date of birth, is needed. After finding the right folio according to the party's identifier, how can third parties know about the content of the transaction and the object involved? It is necessary to describe the type of the transaction and the object involved in the transaction and to have the description recorded in the system. About these three aspects, namely the party's identifier, the type of the transaction, and the object involved, further discussion is offered later.

In the end, it should be noted that not all corporeal movables cannot be uniquely identified. For example, a motor vehicle has a unique identifier, the VIN (vehicle identification number).[121] This creates a possibility of having a central and object-based register. It is interesting that Canadian law and Australian law incorporate this register in the system of registration constructed for secured transactions by enabling "*finance statements relating to security interests in motor vehicles to be registered and searched by reference to the vehicle identification number*".[122] The entire system of registration is constructed generally according to the party's identity, but the secured transaction concerning motor vehicles can be searched with reference to the VIN. In doing so, the system also has an object-based dimension. In this research, we probe into the possibility of constructing a specialized and object-based system of registration for motor vehicles (see 5.6). This system is presumed to be comprehensive: it not only serves for secured transactions, but also for transfer of ownership of and creation of proprietary rights of use on motor vehicles.

A The Party's Identifier

As mentioned above, the index of a subject-based system is the party's identity. Undoubtedly, the party's name is the most important identifier. If the party is a legal person, the registered name appearing in relevant official documents, such as the operating license, is the identifier.[123] However, the name entered by the legal person might be misspelled, inaccurate or later modified. In order to avoid errors and guarantee that searchers can find the right folio, it is advised that the legal person be required to provide additional information, such as the enterprise code (i.e. business number) and the address.[124]

---

121 In addition to motor vehicles, aircraft, vessels and intellectual property also have a unique identifier. In general, these three types of property have already owned a specialized system of registration. Therefore, there is no need to include them in the system of registration for corporeal movables and claims.

122 Walsh 2016, p. 77; Whittaker and Partner 2015, p. 183.

123 UNCITRAL Guide on the Implementation of a Security Rights Registry, p. 72; White and Summers 2012, p. 1225; Whittaker and Partner 2015, p. 193.

124 Whittaker and Partner 2015, p. 193.

If the party is a natural person, his or her full name appearing on official documents is the identifier. Here official documents include the identity certificate, driver's license, and birth certificate. As different natural persons might have the same name, adding extra personal information would be needed. In general, the date of birth should be required to be entered in the system.[125] The natural person's address might also be relevant but should not be considered as very reliable, because the address may change later. As there are multiple sources from which the information concerning the natural person can be collected, the law can, for the sake of certainty, determine the order of these sources.[126]

Partnerships, whether including partners bearing limited liabilities or not, are not a legal person. Nevertheless, they are often viewed as an entity, having a (registered) name and being provided with an enterprise code. Therefore, it is also possible to have a unique identifier for partnerships in most situations. However, some partnerships do not have a (registered) name or a business number. For these partnerships, one solution is requiring them to provide relevant details of the partners, such as the name, the business number in the situation of a legal person partner, and the date of birth in the situation of a natural person partner.[127]

Proposal 1:
The register should be constructed as a subject-based system according to the party's identifier. The identifiers of legal persons include the name, the enterprise code, the address of the legal person and so on. For organizations without legal capacity, the information provided includes the name, the enterprise code (if possible), and the organization's address. The identifiers of natural persons should be the name, date of birth, address and other relevant information included in the identity certificate, driver's license, and birth certificate.

B The Description of the Object

Finding the right folio according to the party's identifier is the first step for third parties to collect proprietary information. As stated above, proprietary information concerns three aspects: the parties of the property right, the object of the property right, and the content of the property right. Usually, the information concerning the parties, at least one of them, was obtained by the searcher. Otherwise, the searcher would not be able to conduct any

125 UNCITRAL Guide on the Implementation of a Security Rights Registry, p. 67; Whittaker and Partner 2015, p. 189.
126 For example, the UCC relies on the driver's license primarily, the Canadian and New Zealand PPSAs take the person's birth certificate in priority, while the Australian PPSAs first rely on the data collected as a result of the operation of the Anti-Money Laundering and Counter-Terrorist Financing Act (2006).
127 Whittaker and Partner 2015, p. 201.

inspection of the register. Therefore, the other two aspects are what the searcher is mainly concerned about. The following discussion centers on how to describe the object of and the content of property rights.

Property rights are subject to the principle of specificity (see 2.1.3.1). Under this principle, only specific things may be validly disposed of. In the field of immovable property, the principle does not trigger any difficulty in constructing the land register because this system is object-based. Because of land survey and delimitation, every individual parcel of land is earmarked and can be identified easily.[128] Differently, the principle, when being understood strictly, might form a hindrance to the construction of a system of registration for corporeal movables and claims. Firstly, most corporeal movables and claims do not have any unique identifier, and this is the main reason why an object-based system is impossible. Secondly, a transaction perhaps involves a bulk of movable assets, such as all the inventories stored at a certain place, and it is often too costly to describe them one by one in detail. Thirdly, it is possible that parties include in the transaction future movables, namely movables that are not acquired or produced yet, and this also makes it difficult to describe the object involved.

However, this difficulty is not insurmountable. The practice in secured transactions of movables, regardless of whether registration has played a role, has offered an inspiration. It suffices that the objects involved are described with adequate accuracy first in the security agreement and then in the register. It is not necessary to describe each of the objects involved individually, nor to provide all details of every object in the register. For example, § 9-504 UCC requires, by reference to § 9-108, that the description of collateral in the financing statement "*reasonably identifies what is described*". A specific listing of each collateral involved is never necessary.[129] This approach is followed by the PPSAs in Canada and the new pledge register (*pandregister*) in Belgium.[130] The UNCITRAL also recommends that "*a description of the encumbered assets should be considered sufficient, for the purposes of both an effective security agreement and an effective registration, if it reasonably allows identification of the encumbered assets*".[131] Under the German law concerning the security transfer of corporeal movables and claims, where registration plays no rule, it suffices that the collateral is able to be clearly distinguished from other property of the security provider by virtue of the agreement.[132] Therefore, if a system of registration is introduced in Germany one day, it seems desirable to require the parties to have the

128 Dekker 2003, p. 171.

129 White and Summers 2012, p. 1228.

130 MacDougall 2014, p. 253-254; Bontinck 2017, p. 211-212.

131 UNCITRAL Guide on the Implementation of a Security Rights Registry, p. 77.

132 Bülow 2012, Rn. 1283, 1381.

description in the agreement of security transfer recorded in this system. This also, more or less, applies to Dutch law.[133]

It should be recognized that a general but sufficiently accurate description can satisfy the requirement of specificity. As a result, the system of registration may fail to inform third parties of each of the specific objects involved. However, with this description, third parties are able to ascertain what objects are involved. The possibility of a general but sufficiently accurate description creates three practical benefits. Firstly, parties do not have to make a specific list by describing each object involved, which guarantees that the system can operate smoothly and cheaply. For some assets, such as inventory, specific description of each item may be impractical. Secondly, a general description caters to the demand for disposing of future corporeal movables and claims. If a specific list has to be provided, then the disposal of future property would become impossible because parties may be unable to describe a thing they do not own. Thirdly, a general description also makes it possible to further dispose of the object without having to alter the registration. If there is a specific list, and one of the objects in this list is transferred later free from the existing property right, then this list needs to be updated to maintain its accuracy. Undoubtedly, this will affect the smooth operation of the system as well as the transaction. In a nutshell, the general description is flexible and can thus accommodate dynamic transactions of corporeal movables and claims.

What description can be deemed as sufficiently accurate? What level of generality of the description can be accepted? For example, is "*all corporeal movables owned by X*" or "*all corporeal movables stored at the place of Steenschuur 25 Leiden*" sufficiently accurate? How about "*all receivables against the debtors whose name starts with X*" and "*50% of all receivables*"? Will "*all present and future assets*" be recognized by law? In general, these are not only a question concerning interpretation, but also an issue depending on legal policy. The "*all present and future assets*" clause is sufficiently accurate itself. However, it is recognized in some jurisdictions but not allowed in other jurisdictions for policy reasons.[134] The "*50% of all receivables*" clause is not sufficiently accurate because it is impossible to identify which specific receivables are involved on the basis of this clause.[135]

---

133 Under Dutch law, it is generally possible to pledge a bulk of corporeal movables and claims, whether future or not, by describing the collateral pledged with sufficient accuracy in the deed of pledge. See Snijders and Rank-Berenschot 2017, p. 470, 483. At present, there is not any public register for general corporeal movables and claims in the Netherlands. It is conceivable that such description would be made visible to third parties if Dutch legislators were to introduce a system of public registration for general corporeal movables and claims one day.

134 This difference is a result of two policy concerns about the disposal of future property: one is the protection of the person who intends to dispose of future property, and the other is protection of unsecured creditors' interest in obtaining satisfaction of their claims. See UNCITRAL Legislative Guide on Secured Transactions, p. 78; Schuijling 2016, p. 53-62.

135 Rakob 2009, p. 98.

It is possible that the law stipulates the classes of movable property and requires parties to indicate the class to which the object involved belongs.[136] Within the framework of this research, corporeal movables and claims are two classes of property, and they might be further classified. For example, the class of corporeal movables might be divided into livestock, crops, inventory, equipment, and others. In addition to indicating the class of property to which the object belongs, the parties also need to describe the object to guarantee that the object can be reasonably identified.[137] The requirement of specifying the class of property serves two purposes: one is to facilitate the accuracy of the description of the object, and the other is to reduce the number of registrations a searcher needs to examine.[138] For example, if a third party wants to know about whether the inventory is encumbered with any security interest, this party does not have to pay attention to registrations concerning, for example, receivables.

Proposal 2:
The description of the object should be sufficiently accurate and third parties should be able to identify the object. The register should provide a classification of corporeal movables and claims, which includes, for example, inventory, equipment, livestock, crops, and receivables. There should also be a free text area so that the object can be further described in a general clause by indicating the name, type, location and other relevant features.

C The Description of the Transaction
In general, the legal relationship of property rights includes three elements: the subject (parties) of the right, the object of the right, and the content of the right. To make the legal relationship visible to third parties, it is necessary that the content of the right be shown by the subject-based register. Otherwise, the purpose of publicity will not be realized to a large extent.

For some registers for secured transactions of movables, description of the transaction or the content of the property right created is unnecessary. This is because the register is, under the functional approach, only

---

136 According to s. 2.3 (1) of Schedule 1 of Australian Personal Property Securities Regulations (2010), movable collateral has nine classes: "*(a) agriculture; (b) aircraft; (c) all present and after-acquired property; (d) all present and after-acquired property, except: (e) financial property; (f) intangible property; (g) motor vehicles; (h) other goods; and (i) watercraft.*" It should be noted that the classification is made for the purpose of registration of secured transactions concerning movables. In New Zealand, s. 8 (1) of Schedule 1 of Personal Property Securities Regulations (2001) divides movables into 13 types: "*(a) goods: motor vehicles; (b) goods: aircraft; (c) goods: livestock; (d) goods: crops; (e) goods: other; (f) documents of title; (g) chattel paper; (h) investment securities; (i) negotiable instruments; (j) money; (k) intangibles; (l) all present and after-acquired property; (m) all present and after-acquired property, except.*"

137 Under Australian law and New Zealand law, a further description of the collateral may have to be provided in the "*free text field*" to guarantee that the collateral can be ascertained. See Whittaker and Partner 2015, p. 168.

138 Whittaker and Partner 2015, p. 172.

established to show one interest: the security interest.[139] Security interest is defined broadly, including both limited property rights of security and title-based security device, such as reservation of ownership. In the aspect of publicity, Canadian law goes even further by treating long-term leases and outright assignment of claims as security interests, despite the fact that these two transactions do not perform any function of security.[140] Under Australian law, these two transactions are known as "*deemed security interests*" and can be entered in the register.[141] As the register is established only to publicize security interests, it is supposed that every registration concerns a transaction giving rise to a security interest. The registration does not show the details of the transaction, nor does it indicate whether the transaction will lead to a "deemed" security interest. The register only indicates that there is a certain proprietary right created on certain movables. The secured creditor might be a pledgee, a transferor who reserves ownership, a transferee who acquires ownership for security purposes, or even an owner who gives up possession to the lessee. Thus, unlike land registers, it does not indicate the content of the property right in detail. Searchers have to conduct further inquiries to know about the details.[142] In this sense, it can be said that the register is, like possession, an "abstract" means of publicity (see 3.2.1.2).[143]

In this research, we advocate that a brief description of the transaction be provided by the register so that searchers are able to have general knowledge about the transaction. This description can be brief to the degree that it is only described by several words. For example, if it is a transfer under a clause that the seller does not lose ownership until the price is paid off, then a simple indication of "*reservation of ownership*" suffices; in the situation where the transferor alienates and leases back the object, a mark of "*sale and leaseback*" is adequate. As has been shown above, it is possible that the law classifies the assets and requires the parties to indicate the class to which the object belongs. Likewise, the law can provide a list of transaction types and require parties to indicate the type of the transaction. For example, the list may include the following types of transactions: non-possessory pledge, reservation of ownership, transfer under other suspensive conditions, security transfer of ownership, lease (including financial lease, sale and

139 Whittaker and Partner 2015, p. 42-43; White and Summers 2012, p. 1153.
140 Walsh 2016, p. 81-84.
141 Brown 2016, p. 153-155.
142 See § 9-210 UCC, s. 275 Australian PPSA (2009), and s. 177 New Zealand PPSA (1999).
143 The UCC financing statement allows the filer to replace the "creditor/debtor" with one of the following alternative designations: "Lessee/Lessor", "Consignee/Consignor", "Seller/Buyer", "Bailee/Bailor" and "Licensee/Licensor" (see UCC Financing Statement 1). In this way, the parties are entitled to show the type of their transaction in the situation of lease, consigment, sale, bailment and license.

leaseback, and operating lease), trust, assignment, and other transactions.[144] With a simple mark, third parties would be able to have a rough understanding of the content of the transaction.[145]

The preceding list is just an example. In reality, legislators have to determine the transaction types according to property law. In general, property law implements the principle of *numerus clausus*, a principle giving rise to a closed list of property rights (see 2.1.1.1). As a result, the list of transaction types would need to be determined without violating the principle of *numerus clausus*. For example, security transfer of ownership is prohibited by Dutch law (art. 3:84 (3) BW), thus any future register introduced in the Netherlands will not include this type of transaction; non-possessory pledge cannot be found in German law, thus it is conceivable that this form of pledge would not be included if German legislators decide to introduce a register one day.[146]

In general, the requirement of indicating the transaction type briefly guarantees that searchers are able to have a general understanding of the transaction from the register. The indication lowers the possibility that the parties of the transaction provide incorrect information to the searcher. Moreover, the indication also helps the searcher determine whether to further inquire with the parties about the transaction. The indication makes the system of registration more than an "abstract" and ambiguous means of publicity. On the other hand, the requirement will increase the costs of operation of the system. In general, the costs additionally involved would not be high, because the requirement only involves a simple indication instead of a detailed description of the transaction. The benefits for third parties can outweigh the costs incurred.

Proposal 3:
The register should include a brief description of the transaction type, so that searchers are able to have a preliminary rough understanding of the transaction. A list of the transaction types should be provided under the principle of *numerus clausus* of the national law, such as by embodying reservation of title, financial lease, security transfer, sale and leaseback, non-possessory pledge, and operational lease. There should be a free text area in which further information concerning the transaction type can be provided.

---

144 Undoubtedly, where a transaction falls in the category of "other transactions", the parties have to describe this transaction briefly.

145 This reminds us of the pledge of order securities, such as bills of exchange payable to order. Where an order document is pledged, a mark of pledge can be recorded on the surface of the document so that subsequent acquirers can be aware of this encumbrance (see 4.2.3.5.B).

146 Moreover, for parties who create a "property right" in violation of the principle of *numerus clausus* and have this right registered, the right cannot bind third parties. The system of registration has to be subject to the principle.

5.3.1.2 A Digital System

After showing that it is possible to establish a subject-based system of registration for corporeal movables and claims, we now turn to the issue of how to construct this system. In general, the system is expected to be cheap, efficient, and user-friendly. To realize these purposes, the system should be digital (see 5.3.1.2), self-service (see 5.3.1.3), notice-based (see 5.3.1.4), and fully open (see 5.3.1.5).

The system should be digital rather than paper-based. Undoubtedly, digital systems are cheaper and more efficient than paper-based systems. For example, the storage of information in a digital database requires less space, and digital information is easier to search.[147] Moreover, the registry with a digital register can maintain a backup storage of the data so that the system can be reconstructed in the event of malfunction or physical destruction of the system. In general, reconstruction of a paper-based system seems much more difficult in the situation where the physical documents are damaged or destroyed.[148] Because of the achievements made in the area of information technology, it is easy and cheap to construct a digital register nowadays. In general, it can be said that digitalization has become an intrinsic feature of modern registers.

For example, Article 9 UCC and various PPSAs build a digital register for secured transactions of movable assets. The UNCITRAL recommends that member states take advantage of modern technology to construct an electronic register for the secured transaction of movables.[149] In the harmonization of the European law concerning secured transactions of movable assets, an electronic register is proposed.[150] In the field of immovable property, where registration is traditionally treated as a means of publicity, original paper-based land registers have been or are intended to be replaced by a digital system.[151] This indicates that making use of new information technology is commonly accepted in the construction of registers in property law.

Proposal 4:
The system should be digital and computerized by taking advantage of new information technologies.

147 UNCITRAL Legislative Guide on Secured Transactions, p. 158; Proprietary Security in Movable Assets 2014, p. 436.
148 UNCITRAL Legislative Guide on Secured Transactions, p. 163.
149 UNCITRAL Guide on the Implementation of a Security Rights Registry, p. 31-32.
150 See art. IX.-3:302 DCFR; Proprietary Security in Movable Assets 2014, p. 436.
151 The Law Commission 2001, p. 4; Wilhelm 2010, p. 250.

5.3.1.3 A Self-Service System

A digital system also allows individuals to register the transaction themselves, without having to rely on a registrar. In this research, we propose that the digital register for corporeal movables and claims should be self-service or direct-entry: parties can accomplish registration directly online, and there is no need to involve any registrar. In the viewpoint of Belgian legislators, this is an essential aspect of a modern register for secured transactions of movable property.[152]

Traditionally, entries in a register, such as the land register, are made by registrars. Parties who intend to have their transaction registered have to submit an application to the registrar. The registrar will verify whether the application satisfies the statutory requirements. The scope of verification varies, and the registrar's authority differs in different jurisdictions. For example, the registrar might play a quasi-judicial role, checking the validity of the transaction.[153] On the other hand, the registrar may only play a passive role and verify whether the document submitted satisfies formal requirements. The validity of the transaction falls outside of the scope of the verification.[154] In general, the registrar's check is not without costs. Even verifying the satisfaction of formal requirements takes time. Moreover, the registrar's verification also leads to a time gap between the application and the actual entry in the system. This time gap often means that a property right created cannot be shown by the system immediately and further affects the reliability of the system. In addition, the verification causes a risk of errors for which the registry needs to bear corresponding liabilities. A self-service system averts these problems because registration can be completed without the involvement of any registrar. Only a small number of technical workers are required to maintain the regular operation of the digital system. In sum, the self-service register is cheaper and more efficient and averts the problem of the time gap and the registrar making mistakes.[155]

A self-service system not only allows direct registration but also direct search. The latter means that third parties can inspect the system themselves, without having to involve any registrar. After becoming a client of the system, third parties can collect the information they want from the system independently. Therefore, the self-service system can reduce the costs of search.

In establishing a register for the secured transaction of movables, the self-service model is recommended by the UNCITRAL,[156] incorporated in

152 Bontinck 2017, p. 205.
153 Dekker 2003, p. 151-152.
154 Dekker 2003, p. 152-153.
155 UNCITRAL Legislative Guide on Secured Transactions, p. 158; Proprietary Security in Movable Assets 2014, p. 435.
156 UNCITRAL Legislative Guide on Secured Transactions, p. 151.

the DCFR,[157] and accepted by Belgian law.[158] The English Law Commission also proposes to restrict the involvement of registrars: "*the Registrar should no longer check the accuracy of the particulars or issue a conclusive certificate of registration*".[159] However, the registrar has to check the application under other systems of registration for secured transactions of movables, such as the Australian personal property security register. According to s. 150 (3) Australian PPSA, the registrar can reject the financing statement that is "*frivolous, vexatious or offensive, or contrary to the public interest*". In this research, we hold that such verification and rejection are not necessary. It suffices that the statement be treated as invalid. Moreover, it is always difficult for the registrar to judge whether a statement is "*frivolous, vexatious or offensive, or contrary to the public interest*". Thus, conflicts might arise between the applicant and the registry.

Proposal 5:
The register should be a self-service system, allowing users to complete registration and conduct investigations without involving any registrar. It suffices that the entire system is maintained by a group of technicians.

5.3.1.4 A Notice-Filing System

In the area of movable property, there are three types of registration. The first is the land-register-like system for some special movable assets, such as aircraft and vessels. These corporeal movables have remarkable similarities with land: they can be easily identified according to a unique index and have high value. Due to these similarities, a comprehensive system of registration is created. In the BW, an individual concept, i.e. "registerable property (*registergoederen*)", is raised to cover certain vessels, aircraft and immovable property. These assets all take registration as the means of publicity and are subject to the same rules of derivative acquisition.[160]

The other two types of registration are the notice-filing system and the transaction-filing system. These two systems mainly exist in the practice of secured transactions concerning movables. They differ in whether the details of the secured transaction have to be recorded in the system.[161] Different from the transaction-filing system which contains detailed information concerning the transaction, the notice-filing system provides third parties with only a simple notice, a warning that a security interest

157 Art. IX.-3:305 (1) DCFR: "*Entries in the register can be made directly by the secured creditor.*"

158 Bontinck 2017, p. 205-206.

159 The Law Commission 2005, p. 50.

160 Art. 3:10 BW: "*Registergoederen zijn goederen voor welke overdracht of vestiging inschrijving in daartoe bestemde openbare registers noodzakelijk is.*" English Translation: Art. 3:10 BW: "*Registerable property is things for which registration in an open register book is necessary for transfer thereof or creation of limited rights thereon.*"

161 Van den Heuvel 2004, p. 91.

might exist on the assets involved.[162] The contract on the basis of which the security interest is created does not have to be registered. At present, English law still has a transaction-filing system, while many other common law jurisdictions have established a notice-filing system, such as Article 9 UCC and the PPSAs.[163] The DCFR also proposes to construct a notice-filing system for security interests in movable assets.[164] The notice-filing model is also accepted by the Cape Town Convention on International Interests in Mobile Equipment which aims to create an object-based register.[165]

The fact that the notice-filing system only provides a simple notice or warning does not mean that third parties are unable to know about the details of the property right involved. The system is necessarily associated with a duty of disclosure.[166] The parties of the property right need to provide information concerning the right when inquired with by searchers.[167] The duty of disclosure guarantees that third parties are able to obtain further detailed information after inspecting the notice-filing system.[168] As the disclosure is central to the functioning of the system, legislators should regulate the time, the way, the language, and the legal effect of the disclosure, instead of leaving these matters to parties. Here it is worthwhile mentioning that the inquirer's reliance on the information disclosed needs to be protected. For example, if the inquirer is told that the object is not encumbered with any property right, but the reality proves to be the opposite, then the inquirer should not be bound by the existing rights; if the inquirer is misled that the object has been encumbered with a property right and thus gives up the transaction, damages should be available to the inquirer (see 5.3.3.5.B).[169]

In general, it is held in this research that a notice-filing system is better than the transaction-filing system. Firstly, the entry of a brief notice guarantees that the notice-filing system can operate smoothly.[170] This alleviates the fear that the burden of registration will unduly affect rapid transactions. This advantage of the notice-filing system has been demonstrated by the problem the present English transaction-filing system is confronted with. Under current English law, "*the weight of documentation*" causes a heavy

162 McCormack 2004, p. 130-131.
163 LoPucki, Abraham and Delahaye 2012, p. 21-24.
164 DCFR 2009, p. 4560; Proprietary Security in Movable Assets 2014, p. 435.
165 Van Erp 2004, p. 97.
166 See § 9-210 UCC, s. 275 Australian PPSA (2009), and s. 177 New Zealand PPSA (1999).
167 UNCITRAL Legislative Guide on Secured Transactions, p. 153; Proprietary Security in Movable Assets 2014, p. 512.
168 In this aspect, the notice-filing system is different from notification, a formality involved in the transaction of claims. In the latter situation, even the debtor is notified and knows about the disposal made by the creditor, the debtor bears no duty to disclose the disposal to inquirers (third parties). This is a reason why notification is not qualified as a means of publicity (see 4.1.1.2.C).
169 Proprietary Security in Movable Assets 2014, p. 524.
170 Van Erp 2004, p. 98.

burden to secured transactions.[171] For this reason, the English Law Commission intends to reform the present system by introducing a notice-filing system.[172] Moreover, the filing of simple notices allows the system to operate smoothly and averts the problem of overload of information. As a result, the system is easy to search for third parties.

However, the transaction-filing system also has its merits. In particular, it can provide more detailed information to third parties by allowing them to access the contract of creation.[173] As to this advantage, it should be mentioned that the notice-filing system also allows third parties to obtain detailed information by inquiring with relevant parties, such as the secured creditor. Under the system, the secured creditor has a duty to provide correct information concerning the security interest, as just presented. Moreover, even under a transaction-filing system, inquiries are often inevitable: "*no matter how perfect the information on the register it would be unrealistic to expect any register to render obsolete inquiries being made of the debtor or of the third party*".[174] Even where the contract creating the security interest is recorded, searchers cannot know exactly what assets are subject to the interest.[175]

Secondly, the notice-filing system alleviates the worry that the information registered might be misused, and the parties' privacy might be interfered with. In the practice of secured transactions of movables, there is always the concern that information collected from the open register might be used for illegal purposes, and debtors often do not want their secured debts to be known by others, especially their competitors.[176] In general, the worry seems justifiable under a transaction-filing system, because this system provides detailed information, for example, by recording the contract based on which the property is created.[177] However, the worry has no firm ground under a notice-filing system. As has been shown above, the notice-filing system only provides a simple notice, and searchers cannot know about details of the transaction from the system. It is unnecessary to fear that the simple notice will be misused. For searchers, the notice provided is just a clue for collecting detailed proprietary information further: the secured creditor bears a duty of disclosing detailed information.

Only at the stage of inquiry and disclosure, is there cause to worry about the misuse of information. This is because the information disclosed will concern details of the property right. For example, the contract creating the property right might be shown to the inquirer. To prevent unlawful use of the detailed information, one solution is to grant a right of approval to the

171 Bridge 2008, p. 188.
172 The Law Commission 2005, p. 4.
173 McCormack 2004, p. 140.
174 McCormack 2004, p. 140.
175 Whittaker and Partner 2015, p. 231.
176 Lwowski 2008, p. 178.
177 Whittaker and Partner 2015, p. 231.

debtor. For example, the DCFR provides that further information will only be provided to the inquirer when the debtor agrees.[178] The main purpose of this restriction is *"to avoid the secured creditor being approached for information concerning its proprietary security by persons who do not have any legitimate interest in this information"*.[179] A similar mechanism is implemented under the Australian PPSA.[180] In general, the restriction will not affect the right of searchers to collect detailed information. If the debtor refuses to give its approval, then prospective counterparties can simply refrain from entering transactions with the debtor.[181]

Proposal 6:
The register should be a notice-filing system without requiring individuals to record the contract or another "title" on the basis of which the property right is transferred or created. Advance registration, registration in the absence of any underlying contract created, should be recognized. However, the requirement of describing the transaction type must be fulfilled.

Proposal 7:
Upon the request of searchers, the parties of the transaction need to provide further information concerning the transaction in the prescribed manner. The disclosure of further information by one party might be restricted by granting the other party a right of approval.

5.3.1.5 A Fully Open System

As to the degree to which the system should be fully open to third parties, different rules exist. Some registers are open to third parties who have a legitimate reason to search the register, while other registers might be open to the public with no requirement of the searcher's qualification.[182] In the law of immovable property, this difference also exists. For example, under the German Land Register Ordiance (*Grundbuchordnung*), only those who have a legitimate interest can access the land register.[183] However, the Dutch land register (*Kadaster*) is, in general, fully open to the public with no restrictions.[184] In the common law, most registers for secured transactions

178 Art. IX.-3:319 (1) DCFR: *"Any registered secured creditor has a duty to answer requests for information by inquirers concerning the security right covered by the entry and the encumbered assets if these requests are made with the security provider's approval."*

179 Proprietary Security in Movable Assets 2014, p. 513.

180 According to s. 275 (6)(a) PPSA, the secured creditor can refuse to provide additional information by claiming that a confidentiality agreement exists between the creditor and the debtor. Therefore, the debtor can prevent the disclosure of details through a confidentiality agreement with the secured creditor. For sure, the creditor needs to provide further information when the debtor authorizes him or her to do so. See Duggan 2011, p. 887.

181 Proprietary Security in Movable Assets 2014, p. 513.

182 UNCITRAL Legislative Guide on Secured Transactions, p. 155.

183 Berlee 2018, p. 297.

184 Berlee 2018, p. 213.

concerning movables are open to the public without limitations: the notice-filing system under Article 9 UCC, the notice-filing system proposed by Book IX DCFR,[185] the PPSAs in Australia and New Zealand.[186] The register under the Belgian Law of Pledge (*Pandwet*) is also fully open to third parties (art. 34).[187] The English Law Commission recommends the construction of a notice-filing system which is fully open to "*any person*".[188] Thus, in the field of secured transactions concerning movables, a common feature of modern registers is that they are open to everyone.[189]

In this research, it is proposed that everyone should be entitled to access the system. This can be seen as an implication of the self-service or direct-entry notion (see 5.3.1.3): third parties should be allowed to search the system on their own. This notion means that no registrar is involved to check whether the searcher has a legitimate reason to inspect the system. The proposal of a fully open system may meet resistance regarding privacy, especially in the field of secured transactions concerning movable assets. In the following discussion, we take the register for the secured transaction concerning movable assets as an example, arguing that a fully open system does not form a threat to privacy.

It is often argued that a completely open system of registration might be undesirable for the business debtor who provides proprietary security: the debtor is often unwilling to let its competitors or clients know about the proprietary security from the register.[190] The information about the proprietary security is commercial information that might form a part of the debtor's business privacy. Moreover, the publicity of proprietary security may give rise to a problem of "*false poverty*": "*everyone is told to assume that the assets in the debtor's possession are not held free of encumbrances*".[191] As a result, potential creditors would become more conservative in granting credits.[192] In the situation of natural-person debtors, a potential problem of registration is that their personal information is exposed to the public, which cause a concern about the protection of personal privacy.

In general, the privacy concern has no sufficient ground and should not be overstated under a notice-filing system. The protection of personal privacy of natural persons is not a sufficient reason to restrict the access to the register by third parties. This is demonstrated below in detail (see 5.3.2.2). Here we give further attention only to the situation where the secu-

185 Art. IX.-3:317 DCFR: "*Access to the register for searching purposes is open to anyone, subject to the payment of fees; it does not depend upon a consent by the security provider or the secured creditor.*"

186 See s. 169 Australian PPSA and s. 171 New Zealand PPSA.

187 Baeck and Heytens 2019, p. 22.

188 The Law Commission 2005, p. 54.

189 See art. IX.-3:317 DCFR, Recommendation 54 (g) UNCITRAL Legislative Guide on Secured Transactions, and s. 170 Australian PPSA (2009).

190 Lwowski 2008, p. 178; Snijders 1970, p. 29.

191 Sigman 2008, p. 158-159.

192 Vriesendorp and Barendrecht 1993, p. 29.

rity provider is a company or business entity. For the following reasons, our conclusion is that the concern about business privacy is not a sufficient reason to restrict the accessibility of the system.

Firstly, subsequent acquirers, whether existing or potential, have a justified ground to know about the information concerning the secured transaction.[193] As a principle, subsequent acquirers will be bound by the proprietary security interest. By granting proprietary security, the debtor gives rise to an information asymmetry to its existing and potential creditors because of the third-party effect of the property right of security. Thus, proprietary security should be made transparent to the public. Otherwise, third parties would be misled. In fact, the statutory requirement of publishing financial reports also indicates that every enterprise should run in financial transparency: the enterprise should disclose its financial condition to the public. Like the financial report, a fully open system helps existing and potential general creditors to know about the overall financial health of the debtor. Unlike the financial report, a fully open system also allows subsequent acquirers to know about the proprietary condition of specific assets.

Secondly, the system of registration proposed is notice-based, which means that the document filed is merely a summary of the secured transaction. There seems to be no need to fear that the disclosure of such summary will be misused to the extent that the debtor's business is influenced. In this aspect, a notice-filing system is different from the transaction-filing system (see 5.3.1.4).

> *"Permitting full public access does not compromise the confidentiality of the relationship between a grantor and a secured creditor. Confidentiality is protected because only limited information about the parties' affairs appears in the registered notice."*[194]

Truly, the notice-filing system is associated with the duty of disclosure, and the information disclosed by the creditor is more detailed than the summary filed in the register. There might be a concern that the detailed information disclosed might be misused illegally. However, it is possible to dispel this worry by allowing the debtor to decide whether details can be offered by the secured creditor (see 5.3.1.4). As has been pointed out in 5.3.1.4, the DCFR grants a right of approval to the debtor who is entitled to request the creditor not to disclose the details of the proprietary security to third parties (art. IX.-3:319 (1)). Therefore, if the debtor thinks that detailed information might be misused by a third party, he or she can require the creditor not to provide any detailed information to this third party. In a word, the fear of the misuse of information should not be treated as an adequate reason to refuse a fully open system of registration.

Thirdly, the concern of false poverty mentioned above is not a convincing counter-argument against a fully open system. The reason is simple. By

---

193 Vriesendorp and Barendrecht 1993, p. 29.
194 UNCITRAL Legislative Guide on Secured Transactions, p. 155.

virtue of commercial knowledge and experience, prudent businesspeople are often aware that there is a high possibility that the asset possessed by the debtor is encumbered with a security interest (see 3.5.2.2.B). Therefore, if there is the problem of false poverty, it already existed before introducing the system of registration.[195] Moreover, the rule of the "ordinary course of business" allows the collateral to be disposed of without being affected by the security interest registered, provided that the disposal arises in the ordinary course of the debtor's business (see 5.3.3.3.B).[196] The rule can address the problem of false poverty in relation to third parties to some extent. For third parties to a transaction arising in the ordinary course of the debtor's business, registration does not constitute a constructive notice. Under the rule, third parties are entitled to acquisition free from the proprietary security. This means that they can carry out the transaction without having to search the register. The debtor's ordinary business will not be influenced, though the register is fully open and allows every third party to know about the proprietary security provided by the debtor. In other words, the problem of false poverty does not arise in the ordinary course of the debtor's business.

Proposal 8:
The register should be fully open to the public.

5.3.1.6 *Summary*

On the basis of the preceding discussion, we can conclude that the system constructed for corporeal movables and claims is a subject-based register, a register indexed according to the party's identifier. The system only provides a simple notice to third parties who can further inquire with relevant parties to collect more detailed information. The system is digital, fully open, and able to be accessed by users directly without involving any registrar. By constructing the register in this way, the costs of operation would not be high. This has been proven by contemporary systems of registration for the secured transaction of movables.

> *"Experience in the United States [...], Canada and New Zealand has demonstrated repeatedly that the costs of creation and installation of an electronic notice filing system are low and quickly recouped, that costs of current operation of such a system are low and are covered by minimal filing fees, and that the business world adapts to the system easily and without great cost or dislocation."*[197]

On the basis of the preceding discussion, we provide a basic sample of the registration below (Figure 15). This sample is just an example and is open to modifications when necessary.

---

195 Secured Transactions Law Reform Project 2013, p. 4.
196 UNCITRAL Legislative Guide on Secured Transactions, p. 202-204.
197 Sigman 2008, p. 158.

Statement				
	01	Registration Time		_ _ (dd) _ _ (mm) _ _ _ _ (yyyy) _ _ (hh) _ _ (mm)[198]
	02	Registration Number		_ _ _ _ _ _ _ _
	03	Registration Duration		☐ 6 Months ☐ 1 Year ☐ 2 Years ☐ 3 Years ☐ 4 Years ☐ Maximum ☐ Specified Duration ______[199]
PARTY 1	04	Natural Person	Name	______ (First Given Name) ______ (Second Given Name) ______ (Family Name)
	05		Date of Birth	_ _ (dd) _ _ (mm) _ _ (yyyy)
	06	Legal Person and Others	Name	
	07		Operation Number	
	08	Address	______ (House Number and Avenue) ______ (City) ______ (Province) _ _ _ _ _ _ (Postcode)	
PARTY 2	09	Natural Person	Name	______ (First Given Name) ______ (Second Given Name) ______ (Family Name)
	10		Date of Birth	_ _ (dd) _ _ (mm) _ _ _ _ (yyyy)
	11	Legal Person and Others	Name	
	12		Operation Number	
	13	Address	______ (House Number and Avenue) ______ (City) ______ (Province) _ _ _ _ _ _ (Postcode)	
OBJECT & TRANSACTION	14	Object 1	Object Description	☐ Equipment ☐ Inventory ☐ Livestock ☐ Crops ☐ Other Corporeal Movables ☐ Receivables ☐ Other Claims[200]
	15			Additional Description:[201]
	16		Transaction Description	☐ Pledge ☐ Reservation of Title ☐ Financial Lease ☐ Security Transfer of Title ☐ Sale and Leaseback ☐ Operating Lease ☐ Others[202]
	17			Additional Description:
	18	Object 2	Object Description	☐ Equipment ☐ Inventory ☐ Livestock ☐ Crops ☐ Other Corporeal Movables ☐ Receivables ☐ Other Claims
	19			Additional Description:
	20		Transaction Description	☐ Pledge ☐ Reservation of Title ☐ Financial Lease ☐ Sale and Leaseback ☐ Security Transfer of Title ☐ Operating Lease ☐ Others
	21			Additional Description:
OTHER INFORMATION	22			

Figure 15

198 The date of registration is not determined by the filer him- or herself. The filer does not need to fill in the date. Instead, the date on which registration is completed is fixed by the system automatically.

199 About the duration of the validity of registration, see 5.3.3.6.

200 There are various classifications of the object, and this sample only provides an example here. For instance, it is also useful to consider the criterion of whether the object is future property.

201 The description by ticking the box is often not sufficiently precise or incorrect. Therefore, it might be necessary for parties to insert an additional description here.

202 There are various ways to classify transactions, and this sample only provides a simple example here. As we have argued above, the classification of transactions is subject to the principle of *numerus clausus* (see 5.3.1.1.C).

5.3.2 The Scope of Registration

After introducing how to establish a notice-filing system for corporeal movables and claims, we turn to the issue concerning the scope of registration. It should be noted first that not all transactions concerning corporeal movables or claims should be required to be entered in the system. In general, there are multiple reasons to exempt a transaction from the formality of registration, and we discuss these reasons here.

5.3.2.1 The Aspect of Object

Registration is used to address the problem of information asymmetry by providing proprietary information to third parties (see 2.2.3.2). Therefore, registration becomes superfluous when the problem does not exist or has been addressed in other ways.

A Impersonal Transactions

Arruñada demonstrates that asymmetry of information mainly arises in the situation of "impersonal transactions", a kind of dealing which does not rely on local knowledge in relation to parties' reputation and characters.[203] "*Personal transactions*", as opposed to impersonal transactions, usually take place in a close-knit community where members know each other quite well and are encouraged to be honest and cooperative.[204] In a tight community, transactions between members are often not asymmetric in information.

> *"When parties know each other well, they suffer less information asymmetry about the value of each other's promises; thus, conflicts are less likely. Moreover, they also know which safeguards will be activated if a conflict eventually arises. This knowledge facilitates economic exchange [...]."*[205]

Possession, as a source of "*cruder signals*", suffices in a close-knit community but is inadequate in a complex society.[206] This is partly because "*close-knit groups have a variety of advantages including low-cost communication, homogeneity of knowledge, opportunity to monitor, and so on*".[207] It seems that history supports this observation: ancient people lived in an acquaintance society and did not have a formal system of registration. It is possession that acted as a basic role in transactions in ancient society.[208] At that time, people were satisfied with possession, though it was an ambiguous means of publicity.

---

203 Arruñada 2012, p. 15-16.
204 Ellickson 1991, p. 167.
205 Arruñada 2012, p. 15-16.
206 Lipson 2005, p. 507.
207 Smith 2003, p. 1122.
208 In general, the importance of possession is indicated by *traditio* under Roman law, *Gewere* in Germanic law, and *livery of seisin* in the history of English law.

Contemporary society is obviously different: transactions take place between strangers frequently. Under the influence of electronic business, the transactions between strangers become more common. Where two strangers plan to enter into a transaction, there is usually a problem of information asymmetry. This is because they do not know each other's personality or characteristics well. In Arruñada's words, the transaction is "*impersonal*". To address the problem of information, it might be desirable to have a formal system of publicity.

However, not all contemporary transactions are carried out on an impersonal basis. For example, Bernstein conducted research into the diamond industry and found that participants of this industry often make use of local information in the course of business.

> *"Smaller dealers, brokers, and foreigners do most of their trading in the club. For them, club membership provides a secure trading place at a modest cost with additional informational benefits."*[209]

Therefore, the possibility exists that individuals in a certain industry still rely on informal methods to address the problem of information. Under this circumstance, there is no need to introduce any formal method of publicity.

> *"Community can be a proxy for more formal methods of gathering and disseminating information, such as notice filing systems. Notice filing may not matter to diamond merchants inter se because they know-or believe they know-all that is important to know about one another in order to trade internally."*[210]

The preceding discussion explains why the desire for a system of registration is not strong in the diamond industry, despite the high value of the object. It can also, more or less, apply to expensive works of art, jewelry and precious animals. Usually, the transaction of these special movables is under the assistance of professionals and involves certain authoritative documents, such as the certificate of title. This largely diminishes the information asymmetry between transacting parties.

The preceding observation is important for constructing a system of registration for corporeal movables and claims. Since whether information asymmetry exists in a type of transaction is not always clear for legislators, registration should not be mandatory. For those who do not face any information asymmetry in a certain community or industry, mandatory registration is not only unnecessary but also unfair. It prevents them from acquiring property rights without involving registration. For this reason, registration should not be treated as a constitutive condition (see 5.3.3.1), and good faith

209 Bernstein 1992, p. 120.
210 Lipson 2005, p. 506.

should be a condition for the acquisition free from an existing property right (see 5.3.3.4). In general, this allows parties in a certain industry to conduct "*personal transactions*" with security, even though registration is not completed. Third parties in the same industry can be assumed to know about the transaction and thus cannot declare the transaction ineffective against them.

B Securities

As a matter of course, where there is a method that has addressed the problem of information asymmetry, registration will be of little use.[211] Registration is not the only means of publicity of property rights. If there already is an appropriate method of publicity, it will be superfluous to replace this method with registration.

A typical example is monetary securities, such as bills of exchange. As has been shown above, this type of document embodies a claim of payment and can serve as a conclusive source of information (see 4.2.3.5.A and 4.2.3.5.B). Third parties are able to be aware of the legal relationship by glancing at the document, and thus there is no need to introduce registration for the claim embodied.[212] In addition, it is undesirable to include monetary securities *per se* in the system of registration, despite the fact that they have a defect of invisibility (see 4.2.3.5.C). Monetary securities position negotiability as a primary goal, and a formality of registration would make this function impossible.

> "*Negotiability necessitates that subsequent acquirers be able to rely fully on a person's possession as indicative of ownership without having to conduct further inquiries. Requiring them to search and file would be inconsistent with that goal.*"[213]

The preceding discussion also applies to another type of document, securities to goods (see 4.2.2.5). Truly, securities to goods are a document embodying a claim of recovery of the goods involved (namely the relationship of indirect possession). However, this type of document can also show some proprietary relationships of the goods, such as the right of pledge. Therefore, the asymmetry of information can be alleviated to a large extent. Moreover, the principal function of securities to goods is, like monetary securities, to streamline transactions. This function will be completely ruined if the law introduces registration into this field. In the process of harmonizing European private law, the DCFR also takes a humble attitude by excluding registration from "*negotiable documents of title*" including securities to goods.[214]

---

211 Baird and Jackson 1983, p. 190.
212 Walsh 2016, p. 87; Gullifer 2012, p. 467.
213 Walsh 2016, p. 87.
214 See art. IX.-3:202 DCFR and IX.-3:203 DCFR.

However, we have to acknowledge that securities cannot provide all necessary information to third parties, which has been shown above (see 4.2). Under contemporary laws, only the property right of pledge is recordable on the document, which seems to be inadequate. It seems desirable that the law allows and requires individuals to show more types of property rights and transactions (such as reservation of ownership) by recording a corresponding mark, at least when the document involved is created to order. Once the document is able to record more property rights and convey more information, the demand for information by third parties can be satisfied to a larger extent.

Proposal 9:
Money, securities to goods and securities of payment should be excluded from the system of registration.

C Corporeal Movables
Nowadays, ownership of corporeal movables is often transferred under a resolutive or suspensive condition, such as security transfer of ownership and retention of ownership. Conditional transfer often implies that ownership and possession are held by different parties. For example, reservation of ownership, a type of transfer under a suspensive condition, leads the transferor to retain ownership, while the transferee obtains possession. More importantly, conditional transfer might give rise to a distribution of interests between the transferor and the transferee in the proprietary sense.[215] The distribution gives rise to relativity of ownership in the sense that the owner is subject to certain proprietary limitations.[216] In the case of reservation of ownership, both the transferor and the transferee enjoy certain proprietary interests. Undoubtedly, this makes the legal relationship of ownership complicated, and third parties cannot be expected to know about the relationship. As a result, conditional transfer of corporeal movables needs to be filed in the system of registration. The same also applies to temporary transfer or transfer subject to a suspensive or resolutive term.[217]

215 Under Dutch law, both parties obtain "conditional ownership (*voorwaardelijke eigendomsrecht*)". According to German law, conditional transfer may allow one of the parties to obtain a proprietary "right of expectation (*Anwartschaftsrecht*)". See Sagaert and Gruyaert 2017, p. 423-426.

216 Rank-Berenschot 1992, p. 225-230.

217 According to art. 3:85 BW, the obligation aiming at transferring ownership under a term is automatically converted to an obligation of creating a right of usufruct. The fundamental rationale behind this statutory conversion is that ownership is perpetual and "temporary ownership", which in essence amounts to a right of usufruct, is unknown in Dutch law. See Snijders and Rank-Berenschot 2017, p. 151. In German law, the rules applicable to conditional transfer can also apply to temporary transfer. As a result, a right of expectation can follow from a transfer of ownership subject to a term. See Wolf and Neuner 2012, p. 654; Bork 2016, Rn. 1286.

In general, conditional transfer forms a contrast to the outright transfer. The latter is usually accompanied by actual delivery: both ownership and actual control pass from the transferor to the transferee concurrently. Outright transfer may occur in commercial transactions and non-commercial situations, such as our daily shopping in supermarkets. More importantly, no distribution of proprietary interests occurs between the transferor and the transferee, and no new property rights are created. The transferee obtains the right of ownership completely. For third parties, the outright transfer is complete: the transferee obtains both ownership and the abstract appearance, i.e. actual possession. Ownership and actual possession are held by the same person. Before the transfer, the transferor is able to dispose of the object. The transferee obtains no property right that can bind third parties and does not have any chance to mislead third parties. After the transfer, the transferee is able to dispose of the object. The transferor no longer has any right that can bind third parties and does not have any chance to mislead third parties.

Truly, outright transfer is not made completely visible by actual delivery. However, the transfer *per se* does not cause any additional information asymmetry to third parties. Registration will only create useless burden to the transacting parties. In this aspect, outright transfer is different from the security transfer of ownership and reservation of ownership. In the latter two situations, ownership shifts under a condition, which implies a distribution of proprietary interests between the transferor and the transferee. More importantly, the proprietary distribution is invisible and thus causes an additional burden of information on third parties. In general, it is desirable to show the distribution through registration. In sum, where ownership is transferred in a way that both the transferor and the transferee enjoy a proprietary position, there is a need for registration.

In line with the preceding discussion, the creation of a limited property right on corporeal movables (such as pledge and usufruct) should also be registered. In essence, creating limited property rights means distribution of proprietary interests between the owner and the acquirer of the right. Limited property rights constitute, in the words of Hugo Grotius, "sliced ownership (*gebreckelicke eigendom*)".[218] Here we take pledge as an example. Pledge implies a proprietary distribution between the pledgor and the pledgee. The pledgor's right of ownership is encumbered with the pledgee's right of pledge. The creation of pledge will cause additional information asymmetry that cannot be eliminated without employing a new means of publicity. Here we cannot rely on possession. Once the pledgor gives up possession of the collateral to the pledgee, the former's right of ownership becomes hidden. If the law allows the pledgor to keep possession and the pledgor does this, then the right of pledge will inevitably become invisible.

---

218 Smits 1996, p. 59.

To overcome this difficulty, registration seems necessary. About the issue of publicity of possessory pledge, a detailed discussion is provided later (see 5.4.3.2).

From the discussion above, we can summarize that where ownership of corporeal movables is associated with indirect possession, there is in principle a need for registration. In general, that the owner only has indirect possession is a result of granting certain proprietary interests to others. In the situation of reservation of ownership, the transferor retains ownership but only holds indirect possession, and the transferee obtains direct possession with a proprietary interest. In the situation of possessory pledge, the pledgor enjoys ownership but only has indirect possession, and the pledgee holds direct possession with a proprietary interest, namely the right of pledge. As has been shown above, both reservation of ownership and possessory pledge should be registered. Here it is worthwhile reiterating that indirect possession is hidden and cannot show ownership to third parties. In the two examples (reservation of ownership and possessory pledge), registration not only makes ownership visible, but also shows the owner's indirect possession to third parties.

If both unencumbered ownership and direct possession are held by the same person, there is no need of registration, despite the fact that direct possession is only an abstract means of publicity. This is not difficult to understand. Registration should be conducted in the situation where possession and unencumbered ownership are separated. If third parties find no registration concerning the object after searching the register with reference to the actual possessor's registration, they can safely presume that the actual possessor enjoys ownership free from any proprietary encumbrance. For this reason, we argue that the transfer of ownership with actual delivery does not need registration.

On the basis of the preceding discussion, we can further conclude that registration precludes *bona fide* acquisition of corporeal movables. Typically, *bona fide* acquisition occurs where the disponer has possession but lacks authority of disposal (e.g. transfer by a lessee) or lacks authority of disposal free from existing encumbrance (e.g. transfer by the owner of a bicycle pledged). In essence, the rule of *bona fide* acquisition is an *ex-post* regime, serving to resolve conflicts that have occurred. As a result, one of the conflicting parties will lose. A system of registration can diminish *bona fide* acquisition of corporeal movables significantly. Third parties can easily know from this system whether the possessor has actual ownership and whether the object is encumbered with any proprietary interest. For example, registration of possessory pledge makes it difficult for the pledgee to dispose of the collateral by misleading third parties, and the conflict between third parties and the pledgor is prevented. Therefore, the introduction of a system of registration will narrow the scope of application of the rule of *bona fide* acquisition, a rule centered on possession.

In sum, where full ownership and actual possession of corporeal movables shift concurrently, there is no need for registration. The transferor gives up all proprietary interests to the transferee, and no misleading or problem of information is triggered to third parties.[219] On the contrary, if the ownership is transferred under a condition or term or encumbered with a limited property right, registration is desirable to make the conditional or temporary transfer or the limited right visible to third parties.

Proposal 10:
As a starting point, the register should be allowed to include all transactions that give rise to a divergence between ownership and actual possession of corporeal movables. Transfer of corporeal movables under a condition or term able to give rise to proprietary effect and creation of a limited property right on corporeal movables should be registerable.

D Claims
In general, claims do not have an outward appearance, and notification to the debtor involved does not qualify as a means of publicity (see 4.1.1.2).

> *"Turning to receivables, the relevance of the publicity principle is less strong. Whereas corporeal movables are at least visible to third parties, receivables are not. Their very creation is the result of a private act. They can be varied or extinguished by private act."*[220]

Nowadays, the transaction of claims remains in a hidden state in many jurisdictions. Indeed, there are some rules granting protection to third parties, such as the notification-first rule (see 4.1.3.1) and the abstraction principle (see 4.1.3.2). However, these rules are an *ex-post* scheme that inevitably sacrifice one's interest for the protection of another's. Because of the serious information asymmetry, individuals cannot determine their priority at the commencement of the transaction.[221]

For this reason, the starting point is that registration should be introduced to the disposal of claims, regardless of whether the disposal is an outright assignment, a security assignment, or the creation of a limited property right. Registration is an appropriate solution for the problem of

---

219 Transfer of ownership in the way of actual delivery might have a problem of information in an important situation: the underlying contract of transfer is defective. Under the causation principle, where the disposal is not independent from the underlying agreement, the transferee obtains no ownership because of the defect. As a result, possession and ownership fall apart: the possessor (transferee) acquires no ownership and bears a duty to return possession of the object. If the transferee disposes of the object to a third party, a conflict will arise between the transferor and this third party. This conflict cannot be prevented by registration. The defect cannot be made visible by the register. As to which side will prevail, this is an issue concerning legal policy: should the third party's interest of reliance be protected in priority to the transferor's interest of preservation of ownership (see 5.1.4.2.E).

220 The Scottish Law Commission 2011, p. 94.

221 Schwarcz 1999, p. 461.

information concerning the transaction of claims.[222] The importance of registration, especially in the situation of cross-border transactions, has been confirmed by empirical studies by the CEAL (Center for the Economic Analysis of Law).[223] By virtue of registration, the legal status of claims can be clearly shown to third parties.

There are various types of claims, and the transactions of claims are diverse. Not every disposal of every claim needs to be registered. It has been demonstrated that registration is unnecessary for the claim embodied with securities to goods and securities of payment (see 5.3.2.1.B). In this part, we further show that registration is useless in other situations where claims are acquired.

D1: Acquisition Through Novation

The first situation examined is novation of the legal relationship of obligations. In fact, novation is not a disposal of claims. Novation arises in two different situations: (1) an old obligation is replaced with a new obligation between the same parties (objective novation); and (2) a new party replaces one of the original parties (subjective novation).[224] In the latter situation, an outsider may step into the shoes of the original creditor, obtaining a claim against the original debtor. The result of this novation resembles assignment but is based on a *tripartite* agreement: the debtor has to be involved in the agreement.[225] In this very situation, the chance that the retreating party (the original creditor) will deceive third parties by disposing of the original claim is very low.[226] Therefore, there is no need to register the novation.

D2: Acquisition Through Merger, Division or Inheritance

The second situation is that the assignment of claims is a result of the merger or division of businesses.[227] In this situation, the original creditor (the enterprise merged or divided) comes to an end, which implies that there is no need to worry about deceptive disposal by the original creditor. For example, company A is merged by company B, and A's claims are obtained by B automatically; A loses its legal capacity after this merger, and thus the possibility of assigning the claims by A does not exist. By the same token, registration is of no use for the acquisition of claims on the basis of inheritance.

222 Just as in the situation of corporeal movables, registration cannot fully prevent conflicting disposal of claims either. For example, in consecutive assignments, should the original creditor (the first-hand) deceived by the second-hand be protected in priority to a third party (the third-hand) acting in good faith? This is an issue of legal policy. In general, registration cannot prevent illegal deception and the like.

223 Schwarcz 1999, p. 466.

224 Black's Law Dictionary, p. 1064.

225 Zimmermann 1990, p. 60; The Scottish Law Commission 2011, p. 29.

226 Cuming, Walsh, and Wood 2012, p. 172.

227 Beale 2016, p. 10.

D3: Giro Transfer and Bank Accounts

The third situation concerns bank accounts. Nowadays, it is common that debtors discharge their duty of payment through a bank account. In the jargon of law, the holder of bank accounts is a creditor of the service bank, enjoying a claim against the bank within the scope of the surplus of the account.[228] With an account, the holder can instruct the service bank to "transfer" a certain amount of money to another person designated. The recipient also has a bank account issued either by the same bank or by another bank. The result of the "transfer" is that the payor's account and the payee's account are debited and credited respectively by the same amount. In general, the entire process of payment not only involves the payor-payee relationship, but also a relationship between the payer and its service bank as well as a relationship between the payee and its service bank.[229] Payment through a bank account is also known as giro payment or giro transfer. This form of payment is not assignment of claim: the result is not that the payee obtains the claim enjoyed by the payor against the service bank.[230] Instead, the payee acquires a new claim against its own service bank. In general, the consequence of giro payment, i.e. debiting the payer's account and crediting the payee's account, can be immediately shown by the balance of the account. There is no chance for the payor (the original creditor) to dispose of the same sum by misleading third parties. Therefore, giro payment should not be subject to the formality of registration. Moreover, the formality will ruin this swift method of payment.

Bank accounts are not only used for the purpose of payment. Holding deposit accounts implies enjoying a pecuniary claim against the depositary bank. Therefore, the holder, as a creditor, is able to dispose of this claim to a third party.[231] For example, the holder can assign the claim in whole or in part. Naturally, similar consequences can be reached through giro transfer. However, this does not mean that the holder cannot assign the claim as an ordinary personal right. To assign the claim successfully, all requirements for assignment of ordinary claims have to be fulfilled. The claim might be used as collateral by the account holder. For example, it can be pledged by the creditor. Because of the giro payment, pledge of this collateral has a feature: "*the deposit account is indeed a floating security interest, which ebbs and flows; one day, the secured creditor might have no security (the account is overdrawn) and the next day it might be oversecured*".[232] To pledge the claim,

228 Bierens 2009, p. 28; Dubovec 2014, p. 121.
229 Van Empel and Huizink 1991, p. 7-13; Rank 1994, p. 173-174.
230 Mijnssen 2017, p. 54; Rank 1994, p. 176; Van der Lely 2008, p. 170.
231 In reality, the holder and the depositary bank may in an agreement restrict the former's right to assign the claim or to create a property right on the claim. In relation to this contractual restriction, different rules are applied: the restriction has proprietary effect in some jurisdictions but cannot bind third parties in other jurisdictions. See UNCITRAL Legislative Guide on Secured Transactions, p. 96.
232 Dubovec 2014, p. 144.

all requirements for pledge of ordinary claims need to be satisfied.[233] It has been demonstrated that, as a starting point, the disposal of claims should be made visible to third parties by a system of registration. In this research, we hold that registration is a useful means of publicity for assignment and pledge of receivables out of a bank account. There is no reason to treat the disposal of this type of claim differently from ordinary claims in the aspect of publicity.

All in all, claims have become a popular type of asset involved in various transactions, such as factoring and securitization. It is said that *"in developed countries the bulk of corporate wealth is locked up in receivables"*.[234] Therefore, it is necessary to include claims in the system of registration to facilitate certainty of the transaction of claims.

Proposal 11:
Assignment of claims and the creation of proprietary rights on claims should be included in the register. Acquisition of claims through novation, merge and division of entities, inheritance, and giro transfer should be excluded from the register.

E Value of the Object

In determining the scope of registration from the perspective of the object, a relevant factor is the value of the object. An important reason why the majority of movables do not have a general system of registration is that

233 Rakob 2009, p. 93; Van der Lely 2008, p. 171. However, there is a tendency to treat the claim as a special collateral and govern security interests on this collateral by special rules. In Europe, the Financial Collateral Directive (Directive 2002/47/EC) stipulates in art. 3 that *"Member States shall not require that the creation, validity, perfection, enforceability or admissibility in evidence of a financial collateral arrangement or the provision of financial collateral under a financial collateral arrangement be dependent on the performance of any formal act."* However, this formality-free rule was amended for bank accounts in 2009. According to art. 2 (6) (a) Directive 2009/44/EC, *"Member States shall not require that the creation, validity, perfection, priority, enforceability or admissibility in evidence of such financial collateral be dependent on the performance of any formal act such as the registration or the notification of the debtor of the credit claim provided as collateral. However, Member States may require the performance of a formal act, such as registration or notification, for purposes of perfection, priority, enforceability or admissibility in evidence against the debtor or third parties."* In the US, Article 9 UCC also provides special rules for creating security interests on bank accounts. Notably, Article 9 UCC stipulates, in addition to registration, a new method of perfection: control. In general, control can arise in three situations: (1) control is automatic if the secured creditor is the depositary bank; (2) the secured creditor substitutes for the debtor as the holder of the bank account involved; and (3) an agreement of control is created between the debtor, the creditor and the depositary bank. See White and Summers 2012, p. 1211. It is often deemed that control of accounts resembles possession of corporeal things. Nevertheless, *"control is not, like registration in a general security rights registry, a transparent method of achieving third-party effectiveness"*. See UNCITRAL Legislative Guide on Secured Transactions, p. 139. In this research, we do not probe into the issue of whether control is an appropriate means of publicity for the claim out of depositary accounts.

234 Schwarcz 1999, p. 455.

their value is too low to outweigh the costs of registration.[235] On the other hand, some special movable things (such as motor vehicles, vessels, and aircraft) have high value and are thus registerable just like immovable property.[236] In the following discussion, we focus on whether the value of the object should be treated as relevant.

Before starting the discussion, it is worthwhile mentioning that in practice one transaction often involves a number of movable assets, rather than only one asset. Moreover, the assets involved are not confined to be existing, and parties may dispose of future property. The "value of the object" does not refer to the value of each single asset, but the aggregate amount of all the assets involved in one transaction. The question is, precisely speaking, whether "*small transactions*",[237] also known as "*low-value transactions*",[238] deserve registration from the perspective of efficiency.

With respect to this issue, different opinions exist. Some argue for recognition of a minimum threshold on the basis of two reasons: one is that excluding small transactions can avoid cluttering up the system,[239] and the other is that such exclusion will assist small businesses that often carry out small transactions.[240] Opponents contend that there is no need to establish any condition regarding the transactional amount under the context of the voluntary registration, since individuals themselves "*would not bother to file in respect of one-off transactions where only a small amount was concerned*".[241] Another reason is that exclusion of small transactions would "*open up opportunities for secured parties to game the system*" by splitting their transaction into several ones so that each is under the threshold.[242]

In this research, we recommend that the law should set up a minimum threshold for the value of the object. The principal reason is that registration of a low-value transaction cannot produce benefits that can outweigh the administrative costs and the adverse effect of registration on the smooth operation of transactions. Indeed, excluding low-value transactions will give rise to an invisible risk to third parties. However, the low value of the object implies that this risk will not cause significant damage to third parties.

In reality, the parties to a low-value transaction would not bother to register this transaction. For this practical reason, the law should positively affirm that these parties will not face any disadvantages because of the absence of registration. If the law requires and allows registration of low-value transactions, treating them and high-value transactions in the same way, individuals would face the following dilemma: registering the low-

235 Clarke and Kohler 2005, p. 388.
236 Mattei 2000, p. 68; Lurger 2006, p. 51.
237 The Law Commission 2002, p. 204.
238 Whittaker and Partner 2015, p. 111.
239 The Law Commission 2002, p. 204.
240 Whittaker and Partner 2015, p. 111.
241 The Law Commission 2002, p. 204.
242 Whittaker and Partner 2015, p. 111.

value transaction is not without costs, but giving up registration triggers the risk of being defeated by third parties who complete the registration on an earlier date. In other words, the inclusion of low-value transactions within the system of registration amounts to forcing parties to fulfill the requirement of registration they usually resist.

Opponents of the minimum threshold might argue that parties to "big" transactions can split the transaction into a number of "small" transactions to evade registration.[243] In general, this problem should not be exaggerated. Firstly, splitting a "big" transaction into a series of "small" transactions is costly. Secondly, the minimum threshold should be fixed at an appropriate level, so that most transactions can be included in the system. Thirdly, it should be noted that "small" transactions are still governed by the rule of possession and the rule of *bona fide* acquisition. The risk of being subordinate to subsequent acquirers acting in good faith will encourage the parties to a high-value transaction to register this transaction, instead of evading registration by splitting the transaction into low-value ones.

Proposal 12:
A minimum amount of the object should be determined as a threshold of entry in the register. A transaction concerning the assets the total value of which is below the minimum amount does not need to be registered.

5.3.2.2 *The Aspect of Subject*

As to the scope of registration, another relevant factor that should be considered is the identity of parties. In general, there are three types of persons: legal persons having an independent legal position (in particular companies), natural persons running a business (whether a partnership or a single tradesman), and natural persons acting as a consumer.[244] The first two types of persons should be entitled to enter the system to register their transactions and search the system. In fact, the principal value of the system is to cater to the demand for information in commercial transactions. However, should a register folio be available to natural persons acting as a consumer, so that the consumer dealing can be made visible to third parties? For example, if a bicycle is transferred to a natural person under a clause of retention of ownership, should registration be a prerequisite for the effectiveness of this clause against third parties? In 5.3.1.1.A, we have dealt with how to determine natural parties' identifier. The following discussion focuses on whether property rights arising from consumer transactions should be included in the system of registration.[245]

---

243 Whittaker and Partner 2015, p. 111.

244 Gullifer 2017, p. 10.

245 A preliminary issue is ascertaining whether a natural person can be treated as a consumer. However, how to identify consumers is a difficult and controversial task and falls outside the scope of this research.

For the purpose of simplicity, we take secured transactions of consumer goods as an example. In this situation, the consumer purchases the goods on credit, and the seller retains ownership or creates a property right of security on the goods. In practice, the most popular form of transaction seems to be hire purchase under reservation of ownership and financial lease. In general, different laws take different approaches to the secured transaction of consumer goods in the aspect of publicity.

Under Article 9 UCC and Book IX DCFR, where an individual person obtains the object for personal, family or household use, thus a consumer, the formality of registration will be irrelevant.[246] In the words of US lawyers, the security interest created on the consumer goods is automatically perfected upon attachment, and publicity is completely irrelevant.[247] It should be noted that the security interest perfected automatically must be created for the very purpose of securing payment of the purchase price. Usually, the transaction takes the form of hire purchase or financial lease, allowing the seller to retain ownership of the goods.[248] In general, the formality of registration is not required for two reasons: one is to keep the register from being overloaded, and the other is that consumer goods often have low value and depreciate quickly.[249]

> *"In the typical case of a purchase money security interest in consumer goods, the value of the collateral would be low, second security interests in such property would be uncommon, and both the cost of filing and the cost of searching the files would be high relative to the value of the property."*[250]

However, PPSAs in Canada, Australia and New Zealand take a different approach.[251] According to the Australian PPSA, a security right granted on *"consumer property"* is registerable but subject to two restrictions for privacy concerns: (1) the maximum period of registration is seven years; and (2) the consumer's identity may not be shown on the register if the consumer property is serial-numbered (such as motor vehicles).[252] The two reasons for refusing registration shown above are not considered to be important

246 Art. IX.-3:107 (4) DCFR: *"Where a credit for assets supplied to a consumer is secured by an acquisition finance device, this proprietary security is effective without registration. This exception does not apply to security rights in proceeds and other assets different from the supplied asset."* § 9-309 (1) UCC: *"A purchase-money security interest in consumer goods, except as otherwise provided in Section 9-311(b) with respect to consumer goods that are subject to a statute or treaty described in Section 9-311 (a)."*

247 White and Summers 2012, p. 1195.

248 Proprietary Security in Movable Assets 2014, p. 411-412; White and Summers 2012, p. 1197-1198.

249 White and Summers 2012, p. 1196-1197.

250 Baird and Jackson 1983, p. 192.

251 Walsh 2016, p. 78-79; Duggan 2011, p. 884; Gabriel 2000, p. 1127.

252 Whittaker and Partner 2015, p. 159.

by Australian legislators. Even the hire purchase of a wide-screen television is registerable.[253] The Canadian PPSAs also allow registration of security interests on consumer goods. However, the two Australian restrictions, as a result of privacy concerns, are not found in Canadian law.[254] The New Zealand PPSA takes the Canadian approach.[255] Therefore, under Canadian and New Zealand PPSAs, the use to which the collateral is going to be put is irrelevant to the period of registration and the disclosure of personal information.

From the preceding introduction on the practice of secured transactions of consumer goods, it can be found that two factors are relevant here: efficiency and privacy. In the following discussion, we examine these two factors in sequence.

Every natural person is a potential consumer, generally speaking. Excluding the secured transaction of consumer goods from the system of registration helps to keep the system from being cluttered up. In addition to this reason, the consumer goods involved might be of low value, which implies that the costs of registration cannot be outweighed by the benefits produced. In general, these two reasons concerning the factor of efficiency are not convincing. The first reason should be re-examined under the context that the technology of registration has gone through significant development. Filing and search can be carried out online directly, without having to go to the registry or involving any registrar. This is why recent PPSAs include the secured transaction of consumer goods in the register.[256] The second reason is not convincing either, because not all consumer goods have low value. The price or value of consumer goods varies.[257] If the value of consumer goods does matter, a minimum threshold suffices.[258] For example, the UNCITRAL Model Law on Secured Transactions takes the acquisition price into account in determining whether registration is necessary for consumer goods.[259] Setting up a threshold is in line with our argument that the system of registration ought not to be clogged by "*low-value transactions*" (see 5.3.2.1.E). In the end, it should be noted that the efficiency aim might be frustrated by the difficulty in differentiating between consumer property and non-consumer property, where the transaction of consumer property needs to be excluded from the system of registration.[260]

253 Duggan 2011, p. 894.
254 Duggan 2014, p. 71.
255 Whittaker and Partner 2015, p. 160.
256 Walsh 2016, p. 78.
257 UNCITRAL Legislative Guide on Secured Transactions, p. 319.
258 Walsh 2016, p. 79.
259 Art. 24 UNCITRAL Model Law on Secured Transactions: "*An acquisition security right in consumer goods with an acquisition price below [an amount to be specified by the enacting State] is effective against third parties upon its creation without any further act.*"
260 Whittaker and Partner 2015, p. 160.

The factor of privacy relates to an issue of legal policy, namely a balance between the consumer's right of privacy and the searcher's right of information.[261] In general, privacy was never thought as relevant when making the New Zealand and Canadian PPSAs. The granting of automatic perfection to the secured transaction of consumer goods by Article 9 UCC is a result of the efficiency consideration and has nothing to do with privacy. Though Australian legislators hold that protection of privacy is relevant, the solution adopted is imposing two restrictions, rather than excluding consumer property from the system. Moreover, even if the protection of consumers' privacy is important, there is no reason to treat individual consumers and individual businessmen differently.[262] The latter's interest in privacy does not become less protective merely because the object is not intended to be put to personal, family or household use.

In sum, the identity of the transacting parties should not be considered when determining the scope of registration. The purpose of the transaction, i.e. whether the object is intended to be put to personal, family or household use, is in principle of no relevance. This is a feature of the contemporary system of registration.[263]

Proposal 13:
A folio should be available to natural persons so that consumer transactions can also be included in the register. The identifier of natural persons should be determined according to *Proposal 1.*

5.3.2.3 *The Aspect of Transaction*

After discussing the scope of registration from the angle of the object and the subject, we turn to another aspect, namely the feature of the transaction. Some transactions should be excluded from the system of registration because of a certain feature of the transaction. In the subsequent discussion, we focus on two features: transactional frequency and duration of the hidden state.

A *Transactional Frequency*

In general, where a kind of property is transacted with a very high frequency, registration cannot be a suitable method of publicity.

> *"However, registration also has a dark side: It certainly hampers the velocity of transfers and is therefore difficult to apply when transfers use to occur very frequently [...]. Recordable property should be relatively valuable and should not be transferred often."*[264]

---

261 Duggan 2014, p. 72.
262 Whittaker and Partner 2015, p. 161.
263 Gullifer 2017, p. 10.
264 Lurger 2006, p. 50.

The formality of registration leads to, at least, two additional requirements: (1) the parties to the transaction have to complete registration, and (2) the register has to be updated to show the transaction. Higher transactional frequency not only implies more costs caused by the operation of the system, but also lower transaction fluency. Therefore, registration does not suit property that takes negotiability as its central function, such as money and securities (see 5.3.2.1.B).

> *"In some situations a filing requirement would be inconsistent with the notion of negotiability that is the essential virtue of certain kinds of property, such as money or bearer instruments."*[265]

Money is paper currency and coins used as circulating medium of exchange and the legal means of payment. The fundamental function of money is negotiability. As a means of payment, money is always in fast circulation from one hand to another, which makes possession a proper means of publicity for money.[266] If registration is required for paper currency and coins, the problem would arise that *"they change hands faster than the registry can record changes in title"*.[267] Nowadays, money has been replaced, to a large extent, with the claim enjoyed by the holder of deposit accounts against the service bank. Though the claim is neither currency nor the legal means of payment, the debtor often discharges its monetary duty through giro transfer. This is why the claim is known as "transferable money (*giraal geld*)".[268] For the sake of swift payment, giro transfer should not be bothered with the formality of registration either.[269] About giro transfer and registration, we have provided a discussion above (see 5.3.2.1.D).

Moreover, a very low transactional frequency also means no need for registration. The system of registration is created to facilitate the certainty of transactions and prevent the occurrence of conflicts. If a type of asset is rarely put into transactions, conflicts with respect to this asset will occur rarely. Thus, the value of a system of registration would be very low. For example, jewelry, such as wedding rings, is often kept by the buyer for personal use and bequeathed to heirs. In general, most movable property does not have a very low transactional frequency, and excluding registration because of low transactional frequency seems unusual.

B Duration of the Hidden State

The duration of the hidden state of proprietary rights should be considered. For a property right which is hidden for a short period, there is no need

265 Baird and Jackson 1983, p. 192.
266 Baird and Jackson 1984, p. 306.
267 Clarke and Kohler 2005, p. 388.
268 De Jong, Krans and Wissink 2014, p. 80.
269 Another reason why the transfer of credits through the bank account needs no registration is that information asymmetry does not arise here (see 5.3.2.1.D).

to register this right.[270] This is not difficult to understand. Short duration of the property right means that registration has to be canceled within a short time after entry in the register. The relevance of the duration of hidden property rights to the problem of registerability has been illustrated by land lease. There is often a distinction between long-term lease and short-term lease. In principle, only the former is registerable. For example, only the land lease with a term of more than seven years can be registered in an independent folio under English law, and the minimum period of registerable lease is 12 years in French law.[271] The rationale behind the distinction is that the register should not be cluttered by transient, though hidden, property rights.

> *"[...] there are some transient interests, too trivial or fleeting or too numerous, that should not be put on the register, either because it would be a waste of resources or because it would impose too heavy an administrative burden on the Land Registry."*[272]

In the field of corporeal movables, where many transactions are expected to be completed within a short period, the duration of the hidden state should also be considered. For example, in the situation of reservation of ownership, the seller who retains ownership often agrees with the buyer that the purchase price will be paid in a short period, such as 20 days.[273] Upon the buyer's discharging the price debt within this period, ownership will pass to the buyer, and the transaction will be completed. Under this circumstance, registration of the clause of retention of ownership seems undesirable.

Here Article 9 UCC provides an example: § 9-317(e) grants a 20-days grace period to the *"purchase-money security interest"*.[274] According to this paragraph, a seller retaining ownership is entitled to keep his or her super priority within the 20 days after delivery of the object. The DCFR takes a similar approach to reservation of ownership by stipulating a grace period of 35 days.[275] In general, the grace period for reservation of ownership can be accounted for by the fact that the purchase price is usually paid within this period.

270 Baird and Jackson 1983, p. 191.

271 See s. 27(2)(b) Land Registration Act (2002) and art. 28 (1)(b) Decree no. 55-22 respectively.

272 Clarke and Kohler 2005, p. 555.

273 Veneziano 2008, p. 92; Faber 2014, p. 35.

274 § 9-317 (e): *"Except as otherwise provided in Sections 9-320 and 9-321, if a person files a financing statement with respect to a purchase-money security interest before or within 20 days after the debtor receives delivery of the collateral, the security interest takes priority over the rights of a buyer, lessee, or lien creditor which arise between the time the security interest attaches and the time of filing."*

275 Art. IX.-3:107 DCFR: *"(1) An acquisition finance device is effective only if registered. (2) If registration is effected within 35 days after delivery of the supplied asset, the acquisition finance device is effective from the date of creation."*

> *"Why has the grace period been fixed at 35 days? This is not an arbitrary decision but takes into account a wide-spread commercial practice. Buyers are very often given a period of 30 days to effect payment [...]."*[276]

In other words, reservation of ownership usually remains hidden only for a short period: the buyer is expected to obtain the right of ownership in this period by paying the purchase price. In general, a shorter hidden state means a lower possibility of conflicts. In the situation of reservation of ownership, it can be expected that the buyer (possessor) will not dispose of the object during the short grace period by breaching the reservation clause. Secondly, since the grace period is short, third parties are able to take protective measures when the hidden interest is registered upon expiry of the period and made visible to third parties.[277] Thirdly, where the hidden proprietary interest has a short term, registering this interest implies that the registration has to be canceled upon the expiry of this term. Undoubtedly, most parties do not bother to conduct registration. For these three reasons, a grace period should be granted to reservation of ownership.

In the situation of the lease of corporeal movables, the length of the leasing term is relevant. Lease with a short term also does not deserve registration for the three reasons stated above. As to the dividing line between short lease and long lease, a specific term has to be fixed. According to the Canadian PPSAs, only the lease with a term of more than one year is registerable.[278] Austrian PPSA and New Zealand PPSA also follow this approach, because the benefits of registration of short-term lease cannot outweigh the administrative costs triggered.[279]

Proposal 14:
The duration of the hidden state should be taken into consideration in defining the scope of registration. Short-term transactions should not be required to be entered in the register. A grace period should be granted to reservation of ownership. The specific length of this grace period should be determined according to the period within which the purchase price will usually be paid. Short-term lease should not be entered in the register. It is up to the legislature to determine what term of lease is short.

5.3.3 The Legal Effect of Registration

5.3.3.1 Declaratory Effect or Constitutive Effect

In general, registration can yield two different legal effects to the acquisition of property rights: the constitutive effect and declaratory effect. In the

276 Proprietary Security in Movable Assets 2014, p. 410.
277 UNCITRAL Legislative Guide on Insolvency Law (2005), p. 133.
278 Walsh 2016, p. 83.
279 Whittaker and Partner 2015, p. 81; Gedye 2016, p. 126.

former, registration is a prerequisite for acquiring the property right, and the lack of registration means that only a legal relationship comes into existence *inter partes*. In the latter, registration has nothing to do with the acquisition of the property right, but registration may affect the legal effectiveness against third parties. The two effects have been discussed in Section 5.1.4.1. In that Section, we have argued that publicity should have declaratory effect, so that it will only restrict parties' autonomy within the necessary scope.

Under the system of declaratory effect, individuals are entitled to decide whether to have their proprietary right shown to third parties. In general, individuals should have an option to balance the benefits of registration and the risks arising from the lack of registration. Under certain circumstances, registration might not be worthwhile in the view of the transacting parties. The option guarantees that the side effects of registration, especially the costs triggered, are not imposed on the transacting parties directly. Moreover, the declaratory effect is also a consequence of the requirement that legislators should be lenient towards private transactions. It is impossible for the legislature to be omniscient and able to regulate every aspect of our private life. As we have mentioned above, the problem of information asymmetry does not exist or has been addressed in some fields (see 5.3.2.1.A), a property right might be expected to exist only for a short period (see 5.3.2.3.B), and the value of a transaction may be, though exceeding the minimum threshold, too low to deserve registration in the view of the transacting parties (see 5.3.2.1.E). In these situations, declaratory registration allows individuals to do what they think suitable: they can acquire the property right even without registering the right. The irrelevance of registration to the acquisition allows the property right to be obtained simply and efficiently.[280]

Under the system of declaratory effect, registration is not useless. It benefits the acquirer. For example, the property right obtained can be effective towards third parties acting in good faith (see 5.1.4.1.D). This benefit encourages individuals to register their property right. In general, declaratory effect of registration is commonly accepted in the field of secured transactions concerning movables: security interests come into existence upon the effect of the security agreement, and registration is only a requirement for the benefit of priority over third parties.[281] In general, the benefit of priority is usually adequate to motivate individuals to register the security interest created.[282] Therefore, the register will include most property rights even when registration only yields declaratory effect.

280 Bazinas 2013, p. 142.
281 Wood 2019, no. 7-001-7-002; Jansen 2017, p. 70; Gedye 2016, p. 130; Brown 2016, p. 156.
282 Gedye 2016, p. 131; White 1993, p. 826.

Proposal 15:
Registration has declaratory effect and should not be treated as a prerequisite of valid transfer or creation of property rights in the law of corporeal movables and claims.

5.3.3.2 *The Scope of Third-Party Effect*

It has been argued that registration should be irrelevant to the acquisition *per se*, but this means of publicity is a prerequisite of the legal effect against third parties. The question discussed next is what specific third-party effects can be yielded by registration. The following discussion is based on the categorization of third parties in this research: strange interferers, subsequent acquirers, and general creditors.

On the basis of the preceding discussion (see 5.1.3), we can draw a secure conclusion first: registration has nothing to do with strange interferers but is extremely important for subsequent acquirers. The lack of registration is not a sufficient reason to deprive proprietors of the right to remedies against third parties committing illegal interference. In contrast, registration is very important for subsequent acquirers.[283] Failure to register will cause the following risk: the unregistered right may be unable to bind a subsequent acquirer who obtains a property right on the same object and completes registration earlier. As a result of this priority rule, the acquirer would need to register the right obtained as early as possible.

A controversial issue here is whether an unregistered property right can be effective against general creditors in the event of the debtor's insolvency. As has been pointed out above (see 5.1.3.2), general creditors usually have no interest in knowing about the status of the debtor's assets and encumbrances over these assets. Thus, registration is, in general, useless for this type of third parties. In line with this reasoning, unregistered property rights can be enforced against the insolvency administrator. This is accepted by the New Zealand PPSA on the ground that "*unsecured creditors could not claim to be detrimentally affected by non-registration*".[284] However, different from New Zealand PPSA, both Australian and Canadian PPSAs provide that registration is a way to make the security interest become effective against the insolvency administrator and to exclude the collateral involved from the distribution among general creditors.[285] The latter approach is also adopted by Article 9 UCC, English law, and the DCFR.[286] Thus, we can say that connecting registration with the legal effect against general creditors (or the insolvency administrator) is common practice.

283 For example, under the Canadian PPSAs, registration can yield a legal effect against not only secured creditors with a competing security interest, but also buyers and lessees of the collateral involved. See Walsh 2016, p. 59.

284 Gedye 2015, p. 131.

285 Brown 2016, p. 174-175.

286 Sigman 2008, p. 147; Beale, Bridge, Gullifer and Lomnicka 2018, no. 1.17; Proprietary Security in Movable Assets 2014, p. 399.

The rationale behind this common practice is that registration is useful to the insolvency administrator and unsecured creditors for the following reasons. The first is that the insolvency administrator can "*benefit from having a list of all interests in the debtor's assets that is accurate and which enables priorities to be ascertained easily*".[287] Registration can be used to make a "*prima facie determination*" of the assets encumbered.[288] The second reason is that unsecured creditors have an interest in knowing the extent to which the assets are encumbered with security interests.[289] The third reason is that registration prevents fabrication and antedating of transactions, thereby functioning as a protective regime for unsecured creditors.[290] For this reason, Dutch law requires notarization or private registration for the undisclosed pledge.[291]

In addition to these three reasons, another two reasons are raised to explain why unregistered property rights cannot be enforced against general creditors. The fourth reason relates to the right of disposal, as pointed out by the DCFR.

> "*Once an insolvency administrator is appointed, the security provider loses the power to dispose of the assets and security rights are effective against the insolvency administrator only if they fulfil the requirements of this Chapter.*"[292]

The fifth reason concerns the connection between the law of secured transactions and the law of bankruptcy in the field of secured transactions concerning movables. Before the occurrence of bankruptcy, an unregistered security interest is subordinate to general creditors who apply for execution and become an execution creditor. The law of bankruptcy deprives general creditors of their right to claim judicial execution by merging this right in the bankruptcy proceedings.[293] Therefore, making unregistered security interests ineffective against general creditors is to compensate execution creditors for the loss of their priority.[294] As the Canadian judgement in the landmark case *Re Giffen* contends, the purpose is "*to permit the unsecured creditors to maintain, through the person of the trustee, the same status vis-à-vis secured creditors which they enjoyed prior to the bankruptcy of the debtor*".[295] In other words, if a general creditor can get free from the unregistered security interest by applying for judicial execution before bankruptcy, this creditor should be allowed to be free from the interest after bankruptcy.

287 Gullifer 2017, p. 3.
288 Walsh 2016, p. 60.
289 Gullifer 2017, p. 16.
290 Gullifer 2017, p. 4.
291 Heilbron 2011, p. 44. It should be noted that the two kinds of formality cannot provide any useful information to subsequent acquirers, since notarization fails to make the contract visible, and private registration is not open to the public. Moreover, the formality of notarization and that of private registration are, as a formality, also costly.
292 DCFR 2009, p. 4536; Proprietary Security in Movable Assets 2014, p. 399.
293 Duggan 2008, p. 114-115.
294 Duggan 2008, p. 115.
295 See *Re Giffen*, [1998] 1 SCR 91.

In general, the five reasons mentioned above are not fully convincing. In this research, we argue that the absence of registration should not be treated as a sufficient ground to deny the legal effect against unsecured creditors or the bankruptcy administrator in the event of bankruptcy.

Firstly, the insolvency administrator is an agent of the insolvent company. There is no reason why this person can qualify as a third party who can undo the transaction made by the insolvent company with another person, namely the acquirer of the unregistered property right. This viewpoint can be found in judicial practice and theoretical discussion in New Zealand, where registration is irrelevant to insolvency issues.[296] Truly, it may not be fully convincing to say that the administrator is merely an agent of the debtor, because the administrator also has to consider the interest of all creditors.[297] Perhaps, it is more proper to deem the administrator as a "*neutral person*" who has to take all interests concerned into account.[298] Nevertheless, from the system of insolvency law, a proprietor should not be divested of its unregistered property right for the benefit of general creditors.

A property right is by its nature proprietary, regardless of whether this right is obtained with registration. Under the declaratory effect, a property right obtained in the absence of registration is still a property right. This allows the right to form an exception to the principle of equality of creditors (*paritas creditorum*). If the right is not effective against unsecured creditors, let alone subsequent acquirers with a competing interest, how can we say that it is a property right?

> "*The undisputed starting point is that security rights created in accordance with the provisions of substantive law are respected in insolvency. If one follows the insolvency-based approach as to the explanations of priority, this notion is a matter of course: If a right is not respected in insolvency it does not qualify as a security right.*"[299]

Even though we concede that an unregistered right is personal, the insolvency administrator has to step into the shoes of the insolvent debtor in the following sense: pursuant to the criterion of maximizing the insolvent property, the administrator is entitled to either perform the contract to obtain the counter performance or breach the contract with bearing a liability of compensation.[300] Regardless of the option made by the administrator, the consequence is by no means that the proprietor loses its unregistered property right straightforwardly and gains nothing.

296 See *Re King Robb Ltd, Sleepyhead Manufacturing Co Ltd v. Dunphy 50* ((2006) 9 NZCLC 264,000); Gibbons 2006, p. 42-43; Gedye 2011, p. 718.
297 Vriesendorp 2013, p. 180-182.
298 MacBryde and Flessner 2003, p. 31.
299 Brinkmann 2008, p. 262.
300 UNCITRAL Legislative Guide on Insolvency Law (2005), p. 120.

Under the distinction between property rights and personal rights, it is difficult to say that a right, which is created validly but cannot bind general creditors, is a proprietary right. The effect of preference over unsecured creditors in the event of bankruptcy is a basic element of property rights.[301] Inevitably, a right lacking the effect is usually doomed to be personal, being subject to the *paritas creditorum* principle. As indicated by the UNCITRAL Legislative Guide on Secured Transactions, proprietary rights only exist *inter partes* and are conceptually problematic.[302]

Secondly, unsecured creditors do not have an interest in the register or concern about whether there are secured creditors.[303] The reason, as has been argued before (see 5.1.3.2), is simple: unsecured creditors are only concerned about the overall financial health of the debtor and can counter-balance the risk of underpayment by other measures, such as adjusting the interest rate or the selling price. The register does not indicate the overall financial health precisely. Moreover, it cannot show how many assets are encumbered with a limited property right or how many assets are owned by the debtor. In reality, unsecured creditors seldom make use of the register.[304] Since unsecured creditors do not rely on the register, protection should not be granted to them to the detriment unregistered property rights.[305] The Canadian PPSAs accept registration as a condition of the effectiveness against the bankruptcy administrator.[306] However, this is contested because "*unsecured creditors do not rely on the public registry in making lending decisions since nothing prevents the debtor from granting a security interest after the credit has been advanced*".[307] Since general creditors do not rely on the register, failure to register does not cause any disadvantage to them.

> "*Thus invalidation of unperfected security interests by the bankruptcy trustee takes from innocent secured parties to give to unsecured creditors who are not prejudiced by the failure to perfect.*"[308]

Under the PPSAs, certain non-security transactions are included in the register, which is created initially for secured transactions of movables, for the purpose of publicity.[309] For example, outright assignment of claims and operational lease can be entered in the system. However, failure to register these non-security transactions has nothing to do with the issue of the legal effectiveness against general creditors. In other words, though security

301 Clarke and Kohler 2005, p. 163.
302 UNCITRAL Legislative Guide on Secured Transactions, p. 105; Bazinas 2013, p. 145.
303 Wood 2019, no. 9-007.
304 McCoid 1985, p. 190; Cuming 1994 (1), p. 27.
305 Beale 2016, p. 11.
306 McCoid 1985, p. 190.
307 Walsh 2016, p. 59.
308 McCoid 1985, p. 190.
309 Whittaker and Partner 2015, p. 55; Bridge, Macdonald, Simmonds and Walsh 1999, p. 599.

interests and non-security transactions are governed by the same rules of publicity and priority, they are treated differently in the aspect of enforcement in the event of insolvency.[310]

> *"Not all security interests will vest in the grantor in this way. Broadly, it was decided that this consequence would be too draconian for 'deemed' security interests such as non-finance leases and consignments, or non-security account transfers. Nevertheless, if they do not perfect, these types of secured parties may lose priority to other security interests."*[311]

There is no reason to treat secured transactions and non-security transactions differently in this aspect. If an unregistered non-security right can survive in the event of insolvency, why is an unregistered security right unable to be enforced against general creditors? The two rights do not differ in terms of publicity.

Thirdly, the problem of antedating should not be exaggerated, and recognizing the link between registration and the effect against general creditors cannot fully address this problem. As has been mentioned above (see 5.3.3.1), the benefit of priority over subsequent acquirers out of registration can motivate individuals to register their transactions as early as they can. The date of registration is, in principle, decisive in solving the conflict between two subsequent acquirers. As a result, parties often have a sufficiently strong incentive to accomplish the registration.[312] The legal practice in New Zealand has proven this conclusion.[313]

More importantly, registration cannot completely eliminate the risk of antedating because of the fact that *"under a notice registration regime there is no necessary connection between the date of registration and the existence or date of a particular security interest agreement"*.[314] In New Zealand law, where registration is not a prerequisite of the effectiveness against general creditors, the dispute concerning the antedating of transactions does arise. However, the real issue relates to *"whether the security agreement had been executed prior to the appointment of a liquidator"*.[315] In practice, the secured creditor usually has completed registration in advance.

Fourthly, the argumentation from the aspect of the authority of disposal is not sufficiently convincing. Truly, the power to manage and dispose of the insolvency property shifts to the administrator upon declaration of insolvency.[316] However, the requirements of valid disposal, including the quali-

310 Bridge 2008, p. 191.
311 Brown 2016, p. 175.
312 McCoid 1985, p. 189.
313 Gedye 2016, p. 131.
314 Gedye 2016, p. 132.
315 *The Healy Holmberg Trading Partnership v. Grant and Khov* [2012] NZCA 451; cited from Gedye 2016, p. 132.
316 Brinkmann 2008, p. 250.

fied authority of disposal, have been fulfilled at the moment of creating the property right. From the doctrine of property law, it is impossible that a property right can be created validly when the grantor lacks valid authority of disposal. Where a property right has been created validly, the grantor must have the authority to dispose of the object. Therefore, in answering whether unregistered property rights can be enforced against general creditors, the authority of disposal should not be considered as a relevant factor.

Now let us examine the last reason presented above. According to this reason, making unregistered property rights subordinate to general creditors is to compensate general creditors who lose the right to apply for judicial execution after the commencement of the bankruptcy. Before bankruptcy, general creditors can realize their claim free from the unregistered property right in the way of judicial execution. This status in relation to unregistered property rights should be preserved in the proceedings of bankruptcy. The way of preservation is conferring general creditors a superior position over unregistered property rights directly.

In general, the preceding reasoning is not persuasive. If the purpose is to preserve the status of general creditors *vis-à-vis* unregistered secured creditors, the logical outcome is that the latter prevails. This is because, as we have shown above, the secured creditor enjoys a property right, despite the absence of registration of this right.[317] Indeed, general creditors can apply for judicial execution and then obtains a superior interest over the unregistered property right. However, the proprietor is able to counter this risk by registering the property right earlier. Therefore, making unregistered property rights subordinate to general creditors is not to preserve the status prior to the bankruptcy, but to reverse the priority in bankruptcy between unregistered property rights and unsecured claims.[318]

It is often held that the commencement of bankruptcy creates a "common pledge (*gage commun*)" or leads to a "*'collective' seizure*" for the benefit of general creditors.[319] Upon declaration of bankruptcy, "*the position of each creditor in relation to all others in the collective proceedings is 'fixed'*", and any attempt to "*strengthen the position of a particular creditor*" cannot bind the other creditors.[320] In other words, if there is any race between unregistered secured creditors and general creditors before the occurrence of bankruptcy, bankruptcy stops the race.[321] In principle, the commencement of bankruptcy should not affect the legal positions owned by the proprietor involved before the bankruptcy.[322] Therefore, the real question here is whether an unregistered proprietary security right can prevail over

317 White 1993, p. 827.
318 White 1993, p. 827; McCoid 1985, p. 192.
319 Dirix 2006, p. 71-72.
320 Dirix 2006, p. 72.
321 McCoid 1985, p. 191.
322 Jackson 1982, p. 860.

unsecured claims before the beginning of bankruptcy. The priority between different interests needs to be determined according to the legal facts which arose before bankruptcy. As we have argued above, the logical outcome is that the secured creditor should prevail over general creditors, because the former has obtained a proprietary right, while the latter enjoys no right with respect to any specific property.[323]

In sum, registration is a condition of the legal effect against subsequent acquirers but has nothing to do with the legal effect against strange interferers, and the absence of registration is not a sufficient reason to deny the legal effect against general creditors.

Proposal 16:
Registration can make the property right acquired effective against subsequent acquirers. The absence of registration does not affect the acquisition against illegal interference and the bankruptcy of the debtor from whom the property right is acquired.

5.3.3.3 *The Issue of Constructive Notice*

In general, third parties, mainly referring to subsequent acquirers, are assumed to be aware of the property right registered, regardless of whether they actually inspect the register. This is the rule of constructive notice.[324] The rule of constructive notice is only relevant in a priority regime that permits a third party without actual knowledge of a property right to take the object free of that right.[325] Under this regime, registration of a property right can preclude the third party from acquisition free of this right.[326] Where actual knowledge or good faith is irrelevant in determining the priority, there is no need to have a rule of constructive notice. In this case, *bona fide* acquisition is not recognized, and the date of registration plays a decisive role: the person who completes registration first will prevail.[327] Nevertheless, we argue that the doctrine of constructive notice is useful for justifying the "first registration, first right" regime.[328] A basis of this regime is that the person who finishes registration later is assumed to be aware of the property right registered earlier. Therefore, it is necessary to discuss the issue of constructive notice. Moreover, as we will demonstrate later, good faith should be relevant in determining the priority between competing property rights (see 5.3.3.4). This also requires us to devote attention to this issue.

323 White and Summers 2012, p. 1279.
324 Gullifer 2015, p. 437; Proprietary Security in Movable Assets 2014, p. 510.
325 UNCITRAL Legislative Guide on Secured Transactions, p. 150.
326 Proprietary Security in Movable Assets 2014, p. 434.
327 Sigman 2010, p. 514.
328 Whittaker and Partner 2015, p. 243.

Registration is deemed to have an effect of constructive notice in this research. As in the situation of land registration, third parties are also assumed to know about the property right registered in the situation of corporeal movables.[329] However, is it fair and reasonable to assume that every third party has knowledge about the registered right in the latter situation? Can the registration give rise to constructive notice to third parties?[330] For example, should a consumer buyer be expected to search the register to ascertain whether the seller has qualified authority to dispose and whether the object is encumbered with any limited property right? If so, will the smooth transaction of corporeal movables be hampered? In general, all of these questions relate to the extent of constructive notice by registration. In the field of corporeal movables, different jurisdictions take different approaches.[331]

A *The Distinction Between Professionals and Non-Professionals*

With respect to the extent of constructive notice, Belgian law distinguishes between professional transactors and non-professional transactors in art. 25 "*Pandwet* (Law of Pledge)",[332] while such distinction cannot be found in the French law of non-possessory pledge (art. 2337 CC).[333] Under Belgian law, only professional transactors are assumed to know about the property right registered. For a transactor acting as a non-professional, registration does not constitute constructive notice.[334] According to the Belgian legislature, non-professional third parties cannot be expected to consult the register.[335] However, this does not mean *mala fide* third parties are entitled to acquisition: good faith is also a requirement for applying the rule of *bona fide* acquisition of corporeal movables under Belgian law.[336] Thus, art. 25 *Pandwet* only means that registration *per se* does not amount to the negation of good faith.

329 Proprietary Security in Movable Assets 2014, p. 434; Snijders and Rank-Berenschot 2017, p. 86-87.
330 Beale, Bridge, Gullifer and Lomnicka 2018, no. 12.04.
331 Proprietary Security in Movable Assets 2014, p. 459.
332 Art. 25 Pandwet: "*De registratie in het pandregister sluit de toepassing van artikel 2279 uit ten aanzien van rechtverkrijgers onder bijzondere titel van de pandgever die handelen in het raam van hun bedrijf of beroep.*" English translation: Art. 25 Law of Pledge: "*The entry in the register of pledge excludes the application of article 2279 with respect to acquirers who have a particular title with the pledgor but act in the field of their business or profession.*"
333 Art. 2337 CC: "*Lorsque le gage a été régulièrement publié, les ayants cause à titre particulier du constituant ne peuvent se prévaloir de l'article 2276.*" English translation: Art. 2337 CC: "*Where the pledge has been properly registered, the particular successors of the pledgor may not apply article 2276.*"
334 Jansen 2017, p. 83.
335 Jansen 2017, p. 83; Baeck and Heytens 2019, p. 21-20.
336 Jansen 2017, p. 83; Dirix and Sagaert 2014, p. 250.

It is worthwhile noting here that the Belgian legislature created a rule of the "ordinary course of business" in art. 21 Pandwet, which will be discussed in detail later.[337] According to this provision, the pledgor is free to dispose of the collateral in the ordinary course of its business, unless there is an express contrary agreement with the pledgee. The rule is to answer the question of whether the pledgor has valid authority of disposal, instead of whether the third party can acquire the collateral free of the pledge registered. If the pledgor disposes of the collateral to a professional third party in violation of an agreement to the contrary with the pledgee, and this agreement is registered, then this professional party will not be able to acquire the collateral free of the pledge because of art. 25 Pandwet.[338]

In French law, the general rule is that registration excludes the possibility of acquiring the object by a third party free of a registered non-possessory pledge.[339] In other words, all third parties, whether or not acting as a professional, are expected to consult the register under French law. Registration forms a constructive notice of a non-possessory pledge. According to French law, after a non-possessory pledge is created, the pledgor who retains possession is no longer able to dispose of the collateral free of the encumbrance, unless the security agreement stipulates otherwise.[340] Unlike Belgian law, an "ordinary course of business" rule cannot be found in French law.

B The "Ordinary Course of Business" Rule

B1: Introduction of the Rule

In most jurisdictions, the law concerning the secured transaction of movable property includes a rule of the "ordinary course of business", as we will see below. Under this rule, a third party is entitled to acquisition free of the security interest registered when the transaction takes place in the ordinary course of the security provider. The rule primarily applies to inventory collateral.[341] In general, the rule confers priority on the third party in the ordinary course of the security provider, facilitating the ordinary transaction with the security provider.[342] The rule implies that the registration

---

337 Art. 21 Pandwet: "*Behoudens anders overeengekomen, kan de pandgever vrij over de bezwaarde goederen beschikken binnen een normale bedrijfsvoering.*" English translation: Art. 21 Law of Pledge: "*Unless agreed otherwise, the pledgor is entitled to dispose of the encumbered property in the ordinary course of business.*"

338 The Belgian register is a "transaction-filing" system: "*all the basic elements of the pledge agreement need to be reported in the register, the consequence is that the instrument creating the security interest itself has to be presented to the register along with the filed particulars*". Therefore, more information is communicated by the Belgian system than the notice-filing system. See Dirix and Sagaert 2014, p. 247; Baeck and Heytens 2019, p. 10. As a result, the contrary agreement can be filed in the register.

339 Riffard 2016, p. 377-378.

340 Riffard 2016, p. 378.

341 Gedye 2013, p. 2.

342 Proprietary Security in Movable Assets 2014, p. 689.

does not constitute any constructive notice, in particular to the buyer of the inventory collateral.[343]

It should be noted here that the secured creditor will not challenge the vast majority of the ordinary transactions because the proceeds out of the transactions can be used to discharge the debt.[344] Usually, the secured creditor is not willing to hamper the ordinary operation of the debtor. The debtor often has implied authority of disposal, and no conflict will arise between the secured creditor and the third party. For example, where there is no express agreement prohibiting the debtor from selling the inventory collateral or requiring the debtor to obtain the creditor's approval, it can be assumed that the debtor is entitled to sell the inventory.[345] Therefore, attention only needs to be given to the situation where the secured creditor does not approve the ordinary transaction of the collateral.

In the English law of secured transactions concerning corporeal movables, the question of to whom the registration of charge forms constructive notice is not answered directly by statutory law.[346] Instead, this question is left to the courts, and conflicting opinions exist.[347] In theory, there are two views with respect to the question: one is that registration is constructive notice to the entire world, and the other is that registration only forms constructive notice to those who would be reasonably expected to search the register.[348] Regardless of these controversies, it is clear that a buyer in the ordinary course of the seller's business is able to obtain the object free of floating charge. A similar rule can also be found in the UNCITRAL Model Law on Secured Transactions (art. 34),[349] the UCC (§ 9-320),[350] the DCFR

343 It is necessary to note that the rule of the "ordinary course of business" discussed here is different from the Belgian rule of the "ordinary course of business" in several aspects. In general, the former rule allows acquisition free of the proprietary encumbrance, while the Belgian rule only concerns the authority of disposal. As to the question of whether a third party is able to acquire the collateral under Belgian law, art. 25 *Pandwet* which includes a provision that makes a distinction between the professional and non-professional, is also relevant. This has been just discussed. Under the rule discussed here, such distinction is irrelevant. Thus, the role applies to consumer buyers and trade buyers without any differences. See Gengaharen 2013, p. 368. Therefore, unlike the Belgian rule, the rule discussed here imposes no duty of inspecting the register on the third party, regardless of whether the party is professional or not.

344 Phillips 1979 (1), p. 9; Gedye 2013, p. 10.

345 Beale, Bridge, Gullifer and Lomnicka 2018, no. 12.05; Gengaharen 2013, p. 369.

346 Gullifer 2015, p. 437-438; Beale, Bridge, Gullifer and Lomnicka 2018, no. 12.04.

347 Beale, Bridge, Gullifer and Lomnicka 2018, no. 12.06-12.12; McCormack 2004, p. 106-107.

348 Beale, Bridge, Gullifer and Lomnicka 2018, no. 12.05.

349 Art. 34 (4) UNCITRAL Model Law on Secured Transactions: "*A buyer of a tangible encumbered asset sold in the ordinary course of the seller's business acquires its rights free of the security right, provided that, at the time of the conclusion of the sale agreement, the buyer does not have knowledge that the sale violates the rights of the secured creditor under the security agreement.*"

350 § 9-320 (a) UCC: "*Except as otherwise provided in subsection (e), a buyer in ordinary course of business, other than a person buying farm products from a person engaged in farming operations, takes free of a security interest created by the buyer's seller, even if the security interest is perfected and the buyer knows of its existence.*"

(IX.-6:102),[351] and the Australian PPSA (s. 46).[352] The Canadian PPSAs and New Zealand PPSA also establish an "ordinary course of business" rule.[353]

In brief, this rule allows the encumbered assets, in particular inventory, to be sold in the ordinary course of the seller's business without being affected by the proprietary encumbrance.[354] For example, the sale of equipment by an equipment dealer is a transaction in the ordinary course of the dealer's business. However, the sale of equipment by a manufacturer, for whom the equipment is not inventory, cannot constitute a transaction in the ordinary course of this manufacturer.[355] In addition to sale, lease of corporeal movables is also, *mutatis mutandis*, governed by the rule.[356] In general, whether a sale or lease is qualified as a transaction in the ordinary course of business is a question that should be answered in two stages: (1) what is the ordinary course of the business?; and (2) is this sale (lease) carried out in the ordinary course of business?[357] To answer this question, all of the circumstances of the transaction have to be taken in consideration, such as the place where the contract is made, the identity of the buyer (lessee), the quantity of the assets sold (leased), and the price (rent).[358] Thus, uncertainty exists in the application of the rule.

In general, the rule of the "ordinary course of business" constitutes an exception to the *nemo dat* rule or the *prior tempore* rule.[359] This is because, briefly speaking, it makes the proprietary security right registered inferior to the subsequent acquisition in the ordinary course of business. Thus, there must be strong reasons to recognize the exception. Before turning to the possible reasons, it should be noted that the rule requires that the purchaser (lessee) must have no knowledge that the sale (lease) is in violation of the proprietary security right.[360] As has been mentioned above, the security agreement might include a clause that restricts further disposal of the collateral even in the ordinary course of business. In this situation, a requirement

351 Art. IX.-6:102 (2) DCFR: "*For the purposes of VIII.- 3:102 (Good faith acquisition of ownership free of limited proprietary rights) paragraph (1)(d) sentence 1, a transferee is regarded as knowing that the transferor has no right or authority to transfer ownership free from the security right if this right is registered under Chapter 3, Section 3 unless: (a) the transferor acts in the ordinary course of its business; or (b) the entry is filed against a security provider different from the transferor.*"

352 S. 46 (1) Australian PPSA: "*A buyer or lessee of personal property takes the personal property free of a security interest given by the seller or lessor, or that arises under section 32 (proceeds-attachment), if the personal property was sold or leased in the ordinary course of the seller's or lessor's business of selling or leasing personal property of that kind.*"

353 Whittaker and Partner 2015, p. 289.

354 UNCITRAL Legislative Guide on Secured Transactions, p. 202.

355 UNCITRAL Legislative Guide on Secured Transactions, p. 202-203.

356 UNCITRAL Legislative Guide on Secured Transactions, p. 204; Gedye 2013, p. 6.

357 Gedye 2013, p. 20.

358 Gedye 2013, p. 24; Gengaharen 2013, p. 372.

359 Gedye 2013, p. 3; Gengaharen 2013, p. 367.

360 UNCITRAL Legislative Guide on Secured Transactions, p. 202; White and Summers 2012, p. 1307-1308.

of applying the rule is that the purchaser (lessee) does not know that the seller (lessor) lacks valid authority to dispose. About this requirement of good faith, a further discussion is provided later (see 5.3.3.4).

B2: Rationale of the Rule

In general, the rule of the "ordinary course of business" can be justified from three perspectives, even when the rule is applied where the authority of disposal is defective. The first is that the rule can facilitate transactions by guaranteeing that the transaction in the ordinary course of business will not be affected by the property right registered.[361] It amounts to stipulating that the third party has no duty to search the register in the ordinary course of business, eliminating the impact of the formality of registration on the smooth operation of the transaction. In the absence of the rule, buyers would have to check the seller's authority of disposal by inspecting the register before entering into the transaction.[362] Moreover, the rule is consistent with the commercial expectation that the security provider will sell the inventory collateral without being affected by the existing encumbrance.[363] As we have demonstrated above, the security provider is usually entitled to sell the inventory collateral in the ordinary course of its business and discharge the secured debt with the proceeds obtained. Otherwise, the debtor's earning ability would be hampered.

The second perspective concerns the assumption of risks. In general, it is expected that the security provider will sell the inventory collateral and then use the proceeds out of the sale to repay the secured debt. In practice, most debts, whether secured or not, are discharged on the basis of the debtor's cash-flow in the ordinary course of the debtor's business. However, there is always a risk that the debtor fails to discharge the secured debt with the proceeds obtained. In this particular situation, who must bear the risk: the secured creditor or the buyer as a third party? In general, it is held that the former *"is in a much better position than the buyer to weigh the risks"*.[364] For example, the secured creditor can avert the risk *"by taking insurance against credit risks, and by raising the costs of borrowing"*.[365] It is unfair to expect the buyer to assume the risk of the seller's default.[366] Thus, the secured creditor loses the right to follow (*droit de suite*), and the property right can no longer exist on the collateral.

The third perspective relates to the rationale of publicity. As the drafter of the DCFR points out, *"the third person [...] cannot be expected to care about any possible entries in the register for proprietary security"* when the transac-

361 UNCITRAL Legislative Guide on Secured Transactions, p. 204; Gengaharen 2013, p. 369.
362 UNCITRAL Legislative Guide on Secured Transactions, p. 202; Gedye 2013, p. 9.
363 UNCITRAL Legislative Guide on Secured Transactions, p. 202.
364 *Fairline Boats Ltd v. Leger* (1980) 1 PPSAC 218 at 220-221.
365 Gengaharen 2013, p. 369.
366 Gengaharen 2013, p. 369.

tion is in the ordinary course of the debtor's business.[367] In other words, registration does not give rise to constructive notice to third parties in the ordinary course of the debtor's business, because they cannot be reasonably expected to search the register.[368] Thus, the third party is able to acquire the collateral free of the proprietary security registered, even though the acquisition is in violation of the proprietary security. For such acquisition, it is necessary that the third party acts in good faith with respect to the violation.

C *Conclusion*

From the preceding introduction, it can be concluded that there are three approaches with respect to the extent of constructive notice of registration in the field of corporeal movables. The first approach is adopted by French law: all third parties are treated as knowing about the property right registered, regardless of whether the third party is professional or not, and whether the transaction with the third party is in the ordinary course of business. The second approach is followed by Belgian law, which makes a distinction between professional third parties and non-professional third parties. Under Belgian law, registration of pledge only forms constructive notice to the professional third parties. The third approach is associated with the rule of the "ordinary course of business". Under this rule, registration does not form constructive notice for third parties in the transaction arising in the ordinary course of business of the security provider.

The preceding introduction also demonstrates the rationale behind the restriction of constructive notice. In general, three reasons are relevant. The first reason concerns fairness. Under the Belgian law, it seems unfair to require a non-professional to search the register. Under the rule of the "ordinary course of business", requiring the third party, instead of the secured creditor, to assume the risk of the debtor's default is unfair. The second reason lies in the concern about smooth commerce. The restriction not only implies a limitation of the duty of searching the register, but also means that certain third parties are entitled to acquisition without being bound by the property right registered. In this way, the smooth operation of transactions, in particular those carried out in the ordinary course of business, is facilitated. The third reason relates to reasonableness. In general, it is unreasonable to expect non-professional third parties or third parties in the ordinary course of their counterparty's business to search the register.

In this research, we hold that the effect of constructive notice of registration should be restricted for the purpose of the smooth operation of transactions in the ordinary course of business. In the field of corporeal movables, it is desirable that the system of registration be associated with a rule of the "ordinary course of business". As we have shown above, most

367 Beale, Bridge, Gullifer and Lomnicka 2018, no. 12.05; Proprietary Security in Movable Assets 2014, p. 511.

368 Beale, Bridge, Gullifer and Lomnicka 2018, no. 12.16.

jurisdictions have established this rule in the law of secured transactions of movable property. At the European and international level, the rule is also commonly accepted.[369]

Apart from the three reasons presented above, the restriction of constructive notice under the rule of the "ordinary course of business" also has its practical basis. This basis is that most transactions in the ordinary course of business are carried out with valid authority. The seller (lessor) is usually entitled to dispose of the object free of the property right registered in the ordinary course of its business. Thus, there is no need to require third parties to search the register in most situations. Truly, the seller (lessor) is not allowed to dispose of the object free of the property right registered in exceptional situations. However, it does not seem worthwhile to impose a general duty on the third party because of such exceptional situations.

It has been shown that Belgian law stipulates that registration is not constructive notice to non-professional third parties. This rule overlaps with the rule of the "ordinary course of business". In general, the transaction with non-professional third parties, in particular consumers, falls within the ordinary course of business. Therefore, the principal difference between the Belgian rule and the rule of the "ordinary course of business" is whether registration forms a constructive notice to trade buyers (in the jargon of Belgian law professional buyers). In this research, we argue that a general duty of inspecting the register should not be imposed on trade buyers for the reasons presented above.

Proposal 17:
Registration should not affect transactions in the ordinary course of the debtor's business. Third parties in the ordinary course of the debtor's business cannot be reasonably expected to search the register and thus cannot be assumed to be aware of the property right registered.

5.3.3.4 The Issue of Good Faith

It has been demonstrated that registration is a condition of the legal effect against subsequent acquirers. With respect to this conclusion, an important issue is whether good faith is necessary for subsequent acquisition free of an existing but unregistered property right. In other words, should a third party who has actual knowledge of an unregistered property right be bound by this right? Should the date of registration be a decisive factor? Is knowledge also relevant in determining the priority between different competing property rights?

369 See art. IX.-5:204 DCFR and IX.-6:102 DCFR, and Recommendation 81 UNCITRAL Legislative Guide on Secured Transactions.

A Notice and Race

With respect to this issue, there are three different approaches: one is the "*notice*" system, another is the "*race notice*" system, and the third is the "*pure race*" system.[370] Under the first system, the subsequent acquirer who has neither actual knowledge nor constructive knowledge will prevail, regardless of whether the acquirer has completed registration. Therefore, if a property right is not registered, which implies that the effect of constructive knowledge is not triggered, then this right is subordinate to subsequent acquisition by a third party acting in good faith. This system has a dilemma: since the subsequent acquirer acting in good faith and the unregistered proprietor do not differ in the aspect of registration, there is no reason to protect the former in priority.[371]

Under the second system, the subsequent acquirer obtains priority only when completing registration earlier in good faith. Registration has the effect of constructive knowledge, implying that subsequent acquisitions cannot arise free of registered property rights. The race notice system grants a secure position to registered proprietors. For subsequent acquisition free of unregistered property rights, it is necessary that the subsequent acquirer acts in good faith at the moment of registration. This implies that the information outside of the register is also relevant. Thus, registration is not decisive in solving the conflict between "older" unregistered property rights and "younger" registered property rights.

Different from the two systems above, the pure race system focuses only on the date of registration: the person who completes registration earlier obtains a higher ranking. In general, it is irrelevant whether the person is aware of other property rights created earlier. For example, A purchases a bulk of bicycles from B who inserts a clause of reservation of ownership; soon A mortgages these bicycles to C, and C knows about B's reservation of ownership. Under a pure race system, C will win when he registers the mortgage earlier, provided that both transactions are registerable. In this case, C's knowledge obtained outside of the register is of no relevance.

The pure race system is commonplace nowadays, at least in the field of secured transactions of movables. The system can be found in Article 9 UCC,[372] the Canadian PPSAs,[373] the New Zealand PPSA,[374] and the Australian PPSA.[375] The principal reason for choosing to construct a pure race system of registration is that this system facilitates the "*certainty*" of

370 Baird and Jackson 1984, p. 313.

371 This reminds us of the dilemma in the English landmark case of double sale and lease-back (*Michael Gerson (Leasing) Ltd v. Wilkinson and State Securities Ltd*, 31 July 2000 [2001] Q. B. 514.). If both of the two competing buyers (here acquirers) do not have possession (here registration), falling in the same situation, then why can the second buyer win (see 3.4.3.1.D).

372 See § 9-322 (a) (1) UCC; LoPucki, Abraham and Delahaye 2012, p. 1795.

373 See s. 30 (1) Ontario PPSA; Bennett 1999, p. 57.

374 See s. 66 (b) New Zealand PPSA; Gedye 2011, p. 705.

375 See s. 55 (4) and (5) Australian PPSA; Whittaker and Partner 2015, p. 308.

transactions.[376] Under this system, there is no need to investigate the question of whether the subsequent acquirer acted in good faith at the moment of registration.[377]

Unlike the legislation mentioned above, Book IX DCFR constructs a notice system of registration by combining the *nemo dat* rule and the rule of *bona fide* acquisition.[378] According to art. IX.-2:105 DCFR, a requirement of granting security rights is that the grantor has qualified authority to do so. As an exception to this requirement, the DCFR provides the possibility of acquisition from an unauthorized grantor (art. IX.-2:108) and the acquisition free of earlier limited property rights (art. IX.-2:109).[379] In accordance with these two provisions of *bona fide* acquisition, the subsequent acquirer has to act in good faith,[380] and the completion of registration by the acquirer is irrelevant.[381] Thus, the system proposed is not a race notice system: whether the subsequent acquirer registers the property right earlier is irrelevant. In the viewpoint of the drafters, "*the mere fact that a secured creditor has filed an entry in the register of security rights does not entitle this secured creditor to have confidence in the security provider's entitlement to dispose of the assets concerned*".[382] However, as has been pointed out at the beginning of this part, a problem of this system is that it is difficult to explain that the subsequent acquirer acting in good faith is protected in priority to the unregistered proprietor. Both parties are in the same position in the aspect of publicity.

B Efficiency and Morality

The controversial issue of good faith relates to two aspects: one is clarity and certainty of property rights, and the other is morality associated with property rights. These two aspects have been pointed out by English scholars in discussing whether the conventional doctrine of notice should be abolished in reforming the system of land registration.

> "*Moreover, the displacement of the traditional equitable doctrine of notice achieves a certain kind of efficiency, albeit at the expense of some moral exactitude. Unlike the 'bona fide purchaser' principle, the registration rule obviates any general inquiry into the state of mind or moral standing of the individual disponee in each transaction.*"[383]

---

376 White and Summers 2012, p. 1281.

377 Baird and Jackson 1984, p. 314.

378 See art. IX.-2:105 DCFR and art. IX.-2:108-109 DCFR.

379 Pursuant to art. IX.-401 (5) DCFR, where a security right is obtained in the way of *bona fide* acquisition (art. IX.-2:108 and IX.-2:109), this security right has priority to the earlier security right or the device of reservation of ownership.

380 DCFR 2009, p. 4488 and 4493.

381 DCFR 2009, p. 4489 and 4492.

382 DCFR 2009, p. 4487. In fact, this reasoning is also found in explaining why delivery is not a requirement of *bona fide* acquisition of security rights on corporeal movables. See DCFR 2009, p. 4487.

383 Gray 2009, p. 1093.

Indeed, good faith concerns the state of third parties' minds, which are difficult to probe. Where good faith is stipulated as a requirement for subsequent acquisition by third parties, the real proprietor might make use of this requirement as a means of defense. As a result, whether the third party is innocent will often become a dispute that courts have to adjudicate. This brings two negative consequences: one is that the activity of adjudication *per se* is costly, and the other is that whether third parties can acquire property rights will become uncertain.

Carol M. Rose observes a distinction of "*mud*" and "*crystals*" in the rules of property law.[384] The feature of the crystal rules (or hard-hedged rules) is that "*they signal to all of us, in a clear and distinct language, precisely what our obligations are and how we may take care of our interests*", while mud rules are so "*fuzzy and ambiguous*" that individuals "*don't know quite what their rights and obligations really are*".[385] Property law should include ambiguous terms (such as fairness and reasonableness) as few as possible, because the legal relationship of property rights should be clear and certain for third parties.[386] This view is also in line with the economic rationale that clear delimitation of property rights is a precondition for efficient utilization.[387] In essence, the requirement of good faith forms a mud rule. It is a difficult question whether the subsequent acquirer knows or should be regarded as knowing the existence of an earlier but unregistered right.[388]

Nevertheless, we argue in the following discussion that certainty of property rights is not a sufficient reason to dispense with the requirement of good faith.

Firstly, a pure race system, under which actual knowledge is completely irrelevant, is not in line with the purpose of registration.

> "*After all, the purpose of notice filing is to make the prior right known. If this prior right happens to be already known to the second-in-time lender, then to continue to make filing the sole determining factor defeats the purpose that such filing intended to serve in the first place.*"[389]

As we have stated above, the purpose of registration is to address the problem of information asymmetry by providing a reliable channel through which outsiders can obtain proprietary information (see 2.2.3 and 5.1.1.2). Once a third party has been aware of the actual legal state, this party is expected to act according to what he knows. Otherwise, the registration system would become a tool taken advantage of by third parties to override the *nemo dat* rule, a cornerstone of the entire legal system of property.[390]

---

384 Rose 1988, p. 577.
385 Rose 1988, p. 577-579.
386 Snijders and Rank-Berenschot 2017, p. 69.
387 Lueck and Miceli 2007, p. 189.
388 Rose 1988, p. 588.
389 Hamwijk 2014, p. 357.
390 Rusch 1995, p. 567.

Secondly, the pure race system causes a moral difficulty. Human beings live in communities and are expected to behave in a way that takes others in consideration. There is not a general rule requiring people to benefit others positively. But the negative duty of not harming others exists on the shoulder of every person. In general, *bona fide* acquisition by a third party is recognized at the cost of earlier property rights, and law must attempt to strike a balance carefully. Allowing subsequent acquisition by *mala fide* persons amounts to encouraging immoral or unfair competition.[391] Indeed, market competition is important. However, this does not mean that a person can overlook others' legal position in the course of pursuing his or her own interests. The pure race system runs counter to "*fairness feelings*".[392]

In the system of private law, good faith is always a condition of conferring priority benefits on a third party, when it is inevitable that the interest of another party will be sacrificed (in particular the original owner in the situation of *bona fide* acquisition and the principal in the situation of apparent agency).[393] In the absence of good faith, the protection of third parties' reliance becomes groundless. In fact, even under Article 9 UCC which aims for a pure notice system, good faith is treated as relevant in judicial practice. For example, the case *In re Davidoff* states that "*it was not good faith to impose a security interest on assets which a debtor had already said were secured to two named banks*".[394] Moreover, in situations where "*something more than knowledge of the subsequent acquirer is involved*" the registration-based priority rules have also been modified by judges.[395] Perhaps, one reason for the "*judicial subversion*" is that the "*race priority itself was probably an accident*", and "*the drafters had no clear intent in this regard*".[396]

Thirdly, the requirement of good faith has both downsides and merits. In the viewpoint of Joseph William Singer, good faith is a "*standard*" (as opposed to a "*rule*").[397] Compared with rules, standards are less predictable because judges have to apply them by considering all relevant factors and circumstances. On the other hand, this comprehensive consideration allows judges to avert unfairness and inefficiency which might be caused by clear and rigid rules.[398]

> *"Rules grant the luxury of indifference. They invite self-interested persons to act like Holmes's 'bad man' and go forward with harmful but lawful conduct. In contrast, standards promote attentiveness to the effects of one's actions on others and may thereby promote an other-regarding altruist ethical stance [...]. For this reason, Seanna Shif-*

391 Carlson 1986, p. 243.
392 Carlson 1986, p. 227-229.
393 Nieskens-Isphording and Van der Putt-Lauwers 2002, p. 17-19.
394 *In Re Davidoff*, 351 F. Supp. 440 (S.D.N.Y. 1972).
395 White and Summers 2012, p. 1321-1322.
396 Carlson 1986, p. 235, 250.
397 Singer 2013, p. 1370.
398 Singer 2013, p. 1376.

frin and Jeremy Waldron argue that standards promote moral introspection and justification."[399]

Truly, the requirement of good faith may cause vagueness and be a drain on judicial resources. However, these two downsides can be largely counterweighed by the preservation of moral justice, a value perhaps having a higher ranking than economic efficiency. In strangers community, commerce is not only a cool and hard activity, but also a means to facilitate morally social interactions.[400] Good faith is a core ingredient of social commerce because it requires practitioners to be "*attentive to the needs of others*".[401]

It is noteworthy that the standard of good faith is not always vague. In fact, it is or can be predictable in two senses. The requirement is informally predictable. Individuals commonly expect that a third party acting in bad faith should not be entitled to subsequent acquisition free of existing property rights. In general, this is a result of our commonly-shared value and social experience, which is also known as "*informal sources of justified expectations*".[402] Just as Carlson argues, "*for the public, certainty is desirable for good faith Bs, but certainty for bad faith Bs is probably undesirable*".[403] In light of this view, the pure race registration seems unpredictable: the irrelevance of good faith under this system does not match with our moral sense and thus may surprise us. Moreover, with the accumulation of judicial experience, the question whether a third party acts in good faith can be answered with predictability and certainty. Granting judicial discretion to judges does not mean that they will make judgements arbitrarily. On the contrary, they are, perhaps informally, bound by precedents and popular understandings of lawyers.

Fourthly, a system of pure race registration may fail to realize the purpose of saving costs. The earlier proprietor can resort to other rules to preserve his or her unregistered property right. For example, the earlier proprietor may claim that the third party acted in bad faith, and the third party and its counterparty jointly harmed the unregistered property right intentionally. In general, this is in defiance of good morality, which provides sufficient ground to invalidate the agreement between the third party and its counterparty.[404] In addition, the earlier proprietor might also resort to tort law, claiming that the third party had an intention to damage the earlier property right through creating a new property right. As we have mentioned above, good faith has been used as a ground to deny subsequent acquisition by *mala fide* third parties in the legal practice of Article 9 UCC. Therefore, the effect of facilitating certainty and clarity of property rights by dispensing with the requirement of good faith is not apparent as it appears.

---

399 Singer 2013, p. 1377.
400 Rose 1988, p. 608.
401 Rose 1988, p. 607.
402 Singer 2013, p. 1380.
403 Carlson 1986, p. 241.
404 About this rule, see § 138 (1) BGB and art. 3:40 (1) BW.

In a nutshell, the requirement of good faith matches the purpose of registration and our moral sense. Though it might be a source of uncertainty, this problem should not be overstated due to the fact that judicial discretion on the issue of good faith is only unpredictable to a limited extent. On the other hand, whether abandoning the doctrine of good faith can save costs and facilitate legal certainty is still unclear.

Proposal 18:
For acquisition by a third party free of the property right which is created but not registered, it is necessary that this third party acts in good faith.

5.3.3.5 *The Issue of Public Reliability*

A *Doubts about Public Reliability of the Register*

In theory, a register can be a conclusive or reliable means of publicity with the legal effect of public reliance (see 5.1.2.3). A third party who relies on the register should be protected, even though the register fails to show the actual status of property rights or the relevant registration is incorrect. In reality, however, whether and to what extent a register book is conclusive is a question the answer to which depends on multiple factors. For example, the land register varies in the aspect of reliability (see 5.1.2.3).

In the field of corporeal movables and claims, it is often held that the register for secured transactions has no effect of public reliance.[405] There are several reasons for this. Firstly, the permission of creating a property right in the absence of registration will undermine the reliability of the register (declaratory effect). The integrity of the register will be hampered due to the existence of property rights created but not registered.[406] Secondly, the register is doomed to be "*negative*" because it operates "*in a purely electronic manner without active intervention of the system or the registrar*".[407] The involvement of registrars, especially those who are responsible for checking the validity of the contract, will reduce errors and defective property rights, facilitating the reliability of the register. Thirdly, the registration might cover future movable property, and the registration can be completed before the property right is created (advance registration).[408] Advance registration hampers reliability of the register.[409] Fourthly, the register is notice-based, which means that only "*minimal information*" is conveyed to third parties (see 5.3.1.4). It seems difficult to say that such minimal information can provide an adequate basis for the register to be reliable.[410] In the following discussion, we examine these four reasons in sequence.

---

405 Sigman 2010, p. 508.
406 Dubarry 2016, p. 631.
407 Dirix and Sagaert 2014, p. 246.
408 Sigman 2010, p. 508.
409 Baeck and Heytens 2019, p. 14.
410 Sigman 2010, p. 509.

B The Possibility of Public Reliance of the Register

In 5.3.3.1 and 5.3.3.2, it has been argued that the register proposed in this research for corporeal movables and claims has an effect against subsequent acquirers. This effect can be explained by the doctrine of constructive notice: in principle, subsequent acquirers are assumed to be aware of the property right registered (see 5.3.3.3). As a result, subsequent acquirers should not be bound by a property right which cannot be found from the register, provided that they act in good faith (see 5.3.3.4). Therefore, it can be concluded that *bona fide* subsequent acquirers are protected against the incompleteness of the register. For third parties acting in good faith, property rights not registered should be assumed to be non-existent. The protection against the incompleteness of the register is an important aspect of the public reliance of the register. Typically, this protection arises in the situation of double disposals ("A-B and A-C" transaction): A disposes of the object to B and then to C. Undoubtedly, the person who registers his or her right earlier will obtain a preferential position, and the searcher should not be bound by the property right falling outside the register. Otherwise, the system of registration would be useless: individuals would not bother to register or search the register.

Now let us turn to the second reason, an argument against public reliability from the perspective of the involvement of registrars. In general, this argument relates to consecutive transactions ("A-B-C" transaction): A disposes of an object to B who further disposes of the object to C. If the A-B transaction proves to be defective, will the transaction between B and C be affected?[411] According to the argumentation, since no registrar is involved in the operation of the self-service system, mistakes and errors cannot be eliminated through formal or substantive check by registrars. Inevitably, the register cannot be treated as reliable, and the reliance of third parties such as C should not be protected.

In general, the argumentation shown above is not fully convincing. This is because whether C deserves preferential protection is a matter of legal policy, having no necessary connection to the involvement of the registrar. In the hypothetical case above, the legislature has to make a choice between static security (A's preservation of his right) and dynamic security (C's reliance on the register), provided that B's acquisition has been filed in the system.[412]

---

411 About this question, it should be first noted that the principle of abstraction is not the only way to provide protection to successive acquirers (C in this case). The principle is not necessary for a means of publicity to be reliable for third parties. As we will see here, the protection of C is a matter of legal policy. Moreover, the principle of abstraction goes too far in safeguarding C and is not fully compatible with the rationale of publicity. It grants protection to C, regardless of whether C acted in good faith. As shown above, the principle of causation plus the rule of *bona fide* acquisition suffices for the protection of third parties (see 5.2.3).

412 About the distinction between dynamic security and static security, see O'Connor 2005, p. 47-49.

As has been argued above, whether a system of registration can serve as a basis of *bona fide* acquisition for third parties is an issue of legal policy (see 5.1.4.2). The role played by registrars is not necessarily relevant. Nowadays, there is not any general register for corporeal movables in many jurisdictions, which implies that no registrar is involved in the transaction of corporeal movables. However, this does not prevent third parties from *bona fide* acquisition on the basis of possession, a defective means of publicity. As we have argued above, *bona fide* acquisition of corporeal movables is in essence a result of legal policy and cannot be justified on the basis of the publicity effect of possession (see 3.4.3.4). The self-service system of registration proposed in this research might include defective filings. As in the situation of possession of corporeal movables, however, it is possible to provide *bona fide* protection on the basis of this system, provided that the legislature determines that dynamic security should prevail.

For example, where a bicycle is transferred under a clause of reservation of ownership, and this reservation has been registered; later the transferee (the second-hand) sells this bicycle to a third party (the third-hand). In this case, the latter disposal is subject to the same condition of payment under the *nemo dat* rule.[413] As a result, the third party is entitled to obtain full ownership upon the fulfillment of the suspensive condition. If the first hand (the original owner) is allowed to revoke the transaction against both the second hand and the third-hand by claiming that the first transfer was made under coercion, then the reliance of the third hand on the registration will fall short of protection. For the third hand, what can be seen from the register is that the bicycle was transferred under the suspensive condition of payment. The defect of coercion is invisible. In this case, both the first hand and the third hand are innocent and deserve protection. However, which one should prevail? This is a question of legal policy. If the legal policy is in favor of the third hand, then its reliance should be protected in priority.

In the end, we turn to the third and fourth reasons. These two reasons are co-related. The register proposed by this research is a notice-filing system (see 5.3.1.4), which allows advance registration. An important feature of this system is that it only indicates that the registered property right "may" exist. The registration might be completed before the conclusion of an underlying contract. Moreover, the system only provides minimal information and may fail to indicate, for example, the specific object involved. Therefore, the information stored in the system is not only imprecise but also perhaps incorrect. It is difficult to say that the system is, like the land register, able to serve as a reliable source of information.

Nevertheless, we contend that *bona fide* acquisition is also possible because of a supplementary scheme. This scheme is that third parties are entitled to further inquire with relevant parties to obtain the details of the property right registered (see 5.3.1.4). If the relevant party fails to answer

413 Snijders and Rank-Berenschot 2017, p. 423.

the inquirer's request, the inquirer can act as if "*the secured creditor had given the information that the assets concerned are not encumbered*", as provided for by art. IX.-3:323 DCFR. More importantly, third parties can rely on the information provided, so that they are able to make decisions with security according to the information. This protection has been pinned down by the DCFR in art. IX.-3:321, a provision concerning disclosure of correct information, and art. IX.-3:322, a provision concerning disclosure of incorrect information. Remarkably, art. IX.-3:322 (1) stipulates that where the incorrect information is that assets are not encumbered, "*the inquirer may within three months acquire a proprietary right in these assets free of any encumbrance in favour of the secured creditor on the basis of a good faith acquisition in spite of the entry in the register covering the secured creditor's rights*". In the situation where the incorrect information is that assets are encumbered, art. IX.-3:322 (2) provides two rules: (1) if the inquirer, typically, refrains from taking the transaction, then he or she is entitled to damages; and (2) if the inquirer, nevertheless, obtains a property right, the secured creditor who provides the incorrect information cannot gain any benefit from the incorrect disclosure.[414]

The supplementary regime of disclosure also implies that a third party is not entitled to acquisition in violation of what he or she knows from the disclosure of the relevant party. For example, when a third party knows from the disclosure that his or her counterparty's previous acquisition has a defective legal basis (such as an invalid or avoidable contract), *bona fide* acquisition will become impossible. This is because the third party knew about the actual state of the ownership of the object. In general, this is in line with our preceding argument that the element of good faith should not be dispensed with in introducing a system of registration (see 5.3.3.4). The DCFR confirms the relevance of good faith in art. IX.-3:321 and IX.-3:322.[415]

In a nutshell, the causation principle plus the rule of *bona fide* acquisition should be adopted in the system of registration proposed for corporeal movables and claims. Because of the general possibility of *bona fide* acquisition, the system of registration can be treated as having public reliance: third parties are allowed to transact on the basis of the information obtained from the register and the disclosure. It should be noted that the protection is in essence an outcome of legal policy of facilitating the certainty of transactions. If a contrary legal policy is adopted by conferring preferential protection over the actual owner, then the protection of reliance on the register would be negated.

Proposal 19:

The register might be a reliable means of publicity for third parties acting in good faith, so that *bona fide* acquisition is possible on the basis of the register. Inquirers, as a third party, should be allowed to rely on the information

414 Proprietary Security in Movable Assets 2014, p. 524-525.

415 Proprietary Security in Movable Assets 2014, p. 521-524.

provided by the relevant parties. If the information provided proves to be incorrect or incomplete, *bona fide* acquisition or damages should be available to the inquirer.

5.3.3.6 Duration of the Validity of Registration

In general, the duration of property rights varies significantly. For example, ownership reserved by the seller may pass to the buyer upon the payment of the purchase price, the property right of security enjoyed by the creditor is dependent on the performance of the secured obligation under the feature of "accessoriness (*afhankelijkheid* or *Akzessorietät*)" of security rights, and the property right of use comes to an end when the term of use expires. From these examples, it can be seen first that some property rights have a definite period of duration, while other property rights will change or end within an uncertain period. It is possible that the parties specify a definite period when creating the property right. For example, the secured creditor and the security provider may agree that the property right of security will exist for two years, regardless of whether the secured obligation is not performed within this period of time.

The variety of the period of duration of property rights gives rise to a problem concerning registration: how long should registration be valid? This problem involves two aspects: (1) can registration be valid for an uncertain period which depends on the duration of the registered property right; and (2) can registration be valid for a period specified by the parties without being limited by a maximum term? The first aspect concerns certainty of registration. If the validity of registration is subject to an uncertain period, searchers will not be able to ascertain from the register whether the property right registered remains existent. The second aspect concerns the smooth operation of the register. If a registration can be valid for a long period as the parties desire, the register would be cluttered with too many registrations.[416] To avert the problems presented above, it is desirable to require the parties to specify a definite period of duration of the property right registered without excessing a maximum term.

Under some PPSAs, Article 9 UCC, and Book IX DCFR, a longest period is recognized for the registration of secured transactions concerning movables, provided that no specific term is determined by the parties.[417]

---

416 Whittaker and Partner 2015, p. 208.

417 Under the Australian PPSA, the longest term is 7 years for the consumer property and the property described by a serial number and 25 years for the other types of property (s. 153 (1)). The New Zealand PPSA prescribes a longest term of 5 years (s. 153). Article 9 UCC and Book IX DCFR also include a longest term of 5 years (§ 9-515 (a) UCC and art. IX.-3:325 (1) DCFR). However, the Canadian PPSAs do not prescribe a longest term in general, and a security interest can be registered for infinity. See MacDougall 2014, p. 257-258.

The UNCITRAL also recommends a maximum period of registration.[418] Therefore, where parties fail to specify a definite period of registration, the registration will expire upon the passage of the maximum period. Truly, the property right might end before the expiry of the maximum period, and the register cannot always show the true condition of the property right. However, prescribing a maximum period improves the reliability of the register to some extent: if a registered property right ends before the expiry of the maximum period, and the parties fail to undo the registration, the registration will become invalid automatically upon the expiry of the maximum period.

Is the term specified by the parties also subject to the maximum period? In other words, is the maximum period only a default rule? With respect to this question, different answers are provided by different laws. According to the Australian PPSA and Book IX DCFR, parties are able to determine a period longer than the maximum period.[419] However, the New Zealand PPSA and Article 9 UCC impose a five-year limitation on the period of registration, regardless of whether the period is determined by the parties.[420] In this research, it is proposed that the maximum term is also applicable to the period determined jointly by the parties. Otherwise, the purpose to avert the clutter of registrations will be easily frustrated by parties specifying an extremely long period or even an infinite period.

Of course, where a maximum period of registration is pinned down, parties should be allowed to terminate the registration before the expiry and renew the registration after the expiry. This is commonly accepted by the law concerning the registration of secured transactions of movables.[421] In general, the termination and the renewal form an amendment of the register to which the parties are entitled.

Proposal 20:
To guarantee the smooth operation of the register, a maximum period of the validity of registration should be prescribed. This maximum period applies not only when no definite period is determined by the parties, but also when the parties specify a definite period. Parties are entitled to undo the registration before the expiry of the maximum period and renew the registration after the expiry of the maximum period.

418 UNCITRAL Legislative Guide on Secured Transactions, p. 182; UNCITRAL Guide on the Implementation of a Security Rights Registry, p. 80.
419 See s. 153 (1) Australian PPSA and art. IX.-3:325 (1) DCFR.
420 See s. 153 New Zealand PPSA and § 9-515 (a) UCC.
421 See art. IX.-3:326 DCFR; s. 154 New Zealand PPSA; § 9-515 (d) UCC; UNCITRAL Legislative Guide on Secured Transactions, p. 182.

5.3.4 Conclusion

In the preceding discussion, we propose a general system of registration for corporeal movables and claims. The register is a subject-based system constructed according to the identifier of parties. Third parties are able to search the register with reference to the identifier. A register folio should be attributed not only to legal persons, but also to natural persons, regardless of whether they act as a consumer. The system is digital and makes use of new information technology. The system is based on the notion of self-service, which means that the transacting parties can complete registration and third parties can search the register without involving registrars. The register is a notice-filing system that provides basic information concerning the property right, and searchers are entitled to further inquire with the relevant parties to obtain details of the property right.

In general, the register should not apply in situations where the problem of information asymmetry does not exist or has been addressed through other means. For example, ships and aircraft usually have a specialist register, and there is no need to include these two corporeal movables in the system of registration proposed by this research. In general, claims lack a means of publicity, and it is desirable to include the disposal (such as assignment and pledge) of claims in the register. Due to concerns about efficiency, a threshold of the value of the object should be set up so that the register will not be cluttered by small transactions. For the object which has a high frequency of circulation, such as securities and money, the formality of registration is undesirable; for the object which has a low frequency of circulation, such as jewelry, registration is also undesirable. Moreover, the duration of the hidden state of transactions is relevant to defining the scope of registration. For the transaction which will usually be accomplished within a short term, a grace period should be recognized.

For the acquisition of property rights, the formality of registration has declaratory effect, which means that registration is not a requirement of the acquisition. In general, registration can give rise the legal effectiveness against subsequent acquirers. A property right validly obtained can be enforced against strange interferers and general creditors, despite the absence of registration. For subsequent acquirers, registration constitutes constructive notice. However, the extent of this effect is restricted for the purpose of facilitating the fluidity of commercial transactions. The effect of registration is subject to the rule of the "ordinary course of business". For third parties to obtain a property right from the unauthorized, it is necessary that they act in good faith. The requirement of good faith guarantees that a fair balance can be reached between the third party and the actual owner (or the holder of earlier property rights).

The system of registration operates without involving registrars, and the information conveyed by the notice-filing register is not fully detailed. However, it is possible that third parties can rely on the system, and their reliance on the system is protected. This is because the protection of *bona fide* third parties is a matter concerning legal policy with respect to the means of publicity. If the legislature puts certainty of transactions in a primary position, the register can also act as a basis for *bona fide* acquisition. In addition, it should be noted that the system is associated with a supplementary scheme: the duty to provide information. Third parties are entitled to rely on the information provided by the relevant parties, which constitutes another aspect of the reliability of the system.

5.4 Registration as a Solution | Case Study I: Secured Transactions

In 5.3, we discussed the adoption of a system of registration from three general aspects: the way of constructing the system, the scope of the system, and the legal effect of the system. The general discussion takes the register for secured transactions concerning movables as an important sample but is also applicable to non-security transactions, such as the outright assignment of claims and the true lease of corporeal movables.

From this part, our attention shifts to three specific case studies. The first case study is secured transactions of corporeal movables and claims (see 5.4), a much debated topic in contemporary academic research and the reform of property law.[422] This case study is part of the preceding general discussion. Nevertheless, it is still necessary to devote further attention to this type of transaction from two aspects: the desirability of registration and the scope of registration. The reason for doing so is that there are controversies about these two aspects, as we will see later. In the following discussion, we mainly examine whether the system of registration proposed in 5.3 can alleviate and even eliminate the concerns about the adverse effect of registration on secured transactions.

The second case study is trust of corporeal movables. Trust is a regime of common law. Publicity of trusts is a traditional issue in the introduction of this regime into the civil law system. The regime has no means of publicity under common law, which runs counter to the principle of publicity in the civil property law. The recognition of trusts (*fiducie*) by French law (in 2007) and the recent plan to translate trust into Belgian law attract our attention to this traditional issue from the angle of publicity. In 5.5, we examine the possibility of including trust of corporeal movables and claims in the general system of registration proposed in this research.

The third case study concerns transactions concerning motor vehicles (see 5.6). A transaction concerning motor vehicles is governed by the traditional rules of possession in many jurisdictions. Different from aircraft and vessels, this type of corporeal movable does not occupy a place in the world of private law registration, despite the fact that an administrative system of

422 Gullifer 2016, p. 1-3.

registration has operated for a long time. The publicity of motor vehicles attracts attention in the course of reforming the law of secured transactions concerning movable property. For example, the PPSAs in Canada, Australia and New Zealand treat motor vehicles as a type of "*serial-numbered property*" which can be found with reference to the VIN.[423] As a result, the subject-based register has an object-based dimension. This induces us to devote particular attention to this special type of corporeal movable.

5.4.1 Setting the Scene

In contemporary financing practice, movable property, including corporeal movables and claims, is becoming increasingly important as collateral. The traditional security device, pledge, cannot satisfy the demand because of its intrinsic drawbacks. For example, the traditional pledge requires giving up possession or notifying the debtor in the situation of corporeal movables and claims respectively, which causes significant inconvenience to practitioners. As a result, the most popular security devices are those that do not require delivery or notification: non-possessory security device and undisclosed security device respectively. Both can be title-based (such as reservation of ownership and security transfer of ownership) or take the form of a limited property right (such as non-possessory pledge of corporeal movables and undisclosed pledge of claims). Moreover, security may be provided under the name of lease (such as financial lease and sale and leaseback).

These security devices, including the traditional possessory pledge, may differ in legal structure, but they all face the same problem of publicity. Whether and how these security devices should be made transparent is an issue under fierce debate, as we demonstrate below. Moreover, the debate on publicity is also related to other issues, in particular the question of whether a functional approach (or unitary approach) should be taken and whether non-security transactions should also be included in the same system of registration. Under the functional approach, the legal form a security device takes is treated as irrelevant to the existence of a security interest. For example, reservation of ownership can give rise to a security interest owned by the transferor under the functional approach. Non-security transactions are those that have no function to provide security, even in the economic sense. Outright assignment of claims and true lease are two typical examples of non-security transactions.

Many common law jurisdictions have initiated a legal reform of secured transactions concerning movable property, and most of them have constructed a system of registration. One inspirational approach is the notice-filing system under Article 9 UCC. According to Article 9, filing a

423 Whittaker and Partner 2015, p. 178-179.

financial statement in the system, in addition to possession and control, is a method of perfection that can make the security interest effective against certain third parties, including subsequent secured creditors, lien creditors, and general creditors in the event of bankruptcy.[424] Influenced by Article 9 UCC, both Canada and New Zealand have established a similar register, known as PPSA systems.[425] In 2012, the new Australian PPSA system came into operation and replaced the old system, a register based on the English system of registration. In these jurisdictions, a functional approach is adopted by having a general concept of "*security interest*".[426] Under the functional approach, different types of security device are characterized under the unitary concept of "*security interest*", irrespective of the legal form taken or whether they are title-based.

> *"After all, pursuant to a functionalist model, the essence of a security interest is not determined by the formal legal framework out of which it arises, but in what it seeks to accomplish. So, a transaction cast in some other form-sale, trust, lease, consignment, etc.-may nonetheless constitute a security interest if it functions to secure payment or performance of an obligation?"* [427]

In the world of common law, another example of registration for secured transactions of movable property is the companies register in English law. According to English law, registration is a way of perfection that "*can make the security effective against other secured creditors, trustees in bankruptcy and company liquidators or administrators*".[428] Different from the Article 9 system and the PPSA system, the English system is not governed under the functional approach: English law does not unify different types of security device under one concept according to their economic function, thereby following a formal approach.[429] Under this approach, there is a group of quasi-security interests, such as retention of title the hallmark of which is that it is not subject to the requirement of registration.[430] By rejecting the formality of registration, "*the associated administrative burdens and unwelcome publicity are avoided*" in the situation of quasi-security interests.[431]

The trend of having a system of registration has met with some resistance in some jurisdictions with a civil law tradition. Some countries, such as France, Belgium and Italy, have introduced a register for secured interests of movable property, especially the non-possessory pledge.[432] But they differ in some aspects. For example, reservation of ownership should be regis-

424 Hamwijk 2014, p. 189-190.
425 Ali 2002, p. 156.
426 Whittaker and Partner 2015, p. 39.
427 Bridge, Macdonald, Simmonds and Walsh 1999, p. 577-578.
428 Beale, Bridge, Gullifer and Lomnicka 2018, no. 9.01.
429 Goode 2013, p. 4-5.
430 Bridge, Gullifer, McMeel and Worthington 2013, p. 14.
431 Beale, Bridge, Gullifer and Lomnicka 2018, no. 7.06.
432 Castellano 2016, p. 542; Dirix and Sagaert 2014, p. 231; Renaudin 2013, p. 385.

tered in Italian law, but not in Belgian law or French law.[433] Other countries, such as Germany and the Netherlands, remain hesitant to introduce a general system of registration.[434] The security transfer, a security device without involving any registration, plays a dominant role in the German financing market. In the course of re-codification of the old BW, Dutch law replaced the security transfer with non-possessory pledge of corporeal movables and undisclosed pledge of claims. E.M. Meijers, the spiritual father of the new BW, proposed the construction of a system of public registration, but this proposal confronted fierce resistance and was not accepted in the end.[435] Nowadays, the non-possessory pledge and undisclosed pledge remain invisible to third parties in the Netherlands.[436] Different opinions exist with respect to the issue of whether a system of registration should be introduced.[437] In German law and Dutch law, reservation of ownership, as a common device of security, is subject to no formality of registration.

To harmonize the laws of secured transactions of movable assets at the EU level, the DCFR takes a quasi-functional approach and requires registration as a condition for "*effectiveness as against third persons*", including holders of proprietary rights in the encumbered assets, execution creditors, and insolvency administrators.[438] It is quasi-functional because the broad concept of "*security rights*" encompasses possessory pledge, non-possessory pledge, security transfer of ownership and reservation of ownership, but the reservation of ownership has a special position in enforcement.[439] In terms of publicity, it is unitary: registration is a method of perfection for both reservation of ownership and the other types of security rights.[440] In general, Book IX DCFR has much resemblance to Article 9 UCC, which is understandable when we realize that the functional approach is useful in harmonizing the current chaotic system of security interests in movables within the EU.[441]

---

433 Castellano 2016, p. 543; Dirix and Sagaert 2014, p. 238; Renaudin 2013, p. 389.

434 Mincke 1997, p. 204.

435 Hamwijk 2014, p. 62.

436 Heilbron 2011, p. 44.

437 Struycken 2009, p. 115; Kaptein 2012, p. 139; Van den Boezem and Goosmann 2010, p. 43.

438 Art. IX.-3:101 (1) DCFR: "*A security right created according to Chapter 2 has no effects against the following classes of third persons: (a) holders of proprietary rights, including effective security rights, in the encumbered asset; (b) a creditor who has started to bring execution against those assets and who, under the applicable law, has obtained a position providing protection against a subsequent execution; and (c) the insolvency administrator of the security provider, unless, subject to exceptions, the requirements of this Chapter are met.*"

439 Proprietary Security in Movable Assets 2014, p. 243.

440 In contrast to the DCFR, the recent Belgian reform takes a just different quasi-functional approach: reservation of ownership is characterized as a security interest in the situation of the buyer's bankruptcy, but registration is unnecessary for this security device. See Sagaert 2017, p. 33.

441 Van der Weide 2011, p. 367; De Groot 2012, p. 138.

At the global level, it is registration plus a functional approach that is commonly adopted. For example, the UNCITRAL Legislative Guide on Secured Transactions advises a *"functional, integrated and comprehensive approach"* and proposes *"to enhance certainty and transparency by providing for registration of a notice in a general security rights registry"*.[442] However, the Guide recognizes that reservation of ownership, which needs to be included in the register, might be prescribed as more than a security interest. In 1994, a preliminary report on the desirability and feasibility of the preparation by UNIDROIT of a model law in the general field of secured transactions, drafted by R.C.C. Cuming, proposed a system of registration and a unitary concept of charge covering various forms of secured transactions.[443] In general, the Cape Town Convention on International Interests in Mobile Equipment, an achievement made by the UNIDROIT, adopts a functional approach by unifying different proprietary interests under the concept of *"international interests"* (art. 2 (2)) and advocates a notice-filing system (art. 16-28).[444] However, it should be noted that, like the DCFR, the Convention treats the chargee and the conditional seller or lessor differently in the aspect of the available remedies in the event of the debtor's default.[445]

The preceding brief description of the *status quo* shows that, at least, two controversial issues exist with respect to the secured transaction of movable property. One issue is whether registration should be introduced to address the problem of publicity. The other issue relates to the scope of registration, especially whether title-based security interests should be registered. Accordingly, the following discussion focuses on these two issues in sequence.

5.4.2 The Desirability of Registration

5.4.2.1 Pros and Cons

A Arguments for the Registration System

In general, the justification of registration lies in the effect of the security device against third parties. It is often held that a system of registration is useful for two types of third party: (1) the potential subsequent acquirer (including secured creditors) who has an intention to have a property right over the collateral; and (2) the general creditor who has an inferior position before proprietary security interests in the event of the debtor's insolvency.[446] Registration can solve the problem of information asymmetry and

442 UNCITRAL Legislative Guide on Secured Transactions, p. 21, 23.
443 Cuming 1994 (2), p. 3, 5.
444 Sagaert 2004, p. 81-83.
445 Sagaert 2004, p. 83-85.
446 Struycken 2009, p. 175; Van den Heuvel 2004, p. 87-88.

perform a function of communication, thereby making the security interest transparent for these third parties.[447]

> *"Een ander, hier wel mee samenhangend, argument was dat de publiciteit van zekerheidsrechten tot waarborg voor schuldeisers dient dat de paritas creditorum niet stiekem wordt doorbroken. Het beginsel van de gelijkheid van schuldeisers zou tot gevolg hebben dat iedere voorrangspositie op de een of ander wijze naar buiten moet blijken."*[448]

The Belgian legislature believes that an effective system of security rights of personal property is a prerequisite for optimal lending, and this system necessitates a register for the sake of predictability: *"conflicts of ranking should be solved in a predictable manner"*.[449] It is worthwhile noting that, as a part of the information-disseminating function, the register can also preclude fraudulence, in particular antedating of secured transactions.[450]

In addition to supplying information for third parties, registration can also provide safety for the secured creditor.[451] In the absence of a register, where a non-possessory security right is created without dispossession, actual control of the collateral is held by the debtor or a third party. As a result, the debtor or the third party has a chance to dispose of the collateral, which will trigger a risk to the non-possessory secured creditor because of the possibility of *bona fide* acquisition by a third party.[452] If there is a system of registration from which the secured creditor's interest can be seen, then the absence of dispossession will, generally speaking, no longer be a source of risk for the secured creditor.

> *"Ten eerste is er de zekerheidsgerechtigde [...]: hij heeft er belang bij om zijn zekerheidsrecht zo veel mogelijk veilig te stellen ten opzichte van eventuele latere verkrijgers van rechten op het onderpand. Indien de wet een vorm van inschrijving in openbare registers mogelijk maakt, wordt de kenbaarheid van zijn recht vergoot. Hiermee wordt zijn recht [...] 'versterkt' en krijgt meer 'zakelijke werking'."*[453]

---

447 Hausmann 1996, p. 432.

448 Van den Heuvel 2004, p. 88. English translation: *"Briefly speaking, another argument is that the disclosure of security rights to creditors ensures that paritas creditorum is not secretly broken. The principle of equality of creditors requires that any prior position should be revealed in a certain way."*

449 Dirix and Sagaert 2014, p. 238.

450 Hamwijk 2014, p. 314.

451 Struycken 2009, p. 175.

452 Heilbron 2011, p. 46.

453 Struycken 2009, p. 175. English translation: *"Firstly, there is the security holder [...]: he has an interest in securing his right of security as much as possible in relation to potential subsequent acquirers of the collateral. Only when the law allows a form of entry in open registers, transparency of the right can be realized. With this, his right can be [...] 'strengthened' and obtain stronger 'proprietary effect'."*

As has been demonstrated above, registration constitutes, though under some limitations, constructive notice to third parties and excludes the application of *bona fide* acquisition to a large extent (see 5.3.3.3).

B Doubts about the System of Registration

However, the system of registration engenders doubts from different aspects. Even in those jurisdictions that have already constructed a system of registration for secured transactions, there is the opinion that this system should be abolished.[454]

In the viewpoint of some scholars, a system of registration is useless for general creditors (see 5.3.3.2). One reason is that "*the quantity of unencumbered assets that prospective creditors can see at the time of supplying credit says nothing about whether they will still be unencumbered in the future, when they have become a creditor*".[455] Moreover, general creditors cannot tell whether a debtor is or will face financial difficulties from the system because it only records the existence of proprietary encumbrances.[456] In practice, general creditors often choose to obtain information regarding the debtor's overall financial health from the latter's financial reports, which are more comprehensive than the system of registration.[457] In addition, involuntary general creditors, such as tort victims, are unable to consult the system before the legal relationship of obligation comes into existence.[458] For these reasons, the system of registration is treated as useful principally for subsequent secured creditors who intend to acquire a security interest.

> "*In fact, benefits to secured creditors may be the primary justification for the present notice-filing system, while the direct benefits to general creditors may be small. Secured creditors benefit from a central file that indicates the existence of a claim in a particular asset belonging to the debtor, and whether that or any subsequent claim would have priority over their claim.*"[459]

In addition to its slight importance for general creditors, another doubt is that the function of publicity of the system might be overstated for subsequent acquirers. Firstly, the system might fail to show third parties the specific collateral involved because of the permission of describing the collateral "*in various levels of generality*",[460] as well as the amount or even the nature of the obligation for which the security is provided.[461] To know the details of a security interest, the searcher has to conduct further inquiries.[462]

454 Alces 1995, p. 679.
455 Hamwijk 2011, p. 619.
456 Baird 1983, p. 60.
457 Van den Boezem and Goosmann 2010, p. 46.
458 Lipson 2005, p. 487.
459 Baird 1983, p. 60.
460 Sigman 2008, p. 153.
461 Sigman 2008, p. 154.
462 Von Wilmowsky 1996, p. 160-161.

Secondly, the information obtained from both the system and the further inquiry might become outdated after a short period. This is because the debtor is entitled to continue disposing of the unencumbered property and terminate the existing security interest by discharging the secured debt.[463] Thirdly, the register for movable property is different from the land register in the aspect of public reliability. The possibility for a registered creditor to enforce his or her security interest is contingent on whether the debtor has ownership of the collateral, and completion of registration is not a sufficient basis for *bona fide* acquisition.[464] As a requirement of creating a security interest, the provider needs to have qualified authority of disposal.[465] However, the question of whether the debtor has qualified authority cannot be answered according to the register.[466] Fourthly, there is a doubt about the practical use of this system: some subsequent acquirers, in particular normal buyers, would not search the system before entering into a transaction with the debtor.[467]

Moreover, a completely open system of registration might be undesirable for debtors: debtors are often unwilling to allow their competitors or clients to know about the commercial information from the register.[468] The publication of the proprietary encumbrances may give rise to a problem of "*false poverty*", and potential creditors would become more conservative in granting credits.[469] In the situation of natural-person debtors, a potential problem of registration is that their personal information is exposed to the public. In addition to the concern about personal or business privacy, another argument against a system of registration is about the smooth operation of commercial transactions. In the view of some opponents, the formality of registration constitutes a "superfluous regulative intervention (*overbodige overheidsinmenging*)" in the secured transaction concerning movable property.[470]

In the end, the actual importance of a register for the market of financing is questionable. For example, the healthy operation of the German banking and business industry proves that a system of registration is dispensable.[471] As has been mentioned above, one striking feature of the German law of secured transactions of movables is that a publicity system is completely absent (see 5.4.1).[472]

---

463 Von Wilmowsky 1996, p. 162.
464 Sigman 2008, p. 156; Proprietary Security in Movable Assets 2014, p. 459.
465 Hamwijk 2014, p. 169-170.
466 Von Wilmowsky 1996, p. 161.
467 Snijders 1970, p. 34; Van den Boezem and Goosmann 2010, p. 53.
468 Lwowski 2008, p. 178; Snijders 1970, p. 29.
469 Sigman 2008, p. 158-159; Vriesendorp and Barendrecht 1993, p. 29.
470 Snijders 1970, p. 33; Vriesendorp and Barendrecht 1993, p. 27-28.
471 Lwowski 2008, p. 179.
472 Brinkmaan 2016, p. 343.

> *"German creditors and German economy survived without perfection and publicity. Creditors know that security interests mostly of banks are already charging the movables or receivables of their clients when giving credit. The lesson to be learnt is that the significance of publicity and perfection should not be overestimated."*[473]

In a nutshell, the desirability of a system of registration for secured transactions of movable property is doubted from different aspects, including the actual usefulness of the system and the potential adverse effect on secured transactions.

5.4.2.2 *Conclusion of the Discussion*

In the following discussion, we examine the question concerning the desirability of including secured transactions in the system of registration proposed above (see 5.3). The question is answered in the affirmative, which in fact has been implied in the preceding discussion in 5.3. The following discussion seeks to dispel or alleviate the aforementioned doubts about a system of registration for secured transactions.

A *The Importance for Subsequent Acquirers*

A1: The Function of Preventing Conflicts
In general, where there is no system of registration, there is the possibility of a conflict between secured creditors and subsequent acquirers, such as the transferee of the collateral. If the collateral is a corporeal movable, the conflict needs to be resolved under an *ex-post* approach by applying the *nemo dat* rule together with the rule of *bona fide* acquisition. This approach faces a dilemma: one of the two conflicting parties has to lose. Behind the *ex-post* approach exists the conflict-resolving notion: instead of attempting to preventing the occurrence of conflicts, the approach focuses on how to resolve disputes.

Compared with the *ex-post* approach, an *ex-ante* approach based on the notion of preventive justice is more desirable. In general, *"prevention of such conflicts is better than having to resolve them"*.[474] Resolving a conflict after its occurrence entails costs.[475] Moreover, the possibility of conflicts gives rise to a problem of uncertainty in transactions. This implies two possible consequences for individuals. One is that individuals are discouraged from participating in the transaction. The other consequence is that individuals have to collect information through other means to avert conflicts. Even if some information is obtained, it remains uncertain whether the information is correct and complete. In other words, what are the circumstances under

473 Stürner 2008, p. 168.
474 Hamwijk 2011, p. 626.
475 In general, the cost results from multiple aspects, including the costs borne by the litigants as well as the resources spent by the court.

which the information obtained can be treated as reliable, so that a party's reliance will be protected?

If the secured transaction concerning movable property is included in a system of registration, the undesirable consequences presented above can be averted to a large extent. Not only does the system provide information, but the information provided can also be reliable (see 5.3.3.5). Potential transactors can rely on the register. Thus, the scope of collecting information is delimited: third parties do not have to be attentive to other sources of information.

> *"Die Registerpublizität erlaubt potentiellen Kreditgebern zu erfahren, ob der Schuldner das betreffende Objekt bereits mit einem Sicherungsrecht belastet hat, so dass sie aufgrund des Wissens über Zeitpunkt, Art und Menge bereits bestellter Sicherungsrechte rational über einen Sicherungsvertrag mit dem Kreditnehmer entscheiden können; und diesen versetzt die Registerpublizität in die Lage, dem Gläubiger eine verlässliche Sicherheit anzubieten."*[476]

A2: The Deficiencies of Informal Means

It is true that potential subsequent acquirers are able to obtain some proprietary information in informal ways, such as the debtor's personal disclosure, the debtor's annual or semi-annual financial reports, and even the local knowledge in a specific industry.[477] However, these ways have their own defects. The defect of the debtor's self-disclosure is obvious: the debtor might cheat or mislead its counterparties.[478] Under a notice-filing system proposed in this research, the secured creditor may cheat when being required to provide detailed information. However, the remedies available for the inquirer will discourage the creditor from doing so to a large extent (see 5.3.3.5.B).

The debtor's financial reports play an important role in the dissemination of information but are far from being adequate. Misrepresentations might be included in the report. Moreover, the report often fails to show what specific assets are encumbered with what security interests. Law, such as art. 2:375 BW, might require the debtor to disclose the assets that are encumbered with a security right in the annual report. However, two problems still exist: one is the access to the report, and the other concerns the timeliness of the report.

---

476 Von Wilmowsky 1996, p. 163. English translation: "*The publicity of the register allows potential lenders to find out whether the debtor has encumbered the collateral with a right of security, so that they can rationally reach a security agreement with the borrower on the basis of the knowledge of the date, type and quantity of the already-created security rights; this enables the publicity of the register to provide reliable security to the creditor.*"

477 Schwartz 1989, p. 219-210.

478 Vriesendorp and Barendrecht 1993, p. 4.

"Unfortunately not every party is in the position to ask and to order the contracting party to let him see the annual report. Besides, the annual report represents the situation as on 31st December of last year. As most annual reports are published in the second quarter of the next year, the situation and which assets are encumbered in the annual report do not reflect the current situation."[479]

An annual report is made once a year and provides some rough information. Thus, it neither shows the instant state of proprietary encumbrances nor supplies the details of security interests, in particular the date of creation. Moreover, failure to record a security interest in the report does not bring any disadvantage to the secured creditor, and no good faith protection is granted to third parties who believe that this security interest does not exist. Therefore, the debtor's financial report cannot completely address the problem of information asymmetry and should not be treated as an adequate alternative to registration.

The asymmetry of information might be alleviated to some extent on the basis of the subsequent acquirer's local knowledge and business experience. For example, in Germany and the Netherlands, neither of which has a general system of registration for corporeal movables and claims, protection will not be granted to a person who deems that the possessor has full ownership if the transaction occurs in a particular industry where retention of ownership is common.[480] Moreover, diligent businessmen and professional banks are expected to know that the debtor's assets are usually encumbered with a security interest.

Nonetheless, the problem of information asymmetry still exists. In general, what third parties can get by virtue of their commercial knowledge and experience is that a proprietary encumbrance might exist. The commercial knowledge and experience can by no means be sufficient for clearly knowing whether and to what extent the encumbrance exists with respect to what specific collateral. Precise information is needed.[481] Moreover, the judgement on the basis of commercial knowledge and experience is unfair to those debtors whose movable property is mostly not encumbered with any security interest. The debtor has to try to convince its potential counterparties that the movable property involved is not encumbered.[482]

479 Zeldenrust 2011, p. 25.

480 In a German case in 1980, *"the BGH decided that in those business sectors where practically all goods are sold under retention of title, purchasers can no longer trust that the goods which the seller possesses are in fact his property."* See Kieninger 2007, p. 653. According to a Dutch case adjudicated by the court of appeal of Hertogenbosch in 1985, *"[...] goede trouw is niet aanwezig indien het eigendomsvoorbehoud in de branche gebruikelijk is en de derde met de mogelijkheid rekening had moeten houden dat de koper zijn verplichtingen jegens leveranciers niet op normale wijze had afgewikkeld."* See Hof's-Hertogenbosch 27 maart 1985, NJ 1986, 431. English translation: *"[...] good faith is not present if the reservation of ownership is common in the industry, and the third party should have taken into account the possibility that the buyer does not dicharge its debt to suppliers in a normal way."*

481 Vriesendorp and Barendrecht 1993, p. 30.

482 Zeldenrust 2011, p. 13.

A3: The Information Provided

As has been presented above, there is some doubt about the usefulness of the register: the information provided is general, and the register is not as reliable as the land register. This doubt is not completely groundless. It is true that the notice-filing system perhaps fails to inform third parties of the details of secured transactions. On the other hand, the register is supplemented by a scheme of disclosure by the secured creditor. Under this scheme, the secured creditor bears a duty to provide detailed information upon the request of third parties (see 5.3.1.4). More importantly, the reliance of third parties on the information provided by the secured creditor will be protected, such as in the way of allowing them to acquire a security interest or claim damages (see 5.3.3.5).

A4: The Search of the Register

Another doubt as mentioned above is based on the fact that some subsequent acquirers, in particular buyers, do not inspect the register before entering into transactions. In fact, this doubt is, to a large extent, in line with our viewpoint that a rule of the "ordinary course of business" should be recognized (see 5.3.3.3). Under this rule, third parties are not expected to search the register because the debtor usually has qualified authority of disposal in the ordinary course of its business. Registration does not constitute constructive notice to third parties in the ordinary course of business. In general, this can be treated as a limitation of the system. However, this limitation is necessary and desirable since it guarantees that the formality of registration will not hamper the smooth operation of transactions and commerce.

In sum, there is information asymmetry affecting subsequent acquirers, including buyers and secured creditors, in the field of secured transactions concerning corporeal movables and claims. This makes it desirable to have a register, under the supplement of a scheme of disclosure, as a reliable source of information. Despite the fact that the German financing market currently operates well, as indicated in 5.4.2.1.B, it is desirable to introduce a system of registration in the future.[483] The traditional system is facing new challenges, such as the growth in cross-border transactions.[484]

B The Importance for General Creditors

In arguing for a system of registration for corporeal movables and claims, some writers also attempt to find justifications from the usefulness for general creditors, as has been shown above. Unsecured creditors have a legal position inferior to secured creditors. Thus, there is a need to allow them to know about the existence of security rights. As an exception to the *paritas creditorum*, the preferential effect of security rights requires a basis of pub-

483 Von Wilmowsky 1996, p. 163.
484 Brinkmann 2016, p. 351.

licity.[485] The register for secured transactions concerning movable property can provide such basis. However, this view is exposed to several doubts mentioned above. In general, we hold that these doubts are tenable, and the register is nearly of no use for general creditors (see 5.1.3.2 and 5.3.3.2).

Firstly, general creditors often rely on the debtor's overall financial health (see 2.2.2.2.C).[486] General creditors do not require the debtor to supply proprietary security because, in many situations, they believe that the debt will be paid off on the basis of the debtor's cashflow.[487] For example, "*small creditors*" often believe that the "*big debtor*" will pay and thus rarely, even if possible, search the system.[488] Compared with a register, the debtor's financial reports are more comprehensive and seems more important for general creditors.[489] Financial reports include information that is of great use for evaluating the overall financial health of the debtor. This is a reason why some writers question that a notice-filing system can sufficiently justify the preferential status of secured creditors over unsecured creditors.[490]

Secondly, even if an unsecured creditor searches the register, the information obtained will become out-of-date in a short period of time. The debtor continues to create new encumbrances and remove the already-created encumbrance by discharging the secured debt.[491] Thus, the state of the debtor's assets and that of the encumbrance over the assets are always in fluctuation, and unsecured creditors cannot be expected to search the system every day. Provided that there is a general creditor searching the system every day and finds out that an asset is disposed of, nothing can be done by this creditor since the disposal has been completed validly.

Thirdly, the system is useless for involuntary creditors and those who have already acquired a personal claim before the creation of the registered security right.[492] Persons, such as a tort victim, might be "forced" to become a general creditor.[493] In this situation, the creditor is unable to decide whether to have an obligational relationship with the debtor since the legal relationship is a result of the operation of law. In this situation, the system of registration provides no help to the creditor.[494] In addition, if a right of pledge is created after granting credit in the absence of any security, registration of this right is of no use for the general creditor. Truly, the unsecured creditor can be expected to know that the debtor might dispose of his or her assets after granting an unsecured credit, thus requiring the unsecured

485 Vriesendorp and Barendrecht 1993, p. 4-5; Finch 2009, p. 634.
486 Van den Heuvel 2004, p. 93.
487 LoPucki 1994, p. 1941.
488 Snijders 1970, p. 34.
489 Van den Heuvel 2004, p. 93.
490 LoPucki 1994, p. 1948; Finch 2009, 640.
491 Hamwijk 2011, p. 619.
492 Snijders 1970, p. 33.
493 Hamwijk 2011, p. 623.
494 Finch 1999, p. 662.

creditor to bear the risk of underpayment does no injustice to him or her.[495] However, this argument just proves that the information out of the system of registration is of little importance: every searcher is expected to be aware that the debtor might conduct further disposals.

However, it is not completely correct to say that registration is of no use for unsecured creditors. As observed by E.M. Meijers, the lack of an objective scheme to determine the date of creation offers a chance for transacting parties to fraudulently antedate their security right at the sacrifice of the general creditor's interest.[496] If there is a system of registration, and entry in such system is prescribed as a prerequisite of the effectiveness against unsecured creditors, the problem of antedating can be avoided.[497] However, as pointed out above, the New Zealand practice has proven that most secured creditors choose to register their legal positions for the sake of priority over subsequent acquirers, which means that the date of creation can be indicated by the registration system in most situations (see 5.3.3.2). Moreover, the notice-based system cannot fully preclude the problem of antedating. This is because the security interest might be registered in advance, which could cause a dispute arises with respect to the question when the security agreement was created.[498] Therefore, to what extent the register book can satisfy the general creditor's demand for certainty concerning the date of the creation of security interests is still open to doubt.

In a nutshell, the information asymmetry between the debtor and its general creditors either does not exist or has been generally addressed by alternative methods, in particular the debtor's financial reports. The purpose of protecting unsecured creditors cannot be realized by virtue of a system of registration. Instead, it seems better to protect general creditors in other ways, such as establishing a "*prescribed part*" rule or granting a privilege to involuntary creditors (e.g., tort victims).[499] It is also proposed by some scholars that companies ought to be compelled to buy liability insurance against tort claims to ensure that tort victims are able to obtain full compensation in the event of the debtor's insolvency.[500]

C The Concern about Fluidity of Transactions

It has been mentioned that opponents contend that the formality of registration forms a regulative interference in transactions and hampers commercial fluidity. Truly, movables have a higher circulation frequency than immovable assets, and registration affects, to a certain degree, the smooth operation of transactions. Nevertheless, we argue that this concern might be overstated. The system of registration proposed in this research

495 LoPucki 1994, p. 1949; Finch 1999, p. 645.
496 Meijers 1954, p. 276.
497 Bridge 2008, p. 186.
498 Gedye 2016, p. 132.
499 Eger 2001, p. 40; Finch 2009, p. 635-636; Leebron 1991, p. 1643-1649.
500 Finch 1999, p. 653-654.

will not exert much influence on the smooth operation of transactions and commerce.

Firstly, the system of registration is proposed to be digital, self-service, and notice-based (see 5.3.1.2-5.3.1.4). By making use of new information technology under the notion of self-service, the system is easy to use and access: both registration and investigation can be done online without involving any registrar. This guarantees that the system will not create much inconvenience to the transacting parties as well as searchers. Moreover, the register is a notice-based system, instead of a transaction-filing system. In doing so, the burden of documentation can be reduced significantly, so that the influence of registration over rapid commercial transactions will be limited to an acceptable degree.

Secondly, the scope of application of the system proposed is limited on the basis of several factors, which also restricts the undesirable influence on smooth commence. For example, the factor of transactional frequency is taken into consideration (see 5.3.2.3.A). The system will not include corporeal movables and claims that have a high frequency of circulation. Moreover, the duration of the hidden state of the secured transaction is also relevant (see 5.3.2.3.B). For those transient and short-term hidden proprietary interests, the requirement of registration will simply hinder the smooth operation of the register and the secured transaction. For short-term secured transactions, granting a grace period offers a chance for the transacting parties to complete the transaction without being exposed to the risk arising from the lack of registration. Here a typical example is reservation of ownership by the supplier.[501] In the end, a threshold is set up for the amount of the collateral value, so that the register will not be cluttered by "small transactions" (see 5.3.2.1.E). This threshold also guarantees that small transactions are not affected by the formality of registration.

Thirdly, the rule of voluntary registration further reduces the effect of registration over transactional fluidity. As argued above, registration is not a prerequisite for the creation of a security interest (see 5.3.3.1). Instead, it is only relevant to the legal effectiveness against subsequent acquirers. This means that if transacting parties think registration is not worthwhile, they can opt not to register the security right by bearing a risk of *bona fide* acquisition by a third party.

> *"In this sense, registration is not compulsory as ultimately it is a? matter of commercial judgement and risk for the creditor to determine whether or not the costs attendant with registration are outweighed by the risk of losing priority or even the extinguishment of security interest."*[502]

If there is not any system of registration, the secured creditor will always face the problem of being defeated by a third party acting in good faith,

501 Veneziano 2008, p. 92; Faber 2014, p. 35.
502 Davies 2004, p. 309.

which will further lead to a burden of monitoring the debtor's activities with respect to the collateral, provided that the secured creditor really desires to preserve its preferential position.[503] If there is a system of registration, the security right can be made effective against third parties after registration. This will save on monitoring costs.[504] In this sense, we could say that registration provides a chance, rather than a burden, for secured creditors to eliminate the risk of *bona fide* acquisition.

Fourthly, the system proposed includes a rule of the "ordinary course of business" (see 5.3.3.3.B). Under this rule, transactions carried out in the ordinary course of the secured debtor's business will not be affected by registration. Particularly, buyers in the ordinary course do not have to search the register before deciding to purchase the collateral inventory. Moreover, the collateral can be acquired free of the proprietary encumbrance registered. Thus, the rule restricts the undesirable influence of registration over the smooth operation of transactions in the ordinary course of business.

D The Concern About Privacy

Another form of resistance against a system of registration comes from the fear that the information out of this system might be misused or would violate business or personal privacy. Company debtors often do not want their secured transactions to be known about by others, especially their competitors.[505] For natural persons, the disclosure of the personal information required for creating a folio forms a threat to their privacy. In general, the fear has no firm ground and should not be overstated under a notice-filing system, as has been argued above (see 5.3.1.4 and 5.3.1.5). The personal privacy of natural persons is not a sufficient reason to deny registration either, which also has been demonstrated above (see 5.3.2.2).

5.4.3 The Scope of Registration

As pointed out above, most systems of registration for secured transactions are constructed under the functional approach, an approach focusing on the economic substance and unifying different types of secured transactions under one concept, such as security interest or charge (see 5.4.1). In other jurisdictions where a functional approach is not taken, some secured transactions, despite their economic function of security, are exempted from the formality of registration. A typical example is reservation of ownership.[506]

---

503 Finch 1999, p. 641.

504 Jackson and Kronman 1979, p. 1152-1153.

505 Lwowski 2008, p. 178.

506 In French law, for example, a system of registration was introduced for non-possessory pledge (*gage*) over corporeal movables and charge (*mantissement*) over claims in 2007. However, retention of title still falls outside this system. See Renaudin 2013, p. 386-390. Under English law, reservation of ownership is not subject to registration either. See Bridge, Gullifer, McMeel and Worthington 2013, p. 14.

In the following discussion, we demonstrate that the problem of the scope of registration is not necessarily connected to the issue of whether a functional approach is adopted. In general, whether a security device should be included in the system is contingent on whether this device triggers a problem of information asymmetry. As a result, both reservation of ownership and security transfer of ownership require registration (see 5.4.3.1). In discussing the scope of registration, possessory pledge of corporeal movables is often neglected. Registration is treated as unnecessary for this classic type of security right, because delivery of the collateral has fulfilled the requirement of publicity. However, we contend that registration is also desirable for possessory pledge (see 5.4.3.2).

5.4.3.1 Title-Based Security

In general, title (including ownership of corporeal movables and "ownership" of claims) might serve a function of security in the following transactions:[507] (1) security transfer of title in the narrow sense; (2) sale and leaseback; (3) retention of title in the narrow sense; (4) hire purchase; (5) financial lease; and (6) consignment.[508] These six secured transactions can be divided into two groups: ownership *transferred* for security (type (1) – (2)) and ownership *retained* for security (type (3) – (6)).

In the situation of corporeal movables, all of these transactions share the feature that ownership is held by the creditor to secure its claim, and the debtor possesses the collateral. In these secured transactions, there is a divergence between ownership and possession. Like non-possessory pledge, they are also a type of non-possessory security device, having a function of security associated with an ownership-possession divergence. In general, transfer of ownership for security amounts to granting a right of non-possessory pledge to the transferee, and retention of ownership for security amounts to reserving a right of non-possessory pledge by the transferor. Therefore, if non-possessory pledge is required to be registered, there is no reason to treat title-based security interests differently (see 5.3.2.1.C). For those jurisdictions where non-possessory pledge is included in a register which excludes title-based security device, it is difficult to explain this different treatment.

In the situation of claims, individuals might provide security in the way of security assignment or reservation of title, instead of creating a disclosed pledge or an undisclosed pledge. Claims are invisible, and notification to the debtor does not qualify as an eligible means of publicity (see 4.1.1.2). Thus, the two types of title-based security device and the two types of pledge should also be made through registration (see 5.3.2.1.D). This is not difficult to understand. In the following discussion, attention is mainly afforded to title-based security in relation to corporeal movables.

507 It should be noted here that title is used in the sense of ownership or "belonging", instead of the legal basis on which the property right is acquired.

508 Proprietary Security in Movable Assets 2014, p. 229-260.

A Security Transfer of Ownership

Security transfer of ownership performs a pledge-like function in the situation of corporeal movables. This explains why this security device was replaced with the non-possessory pledge during the re-codification of the BW.[509] In terms of enforcement, the security owner is treated like a pledgee: different from an ordinary owner, the security owner has no right to vindicate the collateral and, in principle, only enjoys a priority in claiming the proceeds out of the sale of the collateral.[510] Thus, what the individuals intend to create is no more than a right of pledge that does not require dispossession of the collateral from the security provider. In German law, "security transfer (*Sicherungsübereignung*)" is covered under the concept of "non-possessory security over movables (*Besitzlose Mobiliarsicherheit*)".[511]

Usually, where non-possessory pledge is not recognized, individuals will turn to security transfer of ownership in the way of *traditio per constitutum possessorium* in order to avert the inconvenience out of the requirement of dispossession for possessory pledge.[512] However, *traditio per constitutum possessorium* is merely a change of possessory intention which cannot provide any indication to third parties (see 3.4.2.2.B and 3.4.2.3.B). Consequently, the security transfer is in essence hidden to third parties. Although the debtor-transferor might dispose of the collateral to others since the collateral remains in his or her factual control,[513] the creditor-transferee might also dispose of the collateral in violation of its fiduciary duties after acquiring ownership.[514] It seems unusual that German law objects to the secrecy of trusts, as we will see below, but does not require publicity for the security transfer.[515]

In general, registration of security transfer of ownership can preclude potential conflicts from arising to a large extent. Firstly, registration is able to indicate the underlying basis of the debtor-transferor's possession, which helps to avoid third parties being misled by the debtor's possession of the collateral. Secondly, when the creditor-transferee disposes of the collateral, registration provides a chance for the counterparty to know that the ownership held by the secured creditor is subject to fiduciary duties. In both situations, registration avoids or lowers the possibility of conflicts between one of the transacting parties and a third party.

Thirdly, security transfer of ownership sets up a barrier against making the most use of the collateral. Once the debtor-transferor alienates ownership of the collateral to the creditor-transferee, the former loses the author-

509 Vriesendorp and Barendrecht 1993, p. 9-10.
510 Drobnig 2011, p. 1037-1038.
511 Bülow 2012, Rn. 1277.
512 Vriesendorp and Barendrecht 1993, p. 6; Hausmann 1996, p. 455.
513 Bülow 2012, Rn. 1277.
514 Bülow 2012, Rn. 1278; Hausmann 1996, p. 459.
515 Wood 2019, no. 9-009.

ity to use the collateral again to secure other obligations.[516] This is why security transfer of ownership is treated as granting more to the secured creditor than he or she should have.[517] As a result, there is an associated problem of "excessive security (*Übersicherung*)" in German law. To address this problem, German courts positively intervene in the legal relationship of security: the security transfer will be invalidated if the value of the collateral substantially exceeds the amount of the secured obligation.[518] For example, where it unduly restricts the debtor's operation and fails to consider the interest of other creditors, the security transfer might be declared as void on the basis of violation of "good morality (*guten Sitten*)".[519] This positive judicial intervention can be partly ascribed to the lack of publicity.[520] It is conceivable that the intervention becomes less necessary when there is a system of registration from which third parties are able to know about the security transfer: in principle, a decision made on the basis of sufficient information must be respected.

After discussing security transfer of ownership in the strict sense, we turn to two particular transactions that are related to the concept of security transfer: one is sale and repurchase, and the other is sale and leaseback.

Repurchase, also known as "repo" or "*pactum de retroemendo*", is a form of transaction mainly arising in the field of investment securities, such as bonds and shares. It is an important way to obtain finance by using investment securities as a collateral.[521] However, sale and repurchase can also take place in the field of corporeal movables.[522] In a repo transaction of corporeal movables, the seller transfers the object to the buyer for obtaining "credit" in the form of the purchase price. The "debt" is discharged by repurchasing the object or another object of the same species by the original seller, who will pay the agreed price to the original buyer. What legal position is held by the original seller before the repurchase? With respect to this question, there are, in general, two approaches. Under one approach, the original seller has no more than a personal or a contractual right to repurchase.[523] Under the other approach, the seller retains a proprietary interest with respect to the object, such as being able to reclaim the object by paying the agreed price in the situation of the buyer' bankruptcy or to exercise its right of purchase against the third party to whom is disposed of by the buyer.[524] The difference between these two approaches relates to the principle of *numerus clausus*. The second approach is more flexible than the

516 Wilhelm 2010, p. 797-798.
517 Parlementaire Geschiedenis (3) 1981, p. 388.
518 Schwab and Prütting 2020, Rn. 420.
519 Schwab and Prütting 2020, Rn. 420b.
520 Vriesendorp and Barendrecht 1993, p. 16.
521 Keijser 2006, p. 101; Rank 2010, p. 304.
522 Sagaert and Cauffman 2011, p. 218-221; Greco 2008, p. 448-451.
523 Dalhuisen 2016, p. 512.
524 Sagaert and Cauffman 2011, p. 218; Greco 2008, p. 449; Dalhuisen 2016, p. 512.

first in the sense that the former approach allows, in essence, the creation of a proprietary security interest on the basis of the legal relationship of ownership.[525]

In general, where the original seller's right of repurchasing corporeal movables is a personal claim, there is no need to include the transaction in the system of registration. This is because both ownership and possession are transferred to the buyer, and the seller retains no proprietary interest with respect to the object (see 5.3.2.1.C). In this situation, no information asymmetry is caused to third parties. However, it is possible that the original transfer is carried out without involving dispossession, such as in the way of *traditio per constitutum possessorium*, and the seller retains actual possession of the object. In this situation, registration should be used to address the problem out of the divergence of possession and ownership. The transaction amounts to a security transfer of ownership in the strict sense. Under English law, the transaction constitutes a sham repo and should be treated as a charge, a proprietary security interest which is subject to registration.[526] If the right of repurchase is prescribed as effective against third parties, especially subsequent acquirers, under the second approach, there will be a need to register the transaction.

Sale and leaseback might be treated as a form of security transfer of ownership when the security transfer is understood broadly. The main difference of this transaction from the ordinary security transfer is that a legal relationship of lease is created between the seller and the buyer. In many situations, sale and leaseback has a purpose of providing security to the seller (lessee). However, it is possible that the buyer does obtain ownership of the object and then grants a possessory interest to the seller.[527] Undoubtedly, the boundary between security lease and true lease is not completely clear. Nevertheless, this has nothing to do with the issue of registration. In general, sale and leaseback needs to be included in the register, regardless of whether the parties intend to create a security interest. For registration, what matters is that ownership and possession diverge and are held by buyer (lessor) and seller (lessee) respectively. The divergence causes a problem of information to third parties who should be made aware through a system of registration (see 5.3.2.1.C).

---

525 The new BW excludes the repurchase transaction in the proprietary sense because the right of repurchase is in violation of "*het gesloten systeem van de zekerheidsrechten* (the closed system of security rights)". However, individuals are entitled to insert a resolutive condition under the new BW (art. 3:84 (3)). In general, this resolutive condition can perform a similar function as the right of repurchase. See Asser/Bartels & Van Mierlo 2013, nr. 240.

526 *Re Curtain Dream plc* [1990] BCLC 925.

527 Beale, Bridge, Gullifer and Lomnicka 2018, no. 4.28.

B Retention of Ownership

Retention of ownership is an important security device in the situation of corporeal movables.[528] However, the functional approach and the formal approach treat this security device in different ways. Under the functional approach, retention of ownership is no more than a security interest with super priority. In other aspects, it does not give the creditor more benefits than what the other security devices, such as pledge, can provide. Under the latter approach, however, retention of ownership confers on the secured creditor (the seller of the collateral), in addition to an interest of preference, some other advantages. For example, the seller-owner is on the basis of its ownership entitled to reclamation in the event of the debtor's bankruptcy and the execution of the object.[529] It is held that these advantages do no injustice to the buyer or other creditors of the buyer, because the collateral retained comes from the seller and is a new asset that is helpful for the debtor's business.[530] There are controversies, however, as to whether the formal approach should be replaced by a functional approach.[531]

In some jurisdictions, this issue is connected to the problem of publicity. For example, although a charge of corporeal movables needs to be registered under English law, retention of title is usually treated as an outright sale that needs no registration because English law takes a formal approach.[532] However, those retention-of-title transactions with a "*proceeds of sale*" or "*aggregation*" clause might be characterized as a charge, which will be void in the absence of registration.[533] This different treatment in the aspect of publicity is not convincing.

> *"If a codified system of remedies is not seen as a necessary part of a secured transactions reform in Europe, it should be possible [...] to disregard functionality and bring title-based schemes and traditional security under the same roof of a scheme that lays down common rules for priority and publicity."*[534]

For example, the DCFR requires retention of ownership to be registered but treat it differently in the aspect of enforcement, and the UNCITRAL Legislative Guide on Secured Transactions also recommends registration

528 Dirix and Sagaert 2014, p. 252.
529 Drobnig 2011, p. 1035.
530 McCormack 2004, p. 172-173.
531 For proponents of the formal approach, treating reservation of ownership just as a security interest under the functional approach is not appropriate. In essence, this treatment constitutes an intervention in parties' autonomy: after all, the seller does not have an intention to give up ownership before the purchase price is paid. Under the functional approach, the location of ownership is problematic: between the seller or the buyer, which party is the owner before the fulfillment of the suspensive condition? See De Groot 2012, p. 145; Bridge 2017, p. 7.
532 Bridge, Gullifer, McMeel and Worthington 2013, p. 200.
533 Bridge, Gullifer, McMeel and Worthington 2013, p. 315-316.
534 Bridge 2008, p. 214.

for retention of ownership, irrespective of whether this security device is governed under a functional approach.[535]

It is without doubt that retention of ownership has a problem of information asymmetry because of the divergence between ownership and possession.

> *"The reservation of ownership lacks publicity. Since the buyer obtains possession of the goods, he becomes the ostensible holder of unencumbered ownership. Due to the lack of any requirement of public notice, the seller's reservation of ownership and the security interest in the goods may remain a secret in trade."*[536]

The debtor-buyer might dispose of the object in breach of the agreement with the seller-owner.[537] In this situation, the seller-owner's right might be sacrificed for protecting third parties acting in good faith under the rule of *bona fide* acquisition.[538] On the other hand, the seller-owner might also dispose of the same collateral object to a third party by keeping silent on the clause of retention.[539] In this situation, the first buyer faces a risk when the second buyer acts in good faith.[540] In both of these situations, there is a conflict.[541] To prevent the occurrence of conflicts, it is desirable to include the transaction in a system of registration.[542]

Truly, the formality of registration will affect the smooth operation of the reservation-of-ownership transaction, and this is a reason why some jurisdictions refuse to introduce registration.[543] However, this side effect is limited under the system of registration proposed in 5.3. Firstly, registration is a requirement of effectiveness only against third parties, and ownership can be retained validly in the absence of registration (see 5.3.3.1). Individuals have a right of option. Secondly, the way how the system operates guarantees that the formality will not create a heavy burden on individuals.[544] Registration involves filing only a simple summary in the digital system without involving any registrar (see 5.3.1.2-5.3.1.4). Thirdly, the grace period allows the secured creditor, especially suppliers of goods, to preserve its safe position even in the absence of registration (see 5.3.2.3.B). As a result, the creditor cannot register when the obligation is expected to be paid within the grace period.[545] Fourthly, the permission of in-advance registra-

535 Keininger 2008, p. 219.
536 Hausmann 1996, p. 456.
537 Bülow 2012, Rn. 766.
538 Sagaert 2017, p. 40.
539 Bülow 2012, Rn. 801.
540 Sagaert 2017, p. 54.
541 Bridge, Macdonald, Simmonds and Walsh 1999, p. 592.
542 Struycken 2009, p. 178.
543 Dirix and Sagaert 2014, p. 252.
544 Bridge, Gullifer, McMeel and Worthington 2013, p. 316.
545 Veneziano 2008, p. 92; Faber 2014, p. 35.

tion also helps to streamline the transaction since "*a single registration can, in effect, cover all future deliveries within a long-term business relationship*".[546]

In general, the preceding discussion is also applicable to other transactions that embody an element of reservation of ownership, such as financial lease, hire purchase, and consignment. Thus, these transactions need to be included in the system of registration proposed in this research. With respect to financial lease and hire purchase, it should be noted that the term of lease and the installment period are usually long. Therefore, the rule of grace period should not be applied to these two types of secured transaction.

5.4.3.2 Possessory Pledge

From the preceding discussion, we can easily make a conclusion that possessory pledge never resolves the problem of information asymmetry through dispossession of the corporeal and movable collateral. Instead, it gives rise to a new problem. Like many other security devices, possessory pledge also causes a divergence between ownership and possession. For the following reasons, the requirement of dispossession is of no help in making the proprietary encumbrance visible.

Firstly, the factual control of the collateral by the pledgee can only make the property right of pledge visible in an abstract way (see 3.2.1). If the collateral is under control by a third party, which means that the pledgee, at most, has indirect possession, the right of pledge is completely invisible since indirect possession has no function of publicity (see 3.2.2). Moreover, the pledgor's right of ownership becomes completely hidden because possession is given up to the pledgee or a third party. Because of the divergence between ownership and possession, possessory pledge not only creates a chance for the pledgee or the third party to dispose of the collateral in the name of the owner, but also a chance for the pledgor to dispose of the collateral without mentioning the existence of the proprietary encumbrance.

> "*Strictly speaking, pledges of chattels, which were recognized at common law, created ostensible ownership problems as well, because the creditor holding pledged property would appear to own property that in fact belonged to another.*"[547]

Possessory pledge not only means that the pledgor grants an interest of security to the pledgee, but also that the pledgor is exposed to the risk out of *bona fide* acquisition if the pledgee disposes of the collateral to a third party.

Secondly, possessory pledge also causes a difficulty to third parties who want to ascertain which collateral is under the encumbrance of pledge.

546 Faber 2014, p. 35.
547 Baird 1983, p. 54.

> *"In our view, perfection of security by possession creates unnecessary costs and problems. Where a financier takes security by possession, the cost of discovery of such security is unduly high to creditors looking to take further security in the same asset. There is also an increased risk of fraud on such creditors."*[548]

The means of publicity of pledge (dispossession) is advantageous for the secured creditor, who is able to gain factual control of the collateral. However, this means of publicity brings a disadvantage to other creditors of the pledgor: it fails to make possessory pledge easy to discover.[549]

Thirdly, the recognition of possessory pledge by treating possession as a means of publicity might give rise to *"systemic costs"*.[550] For jurisdictions that have a system of registration for secured transactions, the recognition of possessory pledge implies that there are two different means of publicity for corporeal movables.[551] One is registration, and the other is possession. If a conflict between a possessory pledge and a registered security interest arises with respect to the same object, the creditor who completes either of the two means of publicity earlier will win.[552] The permission of dual means of publicity is in violation of the principle that one type of property should have one method of publicity (see 2.3.3.2). This principle is a requirement of efficiency. If both possession and registration are allowed for creating a security right on corporeal movables, then third parties not only have to search the register, but also investigate the possessory state of the collateral involved. Undoubtedly, this will compromise the reliability of the register.[553] Moreover, the investigation is expensive for third parties, especially on account of the fact that it is difficult to discover the possessory pledge.

Fourthly, pledge and lease are treated differently in some jurisdictions. For example, possession is a means of publicity for corporeal movable collateral under the Australian PPSA, and it is possible to create a possessory security interest that is effective against third parties.[554] However, lease of corporeal movables is subject to a requirement of registration, and possession obtained by the lessee cannot make the right of lease effective against third parties.[555] In the situation of lease, possession by the lessee gives rise to a *"'publicity' problem"*, instead of being a means of publicity.[556] There is no reason to view possessory pledge and the right of lease, also a possessory

548 Secured Transactions Law Reform Project 2013, p. 1.
549 Secured Transactions Law Reform Project 2013, p. 4.
550 Phillips 1979 (1), p. 43.
551 For example, Article 9 UCC recognizes both dispossession and registration as a means of perfection or a way to make the security interest effective against third parties. See Sigman 2008, p. 148-149.
552 For example, this is accepted by Article 9 UCC. See Sigman 2008, p. 162.
553 Phillips 1979 (2), p. 227.
554 Whittaker and Partner 2015, p. 127-128.
555 Whittaker and Partner 2015, p. 74-76.
556 Whittaker and Partner 2015, p. 76.

interest, differently in the aspect of publicity. The "prejudice" against lease indicates that possession is a problematic means of publicity, and possessory pledge falls short of the principle of publicity. An appropriate solution to eliminate this systematic incoherence is requiring both possessory pledge and lease to be registered.

For the reasons presented above, we argue that possessory pledge should also be included in the system of registration proposed in this research. This argument is supported by the recent reform in some African jurisdictions. For example, in Ghana,[557] Kenya,[558] Nigeria,[559] and Sierra Leone,[560] delivery is excluded as a means of perfection for the security interest of corporeal movables. The inclusion of possessory pledge in the system does not mean that the secured creditor cannot obtain possession of the collateral. If the pledgor agrees to give up possession to the pledgee, there is no reason for a prohibition. In other aspects than publicity, obtaining possession is beneficial to the secured creditor. For example, the pledgee might be able to use the collateral, and there is no need to fear that the value of the collateral might be reduced because of the debtor's damage or overuse.

The formality of registration will not give rise to a heavy burden to the pledgor and the pledgee. The reasons for positing this have been demonstrated above (see 5.4.2.2). For example, the system is digital, self-service, and notice-based; the absence of registration does not affect the valid creation of possessory pledge because registration only yields declaratory effect; pledge of a corporeal movable having low value does not need to be registered. It is worthwhile mentioning that delivery should be retained as a qualified means of publicity for securities to goods. The reason is simple. Securities to goods take negotiability as the central function, and the formality registration will destroy this function (see 5.3.2.1.B).[561]

In general, two benefits can be achieved by introducing registration to possessory pledge. The first benefit is that the pledgor does not have to worry that the pledgee will dispose of the collateral without any approval. Thus, the risk of *bona fide* acquisition by a third party can be alleviated to a large extent. The second benefit is that subsequent secured creditors of the pledgor do not have to investigate whether the collateral is in the possession of the pledgor and, if not, why the collateral is controlled by others. Simply searching the system of registration suffices. There is no doubt that this will reduce the costs out of collecting information.

---

557 S. 14 (1) Ghana Borrowers and Lenders Bill (2020): "*A security interest is effective against third parties when the security interest has been created and registered under this Act.*"

558 S. 15 Kenya Movable Property Security Rights Act (2017): "*A security right in any movable asset is effective against third parties if a notice with respect to the security right is registered with the Registrar.*"

559 See s. 8 (2) Nigerian Secured Transactions in Movable Assets Act (2017); Igbinosun 2020, p. 364.

560 See s. 12 Sierra Leone Borrowers and Lenders Act (2014); Kanu 2018, p. 145-146.

561 Secured Transactions Law Reform Project 2013, p. 5.

5.4.4 Conclusion

In sum, it is desirable to apply the system of registration proposed in 5.3 to the secured transactions of corporeal movables and claims. Indeed, the system is not important for general creditors but can address the problem of information asymmetry to subsequent acquirers. The registration will not impose an unacceptable impact on the smooth operation of secured transactions. Instead, it is able to reduce the costs of the collection of proprietary information and facilitate the certainty of secured transactions. In general, the worry about the threat to privacy should not be overstated, because the information provided by the system is limited.

The legal form a secured transaction takes is irrelevant to the scope of application of the system. What matters is whether the security interest created is hidden to third parties. Thus, both limited property rights of security and ownership-based security device, such as reservation of ownership, should be included in the register. Moreover, possession does not qualify as a means of publicity in secured transactions concerning corporeal movables. Thus, possessory pledge is a hidden property right and should also be included in the system.

5.5 Registration as a Solution | Case Study II: Trust

Trust is another topic that has a connection with the principle of publicity. As pointed out by some scholars, one obstacle to the introduction of this common law device in a civil law system is related to the principle of publicity.[562] This principle, associated with the idea of preventive justice, is deeply entrenched in civil property law. A proprietary interest should be made transparent to third parties. Otherwise, its broad effectiveness will easily cause a conflict between the proprietor and a third party. Trust is a form of transfer of ownership which can give rise to proprietary consequences, in particular the effect on subsequent acquirers. These consequences need, at least at first sight, to be justified by publicity.

The relationship of trust can be created for either a purpose of security (*fiducia cum creditore*) or a purpose of management (*fiducia cum amico*). The prominent example of the former is security transfer of ownership, which is popular in German law but prohibited to a large extent by Dutch law (see 5.4.1). Security trust is often dealt with under the topic of secured transactions, which has been discussed in 5.4. In that section, our conclusion is that registration should be introduced to secured transactions, including the device of security transfer (see 5.4.3.1). The following discussion focuses on the other type of trust, i.e. the trust for management purposes. In the following discussion, the term trust refers to trust for management purposes

562 Banakas 2006, p. 6-7; Aertsen 2004, p. 162; Matthews 2013, p. 330; Kötz 1963, p. 167.

if there is no contrary indication. The discussion concerns only the trust of corporeal movables and claims since this research confines itself to these two types of movable property. Trust of immovable property will be mentioned as a reference or an illustration when necessary.

5.5.1 Setting the Scene

5.5.1.1 The Obstacle of Doctrines

In general, trust is a legal institution of common law and rejected by the civil law system. It is incompatible with a number of doctrines of Continental property law. This incompatibility creates several difficulties for civil law jurisdictions to accept trust. Even though some countries have a law of trust, they dilute it.[563] In this part, we introduce three doctrinal difficulties and then point out that these difficulties can be overcome to a large extent.

A The Unitary Nature of Ownership

The first hindrance to the introduction of trust is the unitary nature of ownership. Since the enactment of the French Civil Code (1804), ownership is treated as the most comprehensive and thus unitary property right. The unitary nature is partly a result of the fear of the revival of the feudal legal system.[564] Ownership cannot be divided or fragmented, and the distinction between legal ownership and economic ownership is not recognized by Continental property law. However, such division and distinction are seen as natural and useful in common law.[565] According to the prevailing opinion, trust is a legal device which can cause a division of ownership: the trustee is the legal owner in common law, and the beneficiary the economic or equitable owner in equity. It is hard to explain the consequence of the division under the framework of Continental property law under the principle of unitary ownership.

> *"In klassieke analyse van de Engelse trust kenmerkt deze rechtsfiguur zich door dual ownership: zowel degene die belast is met beheer over een goed, als degene in wiens belang het goed wordt beheerd, hebben op dat goed een aanspraak, die in het Engelse recht wordt gekwalificeerd als ownership [...]. Van een absoluut eigendomsbegrip, dat de continentale rechtstraditie kenmerkt, is in het Engelse recht nooit sprake geweest."*[566]

563 Alexander 2013, p. 305.

564 Sagaert 2012, p. 40.

565 Matthews 2013, p. 319.

566 Struycken 2007, p. 513-514. English translation: *"In the classical analysis of the English trust, this figure is characterized by dual ownership: both the person who is in charge of managing a thing and the person in whose interests the thing is managed are entitled as having ownership under English law [...]. An absolute concept of ownership, which is the feature of the continental legal tradition, has never been recognized in English law."*

Truly, ownership has a unitary attribute. However, this doctrine has eroded in legal practice to some extent, on account of the possibility of retention of ownership in almost every jurisdiction and that of security transfer of ownership in some jurisdictions.[567] In these two cases, we can say that ownership is, in essence, divided between the two transacting parties in the sense that one's interest forms a proprietary restriction on the other's right.

In fact, if we do want to maintain the unitary attribute of ownership, the problem of fragmentation can be avoided by shaping the beneficial interest as a limited property right.[568] In fact, this is what Dutch law has already done: (1) using the silent pledge to replace security transfer of ownership, which has been achieved by the new code; and (2) using the *bewind* as an alternative to the management trust, which is in suspension now. In the case of management trust, there is no need to follow the common law approach, having a distinction of economic ownership or equitable ownership. The interest enjoyed by the beneficiary can be treated as a limited right, as a proprietary limitation over ownership.

> *"De 'dual ownership'-gedachte zou in de continentale systematiek kunnen worden uitgewerkt met behulp van de in de continentale systematiek overbekende figuur van een 'moederrecht' waaruit 'beperkte rechten' zijn afgesplitst. Ten overvloede zij in dit verband daarbij nog opgemerkt dat het 'zakelijk karakter' van het recht van de beneficiary voortvloeit uit het feit dat er sprake is van obligatoire aanspraken, die mede ten opzichte van verscheidene categorieën van derden kunnen worden gehandhaafd."*[569]

In fact, some English lawyers have already pointed out that the distinction between legal ownership and economic ownership is misleading, and what is at the heart of the seeming distinction is the right-duty relationship.[570] For example, Maitland noted that the notion of legal ownership and equitable ownership was "*not merely nonsensical but mischievous*" because it might lead to the possibility of conflict between common law and equity, and he also opined that an equitable right was "*essentially jura in personam*".[571]

B The Unitary Feature of Patrimony

The second hindrance results from the singleness of patrimony. Under Continental patrimonial law, one person can only have one patrimony, consisting of future and existing assets and debts. A person is responsible for its debts on the basis of its all assets including those acquired in the future. The

567 Sagaert, Tilleman and Laurent 2013, p. 56-57; Loof 2012, p. 108.

568 Kötz 1963, p. 169.

569 Venema 1985, p. 115. English translation: "*The 'dual ownership' theory could be reconfigured in the continental system with the help of the idea that a 'limited right' is subtracted from the 'mother right'. As a consequence, it has been observed that the 'proprietary character' of the beneficiary's right derives from the fact that the obligational claim can be maintained against several types of third parties.*"

570 Matthews 2002, p. 206, 218-219.

571 Maitland 1936, p. 106-107.

creation of a trust requires separating the trustee's own patrimony from the trust property, which enables one person (the trustee) to have two or more patrimonies and undermines the "*unity and indivisibility of the patrimony*".[572]

> "*By definition, therefore, every living person must have a patrimony, and originally he could only have one patrimony. Accordingly, although a person can alienate assets so that they become part of another's patrimony, he should not be able to segregate assets into a second patrimony of his own [...]. To a civilian it might seem that the trustee [...] has two patrimonies, a private patrimony and a trust patrimony.*"[573]

The singleness of patrimony can be traced to the 18th century when "*a metaphysical concept of patrimony prevailed in the civil law countries*".[574] According to this concept, patrimony is the external and economic manifestation of the subject, and the patrimony must be single and indivisible because one subject has only one indivisible personality.[575]

In general, the singleness of patrimony is not a large problem either. There is no convincing reason why one person cannot have two or more separate patrimonies at the same time. For example, English law deems it as "*in any event unnecessary*".[576] In the early 20th century, the idea of singleness of patrimony was criticized and rejected by more and more scholars.[577]

> "*This is reflected by the very simple objection to the singleness of patrimony doctrine: what is single and indivisible is not the patrimony itself, but rather the right to have a patrimony, which belongs to any individual as an external expression of his personality. As a consequence of this new viewpoint, an individual was no longer identified with his patrimony, nor was the latter considered a unique attribute of the human personality.*"[578]

In fact, civil private law has recognized some exceptions to this conventional notion, such as the one-shareholder company,[579] the "separate property (*Sondervermögen*)" in German law,[580] and the "qualitative account (*kwaliteitsrekening*)" held by notaries in Dutch law.[581] Moreover, some civil law jurisdictions have recognized a trust-like device (such as the French *fiducie*), which has an effect of separation and permits one person to have two or more patrimonies. The DCFR also provides that the singleness of patrimony can be restricted in order to introduce a regime of trust (Book X).[582]

572 Sagaert 2012, p. 32.
573 Matthews 2002, p. 214-216.
574 Elgueta 2010, p. 527.
575 Elgueta 2010, p. 527.
576 Matthews 2002, p. 215.
577 Elgueta 2010, p. 529.
578 Elgueta 2010, p. 529.
579 Sagaert 2012, p. 39.
580 Rehahn and Grimm 2012, p. 94-95.
581 Art. 22 Wet op het Notarisambt (Law of Notary Service); Milo 2012, p. 77.
582 Sagaert 2012, p. 36.

C *The Principle of* Numerus Clausus

Another doctrinal obstacle is the principle of *numerus clausus*. It is commonly held that individuals are not allowed to create a property right as they like. Instead, they have to choose from the list of property rights recognized by property law. The principle is closely related to the unitary feature of ownership: ownership cannot be fragmented, but trust can lead to a division of ownership, which amounts to creating a new form of ownership.[583] Trust is difficult to reconcile with the principle of *numerus clausus* in another sense. The content of trust is flexible and largely determined by individuals themselves, which implies that the principle of *numerus clausus* might be easily circumvented by the device of trust.[584] It is difficult to explain the permission of such broad party autonomy under the principle: after all, the principle of *numerus clausus* takes restrictions as its starting point.

> *"Any new or additional real right (here in the form of the beneficial or equitable ownership of the trust beneficiary) falls outside the closed system (numerus clausus). Acceptance of the numerus clausus principle in the sphere of real rights thus forms an almost insurmountable obstacle to the reception of the English law of trusts into civil law jurisdictions."*[585]

In general, the principle of *numerus clausus* is not a large problem either. The fact that the principle of *numerus clausus* is also accepted by common law indicates that this principle will not be an insurmountable obstacle, if the legislature intends to recognize trust.[586] Moreover, the principle prevents the recognition of a new proprietary right by legislators and, when necessary, by courts.[587] Once trust is recognized in statutory law, as what occurred in France in 2007, we can say that this legal device is included in the closed system of property rights. In fact, there are a number of intermediary rights straddling typical property rights and typical personal rights.[588] In most situations, the reason why an intermediary right can be effective against third parties is that law recognizes it.[589] Therefore, the critical question here is not whether trust can be compatible with the principle of *numerus clausus*, but whether and under what conditions the relationship of trust can bind third parties.

583 Van Erp 2006 (2), p. 1056.
584 Dalhuisen 2010, p. 282.
585 De Waal 2000, p. 442.
586 Ryan 1959, p. 79; Nolan 2006, p. 261-262.
587 Kötz 1963, p. 168.
588 Meijers 1948, p. 276; Van Erp 2013, p. 15.
589 According to Smits, the principle of *numerus clausus* should be interpreted in a new way: it refers to the notion that the situations in which individuals can create a legal relationship that have third-party effect are limited by law. See Smits 1996, p. 54.

5.5.1.2 *The Issue of Publicity*

In addition to the three obstacles mentioned above which, in fact, do not exist or can be overcome, there is a fourth barrier concerning the principle of publicity. Under this principle, property rights should be made transparent for third parties because of the third-party effect. In general, trust has proprietary effect in two aspects: one is the effect against subsequent acquirers of the trust asset, and the other is the effect against personal creditors of the trustee.

> *"In het voorgaande is gebleken dat de trust op zijn minst twee rechtgevolgen heeft die aan derden tegengeworpen kunnen worden, te weten het feit dat de beschikkingsbevoegdheid van de trustee door het trustverband wordt ingeperkt en het feit dat de trustgoederen een afgescheiden vermogen vormen."*[590]

The first proprietary effect arises in the situation where the trustee manages or disposes of the trust asset in a way that violates the fiduciary duty under law or the trust agreement. In this situation, the beneficiary is entitled to trace the trust asset to the place of the transferee and recover the asset, except when *bona fide* acquisition by the transferee takes place. This is known as the tracing effect of trust.[591] The second third-party effect means that the trust property owns an independent position from the trustee's own assets, thus the trustee's personal creditors cannot distribute the trust asset. This is called the function of separation (partition or shielding) of trust.[592] In the reform of the law of property, the Belgian legislature also emphasizes these two proprietary consequences in constructing a regime of "trust (*fiducie*)".[593]

Concerning the issue of publicity in the context of these proprietary consequences, different jurisdictions take different approaches. In the following, we give a brief introduction to English law, French law, Belgian law, German law and Dutch law to show the complexity of this issue. Trust is an essential regime in English law, a representative of the common law system. The other four jurisdictions belong to the civil law system. French law has introduced a general trust (*fiducie*), and there is a move to introduce a general trust (*fiducie*) in Belgium, while both German law and Dutch law do not have a general system of trust. However, there is also discussion concerning the publicity of trust in German and Dutch legal theory, as we will see further below.

---

590 Aertsen 2004, p. 163. English translation: *"In the foregoing, it has been shown that the trust imposes at least two legal consequences that might be against third parties: one is that the trustee's power of disposal is restricted by the trust, and the other is that the trust assets constitute a separate patrimony."*

591 Ramjohn 2004, p. 602.

592 Hansmann and Mattei 1998, p. 438.

593 Wetsontwerp Houdende Invoeging van Boek 3 "Goederen" in het Nieuw Burgerlijk Wetboek (2018-10-31), p. 93.

A English Law

In English law, the proprietary benefits enjoyed by the beneficiary are not supported by any publicity. As a principle, creating a trust does not require any formality, let alone publicity, due to the consideration of respecting the settlor's intention.[594] This fits into the doctrine that *"equity looks at the intent rather than the form"*.[595] It is also pointed out by some English lawyers that the absence of publicity serves the policy of *"the free circulation of assets"*.[596] Only in two exceptional cases, i.e. the trust of land and testamentary trust, there is a requirement of certain formalities, such as making the trust agreement in written form.[597] It should be noted that the purpose of these formalities is to preserve evidence, rather than to provide publicity to third parties. Therefore, a trust is generally hidden under English law. Moreover, trust can be a result of the operation of law, which is known as constructive trust. This type of trust is also hidden to third parties.

There is no doubt that the formality-free approach is in conflict with the principle of publicity, and Weiser deems this principle as the *"public enemy"* of accepting trust by civil law jurisdictions.[598] The English law approach affects the certainty of the relationship of trust and creates a source of conflicts. In the viewpoint of Finch, trust, as an undisclosed legal device, is a source of *"deception"* and informational disparities, which is unfair to actual and potential creditors of the trustee.[599]

> *"The law imposes few formalities on the formation of trusts. A transfer of assets to a person who accepts that the property will be held on trust or a declaration by a person who already holds property that the property is held on trust is normally sufficient. Not surprisingly, such informality may encourage abuse by a dishonest trustee who may claim the transfer to him, or that the property is held by him, as the beneficial owner. There is no doubt that the trustee holds the legal title: the problem is that he may deny the existence of his obligations towards the beneficiaries or that there may be genuine doubt as to the nature of the arrangement."*[600]

Nevertheless, the rejection of publicity is deeply entrenched in common law which takes an *ex-post* approach to trust. In other words, the English law of trust does not prevent the occurrence of conflicts concerning the trust asset, but seeks to resolve conflicts after they take place.

594 *"In fact, the basic rule is along the latter lines: that no formality is required to make trust. Ultimately, therefore, the desire not to frustrate settlors in the making of informal trusts is given precedence over the advantages of a converse rule."* See Gardner 2011, p. 89.

595 Ramjohn 2004, p. 40.

596 Lupoi 2000, p. 173.

597 Gardner 2011, p. 86; Aertsen 2004, p. 262.

598 Weiser 1936, p. 8.

599 Finch 2009, p. 663-665.

600 Goldsworth 1997, p. 15.

B French Law and Belgian Law

B1: *The French* Fiducie

Trust is also recognized, subject to some modifications, in some civil law jurisdictions, such as French law. One achievement of the 2007 law reform is translating trust (*fiducie*) into French law. *Fiducie* is a general concept which can be used for both security purposes (*fiducie-sûreté*) and management purposes (*fiducie-gestion*).[601] In terms of publicity, French law treats immovable property and movable property differently.

If the trust object is an immovable asset, registration is treated as the method of publicity and yields declaratory effect, and the register (*publicité foncière*) is open to third parties.[602] In other words, creating a trust on land is subject to the same rule of publicity as transfer or mortgage of the land. In the case of trust of movable property, registration is a prerequisite for valid creation, but such registration is mainly for an administrative purpose, instead of for the purpose of publicity.[603] The only private-law function is to avoid the risk of backdating.[604] Third parties cannot search the system of registration for the trust of movable property, and the problem of secrecy of *fiducie* still exists. This is considered as *"a weakness of the French legal framework"*.[605]

> *"However, when the fiducie bears upon movables that are not subject to publicity by registration and the settlor remains in possession thereof, the beneficiary of the fiducie faces the risk of competition between her rights and those of the legal successors of the settlor […]. As has already been mentioned, in a case where the property is made available to the settlor and there is no publication of the beneficiary's rights, there is a risk that a third party will seize or acquire the property and then set up her possession in good faith against any subsequent claims."*[606]

Moreover, delivery of the corporeal movable is not necessary for establishing a trust over the asset, which means that the transferor or settlor is entitled to continue using the asset entrusted.[607] This fits with the consensual system in French law: ownership passes upon the effect of the agreement.

Because of the lack of an appropriate regime of publicity, the existence of *fiducie* of corporeal movables leads to a risk to personal creditors of the trustee as well as third parties who contract with the trustee.[608] In the view

601 Mallet-Bricout 2013, p. 143.
602 Fix 2014, p. 211.
603 Likewise, Cyprus also introduced a system of registration for trust in 2013, and this system is not accessible to third parties either. See Aristotelous and Christodoulou 2014, p. 498.
604 Barrière 2012, p. 229.
605 Barrière 2013, p. 123.
606 Barrière 2013, p. 123.
607 Braun and Swadling 2012, p. 573-574.
608 Barrière 2012, p. 233.

of some French scholars, for the purpose of certainty and fluidity of transactions, third parties acting in good faith should be protected from the legal relationship of trust.[609] This amounts to saying that the beneficiary's interest should be respected by the third party who is aware of the trustee's breach of the fiduciary duty. However, French law has no provisions with respect to the scope and conditions of the protection of third parties.[610]

B2: The Belgian Fiducie

Inspired by French law, the Belgian legislature intends to introduce a general concept of trust (*fiducie*) into the Belgian civil code. In the draft of Book 3 concerning "property (*goederen*)", thirteen provisions (art. 3.38-3.50) are proposed for a general system of trust.[611] On account of the third-party effect of the trust, the legislature plans to include a rule of publicity in art. 3.46.

> Art. 3.46: "*De fiducie moet met het oog op de tegenwerpelijkheid aan derden, worden geregistreerd in het nationaal pandregister indien het betrekking heeft op goederen waarvan de verpanding in dat register moet worden ingeschreven, of worden overgeschreven in de registers van de hypotheekbewaarder indien het op onroerende goederen betrekking heeft. Voor roerende goederen kan de tegenwerpelijkheid ook door een buitenbezitstelling plaatsvinden.*"[612]

According to this provision, trust of immovable property takes registration as a means of publicity. Moreover, the register involved is the general register for the transaction of land, namely the "register of hypothec (*hypotheekregister*)". This register is open to general third parties.[613] Thus, the legal relationship of trust is able to be made visible. Trust of corporeal movables has two means of publicity: registration and delivery.[614] To publicize the trust through the former means, the parties need to file basic information in the register constructed for non-possessory pledge, which is also

---

609 "*Hence these third parties will not bear the consequences where the trustee acts wrongly by exceeding his powers: the excess of power cannot be invoked against them, unless they are aware of it.*" See Barrière 2012, p. 233. About similar opinions, see Matthews 2007, p. 22.

610 Braun and Swadling 2012, p. 589.

611 The name of the draft is "*Wetsontwerp houdende invoeging van Boek 3 'Goederen' in het nieuw Burgerlijk Wetboek*" (2018-10-31), which can be translated in English as "Legal draft of incorporating Book 3 'property' in the new Civil Code".

612 English translation: Art. 3.46: "*For enforceability against third parties, the fiducie must be registered in the national register for pledge when the trust involves property for which the pledge needs to be registered; the fiducie must be registered in the register managed by the hypothec manager when the trust involves immovable property. For corporeal movables, delivery can also give rise to such enforceability.*"

613 Sagaert 2014, p. 724.

614 I doubt that delivery can qualify as a means of publicity here. The reason is simple: (1) direct possession is an ambiguous means of publicity (see 3.2.1), and indirect possession has no effect of publicity (see 3.2.2); and (2) visible delivery is ambiguous, and invisible delivery cannot make the trust transparent to third parties (see 3.4.2.4.B).

known as the "pledge register (*pandregister*)". This register is open to third parties, and the trust registered can thus be made visible.[615] It can be seen that the Belgian draft and the French law differ in the aspect of publicity of trust of movable property: the former plans to make the trust visible to third parties by including it in the pledge register, while the French register is not open to third parties.

C *German Law and Dutch Law*

C1: The German Treuhand

For those jurisdictions that are still hesitant to introduce a general concept of trust, publicity is an important consideration. For example, the *Treuhand* is a trust-like device in Germany and straddles property law and the law of obligations. In general, there are three types of *Treuhand* under German law: fiduciary *Treuhand* (*fiduziarische Treuhand*), *Treuhand* by authorization (*Ermächtigungstreuhand*), and *Treuhand* by agency (*Vollmachtstreuhand*).[616] The main difference between the first type and the other two types is that fiduciary *Treuhand* involves transfer of full ownership.[617] This is why fiduciary *Treuhand* is also known as "full-right *Treuhand* (*Vollrechtstreuhand*)". Fiduciary *Treuhand* can be created for the purpose of security and of management, which are known as *Sicherungstreuhand* and *Verwaltungstreuhand* respectively. Security transfer of ownership (*Sicherungsübereignung*) will lead to a legal relationship of *Sicherungstreuhand*.[618] Under *Treuhand* by authorization and *Treuhand* by agency, ownership is not alienated.[619] In the following introduction, we focus only on fiduciary *Treuhand* for the purpose of management.

Under fiduciary *Treuhand*, the settlor (*Treugeber*) enjoys a personal right with some proprietary effects.[620] This right is associated with a partitioning effect and in exceptional cases a tracing effect.[621] For example, where a personal creditor of the trustee attempts to seize or attach the trust asset (*Treugut*), the beneficiary is entitled to release the asset from the attachment in the name of a third party.[622] If the trustee becomes insolvent, the beneficiary

615 Bontinck 2017, p. 216.

616 Braun and Swadling 2012, p. 561-562.

617 Braun and Swadling 2012, p. 561-562.

618 Rehahn and Grimm 2012, p. 101.

619 Rehahn and Grimm 2012, p. 100-101. Between *Treuhand* by authorization (*Ermächtigungstreuhand*) and *treuhand* by agency (*Vollmachtstreuhand*), there is a difference in the legal basis. The former is based on § 185 BGB, while the latter is based on § 167 BGB. Thus, *Treuhand* by authorization arises where the "trustee (*Treuhänder*)" is authorized *ex post* to dispose of the object, and *Treuhand* by agency comes to the fore in the situation where the trustee receives the authority of disposal in advance. See Jacoby 2007, p. 35.

620 Canaris 1978, p. 410.

621 Grundmann 1998, p. 471-477; Kötz 1999 (1), p. 56-57.

622 Kötz 1999 (2), p. 56.

can also prevent the trustee's personal creditors from distributing the trust assets.[623] If the trustee disposes of the trust asset in violation of the fiduciary duty arising from the *Treuhand* contract, third parties can acquire the asset, irrespective of whether they act in good faith. This is because third parties *"acquire the property from the legitimate owner"*.[624] However, it is another thing that a *mala fide* third party conspires with the trustee to harm the settlor's personal right.[625] In this situation, the settlor is entitled to protection under tort law (§ 823 BGB).[626] The protection against *mala fide* third parties is an exception and is subject to strict conditions.

Under German law, there is not any specific requirement of formality on the creation of *Treuhand*. However, as a matter of course, transfer of the entrusted asset requires certain formalities according to the nature of the assets.[627] If the trust property is a parcel of land, registration is a prerequisite of the transfer of ownership, but no indication of *Treuhand* is allowed to be recorded in the land register. The reason is that *Treuhand* forms only an obligational or personal limitation over the owner's right of disposal.[628] With respect to the *status quo*, some writers believe that it is desirable to show the settlor's legal position that is partly proprietary.

> *"Daraus folgt für das Liegenschaftsrecht, dass die Drittwiderspruchsklage und das Aussonderungsrecht nur gegeben sind, sofern die Rechtsstellung des Treugebers aus dem Grundbuch ersichtlich ist [...]. Außerhalb des Liegenschaftsrechts kann die Offenkundigkeit grundsätzlich nicht nur durch Besitz, sondern durch jede beliebige Tatsache, insbesondere durch Gewerbe oder Beruf des Treuhänders gewährleistet werden [...]."*[629]

> *"Voor de Treugeber of een derde-begunstigde kan publicatie van het Treuhänderschap daarentegen wel relevant zijn, met name voor het geval de Treuhänder in strijd met de bepalingen uit de Treuhandovereenkomst over het Treugut heeft beschikt [...]. Voorts kan het ook voor de derden belangrijk zijn om te weten dat hun wederpartij handelt in haar hoedanigheid van Treuhänder."*[630]

---

623 Kötz 1999 (2), p. 57; Jacoby 2007, p. 35.
624 Kötz 1999 (2), p. 60-61.
625 Kötz 1999 (2), p. 61.
626 Jacoby 2007, p. 36.
627 Braun and Swadling 2012, p. 568.
628 Coing 1973, p. 120.
629 Canaris 1978, p. 427. English translation: "*As a result, in the property law of land the third party's claim and the right of segregation are only given if the legal position of the grantor is visible from the land register. Outside of the land law, the disclosure can in principle be guaranteed not only by possession, but also by any other fact, in particular by the trade or business of the trustee [...].*"
630 Van Dongen 1996, p. 162. English translation: "*However, publicity of the relationship of trust might be important for the grantor or a third beneficiary, especially when the trustee disposes of the entrusted asset in breach of the provisions of the trust agreement [...]. Moreover, it may also be important for third parties to know that their counterparty acts in the capacity as a trustee.*"

If the trust property is a corporeal movable, then delivery is necessary for transfer of this asset. According to the first excerpt above, possession (*Besitz*) is treated as being able to made the *Treuhand* visible to third parties. This reminds us that the Belgian draft also includes delivery as a means of publicity for publicity of corporeal movables (see 5.5.1.2.B).

C2: The Dutch Bewind

In Dutch law, trust is generally prohibited by art. 3:84 BW under the recodification of the BW. The then drafters proposed an alternative device: *bewind*, a type of agency (*vertegenwoordiging*).[631] The *bewind*, which was initially intended to be incorporated in Chapter 6 of Book 3 BW, was not recognized as a part of the BW in 1992. It is unclear whether this chapter will enter into force in the future.[632] In recent years, some Dutch scholars have proposed introducing a general system of trust in the Netherlands, but with necessary modifications.[633] In the following discussion, we provide an outline of the Dutch view with respect to the problem of publicity of trust and the alternative device of *bewind*.

In Meijers' viewpoint, the common law trust, a device granting ownership to the trustee for the purpose of management, has a problem of excessive bestowment.[634] This is in line with his opinion on the security transfer of ownership: this security device gives more to the creditor than he or she deserves. On the basis of this opinion, security transfer of ownership has been replaced by silent pledge in Dutch law (art. 3:237 BW). Likewise, Meijers proposed using *bewind* as a replacement for the management trust. In his draft for a new civil code, *bewind* is constructed as a legal relationship of agency existing on property.[635] In the relationship of *bewind*, the manager (*bewindvoerder*) has a proprietary right of management including the authority of disposal.[636] Ownership of the object is not alienated to the manager. In this aspect, the Dutch bewind and the German *Treuhand* by agency (*Vollmachtstreuhand*) do not differ.

In general, *bewind* can give rise to some proprietary consequences. For example, where the owner transfers the object to a third party, the relationship of *bewind* will not be affected and will continue to exist on the object.[637] This is why *bewind* is also considered as a "proprietary burden (*zakelijke belasting*)".[638] Because of the proprietary effect of *bewind*, publicity is involved, at least when the object is registerable property.

631 Struycken 2007, p. 524-526.
632 Snijders and Rank-Berenschot 2017, p. 123.
633 Aertsen 2004, p. 299-300.
634 Struycken 2007, p. 523.
635 Meijers 1954, p. 241.
636 Struycken 2007, p. 525.
637 Meijers 1954, p. 241-242.
638 De Boer 1982, p. 39.

> *"Het doen inschrijven van het bewind over registergoederen, hetwelk door het tweede lid wordt verordend, is van groot belang met het oog op de werking van het bewind tegenover derden. Het kan nochtans zijn dat hij die een bewind instelt, wenst dat die geheim zal worden gehouden. Alsdan zal de bewindvoerder niet mogen inschrijven. Dit brengt het gevaar met zich, dat derden dit bewind kunnen verwaarlozen; de insteller heeft echter dit gevaar boven het bekend worden van het bewind verkozen."*[639]

According to Meijers, where registration is absent in the case of *bewind* of registerable property, third parties acting in good faith will not be bound by this burden.[640] In Meijers' draft, there is no particular provision on the publicity of *bewind* of corporeal movables. In article 3.6.11 of the draft, protection of third parties acting in good faith is recognized: those who neither know nor should know about the existence of *bewind* should not be prejudiced.[641]

Unlike Meijers who proposed a regime of *bewind*, Aertsen argues in his dissertation that a system of common law trust should be introduced in the Netherlands. Under this system, ownership is alienated to the trustee.[642] The beneficiary's right should be treated as a personal right, according to Dutch legal terminology.[643] On the other hand, Aertsen proposes that the Dutch legislature should make a balance between the beneficiary and third parties in the event of a breach of the fiduciary duty by applying a rule of *bona fide* acquisition.[644] In this respect, Aertsen's opinion does not differ from Meijers' proposal. Moreover, both scholars acknowledge a separation of the trust property from the trustee's personal property.[645] In sum, Aertsen holds that the beneficiary's interest is personal in nature but has certain proprietary effects.

Because of the proprietary effects of the beneficiary right, Aertsen advises the Dutch legislature to construct a regime of publicity when introducing trust. Publicity is related to "delineation of trust property (*afbakening van het trustvermogen*)": how to clearly separate the trust property from the trustee's personal property.[646] Moreover, publicity is also relevant to the "protection of third parties (*derdenbescherming*)".[647] For trust of regis-

639 Meijers 1954, p. 244. English translation: "*Enrollment of the administration of registerable property, which is prescribed by the second paragraph, is of great importance from the perspective of operation of administration against third parties. However, the case may be that the person who creates administration wants to keep it as a secret. Then the administrator cannot register it. This brings the risk that third parties may neglect the administration, but the creator has chosen this risk that they do not know about the administration.*"
640 Meijers 1954, p. 245.
641 Meijers 1954, p. 245.
642 Aertsen 2004, p. 203-204.
643 Aertsen 2004, p. 279.
644 Aertsen 2004, p. 525.
645 Struycken 2007, p. 527.
646 Aertsen 2004, p. 222-231.
647 Aertsen 2004, p. 248-249.

terable property, registration is not only a means of delimitation,[648] but also a crucial factor for the protection of third parties.[649] With respect to non-registerable property, Aertsen draws a distinction between claims and corporeal movables. The separation of claims can be realized by notifying the debtor involved.[650] In the situation of corporeal movables, they should be separated from the trustee's own corporeal movables "in physical sense (*in fysieke zin*)" when they are "generic property (*soortzaken*)".[651] In terms of the protection of third parties acting in good faith, Aertsen argues that art. 3:86 and 3:88 BW should be applied. In the situation where the trustee's disposal breaches the fiduciary duty, the corporeal movable can be acquired by *bona fide* third parties (art. 3:86 BW), and *bona fide* acquisition of claims is possible when the requirements in art. 3:88 BW are satisfied.[652]

5.5.1.3 *Summary*

From the preceding introduction, it can be seen that the reception of trust as a notion in the civil law system has some doctrinal difficulties. In general, these difficulties are not insurmountable. With respect to publicity of trust, there are several different approaches in contemporary law and theory. The first approach is that trust is, in principle, subject to no formalities, let alone publicity. English law follows this approach. The second approach is including trust in the existing system of publicity according to the nature of the trust asset involved. If the trust asset is immovable property or registerable property, the trust needs to be registered in the register. This is commonly accepted, as the preceding introduction shows. In the situation of trust corporeal movables, controversies exist in the aspect of publicity. French law only requires registration that is not open to third parties. Unlike French law, the Belgian draft legislation allows trust of corporeal movables to be filed in the "pledge register (*pandregister*)" and, at the same time, recognizes delivery as an eligible means of publicity. In some German and Dutch writings, delivery is also treated as a means of publicity for trust of corporeal movables. In general, the preceding introduction mainly concerns immovable property and corporeal movables, and the issue of publicity is often overlooked in the situation of trust of claims.[653]

648 Aertsen 2004, p. 222.
649 Aertsen 2004, p. 249.
650 Aertsen 2004, p. 227.
651 Aertsen 2004, p. 230.
652 Aertsen 2004, p. 248.
653 For example, the Belgian draft only mentions immovable property and corporeal movables in explaining art. 3.46, a provision on publicity of trust. See Wetsontwerp houdende invoeging van Boek 3 "Goederen" in het nieuw Burgerlijk Wetboek, p. 93.

5.5.2 The Desirability of Registration

After providing a general introduction to publicity of trust, particular attention will be paid to publicity of trust of corporeal movables and claims. In general, the problem of publicity can be addressed easily when the object is immovable property or certain movable but registerable property (such as aircraft and vessels). This is because there is an existing system of registration in which trust can be included. Publicity is often a problem in the situation of trust of corporeal movables and claims. In general, we hold that this problem can be addressed by including trust in the register proposed in this research (see 5.3).

In section 5.3, we contend that a subject-based, notice-filing, self-service, and digital system of registration should be introduced to corporeal movables and claims. In section 5.4, we further argued that secured transactions of corporeal movables and claims should be included in the register proposed. In this section, we examine the desirability of including trust of corporeal movables and claims in the register. In general, it is desirable to publicize the trust for the reasons presented in 5.5.2.1. With respect to registration of the trust, a fear is that this formality will hamper the smooth transaction of the trust asset. In 5.5.2.2, particular attention is devoted to this fear.

5.5.2.1 Arguments for Registration of Trust

A Trust and Information Asymmetry

It is often held that the principle of publicity is not an obstacle to the reception of trust, because this principle has been abandoned in some situations, such as non-possessory pledge and security transfer of ownership in some jurisdictions.[654] The principle is less tenable as it appears in the contemporary law of movable property. Thus, it should not be treated as a barrier against trust being received.[655] Just as the French *fiducie* indicates, trust of corporeal movables is hidden to third parties, albeit that the trust of immovable property is made visible by virtue of the land register (see 5.5.1.2.B). It is acceptable that the law of immovable property has a stronger principle of publicity than the law of movable property.

In general, the preceding view is somewhat evasive. It is not convincing to say that trust can be introduced in the absence of any publicity because some other proprietary rights also lack a method of publicity.[656] On the contrary, as has been argued above, hidden proprietary security interests can cause a problem of information asymmetry and thus should be made transparent through registration, save for some exceptional secured transactions (see 5.4). In the viewpoint of Canaris, abandonment of the principle

---

654 Nolan 2006, p. 263; Kötz 1963, p. 169.
655 Milo 2012, p. 74.
656 Canaris 1978, p. 412.

of publicity can only be tolerated where there is sufficient justification.[657] In general, such sufficient justification does not exist in the situation of trust of corporeal movables and claims. The relationship of trust stands on the borderline between typical property rights and typical personal rights.[658] Ownership is acquired by the trustee, but this acquisition is limited in a proprietary sense for the beneficiary. The beneficiary's interest is not purely personal: the positive claim of access to the benefit out of the trust assets is reinforced to be partly proprietary on the basis of the associated legal effect of separation and tracing. In a word, though the interest might fail to be qualified as a typical property right, its proprietary features, in particular the tracing effect, should be justified by a means of publicity.

Truly, it is possible to choose another solution: denying the proprietary effect of the beneficiary's interest, instead of including the trust in a register. In fact, this is what has been followed by German law and French law, but an important difference exists between these two jurisdictions. In German law of *Treuhand*, the proprietary effect of the beneficiary's interest is restricted: in brief, the interest has an effect of separation but lacks the tracing effect (see 5.5.1.2.C). In the situation of disposal of the trust asset to a third party, the starting point is that it is irrelevant whether or not this third party is aware of the trustee's breach of fiduciary duties. The French *fiducie* grants a stronger position to beneficiaries: they enjoy a right of separation and a right of tracing under the restriction of *bona fide* acquisition by third parties (see 5.5.1.2.B).

In general, both rules are under an *ex-post* approach and differ only in the degree to which the beneficiary is protected. Under this approach, German law and French law choose to resolve conflicts, instead of attempting to prevent the occurrence of conflicts. This is unfair to beneficiaries and subsequent acquirers, as a type of third party.[659] In practice, beneficiaries desire proprietary protection in the event the trustee breaches its fiduciary duties. Here, proprietary protection means that the beneficiary is able to recover the object that was disposed of in violation of fiduciary duties. In general, German law and French law allow a remedy under the law of obligations, namely obtaining compensation from the trustee.[660] The demand for proprietary protection is extensive, and the legislature should not turn a blind eye to this demand. Moreover, the absence of a system of publicity might also cause a disadvantage to third parties. Even when *bona fide* acquisition free of the trust is possible, the subsequent transferee who intends to acquire the trust asset has to be prudent with respect to the trustee's authority of dis-

657 Canaris 1978, p. 412.

658 Merrill and Smith 2001, p. 843; Nolan 2006, p. 233.

659 Coing 1973, p. 123.

660 Truly, the proceeds out of the disposal contrary to the fiduciary duty belong to the trust assets, as a result of proprietary substitution. However, two risks still exist: (1) the proceeds might be mixed with the trustee's own assets; and (2) the transferee who obtains the trust asset from the trustee falls insolvent and is unable to pay the purchase price.

posal. Otherwise, the transferee might be treated as *mala fide*. In general, this often implies a burden of investigation for the transferee.[661] In the absence of an appropriate means of publicity, the investigation is often costly.

Therefore, the best way is to recognize the proprietary effect of the beneficiary's interest and allow the interest to be made transparent to third parties. This *ex-ante* approach can be seen as a consequence of balancing the interests of the parties to the trust and that of third parties: the parties to the trust cause information asymmetry to third parties by creating a proprietary relationship, thus they should be required to show this relationship to third parties.

> *"Perhaps more important than the default rule remedies, moreover, is the way in which trust law facilitates signaling to third parties the existence of the trust-like relationship, and hence helps put them on notice that the Manager lacks the authority to make the transfer."*[662]

In the viewpoint of Coing, the prohibition on entering a "mark of *Treuhand* (*Treuhandvermerk*)" in the land register is not desirable.[663] At the international level, the Convention on the Law Applicable to Trusts and on Their Recognition (1984) recognizes a formality of registration in article 12.[664] This formality is a result of the third-party effect of trusts.

> *"The obligation of the trustee to the beneficiaries in respect of the trust property must, indeed, be a specially preferred obligation conferring on the beneficiaries a preference over the trustee's private creditors, spouse and heirs. Giving effect to such preference in a civil law country will, however, require the existence of a trust affecting property to be discoverable in public registers where ownership of such property has to be registered."*[665]

In a nutshell, the broad effect of trusts and the associated problem of information asymmetry make it desirable to include trust of corporeal movables and claims in the system of registration proposed by this research.

B Trust and Systematic Coherence

From the perspective of systematic coherence, there is no reason to treat the trust for security (*fiducia cum creditore*) and the trust for management (*fiducia cum amico*) differently in the aspect of registration. In some jurisdictions, security can be provided in the manner of transfer: the debtor alienates the collateral to the creditor or a third party for the purpose of securing the

---

661 Snijders and Rank-Berenschot 2017, p. 67.

662 Hansmann and Mattei 1998, p. 455.

663 Coing 1973, p. 123.

664 Article 12: "*Where the trustee desires to register assets, movable or immovable, or documents of title to them, he shall be entitled, in so far as this is not prohibited by or inconsistent with the law of the State where registration is sought, to do so in his capacity as trustee or in such other way that the existence of the trust is disclosed.*"

665 Hayton 2016, p. 3.

creditor's claim. Truly, the "trust for security (*fiducie-sûreté*)" is not made visible to third parties under French law. However, registration open to the public is necessary in many other jurisdictions. For example, the PPSA systems in New Zealand, Canada and Australia,[666] Article 9 UCC,[667] and Book IX DCFR[668] all recognize that trust for security (*fiducia cum creditore*) is a device of security that is subject to the same requirement of publicity as other types of security device. Thus, registration is a prerequisite of the effectiveness against third parties.

In the situation of corporeal movables and claims, the trust for management should also be required to be entered a system of registration. The principal difference between trust for management and trust for security lies in the aspect of economic purposes, rather than their legal structure. In general, both types of trust involve transfer of ownership under proprietary restrictions. Thus, both cause a problem of information asymmetry to third parties. It is interesting that English law requires registration as the means of publicity for mortgage (in essence, trust for security) but exempts trust from the requirement of publicity. In fact, both mortgage and trust give rise to a kind of division of ownership under English law.[669] There seems to be no reason to treat these two types of trust differently in regard to publicity.

It is often said that the special treatment of trust for security is consistent with the fact that reservation of ownership is not subject to registration either in some jurisdictions, such as French law.[670] Security transfer of ownership is a reflection of reservation of ownership, thus the two devices should be treated alike in regard to the aspect of publicity.[671] In general, this line of reasoning is not persuasive. It only compares reservation of ownership with security transfer of ownership and ignores their significant

666 Whittaker and Partner 2015, p. 47.

667 Gilmore 1999, p. 86.

668 "*Occasionally, a trust is used for the purpose of creating a security, e.g. by the debtor or other security provider transferring the assets to be encumbered to the secured creditor or a third person as trustee for security purposes. Another example may be the trust receipt which aims to achieve a similar purpose. The rules of Book X on trusts explicitly provide that in their application to a trust serving security purposes those rules are subject to the provisions of this Book on proprietary security (X.-1:202), so that any conflict is avoided.*" See DCFR 2009, p. 4447.

669 In common law, the transferor-debtor enjoys an equitable interest known as the equity of redemption, rather than equitable ownership held by the beneficiary in the trust. Nevertheless, mortgage might be deemed to create "*a similar distinction between legal and equitable ownership but without concepts of trusteeship*". See Hudson 2003, p. 954. Of course, there is an obvious distinction between mortgage and trusts. Mortgagees hold ownership for their own benefit, namely using the collateral to guarantee the payment, while trustees hold ownership for beneficiaries. Nevertheless, there is a tendency of deeming the mortgagee as "*trustee of the property pending exercise of the mortgagor's contractual or equitable right to redeem*" in English law. See Devonshire 1997, p. 266.

670 Riffard 2016, p. 385.

671 "*The conflict is of the same kind and resolves itself in an equivalent fashion. For both institutions this is thus only a relative disadvantage; since the success of reservation of title is not undermined by this disadvantage, there is no reason to think that it would have any more effect on the success of the security fiducie.*" See Barrière 2013, p. 120.

similarity with the non-possessory pledge. In other words, the question should be: if non-possessory pledge requires public registration, do the two types of ownership-based security also need to be registered? In our opinion, the answer should be in the affirmative, as has been argued above (see 5.4.3.1). The reason is simple: all of the three types of security device cause a problem of information asymmetry. French law has introduced a register for non-possessory pledge for the purpose of transparency, but this purpose can be frustrated easily by turning to the hidden *fiducie-sûreté*. As a result, it is still difficult for third parties to ascertain whether a specific movable asset is used as collateral.

In sum, if trust for security (*fiducia cum creditore*) is subject to a requirement of registration, there is no reason to dispense with this requirement in the case of trust for management (*fiducia cum amico*). For systematic coherence, it is desirable to include trust of corporeal movables and claims, irrespective of the economic purpose served, in the register proposed by this research. Moreover, it is worthwhile noting that if the law requires registration only of trust for security and allows trust for management to remain hidden, then it will raise the question of how to draw the boundary between these two types of trust in relation to the requirement of registration.[672]

C Trust and Public Policy

Introducing a system of registration for trusts is not only desirable in private law, but also in public policy, especially the policy to combat money-laundering and tax evasion. Trust is a legal arrangement of managing wealth. However, it is also a means often used to conceal property for certain purposes, such as tax avoidance: "*one of the most popular reasons for the creation of a trust is to avoid or mitigate the settlor's liability to tax*".[673] This concern about tax is an important reason why many civil law jurisdictions are reluctant to introduce trust as a legal concept. In general, a system of registration is useful for addressing this problem.[674]

As pointed out above, French law requires the trust of corporeal movables to be registered for tax and money-laundering reasons (see 5.5.1.2.B).[675] It is worthwhile reiterating that the register is not accessible to third parties. The FATF (Financial Action Task Force) clearly emphasizes in a report the necessity of transparency of trust (FATF Recommendation 25).[676]

672 Bridge, Gullifer, McMeel and Worthington 2013, p. 203.
673 Ramjohn 2004, p. 14.
674 Sagaert 2012, p. 46.
675 Barrière 2012, p. 231.
676 FAFT Recommendation 25: "*Countries should take measures to prevent the misuse of legal arrangements for money laundering or terrorist financing. In particular, countries should ensure that there is adequate, accurate and timely information on express trusts, including information on the settlor, trustee and beneficiaries, that can be obtained or accessed in a timely fashion by competent authorities. Countries should consider measures to facilitate access to beneficial ownership and control information by financial institutions and DNFBPs undertaking the requirements set out in Recommendations 10 and 22.*"

In addition, registration of trusts is also related to other public policy. For example, according to the World Bank, trusts form *"a hurdle to investigation, prosecution (or civil judgement), and asset recovery that they are seldom prioritized in corruption investigations"*.[677]

In sum, a system of registration can satisfy the demand for transparency of trust for administrative purposes.[678] In addition to providing information to individual third parties, this system also assists the government in the combat against tax evasion, money-laundering, corruption and so forth. As a result, the system will resemble the land register which performs both administrative functions and private law functions.[679]

5.5.2.2 Doubts on Registration of Trust

As mentioned above (see 5.5.2.1.A), the Convention on the Law Applicable to Trusts and on Their Recognition (1984) requires a formality of registration for trusts. However, this requirement is deemed as *"surprising"* and cannot be understood by the Law Society of England and Wales.

> *"We find the existence of this article surprising and do not understand its purpose. It is a fundamental principle of English law that trusts are 'veiled'. The existence of a trust and the fact that the trustee is not the true owner of the assets are irrelevant to the world at large and are not disclosed by registration or documents of title. A trust only concerns trustee and beneficiary (and the tax authorities). In fact, it is regarded as desirable or even necessary for protection of persons dealing with the trustee that they should not be concerned whether it is a trustee or the true owner of assets."*[680]

In light of this viewpoint, invisibility is a merit, rather than a disadvantage. The invisibility of trust facilitates the smooth operation of transactions concerning the trust asset: since trust is invisible, the transferee does not have to be concerned about whether the transferor is a trustee or the real owner.

The above viewpoint is not without problems. Firstly, only knowing that the transferor is a trustee does not harm the transactional liquidity, since the law never denies the disposal by the trustee, provided that the fiduciary duty is not violated. Precisely speaking, what the potential buyer is concerned about is not whether the seller's ownership is subject to a relationship of trust, but whether and to what extent the seller has valid authority of disposal. Secondly, if the disposal breaches the fiduciary duty, facilitation of the transactional smoothness by protecting the transferee means that the beneficiary's interest will be sacrificed. It is conceivable that stronger protection of the transferee implies that the settlor and the benefi-

677 The World Bank 2011, p. 45-46.
678 Reich 2013, p. 351.
679 Dekker 2003, p. 132.
680 Lupoi 2000, p. 173.

ciary will spend more on monitoring the trustee.[681] Thirdly, if law does not grant protection to the transferee acting in bad faith, the transferee has to be prudent and investigate, when necessary, the trustee's authority of disposal. English law has a rule of *bona fide* acquisition: in the situation where the fiduciary duty is violated, acquisition of the trust asset is only possible when the transferee acts in good faith.[682] Therefore, third parties can never transact with a trustee as with a true owner: the buyer, as a third party, should be concerned about whether the seller is *"a trustee or the true owner of assets"*.[683] Just unveiling the trustee's qualification cannot fully guarantee the smooth operation of the transaction concerning the trust asset.

The concern about transactional fluidity has been met in examining the inclusion of the secured transaction of corporeal movables and claims in a register in 5.4.2.2.C. There, we argue that the system of registration proposed in 5.3 can guarantee that smooth transactions will not be affected by the formality of registration to an unacceptable extent. Likewise, the formality of registration will not affect heavily the smooth operation of transactions concerning the corporeal movables and claims entrusted. In general, the concern just presented should not be overstated for the following reasons.

Firstly, the operation of the system of registration proposed by this research guarantees that the formality of registration can be completed easily. Under the system, registration requires individuals to file only a simple notice, namely a summary of the legal relationship of trust. In this summary, detailed information about the subject should be included, the object should be described through a general clause with sufficient accuracy, and a mark of trust needs to be included (see 5.3.1.1.C). In general, this is in line with the requirement of the three certainties of trust: certainty of subject, certainty of object, and certainty of intention.[684] Individuals can register the trust without disclosing the other details of the relationship, which restricts the burden of registration (see 5.3.1.4). Moreover, the system will operate in a digital and self-service manner, without involving any registrar (see 5.3.1.2-5.3.1.3). This further reduces the costs of registration and search.

Secondly, the scope of the application of the system proposed is limited for the sake of efficiency (see 5.3.2). In particular, an object of low value should be excluded from the system, so that "small trusts" will not be

681 Hansmann and Mattei 1998, p. 464.

682 Edwards and Stockwell 2011, p. 13.

683 Lupoi 2000, p. 173.

684 Hudson 2014, p. 91-92. Certainty of subject is known as *"certainty of object"* in English writings. In this research, this certainty requires that the parties of the trust, in particular the beneficiary, should be ascertainable. See Hudson 2014, p. 145; Pettit 2012, p. 54. Certainty of object is known as *"certainty of subject"* or *"certainty of subject matter"* in English writings. In this research, certainty of object means that the trust property must be identifiable. See Hudson 2014, p. 116; Pettit 2012, p. 51. Certainty of intention is also known as *"certainty of words"*, which means that the settlor has a clear intention to create a trust. See Hudson 2014, p. 92; Pettit 2012, p. 48.

registered (see 5.3.2.1.E). In addition, where the trust asset is money and securities that have a high frequency of transaction, registration is unnecessary (see 5.3.2.3.A). Trust often lasts for a long period of time. Thus, there seems to be no need to prescribe a grace period (see 5.3.2.3.B).

Thirdly, registration is not a requirement of creating a valid trust and only yields declaratory effect (see 5.3.3.1). Valid creation of a legal relationship of trust has nothing to do with registration, and individuals are allowed to decide whether to make the trust created visible to third parties. Registration only affects the breadth of effectiveness against third parties: in the absence of registration, the trust has no binding effect on third parties acting in good faith (see 5.3.3.2). In general, settlors and beneficiaries who believe in the abilities of the trustee should be allowed to set aside the formality of registration. In relation to the possible disposal contrary to the trustee's fiduciary duty, if settlors and beneficiaries choose an obligational remedy in advance, there is no reason to deny this choice. However, if the settlor and the beneficiary deem registration as necessary, they can file a summary of the trust in the register. In this sense, registration implies freedom of choice, instead of a burden, for individuals.

Fourthly, it should be noted that searching the register does not constitute an extra burden to third parties. This is because trust is included in the register which also serves as a means of publicity for other transactions, especially secured transactions. In other words, both trusts and secured transactions share the same register proposed for corporeal movables and claims. Needless to say, the centralization of proprietary information makes searching the register much more convenient for the searcher.[685] The prospective buyer who searches the register because of a concern about possible secured transactions can also find the trust registered without much difficulty.

5.5.3 Publicity and the Proprietary Effect of Trust

5.5.3.1 Publicity and the Partitioning Effect

In general, the trust property can be separated visibly from the trustee's personal assets through registration, specifically speaking, the description of the trust property. Thus, registration has a function of visible separation. Here we note that identification of the trust property should be carefully distinguished from visible separation. By proper measures taken by the trustee, it is possible to identify the trust property from personal assets owned by the trustee. However, this does not necessarily mean that third parties will be aware of the scope of the trust property. This identification is called "invisible separation" in this research. For example, a trustee stores

685 Hansmann and Kraakman 2002, p. 401.

the bicycles entrusted to him at one place and puts his own bicycles at another place, and both groups of bicycles are under his factual control. In this situation, the bicycles entrusted are separated from his own bicycles in a physical sense, but this physical separation is of no help to an outsider who wants to ascertain whether the bicycle involved is under a relationship of trust. Therefore, separating the trust property is one thing, and making the separation of the trust property is another thing. Registration has a function of making the separation of trust property visible to third parties.

For subsequent acquirers, making the separation of trust assets visible by registration is of great importance. As mentioned above, the summary filed should include a description of the trust assets with sufficient accuracy (see 5.3.1.1.B). In the preceding case about bicycles, a potential buyer can easily ascertain whether the bicycle to be sold is under a relationship of trust by searching the register. If it is, this buyer should be alert with respect to the scope of the seller's authority to dispose. For example, the buyer can request the trustee to present the trust agreement or inquire with the settlor or the beneficiary. It is possible that a third party is able to be aware that the disposal made by the trustee violates the fiduciary duty after searching the register. For example, the trustee donates the trust property or pledges the trust property for his or her own debts. In these two situations, it is hard to say that the trustee acts for the benefit of the beneficiary.[686]

Trusts have an effect of separating the trust property from the enforcement by the trustee's personal creditors. In this sense, personal creditors of the trustee can be seen as a type of third party in relation to the legal relationship of trust, precisely speaking, the beneficiary's right. In general, registration of trusts has limited value to the trustee's unsecured personal creditors. The main reason for saying this is that general creditors are mainly concerned about the overall financial health of the debtor (see 2.2.2.2). In general, however, publicity is to make the proprietary legal relationships on specific assets visible to third parties. For general creditors, whether a specific asset will belong to the bankruptcy assets, if the debtor becomes bankrupt, is of no importance. This conclusion has been demonstrated in 5.1.3.2 and 5.3.3.2. It is necessary to reiterate here that the debtor's assets are always in fluctuation.

In reality, the debtor may be a professional trustee whose principal business is managing assets for the benefit of others. In this situation, the nature of the trustee's business usually already conveys an indication to general creditors.[687] It can be expected that potential and existing creditors are aware that most of the assets held by the trustee will not be distributed

686 It is possible that the trust is created for the purpose of charity, which gives rise to a charitable trust. In this special case, donation is not in violation of the purpose of the trust, and thus the fiduciary duty is not breached.

687 In the practice of pawn lending, the pawnbroker's identity provides an implicit signal that they are not possessing the goods for their own benefits. See Baird and Jackson 1984, p. 307.

to them in the event of the trustee's bankruptcy. In addition to the nature of the trustee's business, accounting measures can also convey some useful information to general creditors. As a fiduciary duty, the trustee has to make a separate account for the trust assets in order to avoid confusion with the trustee's own property.[688] Making separate accounting books can guarantee that unsecured creditors will not be misled by trusts in the evaluation of the trustee's overall financial health.

> *"In contrast, with the rules of trust law in effect, simple accounting measures can easily signal to the Manager's potential creditors which of the properties in the Manager's possession is held in trust and therefore is unavailable to satisfy the creditors in case of the Manager's insolvency."*[689]

As registration is of no importance for general creditors, failing to register the trust will not affect its effectiveness against the personal bankruptcy administrator (or the personal unsecured creditor) of the trustee. Thus, where a trust is not registered, the trust property remains separated from the bankruptcy assets of the trustee.

5.5.3.2 Publicity and the Tracing Effect

Registration is useful for protecting the beneficiary in the situation where the trustee disposes of the trust asset in violation of its fiduciary duty. In general, English law confers the most extensive right of tracing on beneficiaries.[690] Nevertheless, beneficiaries can only in a few cases recover the trust asset from third parties because the law also grants general protection to subsequent acquirers who act in good faith and obtain the trust asset for value.[691] It is conceivable that it is often difficult for the beneficiary to prove that third parties are aware of the violation in the situation where there is no possibility to register the trust. As a result, tracing the asset held by a third party by the beneficiary will be easily interrupted. In this sense, the rule of *bona fide* acquisition can be treated as an advantage to subsequent acquirers of the trust property. On the other hand, settlors and/or beneficiaries might be motivated to invest more time and energy in monitoring the trustee's management.

In general, registration is a solution to address the preceding problem. After making the trust visible, the trustee will be discouraged from violating its fiduciary duty when disposing of a trust asset to third parties. Moreover, where a trust is registered, it is difficult for third parties to claim *bona fide* acquisition of a trust asset. Correspondingly, the beneficiary has a more secure legal position by registering the trust: registration lowers the possi-

688 Finlay 2012, p. 63-64.
689 Hansmann and Mattei 1998, p. 455.
690 Ho 2013, p. 11.
691 Edwards and Stockwell 2011, p. 13.

bility that the beneficiary's right to trace is excluded by *bona fide* acquisition. In general, this does no injustice to subsequent acquirers: they are provided with a channel, namely registration, through which the relationship of trust can be known.

> *"Under a system of registration the owner of the equitable interest is able to protect himself by registering the interest. Purchasers could never be absolutely certain that they had undertaken a thorough enough investigation in order to take free of any interest which had not been revealed by their searches. The system of registration means that the purchaser simply has to inspect the register to know what interests will bind him."*[692]

In sum, registration provides a basis on which a balance can be struck between the beneficiary and the subsequent acquirer. The beneficiary has a chance to preclude *bona fide* acquisition by the subsequent acquirer by registration. In turn, the subsequent acquirer is able to obtain the information concerning the trust from the register.

5.5.4 Conclusion

There are several difficulties concerning trusts being received in civil law systems, one of which is about publicity of trusts. In common law, trusts do not have any requirement of publicity. In contrast, this legal device is subject to, to a larger or lesser extent, a principle of publicity because of the proprietary consequences triggered. This research argues that, in the situation of corporeal movables and claims, trusts should be included in the general register proposed in 5.3. In general, the problem of information asymmetry can be addressed by the register, and the interests of the relevant parties can be well balanced on the basis of registration. Moreover, the formality of registration will not give rise to unacceptable influence on the smooth transaction of the trust asset.

5.6 Registration as a Solution | Case Study III: Motor Vehicles

5.6.1 Setting the Scene

Motor vehicles are the last specific case study this research plans to examine: whether a system of registration should be introduced to the transaction of vehicles. In some jurisdictions, such as Portugal, Spain, and Denmark, a system of registration is constructed for vehicles, which is, like the land register, able to show ownership, the property right of use, and the

692 Edwards and Stockwell 2011, p. 13.

property right of security to third parties.[693] The system is comprehensive in terms of the scope of the registerable property right. A different approach is adopted by the PPSA systems in Canada, Australia and New Zealand. In these jurisdictions, the secured transaction of motor vehicles is incorporated within the system of registration for secured transactions of movables.[694] For example, the Australian PPSA treats motor vehicles as a typical category of "*serial-numbered property*", and valid registration requires an indication of the serial number of the motor vehicle, namely the VIN.[695] As a result, searchers are able to find the folio of the motor vehicle by entering the VIN. In this sense, we can say that the PPSA systems are not only subject-based but also have an object-based dimension.

In France and Italy, a narrow register is introduced for the pledge of motor vehicles for the purpose of publicity.[696] As the pledge does not involve dispossession, it is known as "movables hypothec (*ipoteche mobiliari*)" in Italian law and "pledge without dispossession (*gage sans dépossession*)" in French law.[697] Under Italian law, registration is a constitutive element for creating a property right of pledge, and the register has "public reliance (*öffentliche Glaube*)" for third parties.[698] According to art. 2351 of the French Civil Code, registration is a requirement to make the pledge opposable against third parties.[699] In both jurisdictions, ownership of motor vehicles can be transferred independently from the formality of registration.[700] The register is only constructed for the pledge of motor vehicles. In the end, it should be noted that the two registers are an object-based system.[701]

In contrast, many other countries use conventional rules of possession to regulate disputes concerning vehicle transactions. In these countries, there is an administrative system of registration. But this system, in principle, has nothing to do with the transaction of motor vehicles *per se* and only serves a function of public administration. In the aspect of publicity, motor vehicles are treated differently from aircraft and vessels: the latter two corporeal movables have, like immovable property, a comprehensive register. In the next part, English law, German law and Dutch law are selected as three examples to show the deficiency of the rule of possession (see 5.6.2).

693 About the Portuguese law concerning the registration of motor vehicles, see Gomes and Nóbrega 2011, p. 651-653; Nóbrega 2014, p. 94-95. About the Spanish law concerning the registration of motor vehicles, see Pacanowska and Soto 2011, p. 516, 522. About Danish law on this aspect, see Pedersen 1993, p. 159-160; Kieninger 2003, p. 337.

694 Walsh 2016, p. 76-77.

695 Whittaker and Partner 2015, p. 178-179.

696 The registration of pledge of motor vehicles is articulated in art. 2810 of the Italian Civil Code and art. 2351 of the French Civil Code.

697 Lipsky 2010, p. 118-120; Winter 2014, p. 191.

698 Lipsky 2010, p. 119.

699 Leavy 2007, p. 109-110.

700 Winter 2014, p. 187.

701 Leavy 2007, p. 118; Veneziano 2007, p. 169.

These three jurisdictions do not have a register for property rights of motor vehicles. For example, motor vehicles are subject to the rule of *bona fide* acquisition of corporeal movables, a rule centering on possession.

After the comparative discussion, the construction of a comprehensive and central system of registration is argued for property rights of motor vehicles (see 5.6.3). In other words, the notice-filing system of registration proposed in 5.3 should not apply to motor vehicles. This is mainly because, unlike ordinary corporeal movables and like vessels and aircraft, motor vehicles have a unique feature (the VIN) according to which an object-based registered can be established. The system proposed in 5.3 is only applicable to ordinary corporeal movables and claims. In 5.6.4, we provide a brief discussion of the legal effect of registration of motor vehicles. A conclusion is offered in 5.6.5.

5.6.2 The Rule of Possession

5.6.2.1 English Law

A General Introduction

In general, the English rule concerning the transaction of motor vehicles is embodied in cases and statutes, especially the Hire-Purchase Act (1964). The starting point is the consensual principle and the *nemo dat* rule. Under this principle, ownership of motor vehicles can be transferred upon the effect of the underlying contract, provided that the transacting parties do not agree otherwise. Delivery of the subject matter is never a prerequisite of the transfer. Next to the consensual principle is the *nemo dat* rule, a rule which was applied in the landmark case *Helby v. Matthews*. In this case, the court held that the hirer who only had an option to purchase could not transfer ownership of the motor vehicle to the third party.[702] The consensual principle and the *nemo dat* rule are disadvantageous to buyers, especially those who buy a used motor vehicle, because "*there was no adequate notification mechanism for discovering the interest of the financier as owner of the vehicle*".[703]

For the purpose of fluidity and security of transactions, English law introduces four rules as an exception to the *nemo dat* rule: (1) s. 27 of the Hire-Purchase Act (1964); (2) s. 24 (seller in possession) of the SGA (1979); (3) s. 25 (buyer in possession) of the SGA (1979); and (4) s. 2 of the FA (1889). Roughly speaking, these four provisions find their justification in the notion that possession serves as an outward mark of ownership.[704] S. 27 Hire-Purchase Act (1964) expressly grants a special protection to "*private purchasers*" of a vehicle which is subject to the "*hire-purchase*" or "*a condi-*

---

702 *Helby v. Matthews* [1895] AC 471.
703 Davies 1994 (2), p. 474.
704 Davies 1994 (2), p. 475.

tional sale agreement".[705] The main requirement of this protection is that the private purchaser acts in good faith without having a notice of the hire-purchase agreement or the conditional sale agreement, and the term *"private purchaser"* implies that the buyer has to acquire the vehicle for value.[706]

The two provisions of the SGA (1979) might apply where the vehicle in question is controlled by a seller who retains possession but has transferred ownership (s. 24 SGA) or a buyer who obtains possession but no ownership (s. 25 SGA). The principal requirement of the two provisions is that the third party has to act in good faith, and the subject matter must be delivered to this party. In addition, gift is not an eligible cause for acquisition by third parties acting in good faith. S. 2 FA (1889) provides another exception to the *nemo dat* rule. Pursuant to this provision, successful *bona fide* acquisition by a third party requires that this party acts in good faith, and the transaction occurs in the ordinary course of business of the seller.

In England, there is an administrative system of registration for motor vehicles, and a certificate of registration is issued to the owner of the motor vehicle. In reality, the certificate is also relevant to transactions concerning motor vehicles. Before turning to the relevance of the certificate to the transaction, it is useful to mention that there are now two private registers for the transaction of motor vehicles in England. One is the HPI (Hire Purchase Inspection), and the other is the AutoCheck.[707] These two systems do not have a statutory law basis and are maintained by several large finance companies. In general, the two systems can be seen as *"a market response to the lack of a statutory registration requirement"*.[708] The two systems provide comprehensive information regarding motor vehicles, and most dealers are members who are entitled to search the systems. Nevertheless, the systems have no legal effect of public reliance, as indicated in the case *Moorgate Mercantile Co Ltd v. Twitchings*.[709] This means that the owner's failure to register his or her right of ownership does not prevent him or her from recovering the motor vehicle from third parties acting in good faith.

B The Role of Registration Certificates

In applying the four exceptional rules stated above, a common and central issue is how to determine that the requirement of *"good faith"* and that of the *"ordinary course of business"* are satisfied.[710] In the context of transactions concerning cars, this issue has a close connection with the registration certificate of motor vehicles. In English law, the registration document is issued by the Driver Vehicle Licensing Agency (DVLA) for the purpose of public

705 The Act draws a distinction between the *"private purchasers"* (i.e. consumers) and the *"trade or finance purchasers"*, and only the former is under the statutory protection. See Macleod 2002, p. 690.

706 Benjamin 2014, p. 410-411.

707 Beale, Bridge, Gullifer and Lomnicka 2018, no. 9.26-9.33.

708 Beale, Bridge, Gullifer and Lomnicka 2018, no. 9.26-9.33.

709 *Moorgate Mercantile Co Ltd v. Twitchings*, [1977] AC 890.

710 Davies 2001, p. 499.

regulation.[711] The registration certificate is not a condition of the transfer of vehicles, despite the fact that there is a duty of altering registration after completion of the transfer.[712] The registration certificate is not, in the wording of English law, a document of title to the motor vehicle: "*the owner of the vehicle does not hold out another as having authority to sell the car merely by giving up possession of the car and its registration book.*"[713] However, it is often treated as akin to the document of title because it can produce some private law consequences.[714] For example, the registration certificate is often taken into consideration in determining whether the third party acts in good faith and whether the transaction occurs in the "*ordinary course of business*".[715]

The requirement of the ordinary course of business is embodied in s. 2 (1) FA (1889). The starting point is that a transaction without involving delivery of the registration certificate is suspicious and should not be treated as taking place in the ordinary course of business of the seller.[716] New vehicles should be treated differently from used vehicles in this aspect. The transferor of new vehicles has no registration certificate, and there is no possibility of delivery of the document.

> "*There is all the difference in the world between a case where an owner of a second-hand car retains the log book while handing over physical possession of the car to a dealer so as to ensure that no-one will suppose that the dealer has authority to sell the car, and the case where a dealer effects a sale of a new car while the registration book is with the registration authority for registration or tax purposes. I find it difficult to see why a sale of the latter type should not be in the ordinary course of business of a motor dealer who holds a car on sale or return terms.*"[717]

---

711 "*Following on from this, a major purpose of registration is fiscally related--that is, mechanically propelled vehicles used or kept on public roads in Great Britain must have an excise license which attracts payment by way of a duty [...]. It is for this reason that the particulars contained in the register are made available for use by a local authority for any purpose connected with the investigation of an offence and also the police or, on the payment of a fee, any person who can show to the satisfaction of the Secretary of State that he has reasonable cause, notably theft, for wanting the particulars to be made available to him.*" See Davies 2001, p. 476.

712 "*I do not see how a registration document, which on its face states that it records the name of the registered keeper and that the registered keeper is not necessarily the legal owner can possibly be said to be a document used in the ordinary course of business on proof of the possession or control of goods or authorising or purporting to authorise, either by endorsement or by delivery, the possessor of the document to transfer or receive goods thereby represented [...].*" See *Beverley Acceptances Ltd v. Oakley* [1982] R.T.R. p. 432.

713 Davies 2001, p. 499.

714 Davies 1995 (2), p. 479.

715 Davies 2001, p. 500.

716 "*A sale to a finance corporation does require in the ordinary course of business that delivery of the car can be given to the proposed hirer. To make that delivery effective, it must be given in such a way that the hirer can license and use the car, and this involves that the registration book must be delivered with the car. A sale involving delivery to the hirer of the car without its registration book would not, in my judgement be in the ordinary course of business.*" See *Stadium Finance Ltd v. Robbins* [1962] 2 Q.B. 665, p. 675.

717 *Astley Industrial Trust v. Miller* [1968] 2 All E.R. 36, p. 42-43.

Here, it should be noted that the requirement of the "ordinary course of business" and the requirement of good faith overlap to a large extent: the absence of delivery of the registration certificate often means that the purchaser does not act in good faith.[718] In a nutshell, delivery of the registration document is, at least in the situation of the transaction of used cars, has a close connection with the ordinary course of business and good faith.

In general, the registration certificate plays a similar role in applying s. 27 of the Hire-Purchase Act (1964) and in determining whether the third party acts in good faith.[719] In particular, the registration certificate is irrelevant in the situation of new vehicles, while it is important for answering the question of good faith when the object is a used vehicle.

With respect to the two provisions of the SGA (1979), delivery of the registration certificate is relevant in determining whether the purchaser acts in good faith, at least when the transaction involves a used car.[720] However, it should be noted that where the buyer steals the registration certificate retained by the seller and delivers the document to a third party, this third party is not entitled to *bona fide* acquisition.[721] In other words, the registration certificate must be acquired by the transferor with the consent of the original owner.[722]

C Mortgage, Charge, and Pledge ofVehicles

Mortgage and charge of vehicles are subject to registration according to the Companies Act (2006), provided that the security provider is a company.[723] Through this means of publicity, the security interest can be made visible to and consequently effective against third parties. However, it should be noted that the registration only has limited effect against third parties, and buyers in the ordinary course of business should not be treated as having constructive notice of the security interest.[724] For the mortgage and charge of motor vehicles, the registration certificate does not play any role since delivery of the collateral is not required.

To create a right of pledge, giving up factual control of the vehicle to the pledgee is a prerequisite since delivery is necessary for pledging corporeal movables under English law (see 3.5.3.1.A).[725] There is no need to give up the registration certificate to the pledgee since the certificate is not a document of title. The pledgee does not have to worry that the pledgor will further dispose of the collateral, as the former has obtained possession of the motor vehicle pledged. Needless to say, the delivery causes severe inconvenience to the pledgor who usually wants to continue using the vehicle.

718 Ulph2000, p. 256-257.
719 Bridge 2014, p. 261.
720 Ulph 2000, p. 256-257.
721 Benjamin 2014, p. 400.
722 Ulph 1998, p. 410.
723 Davies 1994 (1), p. 15.
724 Beale, Bridge, Gullifer and Lomnicka 2018, no. 12.05.
725 Goode 2013, p. 32; Bridge 2007, p. 142.

In a nutshell, it can be concluded that the rule of transactions of motor vehicles is complex and patchy in England. English law takes a piecemeal approach in regulating the transaction of vehicles: it involves common law, equity law, the Sale of Goods Act (1979), the Factors Act (1889), the Hire-Purchase Act (1964), and the Companies Act (2006). In general, the transaction is conducted in the absence of a reliable source of information for third parties, and the applicable law is based on the idea of resolving conflicts, rather than the notion of preventing conflicts. The registration certificate and possession play an important role in resolving a conflict between the original owner and third parties. Truly, mortgage and charge provided by companies can be made visible to third parties through registration, but neither the other property rights nor security interests granted by a natural person are able to be shown to third parties.

5.6.2.2 German Law and Dutch Law

Compared with English law, both German law and Dutch law take a unitary approach to the transaction of motor vehicles: the *traditio* system plus a rule of *bona fide* acquisition. Under the *traditio* system, the transfer of ownership of a motor vehicle requires delivery of this motor vehicle to the transferee. For transfer of motor vehicles, *traditio per constitutum possessorium* is an eligible form of delivery, which means that the transferor does not have to give up physical control. Handing over the registration certificate is neither a prerequisite of valid transfer nor has any effect of delivery.[726] This is because the registration certificate (*Kraftfahrzeugebrief* in German law and *kentekenbewijs* in Dutch law) is merely a tool of administrative regulation. The nature of motor vehicles as a corporeal movable is not altered by the issuance of a certificate. In the terminology of Dutch law (art. 3:10 BW), motor vehicles are not a kind of "registerable property (*registergoederen*)" that takes public registration as the method of publicity.[727]

In the aspect of the legal nature of registration certificates, both German law and Dutch law are not different from English law. The starting point is that the registration certificate is not a document of title or title-conferring certificate. Thus, the transaction of motor vehicles can take place independently from the certificate. Changing the document is merely a requirement by administrative law and has nothing to do with the private law transaction. However, this does not mean that the registration certificate is totally irrelevant to the transaction. In general, it has a close connection with *bona fide* acquisition of motor vehicles in both jurisdictions, despite the fact that statutory law is silent about this connection. It is an important factor that should be considered in determining the issue of good faith: whether and to what extent a third party has to conduct an investigation of the counterparty's authority of disposal.

726 Salomons 2008 (2), p. 78; McGuire 2008, p. 107.
727 Reehuis and Heisterkamp 2019, p. 7.

Under both German law[728] and Dutch law[729], the basic rule is that a third party will be treated as not acting in good faith or as acting with gross negligence, if this party fails to conduct further inquiry where the transferor does not present the registration certificate. In German law, if the transferor is not registered on the certificate, or there is any doubt regarding the certificate, the purchaser bears an obligation of further inquiries.[730] As confirmed by a Dutch case, the mere fact that the transferor's name is not on the document does not necessarily mean that the buyer acts in bad faith, provided that there is a "reasonable explanation (*aannemelijke verklaring*)" with respect to this fact.[731] Therefore, presenting the registration document, paying diligent attention to the information on the document and, when necessary, conducting further inquiry are essential in determining the question of good faith.

However, two important exceptions to the preceding rule are accepted by both German law and Dutch law. The first exception is that failure to present the registration document does not imply bad faith when the motor vehicle involved is new and the seller is a commercial dealer.[732] This reminds us of the practice of English law: the transaction of new vehicles is treated differently in applying s. 2 (1) FA (1889). The second exception is that a purchaser will not be treated as acting in good faith, if this purchaser is by virtue of his or her professional experience able to know that the motor vehicle is under a clause of reservation of ownership.[733]

The preceding introduction concerns only the transfer of ownership. In reality, leasing and pledging of motor vehicles are also popular. Under both German law and Dutch law, motor vehicles can be leased. In this situation, factual control should be surrendered by the lessor to the lessee. During the lease, any further disposal by the owner cannot affect the legal relationship of lease in Dutch law, as a result of the rule of "*sale does not break lease*" (art. 7:226 BW). However, the rule is not accepted by German law in the case of lease of motor vehicles: § 566 BGB, a corresponding provision to art. 7:226 BW, confines itself to the lease of immovable property. Therefore, it is easy to conclude that Dutch law, compared with German law, grants more protection to the lessee of motor vehicles. On the other hand, German law is more advantageous to purchasers of the motor vehicle leased.

728 BGH NJW 1975, p. 735; BGH NJW 1996, p. 2226; Wolf and Wellenhofer 2011, p. 107; Westermann 2011, p. 421.

729 *Apon/Bisterbosch* (HR 4 april 1986, NJ 1986, 710); *Coppes/Van de Kolk* (HR 7 oktober 2005, NJ 2006, 351); Nieuwenhuis 1986, p. 790; Kortmann 2006, p. 288; Van Vliet 2006, p. 191.

730 BGH NJW 1994, p. 2022; Baur and Stürner 2009, p. 674; Wilhelm 2010, p. 401; Wolf and Wellenhofer 2011, p. 107.

731 *Bull's Eye/Chrysler* (HR 11 oktober 2002, NJ 2003, 399); Van Vliet 2006, p. 191; Salomons 2006, p. 121.

732 OLG Düsseldorf NJW-RR 1992, p. 381; Wolf and Wellenhofer 2011, p. 107; Westermann 2011, p. 420; Salomons 2006, p. 121.

733 BGH NJW 2005, p. 1365; Westermann 2011, p. 420; *DFM/Mobiel Lease* (HR 21 oktober 2011, NJ 2011, 494); Salomons 2011 (1); Van Swaaij 2012, p. 125.

For pledging a motor vehicle, giving up factual control by the pledgor is necessary in German law (§ 1205 BGB), while it is not essential in Dutch law because of the recognition of the silent pledge (art. 3:237 BW). In general, German law recognizes, as an alternative to the non-possessory pledge, the security transfer of ownership, a form of transfer in the manner of *traditio per constitutum possessorium*. The security transfer is also a non-possessory security device (see 3.5.3.1.D). Unlike English law, both jurisdictions do not have a system of public registration for the non-possessory security device. As a result, the proprietary encumbrance over motor vehicles is in general hidden to third parties under German law and Dutch law.

5.6.2.3 The Problems Observed

From the preceding comparative introduction, it can be found that all the three jurisdictions lack a comprehensive system of registration for the transaction of motor vehicles. English law allows registration of only mortgage and charge of motor vehicles in the situation where the security provider is a company. There is an administrative system of registration in the three countries, but its purpose and function determine that the transaction of motor vehicles is independent of this system. As an exception, the only private law effect of the system is that the registration certificate, issued by the public registry, is related to *bona fide* acquisition of motor vehicles. Where the motor vehicle involved is used, the certificate is a factor that should be taken into consideration in answering the question whether the third party acts in good faith or is grossly negligent. In general, the proprietary relationship on motor vehicles remains invisible to third parties, and it is still the conventional rule concerning possession that is applied to resolve conflicts after they arise. There is no doubt that the transaction is exposed to a severe risk of uncertainty because of the lack of a reliable source of information for third parties. On account of the high value of motor vehicles, it seems that the conflict is more common in the situation of motor vehicles than in the situation of ordinary corporeal movables.[734]

In the situation of new vehicles, there is no registration certificate that can help a potential buyer to know whether the motor vehicle belongs to the seller. In this situation, the *nemo dat* rule is the starting point, and the rule of *bona fide* acquisition only applies exceptionally. Because of the preferential application of the *nemo dat* rule, potential acquirers have to be very prudential with respect to the legal state of the motor vehicle involved. As German law and Dutch law indicate, a professional trader is often not allowed to claim *bona fide* acquisition because of his or her having commercial experience. Indeed, we can say that commercial experience implies that prudential traders will not assume naively that the possessor of the motor vehicle has full ownership. However, the problem of information asymmetry is not

734 Davies 2001, p. 489.

completely addressed by commercial experience. As has been argued above (see 5.4.2.2.A), commercial experience only allows professional parties to not be misled by possession, but it can never indicate clearly whether the seller has unencumbered ownership. Moreover, the assumption on the basis of commercial experience is unfair to those possessors who have unencumbered ownership of the motor vehicles possessed: those possessors have to persuade their counterparties to believe that they have unencumbered ownership, which is not without costs. In addition, it has to be borne in mind that there are a large number of consumer purchasers who have no professional knowledge or commercial experience.[735] Therefore, it can be concluded that the transaction of new vehicles faces a problem of information asymmetry, as indicated by Roskill L.J. in the case *Stevenson v. Beverely Bentinck Ltd.*

> *"Ever since hire-purchase was invented, round about the turn of the century, there have been hire-purchase frauds, and the books are full of examples of such frauds, which have caused loss to innocent parties. Again and again—and the present case is yet another example—courts have to decide where, as between two wholly innocent parties, that loss should fall. This is particularly so in the case of motor cars, because persons who hire motor cars under hire-purchase agreements persist in selling them or purporting to sell them, to innocent purchasers when as persons in possession they have no right whatsoever to sell."*[736]

For used vehicles, the problem of information asymmetry also exists and cannot be fully addressed by registration certificates or by possession of motor vehicles. In fact, the registration certificate might be a source of misleading information and fraud, since it does not seem difficult to forge a registration certificate.[737] The main defect of the registration certificate is that it only shows the relationship of "*keepership*" rather than the ownership of the motor vehicle.[738] For example, one cannot know whether there is any proprietary encumbrance over the vehicle from the registration certificate. Moreover, the relationship of ownership cannot always be reflected by the registration certificate, on account of the fact that transfer of ownership is not contingent on delivery of the certificate. Truly, inspection of and delivery of the registration certificate are common steps in ordinary transactions. However, this does not mean that *bona fide* acquisition by a third party will be completely excluded when the transferor is not registered on the document, or that the mere fact that the transferor is recorded on the document can supply absolute safety to the transferee. Precisely speaking, registration certificates are at most a factor that should be considered in determining whether the third party acts in good faith. The information derived from registration certificates is never decisive: the document has no legal effect of reliance.

735 Lurger 2006, p. 48.
736 *Stevenson v. Beverely Bentinck Ltd*, [1976] 1 W.L.R. 483, p. 486-487.
737 Davies 1995 (1), p. 42; Baur and Stürner 2009, p. 674; Benjamin 2014, p. 400.
738 Davies 2001, p. 499; Tiedemann 1994, p. 159; Salomons 2006, p. 118.

It should be noted that the information asymmetry presented above is not only a problem for third parties, but also a source of risk for the owner of vehicles (usually the financier of the seller). As has been discussed above, a third party acting in good faith is entitled to defeat the original owner by applying the rule of *bona fide* acquisition. Thus, it is conceivable that the owner, who gives up possession of the vehicle, will invest more resources in monitoring the direct possessor, so that the direct possessor will not dispose of the vehicle in violation of the agreement with the owner.[739] This accounts for the private action taken by English finance companies to establish a system of registration (see 5.6.2.1.A). The failure to provide an efficient means of communication of information by the government motivates individuals to construct a system themselves.[740]

5.6.3 The Desirability of Registration

5.6.3.1 Necessity

The comparative introduction above has shown that where there is not any private law register, the transaction of motor vehicles will be regulated by conventional rules concerning ownership and possession of corporeal movables. Possession, registration certificate, and commercial experience cannot successfully address the problem of information asymmetry existing in the field of the transaction of motor vehicles. In general, regulation is an *ex-post* approach. Instead of preventing the occurrence of conflicts by creating a reliable source of information for individuals, it offers a bundle of sophisticated rules to resolve conflicts after they arise. The approach is undesirable and should be given up for three principal reasons.

The first reason is that motor vehicles are of high value and have become an ordinary commodity in our daily life, and the lack of a preventive regime leads to ubiquitous conflicts and even theft and fraud.[741] This is the main reason why the Danish legislature decided to introduce a register for the transaction of motor vehicles.[742]

The second reason is that the *ex-post* approach always faces "*the dilemma of identifying which two innocent parties must bear the loss*".[743] Here the "*two innocent parties*" refer to the original owner who gives up possession and the third party who acts in good faith. The dilemma has been stated above (see

739 Davies 1995 (2), p. 469.

740 Beale, Bridge, Gullifer and Lomnicka 2018, no. 9.26.

741 "*Ever since hire-purchase was invented, round about the turn of the century, there have been hire-purchase frauds, and the books are full of examples of such frauds, which have caused loss to innocent parties.*" See *Stevenson v. Beverely Bentinck Ltd*, [1976] 1 W.L.R. 483, p. 486-487.

742 "*The Danish media have regularly criticised the fact that bona fide purchasers especially of second-hand cars run the risk that the car is burdened with latent debt and, consequently, they may risk either losing the car or having to pay for it twice.*" See Pedersen 1993, p. 159.

743 Davies 1995 (1), p. 54.

5.2.1). It should be noted that the rule of *bona fide* acquisition confers preferential protection to the third party at the sacrifice of the original owner's interest.

> *"The traditional common law nemo dat doctrine and the civilian 'possession vaut titre' approach cannot provide a satisfactory ex post solution to the ostensible ownership problem that emerges in asset financing and more specifically motor vehicle financing."*[744]

The third reason is that the possibility of *bona fide* acquisition will make the owner conservative in determining whether to give up possession of the motor vehicle. This implies an indirect restriction on the circulation of motor vehicles in the situation where ownership and possession have to be apart. Moreover, to preclude *bona fide* acquisition, the owner who gives up factual control needs to monitor the direct possessor's activities with respect to the motor vehicle. This means that the owner has to incur some monitoring costs.

For these three reasons, introducing a system of registration for the transaction of motor vehicles is needed. This system can address the problem of information asymmetry to a large extent, and the certainty of the transaction of motor vehicles can thus be facilitated. This has been illustrated by the Danish system of registration: the *Bilbogen*.[745] Moreover, the system can eliminate or alleviate the owner's fear of *bona fide* acquisition by a third party.

5.6.3.2 Possibility

A Format: An Object-Based System

In general, it is possible to construct a system of registration for the transaction of vehicles. Motor vehicles can easily be identified uniquely, especially with reference to the plate number or the vehicle identification number (VIN). For the purpose of security, it is preferable to use the latter as the index of the register. One reason is that the vehicle plate can be easily counterfeited, and another reason is that the VIN can uniquely identify the make, model, color and exact specification of the vehicle.[746]

> *"Although there are usually some components, large and small, that is part of the vehicle that has separate serial numbers of their own, the VIN is the unique identifying number that represents the vehicle as a whole. In most cases, the original VIN affixed to a vehicle consistently follows it during an entire service lifetime through periodic license plate updates, transfers of ownership, changes in title and registration from state to state, and eventually even possible replacement of some of the vehicle's original major compo-*

744 Davies 1995, p. 479.
745 Pedersen 1993, p. 159-160.
746 Davies 1995 (2), p. 478.

> *nents due to extensive wear, damage, or even theft. The VIN is the principal identifying number used by virtually all government vehicle titling and registration authorities for issuing ownership and related documents for modern motor vehicles."*[747]

Because of the VIN, each individual motor vehicle can be identified easily and efficiently. Thus, it is possible to construct an object-based register. In this aspect, motor vehicles are different from ordinary movables which can only have a subject-based system, such as the notice-filing system proposed for ordinary corporeal movables and claims in 5.3.

In fact, the present system of registration for administrative regulation of motor vehicles has provided a perfect basis on which a private-law register can be built. In general, two principal changes need to be made. The first change is that the present system needs to be more inclusive: ownership and limited property rights should be allowed to be entered in this system. The second change is that the system should be made accessible to third parties, so that third parties are able to collect relevant proprietary information from the system. After these two changes, the system will not only have a public-law function, but also a private law function.[748]

B Scope: An Independent and Comprehensive System

As indicated at the beginning of this section, there are in principle two patterns of registration of vehicles. One is the central and independent system adopted by China and Denmark, and the other pattern is the PPSA system which incorporates registration of motor vehicles within the notice-filing system for secured transactions of movable property. The PPSA system not only includes motor vehicles, but also other "*serial-numbered*" assets, such as aircraft and vessels.[749] Between these two patterns, this research prefers the former, namely the central and independent system of registration for motor vehicles.

Some of the reasons for this preference have been mentioned above. Firstly, it is possible to build an independent system of registration and allocate a separate folio to each motor vehicle according to the VIN. Secondly, there is already a central and independent system of registration for the purpose of administrative regulation of motor vehicles. This system can be reformed to serve private law transactions at the same time. Thirdly, motor vehicles have become an ordinary commodity in our daily life, and there are a large number of motor vehicles in use and transactions. This means that the costs involved in the operation of the system can be easily overweighed by the benefits of scale the system yields.

In addition, the main deficiency of the PPSA pattern is that the scope of registerable property rights is limited, which can be seen as the fourth reason. The aim of the PPSA system is to publicize the secured transaction

---

747 Smylie 2006, p. 127.
748 Winter 2014, p. 187.
749 Whittaker and Partner 2015, p. 178-179; Walsh 2016, p. 77.

of movable property to third parties. A transaction which has nothing to do with providing proprietary security cannot be entered in the system. Though the PPSA system might include a category of *"deemed security interests"* that have no function of security, such as long-term lease, many transactions remain outside of the system. For example, the outright transfer of ownership of motor vehicles in the absence of a clause of retention of ownership cannot be included in the system, because this transaction does not give rise to a security interest. Another example is that the property right of usufruct, a right with respect to the use of and collection of proceeds of motor vehicles, cannot be entered in the system either.

Aircraft and vessels are entered in an independent register in most jurisdictions and are treated as quasi-immovable property. For example, Dutch law classifies these two special corporeal movables as "registerable property (*registergoederen*)" which are regulated by the rules applicable to immovable property.[750] In Germany, there is also an individual system of registration of aircraft and vessels for the purpose of transactions.[751] In general, there is no reason to treat motor vehicles differently from aircraft and vessels. All of these three types of corporeal movables are a means of transportation that is of high value and durable. This can be seen as the fifth reason to construct an independent and comprehensive register for motor vehicles.

5.6.3.3 Efficiency

Efficiency seems to be the most controversial issue for the introduction of a register for the transaction of motor vehicles. There is always the fear that the formality of registration will hamper transactional fluidity. As has been shown above, an inevitable side effect of publicity is that additional costs will be caused (see 5.1.1.3). However, the formality of registration also yields benefits (see 5.1.1.2): it enhances the certainty of transactions and reduces the costs of investigation and monitoring. Therefore, the issue of whether registration should be introduced is dependent on the result of the cost-benefit test.

> *"It is a highly political decision to introduce or abolish a registration system for the ownership of certain types of movables, because such decisions have an important impact on the trade with such goods. The introduction of a registration system is costly and burdensome, for the parties as well as the state or other institutions involved, and it will be justified only for very few categories of goods—which are valuable, long-lasting, and important for the economy, and trade without registration would be too insecure for the market participants."*[752]

750 Reehuis and Heisterkamp 2019, p. 7.
751 Baur and Stürner 2009, p. 406-407; Rakob 2007, p. 89-90; Steppler and Brecke 2015, p. 55.
752 DCFR 2009, p. 3987.

In general, this research argues that a comprehensive system of registration of motor vehicles is desirable and can pass the cost-benefit test for the following reasons.

Firstly, motor vehicles are valuable. Like aircraft and vessels, motor vehicles have higher value than ordinary corporeal movables.[753] In general, the high value of vehicles makes registration desirable in two aspects: (1) the high value can overweigh the costs triggered by the formality of registration; and (2) the high value often implies a strong incentive to commit fraud and theft, which further means that it is desirable to use registration as a counter device.

Secondly, motor vehicles are durable. In general, the longevity of the object is another important factor that should be taken into consideration. For things of a short lifespan, it is undesirable to have an object-based register for them. Otherwise, the system would have to be updated after the extinction of the things. Motor vehicles usually have a long lifespan, which can justify registration in two aspects. One is that the folio will exist for a long term after being allocated to a motor vehicle, which implies that the folio can be made use of for a long period of time. The other aspect is that long lifespan often implies that a large number of legal relationships might be created on the vehicle, which further means a high possibility of conflict. As a result, the need for having a system of registration to prevent conflicts is strong.

Thirdly, motor vehicles have a moderate transactional frequency. In general, after buying a new car, the buyer will use it for a long period of time before selling it as a used car to another person. Unlike securities, motor vehicles do not take circulation as their fundamental function. This also makes motor vehicles suitable for registration. As we have demonstrated in 5.3.2.3, movable things which have a very high transactional frequency (such as currency and negotiable securities) or a very low transactional frequency (such as jewelry) are not suitable for registration.

Fourthly, a notice-filing system constructed by taking advantage of the new information technology can alleviate the fear that the formality of registration will hamper the smooth operation of the transaction of motor vehicles (see 5.3.1).[754] For example, the system can operate online, so that registration and searching the system can be conducted without having to go to the registry office. Therefore, like the register for the "*international interest*" under Cape Town Convention on International Interests in Mobile Equipment, the register proposed for motor vehicles here is also an object-based notice-filing system.[755]

753 Lurger 2006, p. 51.
754 Davies 1994 (2), p. 479.
755 Van Erp 2004, p. 96-98.

Fifthly, the existing register for administrative regulation can provide a perfect basis for registering property rights of motor vehicles (ownership, the right of use, and the right of security). Nearly every jurisdiction has built a system of registration for administrative purposes. In this system, the vehicle is registered on a separate folio. The system can be modified to be capable of performing a private law function, namely making the proprietary relationship of motor vehicles transparent to third parties. The project of modification is not expensive, at least it is less costly than constructing a new register. After the modification, the system will resemble the land register: both the administrative purpose and the publicity purpose can be realized. For example, when a motor vehicle is stolen, the system can supply a warning of theft, which has an anti-criminal effect and a publicity effect to third parties.[756] The system should be in principle open to public officials and individuals because of its dual function. If there is any sufficient reason, such as confidentiality of public authorities' activities, to restrict inquiry by third parties, a threshold or certain restrictions can be set up.

5.6.4 The Legal Effect of Registration

In general, the register for motor vehicles should yield similar legal effects as the system of registration proposed in 5.3 for ordinary corporeal movables and claims. In other words, registration is not a constitutive requirement of acquiring property rights of motor vehicles (see 5.3.3.1). Instead, it has declaratory effect and can make the acquisition effective against third parties. Thus, individuals are allowed to decide whether to have their transaction registered in the system. There is no doubt that the declaratory effect can ease the impact of the formality of registration on the smooth operation of transactions concerning motor vehicles (see 5.4.2.2.C).

As to the scope of the third-party effect, it is argued by this research that registration is a condition for the acquisition to be effective against subsequent acquirers acting in good faith (see 5.3.3.2). In other words, the absence of registration does not preclude the property right acquired from being effective against strange interferers and general creditors. Moreover, subsequent acquirers acting in bad faith should not be allowed to take advantage of the absence of registration (see 5.3.3.4). The reason why a property right registered is effective against subsequent acquirers is that they are expected to be aware of this property right by searching the register. In the situation of motor vehicles, every subsequent acquirer, including the transferee, the pledgee, and the lessee, should be expected to search the register. Therefore, the legal effect of constructive notice is not limited, which is different from the register for ordinary corporeal movables and claims (see 5.3.3.3).

756 Davies 1995 (2), p. 485.

In the end, the system can be reliable and have the effect of public reliance, provided that the legislature the dynamic security or transactional certainty in a primary position (see 5.3.3.5). For example, A transfers a motor vehicle to B on an invalid basis, and B further alienates this vehicle to C who relies on the registration of B as the owner and acts in good faith. In this situation of consecutive transactions, whether C is entitled to obtain ownership of the motor vehicle is, in essence, an issue of legal policy. If preferential protection is allocated to C, and the system is recognized to be reliable, C will be able to acquire ownership without being affected by A's claim. However, if an opposite legal policy is followed, A can recover the motor vehicle from C despite C's having reliance on the register. This means that the system of registration does not have public reliance.

5.6.5 Conclusion

The existing system rules applicable to the transaction of motor vehicles centers on possession and falls under an *ex-post* approach. Possession and the registration certificate cannot make all transactions of motor vehicles visible to third parties. As a result, information asymmetry exists in the field of motor vehicles ubiquitously. To address this problem, it is desirable to introduce a central and comprehensive system of registration by modifying the present system constructed for administrative regulation. Therefore, the system of registration for motor vehicles is different from the system proposed in 5.3 for ordinary corporeal movables and claims. The modification will make the system perform both a public law function and a private law function, i.e. the publicity function. The formality of registration will not affect the smooth operation of the transaction to an unacceptable extent. This is mainly because the register is a digital, self-service and notice-filing system. Moreover, motor vehicles have a moderate frequency of transaction and are durable and of high value, which enables the formality of registration to pass the cost-benefit test.

In general, registration does not affect the acquisition of property rights of the motor vehicle. It is only relevant to the legal effectiveness against certain third parties, namely subsequent acquirers acting in good faith. Registration of a property right implies a constructive notice of this right for third parties. The absence of registration does not preclude the acquisition from being effective against strange interferers, general creditors, and subsequent acquirers acting in bad faith. This restriction of the scope of the third-party effect is an outcome of the purpose of publicity and the special demand of proprietary information by strange interferers and general creditors. Generally speaking, the restriction of the scope of third-party effect is helpful for easing the impact of the registration on the smooth transactions of motor vehicles.

5.7 Conclusion

After the general discussion (5.1-5.3) and the three case studies (5.4-5.6), a concluding remark is provided here. In general, publicity is a formality that has merits and downsides. Therefore, it should only be treated as relevant when necessary and appropriate. Generally speaking, strange interferers take possession as a system of navigation to guide their conduct, unsecured creditors are mainly concerned about the debtor's overall financial health, and subsequent acquirers have a demand for specific and detailed proprietary information. The strange interferers and unsecured creditors do not need to know about the details of the proprietary right. Because of this difference in the demand for proprietary information by these different types of third parties, the consensual principle and the causation principle are more in line with the rationale of publicity. Under these two principles, transactional certainty can be safeguarded generally by the rule of *bona fide* acquisition on the basis of registration. The rule is underlaid by the rationale of publicity and matches with our sense of morality.

The merits and downsides of publicity also determine that a trade-off should be carefully made in introducing registration in the law of corporeal movables and claims. In general, property rights existing on corporeal movables and claims remain hidden to a large extent, which makes it necessary to introduce a system of registration to have a strong principle of publicity in the law of corporeal movables and claims. In Chapter 5, two different registers are proposed: one is the register for ordinary corporeal movables and claims (see 5.3-5.5), and the other is the register for motor vehicles (see 5.6).

In general, the register for ordinary corporeal movables and claims should be a notice-filing, self-service, subject-based and digital system. The scope of application of the system is limited on the basis of some factors, such as the frequency of transactions, the duration of the hidden period, and the value of the object involved. The registration has declaratory effect, and the acquisition of property rights is a result of mutual agreement. The registration can yield legal effect against subsequent acquirers acting in good faith, save in the situation where the transaction arises in the ordinary course of business. The system can be recognized as reliable for third parties acting in good faith, provided that the legislature puts dynamic security in a primary position. In general, the system should be applied to both secured transactions, regardless of whether they are title-based, and trusts of corporeal movables and claims.

Unlike the register for ordinary corporeal movables and claims, the register for motor vehicles is an object-based notice-filing system. The index is the VIN of the motor vehicle. The system should be introduced by modifying the existing register constructed for the administrative regulation of motor vehicles. By doing so, the system will perform both a public law function and a private law function. The system is central and comprehensive: it applies not only to the transfer of ownership, but also to the creation of limited property rights. In general, the registration yields similar legal effects as the registration for ordinary corporeal movables and claims: it can make the acquisition effective against subsequent acquirers.

In a nutshell, we can say that this research argues for an expansion of registration to the field of corporeal movables, including motor vehicles, and claims. The expansion is backed by the idea of preventive justice and can significantly alleviate the perennial tension observed by Denning LJ.

> *"In the development of our law, two principles have striven for mastery. The first is for the protection of property: no one can give a better title than he himself possesses. The second is for the protection of commercial transactions: the person who takes in good faith and for value without notice should get good title."*[757]

By extending the scope of application of registration, the principle of publicity can be strengthened in the law of corporeal movables and claims.

757 *Bishopsgate Motor Finance Corporation v. Transport Brakes*, [1949] 1KB 322.

6 Implications for the Principle of Publicity under the 2020 Chinese Civil Code

In this chapter, the author, being a Chinese legal scholar, examines the system of publicity in Chinese law. This appears more desirable on account of the enactment of a new Chinese Civil Code in 2020. The examination focuses on four general aspects: publicity of corporeal movables, publicity of claims, publicity of trusts, and the construction of a system of registration for corporeal movables and claims. Before doing this, a brief introduction about the new Chinese Civil Code is given.

6.1 Introduction of the 2020 Chinese Civil Code

The Civil Code of the People's Republic of China was enacted on 27 May 2020. This is China's first civil code and will enter into force on 1 January 2021. Before this code, China had several individual acts to regulate private law disputes. Among these individual acts, the most important are the Law of Marriage (1980), the Law of Succession (1985), the General Principles of Civil Law (1986), the Contract Law (1999), the Property Law (2007), and the Law of Tort Liabilities (2010). These individual acts form the core of the system of civil law.

Historically, the Chinese legislature had initiated creating a civil code for the People's Republic of China four times, in 1954, 1962, 1979, and 2001. However, these four attempts all failed in the end. After the third attempt and failure in 1979, the legislature decided to give up pursuing a "wholesale" strategy and decided instead to pursue a "retail" strategy: adopting individual acts rather than a civil code. This change is a result of the lack of sufficient experience and knowledge about a market economy. In 1978, China initiated the "Reform and Opening" policy and attempted to replace its planned economy by a market economy. The timing, however, was not opportune for making a civil code appropriate for a market economy since China was unfamiliar with the concept of a market economy. After 1979, the legislature began to focus on establishing individual acts. Though another attempt to enact a civil code was made in 2001 after the Contract Law of 1999 was adopted, this attempt also failed because there were too many controversies and China was not fully prepared yet.

In 2015, the legislature decided to unify the individual acts into one civil code. The codification would occur in two steps: the first step would be drafting the general part of the code, and the second step would be drafting the specific parts. In 2017, the General Part of Chinese Civil Law was completed and came into force on 1 October of the same year. During the next three years, six specific parts were proposed, discussed, and revised. In December 2019, the General Part and the six specific parts were incorporated together in one draft, which was to be submitted to the National People's Congress that was scheduled to be held in March 2020. However, the Congress was postponed to May 2020 because of the outbreak of the coronavirus (COVID-19) epidemic. On 27 May 2020, the code was approved by the Congress.

The Chinese Civil Code (CCC) includes seven books with 1,260 provisions: General Part, Property, Contracts, Rights of Personality, Marriage and Family, Succession, and Tort Liabilities. The CCC is mainly based on the previous individual acts with some modifications and new rules. The General Part implies that the CCC follows a Pandectism approach and is influenced by the BGB. Book 2, Property, regulates ownership, property rights of use, property rights of security, and possession. Book 3, Contracts, is very important for the entire system of obligations. Section 1 of Book 3, General Rules of Contracts, applies to both contractual obligations and non-contractual obligations, thereby providing general rules of obligations. Section 3 of Book 3, Quasi-Contracts, regulates two types of non-contractual obligations: unjust enrichment and *negotiorum gestio*. Book 4, Rights of Personality, is completely new and is seen as a prominent feature of the CCC. It provides detailed and systematic rules on the protection of rights of personality in this era of the "explosion" of information and technology. Book 5 and Book 6 concern Marriage and Family and Succession respectively. Book 7 is Tort Liabilities. The main reason for providing for rules on tort in the last book of the CCC is that tort law performs a function of protecting property rights, personal rights, rights of personality, rights of status in families, and the right of succession. Tort is not only a cause of obligations, but also of liabilities. The entire CCC is designed on the basis of a "right-duty-liability" logic. Rights imply duties, and violating duties triggers liabilities.

As to Book 2, Property, the main modifications arise in two areas: one is the recognition of a new property right, the right of habitation, and the other refines the system of publicity for corporeal movables and claims. In the following discussion, I examine this system of publicity in the new Civil Code from the angle of our preceding research into the rationale of publicity in the law of corporeal movables and claims.

6.2 Publicity of Corporeal Movables and Claims in the 2020 Chinese Civil Code

6.2.1 Publicity of Corporeal Movables under the Chinese Civil Code

6.2.1.1 Description of the Status Quo

According to art. 11 CCC, the concept of things includes corporeal movables and corporeal immovables, but the object of property rights can be a right if the law prescribes so.[1] As we will see below, claims, as a type of right, can be an object of pledge. The Chinese law of things insists on the principle of publicity. For corporeal immovables, a comprehensive system of registration is introduced: the Immovables Register. In principle, registration is a requirement of acquisition of property rights on immovables (art. 209 (1) CCC).[2] Moreover, the Immovables Register is reliable, and the reliance of third parties on the register is protected by the CCC under a rule of *bona fide* acquisition (art. 311 CCC).[3] The following discussion focuses on publicity of corporeal movables.

Corporeal movables are divided into two types: special corporeal movables and ordinary corporeal movables. The former type includes vessels, aircraft, and motor vehicles. They are special because the disposal of them cannot be effective against third parties acting in good faith if registration is not completed (art. 225 CCC).[4] The register for these three kinds of special corporeal movables is managed by different public authorities: the Ministry of Transportation is responsible for the registration of vessels, the Ministry of Public Security for that of motor vehicles, and the General Administration of Civil Aviation for that of aircraft. The three registers perform not only an administrative function but also a private law function. Through these central and comprehensive registers, the property rights created on these special corporeal movables are made visible to third parties. In general, this is in line with our discussion in 5.3.2.1.E and 5.6.

---

1 《民法典》第115条："物包括不动产和动产。法律规定权利作为物权客体的，依照其规定。" English translation: Art. 115 CCC: "*Things include immovables and movables. If rights are an object of any property right in accordance with any laws, such laws shall apply.*"

2 《民法典》第209条第1款："不动产物权的设立、变更、转让和消灭，经依法登记，发生效力；未经登记，不发生效力，但是法律另有规定的除外。" English translation: Art. 209 (1) CCC: "*The creation, modification, transfer, or extinction of a property right on an immovable shall become valid after it is registered in accordance with the law; it does not take effect if registration is not completed, except as otherwise provided for by any law.*"

3 《民法典》第311条第1款："无处分权人将不动产或者动产转让给受让人的，所有权人有权追回；除法律另有规定外，符合下列情形的，受让人取得该不动产或者动产的所有权：（一）受让人受让该不动产或者动产时是善意；（二）以合理的价格转让；（三）转让的不动产或者动产依照法律规定应当登记的已经登记，不需要登记的已经交付给受让人。" English translation: Art. 311 (1) CCC: "*Where a person transfers an immovable or movable thing of which this person has no right to dispose, the owner has the right to recover this immovable or movable thing; except as otherwise provided for by any law, the transferee can obtain ownership of the immovable or movable thing when the following requirements are satisfied: (1) the transferee acts in good faith when acquiring the immovable or movable thing; (2) the transfer is made at a reasonable price; (3) the immovable or movable thing has been registered as stipulated by laws, or has been delivered to the transferee if registration is not required.*"

4 《民法典》第225条："船舶、航空器和机动车等的物权的设立、变更、转让和消灭，未经登记，不得对抗善意第三人。" English translation: Art. 225 CCC: "*The creation, change, transfer, or elimination of property rights on vessels, aircraft, motor vehicles and so forth may not challenge any bona fide third party, if it is not registered.*"

For ordinary corporeal movables, possession and delivery act as a means of publicity. According to art. 224 CCC, delivery is a prerequisite of the disposal of ordinary corporeal movables.[5] In art. 226-228 CCC, three forms of fictional delivery (*traditio ficta*) are recognized: *traditio brevi manu*, *traditio longa manu*, and *traditio per constitutum possessorium*. There is no doubt that these three forms of fictional delivery temper the formality of delivery and provide more space for the autonomy of parties. In art. 429, the CCC re-confirms the requirement of delivery for the disposal of corporeal movables: pledge of corporeal movables does not become effective until delivery.[6] The CCC is silent as to whether *traditio per constitutum possessorium* is an eligible form of delivery in the situation of pledge. The prevailing view provides a negative answer, and the Supreme Court holds that return of the collateral to the pledgor will make the right of pledge ineffective against third parties.[7]

In addition to this, possession and delivery are also involved in the situation of *bona fide* acquisition of ordinary corporeal movables (art. 311 CCC). Despite being doubted and debated, *bona fide* acquisition of corporeal movables is usually explained by resorting to the notion that possession is an external appearance of ownership of corporeal movables. For *bona fide* acquisition of corporeal movables, two amongst the requirements relate to possession: one is the transferor has possession of the object, and the other is that the object needs to be delivered to the third party. In the view of most lawyers, *traditio per constitutum possessorium* is a form of delivery that can satisfy the requirement of delivery in art. 311 CCC. This is also supported by the court in judicial practice.[8]

In order to avoid the inconvenience caused by the requirement of delivery in secured transactions concerning corporeal movables, the CCC recognizes a form of non-possessory security interest: hypothec (or charge) of corporeal movables. The collateral includes both existing and future equipment, raw materials, semi-manufactured products and products, and the security provider is limited to enterprises, individual businesses,

5 《民法典》第224条："动产物权的设立和转让，自交付时发生效力，但是法律另有规定的除外。" English translation: Art. 224 CCC: *"The creation or transfer of property rights in a movable thing shall become valid upon delivery, except as otherwise provided for by any law."*

6 《民法典》第429条："质权自出质人交付质押财产时设立。" English translation: Art. 429 CCC: *"Pledge is created upon delivery of the collateral by the pledgor."*

7 《最高人民法院关于适用〈中华人民共和国担保法〉若干问题的解释》第87条第1款："出质人代质权人占有质物的，质押合同不生效；质权人将质物返还于出质人后，以其质权对抗第三人的，人民法院不予支持。" English translation: Art. 87 (1) Judicial Interpretation by the Supreme People's Court on Some Issues Regarding the Application of Security Law of the People's Republic of China: *"Pledge will not be valid if the pledgor possesses the collateral pledged on behalf of the pledgee; the court will not support the pledgee against a third party if the pledgee returns the collateral pledged to the pledgor."*

8 See art. 18 Judicial Interpretation by the Supreme People's Court on the Application of Property Law of the People's Republic of China (I).

and agricultural producers (art. 396 CCC).[9] As both existing and future corporeal movables can be charged, the distinction between fixed charge and floating charge, which was accepted by the Property Law (2007), is not included in the CCC. Both types of charge are regulated by the same rules in the CCC. For a person falling outside the three types of parties, the right of charge also needs to be registered to be effective against third parties.[10] As will be seen in 6.2.4, however, the register is different from the register for the charge created according to art. 396 CCC.

The right of hypothec comes into existence upon the contract taking effect. For the purpose of publicity, the hypothec of corporeal movables needs to be registered to be effective against third parties acting in good faith (art. 403 CCC). Therefore, the registration has declaratory effect.

> 《民法典》第403条："以动产抵押的，抵押权自抵押合同生效时设立；未经登记，不得对抗善意第三人。"[11]

If a corporeal movable is charged to more than one creditor, the priority of the charges is determined according to the date of registration (art. 414 (1) CCC).[12] In art. 414 (1) CCC, a "pure race" rule is established, and good faith is not relevant. This rule is not compatible with art. 403 CCC, a provision that stipulates that registration is to make the right of charge effective against "*bona fide* third parties". Thus, how to reconcile these two provisions through interpretation is problematic. An acceptable solution is that art. 414

---

9 《民法典》第396条："企业、个体工商户、农业生产经营者可以将现有的以及将有的生产设备、原材料、半成品、产品抵押，债务人不履行到期债务或者发生当事人约定的实现抵押权的情形，债权人有权就抵押财产确定时的动产优先受偿。" English translation: Art. 396 CCC: *"Enterprises, individual businesses, and agricultural producers may charge its existing and anticipated production equipment, raw materials, semi-finished products, and products, and if the debtor fails to pay the due debt or falls under any circumstance where charge shall be exercised as agreed upon by the parties, the creditor shall have the priority of compensation made with the movable determined as the charged property."*

10 《中华人民共和国担保法》第43条第2款："当事人未办理抵押物登记的，不得对抗第三人。当事人办理抵押物登记的，登记部门为抵押人所在地的公证部门。" English translation: Art. 43 (2) Security Law of the People's Republic of China: *"The parties who fail to complete registration cannot enforce the right against third parties. Where the parties intend to conduct registration, the registry is the notary organ located in the place of the security provider."*

11 English translation: Art. 403 CCC: *"Where a corporeal movable is charged, the charge is established at the time when the contract of charge becomes valid; if the charge is not registered, it shall not be effective against a bona fide third party."*

12 《民法典》第414条第1款："同一财产向两个以上债权人抵押的，拍卖、变卖抵押财产所得的价款依照下列规定清偿：（一）抵押权已经登记的，按照登记的时间先后确定清偿顺序；（二）抵押权已经登记的先于未登记的受偿；（三）抵押权未登记的，按照债权比例清偿。" English translation: Art. 414 (1) CCC: *"Where the same property is charged to two or more creditors, the proceeds from the auction or sale of the charged property shall be used for payment according to the following provisions: (1) if all the charges are registered, the priority of payment is determined by the date of registration; (2) the registered charge prevails over the unregistered charge; (3) if all the charges are not registered, the payment is made in proportion to the amount of the secured claims."*

(1) CCC is a special rule (*lex specialis*) of art. 403 CCC: the latter provision only applies where a conflict arises between the chargee and parties who are not a chargee.

For the usual operation of the debtor's business, an important restriction is imposed on the legal effect of registration: the registered charge cannot bind the buyer who has paid a reasonable price and acquired the collateral in the ordinary course of business (art. 404 CCC).[13] Notably, the rule of the "ordinary course of business" applies to both floating charge and fixed charge. As mentioned above, floating charge and fixed charge are no longer treated differently in the CCC.

In general, the rules introduced above come from the Property Law (2007), and the legislature just incorporates them in the CCC. In addition to these rules, the CCC also establishes some new provisions concerning the purchase money charge, reservation of ownership, financial lease, and factoring. These new provisions extend the scope of registration.

Inspired by the purchase money security interest (PMSI) in Article 9 UCC, the CCC introduces in art. 416 CCC a charge with super-priority: the purchase money charge (PMC).[14] The PMC is created on the goods supplied to secure the payment of the purchase price by the debtor. This form of charge is recognized to guarantee that subsequent suppliers of goods will not be affected by floating charge created earlier on both existing and future assets. Art. 416 CCC prescribes a grace period of ten days for the supplier to register the charge and allows the charge registered duly to have super-priority in relation to other security interests. The PMC performs a function similar to another form of security device: reservation of ownership. Both security devices can be used to secure the payment of the purchase price by the supplier. However, they are treated with a difference in terms of registration, which will be shown in the following paragraph.

In addition to charge, reservation of ownership is also subject to registration. According to art. 641 CCC, reservation of ownership needs to be registered for legal effectiveness against third parties acting in good faith.[15] In the viewpoint of the drafters, reservation of ownership is a security device that should be governed by the same rules of publicity and priori-

---

13 《民法典》第404条："以动产抵押的，不得对抗正常经营活动中已经支付合理价款并取得抵押财产的买受人。" English translation: Art. 404 CCC: "*Where a corporeal movable is charged, it shall not be effective against the buyer who has paid a reasonable price and obtained the property charged in the ordinary course of business.*"

14 《民法典》第416条："动产抵押担保的主债权是抵押物的价款，标的物交付后十日内办理抵押登记的，该抵押权人优先于抵押物买受人的其他担保物权人受偿，但是留置权人除外。" English translation: Art. 416 CCC: "*Where corporeal movables are charged to secure the payment of the price of these collaterals, the charge holder can obtain performance in priority than other secured creditors, except the lien holder, provided that the charge is registered within ten days after delivery of the corporeal movables.*"

15 《民法典》第641条第2款："出卖人对标的物保留的所有权，未经登记，不得对抗善意第三人。" English translation: Art. 641(2) CCC: "*Where the seller reserves ownership of the object, the ownership reserved is not effective against bona fide third parties in the absence of registration.*"

ties as the charge of corporeal movables. This is why art. 388 CCC provides that the contract of security includes charge contracts, pledge contracts, and "other contracts having a function of security". Moreover, the rules concerning priorities of charge are also applicable to determining the priorities of "other registerable proprietary interests of security" (art. 414 (2) CCC). In doing so, reservation of ownership and charge do not differ in the aspect of publicity: both require registration. However, different from the purchase money charge, no grace period of registration is permitted for the supplier who reserves ownership of the subject matter.

The requirement of registration of reservation of ownership indicates that the legislature intends to address the problem of invisible security interests in the field of corporeal movables. This intention is also manifested by art. 745 CCC, a provision applicable to financial lease. According to this provision, ownership enjoyed by the financial lessor cannot be effective against third parties acting in good faith if it is not registered.[16] Moreover, the contract of financial lease is one of the "other contracts having a function of security" in art. 388 CCC and one of the "other registerable proprietary interests of security" in art. 414 (2) CCC. Thus, it is subject to the rules concerning priorities of the right of charge.

6.2.1.2 A Brief Comment

In general, the CCC takes a big step forward on the way to eliminating invisible security interests. The scope of registration is extended from hypothec (charge) to the purchase money charge, reservation of ownership, and financial lease. There is no doubt that this extension will alleviate the problem of information asymmetry significantly in a secured transaction concerning corporeal movables.

However, the CCC overlooks another two types of transactions: true lease (or operational lease) and possessory pledge. As has been argued above (see 5.3.2.3.B and 5.4.3.1), true lease and financial lease do not differ in terms of legal structure, and both give rise to a divergence between ownership and possession. Therefore, there is no reason to treat financial lease and true lease differently in the aspect of publicity. In fact, lease may perform a function of security in the form of sale and lease-back, but registration of this form of security lease is neglected by the CCC. It is not persuasive to require registration of financial lease but allow other types of lease to remain invisible. It is conceivable that differentiating between financial lease and other types of lease will be particularly problematic in the application of art. 745 CCC.

---

16 《民法典》第745条："出租人对租赁物享有的所有权，未经登记，不得对抗善意第三人。"
English translation: Art. 745 CCC: "*In the absence of registration, the lessor's ownership with respect to the object cannot be enforced against third parties acting in good faith.*"

In 5.4.3.2, it is argued that possessory pledge is not visible to third parties and should be included in the register for corporeal movables and claims. Possession acquired by the pledgee does not make the right of pledge visible. The recognition of possessory pledge causes "*systemic costs*".[17] The CCC follows the traditional path and continues accepting possessory pledge. Because of the possibility of a conflict between possessory pledge and registerable charge, art. 415 CCC stipulates that the ranking is determined by the date of delivery and that of registration.[18] A consequence of this provision is that potential third parties have to investigate both the possessory state of the corporeal movable and the register. It violates the principle that one property should have one method of publicity (see 2.2.3.2).

In the end, the CCC recognizes the purchase money charge (PMC), a security interest able to prevail over other property rights of security when registered within ten days after the time of delivery. This form of charge performs a function similar to reservation of ownership, but they differ as to the grace period. The PMC has a grace period of ten days, while reservation of ownership has no grace period. This different treatment is not correct. In comparative law, it is a common practice to grant a grace period of registration to reservation of title (see 5.3.2.3.B). The PMC is recognized to avoid the supplier's goods to be captured by floating charge created earlier for the benefit of the supplier-creditor or the loan-creditor who provides credit or finance for the purchase. According to art. 414 (1) CCC, the date of registration determines the priority of the right of charge. The recognition of the super-priority for the PMC allows the supplier-creditor or the loan-creditor to be not affected by the floating charge registered earlier.

6.2.2 Publicity of Claims under the Chinese Civil Code

6.2.2.1 *Description of the* Status Quo

Under the CCC, claims can be assigned without notifying the debtor involved. In this aspect, the CCC and the old law do not differ. According to art. 546 CCC, the formality of notification is only related to the issue of performance: the assignment cannot be invoked against the debtor who is not notified.[19] Thus, notification is irrelevant to the assignment *per se*.

---

17 Phillips 1979 (1), p. 43.

18 《民法典》第415条："同一财产既设立抵押权又设立质权的，拍卖、变卖该财产所得的价款按照登记、交付的时间先后确定清偿顺序。" English translation: Art. 415 CCC: "*Where the same property is subject to pledge and charge, the proceeds out of auction or sale of the property shall be distributed according to the ranking determined by the time of registration and delivery.*"

19 《民法典》第546条："债权人转让债权，未通知债务人的，该转让对债务人不发生效力。" English translation: Art. 546 CCC: "*If the creditor who assigns the claim does not notify the debtor, the assignment has no binding force on the debtor.*"

However, the CCC follows the Property Law (2007) by providing a different rule for the pledge of receivables, i.e. the pledge of monetary claims. In art. 445 (1) CCC, pledge of receivables cannot take effect until the pledge is registered and visible to third parties.[20] Two things should be noted. One is that notification to debtors is irrelevant to the pledge of receivables. The other is that registration is constitutive for the pledge of receivables, and only an agreement of pledge does not suffice. Thus, the legal effect of registration here is different from the legal effect of registration of charge, financial lease, and reservation of ownership of corporeal movables. In the latter situations, registration only has declaratory effect.

In addition, registration plays an important role in a type of transaction concerning receivables: factoring. In the CCC, factoring is regulated as a specific contract in Chapter 16 of Section 2 (Specific Contracts) of Book 3 (Contracts). Factoring arises in the situation where the creditor assigns existing and/or future receivables to the factor, who in turn supplies services including provision of finance, management and collection of receivables, or provision of security for the payment by the debtor (art. 761 CCC). Factoring is necessarily connected with the assignment of claims, regardless of whether the factor has a right of recourse against the assignor (art. 766 and art. 767 CCC). The CCC establishes a completely new provision for competing factorings. If a receivable is under multiple factorings, the priority between competing factors is determined first according to registration, and, in the absence of registration, notification to the debtor involved (art. 768 CCC).

> 《民法典》第768条："应收账款债权人就同一应收账款订立多个保理合同，致使多个保理人主张权利的，已经登记的先于未登记的取得应收账款；均已经登记的，按照登记时间的先后顺序取得应收账款；均未登记的，由最先到达应收账款债务人的转让通知中载明的保理人取得应收账款；既未登记也未通知的，按照保理融资款或者服务报酬的比例取得应收账款。"[21]

As a result, neither registration nor notification is relevant to the assignment of claims *per se*, but both formalities are relevant to the ranking of conflicting factorings. Art. 768 CCC is a rule to only regulate a conflict between factorings. In the situation where there is a conflict between a factoring assignment and an ordinary assignment of the same receivable, art. 768 is

---

20 《民法典》第445条第1款："以应收账款出质的，质权自办理出质登记时设立。" English translation: Art. 445 (1) CCC: "*Where receivables are pledged, the pledge takes effect upon the registration.*"

21 English translation: Art. 768 CCC: "*Where more than one factoring contract is made with respect to a receivable, and the factors all claim their right, the factor who completes registration obtains the receivable in priority to the factor who does no registration; if all the factorings are registered, the factor who completes registration earlier obtains the receivable; if all the factorings are not registered, the factor who is mentioned in the earlier notification given to the debtor of the receivable obtains the receivable; all factorings neither have registration nor notification, the factors obtain the receivable in proportion to the finance provided or the reward for the service.*"

not applicable. As a result, which assignment prevails depends on which one arises earlier.

For claims embodied within securities, registration does not apply. For example, where bills of exchange, promissory notes, checks, debentures, certificates of deposit, warehouse receipts, or bills of lading are pledged, the right of pledge comes into existence on the date of delivery of the document (art. 441 CCC). As to the pledge of bills of exchange, promissory notes, and checks, a conflict exists between art. 441 CCC and art. 35 Negotiable Instruments Law of the People's Republic of China. According to the latter provision, pledge of bills of exchange needs endorsement with a mark of "pledge" on the document. The conflict has existed since the Property Law (2007) entered into force, and the CCC does not resolve this conflict. From the perspective of publicity, it is apparent that a mark of "pledge" conveys more precise information than simple delivery of the document (see 4.2.3.5).

In addition to the pledge of securities, the claim embodied can also be transferred on the basis of the document according to relevant laws. For example, bills of exchange, which have to be made to order under Chinese law, are transferred in the way of endorsement.[22] Moreover, the way of endorsement is also applicable to the transfer of promissory notes and checks.[23] The right of recovery embodied within warehouse receipts can be transferred through endorsement plus the warehouseman's signature or seal (art. 910 CCC).[24] Bills of lading are able to be transferred in the way of endorsement or delivery of the bill, depending on whether the bill is made to order or bearer (art. 79 Maritime Law of the People's Republic of China).

6.2.2.2 A Brief Comment

The preceding introduction shows that notification is not treated as a means of publicity for the disposal of claims under the CCC. Registration is applied to the pledge of receivables and the assignment of receivables in the situation of factoring. In general, this is in line with our argument that notification to the debtor does not qualify as a means of publicity (see 4.1.1.2). However, the current system of publicity for claims still needs to be refined.

In practice, receivables may be assigned in many other situations than factoring. For example, securitization often involves the assignment of a bulk of receivables. As has been argued above (see 5.3.2.1.D), it is desirable to include both pledge and the assignment of receivables in the register, except for in such special situations as novation, merger or division, and

22 See art. 27 Negotiable Instruments Law of the People's Republic of China.

23 See art. 80 and art. 93 Negotiable Instruments Law of the People's Republic of China.

24 In general, there is no reason to require the warehouseman's signature or seal. Transfer of the receipt and the claim embodied has nothing to do with the warehouseman. In practice, the warehouseman only bears a liability to return the goods to the holder of the receipt.

bank accounts. Only requiring factoring of receivables to be registered does not suffice: the factor (assignee) cannot ascertain easily whether the receivable involved belongs to the assignor. It is possible that the receivable might be assigned in a way other than factoring. Art. 768 CCC is a rule applicable only to conflicting factorings. Moreover, art. 768 CCC recognizes the formality of notification as relevant in determining the ranking of competing factorings in the situation where none of them is registered. This is groundless from the perspective of publicity, since notification does not qualify as a means of publicity. It can be seen from art. 768 CCC that the legislature does not deny the publicity effect of notification completely.

The legal effect of registration for pledge receivables should be modified. Under the CCC, registration yields a constitutive effect, and the absence of registration makes the pledge of receivables invalid. This is not compatible with the rule that registration only has declaratory effect in the situation of secured transactions concerning corporeal movables. Moreover, the constitutive effect is not in line with the fact that registration does not affect the factoring assignment *per se* and is only relevant in resolving the conflict between competing factorings. As argued above (see 5.3.3.1), registration should be granted with declaratory effect.

6.2.3 Publicity of Trust on Corporeal Movables and Claims

6.2.3.1 Description of the Status Quo

Trust as a legal concept was introduced in China by the Trust Law of the People's Republic of China (Chinese Trust Law) in 2001. According to art. 10 Chinese Trust Law, registration is a condition for creating a trust on "registerable property", namely property that needs to be registered according to laws and administrative ordinances.[25] Lack of registration will render the trust invalid. However, no trust of registerable property has been registered after the Chinese Trust Law entered into force. This is because there is not any law or administrative ordinance indicating how to register a trust, and it is unclear which public organ is responsible for registration.[26] Consequently, art. 10 Chinese Trust Law is useless and has never been applied in practice to date. Moreover, coordinating the registration of trust under trust law and the registration of property rights under property law is always problematic.

25 《信托法》第10条："设立信托，对于信托财产，有关法律、行政法规规定应当办理登记手续的，应当依法办理信托登记。未依照前款规定办理信托登记的，应当补办登记手续；不补办的，该信托不产生效力。" English translation: Art. 10 Chinese Trust Law: "*Where trust property shall be registered according to laws or administrative ordinances for the establishment of a trust, such property shall be registered. If the trust fails to be registered as required in the previous paragraph, it shall be made later; the trust shall be invalid if no trust registration is made.*"

26 Ji 2019, p. 110.

It is often held that a trust of immovable property should be registered in the Immovables Register.[27] However, the Regulation on the Registration of Immovable Property (2014) is silent about registration of trust of immovable property. Likewise, trust of special corporeal movables (vessels, aircraft, and motor vehicles) cannot be entered in the corresponding register because registrars cannot find any provision requiring them to record trusts. Corporeal movables and claims are not treated as "registerable property" under art. 10 Chinese Trust Law. As a result, a trust of corporeal movables and claims does not need to be registered.

The first step has been taken in the field of registration of investment trusts. An investment trust arises in the following situation: individual investors (settlor and beneficiary) entrust their money to the trust company (trustee) which will then invest the money entrusted in the projects designated in advance, and the benefits out of the investment will be distributed to the investors. An investment trust is often called a "trust product" because it resembles a "product" for investors to buy. In 2016, the China Trust Registration Co. Ltd was established for managing the registration of investment trusts. It should be noted that this registration only covers the "trust product" and the beneficiary's rights.[28] It is a register of "trust products", instead of a property register. From the "trust products" register, it is impossible to know whether a thing is under trust.[29] Therefore, the problem of information associated with trust is not addressed by the "trust products" register.

The CCC does not address the issue of how to publicize the legal relationship of trusts to third parties. The Chinese Trust Law (2001) simply requires registration as a condition of creating a trust of registerable property in art. 10. However, this provision is never applied in practice, and it remains problematic as to how to coordinate the registration of trusts and publicity of property rights.

6.2.3.2 A Brief Comment

On the basis of our research in 5.5, it is proposed that trust of corporeal movables and claims should be included in the register for corporeal movables and claims. Where immovable property is subject to a trust, this trust should be recorded in the Immovables Register. Correspondingly, trust of intellectual property should be registered in the register of patents, trade-

27 Ji 2019, p. 112; Meng 2012, p. 123-125.

28 《登记管理办法》第9条：“信托登记信息包括信托产品名称、信托类别、信托目的、信托期限、信托当事人、信托财产、信托利益分配等信托产品及其受益权信息和变动情况。” English translation: Art. 9 Regulation on Registration: *"The information registered include the name of the trust product, the type of the trust, the purpose of the trust, the term of the trust, the parties of the trust, the property entrusted, the distribution of benefits, the information concerning the beneficiary's right and the change thereof."*

29 Ji 2019, p. 111.

marks, and so on. It is time for the government to implement art. 10 Chinese Trust law and to coordinate the registration of trusts and the registration of property rights.

In accordance with art. 10 Chinese Trust Law, registration is a constitutive element for creating a trust. The absence of registration will preclude the trust from coming into existence. However, according to our discussion in 5.3.3.1, declaratory effect is more in line with the rationale of publicity, and registration should only be relevant to the legal effect against *bona fide* third parties. Thus, it is desirable to modify art. 10 by recognizing that registration only makes the legal relationship of trusts effective against third parties acting in good faith.

6.2.4 Construction of a Modern System of Registration for Corporeal Movables and Claims

The CCC not only aims to extend the scope of registration in the field of corporeal movables and claims, but also attempts to reform the old system of registration for secured transactions. On the basis of our discussion in 5.3, several proposals are raised for the future Chinese register for corporeal movables and claims.

6.2.4.1 A Uniform and Comprehensive System

Under the Property Law (2007), three registers are created for the publicity of charge of corporeal movables and the publicity of pledge of receivables. The first register is managed by the State Administration for Market Regulation, which is a part of the State Council. This register is applicable to the charge of corporeal movables provided by *"enterprises, individual businesses, and agricultural producers"*. The second register is managed by notary organs for the charge of corporeal movables provided by the other types of parties. For example, if a consumer intends to charge his or her household appliances or jewels to a creditor, the right of charge can be registered at a notary office located where the consumer resides. The third register is administered by the Credit Reference Center, an organ established by the People's Bank of China. In reality, however, the register administered by the Credit Reference Center covers not only the pledge of receivables, but also financial lease, reservation of ownership, the assignment of receivables, trust of corporeal movables, and hire-purchase of corporeal movables. Among these types of transactions, only the registration of the pledge of receivables has a legal basis under the Property Law (2007).

Apparently, the current triple systems cause inconvenience for individuals trying to conduct registration and to obtain the proprietary information they need. For example, if an enterprise intends to pledge receivables and charge inventories, then two registrations have to be conducted: one relates to the register managed by the State Administration for Market Regulation, and the other relates to the system administered by the Credit Reference Center. If a third party wants to know about the security right on the corporeal movables and receivables, that party needs to search the two registers. In 5.3.2.1, a comprehensive system of registration is proposed for corporeal movables and claims. For the sake of efficiency, the three registers should be unified as one system.

Drafters of the CCC are aware of the problem triggered by the triple systems and are determined to construct one comprehensive system. Unlike the Property Law (2007), the CCC intentionally does not stipulate the registry of corporeal movables and that of receivables. This leaves room for the State Council to construct a unified and comprehensive register in the future. It is more likely that the comprehensive system will be managed by the Credit Reference Center, because the current register administered by the Credit Reference Center is already available to various types of secured transactions concerning corporeal movables and receivables.

6.2.4.2 A Self-Service and Digital System

At present, the registration of the charge of corporeal movables provided by enterprises is governed by the Ordinance of Registration of Charge on Corporeal Movables, when the security is provided by *"enterprises, individual businesses, and agricultural producers"*. This ordinance was promulgated in 2007 and revised in 2016 by the State Administration for Market Regulation. Despite the latest modification, the system is still paper-based in some places, which is different from the digital register for the pledge of receivables administered by the Credit Reference Center.[30] Moreover, the system for the charge of corporeal movables is not nation-wide. Individuals have to submit the documents required to the local Administration for Market Regulation located in the county where the security provider resides.[31] Where the security provider is another party than the *"enterprises, individual businesses, and agricultural producers"*, the right of charge needs to be entered in the register managed by notary organs. In general, this register is paper-based and decentralized.

Undoubtedly, it is desirable to replace the current paper-based and dispersive registers by a digital and nationally central system (see 5.3.1.2). Moreover, this digital and nation-wide system should also be a self-service system (see 5.3.1.3). It would allow parties to file the documents required and update the registration without having to go to the registry. Individuals would be entitled to search the system themselves without involving any registrar. In general, a self-service, fully-open, central and digital system can guarantee that the operation of the system will be fast and efficient, so that the smoothness of secured transactions will not be hampered.

30 Gao 2019, p. 204.
31 See art. 2 Ordinance of Registration of Charge on Corporeal Movables.

6.2.4.3 *A Notice-Filing System*

For the sake of efficiency and to avert the problem of information overload, it is necessary to restrict the information that should be filed. Under art. 5 Ordinance of Registration of Charge on Corporeal Movables, the current register for the charge of corporeal movables is, in essence, a transaction-filing system.[32] The statement required to be filed has to show details of the legal relationship of charge, which affects smooth registration. For example, the statement needs to indicate the quality, location, and even ownership and the right of use of the collateral. This information is useless since the ownership of the collateral might pass to another person, the location of the collateral might change after the charge is granted, and the quality of the collateral has nothing to do with the secured transaction.[33]

In this research, it is proposed that a notice-filing system should be constructed for corporeal movables and claims (see 5.3.1.4). The current register for the charge of corporeal movables should be transformed to be a notice-filing system to alleviate the impeding effect over the smooth operation of secured transactions. The notice filed only conveys a "warning" and "minimum information" to third parties. If searchers want to know more about the secured transaction, they can further inquire with the relevant parties who have a duty to disclose. A notice-filing system is necessarily associated with a duty of disclosure. Under this duty, searchers are able to obtain the detailed information they need.

6.3 Conclusion

Under the Property Law (2007), only the charge of corporeal movables and the pledge of receivables are included in a register. Other types of secured transactions are not visible. The CCC attempts to eliminate invisible secured transactions. It extends the scope of registration to the purchase money

32 《动产抵押登记办法》第5条："《动产抵押登记书》应当载明下列内容：(一)抵押人、抵押权人名称(姓名)、住所地等；(二) 抵押财产的名称、数量、质量、状况、所在地、所有权归属或者使用权归属；(三)被担保债权的种类和数额；(四)抵押担保的范围；(五)债务人履行债务的期限；(六)抵押合同双方指定代表或者共同委托代理人的姓名、联系方式等；(七)抵押人、抵押权人签字或者盖章；(八)抵押人、抵押权人认为其他应当登记的抵押权信息。" English translation: Art. 5 Ordinance of Registration of Charge on Corporeal Movables: "*The Statement of Registration of Charge on Corporeal Movables shall record the following information: (1) the names and domiciles of the chargor and the chargee; (2) the name, quantity, quality, status, location, ownership, and the right of use of the property charged; (3) the type and amount of the secured claim; (4) the scope of the charge; (5) the term of performance by the debtor; (6) the name and the way of contact of the representative designated or the agent entrusted jointly by both parties to the contract of charge; (7) the signatures or seals of the chargor and the chargee; and (8) other information concerning the right of charge deemed by the chargor and the chargee as necessary to be registered.*"

33 Gao 2019, p. 216-217.

charge, financial lease, reservation of ownership, and factoring. Nevertheless, some secured transactions and non-security rights remain outside the register, such as true lease, sale and lease-back, the assignment of receivables in other situations than factoring, and possessory pledge. Moreover, the CCC fails to afford attention to the problem of publicity of trusts of corporeal movables and claims, though trusts may perform a function of security in some situations.

In addition to extending the scope of registration, the CCC also aims to unify the current systems of registration for corporeal movables and claims. Under the Property Law (2007), three separate registers are involved in secured transactions, and some of the registers are a paper-based, decentralized, and transaction-filing system. Unification is desirable, but far from being sufficient. The future unified system should also be a self-service, digital, fully-open, and notice-filing system. Under this system, registration and search can be conducted without having to involve any registrar, minimal information is provided directly, and detailed information can be obtained by through further inquiries.

Summary

In general, this research focuses on the principle of publicity in the law of corporeal movables and claims. It deals with two central issues. One issue is whether and to what extent the principle of publicity is still tenable in the field of corporeal movables and claims. The other issue is whether and how registration should be introduced in the law of corporeal movables and claims to strengthen the principle of publicity. Possession is treated commonly as a means of publicity for corporeal movables, and notification acts as a means of publicity for claims in some jurisdictions. In some special fields, such as goods warehoused and transported, securities perform a function of publicity. Chapter Three and Chapter Four address the following question: whether and in what sense these methods of publicity just mentioned can make property rights visible to third parties. Chapter Five focuses on the issue of whether and how registration should be introduced for corporeal movables and claims. Chapter Six reveals some implications of the preceding studies for Chinese law.

This research begins with an introduction to the concept of property rights. In Chapter 2, property rights are argued as a legal relationship between persons instead of a relationship between persons and things. After a comparison with the other types of rights, especially personal rights, we conclude that property rights have two basic distinctive features: "thinghood" and absoluteness. The first feature denotes that property rights have to exist with respect to a specific thing, whether tangible or intangible. The second feature means that property rights can be enforced against general third parties. Property rights impose a duty of abstention over others than the proprietor and have the effect of preference and the effect of following (*droit de suite*). However, the boundary between property rights and personal rights is not completely crystal. As a result, there are a number of intermediary rights that exist in between property rights and personal rights.

Third parties are a general and ambiguous concept in the law of property. In general, this concept includes three types of third parties: strange interferers, subsequent acquirers, and general creditors. A property right is effective against these three types of third parties. However, it should be noted that some personal rights also have binding force on one or two of these types of third parties. In general, the three types have different interests and demands for information in relation to property rights. Strange interferers only want to know the boundaries between the scope their freedom to act and the property right of others. The details of a property right are often useless for this type of third party. Different from strange interferers, subsequent acquirers have a desire to know about the details of property rights existing on the object because of the *prior tempore* rule. According to this rule, property rights coming into existence earlier will have a higher ranking. General creditors are those parties who are subject to the *paritas creditorum* rule in the event of the debtor's bankruptcy. They have no proprietary rights of security and cannot realize their claim with respect to specific collateral in priority. In general, unsecured creditors are concerned about the overall financial health of the debtor. The main reason why an unsecured creditor does not request proprietary security is that he or she believes that the debtor is able to perform the obligation.

Since property rights are effective against third parties, a problem arises for third parties about how to know about the property right. This problem is known as information asymmetry. To address the problem of information asymmetry, there should be a channel through which third parties are able to collect proprietary information, the information concerning the legal relationship of property rights. In property law, publicity is a way in which proprietary information is communicated. The existence of property rights will give rise to information asymmetry to third parties, thus they should be subject to the requirement of publicity. In practice, there are also other ways in which proprietary information can be obtained by third parties. Compared with these other ways, publicity has special qualities: it is objective, singular and statutory.

CHAPTER 3 discusses the publicity of possession. In that Chapter, we observe that possession is a legal concept designed by the legislature to serve certain purposes. Publicity is not a purpose taken into consideration in the process of defining this concept. In general, it is acquisitive prescription and the protection of factual control that determine the question of how to define the concept of possession in contemporary law. In fact, these two are also important for understanding the concept of *possessio* in Roman law. Without noting the two aspects, it is difficult to comprehend the following fact: one is that a person who has physical control might have no possession, while a person who has no physical control might be treated as a possessor in law.

In general, possession performs a function of publicity through the physical proximity between the possessor and the object possessed. In understanding this function, two aspects should be noted. One aspect is that possession is in practice associated with a great diversity of rights. Thus, possession is an abstract and ambiguous means of publicity. It neither is an outward appearance of ownership, nor does it have any effect of publicity. The other aspect is that indirect possession is invisible and cannot act as a method of publicity to convey proprietary information to third parties. The concept of indirect possession is accepted for other purposes, in particular broadening the scope of possessory protection. Therefore, only direct possession is an ambiguous means of publicity capable of informing third parties that the possessor has a certain right with respect to the thing possessed.

As an abstract and ambiguous method of publicity, possession is a navigating system for strange interferers. Thanks to possession, individuals can easily live with others without interfering with others' property rights in this world crowded with things. In daily life, people can respond to possession quickly and instinctively, which lays a foundation for the order of possession. People should respect the state of possession because the possessor has shown his or her right through possession to the outside world. In this sense, possession has a function to visibly draw the boundaries around the sphere of the freedom to act. Therefore, the abstract indication conveyed by possession can satisfy the demand for information by strange interferers to avoid conducting illegal interference.

However, (direct) possession is not a sufficient method of publicity for subsequent acquirers. As a type of third parties, the subsequent acquirer has a demand for detailed information regarding the property rights of a specific object. For example, a potential buyer has to ascertain whether the seller has ownership and whether the object is encumbered with any limited property rights. Possession cannot satisfy this demand. Under contemporary law, corporeal movables can be disposed of independently from direct possession even under a *traditio* system because of the recognition of invisible delivery, such as *traditio per constitutum possessorium.* An outcome of recognizing invisible delivery is that the right of ownership and of direct possession operate in separate ways. On the other hand, possession remains to be a trigger for *bona fide* acquisition of corporeal movables under contemporary law. However, this should not be treated as a sufficient basis to say that possession is an outward appearance of ownership. In general, the rule of *bona fide* acquisition is mainly a result of legal policy, especially the policy of facilitating the security of transactions. The rule cannot be explained fully from the perspective of the publicity effect of possession. Possession is ambiguous and thus cannot be a reliable outward appearance. In sum, property rights of corporeal movables are generally hidden to third parties, and conflicts are ubiquitous in practice. The rule of *bona fide* acquisition is at most an *ex-post* approach to resolve conflicts after they have arisen.

In general, possession as a means of publicity is not adequate for general creditors either. General creditors are concerned mainly about the overall financial health of the debtor. The quantity of unencumbered assets is only a minor factor for evaluating the debtor's overall financial health. Even in this aspect, possession is incapable of conveying any useful indication about the quantity of unencumbered assets to unsecured creditors. This is because a corporeal movable possessed by the bankrupt debtor might belong to another person, while corporeal movables not possessed by the debtor might fall within the insolvency assets. In practice, potential creditors will not pay attention to the state of possession of corporeal movables by the debtor. Possession is not a reliable indicator of either the bankruptcy assets or of overall financial health. Thus, there is no sufficient reason to say that a divergence between ownership and possession will cause a problem of false wealth or ostensible ownership to unsecured creditors.

In CHAPTER 4, attention shifts to the problem of publicity of claims. This chapter starts with pointing out the double characteristic of claims. First of all, claims are an internal relationship between the creditor and the debtor under the principle of relativity, and the existence of a claim does not cause a problem of information asymmetry to third parties. As a result, the principle of publicity does not exist in the law of obligations. On the other hand, claims have a proprietary characteristic if they are treated as a type of wealth and included in transactions. Like the disposal of corporeal movables, the disposal of claims also has a problem of information asymmetry. For example, a claim might be assigned twice, which will give rise to a conflict of double assignments: which of the two assignees should win in this conflict? Therefore, there is also a demand of publicity in the area of transactions concerning claims.

For ordinary claims, claims not embodied within a document, notification to the debtor is often treated as a method of publicity. By notifying the debtor of the claim involved, third parties are able to know about the disposal of the claim by inquiring with the debtor. However, this research argues that notification is too defective to be a means of publicity for claims. The first reason is that notification does not make the disposal of claims visible to third parties. Even if the debtor receives a notification of the disposal, there is no sufficient reason to believe that he or she will provide correct and full information to third parties. The debtor has no obligation of disclosure in law. Moreover, the debtor might conspire with the assignor or the pledgor to mislead third parties. Even if the debtor is willing to cooperate, he or she might forget the notification or fail to disclose the disposal to third parties correctly. More importantly, as a principle, *bona fide* acquisition of claims is not recognized when the third party has reliance on the debtor's disclosure. Also for some practical reasons, notification is not a suitable method of publicity for claims. For example, notification is too costly in the situation of the assignment of a bulk of claims, on account of the difficulty in notifying each debtor involved. In addition, the formality of notification excludes the possibility of disposing of future claims, which forms an obstacle to the modern transaction of receivables. In fact, notification only relates to the issue of performance: the debtor is entitled to perform to the original creditor before being informed of the disposal.

The lack of a publicity function of notification is in line with current legal practice in most jurisdictions. In principle, notification is either irrelevant or treated as a formality that can be averted by another formality in the situation of the disposal of claims. For example, German law does not require notification for valid assignment of claims. Though notification is necessary for pledging claims, it can be easily averted by choosing the device of security assignment. In Dutch law, the disposal of claims can be realized in the way of, in addition to notification, notarization or private registration. Moreover, where a conflict arises between two disposals of the same claim, it is the *nemo dat* rule that will be applied. In sum, claims remain generally invisible as a type of property, and the transaction of claims has a problem of information asymmetry that cannot be addressed by notification.

In the aspect of publicity, documental claims, a kind of claim embodied within securities, are different from ordinary claims. In practice, documental claims exist in the area of goods in storage and transportation (securities to goods) as well as in the field of payment (securities to payment). In general, these two types of securities can make the right embodied visible to third parties, and the problem of information asymmetry can be resolved to a large extent. Moreover, the reliance of third parties acting in good faith on the documental recordation is generally protected. This forms an important exception to the rule that claims are not an object of *bona fide* acquisition. In addition to the possibility of *bona fide* acquisition, the debtor is not allowed to refuse performance on the ground that there is a defect in the legal relationship between the debtor and the original creditor. These two forms of protection guarantee that documental claims can be disposed of like a corporeal movable.

On the basis of the preceding discussion, CHAPTER 5 seeks to provide a conclusive analysis of the rationale of publicity in the law of corporeal movables and claims. Firstly, publicity is a formality, as a contrast to the substance of parties' will. It has both merits and downsides. For the parties to a transaction, publicity has a function of evidence. For third parties, it has a function of communicating proprietary information. Publicity can facilitate the certainty of property rights. However, it also causes some problems, such as increasing the costs of transactions, causing unfair outcomes, and restricting parties' autonomy. The merits and downsides imply that a careful trade-off is necessary before the introduction of a means of publicity. Under the principle of proportionality, publicity is only justifiable when it is really necessary and appropriate.

In this research, it is argued that the consensual principle (system) and the causation principle are more in line with the rationale of publicity, compared with the formalist principle (system) and the abstraction principle. As a starting point, valid mutual consent is sufficient for the acquisition of property rights between the transacting parties, and publicity should not be treated as an additional condition. In the absence of publicity, the acquisition should not be treated as ineffective against strange interferers, general creditors, or subsequent acquirers acting in bad faith. This is because publicity is of no use for these three types of third parties. By the same token, where transfer is made on the basis of a defective legal ground, the original owner should not be restricted in enforcing his or her right against strange interferers, general creditors or subsequent acquirers acting in bad faith. Inevitably, the consensual principle (system) and the causation principle give rise to a phenomenon of the relativity of property rights: the exclusivity of property rights is restricted for the benefit of third parties acting in good faith.

On the basis of the preceding discussion on possession, notification, and documental recordation, it can be found that many property rights exist in a hidden state in the law of corporeal movables and claims. Among these three formalities, only documental recordation can convey adequate proprietary information to subsequent acquirers for whom *bona fide* protection is available. Possession is an abstract and ambiguous method of publicity that is sufficient only for strange interferers. Notification is too defective to be a method of publicity for claims, and the transaction of claims often has a severe problem of information asymmetry. As a result, it is difficult to say that the principle of publicity is tenable in the law of corporeal movables and claims. The *status quo* induces us to raise the following question: whether and to what extent registration should be introduced to strengthen the principle of publicity. Should registration be used to meet the requirement of publicity in the law of corporeal movables and claims?

In comparison with other types of publicity, registration has advantages and disadvantages. It is clear, comprehensive and reliable. Different from possession, registration is able to clearly communicate comprehensive proprietary information in the form of words. Moreover, the law can provide that the proprietary information derived from the register is reliable and enables third parties to securely make transactions according to the register. However, registration is costly. Constructing and maintaining a system of registration is not cheap. Moreover, entry of creation and acquisition of property rights in the system is not without costs and forms a restriction on parties' autonomy. Because of the advantages and disadvantages of registration, a trade-off has to be made before determining to introduce this formality into the law of corporeal movables and claims.

In CHAPTER 5, twenty proposals are provided to construct a subject-based system of registration for corporeal movables and claims. These proposals concern three general aspects: the way of construction and operation of the system, the scope of application of the system, and the legal effect of registration.

PROPOSAL 1: The register should be constructed as a subject-based system according to the party's identifier. The identifiers of legal persons include the name, the enterprise code, the address of the legal person and so on. For organizations without legal capacity, the information provided includes the name, the enterprise code (if possible), and the address of the organization. The identifiers of natural persons should be the name, the date of birth, the address and other relevant information included in the identity certificate, driver's license, and birth certificate.

PROPOSAL 2: The description of the object should be sufficiently accurate so that third parties are able to identify the object. The register should provide a classification of corporeal movables and claims, which includes, for example, inventory, equipment, livestock, crops, and receivables. There should also be a free text area so that the object can be further described in a general clause by indicating the name, type, location and other relevant features.

PROPOSAL 3: The register should include a brief description of the transaction type, so that searchers are able to have a preliminary rough understanding of the transaction. A list of the transaction types should be provided under the principle of *numerus clausus* of the national law, such as by including reservation of title, financial lease, security transfer, sale and leaseback, non-possessory pledge, operational lease. There should be a free text area in which further information concerning the transaction type can be provided.

PROPOSAL 4: The system should be digital and computerized by taking advantage of new information technologies.

PROPOSAL 5: The register should be a self-service system, allowing users to finish registration and conduct searches without involving any registrar. It suffices that the entire system is maintained by a group of technicians.

PROPOSAL 6: The register should be a notice-filing system without requiring individuals to record the contract on the basis of which the property right is transferred or created. Advance registration, registration in the absence of any underlying contract created, should be recognized. However, the requirement of describing the transaction type must be fulfilled.

PROPOSAL 7: At the request of searchers, the parties to the transaction would need to provide further information concerning the transaction in the prescribed manner. The disclosure of further information by one party might be restricted by granting the other party a right of approval.

PROPOSAL 8: The register should be fully open to the public.

PROPOSAL 9: Money, securities to goods and securities of payment should be excluded from the system of registration.

PROPOSAL 10: As a starting point, the register should be allowed to include all transactions that give rise to a divergence between ownership and actual possession of corporeal movables. Transfer of corporeal movables under a condition or term able to give rise to proprietary effect and creation of a limited property right on corporeal movables should be able to be registered.

PROPOSAL 11: Assignment of claims and creation of proprietary rights on claims should be included in the register. Acquisition of claims through novation, merge and division of companies, and giro transfer should be excluded from the register.

PROPOSAL 12: A minimum amount of the object should be determined as a threshold of entry in the register. A transaction concerning the assets the total value of which is below the minimum amount does not need to be registered.

PROPOSAL 13: A folio should be available to natural persons so that consumer transactions can also be included in the register. The identifier of natural persons should be determined according to Proposal 1.

PROPOSAL 14: The duration of the hidden state should be taken into consideration in defining the scope of registration. Short-term transactions should not be required to be entered in the register. A grace period should be granted to reservation of title. The specific length of this grace period should be determined according to the period within which the purchase price will usually be paid. Short-term lease should not be entered in the register. It is up to the legislature to determine which term of lease is short.

PROPOSAL 15: Registration has declaratory effect and should not be treated as a prerequisite of valid transfer or creation of property rights in the law of corporeal movables and claims.

PROPOSAL 16: Registration can make property rights effective against subsequent acquirers. The absence of registration does not affect the proprietor's legal position against illegal interference and the debtor's bankruptcy.

PROPOSAL 17: Registration should not affect transactions in the ordinary course of the debtor's business. Third parties in the ordinary course of the debtor's business cannot be reasonably expected to search the register and thus cannot be assumed to be aware of the property right registered.

PROPOSAL 18: For acquisition by a third party free of the property right which is created but not registered, it is necessary that this third party acts in good faith.

PROPOSAL 19: The register might be a reliable means of publicity for third parties acting in good faith, so that *bona fide* acquisition is possible on the basis of the register. Inquirers, as a third party, should be allowed to rely on the information provided by the relevant parties. If the information provided proves to be incorrect or incomplete, *bona fide* acquisition and damages should be available to the inquirer.

PROPOSAL 20: To guarantee the smooth operation of the register, a maximum period of the validity of registration should be prescribed. This maximum period applies not only when no definite period is determined by the parties, but also when the parties specify a definite period. Parties are entitled to cancel the registration before the expiry of the maximum period and renew the registration after the expiry of the maximum period.

After getting the twenty proposals, three specific examples are discussed in detail: the secured transaction of corporeal movables and claims, the trust of corporeal movables and claims, and the transaction of motor vehicles. In sum, both the secured transaction and the trust should be included in the system proposed, but a separate system should be created for the transaction of motor vehicles.

In the modern finance market, corporeal movables and claims are gaining increasing importance as a type of collateral. To cater at the same time to the debtor's demand for possession of the corporeal collateral and the creditor's need of priority in payment, various non-possessory devices of security have been used. Some of them take the form of a limited right of security, and others are ownership-based or title-based. A common problem of these security devices is that they are invisible to third parties. In the situation where claims are used as collateral, the problem also exists because claims lack a means of publicity. The ubiquitous existence of hidden security interests raises the question of whether registration should be introduced to make these interests transparent to third parties. Different jurisdictions might differ with respect to this question.

In this research, it is argued that the secured transaction of corporeal movables and claims should be included in the system of registration proposed in 5.3, regardless of the legal form the transaction takes. In other words, the system is to publicize not only limited property rights of security, but also reservation of ownership (including financial lease) and security transfer of ownership (including sale and lease-back). Under the twenty proposals, the formality of registration will not exert an unacceptable impact on the smoothness of secured transactions. Moreover, this research also contends that possessory pledge also falls short of the principle of publicity, because the requirement of dispossession of the collateral fails to make the right of pledge visible to third parties. Possession should not be treated as a means of publicity for secured transactions of corporeal movables. Thus, it is also desirable to include possessory pledge in the system of registration.

The trust of corporeal movables and claims is another specific case discussed in this research. In general, there are four obstacles to the introduction of the trust in the civil law system: the uniformity of ownership, the singularity of patrimony, the principle of *numerus clausus*, and the principle of publicity. Among these four obstacles, only the last seems to be actual. The beneficiary's right is partially proprietary. Thus, there is a need to inform third parties, in particular subsequent acquirers, of the trust. Publicity of trust includes two principal issues: one is the visible separation of the trust assets from the trustee's personal assets, and the other is how to show the content of the trust to third parties.

In this research, it is argued that the system of registration proposed in 5.3 should include trusts of corporeal movables and claims. A sufficiently precise description of the trust property should be provided in the register, so that third parties are able to know which assets are under the trust. In addition to the description of the object, a mark of trust and a short description of the trust should be recorded in the system. There is no need to record the complete agreement of trust. In general, this will guarantee that the formality of registration will not constitute an unacceptable influence on the smooth transaction of the trust property.

The last example concerns the transaction of motor vehicles. Unlike vessels and aircraft, motor vehicles are mainly regulated by the *nemo dat* rule and the rule of *bona fide* acquisition, a rule centering on possession, in some jurisdictions. In general, these two rules fall under an *ex-post* approach: instead of preventing the occurrence of conflicts, they focus on how to resolve conflicts. In practice, possession and the registration certificate of motor vehicles play an important role in determining the priority of conflicting interests. However, possession is ambiguous, and the registration certificate does not qualify as a means of publicity. As a result, the problem of information asymmetry is not resolved in the transaction of motor vehicles.

In this research, it is argued that a comprehensive and central system of registration should be introduced for motor vehicles. It is better to exclude motor vehicles from the subject-based and notice-filing system proposed in 5.3. In most jurisdictions, there is a register for administrative regulation of motor vehicles, and it is possible to modify this system so that it also performs a private law function. In brief, creation and acquisition of property rights are allowed to be entered in the system, and third parties are entitled to search the system. Like the land register and the register for aircraft and vessels, the system for motor vehicles is also object-based with reference to the VIN. There seems to be no reason to treat motor vehicles differently from vessels and aircraft. In the central register for motor vehicles, both ownership and limited property rights are registerable. As a result, the system will perform not only a public law function, such as cracking down on crimes, but also a private law function, namely publicity of property rights of motor vehicles.

Chapter 6 provides a short introduction of the CCC (2020) and a brief review of the system of publicity for corporeal movables and claims under the CCC. In general, the CCC extends the scope of registration and aims to construct a unified system of registration for corporeal movables and claims. Under the Property Law (2007), only the charge of corporeal movables and the pledge of receivables are registerable. The CCC includes reservation of ownership, financial lease, and factoring in a system of registration. However, the extension is insufficient, and some types of invisible property rights remain outside the register. Possessory pledge, true lease, sale and lease-back, non-factoring assignment of receivables, and trust are still not registerable. Moreover, registration has different legal effects under the Chinese Civil Code: registration makes the security interest effective against third parties where corporeal movables are involved, while it has constitutive effect in the situation of pledge of receivables. This different treatment is groundless, and the constitutive effect of registration is not in line with the rationale of publicity. In the end, recognizing a grace period for the registration of the purchase money charge but denying a grace period for the registration of reservation of ownership is not reasonable.

The Property Law (2007) establishes a decentralized system of registration: three registers are involved in the secured transaction concerning ordinary corporeal movables and receivables. Moreover, some of the registers are paper-based. The triple systems give rise to inconvenience to practitioners and increase the costs of obtaining proprietary information. The CCC attempts to unify the three registers. In this research, it is proposed that the unified system should be self-service, fully open, digital, notice-based and supplementary with a duty of disclosure. This is desirable and will reduce the influence of registration on the smoothness of secured transactions.

Under Property Law (2007), a separate register is constructed for motor vehicles. This register, administered by the Ministry of Transportation, includes every property right that can be created on motor vehicles. For example, the acquisition of motor vehicles is ineffective against third parties acting in good faith until registration is completed. In general, the register performs a private law function and a function of public regulation. In the future, the register should be allowed to operate independently without being absorbed in the unified system of registration for ordinary corporeal movables and claims.

Samenvatting

De ratio van het publiciteitsbeginsel met betrekking tot roerende zaken en vorderingsrechten. Registratie als invulling van het publiciteitsbeginsel?

Dit onderzoek richt zich in algemene zin op het publiciteitsbeginsel met betrekking tot roerende zaken en vorderingsrechten. Twee vragen staan hierbij centraal. De eerste vraag is of en in hoeverre het publiciteitsbeginsel ten aanzien van roerende zaken en vorderingsrechten nog steeds houdbaar is. De tweede vraag is of, en zo ja, op welke wijze er een vorm van registratie moet worden geïntroduceerd met betrekking tot roerende zaken en vorderingsrechten teneinde het publiciteitsbeginsel te versterken. Bezit wordt algemeen gezien als vorm van publiciteit ten aanzien van roerende zaken, terwijl bij vorderingsrechten, in verschillende rechtsstelsels, de mededeling als een vorm van publiciteit wordt beschouwd. In specifieke gevallen, zoals bij opgeslagen goederen en goederen op transport het geval is, wordt aan het publiciteitsbeginsel uitdrukking gegeven door middel van waardepapieren. In hoofdstuk 3 en hoofdstuk 4 van dit proefschrift wordt nader ingegaan op de vraag of, en zo ja, op welke wijze de zojuist genoemde vormen van publiciteit goederenrechtelijke rechten kenbaar kunnen maken jegens derden. Hoofdstuk 5 richt zich vervolgens op de vraag of, en zo ja, op welke wijze vormen van registratie moeten worden geïntroduceerd voor roerende zaken en vorderingsrechten. In hoofdstuk 6 worden vervolgens de implicaties besproken die de onderzoeksresultaten hebben voor het Chinese recht.

Dit onderzoek vangt aan met een inleiding op het concept 'goederenrechtelijke rechten'. In HOOFDSTUK 2 wordt vervolgens betoogd dat goederenrechtelijke rechten zien op de rechtsverhouding tussen personen onderling in plaats van tussen personen en zaken. Na een vergelijking te hebben gemaakt met andere soorten rechten, in het bijzonder de persoonlijke rechten, wordt geconcludeerd dat goederenrechtelijke rechten worden gekarakteriseerd door twee fundamentele kenmerken: zij hebben betrekking op objecten en hebben bovendien absolute werking. Het eerstgenoemde kenmerk houdt in dat goederenrechtelijke rechten uitsluitend kunnen bestaan ten aanzien van roerende of onroerende zaken of (andere) vermogensrechten. Het tweede kenmerk houdt in dat goederenrechtelijke rechten derdenwerking hebben. Op goederenrechtelijke rechten mag door derden geen inbreuk worden gemaakt, zij hebben prioriteit en zaaksgevolg (*droit de suite*). De grens tussen goederenrechtelijke rechten en persoonlijke rechten is echter niet glashelder. Met andere woorden, er zijn rechten die zowel goederenrechtelijke als verbintenisrechtelijke kenmerken hebben.

'Derden' vormen een algemeen en ambigu concept in het goederenrecht. In de regel kunnen drie typen 'derden' worden onderscheiden: (potentiële) inbreukmakers (al dan niet te goeder trouw), opvolgende verkrijgers, en concurrente schuldeisers. Een goederenrechtelijk recht heeft werking jegens elk van deze drie typen 'derden', met dien verstande dat jegens een of twee van deze typen 'derden' ook bepaalde persoonlijke rechten bindend zijn. De belangen en behoefte aan informatie ten aanzien van goederenrechtelijke rechten van deze drie typen 'derden' zijn niet dezelfde. (Potentiële) inbreukmakers willen uitsluitend weten waar de grens ligt tussen hun vrijheid van handelen en het goederenrechtelijk recht van anderen. Dit type 'derde' hecht gewoonlijk geen waarde aan de eigenschappen van een goederenrechtelijk recht. In tegenstelling tot (potentiële) inbreukmakers, willen opvolgende verkrijgers juist meer te weten komen over de op een zaak rustende goederenrechtelijke rechten, zulks in het licht van de prioriteitsregel; het oudere goederenrechtelijke recht gaat voor het jongere goederenrechtelijke recht. Concurrente schuldeisers zijn degenen op wie, in geval van faillissement van een schuldenaar, het principe van gelijkheid der schuldeisers van toepassing is. Zij beschikken niet over goederenrechtelijke zekerheidsrechten en hebben ten aanzien van een specifiek zekerheidsobject geen voorrang bij de voldoening van hun vordering. Concurrente schuldeisers hebben er gewoonlijk belang bij dat de debiteur financieel gezond is. De voornaamste reden waarom een concurrente schuldeiser niet om goederenrechtelijke zekerheid verzoekt, is dat hij of zij ervan uitgaat dat de debiteur zijn verplichting kan nakomen.

Aangezien goederenrechtelijke rechten derdenwerking hebben, dringt zich de vraag op hoe derden kennis kunnen nemen van het goederenrechtelijk recht. Derden hebben te maken met een zogeheten informatie-asymmetrie. Om deze informatie-asymmetrie weg te nemen, zouden derden moeten beschikken over een middel waarmee zij goederenrechtelijke informatie, dat wil zeggen informatie met betrekking tot de rechtsverhouding van goederenrechtelijke rechten, kunnen verkrijgen. In het goederenrecht kan deze goederenrechtelijke informatie bijvoorbeeld worden verkregen via publiciteit. Aangezien het bestaan van goederenrechtelijke rechten informatie-asymmetrie creëert voor derden, zouden deze rechten onderworpen moeten zijn aan het vereiste van publiciteit. In de praktijk zijn er inderdaad ook al verschillende andere manieren waarop derden goederenrechtelijke informatie kunnen verkrijgen. Vergeleken met deze manieren beschikt publiciteit over bijzondere eigenschappen: het is objectief, eenduidig en wettelijk verankerd.

In HOOFDSTUK 3 wordt nader ingegaan op bezit als middel van publiciteit. In dit hoofdstuk wordt toegelicht dat bezit een door de wetgever bedacht juridisch concept is, bedoeld om bepaalde doeleinden te dienen. Publiciteit is geen doeleinde dat bij het definiëren van dit concept in overweging is genomen. Gewoonlijk wordt de vraag hoe het concept 'bezit' in het hedendaagse recht gedefinieerd moet worden beantwoord door middel van het concept van de verkrijgende verjaring en de bescherming van feitelijke zeggenschap. Deze twee aspecten zijn in feite ook van belang voor een begrip van het concept *possessio* in het Romeinse recht. Zonder deze twee aspecten is het moeilijk te begrijpen dat een persoon die de fysieke macht heeft niet per se het bezit hoeft te hebben, terwijl er omstandigheden zijn waarin een persoon die niet de fysieke macht heeft in rechte kan worden beschouwd als de bezitter.

Bezit wordt gewoonlijk als middel van publiciteit beschouwd vanwege de fysieke verbondenheid tussen de bezitter en het bezeten object. Voor een beter begrip van deze functie dienen twee aspecten te worden onderscheiden. Allereerst wordt bezit in de praktijk geassocieerd met een groot aantal uiteenlopende rechten. Bezit is derhalve een abstracte en ambigue vorm van publiciteit. Het geeft geen uiterlijke blijk van eigendom, noch kan het dienen als enige vorm van publiciteit. Het tweede aspect is dat indirect bezit onzichtbaar is en derhalve niet kan dienen als vorm van publiciteit voor het overbrengen van goederenrechtelijke informatie aan derden. Het concept van het indirecte bezit wordt toegepast voor andere doeleinden, met name ter uitbreiding van het toepassingsbereik van bezitsbescherming. Daarom is uitsluitend direct bezit een ambigue vorm van publiciteit waarmee derden geïnformeerd kunnen worden dat de bezitter beschikt over een bepaald recht ten aanzien van de zaak die hij bezit.

Als abstracte en ambigue vorm van publiciteit fungeert bezit als een 'navigatiesysteem' voor (potentiële) inbreukmakers. Bezit stelt personen in staat samen te leven met anderen in een wereld vol met voorwerpen zonder de goederenrechtelijke rechten van die ander aan te tasten. Mensen zijn in het dagelijks leven in staat snel en instinctief te reageren op bezit, hetgeen een fundamentele voorwaarde is voor ordentelijk bezit. Omdat de bezitter zijn of haar bezit door middel van feitelijke machtsuitoefening aan de buitenwereld heeft getoond, dienen mensen de status van bezit te respecteren. In dit opzicht fungeert bezit als zichtbare grens waarmee de vrijheid van handelen wordt afgebakend. De abstracte indicatie die het bezit afgeeft, kan derhalve de behoefte van (potentiële) inbreukmakers aan informatie bevredigen en zo onrechtmatige tussenkomst voorkomen.

Voor opvolgende verkrijgers vormt (direct) bezit echter geen afdoende vorm van publiciteit. De opvolgende verkrijger heeft, in zijn hoedanigheid als derde, behoefte aan gedetailleerde informatie ten aanzien van de goederenrechtelijke rechten die rusten op een specifiek object. Zo dient een potentiële koper vast te stellen of de verkoper de eigenaar is van het object en of er op het object beperkte goederenrechtelijke rechten rusten. Bezit is op zichzelf genomen niet voldoende om aan deze behoefte te voldoen. In het hedendaagse recht kunnen roerende zaken zelfs in een *traditio* systeem worden vervreemd, ongeacht het rechtstreekse (directe) bezit ervan, gelet op de erkenning van de mogelijkheid van onzichtbare leveringen, zoals de levering *traditio per constitutum possessorum*. Het gevolg van de erkenning van de onzichtbare levering is dat het recht van eigendom en van direct bezit afzonderlijk van elkaar werken. Aan de andere kant kan bezit volgens het hedendaagse recht leiden tot verkrijging van roerende zaken te goeder trouw. Dit vormt echter geen afdoende basis voor de stelling dat bezit een zichtbare vorm van eigendom is. Het beginsel van de verkrijging te goeder trouw is hoofdzakelijk een rechtspolitieke keuze, in het bijzonder om de rechtsgeldigheid van transacties veilig te stellen. Het beginsel kan niet volledig worden verklaard vanuit het oogpunt van de legitimatie functie van bezit. Bezit is ambigu en vormt derhalve geen betrouwbaar baken. Kortom, op roerende zaken betrekking hebbende goederenrechtelijke rechten zijn gewoonlijk aan het zicht van derden onttrokken, wat in de praktijk vaak tot conflicten leidt. Het principe van de verkrijging te goeder trouw is op zijn best een ex-postconcept, waarmee conflicten kunnen worden opgelost nadat deze zijn ontstaan.

Voor concurrente schuldeisers volstaat bezit als vorm van publiciteit evenmin. Concurrente schuldeisers zijn voornamelijk geïnteresseerd in de algehele financiële toestand van de debiteur. Bij de beoordeling daarvan is de hoeveelheid onbezwaarde vermogensbestanddelen van ondergeschikt belang. En zelfs in dat opzicht is het voor concurrente schuldeisers niet mogelijk om op basis van bezit een bruikbare indicatie te krijgen van de hoeveelheid onbezwaarde vermogensbestanddelen. Immers, het is heel goed mogelijk dat een roerende zaak die in het bezit is van de failliet, feitelijk toebehoort aan een ander, terwijl roerende zaken die niet in het bezit zijn van de debiteur heel goed tot de faillissementsboedel kunnen behoren. Potentiële schuldeisers zullen in de praktijk niet zijn geïnteresseerd in de bezitsstaat van roerende zaken van de debiteur. Bezit is geen betrouwbare indicator voor de faillissementsboedel, noch voor de algehele financiële toestand. Er zijn dan ook geen legitieme redenen om aan te nemen dat een scheiding tussen eigendom en bezit ertoe leidt dat concurrente schuldeisers een verkeerd beeld krijgen van de debiteur.

In HOOFDSTUK 4 staat het vraagstuk van de publiciteit van vorderingsrechten centraal. In dit hoofdstuk wordt allereerst gewezen op de meervoudige eigenschappen van vorderingsrechten. Vorderingsrechten geven in de eerste plaats de interne verhouding weer tussen schuldeiser en debiteur, gebaseerd op het relativiteitsbeginsel; het bestaan van een vordering creëert geen informatie-asymmetrie voor derden. Het beginsel van publiciteit komt dan ook niet voor in het verbintenissenrecht. Tegelijkertijd hebben vorderingsrechten ook goederenrechtelijke kenmerken, voor zover zij worden beschouwd als een vermogensbestanddeel en verhandelbaar zijn. Net zoals de vervreemding van roerende zaken, leidt de vervreemding van vorderingsrechten tot informatie-asymmetrie. Zo kan een vordering dubbel worden gecedeerd, wat kan leiden tot het probleem van meervoudige cessie: welke van de twee verkrijgers gaat daarbij voor? Derhalve is ook ten aanzien van overdrachten van vorderingsrechten behoefte aan publiciteit.

Ten aanzien van gewone, 'niet gedocumenteerde vorderingsrechten' (vorderingsrechten op naam) wordt een mededeling aan de debiteur vaak gezien als een vorm van publiciteit. Doordat de debiteur van de vordering in kennis wordt gesteld, kunnen derden kennis nemen van de vervreemding van de vordering door daarnaar te informeren bij de debiteur. In dit onderzoek wordt echter betoogd dat kennisgeving (enkele mededeling) ontoereikend is als vorm van publiciteit van vorderingsrechten. Dit komt in de eerste plaats omdat een kennisgeving de vervreemding van de vordering niet inzichtelijk maakt voor derden. Zelfs als de debiteur een kennisgeving van de cessie ontvangt, is er onvoldoende reden om aan te nemen dat hij of zij derden hierover juiste en volledige informatie zal verstrekken. Er rust op een debiteur geen wettelijke verplichting tot bekendmaking. Bovendien bestaat de kans dat de debiteur samenspant met de cedent of de pandgever om derden te misleiden. En zelfs al zou de debiteur tot samenwerking bereid zijn, dan nog is het heel goed mogelijk dat hij of zij simpelweg vergeet derden van de vervreemding in kennis te stellen. Van nog groter belang is echter dat wanneer de derde vertrouwt op de kennisgeving van de debiteur een verkrijging te goeder trouw van vorderingsrechten in beginsel niet wordt erkend. Ook om bepaalde praktische redenen is een kennisgeving geen geschikte vorm van publiciteit ten aanzien van vorderingsrechten. Zo zijn aan kennisgevingen van de cessie van een groot aantal vorderingsrechten (zgn. bulkcessies) hoge kosten verbonden, aangezien elke betrokken debiteur afzonderlijk in kennis moet worden gesteld. Bovendien sluit de formele handeling van het doen van een kennisgeving de mogelijkheid van vervreemding van toekomstige vorderingsrechten uit, hetgeen een obstakel vormt voor overdrachten van dergelijke vorderingsrechten. De kennisgeving heeft in feite louter betekenis voor het vraagstuk van de nakoming: de debiteur is gerechtigd tot nakoming jegens de oorspronkelijke schuldeiser voordat hij van de vervreemding in kennis wordt gesteld.

Dat een kennisgeving geen publiciteitsfunctie heeft, is in lijn met de meeste rechtsstelsels. In principe is een kennisgeving irrelevant of wordt deze beschouwd als een formele handeling die in het geval van vervreemding van vorderingsrechten zou kunnen worden vervangen door een andere handeling. Zo vereist het Duitse recht voor een rechtsgeldige cessie geen kennisgeving aan de debiteur. Hoewel kennisgevingen noodzakelijk zijn in geval van verpanding van vorderingsrechten, kan dit voorschrift eenvoudig worden ondervangen door te opteren voor de cessie tot zekerheid. Naar Nederlands recht kan een geldige cessie niet alleen tot stand worden gebracht door middel van een akte en kennisgeving van de cessie aan de *debitor cessus* (openbare cessie), maar ook door middel van een daartoe bestemde authentieke of geregistreerde onderhandse akte, zonder mededeling aan de *debitor cessus* (stille cessie). Bovendien wordt ingeval van een dubbele cessie de *nemo dat* regel toegepast. Kort samengevat: vorderingsrechten op naam blijven gewoonlijk onzichtbaar als goederenrechtelijke entiteit, en goederenrechtelijke handelingen met betrekking tot vorderingsrechten op naam, zoals overdrachten, kampen met een informatie-asymmetrie, een probleem dat niet door middel van een kennisgeving kan worden opgelost.

Vorderingsrechten die zijn belichaamd in een waardepapier verschillen op het punt van het publiciteitsbeginsel juist van vorderingsrechten op naam. Vorderingsrechten die zijn belichaamd in een waardepapier komen in de praktijk voor met betrekking tot opgeslagen goederen of goederen op transport en in het betalingsverkeer. Deze twee typen vorderingsrechten die zijn belichaamd in een waardepapier maken het vorderingsrecht door middel van het waardepapier zichtbaar voor derden, waarmee het probleem van informatie-asymmetrie in belangrijke mate wordt ondervangen. Derden te goeder trouw worden in dat geval beschermd. Dit vormt een belangrijke uitzondering op de regel dat verkrijging te goeder trouw niet opgaat voor vorderingsrechten. Naast de mogelijkheid van verkrijging te goeder trouw is het de debiteur niet toegestaan nakoming te weigeren op grond van een gebrek in de rechtsverhouding tussen de debiteur en de oorspronkelijke schuldeiser. Deze twee vormen van bescherming zorgen ervoor dat vorderingsrechten die zijn belichaamd in een waardepapier op dezelfde wijze kunnen worden vervreemd als roerende zaken.

Voortbordurend op de voorafgaande discussie wordt in Hoofdstuk 5 getracht een sluitende analyse te geven van de ratio van publiciteit met betrekking tot roerende zaken en vorderingsrechten. In de eerste plaats betreft publiciteit een formele handeling; het is geen uitdrukking van de wilsovereenstemming tussen partijen. Dit heeft voor- en nadelen. Voor partijen die bij een transactie zijn betrokken heeft publiciteit een bewijsfunctie. Voor derden heeft publiciteit de functie van verstrekking van goederenrechtelijke informatie. Door middel van publiciteit wordt het bestaan en de hoedanigheid van goederenrechtelijke rechten vastgesteld. Dit gaat echter ook weer gepaard met een aantal problemen, zoals verhoogde transactiekosten, onbillijke resultaten en beperking van de autonomie van de partijen. De voor- en nadelen maken duidelijk dat er een zorgvuldige afweging gemaakt moet worden voordat een vorm van publiciteit wordt geïntroduceerd. Op grond van het proportionaliteitsbeginsel is publiciteit uitsluitend gerechtvaardigd wanneer het daadwerkelijk noodzakelijk en gepast is.

In dit onderzoek wordt betoogd dat vergeleken met het formalistische beginsel en het abstractiebeginsel, het consensusbeginsel en het causabeginsel meer aansluiten bij de ratio van publiciteit. Als uitgangspunt heeft te gelden dat een geldige wilsovereenstemming tussen de contracterende partijen afdoende zou moeten zijn voor het verkrijgen van goederenrechtelijke rechten, en dat publiciteit niet gezien mag worden als een aanvullende voorwaarde. Ingeval van afwezigheid van publiciteit zou een verkrijging van een goederenrechtelijk recht niet als rechtsongeldig mogen worden aangemerkt jegens niet te goeder trouw handelende (potentiële) inbreukmakers, concurrente schuldeisers of opvolgende verkrijgers. Immers, publiciteit is ten aanzien van deze drie typen derden nutteloos. Evenzo dient, voor zover de overdracht plaatsvindt op basis van een ontoereikende rechtsgrond, de oorspronkelijke eigenaar niet beperkt te worden in de uitoefening van zijn rechten jegens niet te goeder trouw handelende (potentiële) inbreukmakers, concurrente schuldeisers of opvolgende verkrijgers. Het consensusbeginsel en het causabeginsel leiden onvermijdelijk tot het fenomeen van relativiteit van goederenrechtelijke rechten: de exclusiviteit van goederenrechtelijke rechten is voorbehouden aan te goeder trouw handelende derden.

Op grond van de voorgaande discussie ten aanzien van bezit, kennisgeving, en waardepapieren kan worden geconcludeerd dat een aanzienlijk aantal goederenrechtelijke rechten met betrekking tot roerende zaken en vorderingsrechten in een verborgen staat verkeren. Van deze drie formaliteiten kan uitsluitend via waardepapieren adequate goederenrechtelijke informatie worden overgebracht jegens opvolgende verkrijgers die bescherming te goeder trouw genieten. Bezit is een abstracte en ambigue vorm van publiciteit en is uitsluitend toereikend ten aanzien van (potentiële) inbreukmakers. Kennisgevingen zijn niet toereikend als vorm van publiciteit voor vorderingsrechten, en vervreemdingen en bezwaringen van vorderingsrechten gaan vaak gebukt onder een ernstige vorm van informatie-asymmetrie. Hierdoor kan moeilijk worden volgehouden dat het publiciteitsbeginsel houdbaar is ten aanzien van roerende zaken en vorderingsrechten. Deze status quo werpt de volgende vraag op: moet er een registratieplicht worden ingevoerd ter versterking van het publiciteitsbeginsel en zo ja, in hoeverre? Moet registratie worden gezien als invulling van het publiciteitsbeginsel met betrekking tot roerende zaken en vorderingsrechten?

Registratie heeft zekere voor- en nadelen ten opzichte van andere vormen van publiciteit. Het is transparant, volledig en betrouwbaar. In tegenstelling tot bezit geeft registratie heldere, volledige en schriftelijke goederenrechtelijke informatie. Bovendien kan bij wet worden bepaald dat de aan de registratie ontleende goederenrechtelijke informatie betrouwbaar moet zijn en derden in staat moet stellen op de registratie gebaseerde transacties uit te voeren. Het nadeel is alleen dat er aan registratie hoge kosten zijn verbonden. Het opzetten en in stand houden van een registratiesysteem vergt investeringen. Ook aan het inschrijven van gevestigde en verkregen goederenrechtelijke rechten in het systeem zijn kosten verbonden, en het beperkt de autonomie der betrokken partijen. Gezien de voor- en nadelen van registratie dient er een zorgvuldige afweging te worden gemaakt alvorens te besluiten tot invoering van deze formele handeling met betrekking tot roerende zaken en vorderingsrechten..

In HOOFDSTUK 5 wordt een twintigtal voorstellen gedaan voor een persoonsgebonden registratiesysteem voor roerende zaken en vorderingsrechten. Deze voorstellen hebben betrekking op drie algemene aspecten: de wijze waarop het systeem wordt opgezet en beheerd, het toepassingsbereik van het systeem, en de rechtsgevolgen van registratie.

VOORSTEL 1: Het register dient te worden opgezet als een persoonsgebonden (*subject-based*) systeem al naar gelang de gegevens van de rechthebbende partij. De gegevens van rechtspersonen omvatten bijvoorbeeld de bedrijfsnaam, het KvK-nummer, het adres, etc. Voor organisaties zonder rechtspersoonlijkheid omvatten de gegevens de naam van de organisatie, het KvK-nummer (indien van toepassing) en het adres. De gegevens met betrekking tot natuurlijke personen zijn de naam, de geboortedatum, het adres en overige relevante gegevens zoals vermeld op het identiteitsbewijs, het rijbewijs of het geboortecertificaat.

Voorstel 2: De omschrijving van het object dient voldoende accuraat te zijn om derden in staat te stellen het object te identificeren. Het register dient een onderverdeling van roerende zaken en vorderingsrechten te bevatten, zoals bijvoorbeeld naar inventaris, gereedschap en apparatuur, vee, gewassen en uitstaande vorderingen. Daarnaast dient er ruimte in het register te worden gereserveerd voor het geven van een nadere omschrijving van het object, zoals bijvoorbeeld opgave van de benaming, type, locatie en overige relevante kenmerken.

Voorstel 3: Het register dient een korte omschrijving te geven van het type transactie, zodat gebruikers in staat zijn een eerste algemene indruk van de transactie te krijgen. Er dient een uitputtend overzicht van de soorten transacties te worden gegeven, overeenkomstig het *numerus clausus* beginsel, zoals eigendomsvoorbehoud, *financial lease*, fiduciaire overdracht, *sale and leaseback*, stil pandrecht, *operational lease*. Daarnaast dient er ruimte in het register te worden gereserveerd voor het geven van aanvullende informatie over het soort transactie.

Voorstel 4: Het systeem dient te worden opgezet in digitale en geautomatiseerde vorm met gebruikmaking van geavanceerde technologieën.

Voorstel 5: Het register dient zo te zijn ingericht dat gebruikers zelf de registratie kunnen voltooien (*self-service system*) en daarin kunnen zoeken zonder tussenkomst van een bewaarder. Slechts een kleine groep technici is nodig om het systeem te onderhouden.

Voorstel 6: Het register dient een systeem te zijn waarbij de gebruiker slechts enkele gegevens hoeft in te vullen (*notice-filing system*), zonder dat van de gebruikers wordt geëist dat zij de onderliggende documentatie registreren waarop de overdracht of de totstandkoming van het goederenrechtelijk recht is gebaseerd. Registratie vooraf en registratie bij afwezigheid van de onderliggende documentatie moet mogelijk zijn, met dien verstande dat wel een omschrijving moet worden gegeven van het type transactie.

Voorstel 7: De bij een ingeschreven transactie betrokken partijen dienen op verzoek van gebruikers, op de voorgeschreven wijze, aanvullende informatie te verstrekken over de transactie. Bekendmaking van aanvullende informatie door een partij kan worden beperkt door hieraan de voorafgaande goedkeuring van de andere partij te verbinden.

Voorstel 8: Het register dient volledig openbaar te zijn.

Voorstel 9: In het registratiesysteem zijn gegevens met betrekking tot contante middelen (geld), waardepapieren in het kader van goederen en waardepapieren in het kader van het betalingsverkeer uitgesloten van registratie.

Voorstel 10: Als uitgangspunt heeft te gelden dat in het register alle transacties met betrekking tot roerende zaken opgenomen worden die leiden tot een scheiding van eigendom en feitelijk bezit. Het moet verder mogelijk zijn overdrachten van roerende zaken te registreren onder een voorwaarde die goederenrechtelijk effect bewerkstelligt, alsmede vestiging van een beperkt goederenrechtelijk recht op roerende zaken.

Voorstel 11: In het register dienen voorts overdrachten en bezwaringen van vorderingsrechten op naam te worden opgenomen. Verkrijging van vorderingsrechten door middel van schuldvernieuwing (novatie), fusies en splitsingen van vennootschappen en girale overdrachten dienen echter niet in het register te worden opgenomen.

VOORSTEL 12: Er dient een drempelwaarde te worden vastgesteld voor de objecten die in het register opgenomen kunnen worden. Transacties waarmee activa zijn gemoeid waarvan de totale waarde minder bedraagt dan deze drempelwaarde hoeven niet te worden geregistreerd.

VOORSTEL 13: Er dient te worden voorzien in een aparte voorziening voor natuurlijke personen zodat ook consumententransacties in het register kunnen worden opgenomen. De gegevens van natuurlijke personen dienen te worden vastgesteld overeenkomstig Voorstel 1.

VOORSTEL 14: Bij het vaststellen van het toepassingsbereik van de registratie dient rekening te worden gehouden met de kenbaarheid van de gegevens. Zolang zij niet zijn geregistreerd, zijn goederenrechtelijke rechten niet zichtbaar en kenbaar voor derden. Kortlopende transacties worden niet geregistreerd. Voor eigendomsvoorbehouden geldt een maximale registratietermijn. Deze maximale registratietermijn omvat de periode waarin de koopprijs normaal gesproken dient te worden voldaan. Kortlopende leaseovereenkomsten worden niet geregistreerd. Het is aan de wetgever om te bepalen wat een kortlopende leaseovereenkomst is.

VOORSTEL 15: Registratie heeft een declaratoir effect en mag niet worden beschouwd als voorwaarde voor de rechtsgeldige overdracht of voor de vestiging van goederenrechtelijke rechten met betrekking tot roerende zaken en vorderingsrechten.

VOORSTEL 16: Door registratie kunnen goederenrechtelijke rechten worden tegengeworpen aan opvolgende verkrijgers. De afwezigheid van registratie heeft geen gevolgen voor de juridische positie van de rechthebbende in geval van onwettige inbreuken of het faillissement.

VOORSTEL 17: Registratie heeft geen rechtsgevolgen voor transacties die plaatsvinden in het kader van de normale bedrijfsuitoefening van de debiteur. Ingeval van normale bedrijfsuitoefening kan van derden in redelijkheid niet worden verwacht dat zij het register raadplegen en dus kan niet van hen worden verlangd dat zij kennis dragen van de geregistreerde goederenrechtelijke rechten.

VOORSTEL 18: Voor de bescherming van de derde-verkrijger van een goed dat is bezwaard met een ongeregistreerd goederenrechtelijk recht is vereist dat deze derde-verkrijger ten tijde van de verkrijging te goeder trouw was.

VOORSTEL 19: Het register kan een betrouwbare vorm van publiciteit zijn voor te goeder trouw handelende derden, zodat op basis van het register verkrijging te goeder trouw mogelijk is. Verzoekers om inlichtingen moeten, als derden, in staat zijn te vertrouwen op de door de bij de transactie betrokken partijen verstrekte informatie. Indien de verstrekte informatie onjuist of onvolledig blijkt te zijn, dient de verzoeker daartegen te worden beschermd en schadevergoeding te ontvangen.

VOORSTEL 20: Teneinde een ongestoorde werking van het register te waarborgen, dient een maximumtermijn van de registratie te worden gehanteerd. Deze maximumtermijn is niet alleen van toepassing wanneer de partijen zelf geen bepaalde termijn hebben vastgesteld, maar ook indien zij dat wel hebben gedaan. De partijen hebben het recht de registratie voor afloop van de maximumtermijn door te halen en de registratie na afloop van de maximumtermijn te hervatten.

Naar aanleiding van deze twintig voorstellen worden drie voorbeelden nader besproken: de gesecureerde transactie van roerende zaken en vorderingsrechten, de trust-achtige instrumenten met betrekking tot roerende zaken en vorderingsrechten, en overdrachten van voertuigen. Kort gezegd dienen in het voorgestelde registratiesysteem zowel gesecureerde overdrachten als de trust te worden geregistreerd, maar zou voor motorvoertuigen een afzonderlijk systeem opgezet moeten worden.

Het belang van roerende zaken en vorderingsrechten als zekerheidsobject neemt in de huidige praktijk steeds grotere vormen aan. Om tegelijkertijd tegemoet te komen aan de behoefte van de debiteur controle uit te kunnen oefenen over het zekerheidsobject en de behoefte van de schuldeiser om bij voldoening van zijn vorderingsrechten voorrang te krijgen, wordt gebruik gemaakt van verschillende stille zekerheidsinstrumenten. Sommige daarvan hebben de vorm van een beperkt zekerheidsrecht, terwijl andere zijn ontleend aan het eigendomsrecht. Deze zekerheidsinstrumenten hebben het probleem gemeen dat zij niet inzichtelijk zijn voor derden. In de situatie waarin vorderingsrechten worden gebruikt als zekerheidsobject bestaat dit probleem tevens, omdat vorderingsrechten op naam geen vorm van publiciteit kennen (niet zichtbaar zijn). De alomtegenwoordige aanwezigheid van verborgen zekerheidsrechten werpt de vraag op of een registratieplicht moet worden ingevoerd om deze rechten inzichtelijk te maken voor derden. Deze vraag wordt in diverse rechtsstelsels op een verschillende wijze beantwoord.

In dit proefschrift wordt betoogd dat in het in paragraaf 5.3 voorgestelde registratiesysteem ook gesecureerde overdrachten ten aanzien van roerende zaken en vorderingsrechten opgenomen zouden moeten worden, ongeacht de vorm van de transactie. Met andere woorden, het registratiesysteem dient niet alleen beperkte goederenrechtelijke zekerheidsrechten te bevatten, maar ook het eigendomsvoorbehoud (inclusief de *financial lease*) en de fiduciaire overdracht (inclusief verkoop en terugverhuur '*sale and lease-back*'). In het kader van de twintig voorstellen zal de formele registratie geen onaanvaardbare gevolgen hebben voor de wijze waarop gesecureerde overdrachten plaatsvinden. In dit onderzoek wordt verder gesteld dat ook een vuistpandrecht niet voldoet aan het beginsel van publiciteit, aangezien omzetting van het vuistpandrecht in een stil pandrecht het pandrecht niet zichtbaar maakt voor derden. Bezit dient niet te worden beschouwd als een vorm van publiciteit bij fiduciaire roerende zaken. Het is derhalve gewenst om ook vuistpand in het registratiesysteem op te nemen.

Een ander specifiek geval dat in deze studie wordt besproken, is de trust van roerende zaken en vorderingsrechten. Er zijn in het algemeen vier obstakels te onderscheiden die de invoering van de trust in het civielrechtelijk systeem in de weg staan: de eenheid van het eigendomsbegrip, het unieke karakter van het eigendomsrecht, het *numerus clausus* beginsel en het publiciteitsbeginsel. Van deze vier obstakels lijkt alleen de laatste actueel. Het recht van de begunstigde van een trust kwalificeert zich als een gedeeltelijk goederenrechtelijk recht. Dit betekent dat er een noodzaak bestaat om derden, met name opvolgende verkrijgers, over de trust te informeren. Openbaarheid van de trust behelst twee belangrijke aspecten: allereerst de zichtbare scheiding tussen de trustgoederen en de vermogensbestanddelen van de trustee; ten tweede hoe de inhoud van de trust inzichtelijk moet worden gemaakt voor derden.

In dit onderzoek wordt betoogd dat het in paragraaf 5.3 voorgestelde registratiesysteem ook trusts van roerende zaken en vorderingsrechten zou moeten omvatten. Het register dient een voldoende nauwkeurige omschrijving te bevatten van het trustvermogen, zodat derden kunnen zien welke vermogensbestanddelen de trust ten titel van beheer heeft. Naast de omschrijving van het object, dient het registratiesysteem een trustaanduiding (*mark of trust*) en een korte omschrijving van de trust te bevatten. Het is niet noodzakelijk om de volledige trustovereenkomst te registreren. Hierdoor wordt gewoonlijk gegarandeerd dat het formele vereiste van registratie geen allesoverheersende invloed heeft op de vlotte afwikkeling van transacties met betrekking tot het trustvermogen.

Het laatste voorbeeld betreft transacties met betrekking tot motorvoertuigen. Anders dan schepen en vliegtuigen worden motorvoertuigen hoofdzakelijk gereguleerd door het *nemo dat* principe en het principe van de bescherming van de verkrijging te goeder trouw, een principe waarbij in sommige rechtsstelsels de nadruk ligt op bezit. Of aan deze principes is voldaan, wordt gewoonlijk achteraf getoetst: in plaats van conflicten te voorkomen worden conflicten opgelost nadat ze zijn ontstaan. In de praktijk spelen het bezit en het registratiebewijs van motorvoertuigen een belangrijke rol bij het bepalen van voorrang in geval van strijdige belangen. Bezit is echter ambigu en het registratiebewijs wordt niet beschouwd als vorm van publiciteit. Hierdoor wordt het probleem van informatie-asymmetrie met betrekking tot transacties met betrekking tot motorvoertuigen niet opgelost.

In dit onderzoek wordt gepleit voor de invoering van een allesomvattend en centraal registratiesysteem voor motorvoertuigen. Het verdient de voorkeur motorvoertuigen uit te sluiten van het in art. 5.3 voorgestelde persoonsgebonden (*subject-based*) registratiesysteem waarbij de gebruiker slechts enkele gegevens hoeft in te vullen (*notice-filing system*). De meeste jurisdicties kennen al een administratief register waarin motorvoertuigen worden geregistreerd. Het zou niet moeilijk moeten zijn om deze registers zodanig aan te passen dat zij tevens een privaatrechtelijke functie krijgen, waarbij – kort gesteld – ook de vestiging en verkrijging van goederenrechtelijke rechten wordt geregistreerd en waarbij derden het recht krijgen om in het register te zoeken. Evenals het kadaster en het scheeps- en het luchtvaartuigregister, is het motorvoertuigenregistratiesysteem, door verwijzing naar de VIN (*Vehicle Identification Number*), een op het object gebaseerd registratiesysteem (*object-based system*). Er lijkt geen reden te zijn waarom motorvoertuigen anders behandeld zouden moeten worden dan schepen en luchtvaartuigen. Zowel het eigendomsrecht als beperkte rechten kunnen in het centrale motorvoertuigenregistratiesysteem worden geregistreerd. Het systeem heeft dan niet alleen een publiekrechtelijke functie, zoals het voorkomen van misdrijven, maar ook een privaatrechtelijke functie, namelijk het inzichtelijk maken van op motorvoertuigen gevestigde goederenrechtelijke rechten.

Hoofdstuk 6 bevat een beknopte inleiding op het Chinese Burgerlijk Wetboek (CBW) (2020) en een korte beoordeling van het systeem van publiciteit met betrekking tot roerende zaken en vorderingsrechten op grond van het CBW. In algemene zin wordt in het CBW het toepassingsbereik van de registratie uitgebreid en gestreefd naar het opzetten van een uniform registratiesysteem voor roerende zaken en vorderingsrechten. Krachtens de Chinese Wet op het Goederenrecht (2007) kunnen uitsluitend verpandingen van roerende zaken en vorderingsrechten worden geregistreerd. Op grond van het CBW worden ook eigendomsvoorbehoud, *financial lease* en *factoring* in een registratiesysteem opgenomen. Deze uitbreiding is echter onvoldoende en bepaalde typen niet-kenbare goederenrechtelijke rechten zijn van registratie uitgesloten. Vuistpandrechten, *true lease, sale and lease-back, non-factoring* cessie van vorderingsrechten en trusts kunnen nog altijd niet worden geregistreerd. Registratie heeft bovendien andere rechtsgevolgen onder het Chinese Burgerlijk Wetboek: registratie maakt het zekerheidsrecht waarbij roerende zaken zijn betrokken afdwingbaar jegens derden, terwijl het constitutieve kracht heeft in geval van een verpanding van vorderingsrechten. Er is geen grond voor deze afwijkende behandeling en het constitutieve gevolg van registratie is niet in lijn met de ratio van publiciteit. Tot slot is het aanvaarden van een maximumtermijn voor de registratie van een *purchase money charge*, maar het afwijzen van een maximumtermijn voor de registratie van een eigendomsvoorbehoud onredelijk.

Het met de Chinese Wet op het Goederenrecht (2007) ingevoerde Chinese registratiesysteem is gedecentraliseerd: er zijn drie registers voor gesecureerde transacties met betrekking tot roerende zaken en vorderingsrechten. Bovendien zijn nog niet alle registers gedigitaliseerd. Het drievoudige systeem is onpraktisch voor gebruikers en leidt tot hogere kosten voor het verkrijgen van goederenrechtelijke informatie. In het CBW wordt ernaar gestreefd om deze drie registers samen te voegen. In dit onderzoek wordt voorgesteld dat het uniforme systeem zo wordt ingericht dat gebruikers zelf de registratie voltooien (*self-service system*), het registratiesysteem volledig openbaar en digitaal is, en waarbij de gebruiker slechts enkele gegevens hoeft in te vullen (*notice-based*). Bovendien dient het verstrekken van informatie verplicht te zijn. Dit is gewenst en leidt ertoe dat de registratie de probleemloze uitvoering van gesecureerde transacties niet in de weg staat.

Krachtens de Chinese Wet op het Goederenrecht (2007) is een afzonderlijk register voor motorvoertuigen opgezet. Dit register, dat wordt beheerd door het Ministerie van Transport, bevat alle goederenrechtelijke rechten die op een motorvoertuig gevestigd kunnen worden. Zo heeft de aanschaf van een motorvoertuig geen werking jegens derden te goeder trouw zolang de registratie niet is voltooid. Het register heeft in algemene zin een privaatrechtelijke en een publiekrechtelijke functie. Het register zal in de toekomst onafhankelijk moeten opereren zonder deel uit te maken van het uniforme registratiesysteem voor roerende zaken en vorderingsrechten.

References

Acquisition and Loss of Ownership of Goods 2011
Acquisition and Loss of Ownership of Goods, edited by Wolfgang Faber and Brigitta Lurger, Munich: Sellier, 2011.

Acton 1909
Baron Acton, The History of Freedom and Other Essays, Toronto: Macmillan, 1909.

Aertsen 2004
Rik Aertsen, De trust: beschouwingen over invoering van de trust in het Nederlandse recht, Deventer: Kluwer, 2004.

Aikens, Lord and Bools 2016
Richard Aikens, Richard Lord and Michael Bools, Bills of Lading, New York: Routledge, 2016.

Akkermans 2008
Bram Akkermans, The Principle of Numerus Clausus in the European Property Law, Antwerp: Intersentia, 2008.

Akkermans and Swadling 2012
Bram Akkermans and William Swadling, Types of Property Rights, in Cases, Materials and Text on Property Law (Sjef van Erp and Bram Akkermans eds.), Oxford etc.: Hart Publishing, 2012.

Akseli 2011
N. Orkun Akseli, International Secured Transactions Law, London: Routledge, 2011.

Akseli 2013
N. Orkun Akseli, The Utility and Efficacy of the UN Convention on the Assignment of Receivables and the Facilitation of Credit, in Availability of Credit and Secured Transactions in a Time of Crisis (N. Orkun Akseli eds.), Cambridge: Cambridge University Press, 2013.

Alces 1995
Peter A. Alces, Abolish the Article 9 Filing System, in 79 Minnesota Law Review, 1995.

Alexander 2009
Gregory S. Alexander, The Social-Obligation Norm in American Property Law, in 94 Cornell Law Review, 2009.

Alexander 2013
Gregory S. Alexander, The Dilution of the Trust, in The Worlds of the Trust (Lionel Smith ed.), Cambridge: Cambridge University Press, 2013.

Alexander and Peñalver 2012
Gregory S. Alexander and Eduardo M. Peñalver, An Introduction to Property Theory, Cambridge: Cambridge University Press, 2012.

Ali 2002
P.A.U. Ali, The Law of Secured Finance, Oxford: Oxford University Press, 2002.

Aristotelous and Christodoulou 2014
P. Aristotelous and E. Christodoulou, Establishment of Trust Registers for Cyprus International Trusts, in 20 Trusts and Trustees, 2014.
Arruñada 2003
Benito Arruñada, Property Enforcement as Organized Consent, in 19 (2) Journal of Law, Economics & Organization, 2003.
Arruñada 2011
Benito Arruñada, Property Titling and Conveyancing, in Research Handbook on the Economics of Property Law (Kenneth Ayotte and Henry E. Smith eds.), Edward Elgar, 2011.
Arruñada 2012
Benito Arruñada, Institutional Foundations of Impersonal Exchange, Chicago: University of Chicago Press, 2012.
Arruñada 2014
Benito Arruñada, The Law of Impersonal Transactions, in The Manufacturing of Markets (Eric Brousseau and Jean-Michel Glachant eds.), Cambridge: Cambridge University Press, 2014.
Arruñada 2015
Benito Arruñada, The Titling Role of Possession, in Law and Economics of Possession (Yun-Chien Chang ed.), Cambridge: Cambridge University Press, 2015.
Ashcroft and Ashcroft 2013
John D. Ashcroft and Janet E. Ashcroft, Law for Business, Australia etc.: Cengage Learning, 2013.
Asser/Bartels & Van Mierlo 2013
S.E. Bartels & A.I.M. van Mierlo, Mr. C. Assers Handleiding tot de beoefening van het Nederlands Burgerlijk Recht 3-IV. Vermogensrecht algemeen, Deventer: Kluwer, 2013.
Asser/Van Mierlo 2016
A.I.M. van Mierlo, Mr. C. Assers Handleiding tot de beoefening van het Nederlands Burgerlijk Recht 3-VI. Zekerheidsrechten, Deventer: Kluwer, 2016.
Augustin and Kregel 1996
Georg Augustin and Wilhelm Kregel, Kommentar zum Bürgerlichen Gesetzbuch, München: C.H. Beck, 1996.

Baeck and Heytens 2019
Joke Rachel Baeck and Lize Heytens, Setting a New Standard for the Harmonization of Secured Transactions Law: The New Belgian Pledge Registry, in Uniform Law Review, 2019.
Baird 1983
Douglas Baird, Notice Filing and the Problem of Ostensible Ownership, in 12 Journal of Legal Studies, 1983.
Baird and Jackson 1983
Douglas Baird and Thomas H. Jackson, Possession and Ownership: An Examination of the Scope of Article 9, in 35 Stanford Law Review, 1983.
Baird and Jackson 1984
Douglas Baird and Thomas H. Jackson, Information, Uncertainty, and the Transfer of Property, in 13 Journal of Legal Study, 1984.

Bamberger and Roth 2003
Heinz Georg Bamberger and Herbert Roth, Kommentar zum Bürgerlichen Gesetzbuch, München: C.H. Beck, 2003.
Banakas 2006
Stathis Banakas, Understanding Trusts: A Comparative View of Property Rights in Europe, in 323 InDret, 2006.
Barrière 2012
Françoise Barrière, The French Fiducie, or the Chaotic Awakening of a Sleeping Beauty, in Re-Imagining the Trust Trusts in Civil Law (Lionel Smith ed.), Cambridge: Cambridge University Press, 2012.
Barrière 2013
François Barrière, The Security Fiducie in French Law, in The Worlds of the Trust (Lionel Smith ed.), Cambridge: Cambridge University Press, 2013.
Baur and Stürner 2009
Fritz Baur, Jürgen F. Baur and Rolf Stürner, Sachenrecht, München: C.H. Beck, 2009.
Baumbach, Hefermehl and Casper 2008
Adolf Baumbach, Wolfgang Hefermehl and Matthias Casper, Wechselgesetz, Scheckgesetz, Recht der kartengestützten Zahlungen, München: C.H. Beck, 2008.
Bayles 1987
Michael D. Bayles, Principles of Law: A Normative Analysis, Dordrecht: D. Reidel Publishing, 1987.
Bazinas 2013
Spyridon V. Bazinas, The Utility and Efficacy of the UNCITRAL Legislative Guide on Secured Transactions, in Availability of Credit and Secured Transactions in a Time of Crisis (N. Orkun Akseli ed.), Cambridge: Cambridge University Press, 2013.
Beale 2016
Hugh Beale, Outline of a Typical PPSA System, in Secured Transactions Law Reform (Louise Gullifer and N. Orkun Akseli eds.), Oxford: Hart Publishing, 2016.
Beale, Bridge, Gullifer and Lomnicka 2018
Hugh Beale, M.G. Bridge, Louise Gullifer and Eva Lomnicka, The Law of Security and Title-Based Financing, Oxford: Oxford University Press, 2018.
Bebchuk and Fried 1996
Lucian A. Bebchuk and Jesse M. Fried, The Uneasy Case for the Priority of Secured Claims in Bankruptcy, in 105 Yale Law Journal, 1996.
Beecher 2006
Susan Beecher, Can the Electronic Bill of Lading Go Paperless?, in 40 The International Lawyer, 2006.
Bell 2015
Abraham Bell, Title in the Shadow of Possession, Law and Economics of Possession (Yun-Chien Chang ed.), Cambridge: Cambridge University Press, 2015.
Bell, Boynton and Whittaker 2008
John Bell, Sophie Boynton and Simon Whittaker, Principles of French Law, Oxford: Oxford University Press, 2008.
Benjamin 2000
Joanna Benjamin, Interests in Securities, Oxford: Oxford University Press, 2000.

Benjamin 2014
Judah Philip Benjamin and M.G. Bridge, Benjamin's Sale of Goods, London: Sweet & Maxwell, 2014.
Bennett 1999
Frank Bennett, Bennett on PPSA (Ontario), North York: CCH, 1999.
Berlee 2018
Anna Berlee, Access to Personal Data in Public Land Registers, The Hague: Eleven International Publishing, 2018.
Bernstein 1992
Lisa Bernstein, Opting out of the Legal System, in 21 Journal of Legal Study, 1992.
Biemans 2007
J.W.A. Biemans, Zeven vragen over de verkrijgende verjaring van vorderingen, in 10 NTBR, 2007.
Bierens 2009
B. Bierens, Revindicatoire aanspraken op giraal geld, Deventer: Kluwer, 2009.
Bisset 2015
Mark Bisset, England & Wales, in Aviation Finance & Leasing 2015 (Mark Bisset ed.), London: Law Business Research, 2015.
Bjerre 1999
Carl S. Bjerre, Secured Transactions Inside Out: Negative Pledge Covenants, Property and Perfection, in 84 Cornell Law Review, 1999.
Black, Hashimzade and Myles 2013
John Black, Nigar Hashimzade and Gareth Myles, A Dictionary of Economics, Oxford: Oxford University Press, 2013 Online Version.
Black's Law Dictionary
Black's Law Dictionary, St. Paul & Minnesota West Publishing, 1990.
Blackburn 2008
Simon Blackburn, The Oxford Dictionary of Philosophy, Oxford University Press, Online, 2008.
Blackstone 1893
William Blackstone, Commentaries on the Laws of England in Four Books (George Sharswood ed.), Philadelphia: J.B. Lippincott, 1893.
Bond 1890
Henry Bond, Possession in the Roman Law, in 6 Law Quarterly Review, 1890.
Bontinck 2017
L. Bontinck, Het pandregister, in Roerende zekerheden na de Pandwet (M.E. Storme ed.), Antwerpen: Intersentia, 2017.
Bork 2016
Reinhard Bork, Allgemeiner Teil des Bürgerlichen Gesetzbuchs, Tübingen: Mohr Siebeck, 2016.
Botchway 2004
Francis Botchway, Paperless Trade: Opportunities, Challenges and Solutions, in 52 International & Comparative Law Quarterly, 2004.
Bouckaert 2006
Boudewijn Bouckaert, Divergences of the Law on Securities, in Divergence of Property Law: An Obstacle to the Internal Market? (Ulrich Drobig etc. eds.), Munich: Sellier, 2006.
Brahn 1985
O.K. Brahn, Ons allernnieuwste 2014, in 5739 WPNR, 1985.

Brahn 1992
O.K. Brahn, Levering en beschikkingsonbevoegdheid, Deventer: Kluwer, 1992.
Braun 2011
Alexandra Braun, Trusts in the Draft Common Frame of Reference, in 70 Cambridge Law Journal, 2011.
Braun and Swadling 2012
Alexandra Braun and William Swadling, Management: Trust, Treuhand and Fiducie, in Cases, Materials and Text on Property Law (Sjef van Erp and Bram Akkermans eds.), Oxford etc.: Hart Publishing, 2012.
Brehm and Berger 2014
Wolfgang Brehm and Christian Berger, Sachenrecht, Tübingen: Mohr Siebeck, 2014.
Bridge 2008
M.G. Bridge, The Scope and Limits of Security Interests, in The Future of Secured Credit in Europe (Horst Eidenmüller and Eva-Maria Kieninger eds.), Berlin/New York: De Gruyter, 2008.
Bridge 2009
M.G. Bridge, England and Wales, in Cross-Border Security over Receivables (Harry C. Sigman and Eva-Maria Kieninger eds.), Munich: Sellier, 2009.
Bridge 2013
Stuart Bridge, *Street v. Mountford* (1985), in Landmark Cases in Land Law (Nigel P. Gravells ed.), Oxford: Oxford University Press, 2013.
Bridge 2014
M.G. Bridge, The Sale of Goods, Oxford: Oxford University Press, 2014.
Bridge 2015
M.G. Bridge, Personal Property Law, Oxford: Oxford University Press, 2015.
Bridge 2017
M.G. Bridge, Secured Credit Legislation, in International and Comparative Secured Transactions Law: Essays in Honour of Roderick A. Macdonald (Spyridon V. Bazinas and N. Orkun Akseli eds.), London: Hart Publishing, 2017.
Bridge, Gullifer, McMeel and Worthington 2013
M.G. Bridge, Louise Gullifer, Gerard McMeel and Sarah Worthington, The Law of Personal Property, London: Sweet & Maxwell, 2013.
Bridge, Macdonald, Simmonds and Walsh 1999
M.G. Bridge, Roderick A. Macdonald, Ralph L. Simmonds and Catherine Walsh, Formalism, Functionalism, and Understanding the Law of Secured Transactions, in 44 McGill Law Journal, 1999.
Bright 2007
Susan Bright, Landlord and Tenant Law in Context, Oxford: Oxford University Press, 2007.
Brinkmann 2008
Moritz Brinkmann, The Position of Secured Creditors in Insolvency, in The Future of Secured Credit in Europe (Horst Eidenmüller and Eva-Maria Kieninger eds.), Berlijn/New York: De Gruyter, 2008.
Brinkmann 2016
Moritz Brinkmann, The Peculiar Approach of German Law in the Field of Secured Transactions and Why It Has Worked (So Far), in Secured Transactions Law Reform (Louise Gullifer and N. Orkun Akseli eds.), Oxford: Hart Publishing, 2016.

Brown 2016
David Brown, Australian Secured Transactions Law Reform, in Secured Transactions Law Reform (Louise Gullifer and N. Orkun Akseli eds.), Oxford: Hart Publishing, 2016.
Brox and Henssler 2009
Hans Brox and Martin Henssler, Handelsrecht, München: C.H. Beck, 2009.
Buckland 1950
W.W. Buckland, A Text-Book on Roman Law, Cambridge: Cambridge University Press, 1950.
Buckland and McNair 1952
W.W. Buckland and A.D. McNair, Roman Law and Common Law, Cambridge: Cambridge University Press, 1952.
Bülow 2004
Peter Bülow, Heidelberger Kommentar zum Wechselgesetz, Heidelberg: C.F. Müller, 2004.
Bülow 2012
Peter Bülow, Recht der Kreditsicherheiten: Sachen und Rechte, Personen, Heidelberg: C.F. Müller, 2012.
Byles 2002
John Barnard Byles, Maurice Henry Megrah and Frank Raymond Ryder, Byles on Bills of Exchange, London: Sweet & Maxwell, 2002.

Canaris 1978
Claus-Wilhelm Canaris, Die Verdinglichung obligatorischer Rechte, in Festschrift für Werner Flume zum 70. Geburtstag, Köln: Dr. Otto Schmidt, 1978.
Cardwell 2000
Michael Cardwell, Milk and Livestock Quotas as Property, in 168 Edinburgh Law Review, 2000.
Carlson 1986
David Gray Carlson, Rationality, Accident, and Priority under Article 9 of the Uniform Commercial Code, in 71 Minnesota Law Review, 1986.
Cartwright 2016
John Cartwright, Contract Law: An Introduction to the English Law of Contract for the Civil Lawyer, Oxford: Oxford University Press, 2016.
Castellano 2016
G.G. Castellano, The New Italian Law for Non-Possessory Pledges, in 4 Butterworths Journal of International Banking and Financial Law, 2016.
Caterina 2004
Raffaele Caterina, Concepts and Remedies in the Law of Possession, in 8 Edinburgh Law Review, 2004.
Chalmers 1919
Mackenzie Chalmers and Kenneth Chalmers, A Digest of the Law of Bills of Exchange, Promissory Notes, Cheques, and Negotiable Securities, London: Stevens and Sons, 1919.
Chang 2015
Yun-Chien Chang, The Economy in Concept and Possession, in Law and Economics of Possession (Yun-Chien Chang ed.), Cambridge: Cambridge University Press, 2015.

Cherry 1966
C. Cherry, On Human Communication, Cambridge: Cambridge University Press, 1966.
Cheshire and Burn 2011
Geoffrey Cheshire, Edward Burn and John Cartwright, Cheshire and Burn's Modern Law of Real Property, Oxford: Oxford University Press, 2011.
Chui 2007
Wing Hong Chui, Quantitative Legal Research, in Research Methods for Law (Mike McConville and Wing Hong Chui eds.), Edinburgh: Edinburgh University Press, 2007.
Claringbould 1998
M.H. Claringbould, Het cognossement in het goederenrecht, in Van beheering, Deventer: Gouda Quint, 1998.
Clarke and Kohler 2005
Alison Clarke and Paul Kohler, Property Law, Commentary and Materials, Cambridge: Cambridge University Press, 2005.
Clarkson, Miller and Cross 2017
Kenneth W. Clarkson, Roger LeRoy Miller and Frank B. Cross, Business Law: Text and Cases, Stamford: Cengage, 2017.
Clerk and Lindsell 2014
J.F. Clerk, W.H.B. Lindsell, Michael A. Jones and A.M. Dugdale, Clerk and Lindsell on Torts, London: Sweet & Maxwell, 2014.
Coarse 1937
R.H. Coarse, The Nature of the Firm, in 4 Economica, 1937.
Coarse 1960
R.H. Coarse, The Problem of Social Cost, in 3 Journal of Law and Economics, 1960.
Cohen 1954
Felix S. Cohen, Dialogue on Private Property, in 9 Rutgers Law Review, 1954.
Coing 1973
Helmut Coing, Die Treuhand kraft privaten Rechtsgeschäfts, München: C.H. Beck, 1973.
Cole 2016
Daniel H. Cole, Origins of Emissions Trading in Theory and Early Practice, in Research Handbook on Emissions Trading (Stefan E. Weishaar ed.), Edward Elgar, 2016.
Corral 2013
Julie del Corral, De leveringsplicht bij de overdracht van roerende lichamelijke goederen, Antwerpen: Intersentia, 2013.
Corral 2014
Julie del Corral, Transfer of Generic Goods in So-Called Consensual Transfer Systems, in 3 European Property Law Journal, 2014.
Critchley 1998
P. Critchley, Taking Formalities Seriously, in Land Law: Themes and Perspectives (S. Bright and J. Dewar eds.), Oxford: Oxford University Press, 1998.
Cuming 1994 (1)
R.C.C. Cuming, Canadian Bankruptcy Law: A Secured Creditor's Heaven, in 24 Canadian Business Law Journal, 1994.

Cuming 1994 (2)
R.C.C. Cuming, Outline of a Modern Legal Regime for the Regulation of Secured Financing Transactions, Rome, 1994.
Cuming, Walsh and Wood 2012
R.C.C. Cuming, C. Walsh, and R. Wood, Personal Property Security Law, Toronto: Irwin, 2012.
Curwen 2007
Nick Curwen, The Bill of Lading as a Document of Title at Common Law, in Mountbatten Yearbook of Legal Studies (P. Park and B. Andoh eds), Southampton: Southampton Solent University, 2007.

Dalhuisen 2010
J.H. Dalhuisen, European Private Law: Moving from a Closed to an Open System of Proprietary Rights, in 5 Edinburgh Law Review, 2010.
Dalhuisen 2016
J.H. Dalhuisen, Dalhuisen on Transnational Comparative, Commercial, Financial and Trade Law (Volume 2), Oxford etc.: Hart Publishing, 2016.
Davies 1994 (1)
Iwan R. Davies, Title Problems and Motor Vehicle Financing: A Call for Reform: Part 1, in 13 International Banking and Financial Law, 1994.
Davies 1994 (2)
Iwan R. Davies, Ostensible Ownership and Motor Vehicle Financing in England: Antipodean Insights, in 9 Journal of International Banking Law, 1994.
Davies 1995 (1)
Iwan R. Davies, Wrongful Dispositions of Motor Vehicles: A Legal Quagmire, in Journal of Business Law, 1995, January.
Davies 1995 (2)
Iwan R. Davies, Wrongful Dispositions of Motor Vehicles in England, in 23 Anglo American Law Review, 1995.
Davies 2001
Iwan R. Davies, Registration Documents and Certification of Title of Motor Vehicles, in 9 Journal of Business Law, 2001.
Davies 2004
Iwan R. Davies, The Reform of English Personal Property Security Law: Functionalism and Article 9 of the Uniform Commercial Code, in 24 Legal Studies, 2004.
DCFR 2009
Principles, Definitions and Model Rules of European Private Law, edited by Christian von Bar etc., Munich: Sellier, 2009.
De Boer 1982
B. de Boer, Het bewind, Zwolle: W.E.J. Tjeenk Willink, 1982.
De Bie 1991
Eric de Bie, Juridische aspecten van de negatieve zekerheidsclausule, in 27 Jura Falconis, 1991.
De Groot 2012
Selma de Groot, Three Questions in Relation to the Scope of Book IX DCFR, in The Future of European Property Law (Sjef van Erp etc. eds.), Munich: Sellier, 2012.
De Jong 2012
Th.F. de Jong, De structuur van het goederenrecht, Deventer: Kluwer, 2012.

De Jong, Krans and Wissink 2018
G.T. de Jong, H.B. Krans and M.H. Wissink, Verbintenissenrecht algemeen, Deventer: Kluwer, 2014.
De Waal 2000
M.J. De Waal, The Uniformity of Ownership, Numerus Clausus and the Reception of the Trust into South African Law, in 3 European Review of Private Law, 2000.
Demsetz 1967
Harold Demsetz, Towards a Theory of Property Rights, in 57 The American Economic Review, 1967.
Dekker 2003
H.A.L. Dekker, The Invisible Line: Land Reform, Land Tenure Security and Land Registration, London etc.: Routledge, 2003.
Dernburg 1894
Heinrich Dernburg, Pandekten: Band 1, Berlin: H.W. Müller, 1894.
Devonshire 1997
Peter Devonshire, The Mortgagee as Fiduciary: Comparative Perspectives on an Emerging Doctrine, in The Reform of Property Law (Paul Jackson and David C. Wilde eds.), Ashgate, 1997.
Dirix 2006
Eric Dirix, Effect of Security Rights vis-a-vis Third Parties, in Divergence of Property Law: An Obstacle to the Internal Market? (Ulrich Drobig etc. eds.), Munich: Sellier, 2006.
Dirix and Sagaert 2014
Eric Dirix and Vincent Sagaert, The New Belgian Act on Security Rights in Movable Property, in 3 European Property Law Journal, 2014.
Dobbs 1999
Andrew Dobbs, Possession and Occupation, in 10 King's College Law Journal, 1999.
Dobinson and Johns 2007
Ian Dobinson and Francis Johns, Qualitative Legal Research, in Research Methods for Law (Mike McConville and Wing Hong Chui eds.), Edinburgh: Edinburgh University Press, 2007.
Donahue 1980
Charles Donahue, The Future of the Concept of Property Predicted from Its Past, in Property (J. Roland Pennock and John W. Chapman eds.), New York: New York University Press, 1980.
Drobnig 1993
Ulrich Drobnig, Das neue niederländische bürgerliche Gesetzbuch aus vergleichender und deutscher Sicht, in 1 European Review of Private Law, 1993.
Drobnig 2011
Ulrich Drobnig, Security Rights in Movables, in Towards a European Civil Code (A. Hartkamp and others eds.), Nijmegen: Ars Aequi Libri, 2011.
Du Plessis 2015
Paul Du Plessis, Borkowski's Textbook on Roman Law, Oxford: Oxford University Press, 2015.
Dubarry 2016
Julien Dubarry, Zum Verhältnis zwischen Grundbuchfunktionen und Leitprinzipien des Sachenrechts, in Das Grundbuch im Europa des 21. Jahrhunderts (Arkadiusz Wudarski ed.), Berlin: Duncker & Humblot, 2016.

Dubovec 2006
Marek Dubovec, The Problems and Possibilities for Using Electronic Bills of Lading as Collateral, in 23 Arizona Journal of International & Comparative Law, 2006.
Dubovec 2014
Marek Dubovec, The Law of Securities, Commodities and Bank Accounts, Glos/Massachusetts: Edward Elgar, 2014.
Duggan 2011
Anthony Duggan, A PPSA Registration Primer, in 35 Melbourne University Law Review, 2011.
Duggan 2014
Anthony Duggan, The Australian PPSA from a Canadian Perspective: Some Comparative Reflections, 40 Monash University Law Review, 2014.

Edwards and Stockwell 2011
Richard Edwards and Nigel Stockwell, Trusts and Equity, Harlow etc.: Pearson, 2011.
Eger 2001
Thomas Eger, Bankruptcy Regulations and the New German Insolvency Law from an Economic Point of View, in 1 European Journal of Law and Economics, 2001.
Eggens 1960
J. Eggens, Over de verhouding tussen eigendom en verbintenis, in Mededelingen der Koninklijke Nederlandse akademie van wetenschappen, Amsterdam: Noord-Hollandse Uitgeversmaatschappij, 1960.
Elgueta 2010
Giacomo Rojas Elgueta, Divergences and Convergences of Common Law and Civil Law Traditions on Asset Partitioning, in 12 University of Pennsylvania Journal of Business Law, 2010.
Ellickson 1991
Robert C. Ellickson, Order without Law: How Neighbors Settle Disputes, Harvard: Harvard University Press, 1991.
Ellickson and Thorland 1995
Robert C. Ellickson and Charles D. Thorland, Ancient Land Law, in 71 Chicago-Kent Law Review, 1995.
Emerich 2014
Yaëll Emerich, Why Protect Possession?, in The Consequences of Possession (Eric Descheemaeker ed.), Edinburgh: Edinburgh University Press, 2014.
Emerich 2017
Yaëll Emerich, Possession, in Comparative Property Law (Michele Graziadei and Lionel Smith eds.), Cheltenham etc.: Edward Elgar, 2017.
Emerich 2018
Yaëll Emerich, Conceptualising Property Law, Cheltenham etc.: Edward Elgar, 2018.
Ernst 1993
Wolfgang Ernst, Ist der gutgläubige Mobiliarerwerb eine Rechtsscheinwirkung?, in Festschrift für Joachim Gernhuber zum 70. Geburtstag, Tübingen: Mohr Siebeck, 1993.

Faber 2012
Wolfgang Faber, Book VIII DCFR on Acquisition and Loss of Ownership of Goods, in The Draft Common Frame of Reference: National and Comparative Perspectives (Vincent Sagaert etc. eds.), Antwerp: Intersentia, 2012.
Faber 2014
Wolfgang Faber, Proprietary Security Rights in Movables, in 22 Juridica International, 2014.
Fairfield 2005
Joshua A.T. Fairfield, Virtual Property, in 85 Boston University Law Review, 2005.
Fesevur 2005
J.E. Fesevur, Goederenrechtelijke colleges, Nijmegen: Ars Aequi Libri, 2005.
Finch 1999
Vanessa Finch, Security, Insolvency and Risk, in 62 The Modern Law Review, 1999.
Finch 2009
Vanessa Finch, Corporate Insolvency Law: Perspectives and Principles, Cambridge: Cambridge University Press, 2009.
Finlay 2012
John Finlay, Trusts, Dundee: Dundee University Press, 2012.
Fix 2014
Christian Fix, Die Fiducie-Sûreté, Tübingen: Mohr Siebeck, 2014.
Frisby and Jones 2009
Sandra Frisby and Michael Jones, National Report on the Transfer of Movables in England and Wales, in National Reports on the Transfer of Movables in Europe Volume 2 (Wolfgang Faber and Brigitta Lurger eds.), Munich: Sellier, 2009.
Füller 2006
Jens Thomas Füller, Eigenständiges Sachenrecht?, Tübingen: Mohr Siebeck, 2006.
Furmston and Chuah 2013
Michael Furmston and Jason Chuah, Commercial Law, London etc.: Pearson, 2013.

Gabriel 2000
Henry Deeb Gabriel, The New Zealand Personal Property Securities Act: A Comparison with the North American Model for Personal Property Security, in 34 The International Lawyer, 2000.
Gallants 2011
Thomas P. Gallants, The New Direction of American Trust Law, in 97 Iowa Law Review, 2011.
Gamble 2013
Andrew Gamble, Hayek and Liberty, in 25 Critical Review, 2013.
Gao 2019
高圣平：《担保法前言问题与判解研究（第二卷）》，北京：人民法院出版社。
English translation: Shengping Gao, Research on Frontier Issues and Judgements of Security Law (Volume 2), Beijing: People's Court Press, 2019.
Gardiner 2008
Caterina Gardiner, National Report on the Transfer of Movables in Ireland, in National Reports on the Transfer of Movables in Europe Volume 2 (Wolfgang Faber and Brigitta Lurger eds.), Munich: Sellier, 2008.

Gardner 2011
Simon Gardner, An Introduction to the Law of Trusts, Oxford: Oxford University Press, 2011.
Gedye 2011
Mike Gedye, The Development of New Zealand's Secured Transactions Jurisprudence, in 34 (2) UNSW Law Journal, 2011.
Gedye 2013
Mike Gedye, A Hoary Chestnut Resurrected, in 37 (1) Melbourne University Law Review, 2013.
Gedye 2016
Mike Gedye, The New Zealand Perspective, in Secured Transactions Law Reform (Louise Gullifer and N. Orkun Akseli eds.), Oxford: Hart Publishing, 2016.
Gengaharen 2013
Rasiah Gengatharen, The Acquisition of Pre-Encumbered Personal Property in the Ordinary Course of the Seller's Business, in 41 Australian Business Law Review, 2013.
Geva 2007
Benjamin Geva, Recent International Developments in the Law of Negotiable Instruments and Payment and Settlement Systems, in 42 Texas International Law Journal, 2007.
Geva 2015
Benjamin Geva, From Paper to Electronic Order: The Digitalization of the Check in the USA, in 4 Penn State Journal of Law & International Affairs, 2015.
Ghestin and Goubeaux 1994
Jacques Ghestin and Gilles Goubeaux, Traité de Droit Civil: Introduction Générale, Paris: LGDJ, 1994.
Gibbons 2006
Thomas Gibbons, The First Four Years: New Zealand's Personal Property Securities Act in Practice, in 14 Waikato Law Review, 2006.
Giese 1948
Friedrich Giese, Einführung in die Rechtswissenschaft, Wiesbaden: Gabler, 1948.
Gilmore 1999
Grant Gilmore, Security Interests in Personal Property, New Jersey: The Lawbook Exchange, 1999.
Ginossar 1979
Shalev Ginossar, Rights in Rem: A New Approach, in 14 Israel Law Review, 1979.
Goldsworth 1997
John Goldsworth, Formalities of Trust Formation and Dealings in Equitable Interests, in 3.6 Trusts & Trustees, 1997.
Gomes and Nóbrega 2011
José Caramelo-Gomes and José Carlos de Medeiros Nóbrega, National Report on the Transfer of Movables in Portugal, in National Report on the Transfer of Movables in Europe Volume 4 (Wolfgang Faber and Brigitta Lurger eds.), Munich: Sellier, 2011.
Goode 1991
Roy Goode, Abstract Payment Undertakings, in Essays for Patrick Atiyah (P. Cane and J. Stapleton eds.), Oxford: Oxford University Press, 1991.

Goode 2010
Roy Goode and Ewan McKendrick, Goode on Commercial Law, London: Sweet & Maxwell, 2010.
Goode 2013
Roy Goode and Louise Gullifer, Goode on Legal Problems of Credit and Security, London: Sweet & Maxwell, 2013.
Goode, Kronke and Mckendrick 2015
Roy Goode, Herbert Kronke and Ewan Mckendrick, Transnational Commercial Law, Oxford: Oxford University Press, 2015.
Gordley 2013
James Gordley, The Jurists: A Critical History, Oxford: Oxford University Press, 2013.
Gordon 1970
William M. Gordon, Studies in the Transfer of Property by Traditio, Aberdeen: Aberdeen University Press, 1970.
Gotzen 1979
F. Gotzen, Zakelijke rechten: plaats en aantal in het Burgerlijk Recht, in 36 Rechtkundig Weekblad, 1979.
Gray 2009
Kevin Gray and Susan Francis Gray, Elements of Land Law, Oxford: Oxford University Press, 2009.
Graziadei 2012
Michele Graziadei, Recognition of Common Law Trusts in Civil Law Jurisdictions under The Hague Trusts Convention with Particular Regard to the Italian, in Re-imagining the Trust Trusts in Civil Law (Lionel Smith ed.), Cambridge: Cambridge University Press, 2012.
Greco 2008
Alessio Greco, National Report on the Transfer of Movables in Italy, in National Reports on the Transfer of Movables in Europe Volume 1 (Wolfgang Faber and Brigitta Lurger eds.), Munich: Sellier, 2008.
Gretton 2007
George L. Gretton, Ownership and Its Objects, in 71 The Rabel Journal of Comparative and International Private Law, 2007.
Grey 1980
Thomas C. Grey, The Disintegration of Property, in Property (J. Roland Pennock and John W. Chapman eds.), New York: New York University Press, 1980.
Grundmann 1998
Stefan Grundmann, The Evolution of Trust and Treuhand in the 20th Century, in Itinera Fiduciae (Richard Helmholz and Reinhard Zimmermann eds.), Berlin: Duncker & Humblot, 1998.
Guest 2016
A.G. Guest, Chalmers and Guest on Bills of Exchange and Cheques, London: Sweet & Maxwell, 2016.
Guest and Liew 2018
A.G. Guest and Ying Khai Liew, Guest on the Law of Assignment, London: Sweet & Maxwell, 2018.
Gullifer 2012
Louise Gullifer, Personal Property Security Law, in 27 Butterworths Journal of International Banking and Financial Law, London: Sweet & Maxwell, 2012.

Gullifer 2015
Louise Gullifer, Piecemeal Reform, in Research Handbook on Secured Financing in Commercial Transactions (Frederique Dahan ed.), Edward Elgar, 2015.
Gullifer 2016
Louise Gullifer, Discussion Paper Series: Registration, 2016.

Haag and Peglow 2008
Hendrik Haag and Oliver Peglow, Germany, in Security over Receivables: An International Handbook (William Johnston ed.), Oxford: Oxford University Press, 2008.
Haentjens 2007
Matthias Haentjens, Harmonisation of Securities Law: Custody and Transfer of Securities in European Private Law, Deventer: Kluwer, 2007.
Hager 1990
Johannes Hager, Verkehrsschutz durch redlichen Erwerb, München: C.H. Beck, 1990.
Hammerstein 1998
A. Hammerstein, Betalingsverkeer (Wissel, Orderbriefje en Cheque), Deventer: Kluwer, 1998.
Hamwijk 2011
D.J.Y. Hamwijk, Public Filing with Regard to Non-Possessory Security Rights in Tangible Assets as Contemplated by the DCFR, in 5 European Review of Private Law, 2011.
Hamwijk 2012
D.J.Y. Hamwijk, The Puzzling Concepts of Publicity and Possession: To the Heart of Property Law, in 1 European Property Law Journal, 2012.
Hamwijk 2014
D.J.Y. Hamwijk, Publicity in Secured Transactions Law, Doctoral Thesis, Amsterdam University, 2014.
Hansmann and Mattei 1998
Henry Hansmann and Ugo Mattei, Functions of Trust Law: A Comparative Legal and Economic Analysis, in 73 New York University Law Review, 1998.
Hansmann and Kraakman 2000
Henry Hansmannt and Reinier Kraakman, The Essential Role of Organizational Law, in 110 Yale Law Journal, 2000.
Hansmann and Kraakman 2002
Henry Hansmann and Reinier Kraakman, Property, Contract, and Verification: the Numerus Clausus Problem and the Divisibility of Rights, in 31 Journal of Legal Studies, 2002.
Hästad 2006
Torgny Hästad, General Aspects of Transfer and Creation of Property Rights, including Security Rights, in Divergence of Property Law: An Obstacle to the Internal Market? (Ulrich Drobig etc. eds.), Munich: Sellier, 2006.
Hausmann 1996
Jens Hausmann, The Value of Public-Notice Filing under Uniform Commercial Code Article 9, in 25 Georgia Journal of International and Comparative Law, 1996.
Hayton 2016
David Hayton, Reflections on the Hague Trusts Convention after 30 Years, 12 Journal of Private International Law, 2016.

Hedemann 1927
Justus Wilhelm Hedemann, Einführung in die Rechtswissenschaft, Berlin/Leipzig: De Gruyter, 1927.
Hedley and Hedley 2001
William Hedley and Richard Hedley, Bills of Exchange and Bankers' Documentary Credits, London: Sweet & Maxwell, 2001.
Hegel 2005
G.W.F. Hegel, Philosophy of Right, translated by S.W. Dyde, Kitchener: Batoche, 2005.
Heilbron 2011
M.A. Heilbron, Bezitloze zekerheidsrechten op roerende zaken naar Nederlands, Duits en Amerikaans recht, in 2 Vermogensrechtelijke Analyses, 2011.
Herrmann 2003
Anne Herrmann, Sicherungsabtretung und Verpfändung der Ansprüche aus dem Lebensversicherungsvertrag durch den Versicherungsnehmer, Berlin: TENEA Verlag, 2003.
Heymann/Horn 2005
Norbert Horn, Heymann Handelsgesetzbuch (ohne Seerecht) Kommentar: Band 4, Berlin: De Gruyter, 2005.
Hijma, Van Dam, Valk and Van Schendel 2016
Jac. Hijma, C.C. van Dam, W.L. Valk and W.A.M. van Schendel, Rechtshandeling en overeenkomst, Deventer: Kluwer, 2016.
Hill 2001
Jonathan Hill, The Proprietary Character of Possession, in Modern Studies in Property Law (Elizabeth Cooke ed.), Oxford: Oxford University Press, 2001.
Hinteregger 2012
Monika Hinteregger, The Protection of Property Rights, in Cases, Materials and Text on Property Law, (Sjef van Erp and Bram Akkermans eds.), Oxford etc.: Hart Publishing, 2012.
Hinteregger and Van Vliet 2012
Monika Hinteregger and Lars van Vliet, Transfer, in Cases, Materials and Text on Property Law (Sjef van Erp and Bram Akkermans eds.), Oxford etc.: Hart Publishing, 2012.
Ho 2013
Lusina Ho, Trusts: The Essentials, in The Worlds of the Trust (Lionel Smith ed.), Cambridge: Cambridge University Press, 2013.
Hohfeld 1917
Wesley N. Hohfeld, Fundamental Legal Conceptions as Applied in Judicial Reasoning, in 26 Yale Law Journal, 1917.
Holdsworth 1935
William Searle Holdsworth, A History of English Law (Volume III), London: Methuen & Co. Ltd, 1935.
Hondius 1982
Ewout Hondius, Recodification of the Law in the Netherlands: The New Civil Code Experience, in 29 Netherlands International Law Review, 1982.
Honoré 1960
A.M. Honoré, Rights of Exclusion and Immunities against Divesting, in 34 Tulane Law Review, 1960.

Honoré 1987
A.M. Honoré, Ownership, in Making Laws Bind, Oxford: Oxford University Press, 1987.
Hudson 2003
Alastair Hudson, Equity and Trusts, London/New York: Routledge, 2003.
Hudson 2014
Alastair Hudson, Equity and Trusts, London/New York: Routledge, 2014.
Hueck and Canaris 1986
Alfred Hueck and Claus-Wilhelm Canaris, Recht der Wertpapiere, München: C.H. Beck, 1986.
Huijgen 1995
W.G. Huijgen, Economische eigendom, Zwolle: W.E.J. Tjeenk Willink, 1995.
Huijgen 2017
W.G. Huijgen, Koop en verkoop van onroerende zaken, Deventer: Kluwer, 2017.
Hutchinson 2013
Terry Hutchinson, Doctrinal Research: Researching the Jury, in Research Methods in Law (Dawn Watkins and Mandy Burton eds.), New York: Routledge, 2013.
Hübner 1918
Rudolf Hübner, A History of Germanic Private Law, translated by Francis S. Philbrick, Boston: The Lawbook Exchange, 1918.

Igbinosun 2020
Betha Igbinosun, Security Interests in Personal Property and the Nigerian Secured Transactions in Movable Assets Act 2017: An Appraisal, in 64 (3) Journal of African Law, 2020.

Jackson 1982
Thomas H. Jackson, Bankruptcy, Non-Bankruptcy, Entitlements, and the Creditors' Bargain, in 91 Yale Law Journal, 1982.
Jackson and Kronman 1979
Thomas H. Jackson and Anthony T. Kronman, Secured Financing and Priorities among Creditors, in 88 Yale Law Journal, 1979.
Jacoby 2007
Florian Jacoby, Das private Amt, Tübingen: Mohr Siebeck, 2007.
James 1991
Jennifer James, Richardson's Guide to Negotiable Instruments, London: Sweet & Maxwell, 1991.
Jansen 2007
C.G.H. Jansen, Fiduciaire verhoudingen in historisch perspectief, in Fiduciaire verhoudingen (S.C.J.J. Kortmann etc. eds.), Deventer: Kluwer, 2007.
Jansen 2017
Ruud Jansen, Algemene beginselen bij de verpanding van roerende goederen, in Roerende zekerheden na de Pandwet (M.E. Storm ed.), Antwerpen: Intersentia, 2017.
Ji 2019
季奎明：《中国式信托登记的困境与出路》，载《政治与法律》2019年第5期。
English translation: Kuiming Ji, On the Plight of Chinese-Styled Trust Registration and Its Solutions, in 5 Politics and Law, 2019.

Kant 1799
Immanuel Kant, The Metaphysics of Morals, translated by Kant's Essays and Treatises, London: William Richardson, 1799.
Kanu 2018
Michael Imran Kanu, Access to Credit and Personal Property Security Law Reform in Africa: Examining the Legal Framework in Sierra Leone with Comparative Perspectives from England and United States, Doctoral Thesis of Central European University, 2018.
Kaptein 2012
F.J.L. Kaptein, Naar een elektronische registratie van onderhandse pandakten? in 5 Maandblad voor Vermogensrecht, 2012.
Kaptein 2016
F.J.L. Kaptein, Pandrecht, Doctoral Thesis: Rijksuniversiteit Groningen, 2016.
Karner 2006
Ernst Karner, Gutgläubiger Mobiliarerwerb, New York/Wien: Springer, 2006.
Kateb 2003
George Kateb, A Reading of On Liberty, in On Liberty John Stuart Mill, New Haven/London: Yale University Press, 2003.
Katz 2008
Larissa Katz, Exclusion and Exclusivity in Property Law, in 58 University of Toronto Law Journal, 2008.
Keay, Boraine and Burdette 2001
Andrew Keay, Andre Boraine and David Burdette, Preferential Debts in Corporate Insolvency: A Comparative Study, in 10 International Insolvency Review, 2001.
Keijser 2006
Thomas Keijser, Financial Collateral Arrangements, Deventer: Kluwer, 2006.
Kelly 2014
Daniel B. Kelly, The Right to Include, in 63 Emory Law Journal, 2014.
Kieninger 2003
Eva-Maria Kieninger etc., Security Rights in Movable Property in European Private Law (Eva-Maria Kieninger ed.), Cambridge: Cambridge University Press, 2003.
Kieninger 2006
Eva-Maria Kieninger, European Regulation of Security Rights, in Divergences of Property Law: An Obstacle to the Internal Market? (Ulrich Drobnig etc. eds.), Munich: Sellier, 2006.
Kieninger 2007
E.-M. Kieninger, Evaluation: A Common Core?, in Cross-Border Security over Tangibles (Harry C. Sigman and E.-M. Kieninger eds.), Munich: Sellier, 2007.
Kieninger 2008
E.-M. Keininger, The Scope and Limits of Security Interests, in The Future of Secured Credit in Europe (Horst Eidenmüller and E.-M. Kieninger eds.), Berlin/New York: De Gruyter, 2008.
Kindl 1999
Johann Kindl, Rechtsscheintatbestande und ihre rückwirkende Beseitigung, Berlin/Heidelberg: Springer, 1999.

Kleyn 2014
Duard Kleyn, The Protection of Quasi-Possession in South African Law, The Consequences of Possession (Eric Descheemaeker ed.), Edinburgh: Edinburgh University Press, 2014.
Kortmann 2006
S.C.J.J. Kortmann, De tweedehands Volvo, in 55 AAe, 2006.
Kötz 1963
Hein Kötz, Trust und Treuhand, Göttingen: Vandenhoeck & Ruprechtht, 1963.
Kötz 1999 (1)
H. Kötz, National Report for Germany, in Principles of European Trust Law (D.J. Hayton, S.C.J.J. Kortmann and H.L.E. Verhagen eds.), Deventer: Kluwer, 1999.
Kötz 1999 (2)
H. Kötz, The Modern Development of Trust Law in Germany, in Modern International Developments in Trust Law (D. Hayton ed.), Deventer: Kluwer, 1999.
Kötz 2010
H. Kötz, Third Party Consequences, in Cases, Materials and Text on Contract law (Hugh Beale etc. eds.), Oxford: Oxford University Press, 2010.
Krier 1990
James E. Krier, The (Unlikely) Death of Property, in 13 Harvard Journal of Law & Public Policy, 1990.
Krier and Serkin 2015
James E. Krier and Christopher Serkin, The Possession Heuristic, in Law and Economics of Possession (Yun-Chien Chang ed.), Cambridge: Cambridge University Press, 2015.
Krimphove 2006
Dieter Krimphove, Das europäische Sachenrecht, Lohmar/Köln: Josef Eul, 2006.

Larenz 1982
Karl Larenz, Lehrbuch des Schuldrechts: Allgemeiner Teil, München: C.H. Beck, 1982.
Larenz 1991
Karl Larenz, Methodenlehre der Rechtswissenschaft, Berlin: Springer, 1991.
Lau 2011
M.W. Lau, The Economic Structure of Trusts: Towards a Property-Based Approach, Oxford: Oxford University Press, 2011.
Law and Martin 2014
Jonathan Law and Elizabeth A. Martin, A Dictionary of Law, Oxford: Oxford University Press, 2014.
Leavy 2007
James Leavy, France, in Cross-Border Security over Tangibles (Harry C. Sigman and Eva-Maria Kieninger eds.), Munich: Sellier, 2007.
Lebon 2010
Caroline Lebon, Het goederenrechtelijk statuut van schuldvorderingen, Antwerpen: Intersentia, 2010.
Lebon 2012
Caroline Lebon, Property Rights in Respect of Claims, in Cases, Materials and Text on Property Law (Sjef van Erp and Bram Akkermans eds.), Oxford etc.: Hart Publishing, 2012.
Lee 1956
R.W. Lee, The Elements of Roman Law, London: Sweet & Maxwell, 1956.

Leebron 1991
David W. Leebron, Limited Liability, Tort Victims, and Creditors, in 91 Columbia Law Review, 1991.
Lilja 2011
Martin Lilja, National Report on the Transfer of Movables in Sweden, in National Reports on the Transfer of Movables in Europe Volume 5 (Wolfgang Faber and Brigitta Lurger eds.), 2011.
Lilja 2014
Martin Lilja, The Relevance of Concepts for the Transfer of Movables under the Uniform Commercial Code, in 3 European Property Law Journal, 2014.
Limmer 2013
Peter Limmer, Property Transactions and Certainty of Title Transfer, in 9 European Property Law Journal, 2013.
Lipsky 2010
Max Lipsky, Statutenwechsel im italienischen Sachenrecht, Frankfurt: Peter Lang, 2010.
Lipson 2005
Jonathan C. Lipson, Secrets and Liens: The End of Notice in Commercial Finance Law, in 21 Emory Bankruptcy Developments Journal, 2005.
Logmans 2011
Huibert Logmans, Zekerheid op lading, Zutphen: Paris, 2011.
Loof 2012
Willem Loof, Contractualisation of Ownership: Creating Beneficial Interests in Civil Law Jurisdictions, in Property Law Perspectives (Bram Akkermans and Eveline Ramaekers eds.), Antwerp: Intersentia, 2012.
Loof 2016
W. Loof, De systematiek van voorwaardelijke eigendom, in 7123 WPNR, 2016.
LoPucki 1994
Lynn M. LoPucki, The Unsecured Creditor's Bargain, in 80 Virginia Law Review, 1994.
LoPucki, Abraham and Delahaye 2012
Lynn M. LoPucki, Arvin I. Abraham and Bernd P. Delahaye, Optimizing English and American Security Interests, in 88 Notre Dame Law Review, 2012.
Lubbe 2006
Gerhard Lubbe, Assignment, in European Contract Law: Scots and South African Perspectives (Hector L. MacQueen and Reinhard Zimmermann eds.), Edinburgh: Edinburgh University Press, 2006.
Lucy 2007
Illiam Lucy, Philosophy of Private Law, Oxford: Oxford University Press, 2007.
Lueck and Miceli 2007
D. Lueck and T.J. Miceli, Property Law, in Handbook of Law and Economics (A. Mitchell Polinsky and Steven Shavell eds.), Amsterdam etc.: North-Holland, 2007.
Lukas 2004
M. Lukas, Effect of Security Rights vis-à-vis Third Person, in Divergence of Property Law, An Obstacle to the Internal Market? (U. Drobnig etc. eds.), Munich: Sellier, 2004.
Lupoi 2000
Maurizio Lupoi, Trusts: A Comparative Study, Cambridge: Cambridge University Press, 2000.

Lurger 2006
Brigitta Lurger, Political Issues in Property Law and European Unification Projects, in The Politics of a European Civil Code (Martijn W. Hesselink ed.), Deventer: Kluwer, 2006.
Lurger 2012
Brigitta Lurger, Transfer of Ownership of Movables in Book VIII of DCFR 2009, in The Future of European Property Law (Sjef van Erp etc. eds.), Munich: Sellier, 2012.
Lwowski 2008
Hans-Jürgen Lwowski, "Quiet" Creation of Security Interests or Filing, in The Future of Secured Credit in Europe (H. Eidenmüller and E.-M Kieninger eds.), Berlijn/New York: De Gruyter, 2008.

MacBryde and Flessner 2003
W.W. MacBryde and Axel Flessner, Principles of European Insolvency Law, Deventer: Kluwer, 2003.
MacCormick 1990
Neil MacCormick, General Legal Concepts, in 11 The Laws of Scotland: Stair Memorial Encyclopedia, 1990.
MacDougall 2014
Bruce MacDougall, Canadian Personal Property Security Law, Ontario: Lexis-Nexis, 2014.
Macleod 2002
John Macleod, Consumer Sales Law, London: Sweet & Maxwell, 2002.
Mackaay 1982
Ejan Mackaay, Economics of Information and Law, Springer, 1982.
Maitland 1936
F.W. Maitland, Equity: A Course of Lectures, Cambridge: Cambridge University Press, 1936.
Mallet-Bricout 2013
Blandine Mallet-Bricout, The Trustee, in The Worlds of the Trust (Lionel Smith ed.), Cambridge: Cambridge University Press, 2013.
Mann 1997
Ronald J. Mann, Explaining the Pattern of Secured Credit, in 110 Harvard Law Review, 1997.
Martinson 2006
Claes Martinson, Transfer of Title Concerning Movables Part III, Frankfurt etc.: Peter Lang GmbH, 2006.
Mattei 2000
Ugo Mattei, Basic Principles of Property Law: A Comparative Legal and Economic Introduction, London: Sweet & Maxwell, 2000.
Matthews 2002
P. Matthews, From Obligation to Property, and Back Again? The Future of the Non-Charitable Purpose Trust, in Extending the Boundaries of Trust and Similar Ring-Fenced Funds (David J. Hayton ed.), Deventer: Kluwer, 2002.
Matthews 2007
Paul Matthews, The French Fiducie, in 21 Trust Law International, 2007.

Matthews 2013
Paul Matthews, The Compatibility of the Trust with the Civil Law Notion of Property, in The Worlds of the Trust (Lionel Smith ed.), Cambridge: Cambridge University Press, 2013.
Matz 2012
Henry Matz, Reforming Personal Property Security Law, in 1 European Property Law Journal, 2012.
McCoid 1985
John C. McCoid, Bankruptcy, the Avoiding Powers, and Unperfected Security Interests, in 59 American Bankruptcy Law Journal, 1985.
McCormack 2004
Gerard McCormack, Secured Credit under English and American Law, Cambridge: Cambridge University Press, 2004.
McFarlane 2008
Ben McFarlane, The Structure of Property Law, Oxford: Oxford University Press, 2008.
McFarlane 2011
Ben McFarlane, The Numerus Clausus Principle and Covenants Relating to Land, in Modern Studies in Property Law: Volume 6 (Susan Bright ed.), Oxford: Hart Publishing, 2011.
McGuire 2008
Mary-Rose McGuire, National Report on the Transfer of Movables in Germany, in National Reports on the Transfer of Movables in Europe Volume 3: Germany, Greece, Lithuania, Hungary (Wolfgang Faber and Brigitta Lurger eds.), Munich: Sellier, 2008.
McKay 2000
Nikki McKay, Seller in Possession: Constructive Delivery of Goods on Site, in Business Law Review December 2000.
Medicus 1984
Dieter Medicus, Gedanken zum Nebenbesitz, in Festschrift für Heinz Hübner zum 70. Geburtstag, Berlin/New York: De Gruyter, 1984.
Medicus 1992
Dieter Medicus, Der Grundsatz der Verhältnismäßigkeit im Privatrecht, AcP 192, 1992.
Medicus 2004
Dieter Medicus, Schuldrecht I: Allgemeiner Teil, München: C.H. Beck, 2004.
Medicus 2010
Dieter Medicus, Allgemeiner Teil des BGB, Heidelberg: C.F. Müller, 2010.
Medicus and Lorenz 2015
Dieter Medicus and Stephan Lorenz, Schuldrecht I: Allgemeiner Teil, München: C.H. Beck, 2015.
Mees 1980
T.J. Dorhout Mees, Nederlands handels- en faillissementsrecht III, Arnhem: Gouda Quint, 1980.
Meijers 1948
E.M. Meijers, De algemene begrippen van het Burgerlijk Recht, Leiden: Universitaire Pers Leiden, 1948.
Meijers 1954
E.M. Meijers, Ontwerp voor een nieuw Burgerlijk Wetboek toelichting: Eerste gedeelte (Boek 1-4), 's-Gravenhage: Staatsdrukkerij- en Uitgeverijbedrijf, 1954.

Meijer 2002
Gerrit Meijer, Influence of the Code Civil in the Netherlands, in 14 European Journal of Law and Economics, 2002.
Meng 2012
孟强：《信托登记制度研究》，北京：中国人民大学出版社2012年版。
English translation: Qiang Meng, Research on the Registration of Trust, Press of Renmin University of China, 2012.
Merrett 2008
Louise Merrett, The Importance of Delivery and Possession in the Passing of Title, in 67 The Cambridge Law Journal, 2008.
Merrill 1998
Thomas W. Merrill, Property and the Right to Exclude, in 77 Nebraska Law Review, 1998.
Merrill 2015
Thomas W. Merrill, Ownership and Possession, in Law and Economics of Possession (Yun-Chien Chang ed.), Cambridge: Cambridge University Press, 2015.
Merrill and Smith 2000
Thomas W. Merrill and Henry E. Smith, Optimal Standardization in the Law of Property: The Numerus Clausus Principle, in 110 The Yale Law Journal, 2000.
Merrill and Smith 2001
Thomas W. Merrill and Henry E. Smith, The Property/Contract Interface, in 101 Columbia Law Review, 2001.
Meyer-Cording 1990
Ulrich Meyer-Cording, Wertpapierrecht, Frankfurt: Metzner, 1990.
Miceli 1997
Thomas J. Miceli, Economics of the Law, New York/Oxford: Oxford University Press, 1997.
Miceli 2005
Thomas J. Miceli, Property, in The Elgar Companion to Law and Economics (Jürgen G. Backhaus ed.), Cheltenham etc.: Edward Elgar, 2005.
Mijnssen 2017
Hein Mijnssen, Verbintenissen tot betaling van een geldsom, Deventer: Kluwer, 2017.
Mijnssen and Schut 1991
F.H.J. Mijnssen and G.H.A. Schut, Bezit, levering en overdracht volgens BW en NBW, Zwolle: W.E.J. Tjeenk Willink, 1991.
Mill 1859
John Stuart Mill, On Liberty, Andrews, 1859.
Milo 2004
J.M. Milo, Contents of Real Rights: Personal or Proprietary, in Contents of Real Rights (Steven Bartels and Michael Milo eds.), Nijmegen: Wolf Legal Publisher, 2004.
Milo 2012
J.M. Milo, Country Report: Netherlands, in 18 The Columbia Journal of European Law Online, 2012.
Mincke 1997
Wolfgang Mincke, General Principles of Property Law: A Traditional Continental View, in The Reform of Property Law (Paul Jackson and David C. Wilde eds.), Ashgate, 1997.

Mollema 2013
Anne Mollema, Het beperkte recht, Deventer: Kluwer, 2013.
Mooney 1988
Charles W. Mooney, The Mystery and Myth of Article 9 Filing, in 39 Alabama Law Review, 1988.
Moshenskiĭ 2008
Sergeĭ Zakharovich Moshenskiĭ, History of the Weksel: Bill of Exchange and Promissory Note, Bloomington: Xlibris, 2008.
Mousourakis 2012
George Mousourakis, Fundamentals of Roman Private Law, Berlin/New York: Springer, 2012.
Mulder 1948
S.J.A. Mulder, Hoofdzaken waardepapieren en tussenpersonen, Deventer: Kluwer, 1948.
Munday 2010
Roderick Munday, Agency: Law and Principles, Oxford: Oxford University Press, 2010.
Müller 2010
Therese Müller, Besitzschutz in Europa, Tübingen: Mohr Siebeck, 2010.
MüKoBGB/Damrau 2017
Jürgen Damrau, Münchener Kommentar zum Bürgerlichen Gesetzbuch: Band 7, München: C.H. Beck, 2017.
MüKoBGB/Joost 2017
Detlev Joost, Münchener Kommentar zum Bürgerlichen Gesetzbuch: Band 7, München: C.H. Beck, 2017.
MüKoBGB/Oechsler 2017
Jürgen Oechsler, Münchener Kommentar zum Bürgerlichen Gesetzbuch: Band 7, München: C.H. Beck, 2017.
MüKoHGB/Langenbucher 2018
Katja Langenbucher, Münchener Kommentar zum Handelsgesetzbuch: Band 7, München: C.H. Beck, 2018.
MüKoHGB/Frantzioch 2018
Fritz Frantzioch, Münchener Kommentar zum Handelsgesetzbuch: Band 7, München: C.H. Beck, 2018.
MüKoHGB/Herber 2018
Rolf Herber, Münchener Kommentar zum Handelsgesetzbuch: Band 7, München: C.H. Beck, 2018.

Nieskens-Isphording and Van der Putt-Lauwers 2002
B.W.M. Nieskens-Isphording and A.E.M. van der Putt-Lauwers, Derdenbescherming, Deventer: Kluwer, 2002.
Nieuwenhuis 1980
J.H. Nieuwenhuis, Uit de ban van hier en nu, Deventer: Kluwer, 1980.
Nieuwenhuis 1986
J.H. Nieuwenhuis, Kopie deel drie: Goede trouw bij de aankoop van een tweedehands auto, in 35 Ars Aequi Libri, 1986.
Nieuwenhuis 2019
J.H. Nieuwenhuis, Hoofdstukken vermogensrecht, Deventer: Kluwer, 2019.
Nieuwesteeg 2015
W.H.B.K. Nieuwesteeg, Voorwaardelijke eigendom, in 4 NTHR, 2015.

Nolan 2006
R.C. Nolan, Equitable Property, in 122 Law Quarterly Review, 2006.
Non-Contractual Liability Arising out of Damage Caused to Another 2009
Non-Contractual Liability Arising out of Damage Caused to Another, prepared by Christian von Bar, Munich: Sellier, 2009.
Nörr, Scheyhing and Pöggeler 1999
Knut Wolfgang Nörr, Robert Scheyhing and Wolfgang Pöggeler, Sukzessionen: Forderungszession, Vertrags-übernahme, Schuldübernahme, Tübingen: Mohr Siebeck, 1999.
Nóbrega 2014
José Carlos de Medeiros Nóbrega, Die Entwicklung des portugiesischen Sachenrechts, Göttingen: Vandenhoeck & Ruprecht, 2014.

O'Connor 2005
Pamela O'Connor, Registration of Invalid Dispositions, in Modern Studies in Property Law – Volume 3 (Elizabeth Cooke ed.), Oxford: Hart Publishing, 2005.

Pacanowska and Soto 2011
Isabel V. González Pacanowska and Carlos Manuel Díez Soto, National Report on the Transfer of Movables in Spain, in National Reports on the Transfer of Movables in Europe Volume 5 (Wolfgang Faber and Brigitta Lurger eds.), Munich: Sellier, 2011.
Palmer 2009
N.E. Palmer, Bailment, London: Sweet & Maxwell, 2009.
Parish 2009
Matthew Parish, The Economic Logic of Formality in Property Law, in European Law & Economics Association Annual Conference, 2009.
Parlementaire Geschiedenis (3) 1981
Parlementaire geschiedenis van het nieuwe burgerlijk wetboek Boek 3. Vermogensrecht in het algemeen, Deventer: Kluwer, 1981.
Parsons 2008
Timothy Parsons, England, in Security over Receivables (William Johnston ed.), Oxford: Oxford University Press, 2008.
Pearson 2003
Gail Pearson, Constructive Possession and Constructive Delivery in Transfer of Title to Goods, in 26 University of New South Wales Law Journal, 2003.
Pedersen 1993
Bjarne Lau Pedersen, Denmark-Chattel Mortgage: Registration, in 8 (8) Journal of International Banking Law, 1993.
Peel 2002
Samantha Peel, The Development of the Bill of Lading, Dissertation, University of Plymouth, 2002.
Penner 1996
J.E. Penner, The "Bundle of Rights" Picture of Property, in 43 UCLA Law Review, 1996.
Pennington 1978
Robert R. Pennington, Retention of Title to the Sale of Goods under European Law, in 27 International and Comparative Law Quarterly, 1978.

Pettit 2012
Philip H. Pettit, Equity and the Law of Trusts, Oxford: Oxford University Press, 2012.
Phillips 1979 (1)
David Morris Phillips, Flawed Perfection: From Possession to Filing under Article 9 – Part I, in 59 Boston University Law Review, 1979.
Phillips 1979 (2)
David Morris Phillips, Flawed Perfection: From Possession to Filing under Article 9 – Part II, in 59 Boston University Law Review, 1979.
Pitlo and Bolweg 1972
A. Pitlo and M.F.H.J. Bolweg, Het zakenrecht naar het Nederlands Burgelijk Wetboek, Groningen: H.D. Tjeenk Willink, 1972.
Planitz 1936
Hans Planitz, Das Deutsche Grundpfandrecht, Wien: H. Böhlaus Nachf., 1936.
Plank 2007
Thomas E. Plank, Assignment of Receivables Under Article 9, in 68 Ohio State Law Journal, 2007.
Pollock and Maitland 1968
Frederick Pollock and F.W. Maitland, The History of English Law before the Time of Edward I, London: Sweet & Maxwell, 1968.
Pollock and Wright 1888
Frederick Pollock and Robert Samuel Wright, An Essay on Possession in the Common Law, Oxford: Oxford University Press, 1888.
Posner 2000
Richard A. Posner, Savigny, Holmes, and the Law and Economics of Possession, in 86 Virginia Law Review, 2000.
Pottage 1995
Alain Pottage, The Originality of Registration, in 3 Oxford Journal of Legal Studies, 1995.
Pound 1999
Roscoe Pound, An Introduction to the Philosophy of Law, New Brunswick: Transaction Publishers, 1999.
Prichard 1961
A.M. Prichard, Leage's Roman Private Law, London: Sweet & Maxwell, 1961.
Principles of European Trust Law 1999
Principles of European Trust Law, edited by D.J. Hayton etc., Deventer: Kluwer, 1999.
Proprietary Security in Movable Assets 2014
Proprietary Security in Movable Assets, prepared by Ulrich Drobnig and Ole Böger, Munich: Sellier, 2014.

Quantz 2005
T. Quantz, Besitz und Publizität im Recht der beweglichen Sachen, Berlin: Duncker & Humblot, 2005.

Radbruch 1929
Gustav Radbruch, Einführung in die Rechtswissenschaft, Leipzig: Quelle und Meyer, 1929.

Radint 1982
Margaret Jane Radint, Property and Personhood, in 34 Stanford Law Review, 1982.
Raff 1999
M.J. Raff, German Real Property Law and the Conclusive Land Title Register, Dissertation, University of Melbourne, 1999.
Rahmatian 2011
Andreas Rahmatian, Intellectual Property and the Concept of Dematerialised Property, in 6 Modern Studies in Property Law (S. Bright ed.), Oxford: Oxford University Press, 2011.
Rahmatian 2018
Andreas Rahmatian, Money as a Legally Enforceable Debt, in 2 European Business Law Review, 2018.
Rakob 2007
Julia Rakob, Germany, in Cross-Border Security over Tangibles (Harry C. Sigman and Eva-Maria Kieninger eds.), Munich: Sellier, 2007.
Rakob 2009
Julia Klauer Rakob, Germany, in Cross-Border Security over Receivables (Harry C. Sigman and Eva-Maria Kieninger, eds.), Munich: De Gruyter, 2009.
Ramjohn 2004
Mohamed Ramjohn, Cases & Materials on Trusts, Cavendish: Routledge, 2004.
Rank 1992
W.A.K. Rank, Het mededelingsvereiste bij cessie nader beschouwd, in BW-krant jaarboek, Deventer: Kluwer, 1992.
Rank 1994
W.A.K. Rank, Geld en geldschulden, Deventer: Kluwer, 1994.
Rank 2008
W.A.K. Rank, Netherlands, in Security over Receivables (William Johnston ed.), Oxford: Oxford University Press, 2008.
Rank 2010
W.A.K. Rank, Repos and Securities Lending, in Financial Law in the Netherlands (Marcel C.A. Nieuwenhuijzen ed.), Alphen aan den Rijn: Kluwer Law International, 2010.
Rank-Berenschot 1992
E.B. Rank-Berenschot, Over de scheidslijn tussen goederen- en verbintenissenrecht, Deventer: Kluwer, 1992.
Rank-Berenschot 1998
E.B. Rank-Berenschot, Overdracht en toebehoren onder tijdbepaling, in Van beheering, Deventer: Gouda Quint, 1998.
Rank-Berenschot 2012
E.B. Rank-Berenschot, Bezit, Deventer: Kluwer, 2012.
Reehuis 2004
W.H.M. Reehuis, Levering, Deventer: Kluwer, 2004.
Reehuis 2013
W.H.M. Reehuis, Eigendomsvoorbehoud, Deventer: Kluwer, 2013.
Reehuis 2015
W.H.M. Reehuis, Zwaartepunten van het vermogensrecht, Deventer: Kluwer, 2015.

Reehuis and Heisterkamp 2019
W.H.M. Reehuis and A.H.T. Heisterkamp, Goederenrecht, Deventer: Kluwer, 2019.
Rehahn and Grimm 2012
Johannes Rehahn and Alexander Grimm, Country Report: Germany, in 18 The Columbia Journal of European Law Online, 2012.
Reich 2013
John Reich, Are Transparency and the Registration of Trusts Necessary?, in 19 Trusts and Trustees, 2013.
Renaudin 2013
Muriel Renaudin, The Modernisation of French Secured Credit Law, in 24 International Company and Commercial Law Review, 2013.
Ritaine 2012
Eleanor Cashin Ritaine, Common Frame of Reference and Property Law, in The Future of European Property Law (Sjef van Erp, Arthur Salomons and Bram Akkermans eds.), Munich: Sellier, 2012.
Rodriguez 2013
Marfa Paz Gatica Rodriguez, Possession and Transfer of Goods in the Draft Common Frame of Reference, in 2 Edinburgh Student Law Review 31, 2013-2015.
Rogers 2012
James Steven Rogers, The End of Negotiable Instruments, Oxford: Oxford University Press, 2012.
Rongen 2002
M.H.E. Rongen, Vorderingen als verhandelbare goederen: Wijzigingen van de onderliggende overeenkomst na cessie of verpanding, in Onderneming en 10 jaar nieuw Burgerlijk Recht (S.C.J.J. Kortmann etc. eds.), Deventer: W.E.J. Tjeenk Willink, 2002.
Rongen 2012
M.H.E. Rongen, Cessie, Deventer: Kluwer, 2012.
Rose 1985
Carol M. Rose, Possession as the Origin of Property, in 52 The University of Chicago Law Review, 1985.
Rose 1988
Carol M. Rose, Crystals and Mud in Property Law, in 40 Stanford Law Review, 1988.
Rosenberg, Schwab and Gottwald 2010
Peter Gottwald, Karl Heinz Schwab and Leo Rosenberg, Zivilprozessrecht, München: C.H. Beck, 2010.
Rostill 2016
Luke Rostill, Fundamentals of Property Law: Possession, Title and Relativity, Doctoral Thesis, University of Oxford, 2016.
Rusch 1995
Linda J. Rusch, The Article 9 Filing System, in 79 Minnesota Law Review 1995.
Rusch 2010
Arnold F. Rusch, Rechtsscheinlehre in der Schweiz, Zürich: Dike, 2010.
Rüfner 2014
Thomas Rüfner, Possession of Incorporeals, in The Consequences of Possession (Eric Descheemaeker ed.), Edinburgh: Edinburgh University Press, 2014.

Ryan 1959
Kevin William Ryan, The Reception of the Trust in the Civil Law, Cambridge: Cambridge University Press, 1959.

Sagaert 2004
Vincent Sagaert, The UNIDROIT Convention on International Interests in Mobile Equipment: A Belgian Perspective, in 1 European Review of Private Law, 2004.

Sagaert 2005
Vincent Sagaert, Het goederenrecht als open systeem van verbintenissen?, in Tijdschrift voor Privaatrecht, 2005.

Sagaert 2008
Vincent Sagaert, Consensual versus Delivery Systems in European Private Law, in Rules for the Transfer of Movables (W. Faber and B. Lurger eds.), Munich: Sellier, 2008.

Sagaert 2012
Vincent Sagaert, The Trust Book in the DCFR: A Civil Lawyer's Perspective, in The Future of European Property Law (Sjef van Erp etc. eds.), Munich: Sellier, 2012.

Sagaert 2014
Vincent Sagaert, Goederenrecht, Mechelen: Kluwer, 2014.

Sagaert 2017
Vincent Sagaert, Het Eigendomsvoorbehoud (en retentierecht) onder de Pandwet, in Roerende zekerheden na de Pandwet (M.E. Storm ed.), Antwerpen: Intersentia, 2017.

Sagaert and Cauffman 2011
Vincent Sagaert and Caroline Cauffman, National Report on the Transfer of Movables in Belgium, in National Reports on the Transfer of Movables in Europe Volume 4 (Wolfgang Faber and Brigitta Lurger eds.), Munich: Sellier, 2011.

Sagaert and Gruyaert 2017
Vincent Sagaert and Dorothy Gruyaert, Retention of Title or the Transfer of Ownership in a Slideway, in 2 European Review of Private Law, 2017.

Sagaert and Jansen 2012
Vincent Sagaert and Ruud Jansen, Goederenrecht: De gestage groei naar een conventioneel vermogensrecht, in 1 Rechtkundig Weekblad, 2012.

Sagaert, Tilleman and Laurent 2013
Vincent Sagaert, Bernard Tilleman and Alain Laurent, Verbeke vermogensrecht in kort bestek, Antwerpen: Intersentia, 2013.

Salmond 1947
John William Salmond, Jurisprudence, London: Sweet & Maxwell, 1947.

Salomons 2000
Arthur F. Salomons, Inpassen of aanpassen, in 6427 WPNR, 2000.

Salomons 2006
Arthur F. Salomons, De Onderzoeksplicht van de verkrijger van een tweedehands auto, in 3 Vermogensrechtelijke Analyses, 2006.

Salomons 2008 (1)
Arthur F. Salomons, How to Draft New Rules on the Bona Fide Acquisition of Movables for Europe, in Rules for the Transfer of Movables (W. Faber and B. Lurger eds.), Munich: Sellier, 2008.

Salomons 2008 (2)
Arthur F. Salomons, National Report on the Transfer of Ownership of Movables in The Netherlands, in National Reports on the Transfer of Movables in Europe Volume 6 (Wolfgang Faber and Brigitta Lurger eds.), Munich: Sellier, 2008.

Salomons 2011 (1)
Arthur F. Salomons, Beschikkingsonbevoegdheid bij de verkoop van een tweedehands auto, in 6907 WPNR, 2011.

Salomons 2011 (2)
Arthur F. Salomons, Good Faith Acquisition of Movables, in Towards a European Civil Code (A.S. Hartkamp and Christian von Bar eds.), Nijmegen: Ars Aequi Libri, 2011.

Scheltema 1993
F.G. Scheltema, Wissel- en chequerecht: Algemeen deel (W.R. Meijer and J. Wiarda eds.), Alphen aan den Rijn: W.E.J. Tjeenk Willink, 1993.

Scheltema 2003
A.H. Scheltema, De Goederenrechtelijke werking van de ontbindende voorwaarde, Alphen aan den Rijn: Kluwer, 2003.

Schlechtriem 2003
Peter Schlechtriem, Schuldrecht: Allgemeiner Teil, Tübingen: Mohr Siebeck, 2003.

Schmid, Hertel and Wicke 2005
Christoph U. Schmid, Christian Hertel and Hartmut Wicke, Real Property Law and Procedure in the European Union, 2005.

Schnauder 1991
Franz Schnauder, Sachenrechtliche und wertpapierrechtliche Wirkungen der kaufmännischen Traditionspapiere, in 1642 NJW, 1991.

Schnauder and Müller-Christmann 1991
Franz Schnauder and Bernd Müller-Christmann, Wertpapierrecht, Berlin etc.: Springer, 1992.

Schuijling 2017
B.A. Schuijling, Pandrecht op voorwaardelijke eigendom, in 1 Rechtsgeleerd Magazijn, 2017.

Schumann 1959
Hans Schumann, Einführung in die Rechtswissenschaft, Wiesbaden: Springer, 1959.

Schut 1976
G.H.A. Schut, Bezit geldt als volkomen titel, Zwolle: W.E.J. Tjeenk Willink, 1976.

Schwab and Prütting 2020
Karl Heinz Schwab and Hanns Prütting, Sachenrecht: Ein Studienbuch, München: C.H. Beck, 2020.

Schwarcz 1999
Steven L. Schwarcz, Towards a Centralized Perfection System for Cross-Border Receivables Financing, in 20 University of Pennsylvania Journal of International Economic Law, 1999.

Schwartz 1989
Alan Schwartz, A Theory of Loan Priorities, in 18 Journal of Legal Studies, 1989.

Sdu Commentaar/Jacobs & Ter Horst 2019
B. Jacobs & M.K. ter Horst, Sdu commentaar vermogensrecht, Den Hagg: Sdu Uitgevers, 2019.

Sdu Commentaar/Van Peski 2019
F.M. van Peski, Sdu commentaar vermogensrecht, Den Hagg: Sdu Uitgevers, 2019.
Sealy and Hooley 2009
L.S. Sealy and R.J.A. Hooley, Commercial Law: Text, Cases and Materials, Oxford: Oxford University Press, 2009.
Secured Transactions Law Reform Project 2013
Secured Transactions Law Reform Project-Working Group A, Case for Reform Paper Series: Methods of Perfection, 2013.
Shartel 1932
Burke Shartel, Meanings of Possession, in Minnesota Law Review, 1932.
Shavell 2004
Steven Shavell, Foundations of Economic Analysis of Law, Cambridge: Cambridge University Press, 2004.
Sigman 2004
Harry C. Sigman, Security in Movables in the United States, in Security Rights in Movable Property in European Private Law (Eva-Maria Kieninger ed.), Cambridge: Cambridge University Press, 2004.
Sigman 2008
H.C. Sigman, Perfection and Priority of Security Rights, in The Future of Secured Credit in Europe, European Company and Financial Law Review (Vol. 2) (H. Eidenmüller and E.-M. Kieninger eds.) Berlijn/New York: De Gruyter, 2008.
Sigman 2010
H.C. Sigman, Some Thoughts about Registration with Respect to Security Rights in Movables, in Uniform Law Review, 2010.
Simpson 1986
A.W.B. Simpson, A History of the Land Law, Oxford: Oxford University Press, 1986.
Singer 2013
Joseph W. Singer, The Rule of Reason in Property Law, in 46 UC Davis Law Review, 2013.
Singer and Beermann 1993
Joseph W. Singer and Jack M. Beermann, The Social Origins of Property, in 6 Canadian Journal of Law and Jurisprudence, 1993.
Smith 2002
Henry E. Smith, Exclusion versus Governance: Two Strategies for Delineating Property Rights, in 31 The Journal of Legal Studies, 2002.
Smith 2003
Henry E. Smith, The Language of Property: Form, Context, and Audience, in 55 Stanford Law Review, 2003.
Smith and Leslie 2018
Marcus Smith and Nico Leslie, The Law of Assignment: The Creation and Transfer of Choses in Action, Oxford: Oxford University Press, 2018.
Smith 2012
Henry E. Smith, Property as Law of Things, in 125 Harvard Law Review, 2012.
Smith 2015
Henry E. Smith, The Elements of Possession, in Law and Economics of Possession (Yun-Chien Chang ed.), Cambridge: Cambridge University Press, 2015.

Smith and Merrill 2007
Henry E. Smith and Thomas W. Merrill, The Morality of Property, in 48 William & Mary Law Review, 2007.
Smits 1996
Jan Smits, Van partijen en derden, in 13 Groninger Opmerkingen en Mededelingen, 1996.
Smits 2002
Jan Smits, The Making of European Private Law, Antwerp: Intersentia, 2002.
Smylie 2006
William T. Smylie, Vehicle Identification, in Forensic Investigation of Stolen-Recovered and other Crime-Related Vehicles (Eric Stauffer and Monica S. Bonfanti eds), Elsevier, 2006.
Snijders 1970
W. Snijders, Bezitloze zekerheid op roerende zaken, in Honderd jaar rechtsleven: De Nederlandse juristenvereniging 1870-1970, Zwolle: W.E.J. Tjeenk Willink, 1970.
Snijders 2014
H.J. Snijders, Modern Property Law: The Dutch Example, unpublished, 2014.
Snijders and Rank-Berenschot 2017
H.J. Snijders and E.B. Rank-Berenschot, Goederenrecht, Deventer: Kluwer, 2017.
Soderstrom 2010
Rachelle Soderstrom, An Imperfect System of Perfection, unpublished, 2010.
Sparkes 2012
Peter Sparkes, Certainty of Property, in 3 European Review of Private Law, 2012.
Spath 2010
J.B. Spath, Zaaksvervanging, Deventer: Kluwer, 2010.
Stake 2004
Jeffrey E. Stake, The Property "Instinct", in 359 Philosophical Transactions of the Royal Society: Biological Sciences, 2004.
Staub/Canaris 2004
Claus-Wilhelm Canaris, Staub Handelsgesetzbuch Großkommentar, München: De Gruyter, 2004.
Staudinger/Beckmann 2014
Roland Michael Beckmann, J. von Staudingers Kommentar zum Bürgerlichen Gesetzbuch Buch 2: Recht der Schuldverhaltnisse §§ 433-480 (Kaufrecht), Berlin: De Gruyter, 2014.
Staudinger/Gutzeit 2012
Martin Gutzeit, J. von Staudingers Kommentar zum Bürgerlichen Gesetzbuch Buch 3: Sachenrecht §§ 854-882 (Algemeines Liegenschaftsrecht 1), Berlin: De Gruyter, 2012.
Staudinger/Wiegand 2017
Wolfgang Wiegand, J. von Staudingers Kommentar zum Bürgerlichen Gesetzbuch Buch 3: Allgemeiner Teil §§ 925-984 (Eigentum 2), Berlin: De Gruyter, 2017.
Steneker 2012
Sander Steneker, Pandrecht, Deventer: Kluwer, 2012.
Steppler and Brecke 2015
Ulrich Steppler and Katja Helen Brecke, Germany, in Aviation Finance & Leasing 2015 (Mark Bisset ed.), London: Law Business Research, 2015.

Stiglitz 1999
Joseph E. Stiglitz, Knowledge as a Global Public Good, in Global Public Goods: International Cooperation in the 21st Century (Inge Kaul etc. eds.), Oxford: Oxford University Press, 1999.
Stiglitz 2000
Joseph E. Stiglitz, The Contributions of the Economics of Information to Twentieth Century Economics, in 115 Quarterly Journal of Economics, 2000.l
Stoljar 1984
Samuel Stoljar, Possession in the Civil Codes, in 33 International and Comparative Law, 1984.
Stranz and Stranz 1952
J. Stranz and M. Stranz, Wechselgesetz Kommentar, Berlin: De Gruyter, 1952.
Struycken 1999
T.H.D. Struycken, De eliminatie van het bepaaldheidsvereiste, in 6366 WPNR, 1999.
Struycken 2007
T.H.D. Struycken, De numerus clausus in het goederenrecht, Deventer: Kluwer, 2007.
Struycken 2009
T.H.D. Struycken, Zekerheidsrechten en registratie, in Zekerhedenrecht in ontwikkeling, Den Haag: Sdu Uitgevers, 2009.
Stürner 2008
Rolf Stürner, Perfection and Priority of Security Rights: Commentary, in The Future of Secured Credit in Europe, European Company and Financial Law Review (Vol. 2) (H. Eidenmüller and E.-M Kieninger eds.), Berlijn/New York: De Gruyter, 2008.
Suijling 1940
J.Ph. Suijling, Inleiding tot het Burgerlijk Recht: Zakenrecht, Haarlem: De Erven F. Bohn, 1940.
Swadling 2005
William Swadling, Rescission, Property, and the Common Law, in 121 Law Quarterly Review, 2005.
Swadling 2013
William Swadling, Property: General Principles, in English Private Law (Andrew Burrows ed.), Oxford: Oxford University Press, 2013.

Tai 2003
E. Tjong Tjin Tai, Schijnvolmacht en vertrouwensbeginsel, in 6 NTBR, 2003.
Tallon 1993
Denis Tallon, The New Dutch Civil Code in a Comparative Perspective, in 1 European Review of Private Law, 1993.
Tay 1964
A.E.S. Tay, The Concept of Possession in the Common Law, in 4 Melbourne University Law Review, 1964.
Tiedemann 1994
Andrea Tiedemann, Germany: Contract: Sale of Goods, in 5 (8) International Company and Commercial Law Review, 1994.

Tiedtke 1985
Klaus Tiedtke, Gutgläubiger Erwerb im bürgerlichen Recht, im Handels- und Wertpapierrecht sowie in der Zwangsvollstreckung, Berlin etc.: De Gruyter, 1985.

Timmermann and Veder 2009
Sander Timmermann and Michael Veder, Netherlands, in Cross-Border Security over Receivables (Harry C. Sigman and Eva-Maria Kieninger, eds.), Munich: Sellier, 2009.

The Law Commission 1993
The Law Commission and The Scottish Law Commission, Sale of Goods Forming Part of a Bulk, London, 1993.

The Law Commission 2001
The Law Commission, Land Registration for the Twenty-First Century, London, 2001.

The Law Commission 2002
The Law Commission, Registration of Security Interests: Company Charges and Property Other Than Land: A Consultation Paper, London, 2002.

The Law Commission 2004
The Law Commission, Company Security Interests: A Consultative Report, London, 2004.

The Law Commission 2005
The Law Commission, Company Security Interests, London, 2005.

The Scottish Law Commission 2011
The Scottish Law Commission, Discussion Paper on Moveable Transactions, Edinburgh, 2011.

The World Bank 2011
The World Bank, The Puppet Masters, 2011.

Thiele 2003
Angélique Thiele, Collective Security Arrangements, Deventer: Kluwer, 2003.

Thomas 1976
Joseph Anthony Charles Thomas, Textbook of Roman Law, Amsterdam: North-Holland Publishing Company, 1976.

Tolhurst 2016
Greg Tolhurst, The Assignment of Contractual Rights, Oxford: Oxford University Press, 2016.

Ulph 1998
Janet Ulph, Good Faith and Due Diligence, in Interests in Goods (Norman Palmerand and Ewan McKendrick eds.), London: Informa, 1998.

Ulph 2000
Janet Ulph, Conflicts of Title and the Obligations of the Seller, in Sale of Goods (Ewan McKendrick ed.), London: Routledge, 2000.

Ulph 2001
Janet Ulph, Sale and Lease-Back Agreements in a World of Title Relativity, in 64 The Modern Law Review, 2001.

UNCITRAL Yearbook 1971
United Nations Commission on International Trade Law, Yearbook (Volume 2), New York, 1971.

UNCITRAL Yearbook 2003
United Nations Commission on International Trade Law, Yearbook (Volume 32), New York, 2003.
Uniform Commercial Code Committee 2008
Uniform Commercial Code Committee, Practice under Article 9 of the Uniform Commercial Code (Stephen L. Sepinuck ed.), USA: American Bar Association, 2008.

Valsan 2013
Remus Valsan, Rights against Rights and Real Obligations, in The Worlds of the Trust (Lionel Smith ed.), Cambridge: Cambridge University Press, 2013.
Van Buchem-Spapens and Pouw 2008
A.M.J. van Buchem-Spapens and Th.A. Pouw, Faillissement, surseance van betaling en schuldsanering, Deventer: Kluwer, 2008.
Van Dam 2013
Cees van Dam, European Tort Law, Oxford: Oxford University Press, 2013.
Van den Boezem and Goosmann 2010
F.E.J. Beekhoven van den Boezem and C.E. Goosmann, Centraal pandregister voor roerende zaken schiet zijn doel voorbij!, in Bancaire zekerheid (N.E.D. Faber ed.), Deventer: Kluwer, 2010.
Van den Heuvel 2004
N.W.M. van den Heuvel, Zekerheid en voorrang, Den Haag: Sdu, 2004.
Van der Lely 1993
Arend Jacob van der Lely, Levering door middel van een ceel, in X Groninger Opmerkingen en Mededelingen, 1993.
Van der Lely 1996
Arend Jacob van der Lely, Levering van roerende zaken door middel van een zakenrechtelijk waardepapier, Deventer: Kluwer, 1996.
Van der Lely 2008
Arend Jacob van der Lely, Cash Collateral, in The Past and Future of Money (W.J. Zwalve and E. Koops eds.), The Hague: Boom, 2008.
Van der Walt 1999
A.J. van der Walt, Constitutional Property Clauses: A Comparative Analysis, Deventer: Kluwer, 1999.
Van der Weide 2011
J.A. van der Weide, (On)zekerheden in het DCFR: Proprietary Security in Movable Assets, in 7 NTBR, 2011.
Van Dongen 1996
R.C. van Dongen, De Duitse Treuhand in de spiegel van het Haagse Trustverdrag, in Vertrouwd met de trust (W.E.J.T. Willink ed.), Deventer: Kluwer, 1996.
Van Empel and Huizink 1991
G. van Empel and J.B. Huizink, Betaling, waardepapier en documentair krediet, Deventer: Kluwer, 1991.
Van Erp 2003
Sjef van Erp, Globalisation or Isolation in New Dutch Property Law?, in 7.5 Electronic Journal of Comparative Law, 2003.
Van Erp 2004
Sjef van Erp, The Cape Town Convention: A Model for a European System of Security Interests Registration?, in 1 European Review of Private Law, 2004.

Van Erp 2006 (1)
Sjef van Erp, European and National Property Law, Munich: Sellier, 2006.
Van Erp 2006 (2)
Sjef van Erp, Comparative Property Law, in The Oxford Handbook of Comparative Law (Mathias Reimann and Reinhard Zimmermann eds.), Oxford: Oxford University Press, 2006.
Van Erp 2012
Sjef van Erp, General Issues: Setting the Scene, in Cases, Materials and Text on Property Law (Sjef van Erp and Bram Akkermans eds.), Oxford etc.: Hart Publishing, 2012.
Van Erp 2013
Sjef van Erp, Contract and Property Law: Distinct, But Not Separate, in 9 European Review of Contract Law, 2013.
Van Lier 1937
R.F. van Lier, Wissels en chèques, Haarlem: W.E.J. Tjeenk Willink, 1937.
Van Maanen and Claringbould 2017
M.A.W. van Maanen and M.H. Claringbould, Aspecten van pandrecht op cognossementen, in 1 NTHR, 2017.
Van Oven 1905
J.C. van Oven, De bezitsbescherming en hare functies, Amsterdam: De Bussy, 1905.
Van Swaaij 2012
J.H.M. van Swaaij, HR 21 Oktober 2011, NJ 2011, 494, in 5 Maandblad voor Vermogensrecht, 2012.
Van Schaick 2014
A.C. van Schaick, Rechtsgevolgen en functies van bezit en houderschap, Deventer: Kluwer, 2014.
Van Vliet 2000
L.P.W. van Vliet, Transfer of Movables in German, French, English and Dutch Law, Nijmegen: Ars Aequi Libri, 2000.
Van Vliet 2006
L.P.W. van Vliet, Goede trouw bij de koop van tweedehands auto's in rechtsvergelijkend perspectief, in 5 NTBR, 2006.
Van Vliet 2010
Lars van Vliet, Acquisition and Loss of Ownership of Goods, in Factual Assessment of the Draft Common Frame of Reference (Luisa Anatoniolli and Francesca Fiorentini eds.), Berlin/New York: Sellier, 2010.
Van Vliet 2012
Lars van Vliet, Transfer of Movable Property, in Elgar Encyclopedia of Comparative Law (Jan Smits ed.), Edward Elgar, 2012.
Van Zyl 1983
Deon Hurter van Zyl, History and Principles of Roman Private Law, Durban etc.: Butterworths, 1983.
Vantomme 2018
Anaïs Vantomme, Bezit en houderschap bij titelomzetting, Antwerpen: Intersentia, 2018.
Veder 2007
Micheal Veder, Netherlands, in Cross-Border Security over Tangibles (Harry C. Sigman and Eva-Maria Kieninger eds.), Munich: Sellier, 2007.

Veenstra 2009
H.M. Veenstra, Uitleg op de grens van het goederen- en verbintenissenrecht, in Uitleg in het goederenrecht (Michael Milo and Steven Bartels eds.), Den Haag: Boom, 2009.
Venema 1985
Uniken Venema, Anglo-Amerikaanse trusts en het Nederlandse recht, in 5727 WPNR, 1985.
Veneziano 2008
Anna Veneziano, A Secured Transactions' Regime for Europe, in 14 Juridica International, 2008.
Verdaas 2008
A.J. Verdaas, Stil pandrecht op vorderingen op naam, Deventer: Kluwer, 2008.
Verhagen 1997
H.L.E. Verhagen, Het mededelingsvereiste bij cessie, in Onderneming en 5 jaar nieuw Burgerlijk Recht (S.C.J.J. Kortmann etc. eds.), Deventer: W.E.J. Tjeenk Willink, 1997.
Verhagen 2002
H.L.E. Verhagen, Vorderingen als verhandelbare goederen, in Onderneming en 10 jaar nieuw Burgerlijk Recht (S.C.J.J. Kortmann etc. eds.), Deventer: W.E.J. Tjeenk Willink, 2002.
Von Gierke 1928
Julius von Gierke, Sachenrecht, Berlin/Heidelberg: Springer, 1928.
Von Savigny 1867
Friedrich Carl von Savigny, System of Modern Roman Law, translated by William Holloway, Madras: J. Higginbotham, 1867.
Von Wilmowsky 1996
Peter von Wilmowsky, Europäisches Kreditsicherungsrecht, Tübingen: Mohr Siebeck, 1996.
Vriesendorp 1994
R.D. Vriesendorp, Bosman/Condorcamp, in 4 Ars Aequi Libri, 1994.
Vriesendorp 2013
R.D. Vriesendorp, Insolventierecht, Deventer: Kluwer, 2013.
Vriesendorp and Barendrecht 1993
R.D. Vriesendorp and J.M. Barendrecht, Zekerheid door wetenschap, Deventer: Kluwer, 1993.

Walsh 2016
Catherine Walsh, Transplanting Article 9: The Canadian PPSA Experience, in Secured Transactions Law Reform (Louise Gullifer and N. Orkun Akseli eds.), Oxford: Hart Publishing, 2016.
Weber 2012
Ralph Weber, Sachenrecht I: bewegliche Sachen, Baden: Nomos, 2012.
Weiser 1936
Felix Weiser, Trusts on the Continent of Europe, London: Sweet & Maxwell, 1936.
Wessels 2012
Bob Wessels, Gevolgen van faillietverklaring (I), Deventer: Kluwer, 2012.
Westermann 2011
Harry Westermann, Harm Peter Westermann, Dieter Eickmann and Karl-Heinz Gursky, Sachenrecht, Heidelberg: C.F. Müller, 2011.

Westrik 2001
R. Westrik, 'Koop breekt geen huur' en het huurbeding, Den Haag: Koninklijke Vermande, 2001.
Whittaker and Partner 2015
Bruce Whittaker and Ashurst Partner, Review of the Personal Property Securities Act 2009: Final Report, 2015.
White 1993
James J. White, Revising Article 9 to Reduce Wasteful Litigation, in 26 Loyola of Los Angeles Law Review, 1993.
White and Summers 2012
James J. White and Robert S. Summers, Uniform Commercial Code, West Saint Paul: West Group, 2012.
Wiarda 1937
J. Wiarda, Cessie of overdracht van schuldvorderingen op naam naar Nederlandsch Burgerlijk Recht, Zwolle: W.E.J. Tjeenk Willink, 1937.
Wibier 2007
R.M. Wibier, Eén vraag over de verkrijgende verjaring van vorderingen, in 7 NTBR, 2007.
Wibier 2013
R.M. Wibier, Eigendomsvoorbehoud en de overdraagbaarheid en verpandbaarheid van "voorwaardelijke eigendom", in 5 Maandblad voor Vermogensrecht, 2013.
Wieling 2006
Hans Josef Wieling, Sachenrecht Band 1: Sachen, Besitz und Rechte an beweglichen Sachen, Berlin etc.: Springer, 2006.
Wieling 2007
Hans Josef Wieling, Sachenrecht, Berlin etc.: Springer, 2007.
Wilhelm 2010
Jan Wilhelm, Sachenrecht, Berlin etc.: Springer, 2010.
William 1998
Joan William, The Rhetoric of Property, in 83 Iowa Law Review, 1998.
Wilson 2007
Geoffrey Wilson, Comparative Legal Scholarship, Research Methods for Law (Mike McConville and Wing Hong Chui eds.), Edinburgh: Edinburgh University Press, 2007.
Winfield and Jolowicz 2010
P.H. Winfield, J.A. Jolowicz and W.V.H. Rogers, Winfield and Jolowicz on Tort, London: Sweet & Maxwell, 2010.
Winn and Wright 2019
Jane K. Winn and Benjamin Wright, The Law of Electronic Commerce, New York: Kluwer, 2019.
Winter 2014
Matthias Winter, Das Lösungsrecht nach gutgläubigem Erwerb, Tübingen: Mohr Siebeck, 2014.
WIPO 2012
WIPO, The Enforcement of Intellectual Property Rights: A Case Book, 2012.
Wolf and Neuner 2012
Manfred Wolf and Jörg Neuner, Allgemeiner Teil des Bürgerlichen Rechts, München: C.H. Beck, 2012.

Wolf and Wellenhofer 2011
Wolf and Wellenhofer, Sachentecht, München: C.H. Beck, 2011.
Wood 2019
Phillip R. Wood, Comparative Law of Security Interests and Title Finance, London: Sweet & Maxwell, 2019.
Wood 2011
Roderick J. Wood, The Structure of Secured Priorities in Insolvency Law, in 27 Banking & Finance Law Review, 2011.

Xie 2011
谢在全：《民法物权论》，北京：中国政法大学出版社，2011年。
English translation: Zaiquan Xie, On Property Rights in Civil Law, Beijing: Press of China University of Political Science and Law, 2011.

Yin 2002
尹田：《物权的定义与本质》，载《中外法学》2002年第3期。
English translation: Tian Yin, On Definition and Essence of Property Rights, in 3 Peking University Law Journal, 2002.

Zeldenrust 2011
R.A. Zeldenrust, Right of Pledge and the Transparency of Debtors' Assets, Master Thesis, Utrecht University, 2011.
Zevenbergen 1951
Christiaan Zevenbergen, Leerboek van het Nederlandse recht der order- en toonderpapieren, Zwolle: W.E.J. Tjeenk Willink, 1951.
Zimmermann 1990
Reinhard Zimmermann, The Law of Obligations: Roman Foundations of the Civilian Tradition, Cape Town: Juta & Co, 1990.
Zöllner 1974
Wolfgang Zöllner, Die Zurückdrängung des Verkörperungselements bei den Wertpapieren, in Festschrift für Ludwig Raiser zum 70. Geburtstag, Tübingen: Mohr Siebeck, 1974.
Zöllner 1978
Wolfgang Zöllner, Wertpapierrecht, München: C.H. Beck, 1978.
Zwalve 1996
W.J. Zwalve, Revindicatie en condictie van geld, in XIII Groninger Opmerkingen en Mededelingen, 1996.
Zweigert and Kötz 1998
Konrad Zweigert and Hein Kötz, Introduction to Comparative Law, Oxford etc.: Clarendon, 1998.
Zwitser 2005 (1)
R. Zwitser, Pandrecht en orderpapier (I), in 6612 WPNR, 2005.
Zwitser 2005 (2)
R. Zwitser, Pandrecht en orderpapier (II), in 6612 WPNR, 2005.
Zwitser 2006
R. Zwitser, Order- en toonderpapieren, Deventer: Kluwer, 2006.
Zwitser 2012
R. Zwitser, De rol van het cognossement als waardepapier in het handelsverkeer, Zutphen: Paris, 2012.

Index

Reference is made to paragraphs.

N

O

P

Q

R

In the range of books published by the Meijers Research Institute and Graduate School of Leiden Law School, Leiden University, the following titles were published in 2020 and 2021:

MI-335 M.R. Bruning e.a., *Kind in proces: van communicatie naar effectieve participatie*, Nijmegen: Wolf Legal Publishers 2020
MI-336 J. van Kralingen, *De ondeelbaarheid van het pand- en hypotheekrecht; deconstructie van een leerstuk. Een historisch-comparatieve studie*, (diss. Leiden), Den Haag: Boom juridisch 2020, ISBN 978 94 6290 782 9
MI-337 J.C.A. van Dam, *Guidance documents of the European Commission in the Dutch legal order*, (diss. Leiden), Amsterdam: Ipskamp Printing 2020
MI-338 F. Jiang, *Greening' the WTO Ban on China's Export Duties. Should WTO law allow China to use export duties to protect the environment and, if so, in what manner?*, (diss. Leiden), Amsterdam: Ipskamp Printing 2020
MI-339 M.J.R. Broekema, *Cognitive Bias in the Judgment of Business Valuations and Valuators. How Systematic Patterns of Irrationality Affect Entrepreneurs, Legal Professionals and Business Valuators*, (diss. Leiden), Amsterdam: Ipskamp Printing 2020
MI-340 H. Horii, *Child Marriage as a Choice. Rethinking agency in international human rights*, (diss. Leiden), Amsterdam: Ipskamp Printing 2020
MI-341 R. de Graaff, *Concurrence in European Private Law*, (diss. Leiden), The Hague: Eleven International Publishing 2020, ISBN 978 94 6236 134 8
MI-342 J.M.M. van der Vliet, *The International Legal Protection of Environmental Refugees. A human rights-based, security and State responsibility approach*, (diss. Leiden), Den Haag: Boom juridisch 2020, ISBN 978 94 6236 139 3
MI-343 M. Samadi, *Normering en Toezicht in de Opsporing. Een onderzoek naar de normering van het strafvorderlijk optreden van opsporingsambtenaren in het voorbereidend onderzoek en het toezicht op de naleving van deze normen*, (diss. Leiden), Den Haag: Boom juridisch 2020, ISBN 978 94 6290 816 1
MI-344 D.J. Verheij, *Credit rating agency liability in Europe. Rating the combination of EU and national law in rights of redress*, (diss. Leiden), The Hague: Eleven International Publishing 2020, ISBN 978 94 6236 144 7
MI-345 P. Rustenburg, *Een algemene normtheorie toegepast op open normen in het belastingrecht*, (diss. Leiden), Amsterdam: Ipskamp Printing 2020
MI-346 J.V.O.R. Doekhie e.a., *Invoering jeugdstrafrecht in Caribisch Nederland. Een verkenning naar een jeugdstrafrechtmonitor*, Den Haag: Boom criminologie 2020, ISBN 978 94 6236 151 5
MI-347 A. Varga, *Establishing State Responsibility in the Absence of Effective Government*, (diss. Leiden), Amsterdam: Ipskamp Printing 2020
MI-348 M. Darouei, *Managing a Sustainable Career in the Contemporary World of Work: Personal Choices and Contextual Challenges*, (diss. Leiden), Amsterdam: Ipskamp Printing 2020
MI-349 N. Strohmaier, *Making Sense of Business Failure. A social psychological perspective on financial and legal judgments in the context of insolvency*, (diss. Leiden), Amsterdam: Ipskamp Printing 2020
MI-350 S. Kouwagam, *How Lawyers Win Land Conflicts for Corporations. Legal Strategy and its Influence on the Rule of Law in Indonesia*, (diss. Leiden), Amsterdam: Ipskamp Printing 2020
MI-351 A.D. Sarmiento Lamus, *The proliferation of dissenting opinions in international law. A comparative analysis of the exercise of the right to dissent at the ICJ and the IACtHR*, (diss. Leiden), Amsterdam: Ipskamp Printing 2020
MI-352 B. Ribeiro de Almeida, *Building land tenure systems. The political, legal, and institutional struggles of Timor-Leste*, (diss. Leiden), Amsterdam: Ipskamp Printing 2020
MI-353 K.A.M. van der Zon, *Pleegrechten voor kinderen. Een onderzoek naar het realiseren van de rechten van kinderen die in het kader van de ondertoezichtstelling in een pleeggezin zijn geplaatst*, (diss. Leiden), Den Haag: Boom juridisch 2020, ISBN 978 94 6290 842 0
MI-354 E.G. van 't Zand e.a., *Bestuurlijke boetes en de Verklaring Omtrent het Gedrag. Een onderzoek naar de realiseerbaarheid en wenselijkheid van het betrekken van bestuurlijke boetes bij de VOG-screening aan de hand van een casestudy naar handhaving en integriteit in de financiële sector*, Den Haag: Boom juridisch 2020, ISBN 978 94 6290 843 7
MI-355 J. Boakye, *Understanding Illegal Logging in Ghana. A Socio-Legal Study on (non)Compliance with Logging Regulations*, (diss. Leiden), Amsterdam: Ipskamp Printing 2020
MI-356 N.N.A. Sánchez Castillo-Winckels, *International law and the sustainable governance of shared natural resources. A principled approach*, (diss. Leiden), Amsterdam: Ipskamp Printing 2020, ISBN 978 94 0282 145 1

MI-357 S.S. Arendse, *De uiterlijke verschijningsvorm in het strafrecht. Een analyse van de jurisprudentie van de Hoge Raad*, (diss. Leiden), Den Haag: Boom juridisch 2020, ISBN 978 94 6290 844 4

MI-358 J. Reef, M. Jeltes & Y.N. van den Brink, *De PIJ-maatregel doorgelicht. Juridische grondslagen, populatiekenmerken, gedragsverandering en recidive*, Nijmegen: Wolf Legal Publishers 2020, ISBN 978 94 6240 608 7

MI-359 S. Guo, *Recognition of Foreign Bank Resolution Actions*, (diss. Leiden), Amsterdam: Ipskamp Printing 2020

MI-360 B. Muscat, *Insolvency Close-out Netting: A comparative study of English, French and US laws in a global perspective*, (diss. Leiden), Amsterdam: IpskampPrinting 2020

MI-361 J.M. ten Voorde, S.V. Hellemons & P.M. Schuyt, *Discriminatie als strafbeïnvloedende omstandigheid bij strafbare feiten, Een rechtsvergelijkende studie*, (diss. Leiden), Den Haag: Boom juridisch 2020, ISBN 978 94 6290 871 0

MI-362 F. Afandi, *Maintaining Order: Public Prosecutors in Post-Authoritarian Countries, the case of Indonesia*, (diss. Leiden), Amsterdam: Ipskamp Printing 2020

MI-363 R.M. Koenraadt, M.M. Boone, S.E. Rap & S. Kappert, *Financieel toezicht binnen het (jeugd) strafrecht. Een onderzoek naar het verloop, de resultaten en mogelijke uitbreiding van verplicht financieel toezicht binnen het (jeugd)strafrecht*, Den Haag: Boom juridisch 2020, ISBN 978 94 6290 933 5

MI-364 J.J. Asscher, Y.N. van den Brink, H.E. Creemers, E. Huls, E.K. van Logchem, N. Lynch & S.E. Rap, *De strafmaat voor jeugdige daders van ernstige gewelds- en zedenmisdrijven in internationaal perspectief*, Den Haag: Boom juridisch 2020, ISBN 978 94 6290 943 4

MI-365 M.P.A. Spanjers, *Belastingbudget. Onderzoek betekenis budgettaire impact belastingen bij parlementaire vaststelling belastingwetgeving*, (diss. Leiden), Den Haag: Flosvier, ISBN/EAN 978 90 8216 072 7

www.ingramcontent.com/pod-product-compliance
Ingram Content Group UK Ltd.
Pitfield, Milton Keynes, MK11 3LW, UK
UKHW051448290926
15471UKWH00008B/1089

9 789462 362109